"THERE IS A NORTH"

"THERE IS A NORTH"

Fugitive Slaves, Political Crisis,
and Cultural Transformation in the
Coming of the Civil War

John L. Brooke

UNIVERSITY OF MASSACHUSETTS PRESS
Amherst and Boston

Copyright © 2019 by University of Massachusetts Press
All rights reserved
Printed in the United States of America

ISBN 978-1-62534-447-2 (paper); 446-5 (hardcover)

Designed by Sally Nichols
Set in Adobe Caslon Pro

Cover design by Thomas Eykemans
Cover art: detail of *Richmond, the Confederate Capital, entered by the Union Army*, c. 1865. Image courtesy of the Miriam and Ira D. Wallach Division of Art, Prints and Photographs: Picture Collection, New York Public Library

Library of Congress Cataloging-in-Publication Data

Names: Brooke, John L., author.
Title: "There is a North" : fugitive slaves, political crisis, and cultural transformation in the coming of the Civil War / John L. Brooke.
Description: Amherst : University of Massachusetts Press, [2019] | Includes bibliographical references and index. |
Identifiers: LCCN 2019019863 | ISBN 9781625344465 (hardcover) | ISBN 9781625344472 (paperback) | ISBN 9781613766903 (ebook) | ISBN 9781613766910 (ebook)
Subjects: LCSH: Stowe, Harriet Beecher, 1811–1896. Uncle Tom's cabin—Influence. | Antislavery movements—United States—History—19th century. | Antislavery movements—United States—Public opinion. | Politics and culture—United States—History—19th century. | Popular culture—United States—History—19th century. | United States—Politics and government—1849–1861. | United States—History—Civil War, 1861–1865—Causes.
Classification: LCC E449 .B869 2019 | DDC 973.7/11—dc23
LC record available at https://lccn.loc.gov/2019019863

British Library Cataloguing-in-Publication Data
A catalog record for this book is available from the British Library

An early version of a portion of this book appeared as "Party, Nation, and Cultural Rupture: The Crisis of the American Civil War," in *Practicing Democracy: Popular Politics in the United States from the Constitution to the Civil War*, ed. Daniel Peart and Adam I. P. Smith (Charlottesville: University of Virginia Press, 2015), 72–95. Copyright © 2015 by the Rector and Visitors of the University of Virginia. Used by permission.

*For my parents, their sense of adventure,
and their stories of the past*

Contents

List of Figures ix
Preface and Acknowledgments xi
Chronology, 1846–1861 xv

INTRODUCTION
Confluence, Creolization, Liminal Crisis, and the Antislavery North 1

CHAPTER 1
Structures Challenged
The Rise of Abolitionism and Antislavery 23

CHAPTER 2
Structure Defended
The Compromise of 1850 65

CHAPTER 3
Liminality Erupting in the First Crisis
Fugitives and the Northern Public 89

CHAPTER 4
Creative Liminality
Writing and Reading Uncle Tom's Cabin 116

CHAPTER 5
Transforming Culture
Commercializing Antislavery 159

CHAPTER 6
Guarantees Violated in the Second Crisis
The Kansas-Nebraska Act 202

CHAPTER 7
Restructuring Coalescence
Nativism and Antislavery Politics   230

CHAPTER 8
Confirming and Consolidating New Structures
The Rise of the Republican Party   276

EPILOGUE
Into the War   295

Appendix of Tables   307
Notes   319
Index   385

Gallery follows page 158.

List of Figures

FIGURE 1. "Slavery" per 10,000 "articles" in free state and abolitionist/antislavery papers, in America's Historical Newspapers, 1830–1870   56

FIGURE 2. "Slave Power" per 10,000 "articles" in free state and abolitionist/antislavery papers, in America's Historical Newspapers, 1830–1870   57

FIGURE 3. United States population and economy, 1790–1870   58

FIGURE 4. Antislavery petitions to the 31st Congress, and "fugitive," "Union," and "meeting" as keyword hits per month, free states, December 1849–1851   94

FIGURE 5. "Fugitive" and "Slave Power": Total hits, 1850–1856   106

FIGURE 6. Liminality and structure in antislavery and proslavery thought   135

FIGURE 7. Liminality and structure in Stowe's *Uncle Tom's Cabin*   136

FIGURE 8. Naming events: Jenny, Joanna, Johanna, and Eva, 1841–1860   147

FIGURE 9. Cultural action and antislavery politics in the early to mid-1850s   172

FIGURE 10. Petitions to the 33rd Congress, Anti-Nebraska language in free state papers   212

Preface and Acknowledgments

THIS BOOK had its origins in the summer of 2010, when invitations to present lectures, participation at a conference panel, and the example of the Occupy movement all came together to make me think about politics, culture, and the shape and trajectory of transformative "events." I wanted to know more about the specific processes that drive critical shifts in public sentiment.

The larger question here is the coming of the American Civil War, and my central premise is that the decisive event in this long process involved a dramatic swing in northern white public opinion in the early 1850s. Three strategic groups controlled the direction of public affairs. A majority of southern whites had been committed to slavery since before the Revolution; African Americans were more than ready for freedom. The critical balance lay with the white North, which, despite a century of abolitionist activism, as of 1850 remained by and large noncommittal. By 1856 a strategic bloc of this northern opinion had shifted, launching a new antislavery party, gaining control of Congress, and almost winning the presidency. If the final struggle was not precisely inevitable, the space for delay and compromise had fundamentally narrowed.

The forces driving matters to this tipping point were the self-liberating actions of African Americans, a constitutional crisis, and the efforts of cultural actors working in the burgeoning arena of entertainment capitalism. This shift in opinion can be called an "event" in the many senses of the word, unfolding as a drama in the public eye, beginning with crisis and ending in a form of resolution. For a large bloc of northerners, the Compromise of 1850, and especially the Fugitive Slave Act, stoked a growing anxiety about an emergent nationalization of slavery, intensified by the recurring dramas of fugitives escaping slavery, sometimes to be recaptured and returned to the South under draconian federal action. This open-ended crisis, what can be called a liminal moment, facilitated the sudden eruption of a new metanarrative. The publication of Harriet Beecher Stowe's *Uncle Tom's Cabin* launched a wave of books, songs, consumer ephemera, and theatrical performance that worked to fill the void, the rupture, left by political failure, and to transform the context for political action. Embedded in this first transformative modern media event in American history was a highly fraught and contested resonance between a cultural connection, a "creolization," and a confluence of political interest that briefly transcended the boundaries separating northern whites and African Americans. These pivotal moments leading to the American Civil War saw a mingling of politics and culture, and of black voices with white; this mingling, however, was contested and ambiguous, and bore within it the seeds of reaction.

I owe many people and institutions a debt of gratitude in the evolution of this book. First, many thanks to Steve Bullock and Sarah Purcell for asking me to comment on a 2010 SHEAR panel that launched my thinking on the dynamics of media events in the public sphere. Bernd Fischer, May Mergenthaler, Adam Smith, and Daniel Peart invited me to present early outlines in 2010 as an offering in the Ohio State University Lecture Series on Public Sphere and Modern Social Imaginaries and the 2011 Commonwealth Fund Lecture at the University of London and the very productive workshop that followed.[1] Subsequently, versions and parts of this project were presented at the 2011 Annual Conference of the Society for Historians of the Early American Republic, the Georgetown University Nineteenth Century Seminar, the University of Tokyo and Doshisha University, Kyoto, and Mike Zuckerman's seminar in Philadelphia. My profound thanks to Adam Smith, Dan Peart, Elizabeth Varon, Chandra Manning, Yasuo Endo, Yoshio Higomoto, and Mike Zuckerman for their thoughts at these meetings that they organized. More recently, in February 2018, the American manuscript seminar at CUNY, led by James Oakes and David Waldstreicher, gave the entire manuscript a rigorous reading, for which I am eternally grateful. My readers for the press were amazingly supportive and generous.

Tyler Anbinder, Emily Arendt, Les Benedict, Mark Boonshoft, Corey Brooks, Joan Cashin, Mary Cayton, Timothy Leech, Sarah Levine-Gronningsater, Lou Masur, Heather Nathans, and Mitchell Snay all provided detailed—sometimes scathing, always encouraging—readings of all or part of the book manuscript in its various manifestations. Richard Bensel, Corey Brooks, Zack Fry, and Sarah Levine-Gronningsater shared vital pieces of evidence. Cameron Shriver undertook many of the grueling database keyword searches. I am greatly indebted—as are all historians—to the work of library staff at a number of institutions, among them the manuscript department at Butler Library, Columbia, the Ohio Historical Society, the Historical Society of Pennsylvania, the Massachusetts Historical Society, the Library of Congress, the National Archives, the Stowe Center, Hartford, the Cincinnati Historical Library and Archive, the Indiana State Library, and the Austin Ransom Center at the University of Texas. And since 2010 the many students in my undergraduate research seminar at Ohio State, "Slavery and Politics from the American Revolution to the Civil War," have, in their wrestling with the historiography and in their excellent research papers, taught me far more than I can acknowledge.

The roots of the publication of this book by the University of Massachusetts Press goes back to a friendship with Clark Dougan forged over thirty years ago, and the promise of a book. Clark and the press were amazingly patient over the years, as the promised book receded into the future; I hope that this effort meets his early expectations. Since Clark's retirement, Mary Dougherty has been as encouraging and patient an editor as anyone could hope for. The staff at UMass Press have been heroically cheerful and efficient.

Finally, and most important, Sara, Matt, Alyssa, Benjy, and Tess may not have the details of the crisis of the 1850s at the center of their attention, but they are an enduring inspiration in their determined engagement with the politics of our own age, which carries powerful and disturbing echoes of that earlier time.

Columbus, Ohio, February 2019

Chronology, 1846-1861

May 1846: war declared with Mexico
August 1846: Wilmot Proviso introduced in the U.S. House
January 7, 1847: Gamaliel Bailey publishes the first issue of the *National Era* in Washington
September 1847: Stephen Foster's song "Oh Susannah" published
  • *December 6, 1847: opening of the first session, 30th Congress*
April 15–16, 1848: attempted escape by slaves from Washington, D.C., on the schooner *Pearl*
summer 1848: California Gold Rush under way after discoveries at Sutter's Mill
August 9–10, 1848: convention of the Free Soil Party in Buffalo
  • *August 14, 1848: end of the first session, 30th Congress*
November 1848: Zachary Taylor elected president
  • *December 4, 1848: opening of the second session, 30th Congress*
  • *March 3, 1849: end of the second session, 30th Congress*
September and October 1849: California statehood conventions, Monterey
September–October 1849: Harriet Tubman makes her escape from plantation near Bucktown, Dorchester County, Maryland
  • *December 3, 1849: opening of the first session, 31st Congress*
January 3–4, 1850: James Mason of Virginia introduces the fugitive slave bill in the Senate
February 5, 1850: Henry Clay proposes his "omnibus" Compromise bill
March 11, 1850: William Seward presents his "Higher Law" speech in the Senate
March–May 1850: peak of the anti-Compromise petitioning campaign to the 31st Congress
July 31, 1850: Clay's omnibus bill defeated
August 21–22, 1850: radical abolitionist convention in Cazenovia, New York

August 29–September 12, 1850: Stephen Douglas's Compromise bills debated in the House; Fugitive Slave Law passed September 12

September 1, 1850: Swedish opera singer Jenny Lind arrives in New York from Liverpool; returns to Europe May 29, 1852

September 18, 1850: Millard Fillmore signs the Fugitive Slave Law

September 28, 1850: James Hamlet arrested in New York, the first arrest under the Fugitive Slave Law; followed by months of protest meetings
- *September 30, 1850: end of the first session, 31st Congress*
- *December 2, 1850: opening of the second session, 31st Congress*

December 1850: Harriet Beecher Stowe begins corresponding with Gamaliel Bailey and starts writing *Uncle Tom's Cabin*

February 18, 1851: Shadrack Minkins rescued in Boston
- *March 3, 1851: end of the second session, 31st Congress*

April 3, 1851: arrest and rendition of Thomas Sims in Boston

May 22, 1851: first two chapters of *Uncle Tom's Cabin* published in Bailey's *National Era*

September–October 1851: publication of pivotal *Uncle Tom's Cabin* chapters in the *Era*: chapters on Eliza and George Harris in Ohio and Uncle Tom's arrival at the St. Clare household in New Orleans

September 11, 1851: Christiana riot

October 1, 1851: Jerry Rescue, Syracuse

October 1851: Foster's song "Old Folks at Home" published; forty thousand copies in circulation by September 1852
- *December 1, 1851: opening of the first session, 32nd Congress*

November 27, 1851–January 22, 1852: publication of *Uncle Tom's Cabin* crisis chapters in the *Era*: the death of Eva, the killing of her father, the sale of Uncle Tom up the Red River to Legree's plantation

March 22, 1852: *Uncle Tom's Cabin* published in two volumes by John Jewett, Boston; print run of 300,000 copies ends in April 1854

April 1, 1852: last two chapters of *Uncle Tom's Cabin* published in the *National Era*

July 1852: Foster's song "Massa's in de Cold Ground" published

August–September 1852: C. W. Taylor's version of *Uncle Tom's Cabin* performed at Purdy's National Theatre, New York

August 26, 1852: Charles Sumner presents "Freedom National, Slavery Sectional" speech in the Senate
- *August 31, 1852: end of the first session, 32nd Congress*

September 27, 1852: Howard-Aiken version of *Uncle Tom's Cabin* opens in Troy for one hundred performances through December 1, followed by a brief run in Albany

November 6–13, 1852: Lemmon family slaves freed in New York City

November 15, 1852: Henry Conway version of *Uncle Tom's Cabin* opens at the Boston Museum

November 1852: Franklin Pierce elected president

• *December 6, 1852: opening of the second session, 32nd Congress*

January 1853: Foster's "My Old Kentucky Home" published

• *March 3, 1853: end of the second session, 32nd Congress*

April 1, 1853: Stowe departs New York for England; returns in September

April 29, 1853: first excerpts of Solomon Northrup's *Twelve Years a Slave* published in *Frederick Douglass's Paper*

May 1853: Harriet Beecher Stowe's *Key to Uncle Tom's Cabin* published by John Jewett

May 14, 1853: Stephen Douglas departs New York for England; returns in October

July 17, 1853: Howard-Aiken version of *Uncle Tom's Cabin* opens at Alexander Purdy's National Theatre for a run lasting until May 1854

September 8 and October 22, 1853: competing versions of *Uncle Tom's Cabin* open at the National Theater and the Chestnut Street Theater, Philadelphia

November 7, 1853: Conway version of *Uncle Tom's Cabin* opens at P. T. Barnum's American Museum in New York

November 11, 1853: first performance of Aiken version of *Uncle Tom's Cabin* in Pittsburgh

November 11–18, 1853: Marsh troupe performs a fusion version of *Uncle Tom's Cabin* at the Cleveland Atheneum after several stands in towns along the Erie Canal and launches a midwestern tour ending the following May, competing with at least five other theatrical troupes and various panorama shows

• *December 5, 1853: opening of the first session, 33rd Congress*

January 4, 1854: the Nebraska bill introduced in the Senate

January 24, 1854: "Appeal to the Independent Democrats" published

February 3, 1854: Salmon Chase presents "Maintain Plighted Faith" speech in the Senate

February 23, 1854: Stowe publishes her "Appeal to the Women of the Free States"

February 28, 1854: Ripon, Wisconsin, meeting forms the Wisconsin Republican Party

March–May 1854: peak of anti–Nebraska bill petitioning to the 33rd Congress

March 4, 1854: Kansas-Nebraska bill passes the Senate at 5:00 a.m.

March 7, 1854: Ralph Waldo Emerson delivers his speech on the Fugitive Slave Act at the New York Tabernacle

March 11, 1854: Joshua Glover rescued in Milwaukee; Marsh troupe begins performance of *Uncle Tom's Cabin* two days later

May 22, 26, and 30, 1854: Kansas-Nebraska bill passes the House, is confirmed in the Senate, and signed by President Fillmore

May 24–June 2, 1854: arrest and rendition of Anthony Burns in Boston

June 17, 1854: constitution of the National Council of the Order of the Star Spangled Banner adopted at New York City meeting

• *August 7, 1854: end of the first session, 33rd Congress*

August 26, 1854: Abraham Lincoln's first antislavery speech, at Winchester, Illinois

• *December 4, 1854: opening of the second session, 33rd Congress*

January–April 1855: Emerson, Douglass, Sumner, and others speak on an antislavery circuit running from Boston, Worcester, New York, and Philadelphia to Rochester and Syracuse

• *March 3, 1855: end of the second session, 33rd Congress*

June 5–15, 1855: Native American Party convention in Philadelphia; secession of antislavery delegates over section 12

August–November 1855: beginning of the crisis and civil war in Kansas

• *December 3, 1855: opening of the first session, 34th Congress*

December 25, 1855: meeting at Francis Preston Blair's Silver Spring mansion to form the national Republican Party

January–February 1856: fugitive Margaret Garner arrested in Cincinnati, kills her child, is returned to slavery

February 2, 1856: Nathaniel Banks elected Speaker of the U.S. House after 133 ballots since December 3

February 22–23, 1856: Republican planning convention in Pittsburgh; nativist convention in Philadelphia

May 19–25, 1856: Charles Sumner presents "The Crime against Kansas" speech in the Senate; sack of Lawrence by proslavery forces; Sumner attacked in the Senate by Preston Brooks; John Brown's raid on Pottawatomie Creek

June 17–19, 1856: John Frémont nominated for president at the Republican convention in Philadelphia

November 1856: James Buchanan elected president

March 1857: *Dred Scott* decision

September 1857–August 1858: Kansas constitutional crisis

August–October 1858: Lincoln-Douglas debates

October 1859: John Brown's raid on Harper's Ferry

November 1860: Abraham Lincoln elected president

December 24, 1860: South Carolina secedes from the Union

April 12–13, 1861: bombardment of Fort Sumter

"THERE IS A NORTH"

INTRODUCTION

Confluence, Creolization, Liminal Crisis, and the Antislavery North

IN THE spring of 1856, newspapers and correspondence across the North triumphantly announced, "There is a North." Over the previous decade the plaintive query had been "Is there a North?" Abolitionists had despaired that the free North would ever unite as a self-conscious collectivity against the slaveholders of the South, what they called the "Slave Power." In 1848 Daniel Webster, the great Union Whig, had dismissed the idea that "a North strong in opinion and united in action against slavery" existed in any form; he would restate this opinion at length in his seventh of March speech in the Compromise debates of 1850.[1] During these debates Thaddeus Stevens, the Pennsylvania antislavery radical, sarcastically praised the South—and mocked his fellow northern citizens. "Even in a bad, wicked cause," said Stevens, the South was presenting "a united front." But as for "the North—the poor, timid, mercenary, driveling North," it "has no such united defenders of her cause, although it is the cause of human liberty."[2] Over the next several years, antislavery activists agonized that Webster and Stevens were right, as the Fugitive Slave Act of 1850 brought a cloud of slave hunters across the North, and the Kansas-Nebraska Act opened the western plains to slavery in May 1854. The North, far larger and more dynamic than the South, was divided, seemingly paralyzed, in the face of southern unity.

But the tide turned in the deep winter of early 1856. Nathaniel Banks of Massachusetts, the antislavery candidate of the emerging Republican Party, won the Speakership of the 34th United States House of Representatives in early February on the 133rd ballot. The correspondent to the *Boston Daily Atlas* wrote from Washington of the three-month struggle for the Speakership "We have fought the good fight, and there is a North at last . . . [F]or the first time in many years, freedom and free men have triumphed." The day after the vote, Senator Charles Sumner of Massachusetts wrote to his friend and ally Charles Francis Adams: "At last Banks is elected. I was present when he was conducted to his chair. It was a proud historic moment. For the first time [in] years there seems to be a North. I fancied I saw a star glittering over his head." The Reverend Theodore Parker, a militant abolitionist leader in Boston, wrote to Sumner a few days later, "Banks election is the first victory for the North I deem since 1787." And five weeks later, applying the triumphant announcement to the immediate crisis, the Reverend Lyman Beecher, for decades the national spokesman for conservative evangelical reform, pledged a subscription for Sharpe's rifles to be sent to arm antislavery settlers in Kansas. His comment (delivered to "great applause") was repeated in papers throughout the free states: "I think Kansas will now know that there is a *North!*"[3]

What created this antislavery North? On the first of December 1860, soon after Abraham Lincoln's election to the presidency, George Templeton Strong, a rising New York lawyer of conservative inclination, sat down to consider the state of the nation. His mind turned first to recent politics: "Why do the people so furiously rage together just now? What has created our present unquestionable irritation against the South? What has created the Republican party?"[4] Looking back in late 1860 on the course of events in his recent past, George Templeton Strong could clearly see a tipping point. He remembered among northerners of his stripe "not hostility to slavery, but indifference to it, and reluctance to discuss it." Through the 1840s the efforts of abolitionists to rouse the North "made little impression on us." But things changed fundamentally between 1850 and 1854. The Compromise of 1850 "opened our eyes to the fact that there were two hostile elements in the country," launching debates that "were unfortunate for our peace." The "fatal blow" came in the spring of 1854, when Stephen Douglas's Kansas-Nebraska Act opened great parts of the West to slavery, overturning the earlier Missouri Compromise of 1821, which had reserved the northern section of Jefferson's Louisiana Purchase for free labor. But as he listed the consequences of the Nebraska bill, Strong was drawn back to the early 1850s. The Fugitive Slave Law, a key element of the 1850 Compromise, had "stimulated sectional feeling by making slavery visible in our own communities"; and "a sentimental romance, *Uncle Tom's Cabin*, . . . [had] set all Northern women crying and sobbing over the sorrows of Sambo."[5] Culture had a role in his analysis.

Frederick Douglass, the great black abolitionist and once a self-emancipated fugitive from slavery, was of a similar opinion, if he used rather different language. In March 1855, addressing the Ladies Anti-Slavery Society in Rochester, New York, Douglass had also turned to *Uncle Tom's Cabin*, in a tone that hinted of things to come:

> Anti-slavery is no longer a thing to be prevented . . . It has grown too large—its friends are too numerous—its facilities too abundant . . . A thousand strong men might be struck down and its ranks still be invincible. One flash from the heart-supplied intellect of Harriet Beecher Stowe could light a million camp-fires in front of the embattled hosts of slavery, which, not all the waters of the Mississippi, mingled as they are, with blood, could extinguish.

Devoting most of his address to assailing northern churches for failing to confront slavery, Douglass had discovered better allies: this was "the age of anti-slavery literature," an age when "supply on the gallop could not keep pace with the ever growing demand—when a picture of a negro on the cover was a help to the sale of a book." Rather than the churches, it was the poets, the scholars, the statesmen who were now aligned with antislavery. And he even extended his embrace to the music that emerged from the blackface minstrel shows proliferating across the country, notorious for their racism:

> It would seem almost absurd to say it, considering the use that has been made of them, that we have allies in the Ethiopian songs; those songs that constitute our national music, and without which we would have no national music. They are heart songs, and finest feelings of human nature are expressed in them. "Lucy Neal," "Old Kentucky Home," and "Uncle Ned," can make the heart sad as well as merry, and can call forth a tear as well as a smile. They waken the sympathies for the slave, in which anti-slavery principles take root, grow and flourish.[6]

Looking back from 1865, Strong and Douglass might have well agreed that the antislavery cause that drove the North to fight and win the Civil War had finally been forged in cultural action in the early 1850s, working in and between the gaps and failures of political action.

THIS IS a book about the essential tipping point leading to the American Civil War and the end of slavery in the United States. It is also a book about the nature of events. I argue that we need to think about *how* important events unfold, and particularly about what is happening *as* events unfold. Certain moments in time matter because the familiar patterns suddenly shift toward new configurations, new possibilities. I make no claim to provide a complete narrative of the period; my book devotes little attention either to the South or to transnational contexts. Rather, I hope to present arguments about the course of events in the 1850s that will be seen as compelling. Argument will not supersede narrative, however, since I am very concerned about the contemporary experience of the sequence and pacing of events.

This book is based on several critical assumptions. First and most obviously, slavery lay at the origins of the Civil War: as Abraham

Lincoln put it in his Second Inaugural Address in 1865, "All knew that this interest was, somehow, the cause of the war." Second, peaceful secession by the slaveholding states to avoid the consequences of an election was impossible. he great body of the northern public, whatever their opinion about slavery, agreed with Lincoln's assertion in his First Inauguration Address that national sovereignty rested with an electoral majority: "Rejecting the majority principle, anarchy or despotism in some form is all that is left."[7] War was inevitable following secession. Third, then, why did the South secede? The South Carolina secession convention spelled out the issues in its December 1860 "Declaration of Causes": the northern states had refused to uphold their constitutional obligations to return fugitive slaves and had raised up a "sectional party" and a president "whose opinions and purposes are hostile to slavery."[8]

If the defense of slavery is one factor in the equation of Civil War causation, the antislavery movement was the necessary and essential, equal and opposite factor. The forging of an antislavery alliance is at least as critical to understanding the causes of the Civil War as the southern white defense of slavery. As much recent literature suggests, the white slaveholding South ever since the Revolution had been ready to defend slavery by secession and even war from any serious threat to its existence. Similarly, this literature also suggests that throughout this period, black Americans, slave and free, struggled against slavery and prayed for its abolition. Their resistance to slavery may indeed have been a fundamental cause of the Civil War. But as an oppressed minority, they needed a large bloc of white allies so they together might pose an existential threat to the slaveholders' interests. For most of the antebellum period, no such alliance and no such threat existed, and indeed the slaveholders had every reason to be confident that the national government would continue to act in the interests of slavery.

Thus the critical question is to define when and how such a decisive antislavery alliance and fundamental threat to slavery emerged. Clearly this threat had to be embodied in the rise of a viable political party organized on antislavery principles. By 1856 such a party had emerged in response to the intensification of slaveholders' demands on the nation in defense of slavery—to what was called across the North "the Slave Power." Before 1856 the antislavery cause could seem hopeless; after 1856 it had established a clear path to power. Given the Republican Party's critical challenge to slaveholders' interests, the options for sectional compromise on the future of slavery narrowed dramatically between 1854 and 1856. While the intensifying grip of the slaveholders on national power has been ably described, I hope to demonstrate that our understanding of the final coalescence of the antislavery movement still needs some work.

Important as timing was, the problem here is less "when" than "how." The transition—the hinge—to irreconcilable conflict and war certainly required the emergence of an antislavery party between 1854 and 1856. But my essential argument is that this political coalescence and consolidation rested on a prior media event, the eruption of cultural antislavery following the Compromise debates and passage of the Fugitive Slave Act in 1850. We know a lot about both politics and culture in the 1850s, but I would propose that they have not been examined carefully enough together in a single arena.[9] As both Frederick Douglass and George Templeton Strong knew instinctively, the pursuit of power and the construction of meaning were deeply entangled in the 1850s. I stress that this was a special entanglement, shaped by a particularly fluid condition, what is called "liminality" by anthropologists, as routine institutions and understandings—structures—collapsed and new ones were constructed.

In addition, as recent work has made clear, this was a moment of entanglement of black and white, of what has been called a "creolization."[10] Antislavery authors led by Harriet Beecher Stowe, the blackface minstrel songwriters, most famously Stephen Foster, and dozens of opportunistic publishers, merchants, and theater producers all brought this entanglement of black and white to an exploding, commercialized popular culture. But this entanglement reverberated against an informal interracial politics that in the end was the critical driver of events. The secession ordinances passed by southern conventions in 1860–1861 all stressed an essential grievance: African Americans were liberating themselves from slavery, and they were being aided by northerners, white and black. Fugitive slaves were central actors in this crisis, pushing the white South toward draconian measures that radicalized growing numbers in the white North. As the country was embroiled in a visceral debate about the future of the territories, and thus the possible economic futures of innumerable families and individuals, the Fugitive Slave Act, as George Templeton Strong put it, made "slavery visible in our own communities."[11] A new literature has reopened the history of the Underground Railroad as an interracial movement. This small but intense zone of interracial coordination was embedded in a much larger public arena, in which many northern whites began to recognize a confluence of political interest: the southern "Slave Power" threatened their own liberties as much as it denied those of the enslaved.

Cultural creolization, interracial coordination, a political confluence: all of these entangling mixtures came into alignment at a particular volatile moment, between the summer of 1850 and the spring of 1854. For the large numbers of previously ambivalent white northerners who would vote Republican and fight for the Union, the nationalizing of slavery legislated in the Fugitive Slave Act in 1850, followed and confirmed by the reversal of the 1821 Missouri Compromise in 1854, undermined the terms of the federal Constitution as written and ratified in 1787–1788. This was a structural rupture of the highest order, and set the conditions in which the liminal entanglements of white and black could set the United States on a course toward the end of slavery.

AMERICAN DEMOCRACY was founded on a paradox. While the country announced its independence with a profound invocation of the natural rights of humanity, slavery loomed over the republic. Slavery was deeply rooted in the colonial past and guaranteed by the Constitution that structured the federal Union. If it seemed headed for inevitable decline in the era of the Revolution, by the 1820s slavery had been revitalized by the cotton boom. By the 1850s, "King Cotton" was surging in economic profitability and political power. It would take a second American revolution to abolish slavery in this land of liberty. When the American Civil War came to an end in 1865, over 700,000 soldiers were dead or dying, 4 million people had been freed from bondage, and $3 billion in the personal wealth of southern white slaveholders had been wiped away. The Civil War was itself the hinge of a profound constitutional transformation. The nation had been forged at the Constitutional Convention in 1787 on a compromise: there would be union with slavery. This compromise began to crack in the early 1850s, as northerners started to question its central premise. In 1860 the white South withdrew from union to save slavery, and the North, white and black, destroyed slavery and re-created union on new terms. Launched in Abraham Lincoln's Gettysburg Address, the Thirteenth, Fourteenth, and Fifteenth Amendments resolved the great contradiction of Jefferson's language that "all men are created equal," establishing a new order of equal national citizenship and confirming the supremacy of the national government in and over the states.[12] The struggle over slavery and the results of this great revolution still reverberate in American political life.

One of the foundational questions in American history involves the causes of this second American revolution. Very broadly, the field of debate has been defined by two schools of thought, fundamentalist and revisionist.[13] The fundamentalist school sees the Civil War as the inevitable result of deep-running structural tensions between a free North and a slave South. Slavery and freedom created such utterly different cultures and interests that they could not be contained within the same political universe. North and South were, as William Seward argued at Rochester, New York, in 1858, "two radically different political systems"; the sectional struggle was "an irrepressible conflict between opposing and enduring forces."[14] Such was the argument of the first historians of the war, mostly northern partisans, writing in the closing decades of the nineteenth century.

But the turn of the century saw the rise of the revisionists, many of them white southerners, who began to argue that the war had been avoidable: that slavery was a benevolent institution that would have eventually disappeared, and that a generation of "blundering politicians" had driven the nation into an unnecessary, destructive conflict. They focused, in particular, on the play of events and personalities through which, they maintained, small groups of sectional extremists had pushed apolitical majorities toward confrontation. This position, dominant into the 1950s, was challenged on a number of fronts by a resurgent fundamentalist school, which in its classic form described the struggle as one between, on the one hand, a modernizing liberal North, committed to the principles of free labor and free soil, and on the other, a traditional agrarian South, defending an old order.[15]

Currently the debate over the origins of the Civil War has three leading elements. First, revisionism has its proponents, both in its traditional form and in a new twenty-first-century literature on the costs of destructive war.[16] Second, a new fundamentalism has replaced that forged in the 1950s and 1960s, arguing conclusively that the South was not an agrarian backwater but stood at the cutting edge of nineteenth-century capitalism. Thus the Civil War was a struggle not between tradition and modernity but between two very different kinds of modernity, one based on freedom and the other on slavery.[17] And third, a very different mode of fundamentalism focuses on the Civil War as the culmination of an ongoing black resistance to slavery—in flight, sabotage, rebellion, and free political action—that endured for its entire history. In this interpretation, the war itself was only an intensified continuation of slavery's permanent state of war.[18]

Edward Ayers has pointed out the problems for the broad camps of fundamentalist and revisionist interpretation, calling for an effort to bridge the gap between them through a reconsideration of the "catalysts that emerged in the two to three decades before the war began."[19] The revisionists have a basic problem: clearly, as contemporaries well understood, the war was definitively caused by slavery.

The popular revisionism, the argument that the Civil War was over "states' rights," is profoundly circular, since states' rights were invoked primarily to protect slavery from a national emancipation. The Civil War fundamentalists focus directly on slavery and sectionalism, as I will show. But the revisionists do have a point: there is an essential problem with the fundamentalist argument that slavery was leading to an inevitable confrontation between North and South; after all, that confrontation took a long while to come to a boil—at least six to seven decades.

Thus Ayers is asking for a fusion of approaches, and particularly for an analysis of what was necessary, and what sufficient, to set in motion a sequence that would end in a decisive confrontation. The absolute language of the fundamentalists' "inevitability" can be restated in terms of *the range of options in a field of political action*. Sometimes there are many avenues for contingency to unfold in a wide field of action; nothing is necessarily "inevitable." But at certain junctures, certain avenues become untenable or impossible, and the field of action progressively narrows into a pathway toward what, in hindsight, will be seen as a reasonably certain outcome.[20] This book seeks to isolate and to examine in depth the critical juncture in which the field of possible outcomes narrowed to such a constrained pathway. It was at this point that room for political maneuver and compromise had narrowed to the point where decisive conflict loomed on the horizon.

Would the slaveholding South have accepted an antislavery party in control of the federal government? Clearly never. Not only were the slaveholders aggressive capitalists set on expanding slavery at all costs, but also they had worked assiduously and effectively since the Revolution itself to control the operation of the common national government of the United States. Southern Democrats had certainly done what they could to undermine the developmental program of the Whigs, opposing a national bank, tariffs, and internal improvements. Many southerners were plainly concerned that a national state might interfere with slavery inside the established states, but they also had a clear picture of what they wanted such a state to do:

suppress slave insurrections, if necessary, and expand the national territory by force, clearing Native inhabitants out of the way for the imperial cotton crop. This position constituted an amplified "federal consensus": the national government suited the purposes of the slaveholding South, but only if it acted as a coercive state rather than as a broadly developmental state, a model pursued by many northern state governments. If the United States government was small, it did one thing very well, and at great cost: fight wars that benefited the interests of the slaveholders. Andrew Jackson's campaigns against the Creeks in the War of 1812 and the sequence of wars against the Seminoles between 1819 and 1842 were fought to secure the southern frontier for cotton agriculture and to suppress the flight of slaves.

The South's national power had a constitutional origin. As one strand of "fundamentalist" literature running back to historian Staunton Lynd has made very clear, the South's membership in the Union was contingent on the primal compromise made in Philadelphia in 1787 that grounded the federal consensus: no union without slavery.[21] When the possible end of slavery was proposed by petition in 1790, southern congressmen made it perfectly clear that the result would be bloody civil war. The slaveholding states had a demographic advantage written into the 1787 Constitution, in the clause stipulating that three-fifths of the slave population would count toward representation in Congress, and thus toward representation in the Electoral College. If the three-fifths clause directly tipped the electoral balance only in the 1800 election, southern political strategy was fairly simple. With a solid proslavery vote from southerners, all that was required to control the federal government was to enlist the swing vote of a northern minority. The result was that the critical national officeholders who determined policy agendas, appointing officials from the postmasters at country crossroads to cabinet secretaries and Supreme Court justices ruling on major points of law, were predominantly proslavery figures. The South's electoral advantage could not last forever, and by 1850, immigrants flooding into the northern states were beginning to undermine the

South's control of the levers of national power. Lincoln's election broke the South's federal monopoly and signaled a turn from a proslavery coercive state to an antislavery developmental state. But until then, the South's grip on the federal government constituted roughly what antislavery critics called it: a "Slave Power."[22]

Thus I would suggest that there is really not that much of a puzzle as to why the South waited until 1860–1861 to secede from the Union. The emergence of a clear and present threat to slavery at any time would have led to secession, and loss of control of the presidency and the executive branch constituted such a threat. But the southern majority was confident in their growing wealth, and in their enduring control of the federal government. Despite occasional challenges over the antebellum decades, most southerners saw their interests protected within the Union by the national political parties and in an enduring southern control of presidential power. Whatever their differences, the two major antebellum parties stood by the 1787 compromise of union with slavery as the pillar of national unity, and the dominance of the Democratic Party in particular seemed to ensure that slavery would expand into new territories, as demanded by the interests of the cotton economy. But when the national parties failed to protect southern interests, when a distinct antislavery majority in the North emerged, and when slave insurrection seemed imminent, southern extremists had a ready-made argument. A decisive bloc of the southern white majority gravitated very quickly to a new sectional party, the Southern Democratic Party. When Lincoln was elected as a clear antislavery candidate, states across the Deep South began to secede from the Union, led by South Carolina, upholding slavery and accusing the northern states of undermining efforts to return fugitives. Deep South secession spiraled in a matter of months to the assault on Fort Sumter, the secession of most of the upper South, and then to all-out war.

So if southern proslavery was a necessary and fundamental cause of the Civil War, it was not a sufficient cause, since it was a constant background condition. Similarly, African American hostility to slavery was another constant, though the spread of railroads aided the flight of fugitive slaves to the North and to Canada. Against this background, the dynamic side of the equation was the rise and victory of a strong antislavery party. Rather than in the South, the causal nexus lay in the North. The central question is when, why, and how did a strategic majority of northern public opinion finally decide that the constitutional compromise of 1787 was no longer tenable, thus setting the stage for the inevitable southern withdrawal from the Union. The reality is that this strategic majority took a very long time to emerge and did not coalesce as a voting bloc until 1856. (See Appendix, table 1.)

Certainly there are problems for both broad schools of Civil War causation. Contrary to the revisionists, slavery did matter, but unfortunately for the fundamentalists, the rise of a decisive northern antislavery coalition was a long drawn-out process. Critiques of slavery began to emerge just before the Revolution, and there were mutterings of hostility to the South's constitutional advantages from the 1790s forward. Black voices raised against slavery all through the early republic were joined by those of radical whites in the early 1830s. The Slave Power argument had been put before northern audiences since the late 1830s, when large constituencies joined in petitioning against slavery. It took on great salience in the wake of the Mexican War, as northern congressmen tried to keep slavery out of newly conquered territories. But in the 1848 presidential election, the Free Soil Party attracted only 291,000 votes, 10 percent of the national vote and 14 percent of the free state vote. In 1852 the antislavery vote was weaker still. Opponents of slavery had been at work for many decades, and had gained signal successes in many of the northern states and in building the architecture of a national movement. But in terms of assembling a critical mass of electoral power on the national stage, they had little to show for their efforts.

What, then, happened in the 1850s? Political historians focus on the Kansas-Nebraska Act as the decisive force. Here, really, lies the core of the revisionist position: "blundering politicians" and "irresponsible agitators" ultimately caused a "needless war" by forcing a destabilizing piece of legislation, and by alerting the northern public to its dangers. On the one hand, they argue, Stephen Douglas, his southern allies, and President Franklin Pierce forced through a major alteration of the near constitutional language of the Missouri Compromise, which had reserved the northern Louisiana Purchase for free settlement. On the other hand, the revisionists condemn a group of six antislavery senators for ginning up northern opposition in "An Appeal of the Independent Democrats in Congress," which vociferously attacked the Nebraska bill. The "Appeal" was—in William Gienapp's account—"a brilliant piece of antislavery propaganda"; it was—Michael Holt argues—a desperate effort by a few Free Soilers to "perpetuate their party and their own political careers." Even Eric Foner, a leading figure in the reemergence of a fundamentalist interpretation in the late 1960s, called it "one of the most effective pieces of political propaganda in our history."[23]

Why was the "Appeal" so effective if, in the preceding years, the northern electorate had been, as Holt puts it, so "unconcerned about slavery"? The political historians describe the "Appeal" in total isolation from its rhetorical context. Could it be that the northern public had been prepared for this moment by a series of events and experiences that fall outside the purview of routine politics and traditional political-historical writing? Was there anything else at work in what has been called the "maniacal reaction of northerners" to the Kansas-Nebraska Act and the "stunning" result of the 1854 congressional elections? Indeed, was the Republican surge in 1856 such an "astounding performance"?[24]

Understanding this pivotal moment in the Civil War crisis requires that we venture well beyond formal politics. By all political indicators, when Stephen Douglas launched his planning for the Nebraska bill in December 1853, the great majority of the northern public seemed inert, disengaged from the issue of slavery. But here, as did George Templeton Strong in 1860, we need to go back to before the "fatal blow" of the 1854 Kansas-Nebraska Act to what Strong said "opened our eyes"—the 1850 passage of Fugitive Slave Law—and to the work of cultural actors in the intervening years. Frederick Douglass had put his finger on exactly the same dynamic and its wider ramifications. The first initial organization of the Republican Party in the summer of 1854 was certainly triggered by the Kansas-Nebraska Act, but it was fundamentally shaped by a four-year experience with "events" that fall outside the traditional definition of politics. Party formation between 1854 and 1856 marked the ending, not the beginning, of the key sequence of events.

Thus what has been assumed to be the most significant cause may simply have been an effect. Rather than the formal politics of party, it was an informal politics of culture during a *liminal rupture* that drove uneasy questioning, even rejection, of the 1787 compromise linking union and slavery. Party formation was thus not the "event" but the restructuring following a profound rupture, a rupture that forced a reshaping of the collective social imaginary, and was literally a revolutionary, nation-building event. This reshaping required cultural action.

The body of this book thus integrates the partisan political history of the early 1850s with the histories of very different forms of action in the public sphere. As formally defined, the public sphere is the arena of media and association, situated between the state and private life, in which public opinion forms and acts. The public sphere has its deliberative and its persuasive dimensions, its formal and informal politics, and I seek to weave them together into a single story. Thus I will be discussing party politics, politicians, and voters, novels and authors, songs, songwriters, and singers, and theater, producers, and stage actors. All were part of a single performative field of action; all were aware of, accessing, and interacting with one another and with their collective audiences. This is, of course, the normal mode of experience from which scholarship typically isolates analytical problems. But the early 1850s are the point where the problem to be analyzed is exactly the connections and interactions between political and cultural domains. In short, as the political actors stalled and failed, and constitutional order began to dissolve, cultural actors stepped into the breach.[25]

BEFORE WE start this story, however, we need to consider key dimensions of public life in the early 1850s and, briefly, a theoretical framework. This was, as I noted earlier, a liminal rupture. *What, exactly, is a "liminal rupture?,"* you might ask. More broadly, *What exactly is an event?* As historians, as citizens, we take events for granted, without much thought about how they work. Arriving at a theory of events requires that we think carefully about the different ways in which events are linked to the maintenance, evolution, or transformation of the social imaginaries that form the basis of consent in human society.²⁶

A significant event, as distinct from what we call a "non-event," is a coherent set of occurrences that change things, to some degree. Its outcome is uncertain, as distinct from that of a "non-event." In this uncertainty the event has the quality of liminality, a condition of being indeterminate and open-ended, of being "betwixt and between." The "things" that are changed by events can be called cultural "structures": routine common assumptions and modes of thought that govern behavior and relationships through time in social space. Structures cannot be liminal, though certain managed rituals and marginalized groups with liminal qualities often are embedded in structured situations. In ways large and small, events work to change structures.

The theory of liminality as transition emerged in the work of Arnold van Gennep, a French anthropologist and folklorist working in the early twentieth century. But van Gennep's concept was rejected and buried by the great structural theorist of the time, Émile Durkheim, whose prime commitment was to patterned and permanent continuities in culture. It was rediscovered in the 1960s by the British anthropologist Victor Turner, who expanded into a broad framework of structure and anti-structure, stressing the condition of what he called *communitas*—of homogeneous, equalitarian conditions in the liminal condition, and describing the dynamism of mythic creation in liminal conditions, through the action of metaphor, in which unauthorized and potentially subversive connections are constructed, in the way that metaphor creates new meaning in the association of dissociated words.²⁷ Whereas van Gennep and Turner were focused on the cultures of small-scale premodern, even tribal, societies, new scholarship in recent decades, much of it inspired by the transformation of eastern Europe following the collapse of the Soviet Union in 1989, has expanded the theory of liminality to encompass both large marginalized groups as well as entire societies undergoing revolutionary change through historical time. Among American political sociologists, William Sewell has advanced the Turnerian model of a narrative drama of breach, crisis, and redressive action most fully in his book *Logics of History*.²⁸

In a given chronological sequence of structure, rupture, and restructuring, it is in the chaos and creativity of the unstructured moment that a new structure—and the new mythology that supports it—is launched. The actual vehicles of this transformation are, Turner argued, the special place of metaphor in the drama of the liminal moment. Metaphor fuses two distinct entities into mutual association, and Turner stresses that the action here is entirely intuitive and emotional, perhaps nonrational. "New ideas" therefore take hold by the breakdown and reconnection of categories and symbols—the cultural system of signs—in processes of metaphoric association. Thus in liminal anti-structural contexts there is openness to metaphoric action, to a slippage between multivocal meanings, statuses, and authorities, to the fusion of previously separated domains of experience. Images and individuals marginalized in structural epochs can take on powerful roles in the liminal moment. In this way the liminal moment offers the opportunity for the assertion of creative agency and the emergence of powerful myth-making texts crystallizing opinion in new forms—literally the building blocks of new structures.²⁹

The idea that events alter structures—Sewell is quick to point out—is a pretty basic assumption among historians. Indeed the structure-altering event in its many forms has long occupied center stage in historical work. We spend a lot of time thinking about the collision of contesting structures in war and colonization, the crises of dominant structures in revolution, regime shift, realignment, and civil war. We may not spend enough time thinking about the specific qualities of life in these disruptions, particularly the way in which the particular emotional conditions that characterize significant events can very rapidly reshape "cultures." Sewell argues that events are cultural transformations characterized by environments of "heightened emotion"; they are contexts of memorable ritual and "acts of collective creativity." These are not, Sewell stresses, moments when "rational choice theory" works particularly well.[30]

In our common and scholarly discourse on the modern world, moments of significant liminal rupture are generally called "revolutions" and are the subject of a vast literature in a political and constitutional framework. But working with Turner's and Sewell's constructs allows us to widen our field of inquiry by recognizing that the liminal cultural action at work in revolutionary moments is just as significant as the formal politics, and may be more significant—even in nonrevolutionary moments—in explaining broad and rapid shifts in popular opinion that underlie consent and legitimacy. Their perspective expands our understanding of the framing of national identities, for the successful revolution forms not just a new government but a new and enduring national culture.

This brief excursion into theory provides an avenue into several recent interpretive approaches to the history of the antislavery movement, African American experience, American culture, and the origins of the Civil War. Historians are seeing both a political confluence and a cultural creolization, mutually reinforcing if not always recognized or acknowledged. Frederick Douglass, in particular, embracing the Liberty, Free Soil, and Republican parties, celebrating Harriet Beecher Stowe, and invoking the "Ethiopian songs" as a "national music," recognized and advanced this complex and contested fusion of political confluence and cultural creolization. It was not by coincidence that proslavery politicians and editors were calling their opponents the "Black Republicans" by the summer of 1854.[31] Between 1850 and 1854, an uneasy, uncertain time, a fraught and uneven creolizing fusion of culture acted upon an equally fraught and uneven convergence of interest linking American blacks and northern whites.

Though it was equally fraught and contentious, it is becoming increasingly clear that a powerful *political confluence* united the interests of black Americans, slave and free, with the interests of the growing numbers of white northerners who were hostile to the power of the southern slaveholders. Here an important new literature is stressing the role of black Americans in the very serious, informal politics of the sectional crisis.

In the North, African Americans from the moment of their own freedom began to raise their voices against the enslavement of their brethren in the South. In the South, African Americans never accepted enslavement, and this resistance undermined southern white slaveholders' pretensions to a contented and happy labor force, and drove a constant undercurrent of anxiety. Across the border running down the Ohio River and along the Mason-Dixon line, slaves were in flight north from Kentucky, Maryland, and Virginia into the lower North, aided by the highly organized network of vigilance committees and support groups known as the Underground Railroad. Northern free blacks played a central role in these committees, but they worked in concert and in coordination with white sympathizers. The Fugitive Slave Law, as Strong remembered, as did large numbers of northern whites, "opened our eyes" to the new reality that the northern states were part of a slaveholding republic and, increasingly, an indeterminate borderland between slavery and the land of freedom, now situated in the British queen's Canadian provinces.[32]

And the willingness of slaves to liberate themselves, along with the effectiveness of blacks and whites in aiding these fugitives, was raising fears among the planter class: fears that slavery would be abandoned in the border states, weakening southern power in Washington, and leading to a political death spiral. The accusations in the ordinances of secession that southern states issued in 1860–1861 that the northern states had failed in their constitutional obligations to remand fugitive slaves is testimony to these concerns. Indeed it has been argued that slave self-liberation was more important in the fears of the white South than the exclusion of slavery from the territories.[33]

From the 1830s the slaveholder response to black and white abolitionism was a series of increasingly extreme measures, most important the House and Senate "gag rules" that suppressed antislavery petitions, demands for the expansion of slavery into western territories, and the Fugitive Slave Act. As these measures were pushed onto the national stage, white northerners began to see the Slave Power of the South as a growing threat to their own personal liberties. While many white northerners were extremely uncomfortable with any hint of an interracial alliance, and vehemently denied any sympathy for enslaved peoples or interest in the abolition of slavery, their hostility to the Slave Power put their interests into alignment with those of black Americans.[34] Frederick Douglass committed himself to powerful vehicles of this confluence when in the early 1850s he threw his considerable influence behind antislavery political parties. Here, and through to the defeat of the white South in battle, black and white were bound together in a common enterprise.

This political confluence of interest and action was the first alignment of black and white in the final antebellum decades. A second, equally fraught and complex, had been building for decades in a creolization of American popular culture that bound and still binds black and white Americans together in an uneasy common cultural domain.[35] Whites and blacks had been living together in the New World for two centuries, living in a volatile reverberation of culture that suddenly intensified in the early 1830s. At the same time that the American Anti-Slavery Society raised a militant and uncompromising voice against slavery, the "Jump Jim Crow" dance craze began to fuel an intensifying racism, and a fascination with whites becoming black, in the blackface minstrel shows.[36] To borrow Eric Lott's formulation, this was a dynamic of hate, love, and theft. Interpretations of these minstrel shows has shifted over the past forty years and more, from an assumption that they were simply raw racism to much more complex and ambiguous understandings of these shows as vehicles also of political critique and vectors of creolization. Quite simply, as much as cultural appropriation, the shape-shifting involved in whites putting on burnt cork and playing music inflected by African idioms was profoundly liminal. Its influences reach down to our own time in the deep structures of American popular music, Douglass's "national music."[37] Indeed, Frederick Douglass was a critical force in the interracial fusion of politics and culture in this final stage of the antislavery movement. For better or worse, this creolizing of culture built the context for the political confluence of hostility to slavery and the Slave Power which came to a head in the early 1850s, suddenly narrowing American pathways toward the future and the Civil War.

My emphasis on the northern public in the early 1850s will undoubtedly challenge some of my readers, but I think the evidence indicates that this was the decisive arena, after which the path to war and the end of slavery was essentially set. The fundamental causal arrow was shaped in the North, in the emergence between 1850 and 1854 of a large, ultimately determinative bloc of northern opinion against the compromise of 1787, which had fused union with slavery. The abolitionists had been the vanguard, but until the early 1850s they were embattled and isolated, unable to mobilize a sectional antislavery majority. I argue that culture in novel, song, and theater in the liminal space between the twin crises of 1850 and 1854 played a powerful transformative role in this final antislavery mobilization. How transformative this impact was will have to be a matter for my readers to decide. But I hope to describe *how* culture worked on politics, helping many to resolve the effects of a profound political breakdown and achieve a new and enduring political structure.

The narrative that follows is organized in terms of the simple three-act model of the liminal crisis. We start with structure, as constituted and defended from the Revolution through the 1840s, and challenged by radical outsiders, who for decades failed to establish a wider claim to the alliances of northern voters and the resources of political actors. The Compromise of 1850 was designed to reinforce and extend the structure established in 1787, effectively nationalizing the reach of slavery with the Fugitive Slave Act. The result was a constitutional crisis and a liminal rupture, leaving people open to the voices of new cultural action that reached a point of political synthesis in the spring of 1854, during the congressional debates on the Kansas-Nebraska Act. Here, I suggest, there was a twenty-one-month period of political coalescence, ending with the election of Nathaniel Banks to the Speakership of the House and the meeting of the first Republican national convention in February 1856. Bold as it may seem, I argue that the events of the next four and a half years acted simply to confirm and expand the cultural-political structure that had emerged for a strategic northern bloc over the previous five to six years. The course was set, and little could move the flow of events from an increasingly narrow channel.

CHAPTER 1

Structures Challenged

The Rise of Abolitionism and Antislavery

IN JANUARY 1827, Martin Van Buren, a senator from the state of New York, wrote a long letter to Thomas Ritchie, in Richmond, Virginia. Van Buren and Ritchie occupied parallel leading positions in the conservative Old Republican factions of their respective states, Van Buren as the head of the Regency faction controlling the *Albany Argus*, Ritchie as the editor of the influential *Richmond Enquirer*. Van Buren wanted to build an alliance to support Andrew Jackson for president; his thinking was shaped by the sectional conflict he had seen when he arrived in Washington late in 1821 following the drawn-out and bitter debates over the admission of Missouri as a slave state. He was not alone. Writing privately from Monticello in the midst of the Missouri crisis, Thomas Jefferson had said, "This momentous question, like a fire bell in the night, awakened and filled me with terror."[1]

Writing to Ritchie six years later, Van Buren wanted this fire bell—any debate about slavery—silenced by "the revival of old party distinctions" between Federalists and Jeffersonian Republicans. "Party attachment in former times," he stressed, "furnished the complete antidote for sectional prejudices by producing counteracting feelings." Party loyalty and discipline had been a national bulwark: "It was not until that defense had been broken down that the clamour agt Southern Influence and African Slavery could be made effectual in the North." Furthermore, "political combinations between the inhabitants of the different states are unavoidable," he urges upon Ritchie, "and the most natural and beneficial to the country is that between the planters of the South and the plain Republicans of the North."[2]

From this initial inquiry, Van Buren and Ritchie would indeed restore party structures and defense of the constitutional compromise of union with slavery forged in 1787. William Freehling has framed the entire period up to the verge of the Civil War as an epoch defined by "secessionists at bay."[3] This construct assumes that the primary issue in Civil War causation was southern secession in the crisis of the Union. I would suggest that "antislavery at bay" was a far more important framework in this brewing crisis. Opponents of slavery were held at bay by national political structures maintained by men like Van Buren, intent on compromise to preserve the Union as it was established in 1787. Voices opposed to that primal compromise were marginalized, even violently suppressed, for decades. And religious and cultural voices were very much a part of the structures that held the abolitionists at bay. It was only after 1850—in a liminal rupture—that antislavery voices would break through and persuade a strategic majority of the northern white population to oppose slavery, despite the ever-present threat of secession and war.

Revolution, Union, Slavery

Of course the American Revolution itself was a great liminal moment, in which empire, king, and old attachments were all swept away and a new order of things seemed imminent. A "contagion of liberty" appeared to sweep America. Town meetings and county conventions proclaimed an abhorrence of slavery in the name of natural rights; black men, mostly former slaves, served throughout the war in the Continental Army and Navy. But the contagion had strict limits and faded quickly. The black soldiers served only from the New England states, where they provided a means of pushing draft quotas onto the poorest of the poor. Blacks in New England did succeed in gaining statewide abolition of slavery, but only after arduous petitioning efforts that essentially embarrassed the white public into accepting the end of the practice.[4] In the mid-Atlantic states, emancipation took much longer and came only in the form of a gradual system that left many enslaved for decades.

The "contagion of liberty" met a virtually solid wall of resistance in the South, where many saw an "untrammeled ability to control slavery as a central part of what the Revolution was about."[5] Here the issue of self-liberating fugitives from slavery was already foundational. A British judicial decision handed down in the summer of 1772 echoed far into the nineteenth century. A slave named James Somerset had been taken from Massachusetts to London and, after attempting to escape into the city's black underground, was chained up in a ship's hold for sale in the West Indies. Ruling in his case, Lord Mansfield decided that since there was no "positive" local or municipal law sanctioning slavery, and since slavery violated natural law, slaves could not be held in England. In this decision he carved out a colonial loophole, as all of the colonies had such "municipal laws."[6] But in 1766, as part of the repeal of the Stamp Act, Mansfield had played a central role in Parliament's passage of the Declaratory Act, which had announced Parliament's supremacy in all matters of law in the empire. Sixty-eight years later, in 1834, Parliament would indeed act on these powers to abolish slavery throughout the British Empire, most dramatically in the West Indies; in 1836, judges in the northern states began to invoke Mansfield's *Somerset* requirement of a positive law in refusing to return fugitives to the South. British authorities in Canada had announced the same policy by 1819.[7]

In the short term, southern mutterings about the *Somerset* decision were confirmed when, as the Revolution began in 1775, Virginia's last royal governor, the Earl of Dunmore, offered freedom to slaves who took up arms on the side of the British. During the Revolution, thousands of slaves fled to British lines in hopes of freedom, and after the war, white slaveholders were enraged when American negotiators failed to get full compensation for lost slaves in the 1783

Peace of Paris. John Jay's inability to secure this compensation in his treaty negotiated with the British government in 1794 reinforced southern anger.[8] In the meantime, fearing an American combination of the Declaratory Act and the *Somerset* decision, southern leaders worked assiduously to ensure that any new central government in America would never threaten slaveholding interests. In the 1776–1777 debates over the powers of the proposed Confederation, southern delegates worked to undermine its national powers and to protect slaveholdings from taxation; Thomas Lynch of South Carolina made it clear that if there were any challenges to the property status of slaves, "there is an end of the confederation." The southerners were so adamant about the quid pro quo of slavery and union that John Adams warned legislators back in Boston to sideline a bill providing for gradual emancipation. Richard Henry Lee of Virginia chaired a committee that worked to prevent an American *Somerset*, protecting the sovereignty of state law from Confederation intervention and ensuring that the Articles of Confederation mandated the interstate protection of slave property and the return of fugitives. He played a similar role in the congressional committee deliberations that inserted a similar anti-*Somerset* fugitive rendition clause into the Northwest Ordinances in July 1787.[9]

The Constitutional Convention was meeting in Philadelphia in the same summer of 1787. Ten days after the Northwest Ordinances were enacted in New York, Charles Cotesworth Pinckney of South Carolina played a role similar to Lee's, "remind[ing] the Convention, that, if [any member of] the committee should fail to insert some security to the Southern States against an emancipation of slaves, and taxes on exports, he should be bound by duty to his state to vote against" the result. A month later Pinckney had a central part in shaping the debate on the fugitive slave clause.[10] The Constitution would contain provisions that would be pillars of the slaveholder interest for decades to come. Fugitives would be returned to slavery, the slave trade would continue without challenge until 1808, the federal government was empowered to suppress insurrection, and three-fifths of all slaves, as enumerated in the federal census, would count toward both representation in Congress and any taxes that body might authorize. Speaking before the South Carolina House of Representatives in January 1788, Pinckney seemed amazed at his handiwork. With regard to the three-fifths clause, he recounted to the delegates, "We thus obtained a representation for our property; and I confess I did not expect that we should have been told upon our return that we had conceded too much to the Eastern States, when they allowed us a representation for a species of property which they have not among them." Admittedly, the southern delegates had not secured an explicit federal guarantee of a right to hold slaves as property. But summing up, Pinckney offered this assessment: "We have made the best terms for the security of this species of property it was in our power to make. We would have made better if we could; but, on the whole, I do not think them bad."[11]

The southern delegates had secured at Philadelphia the elements of a national coercive state that would serve their interests well in the decades to come. This was the amplified federal consensus: union with slavery, and union government to ensure slavery. Ignoring the fact that the South had failed to get a clause in the Constitution explicitly defining slaves as property, Richard Henry Lee's younger brother Henry, as one of the last Federalist representatives from Virginia, spelled out this amplified consensus in Congress in 1800: the property of "the people of the Southern States . . . consisted of slaves, and therefore Congress had no authority but to protect it, and not to take measures to deprive the citizens of it."[12] Better known as Light Horse Harry Lee of Revolutionary War fame, Henry Lee would be the father of another Lee, of Civil War fame. But in 1800, Lee's position was unremarkable, articulating the central argument that would define the slave interest up to the Civil War.

In 1790, when petitions from Pennsylvania, one initiated by Benjamin Franklin himself, had proposed that the United States begin to work out a plan to "loosen the bonds of slavery," two southern representatives, from South Carolina and Georgia, went on the offensive. They forcefully maintained that slavery was a benevolent system sanctioned by religion and tradition. Moreover, it was a matter of internal state regulation in which Congress had no authority, and any discussion of emancipation would "light up the flame of civil discord." The slaveholders of the South would resist such "tyranny," and even if "the other parts of the continent may bear them down by force of arms, . . . they will never suffer themselves to be divested of their property without a struggle." With the threat of disunion and civil war hanging in the air, Congress united to refuse all petitions regarding slavery, establishing a key political structure that would endure for decades.[13] This 1790 struggle over the abolitionist petitions nearly derailed progress that winter on Alexander Hamilton's plan to establish a national financing system.[14] Four years later, Hamilton's passage of a federal carriage tax (at the same time that debates over the Jay Treaty were heating up) restated southern arguments that the powers of a national developmental state threatened the slave interest. John Taylor of Caroline County, Virginia, in an argument before the Supreme Court, declared that the tax was unconstitutional because it might be extended to another "species of property which is peculiarly exposed" to the decisions of an "American Majority," and thus "effect a general emancipation." Southern slaveholders would never have exposed their slave property to such a threat by ratifying the Constitution, and thus, Taylor argued, the federal government was barred from enacting any law that might set a precedent for the abolition of slavery.[15]

Thus, by the middle of the 1790s, the key elements of the entrenched structure that would support the slave interest for decades to come were forged: the constitutional provision of an intersectional agreement in Congress to suppress any discussions of slavery, an image of slavery as a benevolent and positive good, expectations of coercive action but rejections of developmental action, and the simmering threat of disunion and civil war.

Early Abolitionist Liminality

Against these odds, abolitionist voices struggled to be heard. A few delegates in northern ratifying conventions raised hostile questions.

In the South some evangelicals resisted slavery, but by the 1810s they had begun to move en masse to the Midwest. During the 1770s and 1780s associations were formed in Philadelphia and New York City to work toward freedom, playing a role in the gradual emancipations in these states and in the ill-fated 1790 petitions to Congress. They launched decades of careful legal action that would protect the freedoms of free blacks and fugitives; both John Jay and Alexander Hamilton were among the lawyers in the New York Manumission Society.[16] After they lost national power, New England Federalists began to chafe at the political power of the South in Congress and the presidency, mocking Jeffersonian slaveholders, complaining about an executive Virginia dynasty, and challenging the three-fifths clause, disastrously perhaps, in the Hartford Convention.[17] Notably, many northern white political figures opposed to slavery joined the American Colonization Society after it was established in 1816. Seeing no viable path to an abolition of slavery and to civil rights for free African Americans, the colonizationists proposed returning all emancipated slaves to Africa, or sending them to the new black Republic of Haiti.[18]

A more militant, immediatist message developed quickly in the communities of free people of color emerging in northern towns and cities. These communities encompassed small but growing groups of emancipated slaves, Revolutionary veterans, and newly arrived fugitives. Their claim to American equal rights was embedded in their construction of independent black institutions: churches, lodges, and mutual aid and benevolent societies.[19] If Congress had a set policy to reject them, black leaders in these new communities nonetheless organized petitions against kidnapping and the slave trade. Absalom Jones, one of the key figures in the Philadelphia black community, led the 1799 petition to Congress which drew Light Horse Harry Lee's announcement of the amplified federal consensus.[20]

While their petitions were buried in Congress, black abolitionists left an enduring mark in the public sphere.[21] Black publication was designed both to speak to an emerging and oppressed minority but also to witness to all of American society in the national public sphere. From the era of the Revolution, starting with Phillis Wheatley, Benjamin Banneker, and Venture Smith, black writers wrote direct challenges to slavery as part of a wider black corpus published over the course of the next four decades, much of it emerging within the fabric of black institutions.[22]

These efforts, presenting the example of arduous lives and carefully constructed arguments for black freedom, culminated in a series of events in the late 1820s. In 1826 black activists from across the Northeast organized the General Colored Association to coordinate antislavery efforts. In New York City, John Russwurm and Samuel Cornish began to publish the first black paper in the country, *Freedom's Journal*, announcing that there "ought to be some channel of communication, between us and the public" in which "the calumnies of our enemies should be refuted by forcible arguments." All during its short run, *Freedom's Journal* listed David Walker of Boston as an agent, and for a few months ran an ad for his clothing store at 42 Brattle Street. Printing Walker's inaugural speech to the General Colored Association, the *Journal* ended its run before it could print a notice of his *Appeal . . . to the Coloured Citizens of the World but in Particular, and Very Expressly to Those of the United States of America*, or of his suspicious death in August 1830, soon after the publication of the third edition. Walker's *Appeal* stands as the breaking point to a public and militant demand for immediate abolition. Framed in four articles on the causes of African American "wretchedness"—slavery, ignorance, proslavery Christianity, and colonization—the *Appeal* warned white Americans that their "pride, prejudice, avarice and blood, will, before long prove the final ruin of this happy republic, or land of liberty!!!!" In his conclusion Walker quoted at length from Jefferson's Declaration of Independence: "See your Declaration Americans!!! Do you understand your own language? Hear your language, proclaimed to the world, July 4th, 1776—'We hold these truths to be self evident–that ALL MEN ARE CREATED EQUAL!! that they are endowed by their Creator with certain unalienable rights; that among these are life, liberty, and the pursuit of happiness!!'" He closed with the threat that white "Americans may be as vigilant as they please, but they cannot be vigilant enough for the Lord." Dozens of copies of the *Appeal* soon made their way into the South with black sailors working aboard coastal vessels.[23]

While Walker's *Appeal* probably did not play a direct role in Nat Turner's bloody rebellion in Southampton County, Virginia, in 1831, it certainly sent a wave of anxiety across the South, already on edge after two events: a threatened insurrection in Charleston in 1821 and the explosive Missouri crisis debates of 1819–1821.[24] These events had opened up the issue of slavery on the national stage, presenting the raw threat of bloody rebellion and even national dissolution. In some measure the Missouri crisis was the linchpin, since it revealed that white America was actually deeply divided on the issue of slavery. While the rise of the cotton frontier had already united the slaveholding South on the very real profits of chattel slavery, most white northerners were ambivalent to hostile on slavery and its expansion. When James Tallmadge, a Republican representing Quaker-settled Dutchess County, New York, proposed restricting and eliminating slavery in the new state of Missouri, support erupted across the northern states. Missouri would be the second slave state after Louisiana to be carved out of Jefferson's Louisiana Purchase, and northerners were seeing an alarming pattern. The Missouri debates stretched over three congressional sessions, from February 1819 to February 1821, and were finally resolved in a complex exchange. Missouri was admitted as a slave state but balanced against the admission of Maine as a free state. And it was agreed that slavery in the remaining unorganized Louisiana Purchase lands would be restricted to the line running west from Missouri's southern boundary, 36°30'. This was roughly on a line with the meeting of the Mississippi and Ohio Rivers, and thus extended to the west the boundary between freedom and slavery established in the 1787 Northwest Ordinances. The debates were suffused with extreme sectional rhetoric, breaching the wall of comity more or less respected since 1790. Southerners raised the specter of war "profuse in blood," while Senator Rufus King of New York condemned all laws upholding slavery as "absolutely void, because contrary to the law of nature, which is the law of God." Both sides threatened disunion. The great majority of northern congressmen stood together to oppose the admission of Missouri with slavery, stymied by a united South and a small rump of mid-Atlantic Republicans.[25]

Nation, Party, Structure

When King condemned slavery in 1821, it was not quite the national structure that it would become in the decades following. Its future would rest on the expansion of cotton production, which in 1821 was a small fraction of what it would be by 1860. But cotton planting was spreading west across the Deep South and up the Mississippi, and in the 1830s and 1840s would move west into Texas. Its inexorable expansion drove a demand for slaves that brought income to declining planters in the older regions and deepened linkages with northern commerce, banking, and manufacture. Slave ownership was a hugely valuable enterprise. All told, the slaves held in 1860 were worth $3 billion, a value easily converted to cash in the slave markets across the South; fewer than fifty thousand families owned half of this investment in human beings. Slave property was worth more than the total national investment in manufacturing, railroads, and banking capital combined. The result was a great concentration of wealth in the South: Deep South states had three to five times the wealth per white population as many northern states.[26] Slavery was a profound economic structure, and powerfully protected by political structures.

But even in 1821 King was expressing passions that Martin Van Buren feared, coupled with the rising voices of abolition, both its black immediatist and white gradualist proponents. As he clearly saw it, politics could regain control of the public discussion by restoring the "party attachment [of] former times," which would "furnish . . . the complete antidote for sectional prejudices by producing counteracting feelings." Van Buren proposed "the substantial reorganization of the Old Republican Party" around regular nominations by congressional caucus or a national party convention "substituting *party principle* for *personal preference*."[27]

Parties would preserve the nation from its most obvious contradiction: slavery in a land of liberty. They would also, like the national organizations of churches, provide a structural glue holding the Union together. This glue is inherent in the institutional structure and trajectory of a party—in which the personal interest of party notables is bound to both policy and preservation. The origins of American party organization lay with the printers, whose newspapers and printing offices lived and died by party patronage. Newspapers drove the electoral victories that brought in the courthouse printing contracts which in turn allowed the printers to continue to publish their party papers.[28] Beyond the papers lay the entire fabric of patronage and position in a widely ramifying range of administrative and judicial positions. Established politicians simply could not afford to risk their household income—the "bread of office"—that flowed from loyal attachment to party discipline. This simple fact alone powerfully slowed the emergence of effective antislavery politics all through the 1840s. Political parties were and are powerful engines of self-perpetuation, practically inventing their own physical laws of friction and inertia. Joel Silbey has captured the essential features of the antebellum parties in describing them as "wide-ranging management institutions" and arguing that "policy advancement, partisan organization, popular mobilization, and the art of management all went hand in hand."[29] If voter identity was not necessarily quite as tribal as Silbey would have it, party management was closely calculated, since the loss of an election might mean the ruin of many a loyal soldier in the ranks of federal, state, and county leadership. And with this control of party rank and file, party managers could be reasonably confident that they could control the flow of events, or at least restrict them to a narrow channel.

Van Buren's planning was realized in General Andrew Jackson, the slaveholder hero of the Southwest, who in the War of 1812 and its aftermath had broken the power of Creek Indians and escaped slave

Seminoles in north Florida and defeated the British regulars at New Orleans. Jackson had lost the 1824 election to John Quincy Adams through what Jackson saw as a "corrupt bargain" between Adams and Henry Clay of Kentucky.[30] Jackson beat Adams in 1828 by conjuring a populist image that swept the South, the new Midwest states, and the Mid-Atlantic. By 1830 he began to flesh out his image with an assault on the developmental state that Adams and Clay advocated, first vetoing federal money for a road in Kentucky and then going to war with the Bank of the United States, vetoing its re-charter in the summer of 1832. This assault on the "Money Power" was combined with his critical commitment to remove the Cherokee and other eastern tribes from the Southeast, where they stood in the way of the expansion of the white slaveholding cotton frontier. Many southerners had, since the 1790s, argued that the developmental power to create a bank was an extension of the "necessary and proper" clause of the Constitution, which might be extended to the abolition of slavery, but they saw full constitutional grounds for the use of federal coercive power to advance the territorial interests of slavery.[31] Jackson, of course, did not please slaveholders in South Carolina when he stood firm against their plans to nullify the federal tariff, but most of the South stood with him, since his persona and policies all worked to advance what many in the North would soon call the "Slave Power."

Arch-Democrat Duff Green predicted in the year before the 1828 election that Jackson's victory would put the "anti-slave party in the North . . . to sleep for twenty years to come," crushed under "the chariot wheels of Jackson's popularity." More precisely, Jackson's election—and the reactive response of the Adams Republicans and then the Whigs—marginalized but intensified antislavery sentiment in the North.[32] Jackson defined the framework of a partisan political debate in terms that were understood as a contest over the developmental state running back at least to Hamilton's plan for the first Bank of the United States in 1791, producing exactly the "counteracting feelings" that Van Buren had proposed to Ritchie in 1827. There would be no room for any discussion about slavery in the national political arena with Jackson in office. Public antislavery among the white northern majority would have to find a new avenue into the public sphere.

1830s: Abolitionism

William Lloyd Garrison personified and organized this avenue: militant immediatist abolitionism. The rise of Garrison was shaped by the rise of Jackson, but it was also directly informed by the message of David Walker. Garrison, a young printer of impoverished origins who had apprenticed with Federalist and Adams newspapers, was in 1829 working with the Quaker Benjamin Lundy in Baltimore, putting out the antislavery *Genius of Universal Emancipation*. Within weeks of its publication they were reading Walker's *Appeal*, and its stark natural rights militancy aligned with Garrison's developing thinking, grounded in new friendships in the black community in Baltimore. If Lundy was appalled by Walker's proposal for a slave insurrection, Garrison in January 1830 turned more radical, writing a column mocking Georgia's new law quarantining ships with black sailors aboard and criminalizing the teaching of slaves to read and write. But by this time Garrison and Lundy had been indicted for libel for a different article; Garrison spent two months in jail before his fine was paid by a sympathizer, and he headed north to Boston. On the first of January 1831, he published the first issue of the *Liberator*, which would be the leading voice of militant abolitionism for the next thirty-four years. In his inaugural issue he declared: "I do not wish to think, or speak, or write, with moderation . . . I am in earnest—I will not equivocate—I will not excuse—I will not retreat a single inch—AND I WILL BE HEARD." Exactly a year later he and others met in the basement of the Boston African Meeting House to organize the immediatist New England Anti-Slavery Society. In December 1833 he met with abolitionists from throughout the North to form the American Anti-Slavery Society. They too invoked the natural rights language of the Revolution to demand a "general and immediate emancipation."[33]

The Anti-Slavery Society drew on organizational systems developed by contemporary reform movements to build a network of state and local auxiliaries. By May 1836 there were over five hundred local societies; by May 1838 there were almost 1,350. Abolition drew on the explosion of popular reform energy released by a new religious message coursing through the churches of the small-town and rural North, especially in New England and in the Yankee diaspora to the west in New York and the upper Midwest. Charles Grandison Finney, with other theologians, had abandoned the stark terms of predestination Calvinism to preach that sinners had the personal agency to open their hearts to conversion, and once converted, had the responsibility to act to bring perfection to the world. This theology was unleashing optimistic activist energies in the late 1820s. Starting with the issue of the federal delivery of mail on the Sabbath and Jackson's policies of Indian removal, activists began to sign petitions to Congress by the hundreds. In 1831 the temperance movement exploded in a massive network of local societies. The broader membership of the new abolition societies was drawn out of these mobilizations, broadly Sabbatarianism and temperance and very specifically opposition to Indian removal.[34]

Once slaves were emancipated throughout the British Empire in 1834, the Anti-Slavery Society had hopes for a peaceful solution in America. Flush with funds supplied by the Tappan brothers, Lewis and Arthur, merchants in New York City, and by Gerrit Smith, a wealthy landowner in the Adirondacks, and by hundreds of small donations, they began to plan a campaign to persuade southern slaveholders of the national sin of slavery through a barrage of printed materials and to generally revolutionize the American public sphere. By July 1835, making use of expensive new printing technology available in New York, they had sent 175,000 items through the mail to the South. The society launched a campaign in 1835 to petition Congress to abolish slavery in the federal District of Columbia. Dozens of paid agents were sent out to launch canvassing campaigns that mobilized a wave of petitioners. By 1839 more than 8,600 antislavery petitions, each bearing on average about a hundred signatures, had been submitted to Congress.[35]

These petitioning abolitionists included a vast army of women, entering the political arena for the first time in American history. Starting with the campaigns regarding Sunday mail, the rights of the Cherokee, and especially temperance, women had surged into the reform movement. But they typically had joined societies and signed petitions led and initiated by men, and had not overtly challenged the patriarchal gender order. By 1838 there were fifty-one female antislavery societies in Massachusetts, twenty-one in New York, and eighteen in Ohio, three abolition strongholds.[36] And they were signing petitions in the thousands. (See Appendix, table 2.) In the first wave of petitions, sent to Congress between 1833 and early 1837, the roughly 2,500 women signing accounted for only about a quarter of the petitioners. But in the huge surge of petitions to the 25th Congress between 1837 and 1839, women constituted more than half of the almost 600,000 petitioners; all told they made up almost 60 percent of the 173,000 signers petitioning that Congress to abolish slavery in the District of Columbia. Indeed the petition drive took on qualities of a women's movement, as female canvassers recruited significantly larger numbers of their peers than did men, both in meetings and in door-to-door solicitations.[37] A new social force in America was born.

Structural Forces in Action

Huge forces were mobilized against the growing movement. First, there were many people in the urban North who felt threatened by the mobilization of radical men and women who advocated transforming change, and they took action. In July 1834 riots broke out in New York City, aimed at the abolitionist Tappan brothers and their associates. The next year a mob in Boston dragged Garrison through the street with a rope around his neck. Major riots broke out in Philadelphia, Utica, Troy, and Cincinnati, targeting abolitionists, their presses, and free black communities. In Alton, Illinois, in 1837, abolitionist Elijah Lovejoy was killed defending his press from a proslavery mob. In Philadelphia in May 1838, the newly built Pennsylvania Hall, where the Anti-Slavery Convention of American Women was about to meet, was torched by an anti-abolitionist mob. All told, between 1834 and 1840, at least 175 riots broke out in northern cities and towns against abolitionists and black communities, concentrated in 1834 to 1836. These mobs were led by "gentlemen of property and standing"—typically merchants with strong party affiliations who often had business connections in the South. And it has been convincingly argued that these rioters took from Andrew Jackson an assertive violence toward all who stood in the way of a patriarchy of free white men.[38]

Second, the executive branch took action against the onslaught of abolitionist print arriving in southern post offices. The abolitionists had hoped to revolutionize the American public sphere. When hundreds of antislavery tracts arrived by steamer in Charleston in July 1835, they were taken from the post office and burned. Protests—and lynchings—spread across the South.[39] Postmaster General Amos Kendall, after consulting Jackson, issued a statement that allowed the slaveholding states to protect their "domestic police" and "interest in slaves" from outside interference, effectively censoring the mails.[40]

Finally, Congress took action against the antislavery petitions flooding the capital as soon as the 24th Congress convened in December 1835. James Henry Hammond of South Carolina wanted all petitions on the subject of slavery to be immediately rejected by the House; his colleague Henry L. Pinckney proposed an alternative that resulted in the "gag rule." The petitions would be automatically "laid upon the table" without further consideration or notice. Here the northern Democrats in the House played a key role, voting 57–15 for the gag, supporting a solid southern bloc, and opposing virtually all northern Whigs. The gag would be upheld for eight years on the basis of these northern party votes.[41]

If the northern Whigs balked at the gag rule, they did very little to assist the cause of organized antislavery. During the gag rule debates, most of the opposition on the floor had come from two lone congressmen, John Quincy Adams of Massachusetts—the former president now on a second career in Congress—and William Slade of Vermont. The majority of the northern Whigs hung back from directly challenging the South for fear of alienating their southern Whig colleagues. Thus partisan politics as "structure" worked to obstruct abolitionism; so too did organized religion.

Just as on the parties, pressures for national unity came to bear on the Protestant denominations. Presbyterians, Methodists, and Baptists felt the necessity to maintain a union of sentiments across the nation to uphold their denominational interests. Locally, northern ministers were caught between vocal immediatist abolitionist minorities and opposing moderate and proslavery majorities. National schisms did eventually take place. In 1837 the Presbyterians ejected the synods from western New York and northeast Ohio on grounds of their participating in nondenominational reforms. Behind the scenes it was clear that they were unhappy about the abolitionist tendencies in these churches. But even within the Genesee and Western Reserve synods, ministers were cross-pressured by competing antislavery factions, most significantly between the immediatists and the supporters of the American Colonization Society, or an emerging schism between Garrisonians and the Tappan circle. The result was that large numbers of Protestant ministers refused to take a radical stand against slavery until the 1850s.[42]

Race and Music

Another force ranged against the abolitionists was less structural than liminal, but it was put to structural purposes in the 1830s. The blackface minstrel tradition had its origins in the cultural encounters within a wider American underclass, white and black, brewing in the marginalized common cultures of enslaved, indentured, and wage labor circulating broadly around the colonial Atlantic for over a century and specifically around the growing United States since the War of 1812. Fused with and projected by another volatile force in the public sphere—commercial entertainment—the blackface minstrel performance experienced an explosive rise that changed the cultural landscape of the United States in the early 1830s, just as Jackson was challenging the Bank of the United States and Garrison was nationalizing the call for immediate abolition. Where Frederick Douglass would praise the minstrel songs of the early 1850s as "our national music," "heart songs . . . in which anti-slavery principles take root, grow and flourish," in 1848 he had condemned the minstrels of that day as "the filthy scum of white society."[43] This hybridizing, creolizing culture would play an important part in the events of the early 1850s. In the 1830s it was clearly ranged against abolitionism.

The roots of this tradition run back to the first encounters of English and Africans in North America, working and living together in a violent close proximity and exchanging language, worldview, music, and dance. African string and percussion traditions shaped the adoption by black musicians of the fiddle, black performance in eighteenth-century military drumming, and the development of the banjo. Black fiddlers playing British tunes with African inflections were in demand for white dancers throughout the South and mid-Atlantic colonies.[44] This evolving musical fusion became more complex and disjointed with the great movements of labor following the Haitian Revolution, the Louisiana Purchase, and the War of 1812. Slaves from the Caribbean, the Carolina Lowcountry, and the Maryland-Virginia Tidewater region were flung into the cotton and sugar frontiers of the Deep South. Sailors white and black worked together in the coastal and Caribbean trades, and Irish workers dug the narrow canals that connected the East to the western lakes and rivers, waters and shores worked by rough riverboat men and stevedores. Down these western waters, these crews shared space with chained slaves being sold into the Deep South, while in a smaller reverse flow, growing numbers of fugitives moved along these circuits north to freedom, to labor on farms, in rural ironworks, and around the docks in the new river cities and old seaports.[45]

Among other important points along this circuit, the Lower East Side of New York, specifically the markets at Catherine Slip, was a place where this creolization advanced dramatically among poor whites and free blacks (in the largest concentration in the country) mingling with slaves coming across the East River from the truck farms on Long Island. By 1820 Catherine Market was famous for its competitive street dancing; this street culture flowed into theaters nearby, specifically the Chatham Garden Theatre, a rough venue a few blocks away on the Bowery. Here a creolizing hybrid culture was put to the purposes of a commercial appropriation. Micah Hawkins, who kept a tavern and grocery on Catherine Slip and who had written some of the first published black dialect songs, celebrating the defeat of the British on Lake Champlain, in 1824 put on *The Saw Mill, or A Yankee Trick*, filled with German, Irish, and African American dialect and slang.[46] In the autumn of 1828, the players who would forge the commercial minstrel performance were brought together in a great tour of the country. George W. Dixon was performing blackface songs—"Coal Black Rose," "Long-Tail'd Blue"—at the Lafayette Theatre. Noah Ludlow, who had already spent years on rough stages in the West, including the first performance of "The Hunters of Kentucky" in New Orleans in 1822, a song that helped propel Jackson to the presidency, was managing the Chatham Garden Theatre. And a local teenager, Thomas D. Rice, was working pickup jobs at both theaters; for years to come, Dixon's songs would be part of his repertoire. Rice joined Ludlow's company for another tour of the West, starting in a coastal voyage to Mobile, and from there to New Orleans, Nashville, Louisville, and Cincinnati. Here Rice created his great blackface dance routine "Jump Jim Crow."[47]

By the time of Rice's first performance in Louisville in May 1830,[48] his "Jim Crow" was a shuffling, leaping dance extravaganza arranged around his song's chorus: "Wheel about and turn about and do jis so, / Eb'ry time I wheel about I jump Jim Crow." This performance suddenly captured the public imagination, and as Rice moved from Louisville to Cincinnati, and then to Philadelphia, Baltimore, and back to New York by November 1832, it became an early media sensation. Rice had by no means invented it: elements clearly run back deep into African American folklore and the Caribbean-Carolina dance routine of John Canoe, and versions of it were being sung in public in New Orleans by 1830–31.[49] But his success on the stage spawned imitators. All through 1833 and the years following, he would compete with others performing his song and dance, and by late in the year another black-inspired racist dance "extravaganza" was in development. "Zip Coon" mocked the urban black dandy, as Jim Crow mocked the "corn field negro." In particular, George W. Dixon brought Zip Coon up from the South to confront Rice's Jim Crow in New York.[50] From these beginnings in songs performed in mixed variety shows and before and after plays and farces, the tradition would evolve and become far more commercialized with the emergence of full-scale touring groups in the early 1840s, specifically the Virginia Minstrels and Christy's Minstrels. As a measure of the penetration of the genre, we might consider the early life of a later songwriter for Christy's: Stephen Foster. As a boy of nine in 1835 he was organizing performances of all of the genre classics three nights a week, to the "uproarious applause" of neighborhood audiences in Pittsburgh.[51]

The "Jump Jim Crow" phenomenon was full of complicated ironies. Thomas Rice made a good living from this appropriation of black culture, taking it eventually on a wildly successful European tour. He was one of Douglass's "filthy scum," and his performances were read as racist and derogatory. His audiences were rough young white men and boys of the Jacksonian persuasion, certainly not of Whig respectability. But Rice, who had grown up on the Lower East Side of Manhattan in one of the most integrated neighborhoods in the country, also put an artistic form clearly derived from African American culture front and center in the American public sphere. Historians over the last half century have wrestled with this critical ambiguity and its degree of appropriation and creolization.[52]

For antebellum contemporaries, faced with abolitionists demanding total emancipation for slaves and a president destroying the great establishment of the bank, the early 1830s were wild and uncertain times. In 1832 the uncertainties were intensified by the first wave of cholera, a deadly and unknown disease sweeping in by steamship from India. Tens of thousands suddenly died in cities throughout Europe and the United States in the summer and fall of 1832, inspiring a gothic fatalism and even masked balls ruled by "King Cholera." Rice's return to New York was delayed by the epidemic, though papers throughout the country reprinted a short paragraph on partying in the face of death: "Right on the track of the Death Cart, at Montreal, comes a grand Masquerade at the Theatre. In New York, all is frolic and fun . . . in Philadelphia . . . Mr. Rice is exciting laughter with Jim Crow. Tears and smiles, Cholera or No Cholera, the world will roll on much after the old fashion."[53] The fall of 1832 also brought a pivotal election, in which the Whigs hoped to unseat Jackson for killing the bank, the election adding to the liminal feeling of uncertainty in which Thomas D. Rice and his cohorts brought "Jim Crow" and the earliest commercial minstrelsy to the public sphere.

If "Jim Crow" came out of marginality, out of the shadows of slavery, in a particularly fraught period, he was quickly normalized into the structural routines of American public life. There were, on the edges, some hints of radical subversion, echoing Nat Turner and foreshadowing John Brown: in the summer of 1833 in western Georgia, rumors circulated that a "Jim Crow" had launched a "diabolical scheme . . . to have all the slaves set free, and their masters become bond-servants to them."[54] But southern politicos could adopt "Jim Crow" as a pseudonym,[55] and more typically, all over the country, the "Jump Jim Crow" dance step quickly became the label for "any little 'Jim Crow' politician . . . anxious to change sides." Thus the South Carolina nullifiers might mock-toast Martin Van Buren as "a real Jim Crow of a fellow"; differing positions on the tariff were "as they sing 'turn about, wheel about, jump Jim Crow.'"[56]

The most pointed use of the language was the song itself, in racially charged public settings. Such tension was in the air when the Sauk war chief Black Hawk and his companions attended the Chestnut Street Theatre in Philadelphia in 1833. They reacted with "looks of surprise, when *Jim Crow* was called out for a *fourth* song, by a white congregation."[57] And with notable regularity, "Jim Crow" or "Zip Coon" was sung, or otherwise involved, in a striking number of anti-abolitionist riots and disturbances in the mid-1830s.

By the summer of 1834, the geography of entertainment, race, and reform in New York City had become particularly volatile. The Chatham Garden Theatre had failed, and the building had been converted into a temperance chapel by Lewis and Arthur Tappan. On a hot July night a crowd gathered to disrupt a meeting of free blacks, trashing the chapel. The crowd then moved up to the Bowery Theatre on another mission, to prevent an English actor—heard to have insulted Americans—from performing. Men in the crowd started singing and dancing "My Long-Tailed Blue" and "Jim Crow" and demanding that the actor be fired. Once this was accomplished, they suddenly marched on Lewis Tappan's house, broke down the doors, and dumped his possessions in the street and set them ablaze.[58]

The New York riot, with roots in a heated April election and growing unemployment, clearly had echoes of nativism and class as well as race and anti-abolitionism. Nativism and class were certainly at work that summer in Charlestown, Massachusetts, where a Catholic convent was burned by gangs of Protestant workingmen amid calls for a performance of "Jim Crow." In December 1836 an antislavery lecture in New Haven was disrupted by young men (probably Yale students) singing "Jim Crow" and "Zip Coon," and threatening worse.[59] The next January, anti-abolitionists recruited a "wandering ballad singer" to disturb an abolitionist meeting in rural Massachusetts (which had been shut out by the conservative churches) by singing "Jim Crow"; the next year an antislavery meeting in Saratoga County, New York, was similarly targeted. These events continued and intensified. In July 1848 Martin R. Delany, a prominent black leader and co-editor with Frederick Douglass of the *North Star*, was subjected to a massive minstrelized riot in a small town in Ohio: "Halloing, cursing, and swearing, blackguardism—the roaring of drums, beating of tamborines, blowing of instruments and horns, the rattling of bones, smashing of store boxes and boards for the fire—all going at once and the same time, incessantly for the space of four hours, by far exceeding anything of a similar nature which I have witnessed." This riot against his colleague must have been on Douglass's mind three months later when he wrote his angry condemnation of the minstrels as the "filthy scum of white society."[60] Across the Atlantic, Rice's European tour had worked its own magic. An opponent of a petition to disestablish the Church of England apparently signed his name "Jim Crow."[61]

Thus "Jim Crow" minstrelsy was mobilized very quickly against reform of all kinds, but particularly radical abolitionism, which seemed such a threat to young white men facing uncertain futures. Its performers advanced a subtle class critique and were themselves deeply shaped by an interracial world. But despite these origins in marginality, the minstrel culture was naturalized into the structures of Jacksonian America, and its racist overtones were set against the efforts of the abolitionists. Certain key cultural actors in the early 1850s, I will suggest, forged a harmonic resonance between these two dissonant worlds, briefly aligning two outsider cultures in the sudden shift in northern public opinion against slavery. But this resonance—however powerful—would be brief and fleeting, and no such alignment was even faintly visible in the 1830s.

Abolitionist Liminality

Thus the abolitionist movement, armed with a message of radical transformation, was faced with a wall of political, religious, and cultural opposition. The abolitionists were an abused and hounded minority, doubly so if they were black. Assaulted by party politicians, excluded from the churches, and undermined by popular culture, they worked to forge their own separate world, liminal and marginal on a host of measures. The abolitionists certainly succeeded in putting the question of the end of slavery on the national agenda, but they failed to convert the northern public to their cause on their own terms. In some measure, both the survival and the failure of the movement rested in the communities that it developed.

Some abolitionists may have had hopes of a quick triumph—a rapid conversion of the slaveholders to a recognition of the sin of slavery, and the instant emancipation of slaves in America in the 1830s, matching the final success of the British abolitionist movement in 1834. These hopes were in great measure inspired by the liminal conversion experience many white abolitionists experienced in the Yankee revivals of the Second Great Awakening, driving an urge for immediate transformation.[62] But once this initial abolitionist dream faded, if not before, the radical abolitionists separated themselves from the prevailing cultural structures of American society, entering a liminal space of uncompromising condemnation. They were perfectionists, prophets, come-outers. As an earlier broad hostility to slavery dimmed in the Jacksonian North, they stood and acted as visionary outsiders.[63] And while the minstrels superficially race-shifted by blacking up for their performances, some among the abolitionists race-shifted in their hearts, and their efforts to "make myself a colored man" were accepted by their black associates.[64] Taking this outsider stance, they had to create an outsider culture. To survive the hostility, even violence, of the wider society, the abolitionists had to create worlds of their own, sanctuaries that would reinforce their radicalism and stand as testimony to their alternative vision. A tight communion of sentiment ensured the movement's long-term survival—but may have stood in the way of the conversion of a strategic majority in the North. Paradoxically, the most powerfully challenging voices among the abolitionists were the least successful; more accommodating, less challenging voices would have more success with the northern public. Both were essential to the wider character and force of the abolitionist message.

The original core of the abolitionist movement were the Garrisonian immediatists, a tight-knit group centered in Boston, but with small groups of supporters scattered in northern New England, New York City, around Philadelphia, and in northern Ohio and Indiana.[65] Following Garrison's lead in the *Liberator*, they defined the most radical position on the abolitionist spectrum. Rejecting the major political parties, perhaps rightly, as engines of compromise and corruption, they also rejected the churches, even the evangelical churches that were moving beyond Calvinism. The immediatists in the wider Boston area tended to be Unitarian in broad sentiment, often tinged with elements of mystical transcendentalism. Elsewhere many Garrisonians had Quaker connections. Many of the Garrisonians were pacifists and adherents of both non-resistance and—seeing government as utterly corrupted by slavery—forms of antinomian anarchism. Impelled by their perfectionist radicalism and by the women in their ranks, the Garrisonians took up the cause of women's rights in the late 1830s, most dramatically in supporting three abolitionist women—the Grimké sisters, Sarah and Angelina, and Abigail Kelly—as antislavery lecturers, and then in nominating Kelly as a presiding officer in the American Anti-Slavery Society in 1839.[66]

The Garrisonian demand for women's rights broke open an enduring schism in the wider abolitionist movement, as more conservative elements withdrew their membership, and resources, to form the American and Foreign Anti-Slavery Society. Led by Lewis Tappan, the New York silk merchant whose fortune had funded the movement since 1833, this faction was one of two more pragmatic groups that, while still immediatist, were more willing to maintain their ties to relatively mainstream religion and to experiment in the political arena. The Tappan wing, strongest in New York City, in the Burned-Over District in western New York, and throughout Ohio, held the loyalties of the great body of converts radicalized in the Finneyite revivals. In Ohio this wing of the movement was led by Theodore Dwight Weld, who in 1834 had led a group of student rebels who challenged the colonizationist professors at Cincinnati's Lane Seminary, withdrawing to found Oberlin College in northern Ohio, funded by the Tappan fortune. While the Garrisonians were increasingly hostile to organized religion, the Tappan wing were committed to remaining in communion in their churches, typically the Congregationalists and New School Presbyterians expelled from the Presbyterian General Assembly in 1837. But the Tappanites' comfort with evangelical Christianity was tied to their conservative stance on the "woman question." There would be a much more limited and traditional role for women in their movement. This position certainly helps to explain the dramatic drop in the number of women petitioning Congress. From a peak of 52 percent of petitioners to the 25th Congress, women's petitioning plummeted over the early 1840s to 15 percent of the much-reduced petitioning to the 28th Congress.[67]

Women—both Garrisonian and Tappanite—may have receded from their aggressive public activism of the late 1830s, but they remained deeply committed to abolition. They increasingly focused on the means of "persisting in the cause," most centrally in organizing the annual antislavery fairs that were launched in many northern cities and towns in the 1840s to raise money for the movement. The fairs often spanned the divisions between different factions and increasingly became a space in which the aspiring antislavery political leadership could meet and mingle with a broad base of supporters. Women also became the epicenter of an antislavery commerce, supplying needlework, food, paper goods, pamphlets, and books on antislavery themes, practical and sentimental. A generation or more of young northerners came of age flocking to the fairs and grew up in households stocked with their antislavery material culture. Such fairs and artifacts would have enduring influences down to and through the coming war.[68]

While the Garrisonians embraced radical causes and opposed all participation in the political arena, their opponents' conservatism opened the way back into politics. The Tappan wing supported the Liberty Party, committed to antislavery, which ran James Birney for president in 1840 and 1844. Here they were allied with a third abolitionist faction, which revolved around Gerrit Smith, another source of funding for the movement. The Smith faction was really an upstate New York group, with core supporters in Smith's village of Peterboro, in Madison County, and out to the west through Syracuse and Rochester along the Erie Canal, New York's Burned-Over District, so named because it had been swept by the fires of religious revival. The Smith wing focused its attention on the New York State Anti-Slavery Society, on the Liberty Party, and particularly on developing a new understanding of the United States Constitution. William Lloyd Garrison saw the Constitution as fundamentally a proslavery document, written by and for the slave interest. Smith and his allies flipped this argument, constructing an antislavery interpretation from the Preamble of the Declaration, the guarantees of due process in the Fifth Amendment, and the federal guarantee of a "republican form of government" in all of the states.[69]

Each of these three groups of abolitionists made up a circle of connection and reinforcement inside of which their ideals could be supported and nurtured in the face of a hostile or indifferent northern majority. Sealed off from a hostile word, they were to some degree sealed off as well from the other factions in the movement. Though necessary for the survival and development of the movement, these boundaries impeded effective communication with that outside world. This was of course a gradient—with the Garrisonians the most alienated and liminally "other," and the Tappan and Smith factions somewhat more attuned to the mainstream of northern society. Beyond them lay another domain of antislavery thinking, the supporters of the American Colonization Society. Some of the colonizationists—with doubts—were tending toward immediatism, though they were at the far end of the spectrum from the Garrisonians. Here a Connecticut group stands out, led by Leonard Bacon of New Haven—and by Lyman Beecher, who by the 1830s had established himself at the Lane Seminary in Cincinnati. His daughter Harriet, quietly supporting abolitionism while dutifully refraining from asserting herself in public, would eventually play a central role in communicating antislavery sentiment to the northern white public.[70]

Antislavery Victories

Abused and divided "outsiders," the abolitionists nonetheless achieved some real successes in the 1830s. First, they established a vibrant press, building on the example of the black activists of the 1820s and Benjamin Lundy's *Genius of Universal Emancipation*, through which Garrison had his transformative experience. Garrison's *Liberator* was the founding pillar of this abolitionist press. But as the movement took hold, a number of new papers were formed in 1835 and 1836, both by the American Anti-Slavery Society in the postal campaign and as the public faces of the regional and ideological factions: the *Pennsylvania Freeman* in Philadelphia (Garrisonian), the *New York Emancipator* and James Birney's *Cincinnati Philanthropist* (both in the Tappanite wing), and the *Utica (N.Y.)*

Friend of Man (Smith wing). In 1840, with the open schism, competing papers were established in New York: the Garrisonian *National Anti-Slavery Standard* and the Tappanite/pragmatic *American & Foreign Anti-Slavery Reporter*. As some of these papers folded in the 1840s, a new generation of papers emerged. From 1845 the *Anti-Slavery Bugle* was the voice of Garrisonianism in Ohio's militant Western Reserve, while Frederick Douglass's *North Star*, established in Rochester in 1847, was broadly affiliated with Gerrit Smith and an emerging political antislavery. The next year a new paper was launched virtually in enemy territory: Washington, D.C. Gamaliel Bailey had taken over the *Philanthropist* from Birney, but in 1848 he moved to the national capital and began publishing the *National Era*. In their competing multiplicity, these antislavery papers provided a vibrant platform for advocacy and information to a growing abolitionist constituency across the North.[71]

Events in 1836 drove an explosion of petitions to the 25th Congress, but they also began to add new and perhaps less utopian voices to the movement responding to the gag rule and the expansion of slave territory, threats less to black freedom than to white liberties. In contrast to the female majority signing petitions asking for the end of slavery in the District of Columbia, a distinctly male majority (almost 70 percent) protested the adoption of the gag rule, and a slightly smaller male majority signed petitions regarding the admission of new slave states and territories—perhaps a signal shift toward a masculine politics in antislavery. At the center of this new focus was the possibility of the admission of the vast Mexican province of Texas into the American Union. In 1836, the same year that the Pinckney gag rule was imposed, American slaveholders rose up against Mexican rule in Texas and then launched a bid to add this territory to the United States. Wider fears began to grow about slavery's grip on the federal Union, and they began to capture the attention of men in politics.[72]

The purity of the immediatist doctrine on the immorality of slavery was thus diluted in a new sense of the threat of the slave interest to the rights and economic future of northern free whites. Nonetheless, despite its utter neglect by most historians, the anti-Texas petitioning to the 25th Congress was actually a great triumph. The scale of its onslaught intimidated President Martin Van Buren. Terrified by the rout of the Democrats in the 1837 New York State elections, he sidelined the admission of Texas, destined to be a massive slave state, for what would be seven and half years.[73] And the threat of slavery in Texas contributed to the defection of one Jacksonian Democrat. Senator Thomas Morris of Ohio, in a February 1839 speech defending the right of petition, transformed the Jacksonian Money Power into the antislavery Slave Power. Morris declared in the Senate that "the slave power has the assurance to come into this very Hall and request that we—yes, Mr. President, that my constituents—be denied the right of petition on the subject of slavery in this District." He felt himself "compelled into this contest, in defence of the institutions of my own State, the persons and firesides of her citizens, from the insatiable grasp of the slaveholding power as being used and felt in the free States." Morris's articulation of the threat of the Slave Power, if detached from the abolitionists' mission of immediate abolition, laid the groundwork for an emerging, unspoken confluence of the interests of northern free whites and southern enslaved blacks.[74]

During these years, with the surge and petitioning and then the schism—and reordering—in abolitionist ranks, there were further important developments in the national profile of antislavery politics. In Congress, John Quincy Adams, elected to the House in 1832 to a uniquely important post-presidential career, began to take a central role in managing the abolitionist message in Congress. Adams, along with two of his close associates, William Slade of Vermont and Seth Gates of western New York, was elected as an Anti-Mason, a populist party that swept much of the North between 1826 and the mid-1830s. He was outraged by the slaveholder plan to gag northern petitions. In 1836, though not an advocate of immediate emancipation, he began to disrupt the House every year by presenting armloads of petitions and defending the First Amendment rights of the petitioners.[75]

Adams was also deeply involved in a wider project to reassert the terms of Lord Mansfield's *Somerset* decision that slavery existed only in "positive law," meaning actual legislation stating that slavery was legal and spelling out the terms of its enforcement. From 1836 slaves transported to the North were freed by courts in Massachusetts and Pennsylvania, and important arguments were made in cases brought in Ohio under the *Somerset* precedent. In 1838 Theodore Dwight Weld drafted an influential document, "The Power of Congress over the District of Columbia," arguing that Congress, unimpeded by state laws, had the positive power to abolish slavery in the District on the grounds of the Fifth Amendment, in which the federal government pledged that "no person shall be deprived of life, liberty, or property, without due process of law," and the Preamble's injunction to "establish justice." John Quincy Adams and Joshua R. Giddings of Ohio, another of his close associates in the House, also applied the *Somerset* principles to the cases of the slave ships *Creole* and *Amistad*. They argued that slaves on ships in international waters were outside the domain of the positive "municipal" law of any slaveholding state, and "in resuming their natural rights of personal liberty, violated no law of the United States." *Somerset*'s logic of "positive law" had its limits, however, since the Constitution guaranteed that all state laws would be respected by the federal government, and until the Civil War this limitation prevented all but the most radical abolitionists from arguing that Congress could directly emancipate the slaves and abolish slavery. But twice in debate in the House, Adams developed a *Somerset*-based theory of slave law that had first been proposed by Alexander Hamilton in the 1790s, and would in 1862 become the basis of the Emancipation Proclamation: in time of war, slaves could be freed under martial law, superseding state law. This opinion could be and would be the eventual grounds for ending slavery in the United States, confirmed and extended by the Thirteenth Amendment.[76]

Antislavery constitutionalism was the core position of the political abolitionists. While the Garrisonians retained control of the American Anti-Slavery Society and its network of influential newspapers, the more pragmatic factions led by Gerrit Smith and Lewis Tappan coalesced around a new departure, the Liberty Party, which put forward James Birney as a candidate for the presidency in 1840 and again in 1844. In the early 1840s, Liberty activist Joshua Leavitt began to work as a lobbyist in Congress, feeding Adams information for his House speeches and court arguments, taking extended notes of congressional debates, and constructing the network that was starting to build a core of antislavery political activists.[77]

Of course, the slaveholding interest had long feared the impact of an extension of *Somerset* to American soil. The successful defense of *Somerset* principles would make the North a legally protected zone for fugitives. *Somerset* principles were first adopted in Massachusetts in a fugitive case in 1836 and spread across the northern states in the years following in a thicket of legal doctrine, administrative practice, and statute—the personal liberty laws—making the rendition of fugitives more difficult. A major Supreme Court decision in 1842 invalidating some of the personal liberty laws only encouraged northern states to pass additional statutes forbidding state officers from cooperating in the capture of fugitives and denying the use of local jails by slave hunters. In New York, Governor William Seward moved a law through the legislature requiring that fugitives be given a jury trial. In Massachusetts, the case of fugitive George Latimer exploded into state politics, pulling disillusioned country Whig voters to the Liberty Party, which gained a controlling balance of power in the Massachusetts House.[78]

On a closely related front involving many of the same people, an increasingly organized network was emerging to aid fugitives, becoming known over the 1840s as the "Underground Railroad." This system had its origins in informal piecemeal efforts to aid both fugitives and free blacks being kidnapped into slavery, formalized with the establishment of the New York Vigilance Committee in 1835. By the middle of the 1840s, a dense fabric of vigilance committees and "stations" was firmly in place across the North, with active participation of both black and white abolitionists. While many Garrisonians were involved, some hung back, impeded by their doctrines of pacifism and nonresistance and arguing that this work distracted from the long-term goal of total emancipation. Indeed, in New York, Pennsylvania, and Ohio, most of the aid to fugitives was organized by the more political Tappan and Smith wings of the movement. In New York City the Tappans' American and Foreign Anti-Slavery Society became in essence a front for the Vigilance Committee, while upstate Gerrit Smith's New York State Anti-Slavery Society was deeply intertwined with the New York State Vigilance Committee. Confrontations with slave catchers over the 1840s were becoming more organized and violent. The ongoing flight of slaves from the upper South, along with this increasingly coordinated network and the northern personal liberty laws, all intensified southern slaveholders' anxiety that the North was undermining slavery.[79]

The elements of a national antislavery political strategy were certainly under construction. Unfortunately, these were only some of the elements needed for a national political victory. Antislavery was unable to stop either the annexation of Texas in 1844 or the launch of the Mexican War in 1846, both critical victories for the Slave Power. The decade between 1836 and 1846 was an important building period for the antislavery movement. But these were also frustrating and demoralizing years. Press and party—both voters and leadership—stood in the way of a rapid advance of antislavery opinion and organization after the surge of petitioning in the late 1830s. In sum, the mainstream press barely mentioned issues of slavery and abolitionism well into the 1840s, and the abolitionist press really reached only a limited circle around the most committed. As one abolitionist paper put it bitterly, the mainstream "servile, lickspittle press" simply served the interested of the "slave power."[80]

Of the two parties, the Democrats were arrayed more decisively with the South and against the abolitionists. The Whigs played a complicated game with antislavery voters, supporting their cause as far as possible but staying in the national and state party organizations, with their promise of patronage. Thus from 1836, northern Whigs established themselves as friends of antislavery by voting almost to a man against the gag rule, while they continued to work with their southern colleagues on the Whig economic agenda. The opportunity to win the 1840 election with William Henry Harrison stalled any migration of Whigs, either officeholders or voters, to the new Liberty Party. Indeed no antislavery congressman was ever elected as a Liberty Party candidate, and when Free Soilers were elected in 1848, they were a tiny minority. Minorities—when they held the balance of power—could influence the shape of legislation, but they could not control it. Not until the mid-1850s would any state legislatures, and certainly not Congress, be controlled by majority antislavery representation.[81] The Liberty Party itself attracted a microscopic fraction of the national electorate: 6,800 of 2.4 million votes in 1840 and 62,000 of 2.7 million in 1844.

Thus northern Whig leadership and voters showed a strategic reluctance to move toward a third party. But northern Whigs, and increasingly in the 1840s many northern Democrats, were looking over their shoulders at the brewing, if not yet politicized, antislavery opinion manifested in the 600,000 abolitionist signatures on petitions in the late 1830s. In Congress, Adams, Giddings, and Slade were the public core of a small, shifting group of committed antislavery Whigs, who might number as many as thirty-five or so in any given House. But of them only Giddings could be seen as a de facto Liberty congressman. Giddings was censured by the House in the spring of 1842 when he advanced a set of *Somerset*-based resolutions on the case of the *Creole* slave ship rebels. Abandoned by the Ohio Whig Party, Giddings won reelection with Liberty support, though he officially returned to Washington as a Whig.[82]

Such was the power of party in the 1830s and 1840s. Clearly, the rise of abolitionist sentiment, organization, and political mobilization in these decades was a fundamental, necessary precondition for the end of slavery. Persistent radical voices put the cause of the slave before the nation. By and large, as George Templeton Strong remembered in 1860, the nation did not really respond, other than to strengthen the defense of slavery and push for its expansion. Abolitionists—black and white—were outsiders to the two great parties, marginal to the structures and levers of power. While

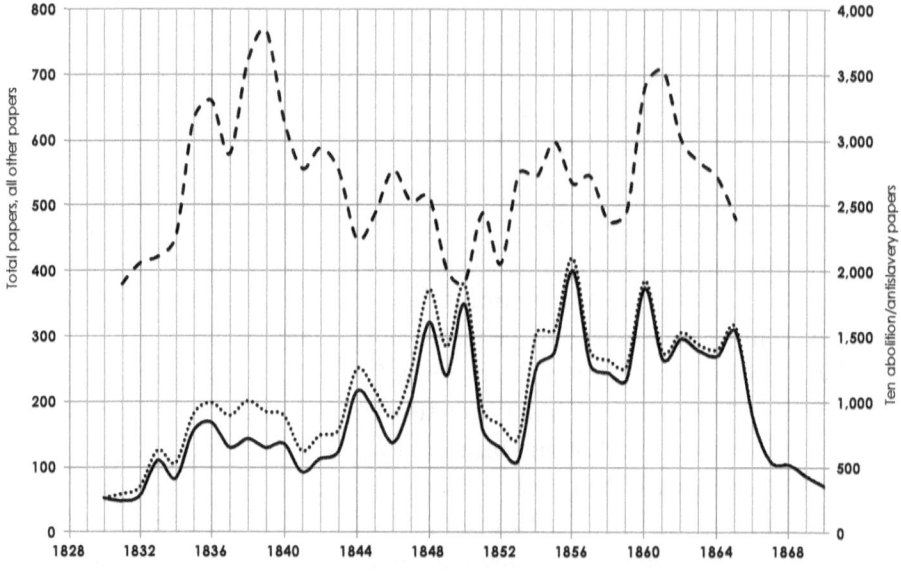

FIGURE 1. "Slavery" per 10,000 "articles" in free state and abolitionist/antislavery papers, in America's Historical Newspapers, 1830–1870

The word "slavery" appeared in ten abolitionist or antislavery newspapers in about three thousand of ten thousand articles, as against roughly two hundred of ten thousand articles in all other free state newspapers. While the term peaked in the antislavery newspapers in the late 1830s and 1856–1857, it peaked in the mainstream press in 1844, 1848, 1850, 1856, 1860, and 1864, with a distinct trough in 1851–1853. (The sample of ten abolitionist/antislavery newspapers includes the daily and weekly *National Era, Emancipator and Republican, Liberator, Emancipator, Frederick Douglass' Paper [North Star], Liberty Party Paper, Friend of Man, Pennsylvania Freeman, Philanthropist*. The *National Anti-slavery Standard* is excluded since its title generates hits on "slavery.")

SOURCE: America's Historical Newspapers (accessed November 2017).

antislavery mobilization was from the mid-1830s more advanced and pervasive than proslavery mobilization in the South, it failed for two long decades to achieve a synthesis that would recruit a northern majority to the antislavery cause. Most important, the antislavery coalition lacked two key and mutually dependent elements denied to them by the maturing of the Second Party System in the

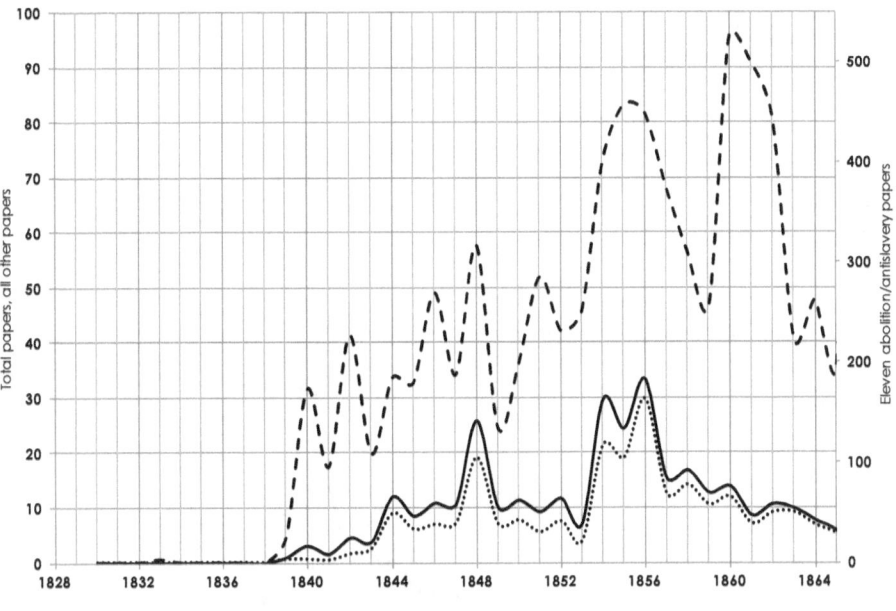

FIGURE 2. "Slave Power" per 10,000 "articles" in free state and abolitionist/antislavery papers, in America's Historical Newspapers, 1830–1870

A comparison of the appearance of the term "Slave Power" in newspapers in America's Historical Newspapers. "Slave Power" rose to peaks of roughly 425 and 525 in articles in abolitionist and antislavery newspapers, while it peaked at far lower levels in the mainstream papers in 1848, 1854, and 1856. (The sample of eleven abolitionist/antislavery newspapers includes the daily and weekly *National Era, Emancipator and Republican, Liberator, Emancipator, National Anti-slavery Standard, Frederick Douglass' Paper [North Star], Liberty Party Paper, Friend of Man, Pennsylvania Freeman, Philanthropist*.)

SOURCE: America's Historical Newspapers (accessed November 2017).

late 1830s at the moment of their greatest triumph: leaders and voters. From 1840 antislavery was able to field a party committed to sectional principles, something that the South would not do for years to come. But effective leaders and voting majorities were both in short supply; they remained committed to the major parties, most significantly the Whigs. Without votes, political leaders would not break from their patronage systems; without convincing leadership,

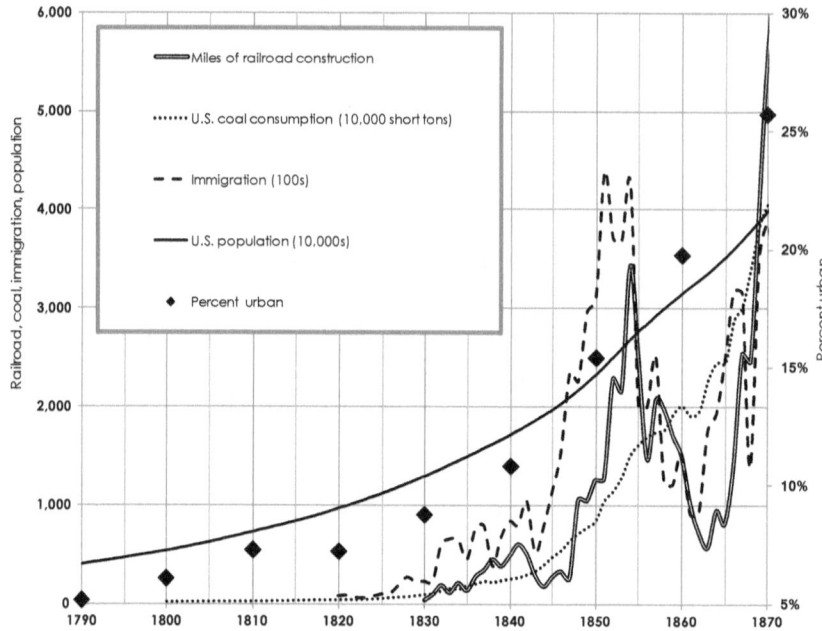

FIGURE 3. United States population and economy, 1790–1870

The late 1840s and early 1850s were years of profound structural shifts in the United States, with urbanization accelerating, immigration peaking between 1851 and 1854, and railroad construction peaking in 1854. This was also a period of the dramatic expansion of the telegraph.

SOURCE: *Historical Statistics of the United States: Millennial Edition Online* (New York: Cambridge University Press, 2006), Aa9, Aa699, Ad1; Db60; Db67, Df882.

voters would not commit their votes. The Liberty Party received symbolic support from only a fraction of abolitionists in 1840 and 1844. Even after the drama of the southern-driven Mexican War, the Free Soil Party, led by a coalition of Whigs, Democrats, and antislavery men and deploying a powerful rhetorical assault on the "Slave Power"—still could not attract even 15 percent of the vote in the free states in the 1848 election. Zachary Taylor, one of the conquering generals of the Mexican War, was swept into the presidency on a tide of Whig support from all sections of the country, as most northern Whigs clung to the party. But the primacy of national parties over the politics of slavery was clearly under stress, and over the winter, spring, and hot summer of 1850, the party politicians made a desperate effort to shore up the structure of the Union as it had existed since 1787.

Structures, Cracking

By 1848 powerful forces were moving, preparing the ground for the decisive turn to a politics of slavery that would come in the early 1850s. Economic crisis and depression were followed by a roaring recovery entwined with technological transformation, and with war, territorial expansion, and European revolution. All of these forces intensified the arena in which the politics of slavery were contested, driving each side in a struggle to reinforce—or transform—the structures that defined the Union.

The 1820s and 1830s had seen a long-running and accelerating economic boom, fueled by the peace dividend of the end of the European Napoleonic Wars, coupled with the settlement of the trans-Appalachian West, both on the cotton frontier and along the northern lakes and rivers. English demand drove up the price of cotton, and two new global systems developed, one linking English factories, southern plantations, and northern farms and shops, and another linking English capitalism, Andean silver, Indian opium, and Chinese markets. Then, in the late summer of 1837, the global boom began to collapse. The American economy fell into a deep six-year depression; the price of cotton fell by almost two-thirds, banks failed by the hundreds, and laboring families in New England survived on clams and dandelions.[83]

The recovery that began in 1843 and surged to new highs to the late 1850s was as traumatic as the depression. On the one hand, cotton experienced a long boom that stretched to the beginning of the Civil War. While cotton prices rose only moderately, the value of the total crop doubled twice between the mid-1840s and 1860, reaching $100 million by the early 1850s and $200 million by 1860. This surge in production was the result of great suffering and new lands to cultivate, as slaves picked faster and faster under the lash, and as cotton planting spread west into Texas.[84] This economic expansion was also fueled by a revolution in steam technology, the first technologically driven "Schumpeterian" surge of modern economic growth. The logic and power of steam overwhelmed the small-town agrarian North. The new technology, well supplied with coal, could operate free of the constraints of distance and friction that had defined the organic economy. Railroad construction jumped in 1848, peaking between 1851 and 1854. Steam-powered factories based on the new high-pressure engine began to multiply on land, while steamships dramatically cut the time needed for the Atlantic crossing. Even before the railroad boom began, and providing the labor for its construction, immigrants, first from Ireland and then from Germany, surged into the northern states, driven from Europe by potato famine on the one hand and failed revolution on the other. Immigrants, native whites, and blacks met in growing cities: the urban population, which had increased nationally from 7 to 10 percent between 1820 and 1840, surged 20 percent in 1860. Counties throughout the North became dramatically differentiated, with what had been moderate-sized centers morphing into small cities, while populations leveled off and fell in smaller towns.[85] With the railroads came the telegraph, sending news and market information in a matter of minutes over distances that recently had required weeks of transit. In January 1846 there had been a total of forty miles of telegraph wire in the entire country; two years later, two thousand miles had been built. In January 1850, as the Compromise debates began, there were twelve thousand miles of wire; two years later there were more than 22,000 miles. Hundreds of cities, towns, and villages had local telegraph stations. Expensive postal rates that had been in effect for decades were suddenly lowered between 1845 and 1851 after a long political campaign. Letters mailed in the United States tripled in volume per capita in the two decades after 1840. The world suddenly got much smaller.[86]

The whiplash of depression and recovery left Americans on edge, nervous about life in a shifting, changing world. Native-born Protestant men, white and black, committed themselves to temperance in the depths of the depression of the early 1840s, only to be confronted with more exuberant drinking behavior among equally stressed populations of Catholic Irish and German immigrants.

While Democrats welcomed immigrants and their votes, a toxic tangle of pro-temperance, anti-immigrant, and anti-Catholic sentiment began to emerge among Whigs of all persuasions from the mid-1840s.[87]

The booming economy of the late 1840s—following constitutional changes in many states—also had a powerful effect on the ideological contest that lay at the center of the struggle between Whigs and Democrats. In essence, that struggle had hinged on the policies advanced by Federalists, National Republicans, and Whigs to blend public authority and private capital in various kinds of corporations whose monopoly privileges were justified as advancing the public good. Starting with the Jeffersonian attack on the Bank of the United States in 1791, the Democratic opposition had seen the threat of corruption, aristocracy, and tyranny in these corporations. Indeed, some of the more complex public-private entities had failed miserably in the depression, dragging entire state governments into bankruptcy. The solution came in a wave of new constitutional changes in states throughout the country, establishing stricter boundaries between public and private, solving problems in financing infrastructure, and mandating general incorporation laws. As these measures took effect, much of the ideological wind in the sails of party died down. Indeed, Democrats jumped into the new economy, especially in railroading, and by 1849 the general expansion had lessened the pressure for a protective tariff, a traditional bulwark of the Whigs' "American System." While the ideological structures dividing the two parties seemed to be crumbling, the behavioral structures remained firmly in place: the pursuit of power through party discipline and party patronage showed no signs of disappearing. But some of the party ties were beginning to fray.[88]

With this profound reshaping of common experience came a literal reshaping of the nation. Texas was finally annexed in the last days of John Tyler's administration, and James Polk's election brought the country into war with Mexico within fourteen months. The Mexican War was a Democratic war, and a slaveholders' war, and was deeply unpopular among northern antislavery Whigs, among them one-term congressman Abraham Lincoln of Illinois.[89] The mid-1840s thus saw a reintensification of sectional stresses, made manifest in the sectional division of the national Methodist and Baptist associations over the issue of slavery in 1844 and 1845.[90] Even some northern Democrats opposed the war. In 1844 they had finally turned decisively against the gag rule, and in August 1846 Democrat David Wilmot of Pennsylvania introduced the first of his "Provisos": that no territory conquered with federally appropriated funds should become part of a slave state.[91]

Wilmot's rebellion was deeply entangled with patronage politics. Wilmot was part of the Van Buren faction of the party, and Van Buren's nominations had been rejected by the Polk administration. But this intraparty squabble had broad consequences. By the summer of 1848, plans were in the works to build a new party based on the premise of the Wilmot Proviso—that there must be no expansion of slavery into federal territory. Meeting in Buffalo in August 1848, a coalition of antislavery Whigs, Liberty Party men, and New York Democrats of Van Buren's "Barnburner" faction, with black activists Frederick Douglass and Henry Highland Garnett in attendance, voted to nominate Martin Van Buren as the Free Soil candidate for the presidency. John Quincy Adams, at his desk to the last, had died of a stroke on the floor of Congress that February. In one of the great symbolic gestures in American political history, the convention nominated his son Charles Francis Adams to be Van Buren's running mate.[92] While Free Soil stood on the platform of the Wilmot Proviso—Congress should allow no slavery in the territories—its opponents took competing positions that would play critical roles in the coming years. The Democratic candidate, Lewis Cass, advanced a new doctrine of popular sovereignty, also known as squatter sovereignty: let the settlers of a territory decide through a constitutional convention whether they would be a slave state or free state. Zachary Taylor, not only a soldier but also a Louisiana sugar planter, seemed to be a proslavery man of the South, though he had quiet reservations as to whether slavery should be imposed on regions where it had been forbidden under Mexican law.[93]

Meanwhile, revolution was in the air in 1848. All across continental Europe people rose in a struggle for liberal democracy. The suppression of the German revolution accelerated mass immigration into the United States. The English Chartist and land reform movements had important echoes in the ideology of free soil, resulting fourteen years later in the passage of the Homestead Act in 1862. But in 1848 the results of the election, though encouraging, were limited for the antislavery movement. Taylor won with strong support in both North and South, and Van Buren received 291,000 votes, about 10 percent of the national vote and 14 percent of the free state vote. While this was a dramatic increase from the Liberty performance in 1844, these 1848 voters constituted a group roughly the same size as the number of men signing antislavery petitions in the late 1830s.[94] Moreover, Taylor and Cass had drawn strong party votes in both the North and the South. This was not a dramatic new departure. As the historian Joel Silbey has concluded, "a sectional crisis had certainly erupted, but the reigning political world, if shaken, had not unraveled."[95]

In April 1820, as the nation was shaken by the Missouri crisis, Jefferson had called the eruption of conflict over slavery a "fire bell in the night." Six months later John Quincy Adams, then serving as James Monroe's secretary of state, had been far more explicit in an evening conversation with a Pennsylvania politician. Slavery was, he predicted, "the destined sword in the hand of the destroying angel." Disunion over slavery "would be followed by a servile war in the Slave-holding States, combined with a War, between the two severed portions of the Union." And "calamitous and desolating" though it would be, this war would bring "the extirpation of Slavery from this Continent," a result "so glorious . . . that as God shall judge me I dare not say that it is not to be desired."[96] Such were the fears and predictions of two of the surviving Founders. But almost three decades later this apocalyptic transformation had not come to pass. Despite the best efforts of a generation of abolitionist activism, Van Buren's mobilization of national parties still held the line against the great rupture.

To a degree. While the national parties prevailed in 1848, antislavery had entered the national arena. Nine Free Soilers had been elected to the House from districts in eight different states, where they would be led by antislavery veteran Joshua Giddings. In the Senate, Whig John P. Hale was reelected by the New Hampshire state assembly as a Free Soiler, and in a dramatic coalition with Democrats, Liberty leader Salmon P. Chase was elected as a Free Soiler from Ohio. If they could not determine policy in Congress, the Free Soilers could disrupt. They would have an immediate impact on the 31st Congress when it first convened in December 1849.

CHAPTER 2

Structure Defended

The Compromise of 1850

EVENTS IN 1848 and 1849 set the stage for the explosive struggle over the "slavery question" that would consume Congress and the nation for the first eight months of 1850. These events of portent literally spanned the nation from coast to coast.

In January 1848 gold was discovered at John Sutter's mill in the Sierra foothills of California; news began to spread in August, and the Gold Rush was on. Thousands of young men flocked to California to seek their fortunes, and by the spring of 1849, the territorial population had met the statehood requirement. There was an obvious need to replace military government with local law and order. Meeting over a period of six weeks in September and October 1849 in the coastal town of Monterey, the California statehood convention drafted a constitution banning slavery. Ratified in November and delivered to Washington just as the 30th Congress was about to convene, California's free state constitution—demonstrating that the Wilmot Proviso could be enacted by local popular sovereignty—would drive new efforts to resolve conclusively the future of slavery.[1]

On the other American coast, a more secret venture was under way. Late that September, under threat of sale following the death of her owner, a slave known as Minty, more famously Harriet Tubman, left her home plantation near Bucktown, in Dorchester County on the Eastern Shore of Maryland. Making her way by night through the open pinewoods of Delaware and along a chain of abolitionist Quaker households north into Pennsylvania to join the free black community in Philadelphia, Tubman would return repeatedly to carry fugitives north along this Underground Railroad.[2] Her life was thus poised between two flows of African American movement—legal, coerced slave trade to the Deep South and illegal, self-liberating flight to freedom in the North and Canada. Each of these trajectories would capture white American imaginations and passions in the coming decade.

Tubman's flight in 1849 and repeated returns in the years that followed were necessarily secret. But events unfolding since spring 1848 on the Potomac had put the issues of fugitives and the slave trade at the center of public affairs in Washington, D.C. On April 13, 1848, as the first reports of revolution in France were circulating, seventy-seven slaves and free people of color—many of them servants of leading Washington families—boarded the coastal schooner *Pearl* to escape the capital's slave regime. When winds died several hours into their voyage down the Potomac, they were recaptured and dragged in chained coffles back to Washington. Held in the city's notorious slave pens, they were sold into the southern trade. Proslavery men rioted against known antislavery figures in Washington, while public meetings in New York City were called to raise money to buy a few of the victims out of slavery.[3]

The very public fate of the *Pearl* captives, reversing Tubman's secret self-liberation, reverberated through life in the nation's capital and in the halls of Congress for months to come. Five days after the *Pearl* fugitives were captured, Massachusetts representative John Palfrey introduced a resolution calling for an investigation of the proslavery rioting of the preceding days. During contentious debate, Joshua R. Giddings and John P. Hale, antislavery leaders in the House and Senate, were grilled regarding their prior knowledge of the escape. While the *Pearl* fugitives were summarily sold off— and a lucky few recovered—the trials of white men captured on board the *Pearl* began in July. Convicted on charges of slave stealing and illegal slave transportation, they were given long terms at hard labor; their cases would drag on well into the following year. They would be pardoned by President Millard Fillmore in 1852, but over the summer of 1848 both the *Pearl* crisis and the news of the impending Free Soil convention in Buffalo was driving conflict in the 30th Congress.[4]

Proceedings in Congress to establish territorial government in Oregon had been under way in the Senate since January 1848, and in late May—in the wake of the *Pearl* crisis—they were swept into a great compromise that potentially opened to the door to slavery in the entire arc running from New Mexico to Oregon. The plan seemed to suggest that slavery might be established along the Pacific coast north of the 36°30′ line that had settled the Missouri crisis in 1820–1821. As the Free Soilers gathered in Buffalo in early August, and in the press of legislation in the final days of the first session of the 30th Congress, northern Democrats joined with northern Whigs to reject this plan and rammed through a free soil bill for Oregon that the Senate was forced to accept.[5]

As soon as the second session of the 30th Congress opened on December 4, 1848, slavery was on the table, and tensions flared. President Polk urged that the admission of new territories be settled in "a spirit of harmony and concession, and of equal regard for the rights of all and for all sections of the Union." In the Senate, Lewis Cass's ally Stephen Douglas announced a bill for California statehood.[6] But things were much more volatile in the House, where two antislavery leaders—both recently involved in the *Pearl* crisis—forced debates on the status of slavery in the District of Columbia. A proposal by Palfrey to repeal all federal laws supporting slavery and the slave trade in the District was quickly suppressed, as was a resolution by Ohio's Joshua Giddings that all adult males, including slaves, be given the right to vote in a convention on the future of slavery in the District. These radical measures failed to gain the backing of many northern Whigs or Democrats. But in the same week these representatives did provide the decisive support for free soil resolutions repeating the Wilmot Proviso language banning slavery in the Mexican territories. Then on December 21 a radical resolution to prohibit the slave trade in the District squeaked through by a 98–87 margin.[7]

This vote and the wave of antislavery resolutions, debated in the context of the *Pearl* rescue proceedings, set off a hostile reaction among southern congressmen. They met on December 23 to defend the amplified federal consensus and to condemn any effort in Congress "to impair or destroy the right of property in slaves." When they convened again on January 15, 1849, they issued an "Address of the Southern Delegates in Congress." Written by a committee of five chaired by John C. Calhoun of South Carolina, their "Address" made it clear that both slave flight to the North and northern "hostility to that part of the constitution which provides for delivering up of fugitive slaves" were uppermost in their minds. They were concerned about the unprecedented number of antislavery resolutions already presented in the first month of the session. Giddings's resolution was a particular threat, with great portent for the future: giving the vote to blacks in the District would be the first step toward revolutionary turmoil. In their minds, the voting blacks would now be the masters: "We would, in a word, change conditions with them—a degradation greater than has ever yet fallen to the lot of a free and enlightened people, and one from which we could not escape, should emancipation take place."[8]

They had reason to be afraid, because, at least for rest of this session, the tide of opinion in the House was shifting strongly against them. A week before, on January 8, one of this southern caucus had introduced a bill in the House to revise and improve the enforcement of the fugitive slave laws. This proposal was swept away (100–79) by a united front of northern Whigs and northern Democrats, who then twice voted (on January 10 and 31) for resolutions calling for an end to the slave trade in the District. These votes were an important departure, as northern Democrats were joining northern Whigs on core issues on the abolitionist agenda rather than simply on the issues of slavery and the territories. But those issues were not off the table, since the more proslavery Senate had been working on a bill to admit California as a state, as proposed by Douglas in

January. The proposal stood in late February as an amendment to an appropriations bill that would replace all Mexican law in California with federal law, once again a de facto advantage for proslavery forces, since Mexico had expressly abolished slavery. Once again the Senate's proslavery-tilted territorial measure was rejected by the House, and as the 30th Congress finally adjourned in early March 1849, it adopted a stopgap measure to extend military rule in California to July 1850.[9]

The 30th Congress had been deadlocked on slavery issues between the Senate, where a united South with some northern backing could support slavery, and the House, where proportional representation was dominated by northern states, increasingly hostile to slavery. The questions of the future of slavery and the slave trade in the federal District of Columbia, of slavery in the territories as they became states, and of the "recovery" of fugitive slaves were all left on the table, unresolved. Zachary Taylor was inaugurated as president as the 30th Congress adjourned in March 1849. The next Congress, the 31st, elected in November 1848, would not convene until December 1849. With word of the suppression of the European revolutions rumbling across the Atlantic and the news from California arriving daily, the details of the California constitution were anxiously anticipated. But this news did not arrive in eastern ports until the middle of November 1849, so the political establishment was caught in a growing anxiety throughout the entire year.[10] A decision was essential, one somehow satisfactory to all parties. The 31st Congress would take up the task of settling the outcome for the new territories acquired from Mexico in 1847. And southerners would take the opportunity to solve the threat to their mobile property posed by Harriet Tubman and the *Pearl* captives.

The coming crisis in Congress in 1850 was intensified by a long struggle over the election of the Speaker of the 31st House. Victors in the 1848 election (which had actually been scattered across the various states between August 1848 and November 1849), the 31st Congress finally convened on December 3, 1849. The first order of business was the election of a Speaker, which in 1847 had proceeded relatively smoothly, with only three ballots required to select Whig Robert C. Winthrop of Massachusetts. But the political landscape in the House had been changed in one small but significant way in the 1848 election.

Democrats maintained a slim 113–107 majority over the Whigs in the new 31st House, but nine Free Soil representatives, elected from districts stretching from New Hampshire to Indiana, held the balance of power. The Whigs were confident that the new Free Soil minority would caucus with them and easily reelect Winthrop, but such was not to be the case. On the first ballot, eight votes for David Wilmot (still officially a Democrat) and two for Free Soiler Horace Mann of Massachusetts, plus ten other scattered votes, denied the majority to either Winthrop or Democrat Howell Cobb of Georgia. The stalemate continued for a week and over thirty ballots, until the Free Soilers cut a deal with an Indiana Democrat to trade votes for key committee assignments and commitment to the terms of the Wilmot Proviso. When this deal was exposed, the balloting continued for days until it was decided to accept a plurality vote rather than a majority vote, and Cobb was elected on the sixty-third ballot on December 22.[11]

The dust had barely cleared when the titans of Congress moved to "end all agitation" with a "final settlement" of all the questions of slavery challenging the country. A grand compromise would restore harmony and unity in a collective confirmation of the federal compromise of 1787: union with slavery. Or so they hoped.

THE DEBATES over the so-called Compromise of 1850 would take more than eight months and destabilize the Union profoundly. As the House struggled over the Speakership, President Taylor's remarks to Congress repeated Polk's lame duck injunction for a territorial solution and sectional peace. Noting the result of the California constitutional convention and the necessity of congressional action, Taylor hoped that Congress would "maintain ... the harmony and tranquility so dear to all" and "abstain from the introduction of those exciting topics of a sectional character which have hitherto produced painful apprehensions in the public mind."[12]

As soon as routine business had been cleared away, two weeks after the end of the long Speakership battle in the House, debate was launched in the Senate, on less-than-friendly terms. Dueling state resolutions were introduced and wrangled over: one from the Missouri General Assembly on January 3 denying Congress any constitutional right to act on slavery in the territories and threatening that the South would take "measures" for "our mutual protection against the encroachments of northern fanaticism"; one from Vermont five days later condemning slavery as "a crime against humanity, and sore evil on the body-politic."[13] With debate over the future of the territories flaring, Senators James Mason of Virginia and Andrew Butler of South Carolina quietly worked to put a draconian revision of the Fugitive Slave Act of 1793 on the agenda, announcing their intention on January 3 and presenting full discussions late in January.[14]

Slaveholders wanted territory, but they particularly wanted control—control over self-liberating slaves, and over the neo-*Somerset* personal liberty laws and organized Vigilance Committees of the northern free states. Over the next eight months, Congress would struggle over the terms of grand compromise that would settle the great questions of the day regarding slavery and reinforce the structures of the settlement of 1787, union with slavery. The first to be proposed and the last to be finalized, the Fugitive Slave Act would inflame northern sentiment against slavery and the Slave Power.

As the Senate began to tangle with these issues, President Taylor sent another message to Congress on January 21 asking for swift action to admit California and New Mexico immediately as states, on the basis of the results of constitutional conventions. This proposal was intended to bypass the coming struggle and to "remove all occasion for the unnecessary agitation of the public mind." California had already voted a free state constitution, and everyone assumed that New Mexico would do the same; nonetheless, Taylor's proposal, if popular among northern antislavery Whigs, was dead on arrival with all of the southern members of Congress.[15]

After almost a month of deadlock, two of the grand old figures in the Senate who had played key roles in the Missouri Compromise thirty years before sat down to work out the details of a new compromise. On the evening of January 26, Henry Clay of Kentucky visited Daniel Webster of Massachusetts to discuss a plan to roll up all of the issues regarding slavery into a single compromise that everyone could accept. Clay had already laid claim to the sentimental origins of the Union several days before. He had introduced two petitions, one for a Revolutionary pensioner's widow and another asking that Congress appropriate funds to buy both George Washington's estate at Mount Vernon, now fallen into disrepair, and a manuscript copy of Washington's Farewell Address. On this last proposal he was supported by Webster but debunked by a suspicious Jefferson Davis. On the twenty-ninth, Clay stood to announce that he had in his hand "a series of resolutions" which he asserted would shape "an amicable arrangement of all questions in controversy between the free and the slave States, growing out of the subject of slavery."[16]

On the fifth and sixth of February, Clay laid out the details of "a great national scheme of compromise and harmony." In its broad outlines, this was the legislation finally enacted months later in early September. California would be admitted as a free state; greater New Mexico would be established as territories "without the adoption of any restriction or condition on the subject of slavery"; and the boundary between Texas and New Mexico (an issue that threatened to flare into armed conflict into the summer) would be established and the state debt of Texas assumed. While "it was inexpedient to abolish slavery in the District of Columbia," as abolitionists had been demanding since 1835, the slave trade in the District would end. This minimal consensus on the slave trade in the District was to be balanced by a drastic revision of the fugitive slave laws.[17]

Clay assumed that these measures would advance on their own, which in the end they did. But after another week of inconclusive debate and Jefferson Davis's blistering demand for slave territories, making an explicit threat of secession and war, his more moderate Mississippi colleague Henry S. Foote interrupted the proceedings.

He proposed that the issues be diverted to a committee to craft an "omnibus bill" that would command universal support, since it would contain something for everyone. It would take until mid-April before this committee—with Clay in the chair—was formed, returning a report in early May. Over the next ten weeks the "omnibus" was amended and battered and slowly bled before it died in the Senate on July 31. At this point Illinois Democrat Stephen A. Douglas emerged as the powerbroker, and in six weeks crafted a series of separate majorities in the Senate and then the House to move these measures forward as separate bills. The last, the Fugitive Slave Act, passing in the Senate on August 23 and the House on September 12, was signed into law by the president on September 18.[18]

This president, however, was not Zachary Taylor but Millard Fillmore. Taylor, whose popularity in the South had utterly collapsed as his "administration plan" for immediate free soil statehood for California and New Mexico became clear, had been sidelined for much of the spring. After a sudden summer illness, he died on July 9. Fillmore, a ticket-balancing northern conservative Whig, saw it as his mandate to support Clay's compromise by whatever means possible. As the spring dragged on and summer heated up, an undercurrent of violence ran through the debates, captured most dramatically when Henry Foote, after weeks of feuding and baiting, drew a revolver on Thomas Hart Benton of Missouri.[19] And while the entire session was filled with grand rhetoric, two speeches in early March powerfully shaped the message of the demand for compromise.

The first of these was by John C. Calhoun of South Carolina, who since the Nullification Crisis of 1828–1832 had been the intellectual architect of southern extremism. Now stricken by a final illness (he would die on March 31), Calhoun came into the Senate on March 4 on Andrew Butler's arm, and his speech was read by James Mason.[20] It included three critical premises: agitation, equilibrium, and fugitives. Calhoun started and ended with agitation. "Agitation on the subject of slavery" had led to "almost universal discontent" in the South, and that discontent was endangering the Union. It had a long history and "an explosive tendency." He used the word "agitation" at least twenty-seven times in his speech, often four to five times in a single paragraph. Echoing Martin Van Buren in 1827, Calhoun appreciated how "the strength of party ties" had acted as an "immense force . . . exerted against agitation, and in favor of preserving quiet." They were, he argued, "the strongest cord, of a political character," consisting of "the many and powerful ties that have held together the two great parties which have, with some modifications, existed from the beginning of the Government. They both extended to every portion of the Union, and strongly contributed to hold all its parts together." But this strength had gradually broken down in the North, as men of "both of the great parties" had given in to "agitation," manifest in the flood of abolitionist petitions. And agitation against slavery, Calhoun argued, was set in the context of the collapse of "perfect equilibrium." As of 1787 the two sections had stood in virtual parity in terms of overall population, but the latest census was showing that the population balance had been disturbed, and the North now had a clear numerical majority, recently manifested in the antislavery House votes at the end of the 30th Congress. Worried about this balance since the era of nullification, Calhoun in 1849 had just finished his *Disquisition on Government*, in which he argued that numerical majorities were illegitimate and tyrannical, and that the just government would be ruled by a "concurrent majority" in which minority interests (meaning slaveholders) would have a veto power.[21] In his eyes the North already had a prevailing power in Congress, and this disequilibrium, coupled with limits on slavery in the territories and ongoing agitation, spelled doom either for slavery or for union.

How, Calhoun asked, could the Union be saved? Not by "eulogies" or invocations of George Washington (a swipe at Clay and Webster), nor by plans to admit territories either immediately as free states (Taylor's plan) or by a form of popular sovereignty (Clay's). Rather, there must be "a full and final settlement on the principle of justice." In such a settlement the North must concede the South's rights to new territories, it must settle the issue of fugitives, it must "cease the agitation on the slavery question," and it must amend the Constitution to restore "the equilibrium between the sections." Echoing his 1849 address and anticipating the articles of secession signed in Charleston ten years later, Calhoun focused on "the delivery of fugitive slaves," since "the violation in this particular" was "too notorious and palpable to be denied."

Daniel Webster had been preparing his address for weeks, and he was clearly stunned to hear Calhoun's. As soon as Mason finished reading, Webster jumped to his feet to ask that a colleague yield his spot so he could—"as early as Wednesday or Thursday . . . have the opportunity to address the Senate."[22] Three days, later on March 7, he began his speech famously, notoriously, "not as a Massachusetts man, nor a Northern man, but as an American." Bowing to Calhoun throughout—figuratively and then literally when the latter shuffled into the Senate chamber—Webster offered at the outset that "it is not to be denied we live in the midst of strong agitations." Trying to review recent history dispassionately, he let it be known that the "abolition societies" were full of "honest and good men" but had "produced nothing good or useful"; rather, "they created great agitation in the North against southern slavery." There was no need to legislate against slavery in California and New Mexico because of their "Asiatic" geographies: "natural law" would preclude slavery. Then speaking as the man who had defended the Union in 1832 against nullifier Robert Hayne, he declared that "peaceable secession is an utter impossibility."[23] But in the end the weight of the Constitution now rested on the North:

> Never did there devolve on any generation of men higher trusts than now devolve upon us, for the preservation of this Constitution and the harmony and peace of all who are destined to live under it. Let us make our generation one of the strongest and brightest links in that golden chain which is destined, I fondly believe, to grapple the people of all the States to this Constitution for ages to come. We have a great, popular, constitutional government, guarded by law and by judicature, and defended by the affections of the whole people.[24]

The central theme running through his address was that of "constitutional duties." The North had a duty and an obligation to return fugitive slaves under the Constitution as written and ratified in 1787–1788:

> I desire to call the attention of all sober-minded men at the North, of all conscientious men, of all men who are not carried away by some fanatical idea or some false impression, to their constitutional obligations. I put it to all the sober and sound minds at the North as a question of morals and a question of conscience. What right have they, in their legislative capacity or any other capacity, to endeavor to get round this Constitution, or to embarrass the free exercise of the rights secured by the Constitution the persons whose slaves escape from them? None at all; none at all.[25]

Webster now stood with Calhoun: the survival of the Union depended on northern whites' sending black men and women living among them back to slavery.

Webster reiterated his position in the desperate days of mid-July, as the omnibus teetered on the brink of collapse. Dismissing the Wilmot Proviso as a "mere abstraction" and burying the fugitives under the Constitution—"the restitution of runaway slaves is not objectionable, unless the Constitution is objectionable"—he departed the Senate to join Fillmore's new cabinet as secretary of state.[26] Two weeks later Henry Clay's omnibus had terminally stalled in the house, and the younger generation took over in the form of the short and rotund Stephen A. Douglas, who managed the roll calls in short order. By August 15 the decisive votes had been taken on the territorial issues in the Senate. A week later he had pushed the fugitive slave bill through. The bill abolishing the slave trade, but not slavery, in the District of Columbia passed as a balancing afterthought in mid-September. Complicated by the byzantine wrangling over the Texas state debt and the interests of bondholders, the House debate finally started in late August. The key territorial votes were taken on September 6 and 7; they were followed within ten days by the linked bills on fugitive slaves and the D.C. slave trade. Fillmore signed all of the bills by September 20.[27]

Celebrated as it has been in some quarters, the Compromise was a sham, a temporary truce, a Band-Aid.[28] Clay's and Foote's omnibus project, if it could have been voted in a package, might have stood as a consensus, perhaps. But such a consensus now was clearly impossible, and in fact the voting under Douglas involved four shifting groups. Two groups, northern Democrats and southern Whigs, stood more or less in the middle and provided the consistent weight of votes for the territorial elements of the Compromise. They fell in and out of alliance with two other broad groups, the southern Democrats on the one hand and antislavery Free Soilers and northern Whigs on the other. (See Appendix, tables 3 and 4.) In one example, the September 7 House vote on admitting Utah as a territory under the terms of popular sovereignty (clearly rejecting the Wilmot Proviso), northern Democrats voted yes (30–17–7) with a strong southern majority (56–15–19), against northern Whigs and Free Soilers (10–57–16). Conversely, on the same day, in the vote to admit California as a free state, southern Whigs voted tepidly (17–10–1) with a free state landslide (122–0–14) again a strong southern Democratic opposition (10–46–6). Another strategy emerged with the two issues most directly connected to freedom and slavery—fugitives and the District slave trade—suggesting that deals were being cut in the final votes to push the entire package through. In the House balloting on these issues on September 12 and 17, there were record numbers of nonvoting members, an indication of the volatility of these issues of black movement—in flight to the North or sale to the South. Almost a third of the northern Whigs (23 out of 77) avoided the vote on the fugitive bill, and a third of all southern representatives avoided voting (27 of 90) on the slave trade in the District. If they had voted with their sections, neither bill would have passed. Similarly in the Senate, over half of northern senators (16 of 30) avoided committing themselves for or against the fugitive bill, including an amazing number of Democrats (9 of 15). Among these, interestingly, was Stephen Douglas himself, who was away on business in New York City when the vote was pushed through the Senate on August 23.[29]

In sum, as measured by votes on popular sovereignty in the Utah territory and on the fugitive slave bill, about 60 percent of northern Whigs voted consistently antislavery; the other 40 percent voted in some measure to advance the Compromise.[30] But that spring, and again in the autumn, pro-Compromise voices dominated the Whig space in the public sphere. As Clay introduced the outlines of his grand Compromise, and after pro-Compromise union meetings called by the Democrats in New York and Philadelphia, Whig-dominated union meetings supporting Clay and Webster were organized in New York and Baltimore and broadcast across the country in the press.[31] Whig speakers at the huge rally at New York City's Castle Garden on February 25 pledged "to the South, we know slavery is recognized by the Constitution . . . We will not infringe or violate those rights; we will not disturb your local laws or institutions; we will not throw barriers in the way of your obtaining all your constitutional rights." General Winfield Scott, Taylor's colleague in the Mexican War, appeared at Castle Garden to "rapturous applause" and hailed Clay's resolutions as "the basis of a harmonious and brotherly adjustment of a most distracted and perilous controversy."[32] After his March 7 speech, Daniel Webster was celebrated in letters signed by hundreds of unionist Whigs in Boston and New York. New York merchants sent him a gold watch, and his Washington banker cleared his debts.[33]

But the last of the measures to be voted, and one over which Fillmore hesitated for two days before signing, had revolutionary implications for the Union. The Fugitive Slave Law effectively nationalized slavery and established the reach of federal law enforcement power into all of the states, in ways that might have reminded people of the imperial commissioners authorized by the Stamp Act and the Tea Act of 1765 and 1773. It empowered federally appointed commissioners and marshals, under the authority of federal courts, to apprehend and return to slavery any fugitives, on the basis of an affidavit of a reputed slave owner, "in a summary manner." There would be no right to a trial by jury for anyone caught up in this dragnet. Northern state authorities were ordered to assist these federal marshals in the recapture of fugitive slaves, and fines were threatened for anyone who impeded such a "rendition." Officers capturing a fugitive slave were entitled to a bonus; officers not arresting an alleged runaway slave were liable to a fine of $1,000. Any person aiding a runaway slave was now subject to six months' imprisonment and a $1,000 fine. The Slave Power had come to the North.

This "final settlement" did not go uncontested. Throughout the long months of debate, antislavery figures in the Senate and the House rose repeatedly to oppose the spread of slavery into the territories, to advocate for freedom in the District of Columbia, and to oppose the Fugitive Slave Law.

The struggle began in the House about a week after the battle for the Speakership ended. On the thirty-first of December, two representatives from Ohio who had voted a straight antislavery position in the previous Congress rose in the House. Whig John Crowell announced a motion to introduce a bill to abolish the slave trade in the District of Columbia, while Joseph Root, now one of the nine Free Soilers, announced a motion for a bill to prohibit slavery in the former Mexican lands east of California. That same day Lucius B. Peck of Vermont had offered resolutions from his state legislature on the territories, the District of Columbia, and a proposed "Department of the Interior," the Vermont resolutions condemning slavery as "a crime against humanity and sore evil" and instructing the state's senators and representatives to work against its extension to the west, and against slavery and the slave trade "wherever either exists under the jurisdiction of Congress."[34] When these resolutions were introduced into the Senate on January 8, southern senators demanded that they be suppressed. John Hale of New Hampshire rose to support his Vermont colleagues, pointing to the "great and growing sentiment at the North at the overshadowing influence which the institution of southern slavery has had ... upon the legislation of this country."[35]

But the antislavery congressmen, Free Soil and Whig, generally bided their time while the outlines of the session's legislation took shape. In the House, representatives held their fire until Clay's early February grand proposal had been assaulted by Jefferson Davis and reshaped by Henry Foote. In the middle of the month, Joseph Root and Thaddeus Stevens of Pennsylvania spoke at length on the territorial issues, but Massachusetts Whig Horace Mann's speech ventured further. Starting with a vigorous defense of abolitionist and free soil principles, Mann developed a detailed argument on the power of Congress over the territories and the imperative of local laws governing slavery. Then he turned Jefferson Davis's threat of disunion against the South: their "riches have legs," he reminded southerners, and secession would put half of the South's slaves "within two days' run" of a 2,500-mile international boundary. After dwelling on the fugitive threat, he pointed out that the territories would remain with the national government, and then gleefully punctured southern hopes of an alliance with the British Empire. Britain was a hotbed of abolitionism, it had freed its slaves in the West Indies, and was governed by "Somersett's case," making it a haven for fugitives.[36]

Mann's speech was published in Boston and distributed widely. This and three other major speeches delivered in the Senate over two weeks in March, and also quickly published, would stand as the great antislavery orations during the Compromise debates. William Seward of New York, John Hale of New Hampshire, and Salmon Chase of Ohio took the floor in the wake of Calhoun's demand for a southern "concurrent" veto and Webster's invocation of the "constitutional duties" of the North. Seward was not known as a great orator, and on the eleventh of March his opening section on the status of California thinned the crowd in the Senate chamber. But turning from California to the demand for compromise, he attacked first Calhoun's insistence on an "equilibrium" and on minority control over the terms of compromise, and then Webster's demand that the northern states participate in the rendition of fugitives—the "extraction of slaves." Famously, Seward invoked a "higher law than the Constitution, which regulates our authority over the domain" defined by the nation's territorial limits. The higher law was manifested in "certain elements of security, welfare, and the greatness of nations . . . [:] the security of natural rights, the diffusion of knowledge, and the freedom of industry." Seward was plain: this higher law demanded the end of slavery, which might come about along one of two paths. Union could prevail and slavery would end "by gradual, voluntary effort," and with compensation. Down the other path lay ruin: "The Union shall be dissolved, and civil wars ensue, bringing on violent but complete and immediate emancipation."[37] Over the next two weeks, on the nineteenth and the twenty-sixth, Seward was followed by Hale and Chase in long set piece speeches rapidly published for the public. If their long historical accounts lacked the rhetorical force of Seward's "Higher Law" speech, they reinforced his challenge to Calhoun's union under minority control and Davis's threat of disunion.[38]

Important as were the rhetorical efforts by the small band of antislavery senators and representatives in Washington, a second track in antislavery politics reopened in the spring of 1850. Petitioning had been a critical force in northern opposition to slavery in the 1830s but had subsided considerably in the 1840s. In 1850 it would surge almost to the level of the 1830s.[39] (See Appendix, table 5.)

The first of the petitions came from a strong free soil county in north-central Pennsylvania. Presented in the House on the fourteenth of January, a week after the fugitive slave bill was announced, this petition asked that the entire 1793 Fugitive Slave Law be repealed.[40] For the next six weeks, through the end of February, 102 petitions were presented in the House and Senate. In the House, where the gag rule had collapsed in 1844, the petitions were shunted off to various committees, eventually discharged of their responsibilities in September 1850; in the Senate, where the gag rule survived, the petitions were summarily tabled.[41]

Of these 102 petitions a total of twenty, most apparently from Pennsylvania Quakers, asked for the total abolition of slavery or the relief of the free states from the burden of defending slavery. One, asking for a peaceable dissolution of the Union, set off a bitter debate in the Senate.[42] Only 19 of the 102 petitions mentioned the territories, in theory the focus of the debate. The majority (57 of 102) were focused on the question of slavery in the District of Columbia, an old issue now renewed by the recapture of the *Pearl*, the sale of the fugitives into the Deep South, and the imprisonment of the white agents Daniel Drayton and Edward Sayres, mentioned in thirteen of these petitions. Another eleven were concerned with the slave trade, but only four mentioned the fugitive slave laws.[43]

Thus, for the opening weeks of the Compromise debates, petitions arriving at the Capitol were concerned with the fate of slaves rather than the fate of territories. The focus was framed by the distant traumas of the slave trade, most recently dramatized in the capture of the *Pearl*. But early in March the thrust of the petitions shifted. Certainly the issue of slavery in the territories surged dramatically, but so too did the other vector of slave movement—the flow of self-liberating people coming to the North. And these petitions demanded that all such fugitives be given one of the most basic rights of citizenship, the right to a trial by jury.

This new direction was launched on January 28 in the Senate after the bill to revise the Fugitive Slave Law of 1793 had been under construction in the Judiciary Committee for several weeks. When it came up for debate on the twenty-eighth, William Seward, drawing upon his jury trial initiative as governor of New York, introduced an amendment that would require that anyone arrested as a fugitive would be "entitled to a writ of habeas corpus," to be issued by a federal judge, and that judge would then be required to ensure a jury trial for that individual. This amendment, which never made it into the final Fugitive Slave Law signed in September, was grounded in terms of hallowed legal tradition and a northern abhorrence for the kidnapping of free blacks. Since the bill as drafted allowed the arrest of so-called fugitives on the simple affidavit of a white claimant, the entire northern free black population fell under the threat of being kidnapped into the domestic slave trade. At the same time, the amendment would have granted actual fugitive slaves one of the basic rights of Anglo-American citizenship.[44]

Seward's amendment was widely reported in the newspapers, and in the following weeks the American and Foreign Anti-Slavery Society developed a circular presenting standard forms for petitions. Their first form was based on the language of his amendment, a "Petition to Secure alleged Fugitives the right of Trial by Jury."[45] The AFASS apparently printed up these forms in great numbers and distributed them widely, because when petitions for a fugitive's right to a jury trial first arrived in the Senate and the House—the first three presented by Seward on March 4—they were written in the precise language of the AFASS forms.[46] Despite the bruising debate over receiving these jury right petitions in the Senate on March 14,[47] they continued to flood into the House and Senate for the next several months, with a final burst between April 15 and May 3. Over these two weeks, 761 petitions were presented, often in great handfuls: 107 by Salmon Chase alone on April 15, and forty-six by Joshua Giddings on May 3, a banner day in the House, with 247 petitions presented by thirty-three representatives.

All told, 2,786 antislavery petitions were submitted to the first session of the 31st Congress, both House and Senate, between December 1849 and September 1850. By contrast, only forty-five proslavery petitions opposed them. Some of these supported either Henry Clay's compromise plan or the fugitive slave bill; others asked for compensation for escaped slaves. Two, as in a petition from Albemarle County, Virginia, presented by Senator Seward, boldly asked "that slavery may be extended by law into the free States of the Union."[48] One antislavery petition from Lunenburg, Massachusetts, presented by Senator Hale equally boldly proposed "that all territory acquired from Mexico, either by treaty or conquest, may be restored to that republic, as the best mode of adjusting all controversies arising out of the institution of slavery."[49]

These were certainly the outliers. The great body of the petitioning centered on the core issues of slavery in the territories, slavery in the District, and the fugitive slave bill. On the one hand, the largest number, almost half, were focused solely on the question of the territories, expressions of the Wilmot Proviso. On the other hand, more than half were focused not on the territories but on the abolitionist priorities of slavery in the District and fugitives from slavery. It is striking that the vast majority of petitions dealing with fugitives (637 out of 675) were signed in support of their basic rights of citizenship in a free state, as advanced by Seward on January 28. At forty signers per petition, these may have involved about 25,000 people. Representing slightly fewer than 25 percent of the petitions to the first session, this was a new but still emerging sentiment.

Overall, the petitioners were embedded in well-established abolitionist and free soil communities, if Ohio is any measure. Strong antislavery sentiment was still very much a minority position in the North, and people concerned about the fugitives were a minority of that minority. But they were emerging from the quiet of the 1840s in a rising militancy. The petitions sent to the 31st Congress suggest that throughout the North the fate of the fugitives under "Mason's bill" was debated and condemned in local meetings of antislavery societies and religious meetings, especially among Quakers, Methodists, and Free-Will Baptists. One such meeting was called in January 1850 among Quakers enraged by the capture of a fugitive by a neighbor in East Nottingham, Pennsylvania, a volatile neighborhood on the Maryland border close to where Harriet Tubman had passed through a few months before.[50] (See Appendix, table 6.)

As the direction of events in Washington clarified, local meetings were amplified by more central, organized efforts. The Ohio Whigs, meeting in Columbus early in February, warned against any changes to the fugitive law, as well as demanding an end to slavery in the District.[51] After the pivotal speeches of early March, antislavery forces in Boston organized a mass meeting at Faneuil Hall for the twenty-sixth. Among his attacks on Webster, Unitarian Theodore Parker condemned his willingness to give up fugitives without a trial as "unworthy of a Senator from Massachusetts." The Reverend Samuel Ward of Syracuse, a leading black abolitionist, was cheered when he hoped "that the bill shall never take effect."

The next day he warned an "anti-Webster meeting of the Colored Citizens of Boston" that as a result of Webster's speech, "slave-hunters were already infesting" cities and towns across the North.[52] On April 2 Ward shared the stage at the Tremont Temple with the fugitive activist Henry Bibb, who assailed Webster and proclaimed to his fellow fugitives that north of the Mason-Dixon line they had gained the "right of self-defense." Three days later the friends of antislavery gathered at the new Corinthian Hall in Rochester, New York, "to protest against the passage of any law in Congress converting the people of the North into bloodhounds to hunt down fugitive slaves."[53]

The most renowned public meeting condemning the Fugitive Slave Law took place in the lakeside town of Cazenovia, New York, near Syracuse, in late August. Organized by Gerrit Smith and Charles B. Ray, the black director of the New York State Vigilance Committee, the meeting brought together as many as fifty fugitives and about two thousand other abolitionists, including two sisters, Mary and Emily Edmundson, who had been ransomed from among the *Pearl* captives. The connection of this convention to the story of the *Pearl* was underscored when the activist William Chaplin, who had helped organize the *Pearl* escape, was arrested in Silver Spring, Maryland, with two fugitives, slaves of a senator and a congressman from Georgia, whom Chaplin had hoped to bring north to the Cazenovia meeting. The convention issued an "Address of the Fugitive Slaves" to the "Afflicted and Beloved Brethren" in the South, offering support, guidance, and warnings, and raised a subscription for Chaplin's defense.[54]

The Cazenovia Convention also issued a radical set of resolves that exposed the boundaries and schisms in the antislavery ranks. Black and white abolitionists in the wider orbit of Frederick Douglass and Gerrit Smith grew increasingly militant and uncompromising, in a trajectory that would lead to John Brown's raids in Kansas in 1856 and at Harpers Ferry in 1859. Their resolves condemned slaveholders as "pirates" and the Free Soilers as deluded: divorcing the government from slavery required either disbanding the government or "wielding it for the overthrow of slavery in every part of the Nation." They were particularly concerned about the fate of the imprisoned rescuers and fugitives in Washington following the *Pearl* and Silver Spring arrests, declaring that "the refusal to liberate these victims of the slave power" was "just cause for Revolution."[55] Over the coming month "Cazenovia" became a byword for violent radicalism, to the point where even Garrison's *Liberator* had to back away, printing a commentary that "fanaticism has its limits, beyond which it cannot go."[56]

Such had been the opinions of the proslavery and unionist public when the Garrisonian American Anti-Slavery Society had met in New York City in May. The abolitionist delegates were hounded from their first venue at the Broadway Tabernacle to the smaller Library Society Rooms on their second day, the crowd cheering for Webster, all gleefully reported in the Democratic press.[57] Things were not that different two weeks later in Boston, when the New England Anti-Slavery Society met at the Melodeon theater. Theodore Parker did present a notable speech condemning Webster, the Slave Power, and the proposed fugitive bill. But this meeting was also taunted by proslavery hecklers, and even the antislavery *Emancipator and Republican* was critical of the radicals of the "old organization," chiding, "We do not wish to see the cause of the liberation of 3,000,000 of men retarded by the insane ravings of fellows who wish to spit their venom out upon the Bible."[58]

If abolitionists were divided on a gradient running from Smith and Douglass at Cazenovia to the Garrisonians to the Tappanite *Emancipator*, antislavery politicians were uneasily divided as well. The nine Free Soilers had entangled the House in what Horace Mann, still in the Whig caucus, complained was "everlasting balloting." Writing to Charles Sumner in January, he worried that depending on Free Soil to stand against the Slave Power in Congress was "setting a mousetrap to catch an elephant."[59] Sumner's close friend Benjamin Silliman was even more caustic several days later. By allowing Massachusetts Whig Robert Winthrop to lose the Speakership, "abolitionism has again given to slavery every committee in Congress. I really begin to think that (you excepted) there is no sincerity in its professions. I am not sure but it intends to increase and perpetuate slavery. No other combination has been or will be so successful in adding and strengthening the peculiar institution. I am sure that Calhoun must consider Giddings, Root, et al., invaluable allies."[60] Joshua Giddings, ever the optimist, stood by his challenge to Winthrop and wrote to Sumner in December and June that the "old parties" were "disbanded" and "entirely broken up."[61]

In the final months of the Compromise debates, antislavery representatives spoke out against the fugitive bill, among them Thaddeus Stevens, mocking both the "wicked cause" of the South and the divisions in the "mercenary, driveling North."[62] But it was increasingly clear that the fugitive law was the essential quid pro quo for the entire Compromise package, and that the House managers were working to suppress antislavery voices. Notably, when Giddings got the floor on August 12, it was to address the volatile issue of the western boundary of Texas, not the fugitives slated to meet ten days later at Cazenovia.[63] When he finally got the floor the following February, Horace Mann complained that during the September fugitive proceedings, "this House was not a deliberative body. Deliberation was silenced . . . [W]e were silenced by force instead of being overcome by argument."[64] In the Senate, Seward briefly brought up the right of fugitives to a trial in his general discussion of the Compromise in July, and Salmon Chase led a minor rearguard action when the fugitive bill was finally pushed through the Senate in August.[65] Apparently under the threat of a duel over the issue of Texas, Seward—like Douglas—left town during the final fugitive bill debates.[66] He returned by the end of the month for the final three weeks of the session in September.

With the bill signed and the session ended, the fate of the fugitives now rested with the northern public. George Julian, a freshman Whig from Indiana, made this point when he took the floor at last on September 25, with a speech sarcastically titled "Healing Measures of Congress." Describing the terms of the Fugitive Slave Act, he was of the opinion that "a tissue of more heartless and cold-blooded enactments never disgraced the legislation of a civilized people"; he was confident that his constituents would never be "base enough to become the miserable flunkies of a God-forsaken southern slave hunter." He closed with a warning: "Sir, these questions are no longer within the control of politicians: party discipline, presidential nominations, and the spoils of office cannot stifle the free utterance of the people respecting the great struggle now going on in this country between the free spirit of the North and a domineering oligarchy in the South."[67] A wider domain of political action was about to open.

CHAPTER 3

Liminality Erupting in the First Crisis

Fugitives and the Northern Public

MUCH OF the northern public was considerably distracted that September of 1850. On the first of September the Swedish singer Jenny Lind arrived in New York from Liverpool on the steamship *Atlantic*, after a ten-day crossing. A crowd of thirty thousand assembled on the Canal Street piers. Having conquered the stages of Europe, Lind had accepted P. T. Barnum's offer of $1,000 a performance, plus expenses, for 150 performances across the country. She would be in New York City for four weeks before moving on to great acclaim to engagements in Boston and Philadelphia. After her first week in Manhattan, "Jenny Lind mania," George Templeton Strong confided in his diary, "continues violent and uncontrolled."[1] Fugitive African Americans had other concerns. On the twenty-eighth of September, two days after Lind departed for Boston and ten days after President Millard Fillmore signed the Fugitive Slave Law, its first victim, James Hamlet, was arrested in New York and returned to slavery in Baltimore. Harriet Jacobs, a fugitive from North Carolina now in New York, wrote sarcastically of these weeks, "While fashionables were listening to the thrilling voice of Jenny Lind in Metropolitan Hall, the thrilling voices of the poor hunted colored people went up, in an agony of supplication."[2] Meanwhile Harriet Tubman, working as a servant in Philadelphia and at Cape May that summer and fall, laid plans for her next move: that December she went down through Baltimore to the Eastern Shore of Maryland to rescue more of her relations from slavery.[3]

Despite the distraction of the great Swedish singer, the signing of the Fugitive Slave Law set off an explosion across the North, a wave of activism and action that flooded the newspapers for months to come. The new and spreading telegraph lines carried the news of fugitives and fugitive meetings far and wide, virtually instantaneously. The "magnetic telegraph" now bound the country together and made the impact of the fugitive law a national media event. The opening moments of this great wave came not in New York but in Pennsylvania, where news of slave catchers assembling spread quickly. By the time word of James Hamlet's arrest began to circulate in the nation's press, events in Pennsylvania were making the rounds by telegraph.

With their long border along the Mason-Dixon line and the Ohio River, Pennsylvania and Ohio constituted a borderland between freedom and slavery. Pennsylvania, with its simple survey line cutting straight west, was a magnet for fugitives making their way north from Maryland and Virginia, and as the Fugitive Slave Law pounded through Congress toward enactment, it rapidly became a battleground.

Along the Susquehanna River, at the state capital in Harrisburg, one drama had been unfolding since the middle of August, when three slaves arrived on horseback from Virginia and were quickly taken into the local black community. Harrisburg was a divided town, in which abolitionists struggled for years with a gang of city constables working as slave catchers. When they were arrested on the seventeenth of August by the constables, the fugitives were charged with horse stealing, since under Pennsylvania law no local officers could act against fugitives, nor could they be incarcerated in city or state prisons. When they came before the county judge on the twenty-third, he freed them on a ruling that the charge was a pretext for slave catching. Released from the courthouse, the three men were assaulted by their owners, who in turn were attacked by local blacks. While one of the fugitives escaped in the melee, the other two—along with eight other people—were arrested on a charge of riot and held for trial the following January. With the signing of the Fugitive Slave Law on Wednesday, September 18, however, a local United States commissioner was appointed, and on the thirtieth the two captured men were returned to slavery, making them—after James Hamlet—among the law's first victims.[4]

These unfolding events, widely published across the country, must have shaped the response to the Fugitive Slave Law in Pittsburgh. On the day President Fillmore signed the bill into law, slave hunters were already in town. Three days later, on Saturday evening, bands of fugitives began to leave for Canada, each organized under a captain, armed, and "resolved to die rather than be again carried into bondage."[5] By the following Tuesday, several hundred people had left, including "nearly all the waiters in the hotels."[6] Forty more left within a few days from neighboring Allegheny City. The Allegheny fugitives caused "quite a sensation" when they arrived 115 miles to the north in the town of Meadville on the evening of the twenty-eighth. "So great was the anxiety of many of the citizens to learn their story," it was reported, "that the fugitives, together with a large crowd, proceeded to the public square, where, in front of the courthouse, they told the story of their wrongs."[7] To the east in the mountains near Bedford, Pennsylvania, another group of fugitives was not so lucky. Discovered and assaulted by white farmers eager for rewards, one was killed and the others were quickly returned to their putative owners without even a hearing before a federal commissioner.[8]

James Hamlet, whose real name was James Hamilton Williams, was arrested on the morning of the twenty-eighth in New York City. Hustled through a hearing before a U.S. commissioner on the evidence of two eyewitnesses and a will, Williams was returned to Baltimore by federal marshals.[9] Harrisburg, Pittsburgh, Bedford, Hamlet: these stories began to flood the nation's newspapers in the first few days of October, transmitted by the "magnetic telegraph" and printed with accounts of the closing of the 31st Congress and Jenny Lind's progress from New York to Boston. They appeared with other stories about fugitives as well. Slave catchers were being spotted in towns throughout the North, and once secure fugitives from slavery were organizing, or already on the run. Those in Ithaca, New York, were on the move; in Utica sixteen armed fugitives were spotted along the Erie Canal; "excitement" ran through the black community in Oswego. In Albany, Springfield, Worcester, Lowell, and Boston, slave hunters were arriving or were on their way; a "great party" of fugitives left Lowell by train for Montreal. In Honesdale, Pennsylvania, slave catchers were hunting a particularly beautiful mixed-race woman, now married with children.[10]

The fears erupting from this sudden arrival of slave catchers, newly empowered under the terms of the revised fugitive law, also drove a wave of what can be called crisis meetings, typically launched by African Americans but often supported by local white abolitionists. The first seems to have been a "Meeting of Colored Citizens" in Springfield, Massachusetts, at the Free Church on September 17. Published under the headline "LIBERTY OR DEATH!," their resolves announced their "disapprobation" of the Fugitive Slave Law, upheld the doctrine that "'he who would be free, must himself strike the first blow,' and that resistance to tyrants is obedience to God," and formed themselves into a Vigilance Committee "prepared to resist" the coming slave hunters.[11] Two weeks later, on October 1, they mobilized a series of mass meetings, reputedly with thousands in the streets, some armed, addressed by local abolitionists active in the Underground Railroad. "Hard fighting" was predicted.[12]

Similar meetings took place in Oswego and Syracuse; in Albany there was a "Great Indignation Meeting among the colored people."[13] In Allegheny, as the first reported exodus began, a late September crisis meeting convened at the Mission Church, an Underground Railroad station, demanding laws to uphold habeas corpus and calling on the local ministers to address the crisis with their congregations.[14] In Boston, the first crisis meeting convened at the African Methodist church on Revere Street on September 30 "to concert measures." At a subsequent meeting on the fifth at the African Meeting House on Belknap Street, after an "address to the clergy" written by William Lloyd Garrison was adopted, a fugitive addressed the crowd, vowing "to defend his liberty with his life." According to one account, "He showed a long knife to the audience and advised them all to buy Colt's revolvers."[15]

The most dramatic of these African American–led crisis meetings took place in New York in the wake of James Hamlet's rendition to Maryland. Early meetings established a subscription fund to redeem him from slavery and asked the mayor for protection from federal agents. On October 1, as many as 1,500 gathered for an "indignation meeting" at the Zion Chapel at Church and Leonard Streets (where Harriet Jacobs's "thrilling voices of the poor hunted colored people went up"). By the end of the week the subscription had been filled and paid, and Hamlet was back in New York and being welcomed at an interracial mass rally in City Hall Park, five to six blocks from Zion Chapel, addressed by the leading men of color in the city. Two more "Repudiating meetings" were held in the next few days across the East River in Brooklyn and Williamsburg, then a separate town.[16]

These crisis meetings of late September and early October were led by those most directly affected—African Americans, both free citizens and fugitives. But as time went by, many of these black voices fell silent, as fugitives across the North departed in great numbers for Canada, and as "colored citizens" retreated in the face of the threat of kidnapping. In their place came a great wave of protest meetings led by white abolitionists and Free Soilers, exploding in October and not tapering off until the following May.

Some of these were meetings already scheduled by societies and parties, such as the annual meeting of the Western Anti-Slavery Society at Salem, Ohio, in mid-September; the Massachusetts Whigs and Free Soil conventions in Boston on October 1 and 2; the Pennsylvania Anti-Slavery Society on the fifteenth.[17] All of these scheduled meetings issued blistering attacks against the Fugitive Slave Act. Reform societies rose to the occasion, as when the American Missionary Association, meeting in Rochester on September

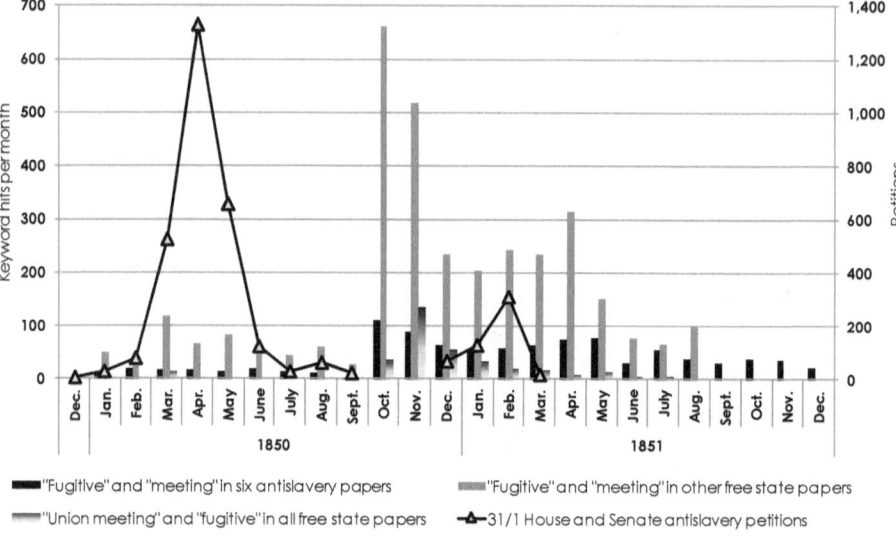

FIGURE 4. Antislavery petitions to the 31st Congress, and "fugitive," "Union," and "meeting" as keyword hits per month, free states, December 1849–1851

During the Compromise debates and the great burst of petitioning, there were relatively few publicized meetings, except for a few antislavery meetings in January 1850 and a few union meetings in February. A small number of hits suggest increasing numbers of antislavery meetings in July and August. Then in October 1850, these data point to an explosion in the number of antislavery meetings focused on the Fugitive Slave Law (more than 650 hits in October), carrying on at a high level through April 1851. Union meetings surged briefly in November 1850 (about 125 hits).

SOURCES: Senate and House journals, 31st Congress; America's Historical Newspapers (accessed December 2017).

24–25, resolved that "the Christianity of this nation is about to be tested in view of the recent act of Congress for making the whole free States a hunting ground for fugitive slaves."[18]

But there were many other more spontaneous abolitionist meetings convened to condemn the law, like those scattered across northern Ohio in late September and throughout the North in the following months.[19] And these grew in scale and reach; the largest after the City Hall Park meeting in New York on October 5 was probably the "immense meeting" in Faneuil Hall in Boston on

October 14, with speeches by Wendell Phillips, Theodore Parker, and Frederick Douglass. The Faneuil Hall meeting established a Committee of Vigilance and Safety, linking black and white abolitionists, a group whose commitment would soon be tested.[20] If the "fashionable" flocked to see Jenny Lind, the committed assembled time and again in towns across the North to protest the Fugitive Slave Law. In addition to innumerable meetings well into the following spring called specifically to protest the law, the antislavery papers from the middle of October offered guidance to the series of lectures and meetings that were available to keep resistance spirits high. In Ohio, the *Anti-Slavery Bugle* listed upcoming local meetings. In Rochester, Douglass's *North Star* promoted a course of lectures to be conducted by a fugitive, David Green Wheelbanks, at twenty-one locations around the surrounding county. Garrison's *Liberator* advertised the meetings of a "one hundred conventions" scheme developed in the 1840s, six lectures supported by the Chaplin Committee (organized to aid William Chaplin, a leader of the *Pearl* escape), and five upcoming events in the "Sixth Course of Anti-Slavery Lectures." And in Ohio, Rochester, and Boston, planning was under way for the antislavery fairs and bazaars that provided yet another opportunity to gather the faithful and to spread the message.[21]

The explosion of antislavery organization and meetings in October was met late in the month and into November by a countervailing pro-Compromise unionism. As in the previous spring, union meetings were held in both larger cities like Hartford, Albany, New York, Philadelphia, New Haven, and Boston, and smaller centers like Utica, New York; Bridgeport, Connecticut; Manchester, New Hampshire; and Bath, Maine.[22] Rallying again at Castle Garden on October 30, New York Whigs and Democrats hailed "*the Union*— THE UNION as it is—THE UNION with all the obligations of the Constitution." Wrapping themselves in the cult of George Washington, they formed a Union Committee of Safety. Among the hundreds of signers to the call for the meeting were many from the city's great merchant houses, which thrived on the southern trade. George Templeton Strong made his way to the rally and was "prepared to hurrah" for the Castle Garden platform. The "Northern

Nullifiers," as he called the antislavery protesters, were "opening a crevasse for anarchy."[23] As the party nominating conventions began to meet in the wake of the passage of the Compromise, the papers again were filled with Democratic and conservative Whig resolves, such as by the Philadelphia Whigs, celebrating "the settlement of the National questions which have recently disturbed this great Republic," and hailing "the noble efforts of Mr. Clay" and "the magnanimous course of Daniel Webster in the senate."[24] Religious authorities, particularly conservative Episcopalians and Presbyterians, joined political party managers across the North in calling for protection of the Constitution and the full enforcement of the Fugitive Slave Act. The support of "law and order," of "government and civil society," was paramount; the Union was "the Palladium of our National Happiness." The people of the North had a "religious duty of obedience to law." Among other voices, the influential Presbyterian *Christian Observer* published a series of articles on the sanctity of the Constitution and the necessity of northern obedience to the Fugitive Slave Law. Conservative northern clergymen gave voice and authority to biblical arguments for the justice of slavery.[25]

Such was the language deployed in 1850 to reinforce the nation's central political structure: the 1787 compromise on slavery and union. The watchword of the unionists was the threat of agitation. At Castle Garden the meeting's president, George Wood, opened the proceedings by expressing concern that antislavery "agitation" had "grown into a magnitude" that threatened "the dissolution of our Union, and the destruction of this glorious Republic." The meeting resolved that "a further agitation of the slavery question in Congress would be fraught with incalculable danger to our Union." And most important, Daniel Webster himself sent a letter to be read to the multitude, widely republished, expressing the hope that "wise and well-disposed citizens will forbear from renewing past agitation, and rekindling the flame of useless and dangerous controversy."[26] President Fillmore's message to Congress in December 1850 was designed to seal this understanding: the laws enacted in 1850 were "a system of compromise the most conciliatory and best for the entire country"; they were "a settlement in principle and substance . . . in its character final and irrevocable." They were, he warned Congress, "beyond your reach." There would be no revisiting these questions.[27]

Or so the president demanded. But abolitionists responded that agitation could not end. When George Julian of Indiana got to speak in the House in late September, he argued in no uncertain terms that "it is vain to expect to quiet agitation by continuing concessions to an institution which is becoming every hour more and more of a stigma upon the nation." The next spring, in a preface to an assault on the constitutionality of the Fugitive Slave Act, Horace Mann reminded the House that agitation had helped build the pillars of American culture, from the rise of Christianity to the American Revolution: "Discussion, or agitation, if you please so to call it, is one of the Heaven-appointed means by which truth is to be spread until it covers the face of the earth as the waters cover the sea." Finding it "remarkable that of the all the 'agitators' in the country, there is none more violent than those who are agitating against agitation," he demanded, "Is the right of agitation to be monopolized by those who denounce it?" Speaking in the summer of 1852, Ralph Waldo Emerson, the transcendentalist philosopher of Concord, considered it "very strange . . . that people supposed that the Compromise measures would put an end to agitation. It was not in the nature of man to be thus gagged."[28]

Abolitionists were clearly not gagged, and agitation continued, both on occasion in Congress but more dramatically outside of political structures. Opinion was being driven by disturbing local and personal dramas, experienced sometimes directly, more typically in print, that were coming to bear on the entire northern public. A sense of unsettling disorder, of the national "calamity" resulting from the Fugitive Slave Law, was at work on many levels, driving a fear that structures of morality and Constitution were suddenly crumbling.[29] The impact of and opposition to the law were marked by a qualitative change—a shift toward the public play of emotion and passion that differentiated the sectional dramas of the 1850s from those of the 1830s and 1840s.

This emotion was driven by the shock of seeing both the enforcement of law and direct action against law. Northern towns and cities were indeed invaded by slave catchers, working with local men who often had been deeply involved in kidnapping free blacks for sale into the southern slave markets. Twenty-one fugitives were arrested in the last three months of 1850 and another sixty-six in 1851. Some were lucky. The first to be arrested, James Hamlet, was redeemed with an $800 subscription, as was a fugitive arrested in Detroit in early October after an armed crowd threatened to storm the jail. One man arrested in Philadelphia, Henry Garnet, was freed for lack of evidence; a riot ensued when police tried to re-arrest him on the courthouse steps.[30] Few were so fortunate. Of the eighty-eight fugitives arrested in these fifteen months, seventy-seven were returned to slavery, of whom thirty-one were not even afforded a federal hearing, including the eight fugitives captured at Bedford, and another group of eighteen captured at New Athens, Ohio. Forty-one of these arrests were in Pennsylvania alone, including a long series in Harrisburg and others in Pittsburgh and Philadelphia. Dozens—perhaps hundreds of others—were targeted and pursued.[31]

Very few of these arrests were made in New England, and all of those that were took place in Boston, where they produced highly publicized dramas. The first such drama actually never got to an arrest. William and Ellen Craft had escaped from Georgia in 1848 by rail and steam packet and had been living in Boston for almost two years when the slave hunters arrived on October 19 and checked in to the United States Hotel. The Boston Vigilance Committee then acted on their pledge "at all hazards, to resist unto death, any attempt on our liberties." A crowd of several thousand crowded around the Georgian slave hunters when they ventured out from their hotel, while Lewis Hayden and Theodore Parker hid the Crafts in safe houses. Parker led a delegation to visit the Georgians in their room, suggesting that they leave town. As the Georgians departed for New York, the Crafts escaped to Portland, Maine, where they boarded a steamer for Halifax and from there on to Liverpool.[32] In February 1851 another posse arrived from Virginia, looking for a fugitive named Shadrach Minkins, who was working as a waiter at the Cornhill Coffee House. Minkins was grabbed and jailed, but the Vigilance Committee first used legal tactics to delay the proceedings, and then an all-black crowd led by Lewis Hayden burst into the courtroom and pulled him away. Hidden in an attic, Minkins was sent on his way to Montreal. Over the next several weeks, the committee helped at least one hundred other fugitives follow him out of Boston.[33] These efforts, however, were not enough to protect Thomas Sims, a bricklayer arriving in Boston as a stowaway the same day that Minkins crossed into Canada. In April, Sims was arrested and quickly remanded to his owner, conveyed to the Boston docks surrounded by police and volunteers.[34]

THE EVENTS of the autumn and spring of 1850–1851 put a host of disturbing images before the public, images that were the essence of liminality, of the condition of transition, of moving between conditions.[35] The crisis raised pervasive questions about settled life, about household and community integrity. It called into question the certainties and securities of northern life, forcing the white population to think carefully about their assumptions regarding the boundaries of respectability and the stability of constitutional order. Indeed some began to talk about revolution. But the majority of the northern public stood in silence, shocked or bemused, caught in the profound dissonance between the structured order in their lives and the disorder erupting around them.[36]

At the center of this disorder lay the dissonance between a language of citizenship and a language of movement in descriptions of African Americans in the northern press. This was—if we might return briefly to the anthropology framing this argument—the dissonance between structure and liminality. On the one hand, northern free blacks were repeatedly described as "colored citizens" in the more antislavery newspapers. Traditionally this term had come into play when black sailors from the North were imprisoned in southern seaports; this issue was debated during the Compromise summer.

But starting in October 1850, these papers repeatedly took notice of meetings of "colored citizens": "A meeting of the Colored Citizens of Springfield, Mass., was held in the Free Church"; "Pursuant to a call, a public meeting of the colored citizens of Trenton assembled in Mt. Zion Church."[37] This was language that resonated with the key demand regarding fugitives presented to the 31st Congress: individuals arrested on the suspicion of having fled slavery must be assumed to be citizens until proved otherwise at a trial by jury. But this core assumption stood in profound tension with an opposed language of motion. Fugitives living in northern towns were now in a state of excitement, in movement, in flight, in "stampede," in "emigration."[38]

This language of liminal disruption pervaded the circulation of accounts in the national press about the events in Pittsburgh in late September. Thus the widely cited notice in the *Pittsburgh Post* of this first exodus opened by stating, "We have heard many stories in regard to the movements of these unfortunate peoples." But it closed with a thought on shifting civic identities: "We had no idea that so many of the colored people of this city were runaway slaves. Many who have stood high in the estimation of the public, and were considered freemen by birth, turn out to be fugitives from the south."[39] The *Cleveland Plain Dealer* (interestingly a Democratic paper), reprinting this story, situated the fugitives' movement in the context of the Atlantic and domestic slave trade which defined the wider frame of African American experience: Africans had been stolen "from their native wilds [and] thrust into the suffocating hold of a ship" and then "sold for life to the cotton planter." Now their descendants were to "be pursued by the hounds of Government, and the alternatives presented as slavery or Death." As important, however, these Pittsburgh fugitives were "leaving their homes, wives and children," were being "driven from their homes and country."[40]

These themes of lost domestic stability and dangerous movement were pervasive in the more committed antislavery denunciations encompassing the fugitive condition, the Atlantic and domestic slave trade, and slavery itself.[41] These themes were captured repeatedly in the simple phrase, deeply embedded in the mid-century culture of sympathy, "torn from family." Slaves were "torn" from their families in both the domestic and Atlantic slave trades, Representative Henry Putnam argued on the floor of Congress in July 1850. "Where is the difference in principle or morals?" In a poem titled "The Land of Slaves" published in the *Christian Citizen* the same month, enslaved women were routinely "torn from husband" and children "for glittering gold, / and the mother from her children into distant bondage sold." In August, abolitionists were enraged that in Washington, D.C., the family of President Fillmore's coachman was suddenly "torn" from him and sold south into the domestic slave trade. "His grief was intense almost to insanity." The story of fugitives William and Ellen Craft, broadcast across the North in late October, was filled with the trauma of slave sale and family rupture: Ellen "was torn from her mother's embrace in childhood, and taken to a distant part of the country."[42]

Remanded fugitives were similarly being torn from their families. Wrongfully arrested as a fugitive, without the right to a trial, a northern free man of color would be "torn from his family," the *Milwaukee Sentinel and Gazette* warned in May 1850.[43] On October 6 Theodore Parker preached a widely reprinted homily on James Hamlet and the Fugitive Slave Law: "Already a man, a husband, has been torn from his family." Six months later, when more fugitives were arrested in Pittsburgh in the spring of 1851, the *Liberator* asked: "Do the people of Pittsburgh endorse the doctrine that a man shall not live with his own wife and support his children? Is the family relation no longer to be sacred in our midst? Can anyone be torn from his family on the oath of one man, and consigned to hopeless slavery, and is there no redress?" Harriet Tubman, on a second rescue mission in December 1850, was resolutely restoring such severed family ties.[44]

In its treatment of human beings as interchangeable commodities, slavery was constantly tearing families apart, constantly violating the structures of domesticity. Thus we can suggest that family and citizenship constituted core dimensions of the stable "structure" of American society, the core expectations of American life. The history of African Americans has been centrally a struggle to achieve these structures of citizenship and family, and in antebellum America they were achieved in some measure in the northern free states. But the passage of the Fugitive Slave Law suddenly highlighted both the difficulties of this achievement and its sudden erosion. Beyond stable civil and domestic structures, individuals moved in a liminal condition, against their will in the two slave trades and now driven in liminal flight to Queen Victoria's Canada. There was also a heroic liminality, captured in the image of the fugitive slave, bag slung on a stick, on the move outside the law, venturing through the dark wilderness to civilization, threatened with death while moving toward life. Fugitives moved from slavery to freedom, across state and national lines; remanded captives returned to slavery. Blacks on the move were liminal figures, outsiders, pariahs, distilling the paradox of American freedom and American slavery.

In 1850 these liminal figures gave form to a wider unease in the northern public. Stumping for John Palfrey in May 1851, Emerson told his audiences around eastern Massachusetts that "there is infamy in the air" and "an immoral law makes it a man's duty to break it at every hazard."[45] The Fugitive Slave Law, for the first time in more than a generation, made slavery a direct and palpable experience for northerners. It also challenged their understanding of their constitutional rights in the federal Union, making ever more real and palpable the threat of the Slave Power, beyond its manifestations in the 1787 three-fifths compromise, and in the 1830s gag rule, still in effect in the Senate. If the Constitution stood as a national structure, the structure of federalism, northerners saw it shifting and changing shape before their eyes. A series of constitutional questions for antislavery northerners became inextricably enmeshed with the image of the fugitive in motion.

President Taylor had argued in his January 1850 message to Congress that the regulation of slavery was an issue "left exclusively to the respective states," and thus not expected to become a topic "of national agitation."[46] But the Fugitive Slave Law nationalized the regulation of slavery. In requiring northern cooperation with fugitive rendition, the law violated the terms of the federalism that

Taylor himself upheld as the pillar of the Union. Whereas southerners had long upheld the internal regulation of slavery as a right under a doctrine of state sovereignty, now the tables were turned and northerners saw their state autonomy threatened. As Emerson put it in an address to a New York audience in 1854, "You relied on State sovereignty in the Free States to protect their citizens," but that sovereignty was overridden by "a hurricane of party feeling and a combination of moneyed interests."[47] The *Cleveland Plain Dealer* was more emphatic: "By this late act of Congress, passed by Southern slave-breeders and Northern compromisers, all the free States are made slavery ground, and all freemen, slavecatchers, if the law is to be enforced." The Western Anti-Slavery Society, meeting in Salem, Ohio, as the bill was signed, resolved that "the passage of the fugitive slave bill is a declaration of war, on the part of Congress, against the people of the non-slave States." The crisis meeting in Springfield, Massachusetts, the same week made the same argument: "The passage of the Fugitive Slave Bill is an encroachment upon the sovereign rights of the Free States." Continuing, the Springfield resolves argued that these states were now thrust out of civilization into an anarchic wilderness: "The soil of Massachusetts is thereby made slave-hunting ground."[48] This dark image of the unnatural violence of hunting down men pervaded the antislavery papers that month: slave catching was now the "Great National Sport," "The Hunt," "The New England's Slave Hunt." The law was the "blood-hound bill," the "man-stealing act," the "man-hunting act."[49]

Civil geography had been destabilized, made darkly liminal; abolitionists—echoing the Cazenovia resolves—moved on to a sense of liminal time. Springfield and Worcester urged nullifying resistance, as did Francis Jackson, president of the Massachusetts Anti-Slavery Society, invoking the doctrine of higher law. Jackson announced that abolitionism was a "revolution which for twenty years has been steadily going on"; abolitionist Parker Pillsbury, back from a spirited meeting in Marlborough, Ohio, was more immediate: "It is revolution now. The Fugitive Slave Law has done its work."[50] A speaker at the city meeting in Worcester warned that "if the attempt was made to take a fugitive here in the heart of Worcester," the result would be "not a rebellion but a revolution."[51] By October 17, The *National Anti-Slavery Standard* ran its crisis news under the headline "THE PROGRESS OF REVOLUTION."[52]

The truly revolutionary force at work in the autumn of 1850 was a renewed, now visceral basis for a political confluence between white northerners and African Americans. Ever since the debates over the federal Constitution in 1787, northerners had been concerned about the gerrymandering force of the three-fifths compromise, and in the 1830s the gag rule and the demands for the annexation of Texas had seen the coalescence of an understanding that the power of the slaveholders in the federal government—the Slave Power—was a threat to the civil equality of northern whites in the federal republic. But these were distant abstractions for most, and separated from the quiet flow of fugitives out of the South. The Fugitive Slave Act changed this equation dramatically. The agency, the self-liberation, of the fugitives in their midst was now directly affecting the lives of northerners. That self-liberation had impelled a nationalizing of the "regulation" of slavery. It put federally authorized slave hunters into northern towns and cities, and it required the cooperation of northern officeholders and citizens alike. It dramatically personalized the threat of the Slave Power, even if editors were keeping the term out of the press. And as the operation of the law unsettled white northerners' understandings of the federal Constitution, it ruptured their society and gnawed at their emotions. Black men and women, entire families long established in northern communities, suddenly disappeared, either in flight to Canada or remanded into brutal slavery. Beginning to shift a deeply entrenched racism pervasive in the North, the image of fellow human beings arrested, chained, and taken back to slavery pushed sensibilities from hostile indifference toward active sympathy. Such sympathy was manifested most obviously when remanded fugitives were freed by public subscription, as when, in at least twelve cases between 1850 and 1854, individuals returned to the South were ransomed in this way. Some were high-profile cases such as that of James Hamlet, apprehended in New

York; others simply involved neighbors in smaller cities and towns, such as Richard Gardiner, arrested in Pittsburgh in March 1851.[53] On occasion northerners expressed their sentiments directly. A fugitive hidden in Medford, Massachusetts, was—according to Lydia Maria Child—called by the firemen to the firehouse, where they "elected him a member of their company, and promised, at a given signal, to rally for his defense in case he was pursued, and to stand by him to the death, one and all."[54] For every rendition and rescue there were probably dozens of quiet, unrecorded acts of assistance to fugitives recently arrived or long resident in northern communities, as hundreds of northern blacks made their way to secure freedom in Canada. By the best estimate, while more than three hundred fugitives were arrested between 1850 and 1860, somewhere between ten thousand and twenty thousand successfully reached Canada. A vast network, black and white, moved fugitives north to freedom.[55]

Was the northern public transformed by the Fugitive Slave Act? Certainly not. We need to maintain a sense of context and proportion. Voting for Free Soil and Republican presidential candidates in the free states, an arbitrary but acceptable measure of antislavery sentiment, rose from 14 percent in 1848, to 45 percent in 1856, to 53 percent in 1860. By this standard, mobilized antislavery priorities captured barely a majority of northern votes in 1860, and accounted for well under 20 percent in 1850. While the South may not have been as united as he thought, John Greenleaf Whittier, both a sentimental poet and an antislavery editor and activist, captured this reality in a letter in 1856: "To my mind the answer is plain. The North is not united for freedom as the South is for slavery. We are split into factions, and the Slave Power, as a matter of course, takes advantage of our folly . . . It could do nothing against a United North."[56] Antislavery would eventually prevail in the North, but never in the emergence of a mass consensus in a contested, closely fought struggle. It would do so by intensifying the resolve of the committed, by sowing doubts among the non-committed, and by eventually adding enough numbers to succeed.

It is clear that the Fugitive Slave Law strengthened the resolve

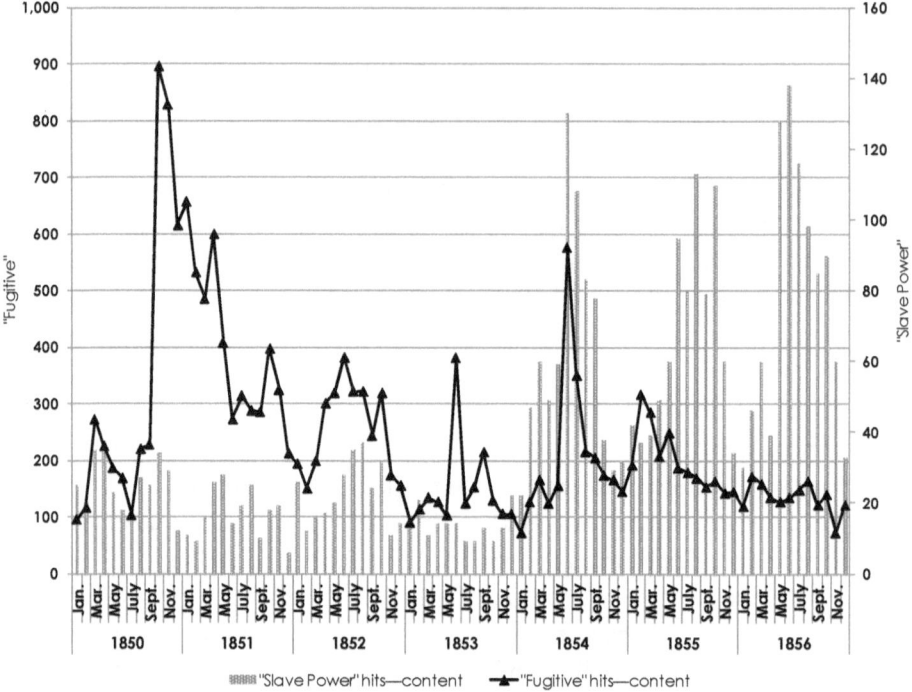

FIGURE 5. "Fugitive" and "Slave Power": Total hits, 1850–1856

Month to month, newspaper attention to the term "fugitive" surged with the signing of the Fugitive Slave Act, the Jerry Rescue, and the rendition of Anthony Burns; attention to the phrase "Slave Power" surged following the debate and signing of the Kansas-Nebraska Act, the rise of violence in Kansas, and the 1856 election.

SOURCE: Gales 19th Century Newspapers (accessed November 2010).

of the committed, whether abolitionists of long standing or recent converts to Free Soil politics. Some of them were already deeply involved in aiding the Underground Railroad. But how the Fugitive Slave Law acted upon the broader mosaic of white northern opinion, of Whig and Democratic persuasion, is the essential question. While strategic figures in the antislavery leadership came from among disaffected Democrats, they were relatively few in aggregate; the Democracy would never be more than a minor source of new voters for the antislavery cause. The majority of antislavery conversion would come from moderate-to-conservative Whigs, and ultimately from a rising generation, too young to vote in the early 1850s.[57] But the editors of the Whig *Boston Evening Transcript* certainly spoke for a majority in October 1850 when they observed, "'How long can the country stand all this?' is a question full of moment, and fraught with consequences formidable to contemplate."[58]

We have a few windows onto the personal thinking of some of those who stood outside the small but intensifying antislavery consensus. They too were affected by the stressful, volatile liminality of these months—by the tensions between a rhetoric of the "sacred obligations of law and constitution" acting on a foundationally law-respecting public and the constitutional and emotional uncertainty injected by the Fugitive Slave Law. Thus George Templeton Strong's diary was shot full of ambiguities in the fall of 1850. He supported the pro-Compromise union meeting at Castle Island, condemned the antislavery leadership, and was confident that slaves were "happier and better off" on the plantation than free blacks in the North. But within days he was deriding the slaveholders for wanting their self-liberated fugitives back "after their six months or six years respectively of independence and citizenship at the North," mocking the "philistines of Virginia," and snarling at the South Carolina nullifiers. On October 9 the dissonance was at a height; "slave-holding was not sin," he believed, but "the expediency of slave-holding, and the policy of upholding the institution, is a very different affair."[59]

Abraham Lincoln was also very much on the fence. Lincoln wrote famously in 1855 to his friend Joshua Speed in Kentucky of how the sight of shackled slaves on a steamboat trip he and Speed took together in 1841 had been a source of "continual torment to me." But in 1850, after a lackluster term in the 30th Congress, where he had supported the arrest of fugitives in the District of Columbia to the disgust of his housemate Joshua Giddings, Lincoln had absolutely nothing to say about slavery.[60] Illinois Whig Orville Hickman Browning, generally ranked among Lincoln's more conservative allies during the Civil War, was on more solid antislavery Whig ground in 1850, stumping in September against the extension of slavery and southern disunionism, and in November handily winning a debate with a Kentuckian over the rights of fugitives to a jury trial.[61]

Calvin Fletcher, an Indianapolis businessman and longtime Whig who committed to Free Soil in 1848, provides another example. Fletcher employed men of color on his large farm. Three born in the South were listed in his household in the 1850 census, and another working for him in the winter of 1849–50 was a "run away negro slave" from Mississippi. Fletcher was still a committed colonizationist, and had arguments about it with his men in the summer of 1851. In 1850 he was too immersed in local affairs—the banks, local deaths, the harvest, a new railroad—to write anything about the Fugitive Slave Act in his diary, but he did record the efforts of a free man of color who came twice to Indianapolis trying to raise money to buy his own children out of slavery in Kentucky.[62]

We also have the perspectives of a few white children. John Davis Long, eventually a committed Republican, was a boy of twelve in 1850, attending an academy in southern Maine and plainly immersed in the civil texts of the age. In March he wrote in his diary that there was "trouble in Washington about the Slavery question." That December he wrote in great expectation of President Fillmore's message to Congress: "I hope that the people will not fuss any more about the slave question; for the people are talking about disunion, and I guess that they have forgotten Washington's farewell address which was to stick to the Union and never dissolve it."[63] Then there were the ambiguous memories of Henry James, the American-born British novelist, looking back on his early childhood in New York City from the turn of the century, and on the two slaves who—he remembered—had been brought north by a Kentucky family from Louisville visiting down the street: "Mother and son had fled, in the dead of night, from bondage . . . taking advantage of their visit to the North simply to leave the house and not return, covering their tracks, successfully disappearing. They had never been to us so beautifully slaves as in this achievement of their freedom; for they did brilliantly achieve it—they escaped, on northern soil, beyond recall or recovery."[64]

This slim evidence suggests that much of the northern white public, even on the edges of the committed antislavery constituencies, was unsettled, but clinging to the Union and unwilling or unable to truly embrace the struggle to end slavery. If, as George Templeton Strong remembered in 1860, the struggles of 1850 had "opened our eyes to the fact that there were two hostile elements in our country," it did not push the northern white majority toward decisive action. They stood on the sidelines, unwilling to plunge into the fray, immersed in enduring routines but struck by the local and personal dramas, experienced sometimes directly but more often in print, in the imagined community of the public sphere. The Fugitive Slave Law jangled against ordinary lives, a threatening discordancy grating against the exciting trajectory of the economic boom, nervously followed by people so recently traumatized by the great depression of the previous decade. And just as the massive petition drive of the preceding spring had unfolded outside the domain of formal politics, resistance to the Fugitive Slave Law lay outside the political routine of election cycles. If the ideological structures that had divided the two great parties were crumbling, their behavioral structures were firmly in place.

News from the South was perhaps equally disturbing as the off-year election for the 32nd Congress got under way in the free states in November of 1850. Inspired by their dying torchbearer John C. Calhoun, southern extremists had met in Nashville in June for a disunion convention, and met again in early November to issue resolves calling for a general southern convention to consider steps toward secession.[65] In the Deep South states of Georgia, Alabama, and Mississippi, the congressional elections—not held until the late summer and fall of 1851—pitted States Rights or Southern Rights candidates against Union candidates. Most of the South ignored the disunionist call, but even so, many northerners were as concerned about disunionism as they were about the assault on the fugitive slaves in their midst. This was certainly a part of the message that young John Long was absorbing at his Maine academy as he hoped "that the people will not fuss any more about the slave question."

Whatever the threats of federal fugitive hunters or southern disunionism, neither translated into an antislavery surge in the northern returns in the 1850 congressional elections. When all the votes were in and runoffs decided, the total vote for Free Soil candidates had plummeted by more than 80 percent across the North. Much of this decline was shaped by the resurgence of the mainline parties, the meager result of efforts to build electoral coalitions. The partisan glue of patronage proved far too strong for the shakily organized Free Soilers of 1848, as did the claim of the union meetings that the Compromise had achieved a "final settlement." With turnout down in an off-year election, in New York the Van Burenite Barnburners abandoned Free Soil to reunite with the conservative "Hunker" Democrats. The Whigs countered to take up Seward's militant stand against the Compromise, shutting out any opening for a Free Soil organization. In Pennsylvania the Free Soilers reunited with the Whigs.[66] Of the nine Free Soilers in the 31st Congress, three were defeated (two by Democrats in three-way races), and six survived, five in two-way races, three of whom ran on Whig or Democratic tickets.

In Massachusetts, where the Free Soil organization survived most strongly, several elections were pushed into runoffs stretching into May 1851. The Fourth District, encompassing Middlesex County, had been represented in the 30th Congress by John G. Palfrey, a Unitarian minister in Boston who had been deeply involved in the struggles in Congress in late 1848. Here the runoff elections for the 31st and 32nd Congresses literally overlapped. Palfrey battled unsuccessfully with Whig Benjamin Thompson through twelve re-votes to decide the seat for the 31st in January 1851, and the two again struggled through four elections until Thompson beat Palfrey for the seat in the 32nd in May 1851. Emerson took his Concord speech on the road to nine events to help Palfrey, to no avail.[67] Palfrey's defeats were bitter blows to the Massachusetts Free Soilers. His close friend Charles Sumner fought a parallel battle in the state legislature for election to Webster's seat in the Senate. Building a coalition with the Massachusetts Democrats led by Henry Wilson, Sumner was nominated for the Senate only to endure three months of ballots in the House until he was finally elected in April 1851.[68]

A similar process put a second strong antislavery figure into the Senate from Ohio that spring. Salmon Chase had engineered an alliance with the Democrats when a Free Soil minority came to control the balance of power in Ohio in 1849. He had been rewarded with a seat in the U.S. Senate for the 31st Congress. In the fall of 1850 another antislavery leader was elected to the Senate from Ohio. Since the Whigs refused to stomach the ardent abolitionist Joshua Giddings, Chase organized a coalition behind the antislavery Whig judge Benjamin F. Wade.[69] Wade, if he did not have the stature of Giddings, was blisteringly angry. He stumped across Ohio's Western Reserve making speeches condemning the Fugitive Slave Act throughout the late fall of 1850, writing to his wife in November, "I cannot and will not swallow that accursed slave bill; it is a disgrace to the nation and the age in which we live."[70]

If antislavery struggled with the old parties for mixed results in the 1850 election, it also acted outside of politics, in the spirit of Wade's letter. Secretly, sometime in December, Harriet Tubman succeeded in rescuing her sister and two children.[71] Publicly, when the second session of the 31st Congress opened on December 2, it was deluged with more petitions. This flood started on the tenth with ten petitions from Ohio alone. A total of 511 antislavery petitions were submitted to the House and Senate during this short three-month session. Petitions were planned at crisis meetings in places such as Honesville, Pennsylvania, and Oswego, New York.[72] Unlike the petitioning to the first session, the petitions to the second session were extremely focused and reflected the new reality of the "final settlement."[73] While a small group of petitions were concerned about slavery in the federal territories, the vast majority—469 of 511—were about one thing, asking in short form for "the repeal of the law, passed at the late session of Congress, known as the Fugitive Law."[74] Thus over the two sessions, petitions regarding slavery in the territories and the Fugitive Slave Law were on the same order of magnitude, while petitions regarding the District of Columbia came in a distant third.[75] All told, if we assume forty signatures per petition, and some duplication, perhaps 75,000 to 100,000 people may have signed petitions to the 31st Congress.

This petitioning was driven by the ongoing meetings now focused on the fugitive issue across the North. Thus the December meeting at White Eyes, Ohio, condemned all representatives from the "free States" who failed to oppose the law as "deserving the highest rebuke from a free, intelligent, and indignant people."[76] At the same time the antislavery leadership kept up the drumbeat of speeches: Giddings and Mann in the House in December and February, Hale and Chase in the Senate in February, Emerson and Mann in Massachusetts and Chase in Ohio in May, and at a host of antislavery conventions, with events in Cincinnati, Chicago, Boston, Philadelphia, and a great "Friends of Freedom" convention in Cleveland in September 1851. The English abolitionist George Thompson headlined a series of meetings that moved across the Erie Canal region to Rochester. There were three meetings in Syracuse alone, an anti–Fugitive Slave Law convention in January, the Thompson event in March, and the American Anti-Slavery Society convention in May. At the January fugitive meeting, organized by many of the same activists who had gathered at Cazenovia in August 1850, Frederick Douglass advocated violent resistance. Then at an AA-SS meeting in May 1851 threw his lot in with the politicians, disavowing the disunionism and pacifism of the Garrisonians, committing himself to a vision of an antislavery Constitution and to political action. In June 1851, after months of planning, Douglass institutionalized this political commitment by merging the *North Star* with the *Liberty*

Party Paper, establishing *Frederick Douglass's Paper*, now with considerable financial backing from Gerrit Smith.[77]

Meanwhile the slave hunters were busy, arresting over sixty people during 1851. But there was some very dramatic resistance that fall, as Harriet Tubman made a third quiet trip down to Maryland, bringing back eleven fugitives from her old neighborhood in Dorchester County. They probably hid at Frederick Douglass's house on their way through Rochester to Canada.[78] Perhaps foolishly, slave hunters came to radical Syracuse as the state Liberty Party convention was gathering, arresting on October 1 William Henry, a fugitive commonly known as Jerry, as he was working at a cooper's shop in the center of town. Here they were venturing into the domain of Gerrit Smith, the central figure at the nexus of the Liberty Party and the New York State Vigilance Committee (the public face of the Underground Railroad), who had co-organized the radical Cazenovia Convention the year before. Charles Wheaton, a local hardware store owner, a Liberty man, and a member of the city's Vigilance Committee who had attended the Cazenovia meeting, saw the arrest and immediately raised the alarm. That afternoon Jerry managed to escape but was roughly recaptured and locked up, battered and bruised. Crowds filled the streets and finally broke down the jailhouse doors, grabbed Jerry, and sent him off toward Oswego, where a few days later he took ship across Lake Ontario for Canada. Wheaton, who had spent the day working on the legal effort, "got home a little after ten," his wife, Ellen, wrote in her diary, "very much fatigued, and yet quite happy." The rescue and the trials that ensued were followed in detail in papers across the country.[79]

Events had been more dramatic and consequential four weeks previously in the border town of Christiana, Pennsylvania. In November 1849 a group of slaves had left Edward Gorsuch's wheat farm in northern Maryland, crossing the Pennsylvania border to Lancaster County, where several settled with William Parker. Parker was a free black farmer and militant member of the local resistance to the "Gap Gang," a criminal posse of whites who had been kidnapping free blacks and fugitives for years. The men at Parker's farm thus were armed and on the alert when Edward Gorsuch, along with his sons, several Maryland neighbors, and a federal deputy marshal, approached on September 11, 1851, Gorsuch demanding "my property." Parker's wife sounded an alarm, which drew eighty men from the neighborhood, and the battle began; in a hail of blows and gunfire, Gorsuch was killed and one of his sons wounded.[80]

Such was the Christiana riot, again covered throughout the country in great detail, as were the trials that followed. Forty-two men, black and white, were tried for treason. When Castner Hanway, a white Quaker who had tried to intervene, was acquitted, all charges against the black rioters were dropped. But the Lancaster County border with Maryland became something of a war zone, with white gangs preying on fugitives and free blacks. A white man from the Pennsylvania town of West Nottingham was lynched in Maryland while traveling to Baltimore to rescue a local girl who had been kidnapped. Just to the west, the Harrisburg constables were hard at work, and in the eight months following Christiana made fugitive arrests no fewer than eight times.[81]

The violence of the Christiana riot brought a wider backlash that put a proslavery Democrat, William Bigler, in the governor's seat that November. The Whig defeat in Pennsylvania in 1851 was matched with losses in other northern states where the Whigs had taken a radical stance on the Fugitive Slave Law. Ronald Formisano describes late 1851 as the last moment of a "dying sectional storm."[82] But if political attention to the Fugitive Slave Law faded, cultural attention began to intensify and ramify in widening circles in American society. Essentially respectful of law, white northerners were witness to the enactment of a law that violated constitutional norms of due process and state sovereignty, as well as common decency and sensibility. Eight months of struggle in Congress over the Compromise drove a steady drumbeat of party rhetoric that a "final settlement" had been achieved, but doubts roiled under the surface. Southern triumphalism rubbed nerves raw. When Thomas Sims was returned from Boston to Savannah, he was publicly whipped on the nineteenth of April 1851, in an explicit insult and challenge to northern honor. Proslavery Democrats and commercial Whigs demanded adherence to the Constitution, but for growing numbers such images fed doubts about the sacredness of the 1787 compromise binding slavery and union.

Most northerners really did not have direct experience of the workings of the law beyond what they read in newspaper accounts. But such reading had a power of its own, as did a wide variety of public entertainments that together shaped the common collective experience of the nation, its imagined community. In a country surging toward modernity, modern forms of collective experience—the telegraph, the weekly magazine, the mass-produced novel, the music industry, the theater—and experimental forms such as the mirror show, the panorama, and the stereoscope, which would coalesce forty-five years later in the first cinema production, were all put to work on the problem of the slave's liminal paths in American society. This cultural commerce, and its impact on American politics in a time of crisis, is the subject of the next two chapters.

CHAPTER 4

Creative Liminality

Writing and Reading Uncle Tom's Cabin

EARLY IN January 1851, Free Soil congressman George Julian wrote an excited letter home to his wife, Anna, in Indiana. Gamaliel Bailey and his wife, Margaret, had issued a standing invitation to all Free Soilers in Washington, opening their house "for talk and a cup of coffee" every Saturday night. Bailey, the editor of the antislavery *National Era*, had just moved from E Street—where eighteen months before he had talked down proslavery vigilantes during the aftermath of the *Pearl* episode—to one of the "finest houses" on C Street. Bailey's new establishment was conveniently several blocks closer to Capitol Hill, where Julian roomed with Joshua Giddings and others among the small contingent of antislavery congressmen. The second session of the 31st Congress had just opened in December, and Julian would be in Washington for only the next few months. In August 1851 he would narrowly lose reelection to the 32st Congress to a Whig. During the previous spring and summer, as the Compromise was being debated in the Senate and House, he along with Giddings, Chase, Hale, and others had met occasionally at the Baileys'. They would now convene every Saturday evening.[1]

These gatherings were part of a multifaceted plan that Gamaliel and Margaret Bailey had pursued to advance the visibility of antislavery in Washington ever since moving from Cincinnati to establish the *National Era* in 1847. This would be a respectable brand of antislavery. The *Era* had been planned and funded by Lewis Tappan and his allies in the American and Foreign Anti-Slavery Society to project a moderate antislavery voice in the capital, a slaveholding, slave-trading city. Its moderation was by design. While William Lloyd Garrison condemned it as "milk-toast abolitionism," the *Era* was strategically situated to attract a particular kind of readership opposed to slavery but also to Garrisonian radicalism. Tappan had considered hiring Joshua Leavitt, the editor of the *Boston Emancipator*, who recently had been deeply involved in lobbying in Washington for Liberty Party positions. But he settled on Bailey, given his refined social skills. Born into a prominent Virginia family, Margaret Bailey—a committed abolitionist—knew how to set the tone for establishing antislavery in the slaveholding national capital. Tappan had consulted with poet and Liberty editor John Greenleaf Whittier, both a key figure in a political antislavery wing and a central cultural figure in the nation at large. Whittier served as Bailey's corresponding editor, publishing hundreds of essays and poems in the *Era* through the early 1850s. Together they recruited notable authors for the paper's literary page, so essential to drawing a respectable subscribership, which topped ten thousand a week as early as September 1847.[2] Nathaniel Hawthorne, Theodore Parker, and William Cullen Bryant appeared in the *Era* in its earlier years. But the Baileys also worked assiduously to recruit rising female voices. Emma (known by her initials, E. D. E. N.) Southworth was a struggling teacher in Washington who had published in the *Baltimore Saturday Visitor*, which Bailey had purchased to expand the *Era*'s subscriber base; Southworth soon became one of the leading female authors in the *Era* and in the country at large. George Julian wrote effusively to his wife about both Southworth and another Bailey protégée, Sarah Jane Clarke, who had recently been fired from *Godey's Lady's Book* in 1850 for writing for the *Era* under the pen name "Grace Greenwood." Clarke's portrait was hanging at the Baileys' on C Street in January 1851, and she, Southworth, and other smart young women were in regular attendance at the Baileys' on Saturdays.[3]

This was the first American age of female cultural celebrity. Jenny Lind, the "Swedish Nightingale," whom P. T. Barnum lured to New York in September 1850 for a two-year tour, had been preceded by another Swedish celebrity, the novelist Fredericka Bremer. George Julian caught a glimpse of her in the House gallery in July 1850.[4] The years 1849 and 1850 were a watershed moment in the rise of a new and immensely popular group of women writers in America. Women of talent, all needing to support themselves and their families, were suddenly producing a stream of essays, poetry, and best-selling novels. Southworth and Clarke combined writing for the *Era* with contributing to the new *Saturday Evening Post*. Throughout 1849 the *Era* featured serials from Southworth's novel *Retribution; or the Vale of Shadows,* published by Harper's in New York in October. Clarke was negotiating a contract with the Boston publishers Ticknor, Reed and Fields, who published her *Greenwood Leaves* late in 1849.[5] In the summer of 1850, when she spent several weeks consulting with her publishers, Bailey wrote her a letter of introduction to Charles Sumner in Boston, noting that "her literary accomplishments have made her a favorite of the reading public."[6] In New York, Susan Warner rose from impoverished obscurity when her *Wide, Wide World* came out in December 1850; she immediately plunged into her second novel, *Queechy*, which appeared in April 1852. In Boston a similarly impoverished Sara Payson Willis got her first essays published in 1851; known as "Fanny Fern," she would become the most prolific female writer for the rest of the century. A new world for women in public was opening in the early 1850s.[7]

The Baileys fused this emerging female celebrity with the aura of respectability they were constructing in order to normalize antislavery in Washington. While shoring up their place in the "structures" at the center of American political life, the Baileys were also laying the foundation for a cultural intervention in the sectional crisis, which would be shot through with liminal transgressions. They opened doors, and the *Era*'s payroll, to rising young women whose skills and success in the public sphere fundamentally challenged patriarchal norms of a woman's place in society. And when they recruited an old acquaintance from Cincinnati, herself already a literary celebrity, to write on slavery in the *National Era*, they unleashed a liminal rupture that would reshape fundamental patterns of opinion in both North and South. It is difficult to see how the politics of the ensuing decade would have unfolded without the hurricane-force impact of Harriet Beecher Stowe's *Uncle Tom's Cabin*. If women's voices—rising so dramatically in the eruption of immediate abolitionism in the 1830s—had been stilled with the emergence of political antislavery in the 1840s, Stowe would restore a female voice and agency to antislavery in the 1850s.

ANTEBELLUM CINCINNATI was a contested border town. Settled in the 1790s, Cincinnati was one of a string of river towns situated between slavery and freedom along the Ohio River to the middle Mississippi. Though the city was formally located in free Ohio, Cincinnati's economy was heavily dependent on the flow of river traffic moving goods and people—including slaves—between Pittsburgh and New Orleans. It lay at the center of a "western country" that seemed destined to shape the future of the United States. It was this sense of western destiny that drew the Reverend Lyman Beecher and his family from New England in late 1832.

What drove Beecher was not the threat of slavery but that of Catholicism. Taking up the presidency of the Presbyterian Lane Seminary in Cincinnati in 1832, Beecher was already famous for reshaping New England Protestant evangelicalism from ancient establishment to a new model of voluntary action—and for his stand against the rise of Catholicism in the United States. He had served as the Congregational minister in Litchfield, Connecticut, where his daughters attended the renowned Litchfield Female Academy, and where he established himself as a leading force in evangelical Calvinism and the early temperance movement. As Unitarianism swept through eastern Massachusetts, he was called to Boston in

1826 to stem the tide. By 1830, however, Beecher was more concerned about Catholicism and its "connection with despotic governments," which seemed to pose a fundamental threat to American "Republican liberty."[8] He was already worried about the spread of Catholic influence in the West, and had a strong connection to Cincinnati in his brother-in-law Samuel Foote, who had arrived there in 1828 and prospered. Meeting with a representative of the new Lane Seminary in October 1830, Beecher announced his intention to move, though he and his family would not arrive until November 1832. The Beechers settled at the seminary in the quiet Walnut Hills neighborhood, a suburban outpost two miles east of the city center. Here he would write his anti-Catholic *Plea for the West*, published in 1835, soon after an early version preached on a return visit to Boston was implicated in the riot in which a mob burned the Ursuline Convent in Charleston in August 1834.[9] His children would carry his anti-Catholicism into the 1840s and 1850s.[10]

But the jumble of people and opinion in the "Queen City" of Cincinnati gradually pushed the Beechers to confront slavery. Lyman Beecher supported the conservative American Colonization Society, which was the standard position among his evangelical peers who considered themselves antislavery. Slavery was a sin, but one that would disappear only gradually, and would require the colonization of Africa by free black Americans.[11] At Lane he was immediately caught between two hostile factions: the young immediatist students led by Theodore Dwight Weld, and the Lane board of trustees, dominated by the proslavery "Old School" wing of the Presbyterian Church, with deep ties to the Kentucky hinterland south of the Ohio River.[12] Starting in the summer of 1833, soon after Beecher's arrival, Weld began to prepare the student body for a great debate about slavery. The debate unfolded over eighteen nights in February 1834, asking whether slavery should be immediately abolished, and whether the doctrines of the Colonization Society made it "worthy of the patronage of the Christian public." Weld then led the radicals in establishing schools of free people of color in Cincinnati, raising a growing condemnation from the conservative majority in the city. The following October, after months of controversy, and while Beecher was east raising money, the board of trustees voted to severely restrict the rights of students and faculty to engage in public action. Dozens of students resigned and became a core group of the radical movement across the West. Over the next year, leading Old School trustees brought charges against Beecher himself in the Cincinnati Presbytery for "New School" heresies, which Beecher fought off as his wife lay dying.[13]

Such was the city in which *Uncle Tom's Cabin* was forged, but the creative fires were only slowly building. Cincinnati was a small city of thirty thousand, but a whirlwind of confrontation. Abolitionist voices were isolated, without the solid support of a hinterland such as lay around Boston, Worcester, Syracuse, Rochester, Pittsburgh, and Cleveland. The nearest militant Yankee abolitionist communities in Ohio's Western Reserve region were two hundred miles to the north. Rural southern Ohio was a sea of indifference and hostility mottled with a scattering of Quaker-abolitionist outposts, barely sufficient to assist in the flight of fugitives along the Underground Railroad.[14] With Weld and the Lane rebels gone, the antislavery movement in Cincinnati was left to a spectrum of careful and conservative voices connected in various ways to Lewis Tappan and his funds. The center of this group was James Birney, once an Alabama slaveholder but now converted to abolition, who moved his *Philanthropist* to Cincinnati in early 1836. Sharing Tappan's funding, Birney would have been on polite and probably cordial terms with Lyman Beecher, and with Beecher's Lane colleague Calvin Stowe, who married Beecher's daughter Harriet in January 1836. He was on much closer terms with another of Beecher's colleagues, Gamaliel Bailey, who was appointed to lecture in physiology in January 1834, a month before the abolitionist debates rocked the seminary. Converting from colonization to abolition, Bailey had joined Birney as an editor of the *Philanthropist* by May 1836. Cincinnati was shattered by rioting that summer, with many among the respectability leading mobs of white laborers to attack free black communities and destroy Birney's press. In 1841 rioting in Cincinnati, led by Kentuckians aggrieved by emerging white support for fugitives, threatened to spread to bucolic Walnut Hills.[15] These violent shocks worked to unite many of the city's leading families and factions, and in this transition a young and well-connected lawyer emerged as a critical associate of the somewhat muted antislavery community. Salmon P. Chase had attended Beecher's sermons and was married by Beecher; he met in the lyceum with Bailey; in 1836 he stood down the rioters and moved in court to get minimal restitution for property damages incurred. By the late 1830s he had become a Democrat of abolitionist, utopian opinions, defended several fugitives on grounds of the *Somerset* decision, and, with Bailey, turned in the 1840s to the Liberty Party.[16]

Harriet Beecher circulated in this orbit of Cincinnati families. She would certainly have known Bailey and Birney, and she and her sister Catharine knew Salmon P. Chase as members of the Semi-Colon Club, a literary circle that met at their uncle Foote's mansion, to which they were admitted on the publication of Harriet's *Primary Geography for Children*.[17] Eliza Stowe was among the Semi-Colon membership, and after she died of cholera in 1834, Harriet married her grieving widower, Calvin, one of the nation's leading classical scholars. Harriet's trajectory toward abolitionist sympathies was constrained by her father's and husband's tenuous position after the Lane debate struggle, as the hostile trustees looked for an excuse to intervene further, and as the fortunes of the seminary plummeted. But she was horrified by the violence of the rioting in 1836. Venturing into the public press for the first time, she wrote an anonymous essay for the city paper being edited by her brother Henry, defending Birney's claim to free speech and the liberty of the press.[18]

The Cincinnati riots, and then the murder of Elijah Lovejoy, an abolitionist editor who was shot while defending his press in Alton, Illinois, in November 1837, began to convert the Beechers, starting with brothers William, George, and Edward, living at various points around the Midwest.[19] Harriet's older sister Catharine had been a leading figure at the Hartford Female Seminary in 1828 in petitioning for protections for the Cherokee. But by 1837 she had withdrawn from such active militancy, issuing a statement against women playing a public role. Catharine's *Essay on Slavery and Abolitionism with Reference to the Duty of American Females* condemned the fusion of abolition and women's rights that the sisters Sarah and Angelina Grimké were announcing on public stages throughout the North. Women should take their stand in the domestic sphere and as schoolteachers, Catharine argued, but not on matters of politics and policy.[20]

Caught in the cross fire between her father's colonization views, her brothers' rising Tappanite abolitionism, her sister's increasing gender conservatism, and Cincinnati's violent politics, and immersed in the stresses and travails of motherhood and housekeeping, Harriet stayed out of the public debate over slavery. Privately, she was apparently boiling. Catharine wrote in a family note during the winter of 1838, "Harriet sometimes talks quite *Abolitiony* at me & I suppose quite Anti to the other side."[21] If Harriet ever spoke "quite Anti," she quietly absorbed a book produced by abolitionists on "other side," Theodore Dwight Weld and Angelina Grimké. This couple, married in 1838, were certainly antagonists of the Beecher family, he for leading the Lane rebels, she for advocating women's rights. Weld and Grimké collaborated in 1839 to put together a book of excerpts from the southern press which described the workings of slavery in bloody detail. Harriet credited their *American Slavery as It Is* as the fundamental inspiration for *Uncle Tom's Cabin*. Presumably she was also reading some of the life stories of fugitive slaves that were being published throughout the decade and into the 1840s.[22]

Antislavery was not thriving in Cincinnati in the late 1830s, as the economic depression settled in and the primacy of the southern market only intensified. Just before the Baileys left for Washington in late 1846, Margaret joined an antislavery sewing circle that served as the opening wedge for a Garrisonian effort.[23] But as Gamaliel Bailey struggled with the editorship of the *Philanthropist* and worked with Salmon Chase to forge an antislavery Liberty Party in Ohio,[24] Harriet Beecher Stowe launched her career as an American writer. As a member of the Semi-Colon Club, she had written a short series of parlor satires for the *Western Monthly Magazine*. In 1839, driven both by ambition and by the pressure of household poverty, she began to write for the national public, and for editors who would pay as much as $15 a page. Under the signature "Mrs. H. B. Stowe," she wrote for two different audiences, the smart, fashionable readers of *Godey's Lady's Book* and the pious Protestant readers of the *New York Evangelist*, in a sequence of essays, poetry, and sermonic discourses that literally put her name on the national map. In 1843 Harper Brothers in Boston published her *Godey's* essays as a freestanding volume, *The Mayflower*, further enhancing her growing reputation.[25]

Even so, the mid-1840s were years of tribulation for Stowe: the Lane Seminary continued to fail, her brother George committed suicide, she suffered a near fatal case of cholera, and pregnancy, miscarriages, and nineteenth-century medical practice all took their toll. In 1843 she had a religious conversion; in 1846 she spent months taking the water cure in Brattleboro, Vermont. And on her return, almost certainly cleansed of the calomel mercury that the regular "allopathic" doctors prescribed so freely, she experienced a great joy, and then a great sorrow. Conceived on her return from Vermont, and born in January 1848, her baby Charles was a healthy, bouncing, blooming child. But 1849 was a cholera year, and the Lane Seminary had rented a few small plots to poor black families, former slaves. One of the workingwomen from this "shacktown" brought cholera into the Stowe household in the summer of 1849, and Charlie quickly died. His story, echoing the death of Eliza Stowe in 1834, would soon be woven into his mother's greatest literary effort.[26]

Soon after Charlie's death, Calvin and Harriet left the failing Lane Seminary and returned to the East. He had been offered a position at his undergraduate college, Bowdoin, and while he finished his teaching commitment at Lane through December, Harriet packed up the children in April and made her way to Brunswick, Maine, to set up a new household. She arrived in Maine as the debate over the Compromise filled the newspapers in the summer of 1850.

Over the late 1840s, the last of the Beecher siblings gradually proclaimed their antislavery sentiments. From 1837, Henry Ward Beecher served in Presbyterians churches in southern Indiana and Indianapolis, where it was best to avoid the topic of slavery. He preached his first sermon on slavery in 1845, the same year when Harriet published her first abolitionist story. While Henry hoped that prayer would solve the question of slavery and tried to stand on moderate ground between slaveholders and immediatist radicals, Harriet was perhaps more advanced, though her narrative had an accommodating touch. "Immediate Emancipation," published early in 1845 on the front page of the *New York Evangelist*, told the story of a trusted Kentucky slave sent on an errand to Cincinnati who escapes with the help of a country Quaker. When confronted with the slave's fear of sale for debt, the pursuing slave master is persuaded and quietly returns home.[27] Soon after Henry began to preach, reluctantly, on slavery, he was recruited to serve the new Plymouth Church in Brooklyn, New York. Moving east in 1847, Henry addressed the Home Missionary Society in the great Broadway Tabernacle in May and was an instant sensation. In the autumn of the next year he returned to the Tabernacle twice to lead massive fund-raising meetings to free two of the *Pearl* captives, the Edmundson sisters. In March 1850, as Harriet was organizing the family's move to Maine, he published stinging attacks on Daniel Webster and the idea of a compromise with slavery in the *Independent*, another moderate evangelical paper in New York. These essays would have been on the living room table when Harriet and her children spent a week in Brooklyn on the way to Brunswick. Here, and in Hartford and Boston, where she stayed with other Beecher families, the Compromise and Webster's invocation of the constitutional duty to return fugitive slaves would have dominated the conversation.[28]

Once she arrived in Maine, though happy to be in the fresh sea air, Harriet was appalled by the detached attitudes toward slavery among her new female acquaintances in Brunswick.[29] She had at hand Weld and Grimké's *American Slavery as It Is*, and certainly a host of memories from her twenty-five years on the borderland with slavery. Two years before, she had worked with her brother Charles on a book of sermons titled *The Incarnation*, contributing an introduction and a number of passages. Radicalized by several years in New Orleans, Charles would have been a source as well.[30] She must have been in touch with Gamaliel Bailey almost immediately, because her first contribution to the *Era*, a poem called "The Freedman's Dream: A Parable," was published on August 1, 1850, the day when Stephen Douglas introduced the bill to admit California to the Union. She began a few other short pieces that autumn. One of these, "The Two Altars," written during the explosion of resistance to the Fugitive Slave Law, juxtaposed the sufferings and sacrifices of two families, one of a Continental soldier at Valley Forge and one of a fugitive arrested in front of his family in 1850, after ten years of freedom in Boston. Planned for the *Era*, "The Two Altars" came out in the *Evangelist* in June 1851, a week after the first serial of *Uncle Tom's Cabin: or, Life Among the Lowly*, appeared in the *National Era*.[31]

Since May, when she had spent a week in Boston with her radical brother and sister-in-law Edward and Isabella Beecher, Harriet had been flooded with letters from Isabella on the fugitive crisis, the mass meetings in Springfield, Worcester, and Boston, the Hamlet arrest in New York City, and the rescue of Ellen and William Craft.[32] Her children remembered one letter in particular, in which Isabella scolded her sister-in-law, "Now, Hattie, if I could use a pen as you can, I would write something that would make this whole nation feel what an accursed thing slavery is." Harriet was said to have risen "up from her chair" and announced, "I will write something, if I live." In her own account, decades later, she wrote that, sitting in a church service in Brunswick in the winter of 1850–1851, she had a vision of a slave being mercilessly whipped.[33] These were the literally liminal beginnings of *Uncle Tom's Cabin*.

She was writing small income pieces for the *Evangelist* and the *Era* in December, but suddenly, the day after Bailey's standing invitation was issued to the Free Soilers in Washington, she had very good news for her husband, Calvin: "I was just in some discouragement with regard to my writing; thinking the editor of the *Era* was overstocked with contributors, and would not want my services another year, and lo! He sends me one hundred dollars, and ever so many good words with it."[34] Bailey was developing prospects: Emma Southworth had published two serialized stories with antislavery themes in the *Era*—*Retribution*, which had concluded in July 1849, and *Hickory Hall: Or the Outcast, a Romance of the Blue Ridge*, which ran from November 1850 to January 1851—and he could use another series by a popular author to improve his sales.[35] By late January 1851 Stowe had made up her mind; she wrote to Calvin that she was "projecting a sketch for the *Era* on the capabilities in liberated blacks to take care of themselves" and asked for details on local black life in Cincinnati.[36] She was clearly well along when on March 9 she wrote to Bailey to announce: "I am at present occupied upon a story which will be a much longer one than any I have ever written, embracing a series of sketches which give the lights and shadows of the 'patriarchal institution,' written either from observation, incidents which have occurred in the sphere of my personal knowledge, or in the knowledge of my friends. I shall show the *best side* of the thing, and something *faintly approaching the worst*." She moved with trepidation, but under the spell of the protest climate of late 1850: "Up to this year I have always felt that I had no particular call to meddle with this subject, and I dreaded to expose even my own mind to the full force of its exciting power. But I feel now that the time has come when even a woman or a child who can speak a word for freedom and humanity is bound to speak."[37]

By April Stowe was far enough along to allow Bailey to mention in the *Era* that the series was in the works, and in early May he announced that it would begin on the fifth of June, describing Stowe as "one of the most gifted and popular of American writers," and subtly suggesting that readers might want to renew their subscriptions.[38] The first two chapters appeared in the June 5 issue, prominently beginning on page one.

Uncle Tom's Cabin: or, Life Among the Lowly was published in the *Era* in forty-one weekly installments between June 1851 and April 1852. Negotiations for the book publication began in the summer of 1851, and John P. Jewett, a publisher in Boston, brought out the first printing of a two-volume set in late March 1852 to coincide with Stowe's "Concluding Remarks" in the *Era*. Six weeks into the serial publication, Bailey started printing letters from readers—he claimed that he received thousands—urging Stowe "*not to hurry through* 'Uncle Tom.'" The first of these letters, printed in July, apparently from a Quaker, suggests the impact that the series was having among women: "None of thy numerous contributors, rich and varied as they have been, have so deeply interested thy female readers of this vicinity as this story of Mrs. Stowe has thus far done, and promises to do." This writer enclosed the subscription cost for three months of the *Era* for a group of readers, and indeed the *Era* did well, rising from 17,000 to 19,000 subscribers between 1851 and 1852, and surging to 28,000 in early 1853, putting it at the upper reaches of newspaper distribution in the United States.[39]

Bailey sent some of these letters on to Stowe, and clearly they helped shape her decision "not to hurry through" her story, in a dialogue of sorts between writer and reader.[40] Stowe's book developed as two entangled stories, encompassing "the *best side* of the thing, and something *faintly approaching the worst*," and the two trajectories of liminal movement for American slaves, particularly those on the borderland: flight to freedom or sale into the Deep South. Throughout, Stowe focused on the impact of slavery on the family: slave marriages broken, children lost, sexual autonomy violated. And as she had suggested in her January letter to Calvin Stowe and stressed in "The Two Altars," one of her purposes was to convince her readers of "the capabilities in liberated blacks to take care of themselves," to be independent productive citizens. At the same time, her careful realism set these stories in real and familiar American landscapes, captured a version of American personalities, and fundamentally gave voices and identities to nameless, voiceless slaves and fugitives. As she put it to Bailey in March 1851: "My vocation is simply that of a *painter*, and my object will be to hold up in the most lifelike and graphic manner possible slavery, its reverses, changes, and the negro character, which I have had ample opportunity for studying. There is no arguing with pictures."[41] This attention to real places and real—if fictionalized—people, rather than the formulaic, vaguely gothic setting and characters in typical American novels contributed to the hold that *Uncle Tom's Cabin* exerted on the northern public, and in fact made it a leading exemplar in a wider mid-nineteenth-century transition from literary romanticism to realism.[42]

The story itself, of course, was central to this hold on the public imagination. Stowe seems to have planned the serial sequence to add to its power. Three times her weekly installment schedule was interrupted, with apologies to her readership citing the very real difficulties of postal delivery from Maine to Washington and the problems of typesetting, not mentioning the household demands on Stowe in Brunswick. Possibly she simply could not get those installments done on time, but it seems likely that she and Bailey may have strategically delayed publication to intensify reader interest.[43] Margaret Bailey and Salmon Chase read the story intently as it appeared, and it is certainly possible that they had a role in these decisions.[44] Similarly, eleven chapters were split between issues, and though it is possible that these decisions were based on space limitations, the pattern of these continuations suggests that strategic decisions were being made.

The "cabin" of the title refers to the Shelby plantation in northern Kentucky and the seemingly benevolent patriarchy that it exemplifies, from which Eliza escapes over the ice to Ohio and Tom is sold south to New Orleans. Of the two trajectories leading away from Kentucky, the northern flight to freedom is the subsidiary story, taking up a total of six chapters, while Tom's progress deeper and deeper into the bowels of the cotton South, to New Orleans and then to the Red River valley in Arkansas, taking up at least twenty-six chapters, is the main drama. The Shelby plantation, apparently drawn from a short visit that Stowe made to Kentucky in 1834, stands as the image of "the best side of the thing": American slavery as a patriarchal institution in which slave families were respected and protected. But such was not to be for Tom, as Colonel Shelby runs into hard times and has to sell a slave, Eliza's son. Eliza's refusal to lose her son to the slave trade and her epic flight across the Ohio means that Tom must go in his place into the southern trade.

The six chapters on Eliza's flight and her movement along the Underground Railroad to certain freedom in Canada dramatized recent events about which northerners had been reading for months. A version of the story of Eliza's dash across the ice had been told to Calvin Stowe by John Rankin, an Ohio abolitionist who had helped dozens of fugitives, and it was repeated by the abolitionist leader Wendell Phillips at the Faneuil Hall meeting in October 1850.[45] From the river, the novel carries Eliza to the Bird household. The fictional John Bird has recently voted for a measure in the Ohio Senate to punish assistance for fugitives as a matter of national policy and politics, but he is overwhelmed by his wife's practical, biblical response to a real living fugitive, a story that would have resonated with Stowe's audience. Eliza is moved along the fugitive network by John Van Trompe, clearly modeled on John Van Zandt, an Ohio Underground Railroad "conductor" whom Salmon Chase had unsuccessfully defended against prosecution for slave stealing five years before.[46] The Halliday household, where Eliza is reunited with her husband, George Harris, is set in a Quaker community north of Cincinnati and painted in terms of the idealized sturdy, self-sufficient free community, a portrait that would have gratified Stowe's northern readership. The episode portraying the hilltop armed stand of the fugitive band against the pursuing slave hunters on the road north to Sandusky, published on October 2, obviously was shaped by the armed defense of fugitives at Christiana, Pennsylvania, publicized throughout the country in mid-September, and the Hungarian revolution of 1848–1849, on the public's mind with the impending arrival in the United States of its hero, Louis Kossuth.

The chapters of *Uncle Tom's Cabin* can be divided into four sequences, as the characters move deeper into slavery or closer to freedom. Stowe's account of the Shelby plantation and the fugitives' escape through Ohio dominate the eleven chapters of the first sequence, published between June and mid-August, when the first of three gaps in the serial sequence interrupted the narrative for her readers. The next sequence, running to the end of October, features Tom's story: his sale to the slave traders, transport down the Mississippi to New Orleans, and sale to the St. Clare family.[47] The St. Clare household, run inefficiently by Augustine St. Clare, who privately is horrified by slavery, is seemingly another manifestation of the benevolent patriarchal institution, but two women complicate the story. St. Clare's wife, Marie, is a hypochondriac who treats her own slaves viciously, and St. Clare's cousin Ophelia, a transplant from Vermont, provides Stowe with a vehicle for depicting moderately conservative northerners like her Brunswick neighbors, opposed in the abstract to slavery yet profoundly racist. "Miss Ophelia's Experiences and Opinions," revealing St. Clare's closet antislavery sentiments, sprawled across three installments before Stowe and Bailey halted publication for a week. These chapters would be split between volume one and two of the Jewett edition.

Starting with the liminal violence of the domestic slave trade along the Mississippi, this second sequence of chapters is dominated by the New Orleans stage setting—but also by programmatic set pieces on the nature of slavery. The third sequence focuses on a different story and relationship. Eva, or Evangeline, had been introduced in the stage setting, but in this third section, published from November to mid-December, the central drama revolves around Eva's friendship with Tom, her announcement that she would carry on a teaching mission among the slaves, her advancing abolitionism, and her slow descent into "consumption" and a heroine's death, surrounded by a weeping family, slave and free. Eva was clearly inspired by Stowe's recently dead child Charles, and her death stands as the primary event in one central thread running through the book: the loss of children, a loss that Eliza has avoided by her own heroic action. But Eva's death, like that of Tom, is virtually Christ-like, transcendentally fusing innocence and sacrifice.[48]

It is not the death of Eva, however, but the death of her father, Augustine, killed in a random knife fight on the street, that precipitates the crisis for Tom and the slaves of the St. Clare household. Here, in a final fourth sequence published i after a gap on December 18, and running till early April, we get Stowe's "something *faintly approaching the worst*," filled with cliff-hangers in the form of chapters split between issues of the *Era*, the great majority of such divided chapters in the series.[49] The St. Clare slaves, having been pampered by Augustine, are sent to the whipping house and sold off by Marie. Tom is sold to Simon Legree, the brutal master of a plantation far up the Red River in Arkansas. This dark and gothic world dominates the final section, hinging on Tom's martyr's death. In Stowe's somewhat rushed and forced wrapping-up of the loose ends of her narrative, she has Legree hallucinating about his sainted mother, and tells a complex interwoven story about Emmeline and Cassie, Legree's quadroon concubines, and George Harris and his sister Emily, once lost in the slave trade but now conveniently free and rich. When Cassie and Emmeline trick Legree by hiding in the attic and "haunting" his mansion, Tom is targeted for refusing to reveal their secret. While the women will eventually escape, Legree brutally kills Tom, just hours before the young George Shelby arrives to redeem him. Kneeling at his grave, Shelby vows to "do *what one man can* to drive this curse of slavery from my land!"[50] Back in Kentucky, he frees all of his parents' slaves. The story, then, is resolved as the son makes good the sins of the father and slavery ends in the Ohio River borderland where the story began.

In her final chapter Stowe shifts from narrator to activist and focuses the reader on her central message: slavery violates the family and defenseless women. In her *Key to Uncle Tom's Cabin*, published early in 1853, the matter is put simply: "The worse abuse of the system of slavery is its outrage upon the family."[51] Here she makes her sources explicit, citing the "public and shameless sale of beautiful mulatto and quadroon girls" after the *Pearl* recapture in 1848, clearly meaning the Edmundson sisters, who recently had been redeemed in part with money raised by Stowe's brother Henry Ward Beecher.

At the close of *Uncle Tom's Cabin* she invoked the stain of the "legislative act of 1850," she appealed to the "mothers of America—you who have learned, by the cradles of your own children to love and feel for all mankind . . . to pity the mother who has all of your affections, and not the legal right to protect, guide, or educate, the child of her bosom!" She called for a revolution in feelings, urging once apathetic people to "see to it *they feel right*" to build "an atmosphere of sympathetic influence."[52]

As a formative generation of literary scholars have argued, this was the central problematic—and purpose—of *Uncle Tom's Cabin*. Feeling and sympathy were going to cut through the pervasive apathy among mainstream northerners. Stowe's cultural work was to generate feelings and sympathies, and she argued that these would have a transformative effect on the sectional struggle. For Stowe, family and sympathy were bound together, one the essential social structure of the republic, the other its unique requirement. Families required loving sympathies, and sympathy built in the family could be extended more widely to the suffering slave. But the operation of these feelings in the public sphere might threaten the other structural pillar of the republic, law and the Constitution. Such was the thinking of state senator Bird when he voted for an Ohio fugitive slave law: sympathy for the fugitives was "a matter of private feeling" that should not interfere with the "great public interests involved," meaning the preservation of the Union.[53] In its 1852 review of the book, the *Southern Literary Messenger*, published in Richmond as the voice of the sophisticated South, made the same argument in more pointed fashion: "The proposition . . . embodying the peculiar essence of Uncle Tom's Cabin is a palpable fallacy, and inconsistent with all social organization . . . It would demonstrate that order, law, government, society, was a flagrant and unjustifiable violation of the rights, and mockery of the feelings of man and ought to be abated as a public nuisance."[54]

Such was the paradox at the heart of Stowe's message: feelings and sympathies grounded in one essential American structure, the family, threatened another, the Constitution.[55] Of course she saw a second paradox as equally important: law and Constitution permitted, indeed protected, the "outrage" on the black family—sexual violation, the domestic slave trade, the rupture of loving familial bonds. Two structures in the anthropological sense of the term, the family and the Constitution, were at odds with each other, and tied via destabilizing vectors to two opposing versions of disorder: sympathy for the slave and the violation of the slave family. These two "disorders" had implications of liminality. The slave market, along with male sexual lust, shattered the structure of the slave family, sending atomized black Americans in motion, in flight to freedom or into the domestic slave trade. The condition of black Americans was one of perpetual marginal liminality. If this was liminality in a destructive mode, sympathy should drive a liberating liminality. Such liminal sympathies were universally linked with the doctrine of the "higher law" against slavery presented formally by William Seward in the 1850 Compromise debates. The opposing acquiescence to slavery on the grounds of constitutional union lay at the core of the "federal consensus" and hampered the spread of a political opposition to slavery. Once slavery had been destroyed by force of war, of course, this double paradox would disappear, and constitutional and familial structures would be realigned and reconciled. And of course these alignments were understandable in antislavery sensibilities, and particularly in Stowe's rendering. Southerners would have had a different view, with slaveholding patriarchy perfectly aligned with a proslavery Constitution, and the North in general, capitalist and radical alike, the source of destabilizing disorder.

This understanding suggests a four-way matrix of constitutional and familial structures and destructive and liberating liminalities, linked by two destabilizing vectors of connection. The characters in *Uncle Tom's Cabin* can be placed in these four positions, with a fifth position for the victims of slavery. Tom, Eva, Eliza, George Harris, and Mary Bird—even Cassie and Emmeline—are most obviously agents of a liberating "higher law" liminality; Simon Legree, Marie St. Clare, the slave hunters and traders, and even the incompetent Colonel Shelby are agents of slavery's destructive liminal force, operating on the "victims": Cassie, Emmeline, Topsy, and the St.

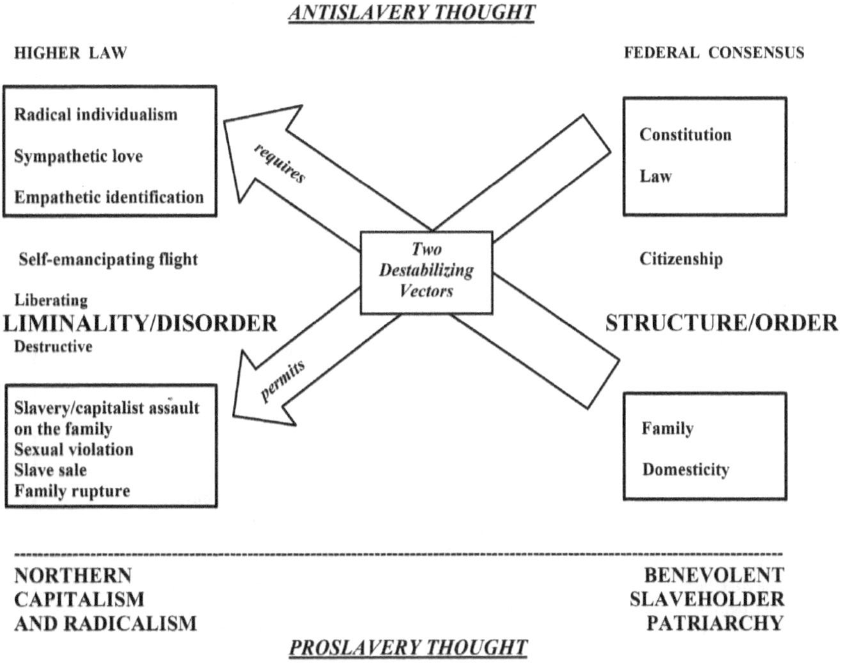

ANTISLAVERY THOUGHT

HIGHER LAW — **FEDERAL CONSENSUS**

- Radical individualism
- Sympathetic love
- Empathetic identification

- Constitution
- Law

- Self-emancipating flight
- Liberating

- Citizenship

LIMINALITY/DISORDER ←→ **STRUCTURE/ORDER**

- Destructive
- Slavery/capitalist assault on the family
- Sexual violation
- Slave sale
- Family rupture

- Family
- Domesticity

Two Destabilizing Vectors (requires / permits)

NORTHERN CAPITALISM AND RADICALISM — **BENEVOLENT SLAVEHOLDER PATRIARCHY**

PROSLAVERY THOUGHT

FIGURE 6. Liminality and structure in antislavery and proslavery thought

Clare slaves. Stowe, reflecting the position of American women denied the right to vote or hold office, gave little space to politics, and Senator Bird is the only character who obviously fits into the constitutional structure category, standing in for the entire tribe of northern party politicians whose names and positions Stowe and her readers could easily rattle off. Finally, the book presents two versions of familial structure: the northern free family and a perhaps mythical slaveholder patriarchy, represented by Mrs. Shelby and Augustine St. Clare.

Uncle Tom's Cabin was not simply an antislavery manifesto; it had a running subtext of tense racial interaction. Indeed, Stowe was writing about the South in a familiar genre, the plantation novel. The earliest work in this plantation tradition, John Pendleton Kennedy's *Swallow-Barn*, dated to 1832, the era of nullification and the intensification of

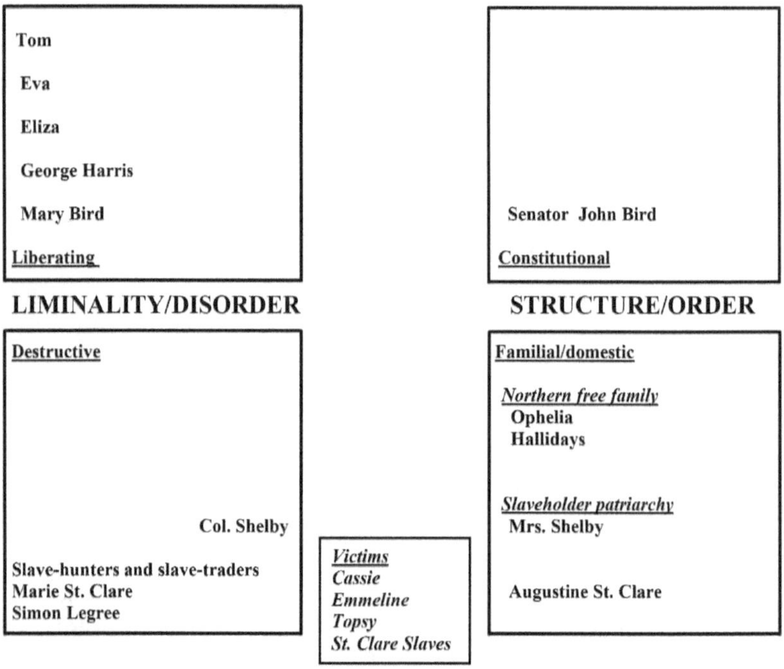

Tom Eva Eliza George Harris Mary Bird <u>Liberating</u>	Senator John Bird <u>Constitutional</u>
LIMINALITY/DISORDER	**STRUCTURE/ORDER**
Destructive	Familial/domestic <u>Northern free family</u> Ophelia Hallidays <u>Slaveholder patriarchy</u> Mrs. Shelby
Col. Shelby	
Slave-hunters and slave-traders Marie St. Clare Simon Legree	Augustine St. Clare

<u>Victims</u>
Cassie
Emmeline
Topsy
St. Clare Slaves

FIGURE 7. Liminality and structure in Stowe's *Uncle Tom's Cabin*

the "positive good" proslavery position, painting a benevolent picture of the master-slave relationship.[56] The figure of Topsy, a slave in the St. Clare household, provides Stowe with the opportunity for a comic interlude, deeply structured by the blackface minstrel tradition. Here Topsy, an orphan slave, plays the role of the minstrel end man, in self-mocking dialect but with subversive intent, to the straight man/interlocutor played by Ophelia, determined to transform a Louisiana slave waif into a proper New England miss. (Later in the century, toymakers would produce a "topsy-turvy" doll that would allow girls to flip their toy between the wild black Topsy and the perfect white Eva.) Earlier in the narrative, the stable hand Sam plays the end man to Mrs. Shelby's interlocutor; they both may be conspiring to underline the slave trader's pursuit of Eliza. In each case, Stowe is playing with powerful racial stereotypes to work a comic routine into her narrative.[57] These blackface interludes are perhaps not as important as two other questions, one implied, one explicit.

Given Stowe's stress on violations of the family as the worst sin of slavery, one wonders whether she would have been satisfied with a truly benevolent slavery, one that did not break up or violate black domesticity. This is unknowable, but it is certain that Stowe was highly ambivalent about the future of free black Americans in the United States. Thus, despite her calls for sympathy for slaves and for the end of slavery, she closed her book by returning to colonization. Eliza and George Harris, along with others among the freed people in *Uncle Tom's Cabin*, have decided to leave for Liberia. "Christian men and women of the North" were to "*pray*," Stowe instructed, but they were also to help educate the freed people coming out of slavery. Her years living "on the frontier-line of slave states" had taught her that the "first desire of the emancipated slave, generally, is for *education*." Stowe urged that they be given "the educating advantages of Christian republican society and schools," but this was not to prepare them for American citizenship but to "assist them in the passages" to African shores. If Stowe's tale centered on the capacities of American blacks to lead free and productive lives, and on the question of sympathy between white and black in American society, she ended her story with the expectation of colonization—not black civil rights and citizenship in a transformed America.[58]

EVER SINCE its publication, the morality of Stowe's narrative has been the subject of intense critique for its underlying racism, blackface tropes, and depiction of the title's hero Tom as meek and humble. The first review, coming out in Garrison's *Liberator* four days after Jewett published the work in two volumes, praised Stowe's "rare descriptive powers" but expressed particularly concern about the "Christian non-resistance" that she was requiring of slaves, and closed with a brief sentence referring to "some objectionable sentiments respecting African Colonization, which we regret to see."[59]

These comments were taken up by black writers over the next two months: in the *Pennsylvania Freeman,* Robert Purvis of Philadelphia assailed the "terrible blow" of the final chapter as *"African Colonization Unmasked"*; William Allen, in Douglass's *Paper,* loved the book but was unhappy with Tom's "non-resistance" and "piety" and wished that the colonization argument in the final chapter "was never written." In June, William Wilson, writing from Brooklyn as "Ethiop," was concerned that shopkeepers were simply changing the window displays, replacing "Zip Coon, or Jim Crow" with *Uncle Tom's Cabin,* written by a white woman; black voices were still "being found in the REAR instead of . . . the VERY LEAD."[60] Martin Delany, who had resigned from his *North Star* editorship in 1851 and was taking an increasingly militant, black nationalist position, hailed Purvis's objections and condemned "Mrs. Stowe's ridicule of Hayti." In the spring of 1853 he renewed his attacks, arguing that Stowe *"knows nothing about us, 'The Free Colored people of the United States'"*; she was "a *Colonizationist*" who celebrated "the little dependent colonization Settlement of Liberia" and sneered "at Hayti—the only truly free and independent civilized black nation . . . on the face of the earth."[61]

Douglass was more restrained. In touch with Stowe since her letter of 1851 inquiring about the cotton South, Douglass's *Paper* published a short non-critical review in early April, and added high praise in the minutes of the American and Foreign Anti-Slavery Society in late May, if contested by a protest regarding the closing remarks on colonization. Starting in August 1852, however, his *Paper* began printing a continuous series of positive, celebratory comments and updates on the impact of Stowe and *Uncle Tom's Cabin.*[62] Douglass had clearly launched a program to quietly forge an alliance with Stowe, a direct extension of his strategic decision to ally himself with the white moderate abolitionism and political antislavery led by Lewis Tappan and Gerrit Smith. Throughout March 1853 he published a four-part serial of his narrative of the Creole insurrection, *The Heroic Slave,* an apparent response to Stowe's model of slave nonresistance. A few days before the series began, he visited Stowe in Andover; they discussed the state of the movement, and he asked her to raise money during her upcoming trip to England to endow an "industrial college" that would contribute to "the elevation and improvement of colored people." Writing to Stowe several days later, Douglass (perhaps in language that he had used in his conversation with her) made his commitment to an American future for those "colored people" very plain: "The truth is dear Madam, we are *here*, and here we are likely to remain. Individuals emigrate—nations never. We have grown up in this Republic; and I see nothing in our character, or even in the character of the American people, as yet, which compels the belief that we must leave the United States."[63] Douglass's alliance with Stowe fast became a flashpoint of conflict with Delany, who since early in 1851 had abandoned white alliances for a plan for a mass emigration to a black republic in Central America modeled on Haiti. But Douglass made his point very clearly: he was committed to citizenship, not colonization or emigration.

These critiques were effective, and by June 1852, Lewis Tappan was circulating rumors that Stowe already regretted her reflexive colonizationist solution at the end of *Uncle Tom's Cabin*. Five years later, smarting from—and educated by—the angry responses of American black leaders, Stowe would abandon her colonizationist trajectory, and her sacrificial hero, for a more militant, insurrectionist story in *Dred: Tale of the Great Dismal Swamp*, just in time for the 1856 presidential campaign.[64] But in 1851 Stowe was still deeply immersed in a conservative, orthodox world, and she knew how large a world that was. Her closest relatives, Lyman Beecher, Catharine Beecher, and Calvin Stowe, were all gradualists and colonizationists. Beyond them lay a wide swath of the northern public: most still Whig, some Free Soil, but still colonizationist. One such was Calvin Fletcher in Indianapolis, who worked closely with Henry Ward Beecher during his New School Presbyterian ministry there, and urged colonization to the skeptical black hired hands working on his farm.[65] To her "left" on the antislavery spectrum, both Garrisonian and Tappanite abolitionists needed no convincing, but in her world and to the "right" there were plenty of converts to be had: people who were appalled by slavery but who tried not to think about it. And when they did, they opted for the colonizationist separation of the races.[66]

But there was a carefully calibrated strategy to her interpretive choices in *Uncle Tom's Cabin*. Under the stress of the Fugitive Slave Law crisis, the northern Whig/colonizationist church constituency was poised to erupt, and reading *Uncle Tom's Cabin* clearly worked to spread private liminal crises across this "imagined community." Framing the transition from gradualism to liberating emancipation in the familiar tropes of sentimental domesticity and devotional piety, presenting a radical message in conservative language, *Uncle Tom's Cabin* was designed to influence opinion among this select audience. Lydia Maria Child commented almost sarcastically in March 1852 on Stowe's "moderate sprinkling of Calvinism" in *Uncle Tom's Cabin*: "Not that I like that fiery medicine . . . but it will make it acceptable to a much larger class of readers."[67] Beyond this Calvinist "sprinkling," Stowe's book was structured as a Christian typology. Shaped by her own conversion in the millenarian 1840s, her husband's enthusiasm for German pietism, her work on Charles Beecher's *The Incarnation* in 1849, and the spirituality of her black servants in Walnut Hills, Stowe, as Joan Hedrick argues, had "concluded that 'bleeding Africa' was the incarnation of Christ in nineteenth-century America." Tom's death at the hands of the demonic Legree for refusing to reveal the hiding place of Cassie and Emmeline was the representation of this second American crucifixion. A radical attack on oppression was structured in the familiar, even conservative frame of Protestant Christianity.[68] And despite the colonizationist message in her "Concluding Remarks," she closed her narrative with the millennial prediction that the Union would be saved by "repentance, justice, and mercy" or it would fall to "the stronger law, by which injustice and cruelty shall bring on nations the wrath of Almighty God!"[69]

Looking back from early 1853, Stowe summarized the effects of *Uncle Tom's Cabin* on public opinion. Boundaries had been crossed, divisions had been blurred. The "bitterness of feelings of extreme abolitionists" had been softened, and "many whom this same bitterness had repelled" had been converted to abolitionism. And "universally throughout the country," there was "a kindlier feeling toward the negro race."[70] While she may have been a bit optimistic, it is clear that *Uncle Tom's Cabin* was eroding boundaries between cultural factions and between races. The means to its success lay certainly in its radical message structured in conservative language, but also in a series of tensions and reversals, driving an entirely new collective experience in the American "imagined community." Stowe's strategy—manifested in the story's movement from familiar to exotically terrifying American spaces—was to gently push conservative evangelical white women and children out of their comfort zone, and to that end she crafted a tale that offered as many comfortable connections as discomforting traumas. Speaking to women in her own biblical voice, Stowe also drove role reversals in a powerfully patriarchal society. Women were actors in *Uncle Tom's Cabin*. Whereas most actual fugitives were men who left women in slavery, Stowe reversed this role, making Eliza—and eventually Cassie and Emmeline—active agents in their own self-liberation, and consigning Tom to the "worst" of slavery.[71] And the boundaries involved personal experience. Ralph Waldo Emerson, in perhaps the only surviving description of serial-reading *Uncle Tom's Cabin*, wrote in his journal: "It is the distinction of 'Uncle Tom's Cabin' that, it is read (in)equally in the parlour & the kitchen & the nursery of every house. What the lady read(s) in the drawing room in a few hours, is retailed to her (week by week) in her kitchen by the cook & the chambermaid, (by) as, week by week, they master (s) one scene & character after another."[72]

Metaphors of a female Christ, of a black Christ, uncomfortable juxtapositions, role reversals, eroding boundaries, trancelike visions, millenarian warnings: all of these are qualities of the liminal experience, of the temporary collapse of structure, of the creation of new structuring mythology. Thus we have in these years two overlapping dimensions of the liminal and anti-structural: the volatile experience of a crisis of legitimacy driven by the Fugitive Slave Law and the rise of extralegal resistance to federal enforcement *and* the volatile tensions within the text of *Uncle Tom's Cabin*. If the Fugitive Slave Act had created an aura of liminal tension, *Uncle Tom's Cabin* constituted liminal action. Stowe herself had a powerful sense of the disruptive liminality that she was igniting. She called for a revolution in feelings, urging once apathetic people to "see to it that *they feel right*" to build "an atmosphere of sympathetic influence." The ability to see others as equals—to see and act beyond structural boundaries—lies at the core of liminal *communitas* as postulated by Victor Turner.[73] Barbara Hochman argues that Stowe pushed her readers beyond feelings of sympathy to flashes of intuitive identification. Working on an audience that thought of slaves and fugitives only in the abstract, she gave them names, voices, and recognizable personalities. Whether manifested as simply sympathy or a more complete identification with the slave, the fugitive, and the abolitionist, such a jolting transition among the majority of apathetic northerners rested on liminal context and liminal text, but also liminal experience. And as Hochman observes, the experience of first-time readers of *Uncle Tom's Cabin*—the first realistic novel directly addressing powerful public anxieties—was a unique experience with an intensity that is difficult to recover at a distance.[74]

With this in mind, we can nevertheless propose that the experience of reading *Uncle Tom's Cabin* worked not unlike a transformative liminal ritual. Readers emerged from their immersion in a different emotional state. Boundaries were disrupted and shattered, assumptions were critically challenged. Practically and politically, Stowe set in motion a tide of personal, private, intuitive epiphanies that dramatically extended the impact of petition, protest, and resistance against the Fugitive Slave Law. In this liminal experience of sympathetic identification, we might see a step in the process of American racial creolization, however contradictory and flawed.

RITUAL EXPERIENCES cannot be dragged out over too many months. A transformative immersion in text would require a book, and

Uncle Tom's Cabin was almost never published as such. Sometime in the summer of 1851, Catharine Beecher had gone to Boston and proposed to the publishing firm Phillips, Sampson that they bring out Harriet's serial as a book. Structures intervened; one partner objected that a novel by a woman, previously printed in an antislavery journal, would never sell, and that the company would lose its southern trade. That September, Calvin Stowe proposed the book to John P. Jewett, also in Boston, and was accepted, though a final contract was not worked out until the following March, about a month before the book went on sale. Jewett was antislavery himself and was a member of the Vigilance Committee formed at the October 1850 meeting at Faneuil Hall. He had published the Beechers before and had probably met the Stowes in 1844, when he set up shop in Cincinnati for several months. Apparently Jewett got a strong nudge from his wife (another Harriet), who was reading the *Era* serial. A bit nervous about the prospective book's growing length and projected two-volume format, he nonetheless paid for the stereotyping of the book plates, enabling quick reprintings, as would become necessary.[75]

If we assume that Gamaliel Bailey's nineteen thousand copies of the *Era* had five readers each, the *Era*'s *Uncle Tom's Cabin* may have reached 95,000 readers. John Jewett published 310,000 copies of the book by April 1854 alone, making it the first best-seller in the modern American book market. And each of these copies was borrowed and re-borrowed in the months and years after the novel's publication. Thus James Birney wrote to Stowe from Michigan early in 1853 that his wife, Elizabeth, had bought *Uncle Tom's Cabin* when it went on sale in Rochester, New York, in April 1852, and "ever since, with very small intermission—although our neighborhood is not distinguished as a *reading* one—rather the contrary I think—it has been loaned out to those around us."[76] If there were five readers per copy, the book could have reached at least a million and a half readers, roughly one reader for every seven inhabitants over the age of nine in the free states and territories.

Some, of course, heard it read aloud. Frances Jocelyn Peck of New

Haven sewed while listening: "Finished my bag this evening while my husband read from 'Uncle Tom.'"[77] In late April 1852, Joseph Sill, a prosperous Philadelphia merchant, recorded in his diary the events of the day with his family: "In the evening we remained at home, and after singing, reading, etc., I was urgently requested to read several chapters of 'Uncle Tom's Cabin' by Mrs. Harriet Beecher Stowe, which is an admirable and truthful picture of life in a Slave State, and the effects of Slavery."[78] By contrast, while the Birneys had planned to read the book aloud to each other on their way back from Rochester to Michigan, they were overcome: "We soon discovered—although, I think, we are not, more than others, given to the '*melting* mood'—that it was a book that no one, having a heart, could read aloud to others. Thus we had to read it separately, and for the most part, alone."[79]

Reading alone often turned into nighttime binge reading, which could shock the readers themselves by this violation of routine and the formalities of life. By April 13, Anna Cushing of Dorchester, just outside Boston, had finished the book in three days, writing guiltily, "I have indulged myself in reading a good deal."[80] Maria Woodbury of Westfield, New York, raved that she had "read Uncle Tom, oh yes, literally devoured it."[81] In Syracuse, Charles Wheaton bought a copy in early April. Ellen Wheaton soon reported that "the children are devouring it"; she may have already read it in the *Era*.[82] Charles Holbrook, a New Englander teaching school in North Carolina that October, also rocketed through the book in three days, in part by finishing it while the children were outside for recess. Fascinated by its "exciting scenes" and weeping at Eva's death, he came away "resolved to be more devoted."[83] In early May, Joseph Sill wrote in his diary about the sermon that the Reverend William Furness had preached that day at Philadelphia's First Unitarian Church. Without mentioning *Uncle Tom's Cabin*, Furness had "alluded to the books which were now publish'd, which would be quietly read & thought of by thousands of people, and prejudice & error gradually overcome." Deep into the second volume with his family, Sill gave in to temptation: "In the evening we remained at home, & after singing some Hymns I read aloud from 'Uncle Tom's Cabin' until past 10 o'clock; but as I did not finish the story, I afterwards sat down alone & completed the perusal before I went to bed. It is difficult to read it without tears."[84] Carrol Norcross, a farm laborer and schoolteacher in Maine, was perhaps more antisocial that August with a borrowed copy of "this ingenious production" which held him "bound captive": "Eagerly I devoured the first volume regardless of the presence of [friends] . . . disregarded all the rules of Ettiquit . . . I read until the flickering lamp and my bedimmed eyes warned me it was time to desist." The next night he was deep into the second volume, reading "until nearly midnight."[85] In July the young James Garfield, studying at a Campbellite Baptist academy in Ohio, binged through a hundred pages one evening before talking with a female friend until four in the morning. Eight months later he went on another binge. Starting in on *Uncle Tom's Cabin* at some point during the day, he reported: "Read after I went to bed. Rested uneasy in night." Despite his tossing and turning, he was up "reading *Uncle Tom's Cabin* in the forenoon."[86] Stowe's brother Henry Ward Beecher had perhaps the most intense experience. He had avoided reading the serialization in the *Era*, but one morning he sat down with the Jewett edition and shut the world out. He "forgot his surroundings entirely, and read until noon. He ate his dinner book in hand and during the afternoon frequently gave way to tears." The afternoon bled into evening, and deep into the second volume, after his wife, Eunice, had gone to bed, there were more tears: "I went and shut all the doors, for I did not want anyone to see me. Then I sat down to it and finished that night," around 4:00 a.m. When he staggered into his bedroom, Eunice reported, "he threw *Uncle Tom's Cabin* on the table, exclaiming 'there I've done it! But if Hattie Stowe ever writes anything more like that! I'll—she has nearly killed me anyhow!'"[87]

Throughout, through the tears, these first-time readers wrote of their personal transformation and hopes for a more general transformation. Anna Cushing "hope[d] that the book will do good."[88] Mary Poor (of Brookline, outside Boston), asked her sister Lucy, "Have you read and cried over 'Uncle Tom's Cabin'?," adding that she "had never read anything so affecting" in her life. She was worried that the experience would kill her sister.[89] Joseph Sill, "hardly able to find utterance in several of its touching passages," considered it "a Book which will open the eyes of many relative to the great curse which seems to be entailed upon this country."[90] Maria Woodbury declared that "it is a book to sink deep into the heart of all readers."[91] Elizabeth Cady Stanton, the great women's rights leader, read it in September in the last stages of pregnancy and told a correspondent: "It is the most affecting book I ever read. I should like to see papa read it. He would cry all the way through. If you have not already done so, read it. That book will tell against slavery; of that you may be sure."[92]

Many of these recording readers were, of course, already among the converted. James Birney was one of the great founders of political antislavery; Charles Wheaton was an associate of Gerrit Smith and recently involved in the Cazenovia meeting and the Jerry Rescue. Elizabeth Cady Stanton was certainly an abolitionist; Joseph Sill had attended the founding meeting of the American Anti-Slavery Society with the minister of his Unitarian church, the abolitionist William Furness. James Garfield probably did have a conversion experience driven in part by his nights with *Uncle Tom's Cabin*. Thus there remains the problem of assessing the breadth of its impact.

One way to measure the effect of the book on the northern public is through naming patterns. Americans had named their children after celebrities since the Revolution, which spawned a generation of George Washingtons and Oliver Cromwells. In the early 1850s (as gauged by names in the 1860 census), there was a minor burst of celebrity naming: the number of baby girls named Jenny doubled between 1849 and 1852, the years of Jenny Lind's tours, and there was a brief bubble of "Jenny Lind" namings in 1850, the year when she arrived for Barnum's tour. But Jennys were overwhelmed by Evas. If the great black figure in the novel was the slave Tom, the mediating figure for northern women was the young—and dying—white girl, Eva, who condemns slavery and engages directly with slaves as human equals as she cheerfully faces a slow death. Eva was an ideal type of pure, female abolitionist sacrifice, and many mothers

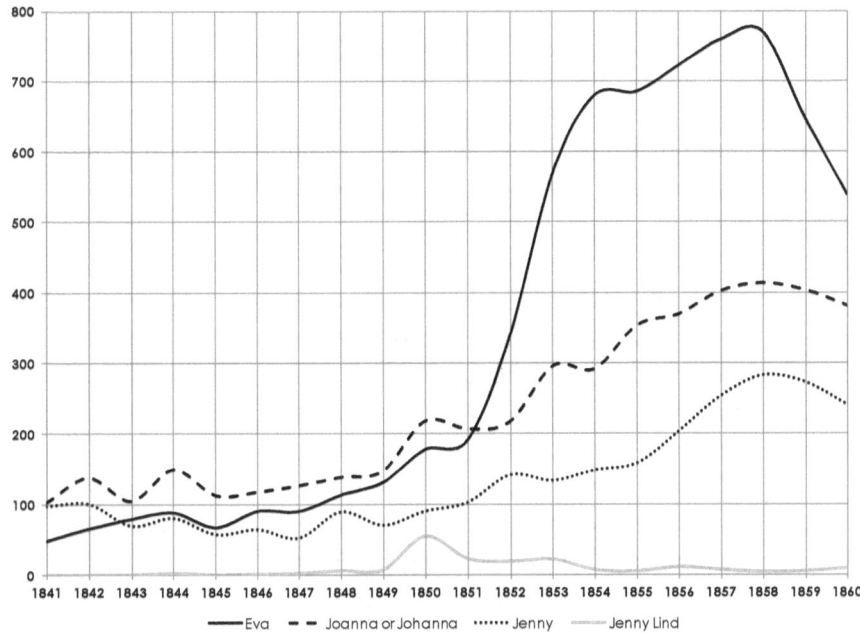

FIGURE 8. Naming events: Jenny, Joanna, Johanna, and Eva, 1841–1860

Whereas parents responded to Jenny Lind's fame with a minor burst of naming events, the name Eva was extremely popular for girls born from 1852 through 1858. Eva was a German name, but it was more popular than Johanna or its alternate Joanna in these years, suggesting the impact of Stowe's Eva in *Uncle Tom's Cabin*.

SOURCE: U.S. Census for 1860.

had to have such a child. The name Jenny peaked in 1852 at about 140 children; the name Eva jumped from fewer than 200 to almost 600 between 1851 and 1853, peaking in 1858 at about 770. This trajectory is complicated, of course, by the surge of German immigration in these years: Eva was a traditional German name. But the history of another German name—Johanna or Joanna—indicates the impact of Stowe's Eva. Slightly more popular than Eva among girls born in the 1840s, Johanna/Joanna could not compete in the 1850s. The comparison suggests that each year between 1853 and at least 1860, several hundred Eva namings across the country may have been inspired by Harriet Beecher Stowe. Disaggregating these national figures by region further suggests—not surprisingly—that the name was not particularly popular in the South in the 1850s, a time when New England families, few of whom were German, suddenly adopted the name for their daughters in dramatic numbers. (See Appendix, table 7.)

Certainly *Uncle Tom's Cabin* had an enormous impact on those who stood on the edge of the antislavery movement, prepared, perhaps, but not yet committed. In broadest outlines, these primary readers were from prepared households: Whig in politics, evangelical in religion, and privately hostile to slavery. They were moved across the line to a public antislavery stance, though many others—the great body of northern Democrats—would never be. *Uncle Tom's Cabin*–reading households certainly produced antislavery voters in the years to come. Decades later, Henry Wilson, the Nativist-turned-Republican senator from Massachusetts, wrote that *Uncle Tom's Cabin* "was both a revelation and a summons." The book had been a "needful preparation for the arguments and appeals of Republican presses and speakers that were soon to follow"; in the 1856 election "many votes cast for [John C.] Fremont were but the rich fruitage of seed broadcast by Harriet Beecher Stowe."[93]

If Wilson had a political reading, Henry James, writing at the turn of the century, looked at the book as a literary critic. He tried to capture the liminal intensity of the impact of reading *Uncle Tom's Cabin* as a boy growing up in 1850s New York. *Uncle Tom's Cabin* reached far and wide in the northern society that he knew:

> We lived and moved at that time, with great intensity, in Mrs. Stowe's novel, . . . my first encounter with grownup fiction. There was . . . for that triumphant work no classified condition; it was for no sort of reader as distinct from any other sort, save indeed for Northern as differing from Southern: it knew the large felicity of gathering in alike the small and the simple and the big and the wise, and had above all the extraordinary fortune of finding itself, for an immense number of people, much less a book than a

state of vision, of feeling and consciousness, in which they didn't sit and read and appraise and pass the time, but walked and talked and laughed and cried and, in a manner of which Mrs. Stowe was the irreversible cause, generally conducted themselves. Appreciation and judgment, the whole impression, were thus an effect for which there had been no process . . . nothing in the guise of a written book, therefore, a book printed, published, sold, bought and "noticed," probably ever reached its mark, the mark of exciting interest . . . [T]he fate of Mrs. Stowe's picture was conclusive: it was simply sat down wherever it lighted and made itself, so to speak, at home: thither multitudes flocked afresh and there, in each case, it rose to its height again and went, with all of its vivacity and good faith through all its motions.

Grappling to capture the scale of Stowe's achievement, James decided that *Uncle Tom's Cabin* was "a wonderful 'leaping' fish," a freak of nature that could inhabit both water and air.[94] In January 1853, speaking at the Anti-Slavery Society meeting in Boston, the long-established abolitionist Wendell Phillips was perhaps more sociologically precise, if somewhat defensive. *Uncle Tom's Cabin* was a "great triumph," he said, and its reception was a "phenomenon," but it was "rather an event than a book." He would prefer to give credit to the "old Anti-slavery movement" as the initiating force, but he recognized that "the unrivalled felicity of its execution has . . . trebled, quadrupled, increased ten-fold, if you please, the number of readers"—and potential antislavery voices. To cheers he situated the literary "event" as an accelerant in an unfolding political context: "Antislavery zeal and the roused conscience of the 'godless come-outers' made the trembling South demand the Fugitive Slave Law, and the Fugitive Slave Law 'provoked' Mrs. Stowe to the good work of 'Uncle Tom.' That is something!!"[95]

Uncle Tom's Cabin, then, was a "revelation," "a wonderful leaping fish," "an event." It was a critically timed cultural intervention in a stalled, sealed-up political process from which there was no exit. If Phillips celebrated the "old Anti-slavery movement," the reality was that the old movement had not made the necessary breakthrough. Stowe's multi-metaphoric, liminoid text crystallized feeling, sympathy, even identification, during a crumbling of certain structure, driving what we might call innumerable private liminal rituals of reading. Under the constitutional and moral anxieties shaped by the Fugitive Slave Law, routine-violating immersion in *Uncle Tom's Cabin* drove readers to transformational private epiphanies, breaking through the barriers that northern majority opinion had erected against the antislavery movement.

On the first of December 1851, as Eva lay dying in the pages of the *National Era* and Harriet Tubman was embarked on a mission that rescued eleven men and women from slavery, the 32nd Congress convened in Washington. The results of the congressional election had not been good for antislavery. Many antislavery Whigs had lost their seats, and declared Free Soilers were down from nine to four. With the election of Charles Sumner to the Senate the preceding spring, joining Salmon Chase and John Hale, there were almost as many Free Soil senators as representatives. Under southern Democratic control, both Senate and House marched to the beat of a proslavery drummer. The Senate was consumed from early December well into the spring with a struggle over the finality of the Compromise. Unionist Henry Foote of Mississippi wanted it "recognized as a definitive adjustment and settlement" to be "acquiesced in and faithfully observed," while Southern Rights senators wanted to leave it open to further gains for slavery. The result was months of debate in Congress.[96] Chase and Hale sputtered on the sidelines. The arrival of the Hungarian revolutionary Louis Kossuth took precedence, and he was feted by all in Washington, like a new Jenny Lind.[97]

In these circumstances, antislavery in the 32rd Congress would be a waiting game. Slowly over the course of the first session, running through August 1852, antislavery politicians began to assimilate the implications of the growing popularity of *Uncle Tom's Cabin*. Being published weekly in Gamaliel Bailey's *National Era*, Stowe's developing story would have been a topic of some conversation at the Saturday evening salon at the Baileys', now working to build morale among the committed and to recruit from the ranks of the "old organizations."[98] Salmon Chase and Margaret Bailey were reading it closely week by week, and Sara Jane Clarke, aka Grace Greenwood, the young star of the salon, was certainly reading it too. In late October she had written a puff piece in the *Era* wishing "long life and prosperity to its author" and suggesting that a scene of Tom and Eva might be engraved for a prospective book.[99]

Connections between the readership and Washington politics were already being made. A writer from Illinois in January 1852 told the *Era* that *Uncle Tom's Cabin* was advancing "Anti-Slavery sentiments" even among those "heretofore violently opposed to everything Anti-Slavery," and hoped that "the faithful few in Congress . . . will not give over their efforts, but nobly sustain" the cause.[100] A Chicago writer, perhaps tongue in cheek, asked, "Can there be finality to the compromise when there is no finality to Uncle Tom?"[101] Immediately after Jewett put out the two-volume set, Charles Sumner received his first letter from a constituent on the subject of *Uncle Tom's Cabin*. It was from Leonard Woods, a professor at Andover Seminary, where Calvin Stowe had just been hired. Woods was an old Calvinist colleague of Lyman Beecher, and his letter was something of an inside job. But on the twenty-sixth of March, he wrote to Sumner: "Mrs. Woods & I have just read the work called Uncle Tom's Cabin by Mrs. Stowe; & I hardly know how to refrain from writing to tell you how deep an interest we have felt in the scenes described, & which I believe do truly set forth the actual evils inherent in the system of Slavery . . . I am sure the publication will have readers in Washington, as well as elsewhere." Three weeks later Dr. Edward Jarvis wrote to his congressman, Horace Mann, to say he had read the book twice and wanted to know if "this book is read at Washington?"[102] In July, Sumner would get another plug from John Jay Jr. in New York, telling him that "'Uncle Tom's Cabin' is revolutionizing public opinion in Circles heretofore inaccessible and slave-catching in the future will be more shuddered at than ever."[103]

Over the previous few years there had been a sea change in language used in debate by northern congressmen. In 1847 Free Soiler David Wilmot had let it be known that he had no "squeamish sensitiveness upon the subject of slavery" or "morbid sympathy" for the enslaved. "The feeling which pervades the North," Congressman James Dixon declared, "is not one of sickly sentimentality."[104] In the spring of 1852, Orin Fowler of the Fall River congressional district in Massachusetts had no such anxieties. Five days (March 31) after Woods sent his letter to Sumner, Fowler celebrated Stowe in his remarks on slavery in the House. Calling it a work "unrivaled" in "descriptive power and truthful delineation of character," he proclaimed that *Uncle Tom's Cabin* "will be read wherever the spirit of liberty beats in the heart of man." His words were gleefully appropriated by John Jewett for a wave of long-form newspaper advertisements published in May and June.[105]

Fowler's comment came at a critical juncture in the "finality" debate in Congress—and the publication history of *Uncle Tom's Cabin*. The renewed debate on the Compromise settlement had shifted to the House, with the discussion revolving around pro-Compromise resolutions. One brought by an Indiana Democrat asked the Congress to "recognize the binding efficacy of the compromises," upholding particularly the provisions of the Fugitive Slave Law, and to "depreciate all further agitation on questions growing out of that provision."[106] On March 16 Joshua Giddings had addressed the House on the Compromise "as a final settlement of the slave question."[107] Petitions had been trickling in during the session, and he had introduced one from Illinois on the fifteenth. Other petitions were brought forward in the House over the next few weeks, and William Seward and John Hale introduced more in the Senate on the twenty-ninth, where they were gagged in two roll call votes.[108] On the fifth of April in the House, southerners and northern Democrats beat back northern Free Soilers and Whigs in eleven grueling votes on the Compromise and on the Fugitive Slave Law.[109] Thus Jewett's late March 1852 publication of *Uncle Tom's Cabin*, actually occurring a week before the serial in the *National*

Era finished with Stowe's "Concluding Remarks" on April 1, came at a critical moment in Congress, marked by Fowler's invocation of the book on March 31.

Over the spring and summer of 1852, the readership for *Uncle Tom's Cabin* grew, as these months were dominated by political affairs. In early and late June, respectively, the Democrats and the Whigs met in Baltimore for national conventions. Franklin Pierce of New Hampshire and General Winfield Scott were finally nominated after long struggles driven by sectional tensions. The Democratic nomination took forty-nine ballots and the Whig nomination fifty-three. Nominating Pierce, the Democrats voted a platform that did not promise "finality" for the Compromise but resolved to "resist all attempts at renewing, in congress or out of it, the agitation of the slavery question." The Whigs, caving in to southern demands, wrote their platform before their nomination, committing in their final plank to the "settlement in principle and substance" of the 31st Congress, to "insist upon" the "strict enforcement" of the Fugitive Slave Law, and to "depreciate all further agitation thus settled." The nomination battle pitted Millard Fillmore, a signer of the Compromise, against Scott, supported by Seward and northern antislavery Whigs. After dozens of ballots, Scott promised to accept the platform, with some oscillation, and was finally nominated.[110]

Five days after the close of the Whig convention, Henry Clay, the greatest of the Whig compromisers, died in Washington.[111] Over the next two weeks, Clay's body was carried by train back to Lexington, Kentucky. The funeral's Whig organizers had several other considerations on their minds. First, there must have been ecological concerns: parading Clay's body through a hot and humid July in the South would have been problematic, especially given that the most efficient transport lay to the North. Then there was the issue of Scott's somewhat ambiguous posture on the Compromise. He was already unpopular in the South, but possibly strong enough to draw Free Soil votes in the North.[112] So Henry Clay was carried in a great Whig-Union ceremony through the North to Philadelphia, then New York, and across the Burned-Over District and the Western Reserve, down to Cincinnati, Louisville, and finally Lexington, with grand manifestations of public mourning along the way, with vast crowds and massive press coverage. Touring Clay's body through the Deep South probably would not have helped Scott in any event. As Americans stood in the liminal moment between Clay's life and his burial, they reflected on the question of Clay's lifework, the preservation of the Union. If the funeral managers hoped to contain liminality in a celebration of Clay unionism, the march of events was far beyond their control. In the end, the stabilizing purposes of this managed media event for a reinforcement of the old order could not overcome the liminal qualities of the event-cluster trajectory; in July 1852 the nation buried the safe past and continued forward into an uncertain future.

A month after Clay was buried in Lexington, with Abraham Lincoln delivering his eulogy in Springfield, Illinois, political antislavery met in convention at Pittsburgh to nominate John Hale of New Hampshire as the candidate of the Free Democratic Party, the inheritor of the Free Soil mantle. With Frederick Douglass in attendance, the party issued a full-throated condemnation of slavery, the Slave Power, and the Fugitive Slave Act.[113] In Congress, where Seward had driven the cause in the early spring, Charles Sumner of Massachusetts, who skipped the Pittsburgh convention, had taken center stage.

Now in Washington for his first full term, Sumner had been playing a calculated game that had not gone particularly well. Hoping to establish himself across the spectrum of opinion in the Senate, he had avoided pressing the antislavery agenda. In December 1851 he gave an ornate speech welcoming Louis Kossuth to Washington which was commended by all parties. In January he rose to advocate for federal funds to support railroad construction in Iowa.[114] He had refused to campaign actively in the fall of 1851 for the coalition of Free Soilers and Democrats who had elected him in the spring, and constituents feared that he had abandoned them, especially when in May 1852 he failed to introduce a petition to free Daniel Drayton and Edward Sayres, the leaders of the doomed *Pearl* rescue. In fact he had been working behind the scenes and had presented a long legal opinion to the president that apparently was a factor in their release in August.[115]

Over the summer of 1852, Sumner was researching, writing, and memorizing a long speech on the national status of slavery, waiting for the opportune moment to address the Senate. But his constituents demanded action, and on May 26 and July 27, with Sumner challenging Senate protocol both times, he first introduced a petition for the repeal of the Fugitive Slave Act and then presented a resolution for the Judiciary Committee to act on that repeal. Both times he was defeated by a four-to-one margin.[116] Finally, on August 26 he gained the floor on a proposed amendment strengthening the fugitive law and delivered a major speech titled "Freedom National, Slavery Sectional." He rejected the concept of a final settlement of slavery as "tyrannical," and then proceeded from the principles of Mansfield's *Somerset* decision to separate the federal Constitution from slavery. There was no positive law of slavery in or following from the Constitution, he argued; thus the federal government should use its power to limit it only to the states where such positive law existed. On these premises, and because of the due process clause, the Fugitive Slave Act was illegitimate, in general and with regard to a fugitive's right to trial by jury. In a long summation, he decried the "interests" who were allied to support slavery's violation of human rights and reminded his audience of new forces in the public sphere. "The literature of the age" stood against slavery:

> A woman, inspired by Christian genius, . . . like another Joan of Arc, and with marvelous power sweeps the chords of the popular heart. Now melting to tears, and now inspiring to rage, her work everywhere touches the conscience, and makes the Slave-Hunter more hateful. In a brief period, nearly 100,000 copies of Uncle Tom's Cabin have been already circulated. But this extraordinary and sudden success—surpassing all other instances in the records of literature—cannot be regarded merely as the triumph of genius. Higher far than this, it is the testimony of the people, by an unprecedented act, against the Fugitive Slave Bill.

Again his proposal was defeated in a roll call, but Sumner's speech was reprinted in key papers and as a pamphlet. Widely read across the nation, "Freedom National" became the political twin of *Uncle Tom's Cabin* in the minds of the growing antislavery North.[117]

Five days later the first session of the 32nd Congress adjourned. Sumner was one of a cluster of at least three Massachusetts members to invoke Harriet Beecher Stowe's efforts that spring and winter. He followed Orin Fowler but also Horace Mann. On August 17 Mann had also rejected "finality" and attacked the Democratic convention's demand for an end to "agitation." This public gag, if enforced, "forbids genius from presenting Truth in the glowing similitudes of Fiction; and that divine-hearted woman, the authoress of 'Uncle Tom's Cabin,' is under the Baltimore ban." Both he and Sumner warned of a coming crisis.[118] Antislavery politicians were sharing the public stage with Stowe and invoked her in their private correspondence as well.

They also shared the public stage with dueling black intellectuals. It is possible that Frederick Douglass's editorial decision to launch a wave of positive coverage of Stowe in August 1852 was synchronized with Mann's and Sumner's performances in Washington. In March 1853, writing in his *Paper* about his visit to Andover, Douglass pulled out all the stops: "The word of Mrs. Stowe is addressed to the soul of universal humanity . . . and thrills the universal heart." She "was our friend and benefactress"; "the friend of all mankind." Over the coming months Douglass's worshipful—though calculated—alliance with Stowe intensified his growing competition with Martin Delany for leadership of the northern free black community. By the spring of 1853 this tension had boiled over, with Delany assailing Stowe's colonizationism as he attacked Douglass's plans for a convention in Rochester, which would center on Stowe's apparent promise of funding for a black "industrial college." When the convention did meet that July, Douglass read into the record his March letter to Stowe, to be published in the convention proceedings and that December in his *Paper*. He also was clearly a shaping force in the writing of the convention's charge, which pointedly referred to "the propitious awakening . . . which has followed the publication of "Uncle Tom's Cabin."[119]

The previous November there had been little to celebrate in the dismal showing of John Hale and the Free Democrats, and in the landslide victory of the proslavery Democrat Franklin Pierce. But several new antislavery congressmen were elected, including Gerrit Smith, the philanthropist and abolitionist leader who had helped organize the radical Cazenovia Convention. Within days of his election he was getting congratulatory letters: his election was "the sequel to Uncle Tom's Cabin," it was "the greatest thing that has happened to us, since our struggle has commenced not excepting Sumner's election and Uncle Tom's Cabin." One of these writers, Barnburner Democrat Bradford Wood, wrote a belated letter to Sumner the same week, congratulating him on "Freedom National."[120] And in early February Garrisonian David L. Child (husband of Lydia Maria Child) wrote a similar letter of praise for "Freedom National" to Sumner, with one catch: "With the exception of Uncle Tom's Cabin, nothing has occurred in the whole history of the slave question in the United States, that has consoled me so much under the sting and shame of Southern usurpation and Northern treachery."[121]

Usurpation and treachery: these were the hallmarks of the Slave Power, which appeared to hold an unbreakable grip on national power. From the autumn of 1852 through 1853 there seemed no question that slavery would determine the fate of the nation for the foreseeable future. With the victory of Democrat Franklin Pierce in November, proslavery forces and Democrats began to beat the drum for the opening of the Louisiana Purchase to slavery. In December, John Jay Jr. wrote Sumner from New York, "'Uncle Tom' has created a New Feeling in regard to slavery, which I am confident will shew itself the moment an opportunity is afforded for its embodiment."[122] That "opportunity" would come, but Jay may have been a bit overconfident in late 1852. *Uncle Tom's Cabin* was reaching an unprecedented audience, certainly, but that audience was still limited relative to the great mass of the northern electorate. There was something in the air, but an even more pervasive cultural action would be required to tip the balance. Over the next two years that balance would be tipped, in a remarkably modern fusion of celebrity, popular entertainment, and commerce, colliding with Stephen Douglas's brash proposal to open up the northern domain of the Louisiana Purchase in the Kansas-Nebraska bill.

THE ANTI-SLAVERY RECORD.

Vol. III. No. VII.   JULY, 1837.   Whole No. 31.

This picture of a poor fugitive is from one of the stereotype cuts manufactured in this city for the southern market, and used on handbills offering rewards for runaway slaves.

THE RUNAWAY.

To escape from a powerful enemy, often requires as much courage and generalship as to conquer. One of the most celebrated military exploits on record, is the *retreat* of the ten thousand Greeks under

"THE RUNAWAY." In 1837 the American Antislavery Society published this image of a fugitive slave used in broadsides in the South, calling attention to the efforts of slaves to escape to freedom.

—Image courtesy of the American Antiquarian Society.

AN UNDERGROUND CORRIDOR. Frederick Douglass was born near Hillsboro in eastern Talbot County, Md., and escaped from Baltimore in 1838. Harriet Tubman escaped from Bucktown, Dorchester County, in September 1849, eighteen months after the fugitives escaping Washington, D.C., on the sloop *Pearl* were recaptured at the mouth of the Potomac. Garland White and another fugitive, heading to the radical abolitionist meeting in Cazenovia, N.Y., were recaptured in Silver Spring, Md., in August 1850. Christiana, the site of a violent battle with slave catchers in September 1851, is located in Sadsbury Township, Lancaster County, Pa.

—*Smith's Topographical Map of Virginia and Maryland,* courtesy of the David Rumsey Map Collection, David Rumsey Map Center, Stanford Libraries.

HARRIET TUBMAN, CA. 1868–1869. Around forty-five years old, Tubman was living in Auburn, N.Y., in 1868 after fifteen years moving people north along the Maryland fugitive corridor and working with the United States Colored Troops in the Lowcountry during the Civil War.

—Image from the Benjamin F. Powelson Collection, courtesy of the National Museum of African American History and Culture and the Library of Congress.

FREDERICK DOUGLASS, ca. 1856. Quarter-plate ambrotype by an unidentified artist.

—Image courtesy of the National Portrait Gallery, Smithsonian Institution; acquired through the generosity of an anonymous donor.

HARRIET BEECHER STOWE, 1852. Sixth-plate daguerreotype by an unknown artist.

—Image courtesy of the National Portrait Gallery, Smithsonian Institution.

TITLE PAGE OF JEWETT'S FIRST EDITION OF *Uncle Tom's Cabin*, 1852. Image courtesy of the Harriet Beecher Stowe Center, Hartford, Conn.

—Image courtesy of the Harriet Beecher Stowe Center, Hartford, Conn.

UNCLE TOM'S CABIN;

OR,

LIFE AMONG THE LOWLY.

BY

HARRIET BEECHER STOWE.

VOL. I.

BOSTON:
JOHN P. JEWETT & COMPANY.
CLEVELAND, OHIO:
JEWETT, PROCTOR & WORTHINGTON.
1852.

TITLE PAGE of Jewett's first edition of *Uncle Tom's Cabin*, 1852.
—Image courtesy of the Harriet Beecher Stowe Center, Hartford, Conn.

FOUR OF TWENTY HAND-COLORED PLAYING CARDS from the 1852 Uncle Tom's Cabin Card Game (W. & S. B. Ives, Salem, Mass.), one example of the wave of *Uncle Tom*–themed consumer goods produced for the Christmas season of 1852.

—Image courtesy of the Harriet Beecher Stowe Center, Hartford, Conn.

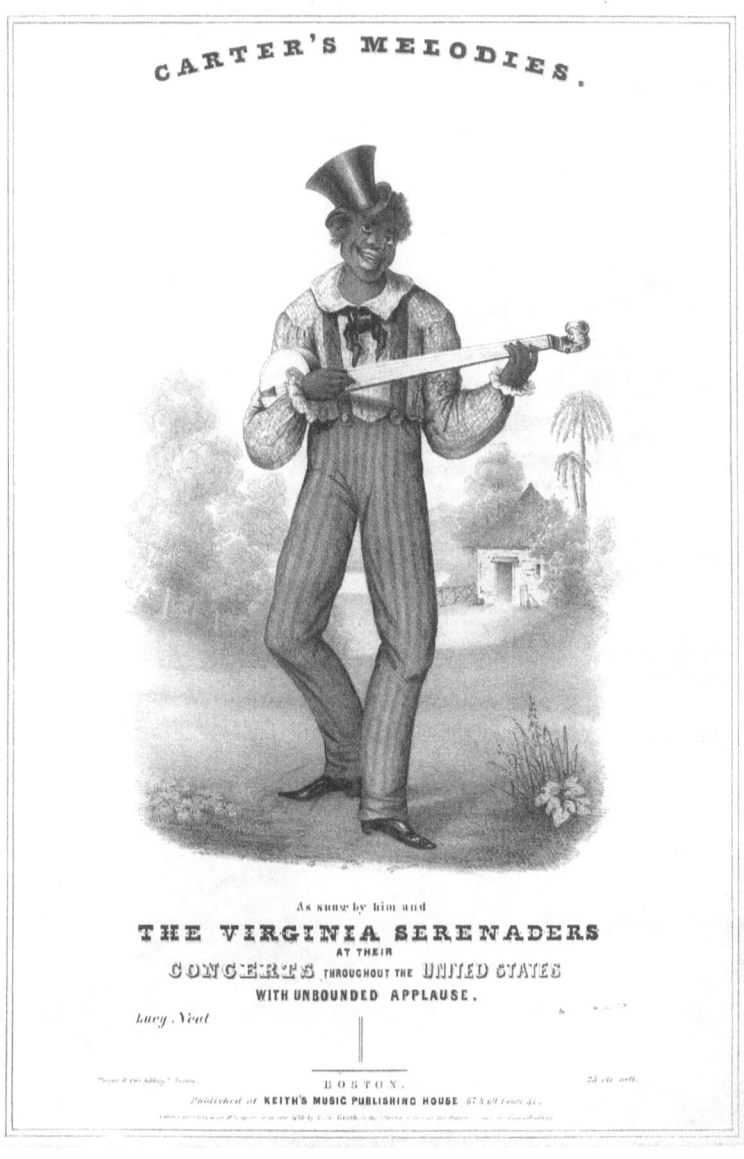

TITLE PAGE, *Carter's Melodies as sung by him and the Virginia Serenaders* . . . (Boston: Keith's Music Publishing House, 1844). James P. Carter's "Lucy Neal" was one of the three "Ethiopian songs" that Frederick Douglass singled out in 1855, though "almost absurd to say it," as constituting "our national music."

—Image courtesy of the Lester S. Levy Collection of Sheet Music, Sheridan Libraries, Johns Hopkins University.

STEPHEN FOSTER of Allegheny, Pa., ca. 1859.

—Image courtesy of the Foster Hall Collection, Center for American Music, University of Pittsburgh Library System.

MARTIN DELANY of Pittsburgh as major, United States Army.

—Image courtesy of the Mollus-Mass Civil War Photo Collection, Army Heritage and Education Center, Carlisle, Penn.

BLACK NATIONALIST MARTIN DELANY probably despised the minstrel songwriter Stephen Foster, but they were both involved in different ways in a common abolitionist circle in Pittsburgh and Allegheny, Pa., centering on Drs. Charles Avery and Francis J. Le Moyne, and poet Charles Shiras.

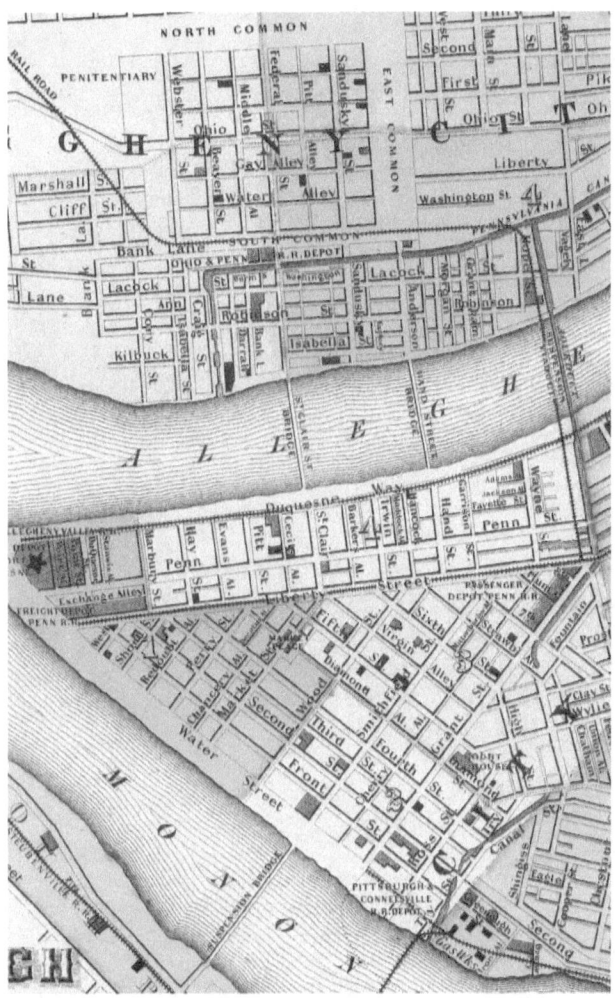

WHILE THEY BOTH MOVED FREQUENTLY, Foster lived for a time at his brother's house at East and South Common in Allegheny, Delany on Hand Street between Liberty and Penn across the river in Pittsburgh. Foster's parents were living in hotels and boardinghouses along Penn Street around 1850. Foster's neighbor Charles Avery, who established the Allegany Institute and Mission Church between Liberty and Ohio, presided over the meeting at the Allegheny Market House, at Ohio and Federal, where Delany spoke in September 1850. When armed bands of African Americans left for Canada over the next few days, the hotels, concentrated along Federal Street in Allegheny and along Penn and Liberty Streets and between Wood and Smithfield Streets in Pittsburgh, lost virtually all of their waiters. The Temperance Arc, where Frank Johnson's band played in 1843, was near Ohio and Sandusky Streets in Allegany; in November 1853 Joseph Foster staged Charles Shiras's *Invisible Prince* and *Uncle Tom's Cabin* at his theater on Fifth Street, just east of Wood Street in Pittsburgh; the 1856 Republican Convention met at Lafayette Hall on Wood Street, between 3rd and 4th. *Colton's Atlas of the World, Illustrating Physical and Political Geography* (New York: J. H. Colton, 1856), no. 40.

—Image courtesy of the David Rumsey Map Collection, David Rumsey Map Center, Stanford Libraries.

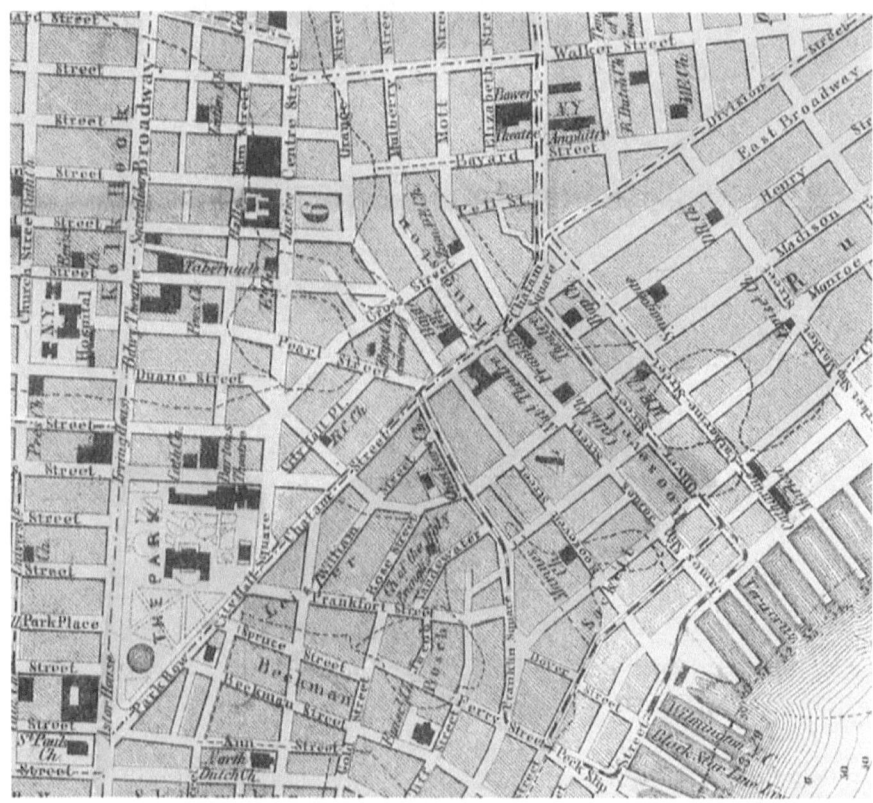

THE EAST SIDE OF NEW YORK CITY in 1855, Catherine Market, Chatham Square, and the Bowery to Broadway. Barnum's American Museum was at Broadway and Ann Street, south of City Hall Park, catty-corner to the Astor House. Up Chatham Street, the National Theatre and the Franklin Theatre were located just south of Chatham Square; the Bowery Theatre was to the north where Chatham turns into the Bowery, beyond the intersection with Catherine Street, running southeast to Catherine Market, the site of Saturday "eel-dancing" earlier in the century. Fugitive Slave Law protests were held in City Hall Park in the autumn of 1850. The Crystal Palace, which Joseph and Jane Sill visited in October 1853 before seeing *Uncle Tom's Cabin* at the National Theatre, was located forty blocks to the north. The Odd Fellows Hall was at Center and Grand, twelve blocks north of the City Hall Park. *Topographical Map of New York City . . .* , Matthew Dripps, No. 103 Fulton St., New York, 1855.

—Image courtesy of the David Rumsey Map Collection, David Rumsey Map Center, Stanford University.

CHATHAM THEATRE.

THE CHATHAM GARDEN THEATRE in 1831. The site of some of the earliest blackface performances in New York, the Chatham Garden was converted into the Tappan Temperance Chapel, serving the Five Points, and damaged in the 1834 rioting.

—Image courtesy of the Eno Collection of New York City Views, New York Public Library.

CHATHAM THEATRE, renamed the National Theatre, New York City. Built in 1839, the Chatham Theater was a venue for minstrelsy in the 1840s. Alexander Purdy purchased the building in 1850 and renamed it the National Theatre, producing an early Charles Taylor version of *Uncle Tom's Cabin* in 1852, followed by the record-setting eleven-month run of the George Howard version in 1853–1854. From *Century Illustrated Magazine* 3, no. 39 (January 1890): 269.

—Image courtesy of the American Antiquarian Society.

P. T. BARNUM'S AMERICAN MUSEUM, 1859, at Ann Street and Broadway. This photo may have been taken from an upper floor at the Astor House Hotel. *Barnum's Museum,* published by the London Stereoscopic Company, featured in the Edward Jackson Holmes Collection.

—Photograph © 1859 Museum of Fine Arts, Boston.

ODD FELLOWS HALL at Grand and Center Streets, New York. Built in 1848, this building was the site of the organizational meetings of the nativists in 1854.

—Image courtesy of the Eno Collection of New York City Views, New York Public Library.

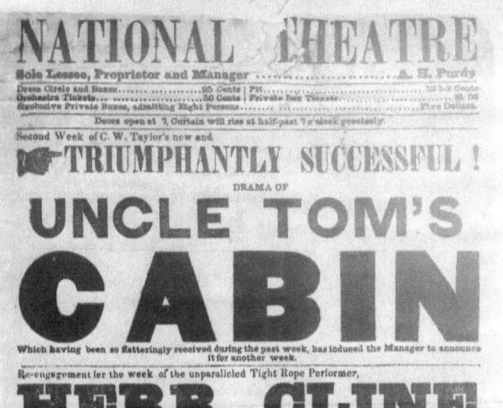

PLAYBILL FOR THE TAYLOR version of *Uncle Tom's Cabin*, Purdy's National Theatre, August 30, 1852. In this early version of the play, Stowe's character George Harris has been turned into "Edward Wilmot," described as "a young mechanic in Bondage," linking him to the antislavery Wilmot Proviso of 1847–1848. During these weeks, *Uncle Tom's Cabin* was followed by Thomas D. Rice playing "Otello."

—Image courtesy of the Harry Birdoff Collection, Harriet Beecher Stowe Center, Hartford, Conn.

SPRINGFIELD, OHIO, CITY HALL and Marketplace, constructed 1848. Harford Toland saw William Shires's production of *Uncle Tom's Cabin* at Springfield City Hall on March 9, 1854. Later that month and into April, Toland went to various Nebraska meetings, and in June had a "little Nebraska talk" with his friend Box Betts.

—Image courtesy of the Archives of the Clark County Historical Society, Springfield, Ohio.

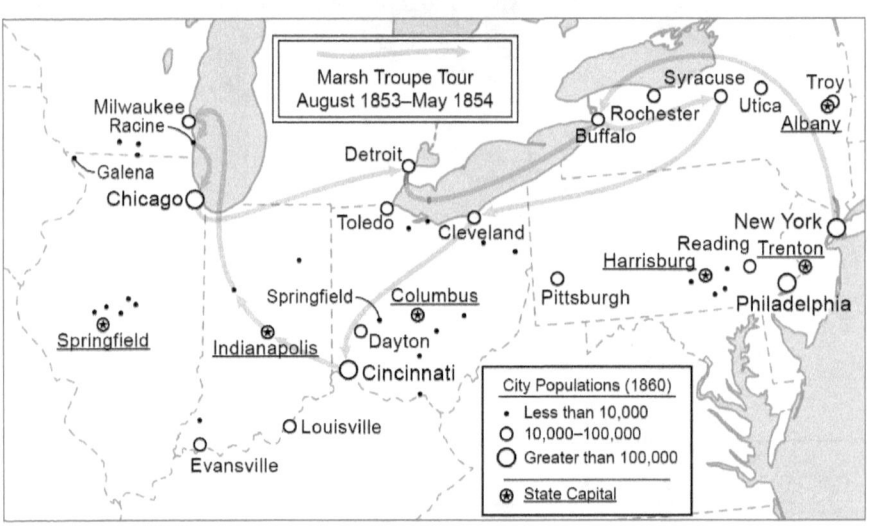

CITIES AND TOWNS in the Mid-Atlantic and Midwest where *Uncle Tom's Cabin* is known to have been performed, 1853–1854.

—Map by James DeGrand.

STEPHEN A. DOUGLAS, ca. 1850–1852, as he would have appeared during the Compromise debates and on his European tour.

—Image courtesy of the Prints and Photographs Division, Library of Congress.

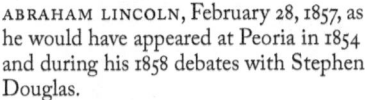

ABRAHAM LINCOLN, February 28, 1857, as he would have appeared at Peoria in 1854 and during his 1858 debates with Stephen Douglas.

—Image courtesy of the Prints and Photographs Division, Library of Congress.

NATHANIEL P. BANKS, ca. 1861. After serving as Speaker of the U.S. House of Representatives, Banks was elected governor of Massachusetts, serving through January 1861. He was appointed major general of volunteers in May 1861 and commanded troops in Maryland and western Virginia through September 1862, when he was sent to command forces in Louisiana.

—Image courtesy of Civil War Photographs, Prints and Photographs Division, Library of Congress.

RICHMOND, THE CONFEDERATE CAPITAL, ENTERED BY THE UNION ARMY.

RICHMOND, THE CONFEDERATE CAPITAL, entered by the Union Army. A depiction of black troops of the Twenty-fifth Army Corps entering Richmond on the morning of April 3, 1865. Hours later Garland White, once a fugitive and now the chaplain of the Twenty-eighth United States Colored Troops, addressed crowds in the streets and was reunited with his mother after having been separated for over twenty years.

—Image courtesy of the Miriam and Ira D. Wallach Division of Art, Prints and Photographs: Picture Collection, New York Public Library.

CHAPTER 5

Transforming Culture

Commercializing Antislavery

EARLY IN July 1852, Harriet Beecher Stowe received a check for $10,300, the first installment of the $30,000 that she would be paid by Jewett and Co. for *Uncle Tom's Cabin*. Given the explosive success of the book, she was already unhappy with the terms of her contract, and her sister Catharine was pushing a plan to sue. Eventually Stowe would cut her ties with Jewett. But in the meantime her July payment was the largest on record for the first three months of a book's sales. She was on her way to be becoming a wealthy woman, her royalties far outstripping her husband Calvin's meager income from Andover Seminary.[1]

The liminal impact of her text was intensified by the fact that Stowe was a woman in public, and highly successful. The sheer commercial success of *Uncle Tom's Cabin* further reinforced the gender violation represented by Stowe's authorship. Starting with the arrival on the scene of social reformer Frances Wright in the 1820s and then the emergence of female abolition lecturers in the 1830s, conservative voices in America had condemned female public performances as disorderly violations of social norms.[2] Jenny Lind's rave reception in 1850 may well have begun to normalize the sight of women earning money in public performance. So too did Stowe's female peers in the literary world. Not an insignificant figure before she began to write *Uncle Tom's Cabin* in January 1851, Stowe was suddenly a celebrity of means, and deeply involved in the greatest public struggle of the day.

Stowe thus plunged into a new world of wealth and celebrity, a world that looks quite familiar to us today. With roots in the previous two or three decades, certainly, entertainment capitalism was exploding in the early 1850s, accelerated by new technologies of mobility and communication: the steam engine and the telegraph. This entertainment industry took the productions of writers and artists and turned them into commercial ventures for mass audiences. It encompassed book publication, newspapers, the song-sheet music industry, the theater, vaudeville, and a host of evolving technologies like the magic lantern, panorama, and diorama shows and the silhouette and daguerreotype parlors that would lead in less than half a century to the film industry.[3] It was also a world of direct personal performance by celebrity authors, inaugurated by Charles Dickens in his lecture tours of the United States in the 1840s.[4] The phenomenon was transnational, and Stowe would partake, spending five months in England and on the Continent in 1853, raising the profile of her book in a great mass market and reinforcing the British commitment to antislavery. Her success bred imitation, and a flood of long, well-funded antislavery books—and proslavery books—followed in the years immediately after the publication of *Uncle Tom's Cabin*.

The blackface minstrel show and song-sheet industries were well poised to capitalize on this trend. In the highly contradictory circumstances of American "creolization," a songwriter equal to Stowe's caliber, if not her personal success, Stephen Foster, composed his most highly acclaimed songs—songs that were immediately incorporated in productions of *Uncle Tom's Cabin* in American theaters. Fusing with and extending the readership of Stowe's novel, these vectors of entertainment commerce put race and slavery at the center of the American public sphere. This cultural eruption was accelerating in a spiraling synergy when Stephen Douglas introduced the Nebraska bill in the Senate in January 1854. When great swaths of the northern public rose up in opposition to the Kansas-Nebraska

Act, it was thus in the wake of the first great modern media event in American history.

PERHAPS INEVITABLY, within two months of the publication of *Uncle Tom's Cabin*, Stowe was embroiled in a series of public controversies that would roll into the autumn and inspire her next publishing venture. In chapter 12 of the novel she had identified a minister in Philadelphia, Joel Parker, as the source of a passage supporting slavery, and that May, Parker launched an attack in the press, threatening to sue. Things rapidly deteriorated. Stowe, commissioned to write a new series in the *New York Independent*, had started with a critique of an article attacking Louis Kossuth in the *New York Observer*, a proslavery Presbyterian paper. Stowe and her brother Henry Ward Beecher exchanged heated letters with Parker during the summer, which were published in the *Observer*. Parker argued that Stowe had violated standards of gender decency in her defense of Kossuth.[5] With a tangle of charges against her, Stowe began a process of documentary investigation to defend herself against Parker and the *Observer* but also against a rising critique from proslavery writers south and north who were beginning to launch counterattacks of their own.[6]

Early in October, in a final volley in the *Independent* to which the proslavery *Observer* failed to respond, Stowe unloaded her documentary research on Parker and his defense of slavery.[7] The model for her work was by her side, *American Slavery As It Is: Testimony of a Thousand Witnesses*, published in 1839 by Theodore Dwight Weld and Angelina and Sarah Grimké to inform the world of the true conditions of slavery. Legend had it that Stowe "kept that book in her work basket by day, and slept with it under her pillow by night, till its facts crystallized into Uncle Tom."[8] Stowe clearly had a copy, but *American Slavery As It Is* was by now out of print and certainly needed updating, and this was the task to which she set herself in late October 1852.[9]

On the twenty-fifth she wrote to Gerrit Smith in Peterboro, New York, with the kernel of what would become *The Key to Uncle*

Tom's Cabin well in mind, if not in final form. In a detailed letter, she told Smith that she had "been solicited both in England & this country to give some forty or fifty pages of notes in addition to my book to supply facts & statistics to show that it is not an overdrawn picture of slavery."[10] The bulk of her letter asked for confirmation of a series of those "facts & statistics." Stowe had launched a fact-finding campaign. Her letter to Smith was one of many that she, Calvin, and her assistant Leonard W. Bacon (the son of Leonard Bacon, an old Lyman Beecher colleague who edited the *Independent*) sent out from Andover to the antislavery leadership across the North, some of which looped through her publisher, John Jewett in Boston, and various other channels.[11]

A wide circle of antislavery politicians and intellectuals was drawn into Stowe's research. Senator Charles Sumner was in communication with Stowe during the autumn election recess between sessions of Congress, and he attended a gathering at her house (known as "Mrs. Stowe's Cabin") in Andover sometime late that autumn, as she was launching her research. When he wrote to her on November 12, the week after the election, he was clearly fully informed about her project: "Let me urge you to special care in your statements of facts & law in your forthcoming tract. You have at this moment a marvelous power, which the enemy will try to break down, by cant and criticism. Your pamphlet will carry a knowledge of the legalized enormities of slavery . . . Let me be of service to you if I can. I leave for Washington in the last week of the month."[12]

By January, proofs of the *Key* were on their way to Washington, with a request that they be reviewed carefully by Sumner, Salmon Chase, and John Hale.[13] Despite promises from Jewett, however, there were delays into March, and the *Key* did not come out until April. Jewett was printing sixty thousand copies and exulting to Sumner, "If the croakers don't find the nails clinched there, I'm mistaken."[14] Antislavery politicians were eager to see it in print. John Jay was confident that it would "materially strengthen and deepen the impression she has made"; James Birney felt that it would "be most needed by those who are strangers to Slavery." Sumner inquired from Washington of a Boston associate: "I am anxious to know about Mrs. Stowe's book? When will it appear? And what impression will it make on the public?"[15]

The excitement around Stowe's efforts stood in sharp contrast with the prospects of politics. The old order was literally dying off, but a new political structure was nowhere in sight. Clay had died in June, and in October Daniel Webster died suddenly and was buried in a somber Whig funeral in his hometown of Marshfield, Massachusetts. While unionist Whigs made an effort to celebrate his life, abolitionists were savage in their condemnation of his performance during the Compromise, virtually dancing on his grave.[16] In the November presidential election, Whig Winfield Scott had lost—and the Whig Party had been set adrift—with the collapse of the party vote in the South, where Scott received 69,275 votes (16 percent), less than Zachary Taylor had won four years earlier. Scott had not done well in New England, either, dropping 10,485 votes (6 percent) from Taylor's total. These declines made 1852 the lowest-turnout election between 1840 and the turn of the twentieth century.

In the meantime, the fugitive crisis continued to heat up. Stowe's *Key* updated Weld and the Grimkés' *American Slavery As It Is* with a detailed account of the recapture of the *Pearl* in 1848 and the tribulations of the Edmundson sisters; Stowe met with their mother in New York in May. Her excerpts from southern papers were all new, running from October 1852 to January 1853.[17] But she was not able to add the case that was roiling New York City in November 1852, when a slave family from Virginia being transported to Texas was rescued on the docks by the Vigilance Committee and freed under New York State law. The Lemmon case, known for the slave owner's name, involved people in Stowe's intimate and wider circles, including her brother-in-law John Hooker as well as John Jay. The Commonwealth of Virginia would pursue the case vigorously in New York courts in the hope of overturning northern emancipation laws. And all through 1852 and 1853 fugitives continued to be arrested and remanded, fifty-one in all, with or without the minimal federal hearings. Three were rescued in Sandusky, Ohio, in September 1852, however, and at least two thousand others made it to freedom in these two years, supported by the network of vigilance committees, the Underground Railroad.[18]

This was the climate, and these were the stakes, as Stowe researched, compiled, and wrote her *Key to Uncle Tom's Cabin*. The *Key* was a strategic effort to intervene again in the public sphere to advance the antislavery cause and to build a common consciousness among those so inclined. These now constituted a coherent and growing "imagined community," a mass of readers aware of their private participation in a wider public experience.[19] Abolitionists had been hoping to build such a community for decades, and clearly Stowe was reaching many more people, and much more quickly.

But text would not have to stand alone. The readership of *Uncle Tom's Cabin* was a mass audience, and a mass-marketing opportunity, and Jewett's success in selling the book, and then its follow-on *Key*, opened the doors to commerce. For the next eighteen months it was, for better or worse, the men of commerce who would drive the message in the market.

Jewett himself was the first of these drivers, beginning with his hard bargaining with Calvin Stowe. The Stowes had wanted 20 percent of sales, but he convinced Calvin that if they accepted 10 percent, he would push sales with an aggressive marketing campaign. Certainly his co-partnership with publishers in Cleveland helped to accelerate sales in northern Ohio and the Midwest in general, beyond the established Boston–New York–Philadelphia axis. He commissioned John Greenleaf Whittier to compose a ballad, "Eva," which Jewett had set to music and sold as a song sheet. He put out a standard two-volume set in a variety of colors and bindings, including a gilt-embossed gift edition, and in October 1852 announced that he would publish an ornately illustrated single-volume luxury edition for the Christmas season.[20] The Christmas season of 1851 had been filled with toys, crockery, and clothing celebrating the Hungarian revolutionary Louis Kossuth; 1852 would be the Christmas of *Uncle Tom's Cabin*.[21] *Uncle Tom's Cabin*–themed engravings, decorative plates and figurines, toys, even clothing were all spun off in vast quantities, including a card game on the division and unification of slave families called "Uncle Tom and Little Eva." This commerce was just as strong in England if not more so. Visiting England in the spring of 1853, Anna Whistler, the mother of the famous painter, complained that "Uncle Tom is stamped on everything all over the kingdom."[22] By the next year Jewett was advertising *Pictures and Stories from Uncle Tom's Cabin*, part of a series of "Anti-Slavery Picture Books" with which to "Indoctrinate the Children, and when they grow to be Men and Women, their Principles will be Correct!"[23] Salmon P. Chase of Ohio was reading his Christmas edition of *Uncle Tom's Cabin* in January 1853. He had followed it in the *National Era* the year before but could still summon up strong emotions: "What a character & the book what a sermon. I cannot read it without tears. Surely it is *'tuba, mirum spargens sonum* [bugle, spread the wonderful sound].'"[24] Perhaps more prosaically, James W. Stone, a Massachusetts Free Soiler, reported to Sumner from Brooklyn in December that *Uncle Tom's Cabin* "is doing a vast amount of good. A bookseller here assures me that he still sells more of that work than of any other in the Market."[25]

IN DECEMBER 1852 Stowe was at a crossroads. Her novel was being hailed as the "great book of the year." Ellen Wheaton in Syracuse wrote in her diary in January that "almost every paper, contains something about the success of Uncle Tom's Cabin, both in this, and foreign lands."[26] In particular, *Uncle Tom's Cabin* was sweeping through England and Scotland. Hundreds of thousands of copies were being sold; by April 1853 the figure was up to roughly a million and a half copies.[27] But by December Stowe was already exhausted with the effort and stress of compiling the *Key*, as she told Sumner in a series of letters. Writing about some of the current controversies, she announced her plans: "If God spares my life I shall visit England soon. I hope this visit will bring me some rest and relief." She had "hope of doing good by going to Europe." Despairing for her country, "she had concluded that "the public opinion of the world is our last hope. The public sentiment of our country is corrupted."[28]

The grounds for her hopes in "the public opinion of the world" rested in communications she received that month. From Glasgow, the New Ladies Anti-Slavery Society issued an invitation for her and Calvin to visit Great Britain at their expense.[29] She also received letters from men in high stations: Lord Carlisle and the Earl of Shaftesbury wrote her glowing letters to which she wrote careful responses. Shaftesbury had in November composed and published an "affectionate and Christian Address" for the women of the British Isles to sign and present to Stowe. Eventually over a half million would sign this address.[30] Stowe was clearly a bit dazzled by the aristocracy, writing to Sumner (in a snipe at the decidedly middling Garrisonian radicals) that "the men of England who now have hold of the matter are of a different class from the George Thompson school."[31]

One has to wonder if there was not a bit of calculation. The cost of her trip would be covered by the antislavery ladies in Glasgow, and her book was selling out across Great Britain. Since it was not protected by copyright laws, an author's tour might bring some further benefit. A collection was already under way, the "Penny-Offering," in which readers paid a penny as a contribution to the author, and one or two publishers did eventually write her modest checks. Stowe would return from England with another $20,000 for her efforts.[32] There is a hint of the fusion of cause, celebrity, and personal benefit in her early letter to Gerrit Smith, when she had written, regarding the *Key*, "I am pressed for time it being thought desirable that it should appear in England during the height of the Uncle Tom fervor."[33] In the end, she never quite found time or opportunity to raise much money for Frederick Douglass's "industrial college."

On April 1, 1853, a little more than a month before the *Key* appeared in bookstores, Stowe left New York Harbor with a large family entourage aboard the steamer *Canada* and arrived in Liverpool after a ten-day voyage.[34] Five days later she met with the Ladies' Anti-Slavery

Society and a vast concourse of people at the Glasgow City Hall, and then moved on to Edinburgh and up the coast to Aberdeen. By early May the Stowes were in London. Feted at a grand affair at Stafford House, the seat of the Duke and Duchess of Sutherland, she was presented with the signed "Address" in twenty-six volumes in black leather bindings, each embossed with a golden American eagle. Soon it was a mass antislavery meeting at Exeter Hall in London, then a departure for the Continent, where she toured for the summer before returning, again through Liverpool, on the steamer *Arctic*.[35]

There was some considerable advance work behind these efforts. Stowe had sent copies of *Uncle Tom's Cabin*—with personal letters—to the English antislavery aristocracy, and to Charles Dickens, in March 1852, an effort that had certainly paid off. She had celebrated Kossuth, the Hungarian hero, and she had corresponded with Jenny Lind in the summer of 1852 as she worked to raise money to liberate the entire Edmundson family from slavery.[36] She then reversed their transatlantic celebrity-building passage, and those of Harriet Martineau and Charles Dickens. Unlike Dickens she did virtually no public speaking, with the exception of a conversation with the ladies at Stafford House, maintaining a careful adherence to the doctrine of the "women's sphere."[37] But she was very much in the public eye everywhere she went, and the entire British tour incalculably reinforced the visibility and legitimacy of the American antislavery movement, followed in every American paper, for good or for ill. Steam and the telegraph were driving a wider Atlantic reintegration, and Americans had read all of the details of the 1848 European revolutions, as they would in 1854 the details of the Crimean War. Stowe followed to England Americans as different as Thomas D. Rice, the minstrel inventor of the "Jump Jim Crow" mania of the 1830s, and Frederick Douglass, who had literally found his freedom on the lecture tour in the 1840s. And interestingly, as we will see, Stowe overlapped with another Douglas in Europe. Stephen Douglas, the aggressively ambitious Democratic senator from Illinois, embarked in May 1853 for Liverpool for his own grand tour of the great European capitals, which occupied him into October. Over these five months he would miss a subtle shift in American culture.

HARRIET BEECHER Stowe and John P. Jewett both did very well with *Uncle Tom's Cabin*, and others saw possibilities. In particular, well-funded book publishers in Philadelphia, New York, and Boston, seeing real opportunities, struck while the iron was hot. Books on slavery would sell, and they wanted part of the action. As they did in the Christmas extravaganza of 1852, men of commerce and capital acted to strengthen their bottom line. This commercial action worked, like Stowe's triumphal British tour, to draw attention to—indeed legitimize—the antislavery argument and the antislavery cause.

Before Jewett took a calculated risk in 1851, book publishers had avoided making significant investments in books relating to slavery. These were typically narratives of the trials and tribulations of a fugitive who had carved out a life in the North after grueling years in slavery. Many were pamphlet-sized, self-published or published by small local presses, minimally supported by advertising, if at all, and otherwise barely noticed in the press.[38] But as the success of the publication of *Uncle Tom's Cabin* in the *National Era* sank in and rumors spread about Jewett's plans, major publishers began to make their own plans to catch the commercial wave and to invest in both full-length books and the advertising to support them. Three months after Jewett put out *Uncle Tom's Cabin*, another Boston publisher reprinted Richard Hildreth's four-hundred-page, two-volume *Archy: The White Slave*, a book that had failed to make much of an impression when it first came out in 1839.[39] In March 1853, probably delaying the publication of Stowe's *Key*, Jewett put out two long volumes: Frederick Douglass's *The Heroic Slave* and Charles Sumner's republished *White Slavery in the Barbary States*. When it was first published in 1847, Sumner's *White Slavery* had faded quickly; in 1853 Jewett publicized it heavily. By contrast, a book in the simple narrative tradition, *The Life, Labors, and Travels of Elder Charles Bowles*, from a steam printer in Watertown, Massachusetts, passed unnoticed in the press, and certainly was unadvertised. In sum, while over the previous several decades longer books of more than two hundred pages had accounted for roughly 10 percent of the books produced on slaves, this proportion jumped to over 60 percent in the five years after the publication of *Uncle Tom's Cabin*, and the works were far more heavily advertised. (See Appendix, table 8.)

Throughout the autumn of 1852 and into the winter, Sumner was in nervous communication about his book with Stowe, Jewett, and William Seward's wife, Frances. Stowe assured Sumner that it would appeal to "a high class of mind, just that class which it is exceedingly difficult to reach"; Jewett kept him up to date on his "beautiful . . . splendid book."[40] The publishing tide rolled on. James W. Stone extended the frame of antislavery print, noting to Sumner in December that he has seen the fifth edition of his "Freedom National" speech for sale, suggesting that "it bids fair to have a run nearly equal to that of Uncle Tom's Cabin."[41] The next summer, after excerpts had appeared in *Frederick Douglass's Paper* (formerly the *North Star*), Solomon Northrup's *Twelve Years a Slave* was published in Auburn and Buffalo to widespread attention. In Palmyra, New York, James Lakey, a local physician and antislavery supporter, read both Sumner's *White Slavery* and Northrup's *Twelve Year a Slave*. Both he considered "well done," but he had sarcastic comments about Northrup's judgment in having let himself be lured to Washington in 1841, where he was kidnapped and sold south.[42] Late in 1853, news of *Clotel: or the President's Daughter*, the first novel written by an African American, began to filter in from London, where its author, William Wells Brown, was in hiding from the Fugitive Slave Act.[43]

The impact of these publications was well recognized by both sides of the debate. By late June the *Washington Star* was complaining about the evil influence of "Mrs. Stowe and her compatriots, Solomon Northrup and Frederick Douglass," and the vehemently proslavery *New York Herald* was in a panic: "The northern States will soon be inundated by a flood of abolition novels, and the effect upon the opinions, the politics, the peace and happiness of the country, is beyond calculation." On the other side, an orator told the Massachusetts Anti-Slavery Society in February 1854 that even if this generation of abolitionists were to fail, the next generation would "get hold of some 'Uncle Tom's Cabin,' or 'White Slave,' or Life of Solomon Northrup,' and begin the work again."[44]

If antislavery voices were suddenly getting the attention of well-financed publishers, so too were proslavery voices. Writing in the plantation novel tradition directly in response to *Uncle Tom's Cabin*, these authors painted a picture of tranquillity and harmony among slaves and masters in the plantation South.[45] The first of these "anti-Tom novels," *Aunt Phillis's Cabin; or, Southern Life as It Is*, written by a Virginia-born army wife in Washington, was hastily published in August 1852.[46] In sheer page count these anti-Tom novels were published on the same scale as the antislavery literature, and they had healthy advertising and received general notice in the press.[47] Through 1854, the majority of the anti-Tom authors (eleven of eighteen) were proslavery northerners, often writers who had relocated to the South. Of the eighteen works published through 1854, sixteen were published in Philadelphia and New York, and one published in Charleston was republished in New York by Harper's. Jewett in Boston led the field among the antislavery publishers, putting out eight books between 1852 and 1856, followed by three by another Boston firm, Phillips & Sampson. Lippincott and Grabo of Philadelphia led among the anti-Tom novels, putting out four through 1856 and seven through 1860, followed by three from J. W. Randolph of Richmond between 1853 and 1856. The dominance of northern publishers of the anti-Tom genre faded after 1854, with half of the imprints coming from presses from Richmond to Mobile to Nashville, while southern authors also came to dominate. But the scale of publication, their visibility in the press, and their northern authorship and publication suggest strongly that in the first few years following publication of *Uncle Tom's Cabin*, the proslavery novels were being produced in a well-financed battle for northern public opinion. Whether they were winning this battle is an open question. James W. Stone thought otherwise in December 1852. His source in Brooklyn had told him that "all the imitations . . . fall still-born upon the public."[48] Nonetheless, publishers in New York and Philadelphia thought they could sell proslavery material and rushed to get it into print to capitalize on that market. But by giving personas to African Americans, Stowe forced the proslavery writers to do the same, and the result put not just slavery but enslaved people before the public.

The explosion of print publication about slavery and slaves reverberated with an equally powerful force in the American public sphere. Music and race were deeply intertwined in both public and private across mid-nineteenth-century America. Abraham Lincoln closed a speech in August 1852 at a Whig rally for Winfield Scott by quoting a sea chantey to mock Franklin Pierce's mixing of Democratic and Free Soil messages: "Sally Brown is a bright Mullater, / Oh Sally Brown, / Pretty gal, but I can't get at her." Lincoln concluded, "Should Pierce ever be President, he will, politically speaking, not only be a mulatto; but he will be a good deal darker one than Sally Brown."[49] On a much less harsh and mocking note, Calvin Fletcher in Indianapolis wrote at the end of 1849 that on Christmas Eve, "Londen the negro runaway slave plaid [sic] marches" while Fletcher's sons Ingram and Billy "promenaded" behind him. Londen performed again on Christmas Day and on New Year's, playing the Washington Grand March "round the house and through the rooms." Declared Fletcher, "Those who heard it said it was exquisite."[50]

These experiences, and their ambiguously creolizing effects, penetrated every corner of society; they had deeply influenced Stowe's writing of *Uncle Tom's Cabin*. We rarely catch a glimpse like this one of the experience of race and music in the Fletcher household.[51] But the song-sheet industry rivaled that of book publishing in its influence, and—if ads in the newspapers are any measure—its reach in American society surged between 1851 and 1853.[52] Before the advent of radio seventy-five years later, the song-sheet and concert business was a central force in shaping a common national popular culture. While the expansion of the early 1850s was driven by the craze

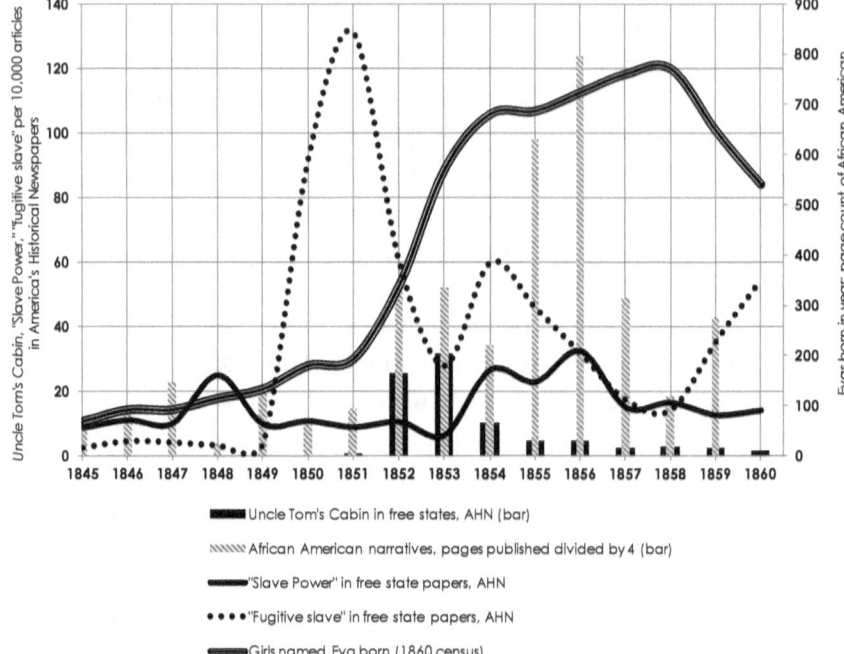

FIGURE 9. Cultural action and antislavery politics in the early to mid-1850s

The issue of fugitive slaves, surging in public consciousness in 1850–1851, setting the stage for *Uncle Tom's Cabin*, is measured here in newspaper publicity and the page count of published antislavery literature. The surge in incidence of the name Eva for girls born between 1851 and 1854 indicates the scale and timing of the public response to *Uncle Tom's Cabin*. The publicity for *Uncle Tom's Cabin* in the newspapers in 1852 and 1853 matched references to the "Slave Power" in 1854 and 1856.

NOTE: The counts from the three series from America's Historical Newspapers are the raw counts divided by the estimated number of articles in these papers, which include the *National Era*. The published page count for African American narratives is divided by 4 to fit this count in this figure. Sources: America's Historical Newspapers (accessed November 2017); African American Narratives and Antislavery Literature database (see table 8); U.S. Census, 1860; Theodore Weld, *American Slavery as It Is: Testimony of a Thousand Witnesses* (New York: American Anti-Slavery Society, 1839); Stowe, *Uncle Tom's Cabin* and *Key to Uncle Tom's Cabin;* Charles Sumner, *White Slavery in the Barbary States: A Lecture before the Boston Mercantile Library Association, Feb. 17, 1847* (Boston: W. D. Ticknor, 1847) and *White Slavery in the Barbary States* (Boston: John P. Jewett, 1853).

for Jenny Lind, she shared the American stage with the blackface minstrels.

The minstrel troupe was a recent invention. During the 1830s the early blackface performers soloed in variety shows and as interludes in theaters, but during one of the last winters of the depression, a group of four minstrel players joined together as the Virginia Minstrels. Having knocked around on the circuit, while doing occasional stints as printers, this group was led by Dan Emmett, who had learned drumming from a black drummer in the army and the banjo from a man he met in western Virginia in 1840 "by the name of 'Ferguson,' who was a very ignorant person, and 'nigger all over,' except in color." Practicing at his rooming house on Catherine Street in New York, they went public as a featured act as the Virginia Minstrels at the Bowery Amphitheatre on February 6, 1843, performing among other numbers Emmett's version of "Old Dan Tucker."[53] Playing fiddle, banjo, bones, and tambourine, they mixed songs, dances, and a mock-formal address broken by a stream of chatter between the "end man" and the "straight man," routines that Stowe used to structure scenes on the Shelbys' farm and between Topsy and Ophelia in New Orleans.[54] The minstrel show format erupted in the next two years, and by 1850 there were probably as many as twenty groups on tour, with constantly shifting membership blending and unifying the repertoires. While the original Virginia Minstrel group broke up after their first season, Christy's Minstrels solidified their model and launched a song-publishing industry under Edwin Christy.[55] To summarize the work of many scholars, this repertoire was a bizarre reflection of the self-identity of laboring and many middling white northerners. Its raw racism masked the fundamental point that whites of different ethnicities were presenting themselves as Americans—on stages where European actors often got top billing and top dollar. And the vehicle of that presentation was the African American "other" in their midst, simultaneously a target of jokes but also the speaker of truths. From "behind the burnt-cork mask," white Americans cast a sarcastic eye on powerful forces in the world around them, and that world included slaveholders and the Slave Power.[56]

The contradictory, creolizing messages of blackface allowed it to serve as a bridge of sorts between popular culture and the antislavery movement. The first important and obvious such bridge was forged by the Hutchinson Family Singers, a group supporting temperance, reform, and abolition, first performing in New Hampshire as the Granite State Singers in 1840. They were already touring widely when the blackface minstrel shows emerged in New York in 1843, and their commercial success in 1842, along with that of the Swiss Rainer Family Singers, seems to have inspired the formation of the Virginia Minstrels. A competitive cross-fertilization developed quickly. The Congo Minstrels advertised that some of their pieces would be "sung in harmony in the style of the Hutchinson family." Mocked by the "Albino Family," the Hutchinsons borrowed from the Virginia Minstrels, setting their powerful abolitionist song "Get Off the Track for Emancipation" to the tune of Dan Emmett's "Old Dan Tucker." Written as a campaign song for the Liberty Party in 1844, "Get Off the Track" became a national sensation the next year when—despite the threat of anti-abolitionist mobbing—the Hutchinsons performed it before huge crowds at Niblo's Garden on Broadway.[57]

These tensions were expressed in Frederick Douglass's changing opinion of minstrel music. In 1848, writing in the *North Star* to defend the Hutchinson Singers from New York State's proslavery "Hunker" Democrats, he condemned the Virginia Minstrels and Christy's Minstrels, among others, as "the filthy scum of white society, who have stolen from us a complexion denied to them by nature, in which to make money, and pander to the corrupt taste of their white fellow-citizens."[58] Seven years later, addressing the antislavery ladies in Rochester in the summer of 1855, he had shifted his position:

> The poets are with us. It would seem almost absurd to say it, considering the use that has been made of them, that we have allies in the Ethiopian songs; those songs that constitute our national music, and without which we would have no national music. They are heart songs, and finest feelings of human nature are expressed

in them. "Lucy Neal," "Old Kentucky Home," and "Uncle Ned," can make the heart sad as well as merry, and can call forth a tear as well as a smile. They waken the sympathies for the slave, in which anti-slavery principles take root, grow and flourish.[59]

Douglass's three "heart songs" were indeed ringing through the country's band halls and parlors. One was composed by James P. Carter, a minstrel performer, and two by Stephen Foster, celebrated by Bob Dylan as American's first modern singer-songwriter. Interpreting these songs and the motives of their composers is a slippery process. Here again, expressive art and commercial profit were interwoven in complex ways, and wakening "sympathies for the slave" was becoming a means of making a living.

James Carter seems to have been a typical blackface minstrel, performing for a season with the Virginia Serenaders in 1844 and the Ethiopian Serenaders in 1847. It is possible that he was the same James P. Carter, born in Virginia in the 1820s, who was living in New York in 1850.[60] During or after his 1844 season, Keith's Music Publishing House published *Carter's Melodies. As sung by him and The Virginia Serenaders at their Concerts Throughout The United States with Unbounded Applause,* comprising two songs, "Lucy Neal" and "Alabama Joe," with a top-hatted, banjo-playing plantation slave on the cover. Both songs had messages that would have resonated with antislavery audiences: Alabama Joe lives in a state "Where dey don't get their freedom then when dey are one and twenty," referring to the gradual emancipation laws in the northeastern states. Lucy Neal is the narrator's true love, and the message of the final stanzas is a direct statement of Stowe's condemnation of slavery's "outrage upon the family":

> Oh dars the white man comin,
> To tear you from my side;
> Stan back, you white slave dealer
> She is my betrothed bride.
> De poor nigger's fate is hard,

> De white man's heart is stone,
> Dey part poor nigs from his wife,
> An brake up dare happy home.[61]

Was Carter antislavery? Or did he and the Virginia Serenaders simply see profit to be made in critiques of slavery? Perhaps both. *Carter's Melodies* was one of two song sets printed by Keith's for the Serenaders in 1844; their *Songs of the Virginia Serenaders*, a fifteen-piece compilation arranged for the piano with songs like "Yellow Gals" and "Nigger put down dat Jug," was being noted in the Boston papers in March.[62] Was *Carter's Melodies* an appendix or a breakaway? The Serenaders were performing in Boston and Salem in March and April, and Carter was specifically named in an ad for the performances in Salem.[63] But he seems to have dropped out as the band moved south, unless he was "Master James, the celebrated bone player" listed in a notice for the Serenaders in the Philadelphia papers in June.[64] But he was not in the lineup when the Serenaders got to Baltimore under the leadership of Old Bull Myers, the master of an earlier version of the group.[65]

THERE IS a lot that we do not know about James Carter, composer of "Lucy Neal." We know a lot more about Stephen Foster. And here the balancing of message and profit was particularly obvious. The arc of Foster's life, from his birth in a prominent Democratic family in Pittsburgh in 1826 to his early death in New York City from alcoholism in 1864, encompassed the history of antebellum minstrelsy. Throughout, Foster was caught between two worlds, on a series of intersecting boundaries—between family respectability and family poverty, the parlor ballad and the minstrel show, the North and the South, the Pennsylvania Democratic establishment and the movement culture of Liberty and abolitionism. These stresses helped send him to an early grave.

Foster had his start in blackface in its early informal period and came of age with the commercializing trajectory. He first sang his songs at the age of nine in a neighborhood blackface group, and as a teenager he offered songs to T. D. Rice after seeing one of his shows in Pittsburgh. Nonetheless, this enthusiasm clashed with his family's sense of place and priority. Coming from a line of families in early Maryland and Scots-Irish Pennsylvania, the Fosters had been an important family in Lawrenceville, just upriver from Pittsburgh, until the Bank of the United States foreclosed on all of their property—including their homestead, the White Cottage—two months before Foster was born. This loss hung over Foster, born into a new and sudden poverty, while the family moved and scattered, before coalescing in Allegheny City in the early 1840s.[66] Though briefly defecting to the Whigs in 1840, the Foster family maintained a close connection to the Democratic Party; indeed, income from patronage positions provided the margin against complete penury. This connection was solidified when Stephen's sister Eliza married Edward Y. Buchanan, the youngest brother of James Buchanan, the towering figure of the Pennsylvania Democratic Party.[67]

If Foster's enthusiasm for minstrelsy clashed with familial respectability, it connected naturally with the family's adherence to proslavery democracy. But racial animosity may not have been so deeply engrained in the Foster family if an incident in 1843 is any measure. Frank Johnson led a noted all-black brass band which had performed in London in 1835. In May 1843 they were touring up the Ohio River; Stephen's brother Morrison accompanied them from Cincinnati to Pittsburgh, where they played to great acclaim for several evenings. Foster's father, William, as mayor of Allegheny City and a strong temperance advocate, invited them to perform at the "Temperance Arc." On leaving the hall, the band members were assaulted by a white gang. Mayor Foster intervened and tried to escort them to safety, and was caught with them in a hail of rocks and stones.[68]

As with Stowe, the border town of Cincinnati played an important role in Foster's emergence. In 1846 he agreed to keep the books for his brother Dunning's mercantile partnership. He spent just over three years living on the Cincinnati docks, actively recording, tradition has it, the songs and chants of black dockworkers and rivermen, in a world where the sound of black field singing could be heard from across the river. He also must have attended the minstrel shows that toured through Cincinnati's theaters in the late 1840s, including the Sable Harmonists and Christy's Minstrels, with whom he signed a contract in 1851.[69]

Two of Foster's earliest songs, which Frederick Douglass did not celebrate, nonetheless were clearly written in the environment shaped by Carter's "Lucy Neal" and its assault on slavery's "outrage" against the black family. "Lou'siana Belle," probably written in 1845, ties the implications of "Lucy Neal" to the sexual power inherent in slavery, as a bondsman promises the master's slave-concubine that they will eventually marry: "Oh! Belle don't you tell, / Don't tell Massa, don't you Belle . . . / I's gwine to marry you / Lou'siana Belle." Foster's manuscript is more penetrating: "He put her up to sell, / I thought I's pine my life away."[70]

Foster's infinitely more famous "Oh Susanna" was also obviously within this "outrage" genre. Set in ambiguous nonsense terms ("The sun so hot I froze myself"), the story tells of a separated couple and a runaway searching for a love lost to the New Orleans slave trade: "I come from Alabama, / With my banjo on my knee, / I's gwyne to Louisiana, / My true lub for to see." It also, Ken Emerson stresses, is about dangerous and confusing new technologies: in the second stanza the telegraph is transmuted into a steamboat, where "the 'lectric fluid magnified," exploded, and "kill'd five hundred Nigga."[71]

Ironically the telegraph would play a role in Foster's own world turned upside down. In July 1850 (as the Compromise debates were raging in Washington) Foster married Jane McDowell at his brother's house in Allegheny. But within two years they separated, Foster spending more and more time in the alcohol-soaked musical world of Broadway, while Jane became part of the first generation of women employed in business: after taking a short course, she took a job as a telegraph operator for the Pennsylvania Railroad. Occasionally, the story went, Foster would arrive at her office on the midnight train from New York; she would lock him out until her night shift was over, while he sat playing the violin—and probably drinking—on the stoop.[72]

Appropriated by the Gold Rush miners, and reworked in many versions to celebrate westward expansion, particularly by northern white men, "Oh Susanna" was not one of Douglass's "heart-songs." "Uncle Ned"—written soon after "Lou'siana Belle"—was among Douglass's chosen examples. It mourned the death of an old slave: "No more hard work for poor old Ned / He's gone wha de good niggas go." These songs can be seen as transitional in Foster's repertoire: he presents black personal and familial tragedy, though still set in stylized minstrel diction. But in 1849 Foster shifted more decisively toward the respectable parlor ballad genre with "Nelly Was a Lady," the story of a black steamboat woodcutter mourning the death of his "Virginia bride," written in a slow and dignified adagio rather than the fast-paced andantino of the classic minstrel songs.[73] This shift is seen as resolving the class tensions, but also, perhaps, toning down the racism, of the minstrelsy while also solidifying Foster's reputation with middling audiences who would have shunned the minstrel theaters. In 1852 he wrote to Edwin Christy, who had been publishing Foster's songs under his name, "I find that by my efforts I have done a great deal to build up a taste for Ethiopian songs among refined people, by making the words suitable to their taste, instead of the trashy and really offensive words which belong to some songs of that order."[74] Between 1851 and 1853 this shift included three of his classics: "Old Folks at Home" ("Way Down Upon the Suwannee River"), "Massa's in the Cold Ground," and "My Old Kentucky Home." Foster was certainly more of an aspiring careerist than an abolitionist, but—as Steven Saunders has put it—his sense of commercial and personal advantage provided the vehicle for many others, in different degrees, to "waken" their "sympathies for the slave."[75]

And yet there remains the question why Foster injected as much sympathy for slaves in his songs as he did. It appears that he was indeed caught between two worlds in his years in Allegheny, and perhaps a careerist veneer was his means of resolution. His family was literally dependent on the most conservative Democratic faction in the entire North, though of the temperance persuasion and not implacably hostile to black Americans. In addition, there were his childhood and teenage acquaintances in the comfortable world of Allegheny City whom he gathered as a singing group he called the "Five Nice Young Men," testing out his earliest original compositions with them. Some of them were just friends, about whom we know little or nothing.[76] But others connected him to a remarkable network of black and white abolitionists in Pittsburgh and Allegheny City.

Robert P. McDowell and his sister, Foster's future wife Jane, were the children of Dr. Alexander P. McDowell, and through him they were connected to a major force in the Pittsburgh black community, Martin Delany. Dr. McDowell had tutored the young Martin Delany in medicine in the 1830s. By the late 1830s Delany was a rising figure in Pittsburgh's black and abolitionist communities; between 1843 and 1847 he published the *Mystery*, a paper devoted to "the Moral Elevation of the Africo-American and African race, civilly, politically, and religiously." In August 1847 Delany and others in both the black and white abolitionist circles in Pittsburgh met with Garrison and Douglass and joined their tour of the Western Reserve of Ohio, speaking at abolitionist meetings. Early the next year Delany joined Douglass as a roving editor of the new *North Star*, traveling through Ohio and Pennsylvania lecturing and raising subscriptions, in the face of virulent white hostility, including the minstrel riot in Ohio in July 1848. He would turn sharply toward militant black nationalism in early 1851 after the double blow of the Fugitive Slave Act and his ejection from Harvard Medical School following complaints by racist white students.[77]

McDowell was presumably among the seventeen white doctors in Allegheny County who recommended Delany for admission to Harvard Medical School in 1850, an effort led by Dr. Francis Julius LeMoyne of nearby Washington, Pennsylvania. LeMoyne, who had founded the early abolitionist organizations in western Pennsylvania, had run for governor as the Liberty candidate three times in the

1840s. His house was a major way station on the Underground Railroad, and his wife and children must have been deeply involved, and others around the family may have suspected. His son John married Julia Murray, a local beauty whom Foster's brother Morrison had courted for years. Stephen dedicated a song to her, "Wilt Thou Be Gone, Love?"[78]

Among those in Foster's musical circle of "Nice Young Men," Charles Shiras was his closest friend and also a deeply committed abolitionist. Shiras was invited with Delany to join the 1847 tour into Ohio with William Lloyd Garrison and Frederick Douglass, the events that led to the brief Douglass-Delany partnership in the *North Star*. Shiras briefly published a small abolitionist paper called the *Albatross*, as did another in this Pittsburgh circle, the abolitionist and feminist Jane G. Swissholm. During the great protests against the Fugitive Slave Law in the fall of 1850, he wrote a protest poem called "The Blood Hound's Song," which was widely published in Pittsburgh and Ohio. He and Foster collaborated on musical and theatrical productions before Shiras's early death in the summer of 1854.[79]

The October 1850 protests against the Fugitive Slave Law at the Allegheny City Market House were led by Charles Avery, a neighbor of the Fosters who had recently established a black school, the Allegheny Institute (a station on the Underground Railroad), after a campaign by Martin Delany in the *Mystery*. Delany delivered a rousing speech at the Market House on the right of self-defense. Charles Shiras and Stephen Foster, who was living with Jane at his brother's house several blocks away, may well have been at this meeting, and Foster probably proofread Shiras's poem. Foster was certainly a familial Democrat and saw himself as a songwriter to the respectability. But he was deeply immersed in a personal network including people profoundly involved in the antislavery movement, and clearly these relationships shaped the direction of his work in these years.[80]

Foster's songs also, of course, tracked the arc of the fugitive slave drama and then the rising popularity of *Uncle Tom's Cabin*. There was mutual borrowing: Stowe's novel borrowed from the minstrel tradition, inasmuch as it offered for the first time in formal prose a rendition of African American dialect; and Foster's original model for his "Kentucky Home," as indicated in his manuscript, was Uncle Tom's cabin (not a mansion in Bardstown, as Kentucky mythology would have it). If Frederick Douglass celebrated "My Old Kentucky Home," it was in the shadow of Stowe's popularity, and her argument that the benevolent patriarchy of the Shelby plantation was a hollow shell, doomed as soon the "massa" might be put in the "cold ground" and his slaves put up for auction. Douglass drew the connection between Stowe and the minstrel tradition in his 1855 Rochester address. In the same paragraph where he found "allies in the Ethiopian songs," he declared that "one flash from the heart-supplied intellect of Harriet Beecher Stowe could light a million camp-fires in front of the embattled hosts of slavery."[81]

Douglass drew the connection, but the connections were there to be drawn already. Both Stowe and Foster had spent formative years on the Ohio River in Cincinnati. Both also shared a sentimental, increasingly nostalgic culture, ironically driven by the same commerce that was overturning a supposedly better past. And both Stowe and Foster were being brought together in theaters across the North.

THERE WAS trouble at Mr. Robbins's preparatory school in Springfield, Ohio, in March 1854. Some of the boys had been stealing food, and all were in trouble. A traveling theatrical production of *Uncle Tom's Cabin* was playing at City Hall, but permission to go was denied. Harford Toland had other ideas: he had a boot that needed repairing, and a business errand to run for his father, or so he claimed. Heading into town, he and a friend dropped off the boot, skipped the business errand, and "went to see 'Uncle Tom's Cabin' performed last night at the 'City Hall,'" he noted the next day. "Although there was a good turnout," he complained, "it was not performed very well." Already the opinionated critic, Toland had probably read the book, and his staunchly antislavery family was reminded of its story daily, since his young niece was nicknamed "little Eva."[82]

By the spring of 1854, theatrical productions of *Uncle Tom's Cabin* had spread deep into the northern hinterland, reaching wider and wider audiences. The anthropologist Victor Turner saw theater and entertainment as an inherently liminal experience, taking the audience out of their routines, suspending them "betwixt and between" in an alternative reality, and returning them somehow changed.[83] And in the antebellum United States, novel readers and theatergoers were overlapping but by no means identical audiences. Very broadly, this was a gender divide: women and girls were novel readers, and men attended the theater. This division was violated as much as it was observed, and theaters throughout the country were called "museums" to distance them from the disreputable, immoral connotations that theater had had for centuries.[84] Theater would indeed reach a far broader, more diffuse audience than Stowe's novel, most significantly, working-class men. The *New York Evening Post*, in a review from 1854, argued that

> the book, wide as its power was felt, was limited to the reading and comparatively reflective portion of the public; while the play with its scenic effects, addressing itself to the eye and the popular observation, has worked among a different class. The unsettled masses of the large cities, chiefly the young, . . . have yielded to the power of the wonderful Uncle Tom. We believe that the general moral effect has been in proportion to the popular interest in the play; and in regard to slavery, there can be no doubt that public feeling has been powerfully guided by it toward the side of humanity.[85]

In December 1852, Congressman Joshua Giddings thought that he was already seeing this impact. *Uncle Tom's Cabin*, he told the House, "has been dramatized, and both in this country and in Europe, the play-going public listen with interest to the wrongs, the revolting crimes of slavery. Thus," Giddings continued, "the theater, that 'school of vice,' has been subsidized to the promulgation of truth, and the hearts of thousands have been reached, who were approachable in no other way."[86] He might have been horrified by the minstrel versions that were playing in many northern towns, but he was certainly prescient. Theatrical adaptations of *Uncle Tom's Cabin* were beginning to sweep across the North, and these performances would be filled with music and song. By the time the 33rd Congress first convened in December 1853 and took up the Kansas-Nebraska bill, Stowe and Foster had been fused together in the theaters and soundways of the North.

The first proposal to produce *Uncle Tom's Cabin* on the stage came from the antislavery Hutchinson Family Singers, but Harriet Beecher Stowe refused their overtures in the summer of 1852, citing the immorality of the theater.[87] Stowe may well have been right about this, since a host of stage managers less moral than the Hutchinsons simply pirated her work. The first theatrical performance was a short *Southern Uncle Tom* put on at the Baltimore Museum in January 1852, while the novel was still being serialized in the *Era*. The performance was titled *Uncle Tom's Cabin As It Is*, a play on Weld and the Grimkés' *American Slavery As It Is*. Sometime in the summer of 1852 a performance of an early British adaptation at Welsh's National Amphitheatre in Philadelphia set off a riot by southern medical students.[88]

In late August another short production was put on in New York for a ten-day run, in the former Chatham Theatre in the Bowery, purchased in 1850 by Alexander H. Purdy and renamed the National Theatre. The Chatham Theatre had been built in 1839, replacing the Chatham Garden Theatre, which had been turned into the Tappans' Temperance Chapel and damaged in the 1834 anti-abolitionist riots. The rebuilt Chatham Theatre soon returned to the minstrel tradition forged in the nearby Catherine Street Market, and had a checkered career through the 1840s, until it was revived by Purdy as the National. It now was about to launch another celebrated phase in Chatham Street's theatrical history, in two steps.[89] The first, if not as triumphant, was suggestive of what was to come.

In August 1852 Purdy produced a short three-act melodrama version of *Uncle Tom's Cabin* written by his house dramatist, Charles W. Taylor. The performance was part of a longer series of routines, including Thomas D. Rice, back on this stage thirty-odd years after he first appeared there, doing a blackface version of *Othello*. But Rice's *Otello* had a happy ending: the black Othello and the white Desdemona were alive, married, and the parents of an interracial child at the end of the performance. And Purdy's 1852 *Uncle Tom's Cabin* contained an explicit antislavery message, to judge from the playbill, a reference aligning creolization with political confluence. The character of George Harris was headlined, transformed into "Edward Wilmot, a young Mechanic in Bondage." Everyone in the audience would have connected him to the Free Soil congressman David Wilmot, whose Proviso banning slavery had so divided Congress in 1846.[90]

The proslavery Democratic *New York Herald* expressed alarm at the "repeated rounds of applause" Purdy's play "received nightly" and condemned it in political terms as a challenge to "the institutions of slavery," the Constitution, and the "two Baltimore platforms," in which Whigs and Democrats had promised to uphold the Compromise: "It is a sad blunder; for when our stage shall become the deliberate agent in the cause of abolitionism, with the sanction of the public, and their approbation, the peace and harmony of this Union will soon be ended." Any further dramatization of *Uncle Tom's Cabin*, the *Herald* warned, would be "a firebrand of the most dangerous character to the peace of the country." Perhaps to spite the *Herald*, Purdy revived this version of the play four times over the winter.[91] The *Herald*'s dictum would have encompassed the next *Uncle Tom's Cabin* performed in the North, a proslavery version put on in Detroit in October, condemned after runs in Buffalo and Cleveland as a "miserable burlesque upon the dramatic" and an "insufferable piece of trash," as well as the revival of *Uncle Tom's Cabin as It Is* in Baltimore in December.[92] A correspondent in the *Liberator*, mocking the *Herald*'s proslavery panic, gave the New York play a nod, asking: "Strange, is it not? A few years since, and the crowd at the National would have mobbed an anti-slavery speaker. Now it cheers—'rounds of applause,' we are told."[93]

The autumn of 1852, however, saw the launch of two productions that would have long and celebrated runs and far-reaching influence on the history of *Uncle Tom's Cabin* in the American theater. Despite the quick collapse of the play in New York, George Howard, a theater master who had worked in Boston, Providence, and Worcester, saw financial opportunities. In the late summer of 1852, he asked his cousin George Aiken to write a four-act adaptation, and, finding space at Peale's Museum in Troy, New York, he launched this production on September 27. Featuring Howard, his wife, Caroline, his daughter Cordelia—playing Eva—and various cousins, the play ran in Troy for a hundred days. Although their version originally ended with the death of Eva in New Orleans, Howard and Aiken whipped up a four-act sequel in October titled *The Death of Tom; or Religion of the Lowly*, and then finally revised both parts into a single six-act production by the middle of November. Described by his daughter decades later as having "warm sympathies enlisted in the antislavery cause," Howard was probably concerned about violence in a tough iron-manufacturing city, but as in New York, there were no riots. Rather, the turnout was clearly enormous. If the play had audiences of one hundred per night, perhaps ten thousand people saw it, including people from Troy (a city of thirty thousand) and surrounding towns, and arriving by the trainload from nearby parts of Vermont and Massachusetts. By one account, when a Baptist minister called a meeting to chastise church members who had seen the play, two-thirds admitted that they had gone, and the rest dropped their resistance and attended soon.[94] Howard would take Aiken's *Uncle Tom's Cabin* very briefly to Albany, then down to New York City to Purdy's National Theatre, for a record run of nearly a year, starting in July 1853.

The second long-running version had already been launched at the "Boston Museum and Gallery of Fine Arts" in November 1852. The Boston Museum was owned and operated by Moses Kimball and designed to suit the tastes of a wide spectrum of Bostonians, with its collections of art and curiosities, and a third-floor auditorium. Here Kimball had put on a series of moral dramas—*The Drunkard, The Gambler,* and *The Mechanic, or Another Glass*—and on November 15, 1852, he added *Uncle Tom's Cabin*, which the house playwright, Henry J. Conway, had been working on since the spring.[95]

The first ad for Kimball's production highlighted its special effects as much as the text. Among other wonders, the "New and Extensive Scenery by Geo. Curtis" included a "Grand Panorama of a portion of the Mississippi River down to New Orleans."[96] Panoramas were an important dimension of the wider urban and traveling entertainment industry, sharing audiences with the theaters, minstrel shows, circuses, and magic lantern shows. The original panoramas, starting in the late 1780s in London, were fixed circular installations in specially constructed buildings. A few were constructed in the United States at the turn of the nineteenth century. But the form was popularized in 1848 with the adoption of the "moving panorama," in which great rolls of painted canvas mounted on a framework of geared rollers unfurled before a seated audience, with a lecturer explaining the sights. Suddenly erupting on the American scene in the later 1840s, these exhibitions would endure almost until the arrival of the cinema.[97] As would the movies, their ads stipulated, along with the price of admission, "Doors open at 7 o'clock; Picture moves at quarter before 8."[98]

Like the rest of a highly mobile American entertainment industry, the moving panoramas literally moved—easily transported by showmen from town to town. In August and September 1852, there were a number of shows in motion across the United States: "Bayne's Voyage to Europe" was showing in Washington and Baltimore; "Pratt's Panorama of the Garden of Eden" moved from Newark to Burlington, Vermont, to Milwaukee; "Bullard's Panorama of New York City" from New London to Newport to Schenectady; "Folger's National Panorama of the Battles of Mexico" from Detroit to Columbus to Kalamazoo; and—most spectacularly—"the wonderful extraordinary exercises of Herr Von Spinhalen," concluding "with Mechanical, Myrioramic Tableaux Panorama of Balbec and Kaleidoscopical Illusion," careening from Brooklyn to Albany to Boston and ending up in Cincinnati. In Augusta, Maine, hundreds of people piled onto a specially commissioned train for an excursion to see the "Seven-Mile Mirror" of Niagara Falls and the Ontario shoreline showing in Portland.[99] In Troy, Howard's *Uncle*

Tom's Cabin briefly competed with a panorama of the Crystal Palace in New York.[100]

Thus panoramas blended entertainment with the newsreel, and the panorama in act two of Kimball's *Uncle Tom's Cabin* was part of the wider mobilization of the form in the growing northern examination of slavery. Henry "Box" Brown, who had escaped slavery in Virginia hidden in a shipping crate, had toured New England with his panorama "Mirror of Slavery" in 1850, and after fleeing to England reopened his tour in Liverpool and Manchester in 1851.[101] The greater Midwest seems to have been fertile ground for panoramas of *Uncle Tom's Cabin*. One of the first was in a production by a Mr. Leslie in Cincinnati in April 1853, and by August it had been shown in Cincinnati, Columbus, Cleveland, Zanesville, and as far east as Syracuse, New York. It was apparently in circulation in northern Ohio through November.[102] Others were in development or in circulation over the next year in Illinois, Indiana, upstate New York, and western New England.[103] Like the magic lantern show running at New York's Franklin Theatre in September 1853, the panoramas were down-market entertainments, cheaper to produce than theatrical productions, and more mobile.[104] They were showing in every major city, but also in smaller towns and even villages for short runs, and for better or worse, they put images of slaves and slavery before a wide public.

Theater in New York City, however, was the center of the entertainment industry, and in 1853 both the Troy and the Boston versions of *Uncle Tom's Cabin* settled in for long-running performances in New York. George Howard made arrangements with Alexander Purdy at the National Theatre (the old Chatham) and moved his entire troupe downriver to New York by paddlewheeler and train in July 1853. Since the minstrel *Uncle Tom* he had put on in August 1852, Purdy had turned from a medley of "sterling Dramas, Comedies, Burlesques, Spectacles" toward moral reform dramas. The Howard-Aiken *Uncle Tom's Cabin* drove another turn toward respectability, and he invested in new decorations for his theater and replaced much of the seating. The Howard troupe, with some additions and fine-tuning, had their New York debut on July 18. Purdy had to accommodate immense crowds by adding matinee performances, and on August 15 he increased those crowds by specifically inviting black New York, announcing that "a neat and comfortable parquet" had been reserved "for the accommodation of RESPECTABLE COLORED PERSONS." In November he added a brass band to welcome the audience; in January he revamped the scenery and the set-piece tableaus that illustrated key moments in the play in stop-motion, in particular a "Grand Allegorical Tableau," a final extravaganza in which Eva was raised to a dazzling heaven followed by Tom. The play would run for 325 days, a New York record.[105]

These improvements were driven in large measure by the competition. Up the Bowery, P. T. Barnum, seeing profits to be made, acquired the rights to the Henry Conway version that had been playing in Boston, with runs in Providence and Hartford. Audiences entering Barnum's American Museum, a huge, gaudily painted building, would thread their way through a constantly shifting collection of sideshows and exhibitions to Barnum's lecture room, where he also was shifting toward moral dramas. On November 7 the Conway version of *Uncle Tom's Cabin* opened with great fanfare, a huge cast, and panoramas painted anew for this production. Henry James remembered Barnum's American Museum as "above all ignoble and awful"; a young Norwegian immigrant wrote of the huge giraffes and the bearded lady, "much to see, good and bad, all mixed together." The theater was "attractive," and she appreciated the new panorama of the Mississippi, but Conway's *Uncle Tom's Cabin* "was frightfully distorted of course; but it was quite amusing . . . to observe the Americans' taste."[106] Barnum's version would run through January 2, 1854. Nine weeks later it would be followed by yet another production, at the Bowery Theatre, featuring Thomas D. Rice as Uncle Tom, running for about two months.[107]

That same fall two productions of *Uncle Tom's Cabin* started up in Philadelphia. Samuel E. Harris, the stage name of actor Wesley Barmore, had written and rehearsed his own adaptation over the summer, which opened at the National Theatre on September 8, running through October 31. Seven blocks away at the Chestnut Street Theatre, cousins of the Howards were authorized to mount the Aiken-Howard version, which opened on October 26, running well into the winter of 1854.[108]

For the autumn of 1853, then, this was the main geography of *Uncle Tom's Cabin* in the theater: long-running productions, after Troy, in Boston, New York, and Philadelphia, with occasional spinoffs in small New England cities. And people flocked to the plays. Ellen Emerson wrote gaily to her father, Ralph (who was on a western lecture tour), that the family were planning a trip to Boston for Christmas and were "going to see Uncle Tom's Cabin acted at the museum." In Philadelphia, Susan J. Baily, a young woman from a prosperous Quaker family, was so "much pleased" with the performance that she saw on October 8, 1853, that she went again a week later; the next week friends came from out of town, went to see the play, and then spent the night.[109] Joseph Sill, who had read the novel to his family and was a constant attendee at both Philadelphia theaters, made different plans that month. Traveling by train to Brooklyn for a Unitarian ordination, he and his wife Jane took the East River ferry to Manhattan several times for some "sight-seeing" (including the "Crystal Palace"). One evening after dinner, he noted, they went across to see *Uncle Tom's Cabin* at the National Theatre and "were much gratified," finding that in "some of the scenes Uncle Tom, St. Clair, and Eva were touchingly portrayed, producing tears in almost every eye." Returning by ferry after midnight, they "tried to renovate ourselves by Oysters & ale" at their lodgings.[110]

Emerson, Baily, and Sill, writers of detailed letters and diaries, were among the respectability flocking to the shows in Boston, Philadelphia, and New York. Henry James remembered this newfound interest among the respectable, celebrating "the fine free rendering achieved at a playhouse till then ignored by fashion and culture, the National Theatre, deep down on the east side, whence echoes had come faintest to ears polite, but where a sincerity vivid though rude was now supposed to reward the curious."[111] Accounts stress the mixture of classes at these shows. In Philadelphia, reviews of the

Harris/Barmore production remarked on this blending of class and race, and of a major transformation: "The rough, stern and sinewy democracy were there in great numbers, filling the best seats and quietly awaiting the progress of the exhibition, in company with the more polished and educated. They were present in their popular summer apparel—shirts and trowsers, without the embarrassment of coats or vests, their nether habilliments rolled up above their boots, and the fashionable cloth skullcaps upon their heads. Every bench and alley was crowded." The galleys were reserved for the black audience. The reviewer was struck by the change from fifteen years before, when Philadelphia's white working class had driven the "Abolition riot": "Extraordinary mutation indeed, which in less than the cycle of a single generation transforms the rioter into a sympathiser."[112]

Observers attending the National Theatre in New York were of the same opinion, perhaps nervously remembering the riot at the Astor Place Theatre in May 1849, when Bowery thugs had attacked a noted British actor. William Lloyd Garrison saw the show on September 3, after spending an afternoon at the Crystal Palace, and was impressed by the audience. Apparently it was Garrison who commented in the *Liberator* that Purdy's *Uncle Tom's Cabin* presented "the strongest antislavery impression" and that "it was a sight worth seeing, those ragged, coatless men and boys in the pit (the very material of which mobs are made) sharing the strongest and sublimest anti-slavery sentiments."[113] The *New York Tribune* claimed that—in contrast to anti-abolition rioting of the previous decades—this time the "b'hoys" in the audience "were on the side of the fugitive. The pro-slavery feeling had departed from among them. They did not wish to save the Union. They believed in the higher law."[114] John Jay must have read one of these articles before writing to Horace Mann: "I was very pleasingly struck this morning with an account of the presentation of Uncle Tom's Cabin at 'The National,' one of the lowest I believe of our New York theaters. It seems to me so cheering a sign of the irreversible progress & certain triumph of our principles." By August he had seen the play at the National and predicted to an antislavery meeting that in a few years the boys in the audience "will be the voters before whom our aspiring statesmen bow." In September he assured Charles Sumner that "Uncle Tom at the National has been making converts for us."[115] While it is unlikely that New York's roughnecks and men of the town were converted to outright abolitionism in one night, opinion was clearly shifting.

What exactly was in these performances, and how might that have been converting the audiences? The question of the faithfulness of the plays to the novel, and to abolitionist doctrine, has been a subject of considerable debate, made all the more problematic by the spotty survival of the text of the plays. Thus the Harris/Barmore text no longer exists, but an early review in a Philadelphia paper was generally positive, though complaining that the playwright might have lost some of his audience by following his original "minutely" and overdoing "the piety of Uncle Tom."[116] The Aiken and Conway texts do survive, and traditionally the Aiken play has been seen as the abolitionist version and the Conway play as the proslavery version. Clearly Harriet Beecher Stowe liked the Aiken version better; she walked out of a Conway performance in Hartford, but watched right through the Aiken version performed by the Howards in Boston, seemingly mesmerized by Mrs. Howard's Topsy.[117] Calvin Stowe beat the drum for the Aiken-Howard version at Purdy's: "The drama of 'Uncle Tom' has been going on in the National Theatre of New York all summer with most unparalleled success. Everybody goes night after night and nothing can stop it. The enthusiasm beats that of the run of the Boston Museum out and out."[118]

There were important differences between the Aiken and Conway productions, in particular Conway's minstrel/Jim Crow depiction of slavery on the Shelby plantation in Kentucky.[119] Opinion has been shifting regarding their message and political impact. The difference may well have been in tone rather than substance, rooted in the "Uncle Tom War" between Purdy's National and Barnum's American Museum when both plays were in competition in New York. Both versions shared common features that separated them from the novel. Both ignored and even reversed Stowe's critique of

American capitalism, and whereas Stowe had foregrounded female agency, both plays sidelined female characters. Both plays, however, did convey a mild antislavery sentiment. But they pulled their punches in their introduction of comedic actors and in their endings. Both plays added men in the stock role of the New England Yankee, a comic, ironic, equalitarian figure dating back to the beginnings of American theater in the 1780s. But these stock Yankees serve different functions. George Aiken's "Gumption Cute" was the more objectionable, perhaps by design, speculating in the slave trade and trying to blackmail Legree for killing St. Clare (another Aiken fiction); he was a foil for the sentimental focus on the saintliness of Eva and Tom. Conway's Yankee, "Penetrate Partyside," is roaming the South taking notes for a book on slavery, and uses his ironic distance to editorialize on the "general" and the "particular" in stinging critiques of slavery. His sarcastic asides to the audience set off act two from a minstrel show act one. Stumbling over chained slaves on a Mississippi steamer destined for sale in New Orleans, he observes:

> *Penetrate:* Oh! They aint done nothing—they're only chained, because they are going to be sold. *(takes out tablets)* Penetrate, put that down in your remarks on the wisdom, mercy, and justice of the laws of the United States, the home of the free and the land of the brave! *Mem. (writes)* Niggers chained like dogs ginerally; because they are going to be sold according to law particularly. Queer! Who deserves to be chained most: the niggers to be sold, or the owners who sell them? That's a nice pint and will admit of considerable argument ginerally. Gess I'll soon get a chance to try the case particularly.[120]

Conway's story contains an edge of the violence that had already erupted at Christiana: in an early version Partyside is threatened with hanging and peels off his jacket for a fight; several scenes later Conway features the violent confrontation in Ohio between George Harris and the slave catchers, a story that Aiken skipped over.[121]

Both endings are as problematical as Stowe's in the novel, with its colonization message. Aiken ended first with Eva's death, then with Tom's death, and eventually both were cobbled together in a "Grand Allegorical Transformation" of an ascension to a glorious heaven; there was no solution to slavery on earth. In Conway's version, Tom is rescued and is granted a plot of land to live a life of independence in New England, a free soil emancipation following a false enslavement, but not the end of slavery, or even a challenge to the Fugitive Slave Act. The pious message of the Aiken version marks the key differences between the productions. Aiken's tone was religious; Conway's was profane. Stowe is reported to have walked out of Conway's version after Partyside's entrance and his acerbic commentary on slavers and enslaved. Just as important, Conway's version included far more links to the minstrel tradition, both in its text and in its musical production, attributed the Boston Museum stage manager William Smith, who was a Webster Whig and initially supported the 1850 Compromise.[122]

Aiken's *Uncle Tom*, then, was a sentimental moral drama; Conway's *Uncle Tom* was a minstrel-inflected moral drama. One probably appealed to a middle-class sensibility, while the other could reach out further toward the rough, unsentimental world of the workingman. Though there were certainly abolitionist critiques of Conway's version, it may well be that Sarah Meer has the right balance: abolitionists preferred Aiken, but slaveholders disliked both.[123] Indeed, for all of the abolitionist praise heaped upon the Aiken version at Troy and at Purdy's, Conway's version got its praise as well. The *Boston Commonwealth* concluded, "We think it will drop many grains of good upon what may be called, politically speaking, a very barren soil."[124] Parker Pillsbury, one the most radical of the abolitionists, was thrilled that Conway's version had proclaimed, "*Slavery is of the Devil*," noting: "Now we have got the Theatre versus the Church, on the question of slavery. The Theatre says it is of the Devil. The Church claims that it is of God. Let us wait patiently for the verdict." Theodore Parker, one of the leaders of the Boston Vigilance Committee, speaking before the Massachusetts Anti-Slavery Society in January 1853, was of the same mind, condemning the conservatism of the churches and heaping praise on Moses Kimball for putting on "an antislavery play," Conway's *Uncle Tom's Cabin*. Strikingly, William Lloyd Garrison, two days after seeing the pious Aiken version in New York, admitted to his wife, Helen, "In some respects, I like the Boston [Conway] performance better."[125] In one of the best analyses of these two theatrical versions, the literary scholar Les Harrison makes a critical point: Aiken's play was a sentimental sermon; Conway's was an argumentative, confrontational debate. In his account, Conway produced the more prescient story: "Whereas Aiken normalizes Stowe in the production of a sermon on the need to 'feel right,' the Conway adaptation dramatizes the violent consequences of acting on those feelings, disrupting the tense peace of compromise politics."[126] Each play worked differently on different audiences. In the end, what may have mattered was a dramatic impression, a burst of vivid exposure and thoughts and conversations on the reflections between performance and novel—and what was known of lived reality. From such exposure, thought, and conversation came evolving sensibilities.

By late 1853 the theatrical *Uncle Tom's Cabin* was spreading to the west. In Chicago a version had run in December 1852 for three weeks, and a year later it was back on the Chicago stage with "R.D. Smith's Mississippi Panorama," playing into the first months of 1854.[127] Local productions of *Uncle Tom's Cabin* popped up in cities along the Erie Canal in the spring and summer of 1853; there was a production in Buffalo in April and another in Rochester in July.[128] More important, however, shows from New York and Philadelphia or their offshoots began to pull up stakes and take to the road in the fall of 1853. With advance work sped by the proliferating telegraph lines and transport sped by the railroad, they would crisscross the greater Midwest over the coming months, inflecting the cultural landscape as the country passed through one of the most consequential political debates in its entire history.

Wesley Barmore's production at Philadelphia's National Theatre closed at the end of October after a two-month run, leaving Philadelphia to the Aiken show at the Chestnut Street Theatre. Barmore reappeared in Cincinnati in mid-December at yet another National Theatre, again playing his old role of Uncle Tom.[129] This production continued into January, and here too it ran into competition, from a company that had been on the move since September, in an epic circuit that would carry into the following spring.

This was the Marsh troupe, which had been playing the Aiken-Howard version of *Uncle Tom's Cabin* at Cincinnati's Melodeon Theatre since early December, in a two-month run ending in early February.[130] Robert Marsh may well have been the "Mr. Marsh" playing a minor character in the 1852 Taylor version at Purdy's National Theatre in New York. In August 1853 he launched a production clearly based on the Aiken script at the Odeon Theatre in Williamsburg, across the East River from the Bowery. This was a rehearsal for their traveling show. In late September the new Marsh troupe was in Buffalo, and in late October they were playing Syracuse for ten days, not long after the second annual celebration of the "Jerry Rescue."[131] By early November they were in Cleveland, performing *Uncle Tom's Cabin* at the Athenaeum through the end of the month, heralded "as played in New York for the last twelve weeks with unabated success." In early December they arrived in Cincinnati, where they would perform into February, before a three-month traveling circuit that in May 1854 would bring them back to Buffalo, playing there as the Kansas-Nebraska Act passed the U.S. House.[132]

The Marsh troupe was a family affair. Robert Marsh played Uncle Tom in Williamsburg, with his daughter Mary Guerneau Marsh, the star attraction soon called the "Flower of the South," playing Eva all the way through the eight-month circuit. Mary's mother began playing Ophelia in Buffalo, and carried on at least through Indianapolis. But the Marsh troupe was performing the Aiken version of the play and had strong connections running back to George Howard's production at the Troy Museum the previous autumn. Marsh may have worked with Howard and a cousin in 1851–1852, and he recruited key members of his cast from Howard's troupe. William J. Le Moyne played Deacon Perry, one of Aiken's invented Yankees, at Troy and all the way around the Marsh circuit. Marsh himself played Uncle Tom in Williamsburg and was then replaced by a series of players, most significantly Greene C. Germon, who had played the role in Troy and then in the first months at Purdy's National Theatre. He joined the Marsh troupe in Cleveland, performing at least through Indianapolis.[133] If the Aiken version of *Uncle Tom's Cabin* was a sentimental sermon, the Marsh troupe was an important vehicle for conveying it to a wide swath of the northern public.

When the Marsh troupe arrived in Cleveland in November, they pushed a local company down to Pittsburgh. Joseph C. Foster had managed theaters in Baltimore and Philadelphia, and he had interests in theaters in Cleveland and Pittsburgh. Leaving one cast in Cleveland, Foster moved another to his theater in Pittsburgh, and ten days after the Marsh company started up in Cleveland, Foster was running another Aiken *Uncle Tom's Cabin* production at his Pittsburgh theater, complete with the final "Allegory—Little Eva in Heaven," running through December 3. While they were in rehearsal, the abolitionist Charles Shiras was putting on a play of his own, with music by Stephen Foster (no relation to Joseph), a "Grand Original Fairy Spectacle," titled *The Invisible Prince, or the War with the Amazons*.[134]

The Invisible Prince had less to do with Shiras's abolitionist agenda than with his literary dabblings and his health: he was dying of tuberculosis, and it was hoped that the play would bring in some money for his young family. Stephen Foster had written the music, but he had abandoned his own family and was living in New York. Shiras certainly knew Foster's songs by heart, and had to have known what he was hearing in the rehearsals and performances of *Uncle Tom*. Joseph Foster staged his play in the same theater with three of Stephen Foster's recent hits, licensed under the Christy name: "Old Folks at Home," "My Old Kentucky Home," and "Massa's in the Cold Ground."

It had been over a year since Stephen Foster's songs had first been heard on stage in productions of *Uncle Tom's Cabin*. Greene Germon had sung "Old Folks at Home" in the Troy production in the fall of 1852, and retained "Old Folks" in the Purdy production at the National Theatre, and then in the Marsh tour starting in Cleveland in December. In Philadelphia that same fall, "Old Folks at Home" was sung at the Chestnut Street Theatre, but also in a proslavery minstrel show version of *Uncle Tom* at Sanford's Opera House, along with Foster's "Camptown Races" and Dan Emmett's "Old Dan Tucker." George Howard was writing a series of his own songs—"Uncle Tom's Religion," "To Little Eva in Heaven," "Oh I'se So Wicked," "Eva to Her Papa"—and these along with many other songs from the intersection of the ballad and minstrel traditions were performed over the coming months in productions throughout the North.[135]

Literally from its publication, *Uncle Tom's Cabin* was tied to the music industry, starting with John Jewett commissioning verses from John Greenleaf Whittier, set to music and sold as "Little Eva."[136] Foster's "My Old Kentucky Home," composed in September 1852, was directly inspired by Stowe's depiction of Tom's cabin on the Shelby plantation. It was sung in Joseph Foster's theater in Pittsburgh and moved quickly into the repertoire.[137] If Foster's songs also appeared in proslavery "Happy Tom" shows, the wider antislavery movement was not averse to working with these vehicles in a multivocal, perhaps ambiguous climate of opinion and sensibility. The antislavery Hutchinson Family Singers eventually did perform music derived from *Uncle Tom's Cabin*, and Republicans borrowed Foster's tunes such as "Camptown Races" and "My Old Kentucky Home" for campaign songs in 1856.[138] Two decades later a nostalgic article on "Old Songs" appearing in many papers echoed Douglass on the effect that Foster's songs and Stowe's novel-turned-play had on the public: "And there was another that we all remember—the 'Old Kentucky Home.' To theatre goers the name will recall a scene in Uncle Tom's Cabin; an old man sitting with bowed head, singing of the home that he should never see again. And looking at the bent figure, listening to the words so mournfully sweet, one realized what a slave may feel."[139]

Thus there were very complex and ambiguous interactions between the culture of race and the politics of slavery in the greater Civil War era. Historians have traditionally seen blackface minstrel culture as fundamentally linked to the racism of the Democratic Party. But it clearly had a much broader, more complicated resonance, functioning as a sounding board for a wide spectrum of white American attitudes. There were complex multivocal interactions between Stowe's novel, Foster's songs, and the theatrical *Uncle Tom*. They played on a near obsession with race among whites in the 1850s; they worked together to draw attention to linkages between slavery, domesticity, sentiment, and nostalgia in bourgeois culture; and they were involved in an explosion of cultural discourse on race and slavery that was unprecedented in scale and scope. This multivocal and contested discourse made the figure of the slave, indeed the figure of the slave in action as a fugitive, the central figure of the American imagination in these years. While the white North was by no means suddenly converted to Garrisonian abolitionism, many white northerners for the first time were moved to sympathy for the slave. The constant presence and power of the narrative, imagery, and sound created by Stowe and a host of other writers, Foster and a host of songwriters and performers, and the theater companies almost inadvertently forced a shift in the white collective social imaginary, in which the metaphoric action of the mid-century popular culture of race raised the political stakes of the slavery debate to new heights.[140]

Of course what was at work here was the sudden intersection of profit and morality. In the wake of the Fugitive Slave Act, perhaps with a sense of the explosive reaction to it in October 1850, men of commerce began to see money to be made in working the boundary of white and black in America. Forty years later, Foster's brother Morrison thought that he had finally identified the dynamic at work in Stephen's musical and political legacy, which may stand in some respect for the way in which commerce in search of a market, and artists for an audience, helped to reshape the wider climate of opinion, literally the soundtrack, in the free states in a little more than a year and a half. Looking at his brother's life, Morrison focused on the impact of "Old Uncle Ned" and "Oh Susanna," writing:

> The fame of these two songs went round the world, and thousands sang and played them who never heard the name of the author or knew whence they came. In these two songs Stephen showed his intuitive knowledge of negro melody and pathos. He founded a new era in melody and ballad. The grotesque and clownish aspect of negro songs was softened, and ridicule began to merge into sympathy. Unknown to himself, he opened the way to the hearts of the people, which led to actual interest in the black man.[141]

How did African Americans feel about this attention in commercial culture? In 1848 Frederick Douglass had condemned the minstrels, as had Martin Delany, Foster's neighbor, in "very severe style," in the pages of the *Mystery*.[142] Douglass had changed his mind by 1855, if he was somewhat amazed at the absurdity of finding "allies in the Ethiopian songs." A moment of cultural creolization was working to solidify an essential confluence of black and white in antislavery politics. He saw the power of commerce in the struggle with slavery: "The present will be looked to by after coming generations, as the age of anti-slavery literature—when supply on the gallop could not keep pace with the ever growing demand, when a picture of a negro on the cover was a help to the sale of a book."[143] Utterly rejecting Douglass's strategic creolizing alliances, Delany would never have made this move. But in his 1852 tract *The Condition, Elevation, Emigration, and Destiny of the Colored People of the United States*, announcing his militant black nationalism in May 1852, Delany celebrated the accomplishments of eminent black musicians, including Frank Johnson and his brass band.[144]

Perhaps some of the most dramatic evidence comes from the enslaved themselves, as reported in papers along the Ohio River in 1853. As Douglass was arguing, *Uncle Tom's Cabin* was a celebration of, even a handbook for, freedom from slavery. That April, word began to circulate about an escape from Boone County, Kentucky.

The slave of a white minister had secretly learned to read. After he read *Uncle Tom's Cabin* to his friends, they plotted and executed their escape across the Ohio on April 2.[145] That Christmas, it was theater that was the attraction. According to the *Louisville Courier*, fourteen slaves had escaped over the river to Cincinnati in December 1853, where they "determined to go and see the representation of Uncle Tom's Cabin at the National Theatre." Their cheering, "boisterous and 'African,'" at Eliza's crossing and George Harris's stand against the slave hunters gave them away, but the men slipped out after the curtain fell, into Cincinnati's streets and alleys. And two and a half years later the African Methodist Episcopal Church in Brooklyn, New York, decided to present a "Diorama of Uncle Tom's Cabin."[146] Despite its many flaws, *Uncle Tom's Cabin* and its commercial spinoffs were opening a path out of slavery.

CHAPTER 6

Guarantees Violated in the Second Crisis

The Kansas-Nebraska Act

ON DECEMBER 5, 1853, as the Marsh troupe's production of *Uncle Tom's Cabin* was opening in Cincinnati, the 33rd Congress opened its first session. Elected in the 1852 electoral sweep (in which voting in many states extended well into 1853), both the House and Senate had huge Democratic majorities. In the House, Democrat Linn Boyd of Kentucky was easily reelected to the Speakership.[1] This easy victory may well have set the stage for a second crisis over slavery, one for which the northern public was now well prepared.

American slavery had depended on a compromise forged in Philadelphia in 1787: there would be a national union, and slavery would not be questioned. A vocal minority of voices testified against this accommodation with tyranny, a framing structure of the republic, through the following decades, rising in the 1830s and beginning to gain political traction in the 1840s. The crisis of 1850 had mandated a "final settlement," including the draconian requirement that northern authorities and the public act to return men and women fleeing southern slavery under penalty of law. The result was, I have suggested, that northerners, some loudly, some quietly, some not sure, began to question the morality of both compromises, of 1787 and of 1850. While political institutions did not respond to this sense of liminal rupture, cultural actors stepped in. Amplified by those seeing a profit to be made in the marketplace, by December 1853 they had framed a decisive shift in the climate of northern opinion and in the soundtrack of popular culture—stated and restated in myth-making terms. Not all agreed, to be sure, including most northern Democrats, but there was now a collective reference point for the spectrum of opinion: the argument that slavery was a national sin, that African Americans in and out of slavery might have personalities and aspirations similar to those of white northerners, and that freedom was the natural condition of humanity.

Perhaps it was hubris; perhaps it was the failure to see the growing disjunction between the terms of politics as usual in Washington and shifting collective opinion in the public sphere. But Democrats in the new 33rd Congress, led by Stephen A. Douglas of Illinois, launched a debate that resulted in the repeal of the ban on slavery in the northern section of the Louisiana Purchase and the adoption of a policy of local popular sovereignty. The focus of that debate would be the new Kansas territory. The first result was a massive response from the newly expanded antislavery public in the North. Ultimately, if not immediately, the second result would be the formation of the Republican Party.

John Jay had written Sumner in December 1852, "'Uncle Tom' has created a New Feeling in regard to slavery, which I am confident will shew itself the moment an opportunity is afforded for its embodiment."[2] In terms of an election, that moment would come in November 1854, but it would take another fourteen months for the results of that election to be manifested in the form of political power. A party realignment, with the emergence of a new party, would complete the restructuring of the American political landscape. But it required a lot of moving parts to coalesce.

As THE 33rd Congress opened, the plans and the hubris of the victorious Democrats hinged on two stories, one a transcontinental story and the other transatlantic. Stephen Douglas, swept up in the vision of the Manifest Destiny of the American republic of the Polk years, had long been an advocate of building a railroad spanning the continent. He had tried to drive this legislation through three times before, in 1844, in 1848, and in the final session of the 32rd Congress in the spring of 1853. Each time it failed on sectional ambitions and suspicions. The development of northern and southern routes across the plains and mountains to the Pacific would have huge economic consequences for the states along the Mississippi valley and their respective sections. In February and March 1853, following the slow, lingering death of his wife, Martha, Douglas had pushed hard for a middle route to San Francisco, a plan that passed the House, 93–43. But it failed in the Senate because Senator David Atchison of Missouri was unhappy with the prospect of free state settlers filling the territory just west of his state, preserved in 1821 against slavery by the terms of the Louisiana Purchase.[3] Douglas would be eager to take up this legislation again, and to cut the necessary deals, when the 33rd Congress convened in December.

In the intervening months he took a rash—if conventional—detour. Mourning his wife, but also eager to be seen in foreign capitals, Douglas booked passage on the Collins Line steamship *Pacific* and left for a grand tour of Europe, via Liverpool, on May 14, 1853. After spending three weeks in London in May and June, he departed for a great circuit of the Continent, first through France and Italy to Greece and Turkey, then to Odessa, the Crimea, Moscow, and St. Petersburg. Perched uncomfortably on horseback, he reviewed the troops with the tsar, then returned to England by way of Denmark, Prussia, Austria, and Paris again. He arrived in New York on the steamer *Arctic* after five and half months abroad.[4]

Seven weeks before, Harriet Beecher Stowe had returned from Liverpool on the *Arctic* after her own exciting European sojourn. Stowe and Douglas both had been in London and Paris in late May and early June, though it is unlikely that their paths crossed. In London, where they overlapped by two and half weeks (May 14–June 4), while Stowe was feted by the antislavery aristocracy, Douglas was welcomed in Parliament and by great financiers. He dined with the banker Thomas Baring in the company of Martin Van Buren, who was on his own tour of the European capitals.[5] Douglas and other Americans on the tour that summer heard a lot about Harriet Beecher Stowe. Douglas might well have been in sympathy with Anna Whistler, in England for a few months, when she complained to her sister: "I hear much of the popular mania—Mrs. B. Stowe's travel in England . . . I am oftener questioned than I like as to my opinion of her work. I am no advocate for slavery, but I can witness to the humanity of the owners of the southern Atlantic states & testify that such are benefactors of the race of Ham" She hoped that "Uncle Tom" would advance the cause of colonization of free blacks to Africa, but was disgusted that "so much romance & poison is mixed up with the abolishionist [sic] prejudices of the writer."[6]

If he'd given it much thought, Douglas certainly would have agreed with Anna Whistler. And if the New York he left in May 1853 had a different tone upon his return on October 30, Douglas paid it no mind. It is unlikely that he saw the crowds at New York's theaters on his quick stop before rushing south to Washington. The Collins Line kept a hotel at its dock on the Hudson River, on the far side of Manhattan from the Bowery; this would have been convenient to the New Jersey ferry that Douglas would have had to take to catch the train south. Of course Douglas was partial to the Astor House on lower Broadway, which was across the street from the American Museum, where Barnum opened *Uncle Tom's Cabin* on November 7. But by then Douglas was gone. Perhaps he had taken in the mood of the New York theater crowds; but the *Washington Union* reported his arrival in the capital on November 3, four days after he landed at the Collins dock in New York.[7] He could not have known—or cared—that a series of antislavery lectures by prominent figures was being planned to open at the Broadway Tabernacle Congregational Church (founded by the great evangelist Charles Finney) in December, to run deep into the winter of 1854. Much more concerned about being totally out of touch with what was happening in Washington and in Illinois, on November 11 he wrote a panicked letter to Charles H. Lanphier, the editor of the *Illinois State Register*, asking: "Why don't you send me a copy of the Register? I have not seen a copy in more than six months." Lanphier wrote back that "these days six months is a long time" to be out of contact with fast-paced national politics. Given the fragility of the nation in 1854, the fact that the Kansas-Nebraska Act was advanced so ardently and recklessly has seemed somewhat mysterious. It may well be that Douglas's absence in the capitals of Europe during the congressional recess, far from American newspapers and his regular correspondence, sheds some light on this mystery.[8]

As HAPPENS with many parties when they gain complete control of the federal government, the Democrats in the 33rd Congress were riven by faction, some shaped by sectional differences, some by jealousies over patronage. Douglas and others felt that Franklin Pierce, still mourning the death of his son in a railroad accident the previous year, was not up to the task of leadership. Strong action was required to advance the Democracy. Douglas decided to link the issue of the transcontinental railroad with the future of the northern section of the Louisiana Purchase. He would pay a steep price.[9]

As speculation swirled in the newspapers, Douglas was reappointed chair of the Senate Committee on Territories and immediately took up the issue of organizing a Nebraska territory (the future states of Kansas and Nebraska) based on the legislation that had stalled at the end of the previous session. There would be one critical change, however. Senator David Atchison of Missouri had agreed in February that this territory could be organized only under the terms of the Missouri Compromise of 1821, which had reserved the entire Louisiana Purchase north of 36°30′ for free settlement. But 36°30′ was also the southern boundary of the slaveholding state of Missouri, and over the recess between Congresses, Atchison had been pressured into changing his position. When he returned in December, he and the rest of his "F Street Mess" made it clear to their mess-mate Douglas that the vast Nebraska territory would have to be opened to slavery. On January 4 of the new year, Douglas's committee presented the first version of the new bill, with an extended report. The territory defined was enormous, essentially the entire Louisiana Purchase north of 36°30´, based on the argument that the Compromise of 1850 should be applied retroactively to the 1803 Louisiana Purchase. The proposed bill applied the doctrine of popular sovereignty as it had been formulated for Utah and New Mexico: the question of slavery or freedom in these lands would be decided by the voters once they were "admitted as a state or states."[10]

Six days later the language suddenly changed. Supposedly on account of a "clerical error," the bill was reprinted to stipulate that "all questions pertaining to slavery in the Territories" to be created would be decided by the territorial voters *before* statehood. None of this actually stated that the Missouri Compromise was being repealed, and that was not good enough for many southerners. And so on Monday January 16, Archibald Dixon of Kentucky proposed an amendment that would do exactly that. Douglas equivocated for a day or two, accepted the amendment, and then took the F Street Mess to strong-arm the president. On Monday the twenty-third of January, Douglass introduced another, essentially final version of the bill in the Senate, repealing the Missouri Compromise and now dividing the territory into two sections, Kansas and Nebraska, for which slavery would be possible through a territorial popular vote. Southern pressure and Douglas's obvious ambitions for the presidency were driving the reversal of a sectional agreement that had virtual constitutional standing among most northerners.

The small antislavery cadre in Washington was ready. Gamaliel Bailey, seeing the need for more rapid communication of affairs in Washington to the country, announced on December 15 that, starting in early January, the *National Era* would be issued as a daily rather than a weekly. This move eventually ruined him financially but otherwise worked as intended. Charles Sumner, Salmon Chase, and Joshua Giddings were all involved in this decision, and Sumner was quick off the mark on January 17, introducing an amendment to reverse Dixon's assault on the Missouri Compromise. Giddings began to work on an address to the people.[11]

The "Appeal of the Independent Democrats," published in Bailey's *National Era* on January 24, was originally aimed only at

Ohio. Giddings and Chase saw the opportunity to divide the state's Democrats with a stark condemnation of the machinations of the Slave Power, and to unite Ohio's Free Soilers and Whigs. Giddings started the draft early in the week of the sixteenth, with Chase rewriting and expanding it and Sumner giving it a final going-over. By the end of the week, after some backroom persuasion involving Seward, Hale, and several others, Giddings, Chase, and Sumner were joined as signers by Edward Wade of Ohio, Alexander DeWitt of Massachusetts, and abolitionist Gerrit Smith of New York, newly seated after his triumphant victory in 1852.[12] Newspapers all over the country that week and the next printed notices that the "Appeal" was in the works, and an early copy was given to the *New York Times*. Douglas announced the final version of the Nebraska bill on Monday January 23, but the next morning, when he began a formal consideration of its terms, Chase and Sumner asked for a week's delay to give the Senate an opportunity to study it. Their "Appeal" was published in the *Era* and the *New York Times* that afternoon.[13]

There was certainly an element of trickery in the plotting of the "Independent Democrats," fully matching that of the Douglas–F Street Mess cabal. And the strident language of the "Appeal" was shocking to the sensibilities of the Senate, so dominated by proslavery and moderate unionist positions.[14] The "Appeal" was a free soil document wrapped in the tone of abolitionist culture. "Shall slavery be permitted in Nebraska?," it asked. Briefly reminding the public of the events at the end of the last Congress, and bringing them up to date on the maneuvers of the preceding week, the "Appeal" presented its basic premise in a single sentence: "We arraign this bill as a gross violation of a sacred pledge; as a criminal betrayal of precious rights as part and parcel of an atrocious plot to exclude from a vast unoccupied region, emigrants from the Old World and free laborers from our own states, and convert it into a dreary region of despotism, inhabited by masters and slaves." Giddings and Chase then developed the geo-constitutional case: the scale of the land involved, the history of the Louisiana Purchase, the settlement of the crisis of 1820–1821, and the "monstrous wrong" of claiming that the Utah–New Mexico settlement in 1850 overturned this agreement. The overturning of a "sacred prohibition," the subverting of a "solemn compact," was an act of "bad faith" that the great Whig Henry Clay would have denounced. Their purpose here was free soil for white men—immigrants and native-born alike—not freedom for black people, but they were well aware that it was a halfway measure: "Perhaps apologies can be offered for the toleration of slavery in the States, none can be urged for its extension into Territories where it does not exist, and where the extension involves the repeal of ancient law, and the violation of social compact." They closed with an exhortation, an "appeal to the people" to "be mindful of the fundamental maxim of Democracy—EQUAL RIGHTS AND EXACT JUSTICE FOR ALL MEN"—and remember that "the cause of freedom is the cause of God."[15]

Thus the "Appeal" was a political document written in moral language. The 1821 Compromise was not only "ancient law" but also a "sacred pledge." In some way it had been bound up in constitutional and religious meaning. Political maneuvers to change it by statute were a "gross violation," "a criminal betrayal," "an atrocious plot." Slavery would turn the "rich lands of this Large Territory" into "a dreary region of despotism." If they were not calling for immediate abolition, they were condemning slavery in the moral language of abolitionists and in the religious language of Rufus King—and William Seward—who in 1821 and 1850 had spoken of the "higher law" standing in judgment of a slaveholding nation.

Historians have for decades seen the "Appeal" as a dramatic rupture in national politics, in which a condemnation of the Slave Power suddenly erupted on the national stage and gripped the political imagination of the northern public.[16] Certainly the language of the "Appeal" had rarely been heard in Washington. But seen against the backdrop of cultural politics over the previous eighteen to twenty months, still unfolding on stages throughout the North, the "Appeal" was less a dramatic departure than a political inflection. The cultural action of novels, song, and theater all had prepared northerners for the rhetoric of the "Appeal." This religious language had an obvious resonance for those still enveloped in the culture that Harriet Beecher Stowe had created with *Uncle Tom's Cabin* and that was reinforced in multivalent ways by the commercial wave that had been washing over the free states in the previous twenty months. The "Appeal" was a critical "event" in the emergence of a viable antislavery politics, but it did not stand alone. It has to be seen in the context of the stream of events unfolding from 1850—the Fugitive Slave Act, the protests and rescues of 1850–1851, and then the commercial intervention of cultural actors. Since the fall of 1850 there had been a disconnect between growing numbers of people in the North and the structure of their politics. What had been implicit but not fully articulated was now being openly stated: the actions of the minority Slave Power to defend and expand slavery involved "a violation of the social compact," a fundamental constitutional crisis.[17]

Did the "Appeal" achieve this transformative result on its own in the winter of 1854? It was certainly influential, but it was quickly reinforced ten days after it was first published.[18] On February 3, Salmon Chase—who had a hand in the final rhetoric of the "Appeal"—presented a major speech in the Senate, restating its argument and its key language. Chase's "Maintain Plighted Faith" would have a great impact. Referring to proslavery complaints about abolitionist agitation, he declared that the "the finalists have become agitators." Slavery was now demanding the reversal of "a time-honored and sacred compact," the Missouri Compromise. Reviewing not only the shift in policy between March 1853 and January 1854, which now reversed the Compromise of 1821, Chase went back to the history of the 1820–1821 crisis, stressing that proslavery forces had originated and voted through the Missouri decision that had made the "prohibition" of slavery north of 36°30´ "absolute and perpetual." He could not believe that Americans had so lost sight of the obligations assumed at the forging of the Union in the Revolution "as to acquiesce in the violation of this compact." In closing he wove together frameworks of sanctity with those of honor: preserving "plighted faith and solemn compacts" were "the ways of honor" rather than "temporary expedients." Indeed "honor and conscience" were "more sacred than constitutional obligation."[19] If sanctity echoed the feminine tone and message of Stowe's *Uncle Tom's Cabin*, Chase's pivot to honor would have struck a chord in male culture. Each resonated with the wider framework of the contemporary meaning of "faith," which had its religious meanings but also its specific understandings regarding contracts and compacts entered into by honorable men.[20]

This language erupted in two contexts, the press and petitions. It would appear that in the end Chase's speech was perhaps more influential than the "Appeal." In hundreds of articles in the national press relating to the Missouri Compromise, mentions of Chase's "sacred compact" and "plighted faith" appeared twice as frequently as references to the "Appeal's" "sacred pledge."[21] But really these terms were interchangeable, and they surged to a peak in February and March 1854, with a secondary echo in May at the final passage of the bill. The prominence of these terms faded, and they were replaced with the term "Anti-Nebraska" as the movement moved sharply into the political domain. But Anti-Nebraska meetings that January and February—in Cleveland, in Boston, in New York—certainly mobilized the moral language of both the "Appeal" and Chase's "Maintain Plighted Faith."[22]

These months offered the "opportunity" for the "embodiment" of John Jay's "New Feeling,"[23] and he had a hand in its emergence in New York. The "Appeal" urged the northern public to "protest, earnestly and emphatically, by correspondence, through the press, by memorials, by resolutions of public meetings and legislative bodies, . . . against this enormous crime." That January, Jay was in close communication with Sumner in Washington. While he was sending petitions on other issues, Sumner urged him on January 12 that "for the present, it is important that petitions should be pointed at Nebraska—& against the violation of the Missouri Compromise. Let petitions against the enormity be circulated." Four days later Jay wrote to Sumner of plans afoot for the New York meeting to be held at the 1,600-seat Tabernacle Church on Broadway; Sumner rejoiced.[24] A grand total of 2,210 petitions were presented during

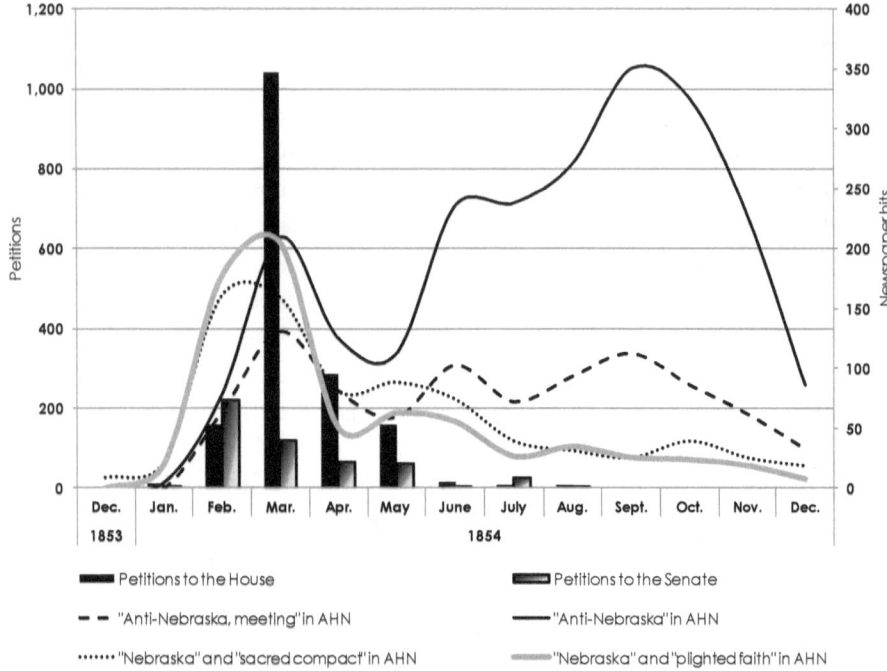

FIGURE 10. Petitions to the 33rd Congress, Anti-Nebraska language in free state papers

The explosion of petitions and items in the press referring to violations of the "sacred compact" and "plighted faith" gave way to a long arc of Anti-Nebraska meetings focused on the 1854 election.

SOURCES: Senate and House journals, 33rd Congress, 1st session; America's Historical Newspapers (accessed July 2017).

the first session of the 33rd Congress.[25] (See Appendix, table 9.) Opposing them, only twelve petitions supported slavery in the territories. Of course, many of the antislavery petitions were duplicates; Sumner had advised Jay that petitions should "be prepared in duplicate, to be presented contemporaneously in both bodies." Nonetheless, petitions to the Senate tapered off after the Nebraska bill was passed in that body early on the morning of March 4, with the effort refocusing on the House. By themselves, the 1,700 petitions to the House were an enormous effort and marked one of the great moments in antislavery activism, along with the petition drives of 1837–1839 and 1850.

Of the 1854 petitions, more than four-fifths (86 percent) were directed—as Sumner had suggested—at the Nebraska bill, and of these almost three-quarters specifically demanded the preservation of the Missouri Compromise, most often as the single focus of the petition.[26] Many petitions were, of course, signed on printed forms, but many others were handwritten and reflect the deliberations of meetings large and small. A sample from Ohio suggests continuities with the language of the "Appeal" and Chase's "Maintain Plighted Faith." On February 18 citizens of Canal Dover wrote a petition, presented a month later in the House, protesting the virtual repeal of the Missouri Compromise as "a violation of good faith, justice, and honor, on the part of the South." Citizens of Lorain County wrote of the "immense territory which has been consecrated to freedom by our forefathers by a solemn compact between the North and the South." A meeting in Hopewell, Muskingum County, agreed, "believing slavery to be a gross violation of man's dearest rights & a curse to any country." Meeting on April 5, the presbytery of Portage, Ohio, protested against the bill "as a gross violation of solemnly plighted faith." Whereas the Portage presbytery virtually quoted Chase's speech, their colleagues in the Pataskala presbytery, meeting the same day, did not refer to the Missouri Compromise but echoed Harriet Beecher Stowe's indictment of slavery's "outrage against the family" and her prediction of divine wrath. The Nebraska bill would "lend the sanction of the Government of the United States to the sundering of all family ties, & to an exclusion of the Bible from a large portion of the future population of Nebraska, & to a withholding from them the enjoyment of the rights guaranteed in the Scriptures . . . thereby exposing us as a Nation to the just indignation, & the swift judgments of Almighty God."[27] Some meetings were not so pious; reports of Senator Douglas being burned in effigy circulated around the North in March and April.[28]

There were of course many echoes of Harriet Beecher Stowe, and some active initiatives. First and foremost, the entire framework of "sacred pledge," "sacred compact," and "plighted faith" all had resonances with a female, religious domain, and it had direct gender implications, since this was the language of the marriage contract.

Here Salmon Chase, who had known Stowe for decades and followed her publication in the *Era* closely, had shaped this critical language in the "Appeal" and his own February 3 speech. Though it was never spelled out specifically, there was the implication that in abandoning the Missouri Compromise, the male South was violating the marriage compact of 1787 and 1821 with a female North. For the close reader, the "Appeal's pronouncement" that "Freemen . . . will not, and should not, work beside slaves" would have resonated with Harriet Beecher Stowe's description of fugitives in the North as "freemen" in *Uncle Tom's Cabin* and throughout her *Key*, published just nine months before the opening of the Nebraska debate.[29] And in the newspapers, exhortation to the public could suggest the ongoing family reading experience of *Uncle Tom's Cabin*. In Chicago, the *Free West* urged its readers:

> Gather the family around the cabin fireside, put the bright light on the stand, and read the document to every member of your family . . . [M]ake every one of the household familiar with the principles of freedom . . . Go with the document to your neighbors, and read it by their firesides. Assemble the people together in every school-district, and let every school house . . . hear the reading of that appeal, to the parents and the children . . . Friends, call then your neighborhood meetings, read the Appeal instead of a speech, discuss the subject until well understood—then let the remonstrance published in the last *Free West* be offered for signatures . . . This is the only effectual way now to vote against the extension of slavery to Nebraska.[30]

There were more than just hints of Stowe's involvement in the Nebraska protests in February, when she was putting the final touches on her memoir of her 1853 European trip, *Sunny Memories of Foreign Lands*.[31] On February 23 she jumped into the deliberative public sphere, publishing "An Appeal to the Women of the Free States" in the *New York Independent*. She opened with her established pious sentimental themes of the violence, the outrage to the family posed by slavery, and then pivoted to the extension of slavery into the territories and beyond toward the threatening specter of national slavery: "Women of the Free States! . . . are we willing to receive Slavery into the free states and territories of the Union? Shall the whole power of these United States go into the hands of slavery?" Her question, then, was: What was the role of "women's influence"? Recounting what she had learned during her recent travels in Europe, she advised the American woman "to give her influence on the right side," to pray, and to circulate petitions, to distribute copies of speeches, to organize lectures. Her central message was to "communicate information" in the public sphere.[32]

Stowe was already deeply involved on most of these fronts. She was organizing a lecture series on the Nebraska crisis that brought a host of antislavery figures—though decidedly of the Tappanite wing, and including two of her brothers—to the Tremont Temple in Boston in March and April.[33] On February 18 she wrote to Garrison that she and her husband were "starting two petitions from Andover," one for the men and one for the "ladies" of the seminary, "remonstrating against the repeal or violation of the Missouri compromise." By then the petitions had finished circulating, but it wasn't until two days later that Calvin Stowe sent them off (with mutterings about "that heartless, soulless, fiendish demagogue & traitor, S. A. Douglas") to Sumner in Washington, who presented the women's petition in the Senate on the twenty-fourth.[34] Stowe's larger project was in motion, fueled by her profits from *Uncle Tom's Cabin*. In her letter to Garrison and, a few days later, another to Sumner, she detailed plans that were in motion for a massive petition. Her brother Edward was meeting with ministers throughout New England and eastern New York State, gaining commitments.[35] Once it was signed, she hoped that Sumner could arrange for the "clerical committee" to present the petition themselves on the floor of the Senate. In 1850 the ministers had hung back from the protests against the Fugitive Slave Act, but now they were pivoting to the antislavery cause. Stowe may have been critically positioned to take part in this effort, since she had just finished a long public exchange with Garrison, debating whether the churches were fundamentally proslavery. Certainly the ministerial networks of her brother Edward, husband Calvin, and her father, the venerable Lyman Beecher—who signed the circulation letter—combined with the clout of the Andover Seminary, all played a key role.[36]

The result was a document signed by 3,050 ministers, shifting this critically influential bloc away from the "structure" of union and slavery. Their short remonstrance, "in the name of Almighty God," condemned the Nebraska bill as "a great moral wrong; as a breach of faith eminently injurious to the moral principles of the community, and subversive of all confidence in National engagements; as a measure full of danger to the peace and even the existence of our beloved Union, and exposing us to the righteous judgments of the Almighty." When it was introduced on March 14 by Sumner's senatorial colleague Edward Everett of Massachusetts, Stephen Douglas jumped up to condemn the petition and the petitioners for perpetrating "an atrocious falsehood" and demanding that the petition be rejected. This in turn set off a hue and cry in the northern press.[37]

Less than a month later Stowe was in Washington, watching her brother Henry preach at the installation of a minister at the Congregational church and dining with the antislavery caucus in Congress at the Baileys' fine house on C Street.[38] But by then, and indeed by the time the ministers' petition arrived, it was too late. After a marathon session, the Senate had passed the Nebraska bill, 37–14, at five in the morning on March 4.[39] It now went over to the House, from where on March 21 it was sent to the purgatory of the Committee of the Whole by a vote of 111–95, where it might have lingered and died. Such was not to be. But the ministers' petition was one of several signs of radicalization in the North that March. On March 11, at a meeting in Worcester, Massachusetts, called to protest the Senate vote, Eli Thayer proposed sending free state settlers to a future Kansas territory. This was the origin of the New England Emigrant Aid Society and a harbinger of the armed struggle in Kansas that would erupt the following year.[40]

Four days earlier, on March 7, Ralph Waldo Emerson had taken his turn at the podium at the Broadway Tabernacle in a series of antislavery lectures that had started in January. Emerson and other transcendentalists had held themselves aloof from abolitionism into the 1840s but had been radicalized fully by the Fugitive Slave Law. He now made that law the centerpiece of his address, focusing his assault on Daniel Webster's betrayal of the North in 1850. Emerson had planned this speech several months earlier, in November, and was worried that it would miss the mark in the midst of the Nebraska debates. But the audience was receptive, and the timing was right, coming four days before another fugitive drama, the rescue of Joshua Glover in Milwaukee. Emerson pushed his audience to remember the personal impact, the shock, of the Compromise debates of four winters previous. "I have lived all my life without suffering any inconvenience from American Slavery," he noted to his audience. "I never saw it; I never heard the whip; I never felt the check on my free speech and action, until, the other day, when Mr. Webster, by his personal influence, brought the Fugitive Slave Law on the Country." Connecting 1850 and 1854, he resorted to bodily metaphors: "The Fugitive Law did much to unglue the eyes of men, and now the Nebraska Bill leaves us staring." He argued that "the events of this month are teaching one thing plain and clear, the worthlessness of good tools to bad workmen." The people of the North had relied on the Constitution and the Supreme Court, "but what if, unhappily, the judges are chosen from the wolves"? Then he took these constitutional questions to the heart of the northern disquiet in 1854:

> You relied on the Missouri Compromise: that is ridden over. You relied on state sovereignty in the free states to protect their citizens. They are driven with contempt out of the courts, and out of the territory of the slave states, if they are so happy to get out with their lives. And now you relied on those dismal guarantees infamously made in 1850, and before the body of Webster is yet crumbled, it is found that they have crumbled: this eternal monument at once of his fame and of the common Union, is rotten in four years. They

are no guarantee to the free states. They are guarantees to the slave states: that as they have hitherto met with no repulse, they shall meet with none.[41]

Reported in New York and Boston newspapers,[42] but not printed until the 1880s, Emerson's Tabernacle address perhaps was less an influence than a symptom; he articulated the sense of a constitutional trap that growing numbers of northerners now felt in the trajectory from 1850 to 1854. Slavery was deeply entrenched in national governance and was spreading its tentacles into free spaces. Now it was the territories; the states were next. There was, Emerson told his audience on the seventh of March, "no reliance to be had in any form of covenant—no, not on sacred forms." Constitutions, churches, Bibles all stood with slavery, and "the devil nestles comfortably into them all." Clearly a great struggle lay over the horizon, between a nationalized slavery or "freedom national."[43]

AT THE same time, there was another force at work that, if in a frenzy of promotion and commerce, was keeping a semblance of a sacred story in motion among the northern public. Between December 1853 and August 1854, during the Nebraska debates and the entire length of the first session of the 33rd Congress, theatrical productions of *Uncle Tom's Cabin* across the free states moved through peak, decline, revival, and dispersal. These performances—and the constant stream of advertising and commentary in the press—were interwoven with coverage of the ongoing congressional debate about freedom and slavery in the plains West, now virtually instantaneous with the accelerating pulse of the "magnetic telegraph." Common memories of the spring of 1854 would weave together Nebraska and *Uncle Tom* into an inseparable experience. And as they made their way deeper and deeper into the northern hinterland, performances of *Uncle Tom's Cabin*—in a remarkable number of instances—were embroiled in local dramas involving the enforcement of the Fugitive Slave Act. National politics, performance of mythos, and real personal struggles all swirled together to crystallize new cultural structures out of the liminal uncertainties of the preceding four years.

This sequence unfolded in part in the great theater towns on the northeast coast: Boston, New York, and Philadelphia. Having run at Moses Kimball's Museum from November 1852 to early July 1853, *Uncle Tom's Cabin* was played out in Boston by the late fall of 1853. A revival in September had raised a caustic note from the *Atlas:* "We supposed that Uncle Thomas 'had died long ago,' and had been decently buried, but it seems that we were mistaken." This Boston revival closed its doors in mid-November.[44]

In New York, where the antislavery series at the Tabernacle on Broadway—four blocks from the National Theatre on Chatham Street—was starting in mid-December, things were more dramatic. P. T. Barnum had launched his own version of the Conway production in November, and as the 33rd Congress opened in Washington, he was going head-to-head with Alexander Purdy's Aiken version at the National Theatre. Rumors may have been afloat that the Bowery Amphitheatre would start its own minstrel show version of *Uncle Tom's Cabin* with Thomas D. Rice in the lead role of Uncle Tom. Purdy made changes starting on December 5. He staged a concurrent production of *Little Katie, the Hot Corn Girl*, a temperance melodrama set in nearby Five Points that had been put on at Barnum's, while he made improvements to the main production. On January 9, 1854, five days after Douglas introduced the Nebraska bill, Purdy launched his revised *Uncle Tom's Cabin*, with expensive new scenery and backdrops, and expanding the production to thirty-four scenes. New material depicted the argument between Mrs. Bird and the senator over the Fugitive Slave Act.[45] Purdy did so well at the National that he was able to raise his prices, and before T. D. Rice started prancing at the Bowery on January 16 (the day Henry Ward Beecher spoke at the Tabernacle), Barnum had pulled his production at the Museum. In the end Purdy prevailed: Rice's *Uncle Tom* at the Bowery closed on March 11, a week after Emerson's address at the Tabernacle. That day one of the city's sporting journals, the

Spirit of the Times, suggested some of the linkages: "The slavery agitation has been augmented by the passage of the Nebraska-Kansas Bill, and a little zest is given to the votaries of negro freedom by an attendance at the Bowery or National . . . We have nothing to do here with the matter, politically, but we can perceive what the drama may do to foster or eradicate passions and prejudices of high or low degree."[46] For the moment Purdy's show, with its spectacular closing scene of the "Apotheosis" of Eva and Tom, reigned supreme.

Uncle Tom's Cabin also hung on in Philadelphia, with a brief break. When Wesley Barmore closed up at the National to head west to Cincinnati, the Aiken version was running at the Chestnut Street Theatre, in competition with a minstrel house takeoff by the New Orleans Opera Troupe at Sanford's Opera House. On January 4, the day Douglas introduced the Nebraska bill, the papers announced the play's demise at the Chestnut Street Theatre, but a month later it was revived, competing with another production at Welch's National Amphitheatre and performances by the Hutchinson Family Singers at Concert Hall.[47] The Chestnut Street Theatre had moved on to other entertainment by March 1, but *Uncle Tom's Cabin* continued at Welch's until late April, when it was revived in Boston. In New York, Purdy's production at the National was challenged briefly by a performance by Wood's Minstrels. Purdy finally ended his record run in New York on May 13.[48]

The dispersal of *Uncle Tom's Cabin* to secondary cities and towns had already started with Barmore's migration to Cincinnati and the launch of the Marsh family's trek to the West. In New England there had been runs in Bangor, Providence, and Hartford, and in January 1854—perhaps with Boston actors—it was playing in Lowell. In April there would be a run in Burlington, Vermont.[49] In January there were performances around Philadelphia, in Trenton and Reading, where Rose Merrifield played the role of Topsy, which she had developed in Philadelphia in the Barmore production and at Chestnut Street.[50] In February a troupe led by an A. Keenan from New York began to play across south-central Pennsylvania, circling through Harrisburg, Carlisle, York, Columbia, and Lebanon till the end of March.[51] This was borderland territory and highly contested.

The Pennsylvania state capital, and a Democratic stronghold for decades, Harrisburg had been the site of twelve slave renditions at the hands of a gang of Democratic constables, starting immediately after the signing of the Fugitive Slave Law. Public opinion in Harrisburg generally supported the fugitive law, and the white population stood by when slave renditions, bitterly opposed by the black community, unfolded from September 1850 into 1852. Then in the summer of 1852 a series of incidents, including the apparent kidnapping of a black teenager, the killing of a fugitive, and the capture of a popular black teamster (who was ransomed after a public campaign), began to turn the political tide. The slave-catching constables had barely been reelected in the spring of 1852, but in the spring of 1853 they were defeated at the polls, and slave catching in Harrisburg came to an end. In late February 1854 Keenan's production of *Uncle Tom's Cabin* arrived in Harrisburg, playing in a volatile atmosphere, competing with the minstrels of the Sanford New Orleans Opera Troupe at another hall. The *Morning Herald* reported enthusiastically of Keenan's show that "the Hall literally crammed, and the sale of tickets stopped long before the performance commenced." Such was the context when proslavery Democrats called a meeting to support the Nebraska bill: antislavery men packed the hall, voted down any proslavery resolutions, elected antislavery officers, and voted to condemn the bill putting the territories "within the reach of slavery." A second attempt at a pro-Nebraska meeting failed six days later, and *Uncle Tom's Cabin* played Harrisburg for almost another two weeks before Keenan folded up and moved on.[52]

Cincinnati, one of the great borderland cities of the antebellum United States, attracted the greatest number of dispersing productions of *Uncle Tom's Cabin*. In addition to the Wesley Barmore troupe at the National Theatre and the Marsh family at the Melodeon, there was a mysterious Colonel Robert E. J. Miles of Culpeper Court House, Virginia, putting on another production in Cincinnati that December into January from a pirated Aiken text. There would be considerable reorganization in late January. The Miles troupe became the Matthias and Co. American Dramatic Company, and in February began to move north through Ohio, performing at Chillicothe, Columbus, and Cleveland with "Mr. Gulick's Panorama of the Mississippi." Settling in Columbus for the summer, the Matthias company toured to Portsmouth, Lancaster, Akron, and back to Chillicothe, performing under "a Mammoth Tent."[53]

The National Theatre company in Cincinnati closed its production on the twenty-first of January, and Wesley Barmore took on another venture: by April he was running "Wesley Barmore's Great Adriatic Circus." Moving from Cincinnati through Dayton and into Indiana, across northern Ohio to a two-week run in Buffalo, and back to Cincinnati via Akron, Barmore's "Monster Circus" always closed with an "interesting equestrian sketch of Uncle Tom's Cabin."[54] A few members of the National company, including the treasurer and, most important, "little Viola Plunkett Grattan" as the "gentle Eva," joined a traveling company organized by the National's proprietor, William Shires, that took the "moral drama" all over the state. Competing with the Matthias troupe, Shires's company moved north to Columbus in early February, touring out east to Zanesville before heading west to Springfield and then north to Sandusky and Toledo.[55] In the last two towns, Shires was competing with two other troupes, Kinney & Co. and Kothe & Co., Kinney traveling with another "Mammoth tent."[56]

The Marsh family troupe would tour through a Midwest resounding with struggles over fugitives, as the Nebraska news pounded in over the wires every day. They closed their last performance in Cincinnati on February 4 and moved up to Indianapolis. Their scenery alone nearly filled a railroad car. Beginning on February 8 they played in Indianapolis at the Masonic Hall for twelve nights, with Greene C. Germon singing Foster's "Old Folks at Home." They competed head-to-head for virtually the entire run with another production by Robinson's Atheneum and with various minstrel shows. Indianapolis was sharply divided between Whig-Temperance voters of antislavery sympathies and the proslavery Democrats typical of rural southern

Indiana. On February 7, the Whig-Temperance faction on the city council pushed through the stage license for the Marsh production, with few Democratic councilors in attendance, cutting the municipal fee from $25 to $10. The white elite of the city, regardless of party, had united to defend a free black man, John Freeman, from false arrest under the Fugitive Slave Act. Calvin Fletcher, as the cashier of the local State Bank, was taking cash commitments for Freeman's case against the federal marshal when the two productions started up. On the ninth, four of his sons went to see one of the performances, but Fletcher asserted in his diary: "I did not nor shall not see it. I am sufficiently [consumed] with hatred of the slave system." Over the next ten days he recorded both collections for Freeman and his children's and farm laborers' trips to town to see the play. Among them was a Mr. Green, a black farmhand.[57]

From Indianapolis the Marsh troupe moved on to Lafayette (where they were "the most important topic of conversation . . . the Nebraska bill not excepted"), and, passing quickly through Chicago, they took a steamer to Milwaukee, where they opened on Thursday March 9 to "large crowds" and "great satisfaction."[58] The next day, federal officers and a slaveholder from St. Louis arrived in Racine, some twenty miles south, and that night grabbed a fugitive, Joshua Glover, living on the edge of town. On the morning of Saturday the eleventh, the city of Milwaukee awoke to the news that Glover was confined in the town jail, awaiting steamer transport south along the lakeshore. Abolitionists white and black assembled by the hundreds, perhaps thousands, at Courthouse Square; in the late afternoon a committee of a hundred arrived on the ferry from Racine. Federal officers were served with writs of habeas corpus, to no avail. Soon after dusk the crowd made its move, breaking down the jail door with a battering ram, rescuing Glover, and sending him off—to his shouts of "Glory, Hallelujah"—to a secret Underground Railroad station, and soon to Canada via Racine.[59] At 7:30 p.m., perhaps an hour later, the Marsh troupe started their third performance of *Uncle Tom's Cabin*, at Young's Hall, four blocks south and west of the courthouse.[60]

For the next ten days the Marsh troupe would put on alternating afternoon and evening shows, their ads in the Milwaukee papers running alongside blistering coverage of the arrests of and hearings for those involved in the rescue, reports of the Senate vote on the Nebraska bill, and the rumble of Anti-Nebraska meetings. On the sixteenth, the *Daily Free Democrat*, edited by Sherman Booth, one of the accused rioters, published a short satirical piece directly connecting the Marsh performances with the courthouse rescue:

> The Marsh troupe are here playing Uncle Tom's Cabin every evening in Young's Hall, and preaching up the old Patrick Henry doctrine of Liberty or Death—the very doctrine carried out by the people at the Court House, in rescuing Glover. They go so far as to justify the Fugitive in shooting down the Slave-Catchers, rather than surrender, and be carried back to Slavery. And what is still worse, the people flock in crowds to hear these performances, and cheer them to the very echo.

Mocking the hardline pro-Compromise judge, the editors suggested that he "arrest the troupe at once, and have them tried for riot, and for aiding Glover to escape." *Uncle Tom's Cabin* in the theater was not just an implicit sounding board but was directly involved in antislavery action in Milwaukee during the Nebraska spring.[61]

In early April the Marsh troupe moved south to Racine for several nights, where they played again as the press was filled with news of the arrests of Racine citizens for their part in the rescue, notices of other rescues, and the endless Nebraska debates.[62] From Racine they played Chicago, Detroit, and finally a two-week run in Buffalo, where they had performed in September, now against the backdrop of the final debates on and passage of the Kansas-Nebraska Act.[63]

As these companies moved across the Midwest in the late winter and spring of 1854, they performed to the constant din of coverage of the Nebraska debates as well as the first Anti-Nebraska meetings. There were critiques: in Akron, the *Summit County Beacon* complained of characters being "miserably butchered" and the "extraordinary liberties taken with the most popular book of the day." A writer in the *Anti-Slavery Bugle* thought that "on the whole it was not the drama that the name stands for." But in September in northwest Illinois, the *Galena Jeffersonian* reported a different reaction among the huge crowds at an evening tent performance by the traveling Robinson Atheneum: "The playing ... was anything but satisfactory, the seats were uncomfortable, and the weather intensely hot," but the audience was patient and receptive. In recent years the performers might have been mobbed out of town. But the tide had turned: now it was Senator Douglas who "was hooted from the stand and driven to his hotel" for his plot to "destroy" the "compact" of 1821. Now it was *Uncle Tom's Cabin* that was "listened to and applauded with unmistakable zest and sympathy *by those who vote*," noted the writer. "Silent tears ... rolled down many a manly cheek, when Uncle Tom was hurried from his home to the hard fare and brutal treatment of the far south." The column closed with the threat of elections to come: "The rough hands that wiped away those tears can deposit ballots!"[64] Noting the close of the play at the National in New York, the antislavery *New York Evening Post* opined that "its influence in extending the sympathy for the suffering African can hardly be exaggerated." The American and Foreign Anti-Slavery Society, deeply involved in fugitive rescues in New York City, was of a similar mind, hailing the long run of *Uncle Tom's Cabin* at Alexander Purdy's theater as "a remarkable sign of the times."[65]

THE EVENTS of May 1854 would undercut and intensify the resonance and influence of *Uncle Tom's Cabin*. The Kansas-Nebraska Act suddenly surged to passage in the House on the twenty-second, was confirmed in the Senate on the twenty-sixth, and was signed by President Pierce on the thirtieth. But on May 24 the arrest and subsequent rendition of the fugitive Anthony Burns in Boston reintensified the political confluence uniting black Americans and white northerners, reinforced by the subtle creolizing effects of the book, the play, and its music.

There were hopes in April that the Nebraska bill might die in the House, buried under dozens of bills in the Committee of the Whole. On April 3, people in Racine read about more arrests in the case of the rescue of Joshua Glover and flocked to *Uncle Tom's Cabin* to hear Greene Germon sing Stephen Foster's "Old Folks at Home" and George Howard's "Uncle Tom's Religion." The *Weekly Racine Advocate* was optimistic about events in Washington, observing, "Every hour's delay now increases the probability of the defeat of this nefarious bill."[66] Starting with Gerrit Smith on April 6, antislavery representatives stood up to attack the bill. Joshua Giddings took his turn on May 18, seeing a decisive moment in "the long-pending struggle between liberty and oppression, under this government."[67] But the Nebraska bill moved forward. The house managers organized by Speaker Boyd sidetracked competing legislation, while the president applied patronage pressure, and Alexander Stephens of Georgia invoked a House rule that allowed the Senate bill to be put to a vote without amendment.[68]

In late March the Senate bill had been shelved in the House Committee of the Whole by a vote of 111–95, but it suddenly passed the House on May 22 by a narrow margin of 113–100. Southerners, both Democrats and Whigs, had voted to advance the bill. (See Appendix, table 10.) Northern Whigs, Free Soilers, and Anti-Nebraska Democrats—clustered in New England, western New York and Pennsylvania, and the upper Midwest—were opposed. In March, fifty-three northern Democrats had voted to slow down the bill, with twenty-six supporting Douglas and eleven not voting. When the tide turned in May, the swing group was made up of two sets of northern Democrats. One, mostly from the lower Midwest, stood with Douglas and his position that slavery could expand through local popular sovereignty, voting against the delay in March and for the bill in May. These twenty-six northern "Douglas Democrats" of March 21 were joined by eighteen others, eleven of whom had voted to delay the bill, but were now enticed by patronage jobs. Some of these shifting Democrats were from the upper Midwest, but the largest bloc were from the "old Mid-Atlantic," running from the Hudson Valley south through New Jersey and eastern Pennsylvania, including the booming and conflicted cities of New York and Philadelphia.[69]

These northern Democrats who voted for the Kansas-Nebraska Act were decisive in two ways: they forced the bill through, and their votes would destroy the party in the coming midterm election. But in the meantime, antislavery forces were stunned and deeply pessimistic. Seward and Sumner rose in the Senate to oppose and condemn the bill on the twenty-fifth,[70] but it passed nonetheless, and Kansas would be opened to settlement as soon as the president signed the bill on the thirtieth of May. The passage of the bill was insult enough, but the injury was compounded by events unfolding at the same time in Boston.

Anthony Burns had escaped slavery in Virginia and landed in Boston in February 1854. He had recently begun work washing windows at the Mattapan Iron Works, where he was arrested on May 24, just as Democrats were firing cannon on Boston Common to celebrate the passage of the Nebraska bill by the House. An attempt was made to free him on the twenty-sixth, and a deputy marshal was shot dead. Burns's hearing went ahead on May 29. Unwilling to allow a rescue like those of Thomas Sims and the Crafts, on June 2 the federal government assembled a brigade of marines and Irish militia to carry Burns from the courthouse to the docks, at a cost of $100,000. Crowds of twenty thousand people surged through streets hung in black bunting, booing and hooting at the soldiers. One group carried a coffin labeled "LIBERTY."[71]

Elite conservative Whiggery in Boston felt utterly betrayed by this sequence of events. Promises had been made, first in 1821 and then in 1850, promises that virtually had the status of constitutional settlement. With these promises in hand, conservative Whigs had, in the face of widespread outrage, defended the finality of the 1850 Fugitive Slave Law. Now they were being undermined by the passage of the Kansas-Nebraska Act and insulted in their own city by Burns's rendition to slavery. The result, as Jonathan Earle suggests, "dramatically altered the mood in Boston," driving a veritable antislavery conversion among Massachusetts conservative cotton Whigs who had stood by the compromise of 1787. One of them, Amos Lawrence, who had sided with the government in the Sims rendition in 1851, wrote, "We went to bed one night old fashioned, conservative Union Whigs & and waked up stark mad abolitionists."[72]

News of the riot to free Burns spread across the country quickly, mixed with news of the final vote from Washington on the Kansas-Nebraska bill. Readers in Brooklyn and Burlington were reading both on that same Friday, Hartford and Philadelphia on Saturday, Milwaukee and Indianapolis on Monday and Tuesday. The entire event coincided with the final passage and signing of the Kansas-Nebraska Act, fusing them in popular experience. The *Milwaukee Sentinel* headlined the attack on the courthouse in Boston "The First Fruits of the Nebraska Bill."[73] Emerson's decision to speak on the Fugitive Slave Act at the Tabernacle in March was fully vindicated by events. As the session moved into its final months, petitions against the Fugitive Slave Law picked up slightly. There had been sixteen in the Senate between January and May 25; twenty-seven were presented during the summer. The very last, on August 1, came from citizens of Harrisburg, Pennsylvania, which had not sent a petition to either the House or the Senate that session.[74]

But Massachusetts, given the Burns rescue attempt, was suddenly the focal point. On June 22, Senator Julius Rockwell presented one of these petitions, from 2,900 citizens of Boston, asking for "the repeal of the fugitive slave act," leading to two days of bitter debate in the Senate.[75] While Rockwell argued that most were conservative Whigs who had stood by the Compromise in 1850, southerners challenged him, angrily pointing to signers Theodore Parker and Wendell Phillips as abolitionists and key players in the effort to rescue Burns. Sumner intervened, and a snarling struggle ensued over "constitutional obligations . . . to reduce men to slavery." Southern senators denounced him as a "serpent," "a filthy reptile," "a leper."[76] Having announced his intention to introduce a repeal, Sumner got the floor on July 31, at the end of the session; after a brief procedural struggle, his motion was defeated. But the issue had been brought before the Senate, and he could return to Massachusetts having represented his antislavery constituents. A similar vote in the House had failed, 45–120, on July 28, supported only by northern Whigs, Free Soilers, and a few Anti-Nebraska Democrats.[77]

So ended the first session of the 33rd Congress. It would not meet again until after the autumn election, for a second session running from December 1854 to March 1855; the 34th Congress would not meet until December 1855. At this juncture, as congressional politics effectively halted for the next seventeen months, antislavery cultural politics also began to fade into the background. Center stage would be occupied by the politics of party organization, at the grass roots and in the leadership. Though most abolitionists despaired for the future, the liminal moment was effectively over. What lay ahead was the restructuring phase of the event cluster beginning in 1850. In the short run, it was clear to most observers that the Whig Party was finished, and that the northern wing of the Democratic Party was severely damaged. What was not clear was what kind of geometry would be able to establish a political coalition that could prevail in national politics.

CHAPTER 7

Restructuring Coalescence

Nativism and Antislavery Politics

RALPH WALDO Emerson had been critical of the growing role of civil associations in American life in years past, so some of his thoughts in his address at the Broadway Tabernacle on March 7, 1854, had the quality of a *mea culpa*. "I respect the Anti-Slavery Society," he stated in his closing. "It is the Cassandra that has foretold all that has befallen, fact for fact, years ago." He then did a bit of foretelling himself. "The Anti-Slavery Society will add many members this year. The Whig Party will join it. The Democratic Party will join it. The population of the Free States will join it." He was suggesting—in effect—that an alternative political structure would emerge. He called it the "Anti-Slavery Society" because the label "Republican Party" was only just emerging in distant and obscure county conventions in Wisconsin.[1] A few months later, with the passage of the Kansas-Nebraska Act and the passions surrounding the rendition of Anthony Burns from Boston, his suggestions seemed even more likely. Discussions and condemnations of the Slave Power in the press peaked that summer at a level almost twice that of the last peak in 1848, and press attention to fugitives peaked in June at a level not seen since the spring of 1851. Circumstances looked promising for the rise of an antislavery party.

There were hints to the west that this might be the case, but also signs of trouble. Orville Browning, an antislavery Whig lawyer from Quincy, Illinois, who had overcome a Kentuckian in debate over the injustice of the Fugitive Slave Law in 1850, spent a few days in Louisville in the spring of 1854 as the Nebraska debates were winding down in Congress. Seeing slavery up close, he felt a "much more vivid impression of wrong." In March he had been involved in meetings against the Nebraska bill, and during the fall he spoke frequently on the stump. On the thirty-first of October he sat down for supper with a noted competitor, Abraham Lincoln of Springfield, who was in Quincy for court. After dinner, Lincoln "addressed the People at Kendall's Hall on the Nebraska question."[2]

Lincoln would become the central and decisive figure in the rise of the Republican Party, but in 1854 he had been out of politics for five years. He had gone home to Springfield after his term in Congress and attended to his law practice. In these years he was out of the limelight, and apparently depressed, perhaps going through a midlife crisis, as his major biographer, Michael Burlingame, has argued. As had both Harriet Beecher Stowe and President Pierce, he lost a favorite son in these years; he started going to church. But when Stephen Douglas drove the Kansas-Nebraska Act through Congress, Lincoln emerged from his funk. It is possible that he took his family to see the Robinson Atheneum production of *Uncle Tom's Cabin*, "Re-organized, Enlarged, and Improved for the Campaign of 1854," playing in Springfield and surrounding towns in late July and early August.[3] He did spend the summer in the state library, and that autumn launched a series of speeches challenging Douglas, culminating at Peoria on October 16, the first of his major addresses of the pre–Civil War decade. Here he not only defended the Missouri Compromise but also connected the exclusion of slavery from the territories to the Declaration of Independence, assailing slavery as an inherent violation of the message of the Declaration. Slavery was "a total violation" of the principle that a government derives its "just powers from the consent of the governed," he argued, and proslavery forces were in "an open war with the very principles of civil liberty." His call to "re-adopt the Declaration of Independence" prefigures his language in the Gettysburg Address nine years later. But

Lincoln also qualified his binary opposition of slavery and liberty at Peoria in ways that echoed Harriet Beecher Stowe in *Uncle Tom's Cabin* and that were grounded in his own colonizationist instincts. By invoking the Declaration, he was not "contending for the establishment of political and social equality between whites and blacks." Working his way toward accepting a pure binary of slavery and full civil equality would take the rest of his life.[4]

Lincoln already had in mind challenging Douglas for his Senate seat, an ambition that would consume much of the next half decade and launch him into national prominence. He declared his intentions publicly in November, but subsequently—and somewhat bitterly—withdrew his candidacy in favor of an upstate champion, Lyman Trumbull. Lincoln's emergence would eventually be critical to the success of the Republican Party, but in the summer and fall of 1854, he fell to unresolved factionalism. In Illinois, and across most of the North, opponents of the Slave Power were finding it difficult to abandon their long-held political affiliations: Whig, Anti-Nebraska Democrat, or Free Soil. Lincoln himself was guilty, declining his nomination to the state central committee of the struggling new Republican Party in Illinois.[5]

The surge of voters across the free states into Emerson's "Anti-Slavery Society" would be a complicated story, taking until 1856 to settle out. If the liminal re-creation of culture had crystallized by the late spring of 1854, the coalescence of a new political structure would take another seventeen months at minimum. Liminal epiphanies in novel reading and theatergoing might shift political culture, but they could not by themselves create new political institutions. Without those institutions in place, there would be no opportunity for John Jay's "New Feeling" to "shew itself" in an election.[6] While antislavery politicians failed to move decisively in the summer of 1854, proslavery union Whigs, driven by a terror of extinction, did act quickly, and they exploited the explosive rise of the lodges and associations that were sweeping up white Protestant men in an age of rapid and dislocating urbanization. For a brief interval it was not clear what would fill the space left by the collapse of the Whigs, a northern antislavery party or a national nativist party. But by the summer of 1855 it was clear that nativism would not be an option, and by February 1856 an antislavery coalition had taken control of the U.S. House of Representatives. The essential lines of a new political structure were in place, and would be progressively confirmed over the next four and a half years. Despite the importance of events that would unfold in Washington, Kansas, Illinois, and Harpers Ferry between early 1856 and the 1860 presidential election, these would simply confirm the antislavery structure that coalesced after the passage of the Kansas-Nebraska Act. Perhaps secession and war were not "inevitable," but the ground on which contingent factors might have altered the course of events had dramatically narrowed between September 1850 and February 1856, and probably closed thereafter. So civil war may not have been inevitable in February 1856, but the margin for alternatives suddenly shrank. But none of this was clear to contemporaries in May 1854.

THE GREATEST complication of the intervening year and half came from an alternate political voice. In June 17, 1854, eighteen days after the signing of the Kansas-Nebraska Act, the National Council of the Order of the Star-Spangled Banner voted on a constitution formally establishing anti-immigrant nativism as a national political movement.[7] This National Council nominally began to direct a burgeoning eruption of nativist organization and voting—The Native American Party, the Know Nothing movement—that arose suddenly in the summer of 1854, crested in 1855, and collapsed in 1856. But well before its rout in the 1856 election, it was clear that nativism would not overtake antislavery as the organizing principle of a party opposed to the Democratic Party. Thus antislavery forces confronted two obstacles, their own factionalism and a completely different ideological agenda: the cultural—and economic—threat of surging immigration to descendants of the seventeenth- and eighteenth-century British Protestant emigrations.

Historians have struggled for decades over the causal role of the nativist movement in the shaping of the Republican Party. Fundamentalists see nativism as a sideshow; revisionists see it as central to the disruption of the Second Party System.[8] Out of this interpretive struggle has emerged a broad consensus that northern Protestants who stood opposed to the Democratic Party shared three strands of a common heritage that ran back to the Federalists: a sentimental and programmatic unionism, free soil antislavery, and a deep unease with immigrants, especially Catholics.

Union was the inheritance of the Revolution, interpreted in a Hamiltonian tradition to include the vigorous intervention of government to enhance the conditions for economic expansion.[9] Antislavery sentiment had been broad, if not particularly deep, since the days of the slaveholding Virginia dynasty—indeed, since the 1787 debate over the Constitution. And American Protestants, who understood the country as a Protestant nation, could still recite the travails of the martyrs of the Reformation.

Most non-Democrats in the North harbored all three impulses—in qualities and quantities that we can get at only impressionistically. Thus Calvin Fletcher in Indianapolis, long a Whig, announced his commitment to free soil antislavery well before the Marsh troupe brought *Uncle Tom's Cabin* to town. He would become a stalwart of the Republican Party, but in the ensuing summer and fall of 1854 he was clearly fascinated by the nativist agenda, and several of his sons joined Know Nothing lodges.[10] Yet many northern Know Nothings might have been called "doughface Whigs," eager to suppress the "agitation" over the "slavery question" and maintain the Union at all costs. In essence, we need to think of these three ideological strands on their own sliding scale, each having a different salience for individual voters. Whereas Fletcher was cross-pressured but eventually settled into antislavery, and his Know Nothing sons rallied to the Republicans in 1856 and the Union in 1861, radical abolitionists denounced slavery, nativism, and a proslavery Union in equal measure. Similarly, there was a hard core of unionist nativists who were happy to join Union Whigs in the South to build a nativist-union-proslavery party that would have the same national reach as the old

Whig Party. So for a few years there was a potent uncertainty as to who would form the new national anti-Democrat coalition, and on what terms. The coalition options fell into four categories:

1. northern nativism with an antislavery plank;
2. a national nativism united north and south and supporting slavery expansion;
3. an antislavery Republican Party rejecting nativism; or
4. an antislavery Republican Party with nativist tendencies.

Each would have its day, the first in 1854, the second in 1855, the third in 1856, and the fourth in 1860. In the long term the Republican Party would harbor nativism within its cultural orbit, but from the 1850s into the 1870s, antislavery and national racial justice prevailed as a dominant ideological force.

IN THE fourteen years between the Log Cabin election of 1840 and the Kansas-Nebraska year of 1854, the northern United States went through a world-historical structural shift. In 1840 there were few railroads and no telegraph, the prevailing source of industrial energy was waterpower, and westward expansion in the Midwest was stalled, scattered along the lakes and rivers for lack of easy overland transportation. Despite the cultural and economic prominence of larger cities, most people lived in small towns and farming districts, and most were Protestants of various denominations. By 1854 this world was experiencing rapid change, driven by technological advances and Atlantic migrations. The year 1853 had seen the peak of a boom in railroad construction which had started from virtually nothing in 1847. Immigration peaked between 1851 and 1855 in an expansion that began in 1846, sparked by potato famines in Ireland and revolution in Germany. The very shape of the landscape was changing, carved up and channeled by the railroads, which opened up the new prairies and bypassed older villages, driving a vortex of positive feedback that drew people into growing cities, ramshackle boomtowns that had a decided tendency to burn in terrible urban fires. The new steam technology of the small high-pressure engine, first applied in the textile mills, was spreading rapidly in other trades. And while there was no economic shock in 1854, there had been one unfolding over the previous decade and a half, as native white northerners endured the long depression of 1837–1843, only to be buffeted by the new technologies and competition with floods of immigrants.[11]

Immigrants, whether they lived in the cities, and whether Catholic or not, liked to drink beer and whisky, while native Protestant whites, middle-class and workingmen alike, had been subjecting themselves to a campaign of self-denial in the temperance movement. But Catholicism was as significant a difference as drinking liquor, perhaps more significant. For the most part, American Protestants had known of Catholics through a screen of confessional hatred dating to the Reformation and the early modern empire-building era, in which a common Protestantism had shaped loyalties to the British Empire until the Revolution.[12]

These confessional animosities were intensified by both confrontation and poor judgment in the early 1850s. The Catholic Church, and Catholic families, in many cities had demanded in 1853 that public funds be set aside for parochial schools out of the common school funding. At the same time, both Whigs and Democrats courted the immigrant vote, the Whigs in the 1852 election, the Democrats in their general embrace of newcomers, and specifically in President Pierce's appointment of Catholic James Campbell as postmaster general. Tensions were already high when Cardinal Gaetano Bedini arrived as the papal nuncio in June 1853 to assert papal control over church properties, ending an American Catholic tradition of lay trusteeships. Anti-Catholicism was already surging, driven by the arrival of an ex-priest, Alessandro Gavazzi, who spoke to crowded meetings in a number of cites about Bedini's role in the suppression of Garibaldi's revolution in Italy. A reputation as "the bloody butcher of Bologna" and "a known enemy of Republican principles" spread before Bedini as he took a long and ill-managed tour of the country through February 1854. German revolutionaries rioted against him in Cincinnati, events about which Calvin Fletcher had strong and enthusiastic opinions.[13]

The revisionists stress that growing nativist hostility toward Catholicism, immigrants, their drinking habits, and their threat to wages was the decisive factor in the Civil War party realignment. Clearly, nativism did play a role. Under these pressures, and given the salience of ethnic hostility in later nineteenth-century politics, it is not all that surprising that many in a deeply Protestant culture lashed out against Catholic immigrants. What is surprising is how quickly the nativist impulse was reduced to a background issue, sidelined by the antislavery imperative. And what is striking is the way in which the native impulse was channeled through new and explosively growing patterns of culture and social organization.

IN THE spring of 1854 people throughout the North began to find odd bits of paper strewn in the streets or pasted on buildings, usually heart-shaped, sometimes diamonds. These were signals to the informed: a secret council of local nativists was calling a meeting. By May, with the closing arguments on the Nebraska bill resounding in Washington, there may have been fifty thousand nativists organized across the country.[14] That same month a faction of New York City nativists, conservative Whigs known as the "Silver Grays," reorganized their state organization and held a preliminary national caucus. In June they assembled a national meeting of nativists, with delegates from thirteen states. On June 17, eighteen days after the president signed the Kansas-Nebraska Act, these delegates ratified a constitution establishing a "National Council of the Supreme Order of the Star Spangled Banner," committed to coordinating a national policy to secretly determine the outcome of conventions of the major parties.

Out of these origins would emerge the brief-lived Know Nothing movement, the "American" Party, whose stated purpose was to unite white Protestant Americans against a primary threat of Catholic immigration. Rightly or wrongly, antislavery figures had their suspicions about the ultimate motivation of the organization of nativist sentiment. Decades later George Julian, the Indiana Free Soiler, wrote bitterly that this was "a well-timed scheme to divide the people of the free states upon trifles and side issues, while the South remained a unit in defense of its great interest . . . By thus kindling the Protestant jealousy of our people against the Pope, and enlisting them in a crusade against the foreigner, the South could all the more successfully push forward" its relentless expansion of the power and scope of slavery.[15] For the moment, however, nativism had the advantage over antislavery. A vast and ready-made network of white Protestant fraternal orders was better poised to mobilize the voting men of the North than was the experience of sentimental reading and theatrical performance. The "American" Party got off to a quick start in the summer of 1854.

The driving force behind the National Council of the Know Nothings was James W. Barker, a New York merchant and sometime Whig, and formerly a common school trustee in the tenth ward. Barker was a member of the Order of United Americans (OUA), a nativist organization led by Thomas R. Whitney, a conservative Whig who published a polished-looking nativist magazine, the *Republic*. Barker and other members of one of the lodges of the OUA joined the smaller Order of the Star Spangled Banner (OSSB) in 1852, and by 1853 had transformed it into a popular political vehicle for the OUA. In May 1854 Barker engineered the reorganization of the OSSB state council, got himself elected president, and repeated this performance in forming the National Council in June.[16]

He had a lot of practice in the management of secretive fraternal groups. In 1846 Barker seems to have been in Syracuse, where he ranked as the "Vice Grand" (deputy to the presiding officer) of the Onondaga Lodge 79 of the Independent Order of Odd Fellows, a national fraternal organization modeled roughly on the Freemasons. The next year he was back in New York City parading as an assistant grand marshal in the massive annual procession celebrating the laying of the cornerstone of the Odd Fellows Hall on Grand Street, between the hotels on Broadway and the theaters on the Bowery. That same year he was appointed to the Hall's board of managers, and in June 1854 he was well situated to hold the OSSB National Council meeting in the same New York Odd Fellows Hall. There would be many others with the same kind of fraternal experience in the leadership of the nativist movement.[17]

The New York Odd Fellows Hall stood at the center of vast national network of over three thousand lodges and 200,000 members in 1854. It was also the nexus of a lot of money. Fraternal organizations operated on two levels—an elaborate ritual space of theatrical fraternalism, and a mutual benefit society. The Odd Fellows Hall on Grand Street represented the pinnacle of the theatrical opulence of the fraternal order, with its polished brownstone exterior, its elegant meeting rooms (most spectacularly the Egyptian Rooms), and its $125,000 price tag. The order's offices were on the second floor, handling 25,000 letters a year and the records pertaining to $1.2 million in revenues and almost $500,000 in relief, in the form of payments to widows and orphans, and for the burial of lodge members. In the early 1850s there were Odd Fellows lodges in every state of the Union, from Maine to Florida and Wisconsin to Texas, though two-thirds of the membership was concentrated in five states—New York, Pennsylvania, Ohio, Maryland, and Massachusetts—roughly mapping the largest urban centers: New York, Philadelphia, Pittsburgh, Cincinnati, Cleveland, Baltimore, and Boston.[18] But Odd Fellowship had doubled across the country between 1846 and 1850, and the organization's growth was certainly paralleled by that of other groups, such as the long-established Freemasons, only now recovering from the anti-Masonic assault on their secrecy, or the newer Improved Order of Red Men. Together these three groups may have comprised a membership of 400,000. Quite simply, as movement from farming districts and villages toward towns and cities accelerated, the fraternal societies filled a need for instant familiar community, wrapped up in an exciting theater of fraternal mysteries and secrets. Ambitious young men on the move could carry letters of recommendation from lodge to lodge and gain immediate entry into a community of like-minded men. They could expect assistance in time of need, or at least a decent burial. Something about the promise of organic mysteries and profound secrecy captured their imagination. And their expanding fraternal circles provided confidential spaces for conversation and collaboration.[19]

Nativism was clearly interwoven with this growing fraternal culture in urbanizing mid-nineteenth-century America. With the exception of the increasingly isolated world of black Prince Hall Masonry, these fraternal orders were white, and they were overwhelmingly Protestant. Their Protestantism was de facto, hidden behind a screen of universal brotherhood; Catholics, who were forbidden by papal injunction from joining secret lodges, were forming their own authorized Catholic fraternal orders. Building a network of connections and income spanning both North and South, the Protestant fraternal bodies took an ostensibly neutral position on slavery and projected an ambiance of sentimental nationalism. The Odd Fellows in particular had room for expansion in the South. Apparently to reinforce this national commitment, the Odd Fellows added the phrase *Gazette of the Union* to their monthly *Golden Rule and Odd Fellows Family Companion* in the Free Soil year of 1848. In 1850 the *Gazette of the Union* published nothing regarding slavery that would offend conservative Whiggery, placidly noting the seeming progress of Webster's compromise politics.[20]

In effect, they sought to re-create the unifying national role that the Protestant churches had held until Presbyterians, Baptists, and Methodists divided on sectional grounds over slavery in 1837 and 1844–1845.[21] By contrast, many antislavery leaders, including William Lloyd Garrison, Charles Sumner, and Thaddeus Stevens, had cut their teeth in politics with the rise of anti-Masonry in the 1830s and were clearly at odds with the culture of the secret societies.[22] Among the tangle of associational culture that reemerged in the early 1840s were organizations with explicit political-cultural projects: the temperance Washingtonians and the nativist Order of United American Mechanics, the Patriotic Daughters of America, the Order of United Americans. Nonetheless, they shared a common structure with the fraternal societies. Some, certainly, were aligned with the Democrats, but many—if not most—of them were situated in a conservative nationalist Whig political culture that also stood opposed to antislavery. They broadly shared the nativist agenda, and as significantly, they provided a model of organization, and a reservoir of organized men, and some women, for a like-minded political movement to mobilize.[23]

Antebellum nativist hostility toward Irish and Catholics had immediate roots in the 1830s, with the Charlestown Convent riot in 1834, and the forming of an early nativist association in New York, in 1835, by Samuel F. B. Morse, later credited with inventing the telegraph. Religion in the common schools became a focal point in the 1840s for the eruption of nativist organization and violence in Philadelphia, and in New York, where Whigs divided between nativism and William Seward's emerging political antislavery.[24] The fraternal Order of United Americans was founded in New York City in 1844 during this nativist agitation, growing with a secret lodge structure, as did the Order of the Star Spangled Banner, founded in 1850. The OUA was essentially the parent organization of the Know Nothing movement of the 1850s, infiltrating the OSSB in 1852 and 1853 and using it to launch a statewide and then a national secret movement. This was the national movement that emerged in the spring of 1854, with its scattering of secret paper messages in streets and alleys. As in the fraternal associations, membership was sealed with oaths to what would eventually be three degrees of nativism, and organized in lodges reporting to a state council and a grand national council. In November 1853 Horace Greeley called the movement the "Know-Nothings" in print for the first time, probably reflecting common talk in the street. The name stuck.[25]

The secret order—now the Know Nothings—exploded in numbers in 1854. There may have been fifty nativist lodges in 1853; ten thousand would be formed before the movement fizzled out. James Barker claimed that there were five thousand members in sixty lodges in the state of New York in May 1854; the following March he reported 960 lodges. That November there were over 122,000 votes for nativist Daniel Ullman, one of Barker's associates in the OUA, for governor of New York. Across the North, there may have been fifty thousand organized nativists in May 1854, but over 670,000 voters chose Know Nothing candidates for the 34th Congress later that year. Not all of these voters were lodge members, but the movement clearly had erupted overnight.

Riding the Know Nothing surge, Barker had tried to strong-arm the September Whig state convention in Syracuse into supporting his candidate, Ullman. Failing to block the candidacy of an antislavery candidate, Myron Clark, he called the first Know Nothing nominating convention at the New York Odd Fellows Hall, a meeting later condemned as fixed by the secret powers made up of high-ranking lodge delegates and controlled by "rowdies and bullies." An entire slate of nativist candidates was nominated, including Barker for mayor of the city and Ullman for governor.[26]

What role did the fraternal orders play in shaping the political ground for the 1854 election? Many of the men who filled the Know Nothing leadership had, like James W. Barker, long experience with the fraternal orders; such was particularly notable in the National Council formed in June 1854. Charles Deshler of New Brunswick, New Jersey, corresponding secretary of the council, was a former master of the Masonic Union Lodge in New Brunswick. Henry Crane of Cincinnati was the treasurer; he, like Barker, had been an active Odd Fellow officer in the 1840s. Alfred B. Ely was not on the council, but he was the leading nativist ideologue in Massachusetts; he had been an Odd Fellow in the 1840s as well.[27] Of the two new officers elected to the National Council in June 1855, Charles D. Freeman was both a Mason and an Odd Fellow. Like Barker, he was involved in the pageantry of the order, as an aide to the grand marshal in the Philadelphia IOOF parade in 1849 and a lodge officer. A Mason of high renown, Freeman was elected representative to the United States Grand Lodge from Pennsylvania in May 1855, a month before he was elected vice president of the Know Nothing National Council.[28] In the ranks of the New York state council that Barker organized in May 1854, he brought along a young protégé.

Barker's senior mentor in the Odd Fellows was Joseph R. Taylor, deputy grand master in 1846, grand master at the 1847 procession, and serving with Barker on the Odd Fellows Hall committee. He appears to have stepped down from his fraternal duties in 1850 after he was appointed comptroller of the city of New York under a Whig administration. His twenty-three-year-old son, Joseph S. Taylor—an active Whig—was appointed treasurer of Barker's Know Nothing state council in May 1854. While Taylor won his election as almshouse governor on Barker's ticket in November, Barker's run for mayor may have been undermined by an accusation of setting fire to his Catherine Street store for an insurance payout in 1845. Both Taylors joined with Barker over the next few years in various insurance companies. Fraternalism, politics, and commercial schemes moved easily together in Barker's nativist circle.[29]

Thus it is clear that the Know Nothing leadership included well-situated players with long experience of the fraternal orders. What of the voters? Looking at the statistics of the Odd Fellows lodges in New York, one could make a case that the distribution of lodges contributed broadly to the strength of nativist voting. At least such appears to be the case for New York State, where voting for Daniel Ullman in the governor's election broadly tracked the strength of the Odd Fellows, anchored in New York City and surrounding counties, but also in an orbit around Buffalo.[30]

We occasionally get a direct view into this connection; the diary of Joseph Tucker of Millville, New Jersey, gives us such a picture. A twenty-three-year-old clerk at a local glassworks, Tucker was a loyal temperance Whig, and in the early 1850s was gradually making a commitment to the Methodist Church. He took in panorama shows and the circus when they came to town, and on occasion he and his friends "cruised about through the day, rolled some ten pins, and enjoyed ourselves very much." He appears to have joined the Odd Fellows in April 1853; over the next several years he would serve as a lodge inspector, traveling up to Philadelphia on a regular basis. He also went to his first Native American Party mass meeting in late June 1854, and reported to the local nativist nominating committee in October. In late November, after the election, he happily reported on the "grand parade of the American party" in Millville: "Torches to a considerable number were visible, bearing all sorts of mottoes, characters, etc. The whole affair was pleasing, every thing passed off quietly. Something new."[31] While it is difficult to get inside the experience of nativism throughout the North, Joseph Tucker may provide some idea of the basic patterns.

Political nativism was on a fast track in the summer of 1854. It had all of the ingredients needed for a rapid ascent: alienation from a collapsing major party, an ambitious leadership, and (male) voters already organized and requiring only that the right connections be made and strings be pulled. Political antislavery was a different beast, its leaders riven by factionalism or reluctant to break with their parties, along with a base of support suspicious of party and organized, if at all, by churches rather than associations. So, too, novel reading and theatergoing could not translate as quickly as fraternal groups into a political party. Whereas the nativists got off to a fast start, Emerson's "Anti-Slavery Society"—eventually the Republican Party—was slow to get going.

THE UNCERTAINTY of the emergence of the Republican Party was in some measure a function of the mixed feelings of so many northerners who traditionally opposed the Democratic Party. The majority of the political antislavery leadership—John Quincy Adams, James Birney, William Seward, Charles Sumner, John Palfrey, Horace Greeley, Abraham Lincoln—despised nativism and worked to hold the line against its influence.[32] But many others were much more accommodating, deferring to the volatile mixture of antislavery and nativist sentiment in much of the northern electorate. Like Calvin Fletcher in Indianapolis, they were hostile to both slavery and Catholicism, in almost equal measure. More precisely, their opinions ranged along a gradient: at each extreme stood people of reasonably exclusive antislavery and anti-immigrant opinion; but in the vast middle, opinion was mixed. Again, what is striking is that antislavery soon prevailed over nativism. If Fletcher could express nativist views in his diary, Henry Ward Beecher, the minister of Fletcher's church in the 1840s, had expressed them in public a decade before. As the editor of the *Cincinnati Journal*, Henry had repeated his father, Lyman's, well-known opinions, which may have helped to stir up the Charlestown Convent riot. And if Harriet Beecher Stowe's theology in *Uncle Tom's Cabin* had been informed by her editing of her brother Charles's *Incarnation*, she had to have read her brother Edward's anti-Catholic treatise—*The Papal Conspiracy Exposed, and Protestantism Defended*—when it came out in May 1855. She herself clearly harbored similar sentiments.[33] This delicate boundary between antislavery and anti-immigrant opinion was clearly ruptured in May 1854, when Irish militia companies marched with marines to carry Anthony Burns through the streets of Boston to slavery.[34]

There was a different impediment to antislavery organization visible in Washington in May 1854: loyalty to party. Five days before the final vote on the Nebraska bill, and just after the first national meeting of the Know Nothing council in New York, on May 20 Gamaliel Bailey took the lead, organizing a small group of antislavery congressmen for a preliminary meeting. Reconvening after the vote, thirty congressmen led by Israel Washburn of Maine agreed that the time was ripe for a national anti-Nebraska coalition, for which Washburn proposed the name "Republican." After further prodding from Bailey, the group met in June and issued an "Address," published in papers across the North, condemning the Kansas-Nebraska Act but failing to call for a new party.[35] Clearly the majority in Congress, deeply immersed in commitments to a wide range of policy positions in broad party coalitions that had deep and enduring claims, were not going to move quickly—certainly not as quickly as the ambitious men in New York, who were building on efforts going back a decade.[36] The responsibility for moving antislavery politics forward quickly would have to lie in the states.

Such efforts were already under way in the Northwest. State and local meetings had convened in February in Michigan and

Wisconsin (the latter the famous Ripon meeting) to condemn the Nebraska bill and to declare new Republican parties in these states. Republican state conventions met in both states in July, carefully managing to unite Whigs, Free Soilers, and anti-Nebraska Democrats. In both states the Know Nothings failed to gain a foothold, and the Whigs failed to hold nominating conventions, leaving the fall election a clear two-party competition between antislavery—with touches of nativism—and the Democrats.[37]

In Ohio and Indiana the emerging state parties were less antislavery and more "fusion." Again, the Whigs collapsed in both states, but the nativists were reasonably strong and forced a coalition on their terms. Of the two, Ohio emerged as more clearly antislavery, as the nativists were particularly dominated by Cincinnati conservatives (among them Odd Fellow Henry Crane), and the antislavery forces better managed by Salmon Chase. Indiana's party was really nativist in disguise; the July convention at Indianapolis had been secretly managed by the Know Nothing leadership.[38] But in both Ohio and Indiana the elections would pit the Democrats head-to-head with these new fusion parties. The situation in Illinois, as we have seen, was more muddled. Here the Whigs were divided regionally, with those in the central counties, like Lincoln, trying to maintain their old organization, while those in the North around Chicago gravitated toward a new Free Soil Republican Party. The result would be a three-way contest more typical of the eastern states in the Mid-Atlantic and New England.[39]

Across the Northeast the established Whig Party refused to go quietly, and a four-cornered competition among Whigs, Democrats, Free Soilers, and Know Nothings in various combinations created a wildly disordered political landscape. In Maine, temperance issues split the Democrats, and the Know Nothings were slow to emerge; Whigs, Free Soilers, and two factions of Democrats all held conventions. In Vermont, the Whigs worked hard to take an anti-Nebraska stand, and to absorb the Free Soilers; Know Nothings made little headway.[40] Elsewhere the hand of James W. Barker was clearly evident and the rise of the Know Nothing lodges decisive. In the end, however, the meaning of the Know Nothing landslide in these states was and still is highly contested.

A brief look at the convention struggles in the three largest states, Massachusetts, New York, and Pennsylvania, suggests the dynamics at work. In each state, the long-established Whigs saw no reason to abandon the field, as they had in the Midwest, and the Free Soilers failed to construct convincing tickets. Everywhere the secret Know Nothing lodges grew like mushrooms. In some states there were public contests between Whigs, Democrats, and Know Nothings; in others the nativists secretly threw their numbers behind lodge members among the major party nominees.

In New York, Thurlow Weed, the veteran Whig editor and William Seward's close adviser, pulled the strings to manage political affairs that summer. Deciding that there was too much of a threat of a secret Know Nothing fifth column in the emerging anti-Nebraska movement, he suppressed all nominations at an anti-Nebraska convention at Saratoga Springs in August. He then fought off a Know Nothing takeover at the Whig convention in Syracuse in September, nominating the eventual winner in the governor's race, Myron Clark. The Know Nothings, as we have seen, met at the New York Odd Fellows Hall on October 4 and nominated Daniel Ullman. New York would have candidates from the Seward-Weed Whigs, the Know Nothings (allied with the Silver Gray Whigs), and two factions of Democrats (the "Hards" or "Hunkers," and the anti-Nebraska "Softs").[41]

Massachusetts would have a three-way struggle shaped by a similar politics of elite calculation. Politics in Massachusetts was driven by an insurgency against both the Whigs and the Democrats by small-town and rural Yankees, shaped by anti-immigrant sentiment, the failure of a complex politics to reform the state constitution, and a strong anti-Nebraska antislavery faction. The Whigs, the party of the Boston elites, met in August and, in an effort to maintain their historic preeminence, adopted an anti-Nebraska platform. This failed to dissuade a Free Soil–led convention from meeting in Worcester in September, calling themselves "Republicans," and nominating for governor Henry Wilson, a self-made businessman known as the "Cobbler of Natick." Wilson, however, had already joined a Know Nothing lodge and had hopes of creating a Free Soil–Know Nothing fusion. When the Know Nothings met in Boston on October 18, they followed New York in nominating a conservative Whig, Henry Gardner, for governor. Wilson, either strategic or opportunistic in his thinking, agreed to withdraw from his "Republican" candidacy in exchange for Know Nothing votes in the state legislature for his candidacy for the U.S. Senate. Antislavery in Massachusetts was split between the Whigs and the Know Nothings, with no viable party in the field.[42]

In Pennsylvania, a different combination of the same elements gathered behind the Whig label. The Democrats, notoriously known as "doughfaces," restated their adherence to the Compromise of 1850 as a final settlement. Meeting in March, the Whig convention condemned the Nebraska bill, undermining an emerging fusion movement. The proto-Republican Party met in May with hopes of nominating David Wilmot of 1848 fame, but settled for the Whig candidate, James Pollock, a lawyer without much of a record on slavery, who had to be induced to write what Gamaliel Bailey called a "stiff antislavery letter." The Know Nothings, in a strikingly modern touch, held a primary election in their lodges, and Pollock's victory in this secret vote (roughly 56,000 to 24,000) was announced at the state council meeting in early October, along with nominations for other offices scattered between the two major parties.[43] As elsewhere in the Northeast, the enduring strength of Whig commitment and organization, a force still kept moving by an inertial weight and density, combined with the secretive machinations of the nativists to block the emergence of a party founded on antislavery principles.

The election brought a series of great victories for the Know Nothings, who seemed to be poised to define the future of half of the two-party system in the United States. As were all elections in the antebellum period, this was a long election, running from August 1854 to November 1855, as determined by the various laws of the several states. Results in one state became news and a causal force in another. Such had been the case for decades, but in the disordered politics of 1854, this electoral sequence took on a life of its own. When the election began, the Whig Party appeared to have a viable future. By the time it finally came to an end, the Whigs were completely finished. But how American politics would be restructured remained a matter of much conjecture and uncertainty.

Voting in the northern states unfolded in three blocs: four elections in August and September, nine elections on October 10 and November 7 and 12, and three in March and April 1855. Very broadly, the earlier the state election, the more likely it was that Whigs would make a good showing; the later the election, the more likely the Know Nothings would sweep. None the four northern states voting early saw independent Know Nothing nominations, and only in Maine, on September 11, did a "Fusion" party emerge to undermine the Whigs. The core of the election took place in October and November, with the bulk of the "Fusion" voting (430,000 out of 479,000 votes), whether managed by the Know Nothings, as in Indiana, or the first manifestations of the Republican Party, as in Michigan and Wisconsin. While the Whigs fielded candidates in the Northeast, they were challenged by organized Know Nothings in New York and utterly swept away by the Know Nothings in Massachusetts, who won all eleven congressional districts. In Pennsylvania and New York, much of the sizable Whig vote for Congress was managed by the Know Nothing organizations. In the final three elections in the spring, in New Hampshire, Connecticut, and Rhode Island, the Whigs disappeared, and the Know Nothings swept the Democrats in two-way races. (See Appendix, table 11.)

While the early elections did not shift the balance of seats in the House much, the result of the election was beginning to be apparent with the voting in three big states on October 10. Indiana, Ohio, and Pennsylvania had been represented by thirty-eight Democrats, seventeen Whigs, and two Free Soilers; the result of the October 10 election cut Democratic seats to eight, from 67 percent to 13 percent. The jeopardy to Democratic control of the House was confirmed in the November voting and redoubled in the spring vote (when nine Democrats were replaced by nine Know Nothing nominees). Overall, about a fifth of Democrats in the 33rd House were returned to the 34th, while roughly half of the Whigs and Free Soilers returned. Voting on the Kansas-Nebraska Act made a difference: of the forty-four northern Democratic representatives who had voted for the act, only eight were reelected, mostly from lower North districts in Illinois, Indiana, and Pennsylvania. By contrast, twenty-six of the forty-nine Whigs and Free Soilers opposing the Kansas-Nebraska Act were reelected. But the Democrats voting against the bill suffered by association and were replaced by Fusion and Know Nothing representatives.

If the 1854–1855 election in the free states swept away the Democrats, it was not, perhaps, a participatory triumph. Across the country, turnout in the House elections dropped from 61 percent in 1852 to 57 percent in 1854–1855, not atypical for an off-year election. But turnout shifted quite differently in the North and the South, hinging on the surge of the nativists in the late autumn. Free state turnout dropped from 63 percent to 53 percent, and this drop was particularly notable in the states voting after October 10, when the trajectory of the election suddenly became apparent. Voting in the slave states took quite a different direction. Turnout had fallen in 1852 in the South as voters cooled to the candidacy of Winfield Scott and to the Whig Party in general. The elections for the 34th Congress were skewed toward the later dates in the South, with ten of the fifteen slave states voting after mid-May 1855. Turnout rose in the South as it became apparent that the nativists were doing well in the North. Overall, southern turnout rose from 52 percent in 1852 to 68 percent in 1854–1855. The South elected a total of fifty-eight Democrats, six Missouri Whigs, and twenty-seven Know Nothings, all but one of whom were elected in 1855. Southern Whigs had come home—to a new party, the nativist American Party, which offered a bulwark against the threat to their peculiar institution.[44]

The nativist leadership, united North and South, stood firmly on the proposition that they could build a national party that would maintain the Union by focusing the attention of former northern Whigs on the threat of Catholicism and immigration rather than the Slave Power. They clearly almost had voters like Calvin Fletcher of Indianapolis, a colonizationist Free Soiler. In November 1854 Fletcher wrote of a conversation with E. H. Barry, a local merchant and the secretary of the Indiana state temperance society. Barry, Fletcher recorded in his diary, had "recently attended a Know-Nothing encampment of the U. States at Cincinnati where he met Southerners. They [have] no notion of dissolving the union but of preserving it. That gives me great pleasure. He invites me to join the order."[45]

What exactly was the meaning of the "fusion" and Know Nothing voting across the North? Where did the voters and their elected representatives stand, as they waited for Congress to convene in December 1855? We don't know much of Fletcher's thinking in these months. In July 1855 he was pleased with the "mixture of Abolition, Temperance, Know nothing, & Anti Nebraska feeling" evident at the state convention in Indianapolis; in January 1856 he found it "lamentable" that the 34th House was deadlocked in its election of a Speaker.[46] Why did northerners cast votes for the Know Nothings? They were of mixed opinions. Many were indeed very hostile to the wave of immigrants who had just arrived, but they were also angry about the Kansas-Nebraska Act, and the Democratic Party had a role in both, wooing immigrant votes and working with the Slave Power in Congress.

But why would the Whigs not be a sufficient vehicle for their wrath? In great measure, the voting in 1854–1855 was a rejection of both parties, a middling insurgency, and a convenient means of clearing the road of old institutions. Thus, particularly in New England, where the Whigs refused to abandon their local party structures, Know Nothing voting was the only available mechanism for opposition to the Kansas-Nebraska Act and functioned as a mask for anti-Whig antislavery insurgency. As the Rhode Island Know Nothings put it, "The people of the North had got heartily sick of the old organizations, and chiefly because they had truckled with the

South in every matter of great interest."[47] In Massachusetts, George Frisbie Hoar was of the opinion that great numbers voted nativist for an election or two "simply in order that they might get rid of the old parties, and prepare the state as with a subsoil plow."[48]

Others were angry that the northeastern Whigs would not give way to a new antislavery party. As the results in November became clear, Horace Greeley, writing in his *Tribune*, condemned the Whigs: "Here was the popular feeling demanding action; here was the opportunity for patriotism." But the demand for an antislavery party went unheeded. And for what? "The voice of public sentiment, and the circumstances of the emergency," the explosion of anti-Nebraska opinion on the signing of the Nebraska bill, "were thus disregarded for the purpose of keeping up an essentially extinct party," the Whigs.[49] Gamaliel Bailey in the *National Era* focused on the result: the Know Nothings were now a "distinct, manifest, and powerful political party," with national reach and purpose. To Bailey, reviewing the returns from Massachusetts, it was clear that many antislavery voters had voted for the Know Nothings. But the central nativist goal involved federal power to change naturalization laws, and the Know Nothing party was falling into a national alliance with slaveholders using federal power to expand the reach of slavery.[50] Joshua Giddings, now carefully adjusting to the complex politics of fusion in Ohio, took a little more time to come to the same conclusions. Speaking of Know Nothingism, he acknowledged that he had "treated it with forbearance," since it seemed a convenient "screen—a dark wall . . . behind which members of old political organizations could escape from party shackles." But his assumptions had been that the Know Nothing movement could be turned against slavery. Such was plainly not the case, however; it was "evident that many of its members at the North, and in some states a majority of them, are trying to turn its influence in favor of slavery."[51]

There was clearly an irreconcilable paradox in the rise of the Know Nothings. The better part of its support in the North was also antislavery and anti-Nebraska, but its northern leadership, entrenched in Barker's National Council, were conservative Whigs fully committed to a union of North and South against Democrats and foreigners in a national anti-immigrant party. By the end of the summer of 1855, this alliance would be manifested in voting strength in the South; whereas the Know Nothings had received 210,000 free state votes, they ultimately received almost 420,000 votes in the South. Gamaliel Bailey had pinpointed the problem in November: "Who will give an authoritative answer to these questions—How are Anti-Slavery and Pro Slave Know Nothings to act together, in the selection of a Presidential candidate? If a non-committed or Pro-Slavery candidate be selected by the vote of a majority, what is the Anti-Slavery minority to do?"[52] The answer would come quickly. And if James W. Barker was something of a political street fighter, he met his match in Henry Wilson, the "Cobbler of Natick."

BAILEY'S SUSPICION that a national nativist movement would break on the issue of slavery would be confirmed in the summer of 1855, though the nativist leadership made every effort to achieve their goal. In mid-November, just after the Massachusetts election, reports had begun to swirl about the second National Council of the American Party—the Know Nothings—set to meet in Cincinnati, what Fletcher had revealingly labeled an "encampment," a term used by the higher order of the Odd Fellows. In particular, Bailey may well have been reacting to the speculation that this nativist "encampment" would make nominations for president for the 1856 election. Sam Houston of Texas was a favorite.[53]

The twenty-two state delegations that met at the Cincinnati "encampment" did not make nominations for 1856, but they did change the ritual of the order. The National Council had—in true fraternal style—adopted an initiation ritual with two degrees of members at their first meeting in New York in June: the first degree bound the member to vote nativist; the second bound the officeholder to advance nativist policies. In Cincinnati, southerners and northern conservatives insisted that the order adopt a third degree, the Union degree, which was aimed to suppress "agitation." The third degree enjoined its holders with your hands joined in token of that fraternal affection which should ever bind together the states of this Union . . . that so far as your efforts can avail, this Union shall have no end." They were to promise to work "to procure an amicable and equitable adjustment of all political discontent or differences which may threaten its injury or overthrow." They were to "not vote for any one" who threatened the Union, and they were to "vote for and support for all political offices Third or Union degree members of this Order in preference to all others."[54]

Clearly aimed to suppress the antislavery membership, the proscribing Union degree had an immediate purpose for James Barker: the defeat of William Seward's bid for reelection to the Senate. Seward, even if he had avoided leading an anti-Nebraska movement in New York to sustain the Whig Party, was notorious in proslavery circles for his "Higher Law" speech in 1850. He was the first of several of Know Nothing targets that spring. Barker's state council adopted the Cincinnati Union degree in early January, in hopes that it would block Know Nothings in the New York legislature from casting their votes for Seward in early February. It failed: of the thirty-two Know Nothings in the Senate and House, twenty-four voted for Seward, an early indication that the "Order" could not hold the line against antislavery.[55] Antislavery had already been successful in Massachusetts (where the state council refused to adopt the third degree); the abolitionist Theodore Parker was elected as the nativist-controlled legislature's chaplain, and Henry Wilson was voted into the U.S. Senate, despite conservative Whigs in the state Senate throwing their votes to nativist leader Alfred B. Ely. The legislature proceeded to enact a wide array of antislavery statutes, in particular forbidding any state or local action to enforce the Fugitive Slave Act. Antislavery leaders John P. Hale and James Dixon similarly were voted through to the U.S. Senate by Know Nothing legislatures in New Hampshire and Connecticut. Only in Pennsylvania did the Know Nothings fail; when they nominated moderate Simon Cameron, the legislature was deadlocked, and the position was not filled. Elsewhere the rise of a "Know Something" movement, antislavery and anti-Catholic (rather than anti-immigrant), gained some traction, confusing the political field to a degree.[56]

The critical moment came in June 1855, when the National Council of the Know Nothings convened in Philadelphia. Key players had been laying the groundwork for some time. James Barker managed the appointment of New York's delegates at the state council meeting in Syracuse in February and reiterated the proslavery unionism implicit in the third degree in his May 1855 address to the order, signed "Fraternally." The council's platform, he announced, was not only nativist and anti-Catholic but also pro-union:

1. Americans shall rule America!
2. The Union of these States!
3. No North, no South, no East, no West!
4. The United States of America as they are—one and inseparable![57]

For his part, Henry Wilson after his Senate win began to let it be known that he was backing away from Know Nothing allegiance, and he clearly was recruiting antislavery delegates to the Philadelphia convention in Massachusetts and around New England.[58] Barker and Wilson went head-to-head in Philadelphia that June, and Wilson won.

As the convention started on June 5, these tensions were already in the air, as reported by secret correspondents, antislavery for the *New York Tribune* and proslavery for the *New York Herald*. In the eyes of the *Tribune* reporter that day, "the Slave interest is predominant here, and will control the Council."[59] Barker initially blocked the admission of the Massachusetts delegation as a "snub for their boldness on the slavery question." Virginians were already muttering dark and murderous comments about Senator Wilson, who had addressed the American Anti-Slavery Society in the spring, promising to oppose all threats to the antislavery movement.[60]

By the end of the second day, with Massachusetts admitted, the *Herald* reported presciently that "Wilson desires a split" in the movement. Wilson had announced his unequivocal support for the antislavery agenda: repeal of the Fugitive Slave Act, abolition of slavery in the District of Columbia, exclusion of slavery from the territories, and admission of Kansas as a free state.[61] Early on, the *Herald* claimed, "no reasonable doubt" had existed "whatever, of the reelection of James W. Barker." But on the evening of the fourth day, June 8 (after northern delegates had boycotted the order's banquet), the knives came out in the election for officers of the order. Barker was sick but had his address read to the council. The *Tribune* reported that "it was Hunkerish [pro-slavery] to the dregs; he fairly crawled to the South; he spit upon the Higher Law and denounced Seward's election. The North got mad and paid him off by defeating his reelection." It took six ballots, but he was eventually replaced by Edward B. Bartlett of Kentucky. The southerners took some solace in a slaveholder as president of the order, until it was revealed that Bartlett was a member of the northern, moderately antislavery branch of the Methodist Episcopal Church; they fumed about a "Massachusetts trick."[62] Several days later, Wilson took the stage and mocked Barker and the New York delegation, rejecting their obvious alliance with the slaveholders, saying, "We wanted a man who knew something more than to repeat the parrot phrase—'No North, no South, no East, No West,' and would not have one that blasphemously sneers at the higher law." Seward, the champion of the higher law, and now Wilson's close colleague in the Senate, had "trod upon the necks of the rampant gentlemen from New York" and "would look down into their political graves."[63]

On Monday June 11 the platform committee reported a split decision. The majority report included a "section 12," which specifically committed the party to support the Kansas-Nebraska Act and to deny the federal government's authority to legislate on slavery in the territories and the District of Columbia. The antislavery minority rejected these proslavery planks. The Ohio delegation had presented their state platform two days before, which had declared that "slavery is local, not national" and condemned the Kansas-Nebraska Act—and the introduction of slavery into Kansas—as a "violation of law." This became the template for the antislavery "minority report" on the eleventh, which echoed Salmon Chase in calling the Kansas-Nebraska Act "an infraction of the plighted faith of the Nation."[64]

The convention's pivotal moment came late in the evening on the thirteenth, after two days of debate, in a climate of "wild and terrible excitement" in which both New York correspondents were exposed. The convention split that evening, 91–52, to support the majority report with its proslavery section 12, with the New York and Pennsylvania delegations, led by Odd Fellows Barker and Charles D. Freeman, the latter now vice president of the order, voting with the South. Wilson led the northern seceders to a meeting in the Girard Hotel, hoping to move them to the Republicans. The Girard meeting issued an "Appeal to the People" combining planks demanding the restoration of the Missouri Compromise, the admission of Kansas and Nebraska as free states, and federal protections for the franchise in the territories, with nativist planks on naturalization and exportation of paupers and convicts. This was essentially the "Know Something" position, but these delegates did not secede from the order, nor did they call for a new party, blunting Wilson's triumph.[65]

The Know Nothing majority moved on to celebrate, first at a mass meeting in City Hall Park in New York, where James Barker was honored to make up for his presidential defeat, then on to Washington for a final "ratification." Here a Maryland correspondent to the *Tribune* found the essential message coming out of what was being called the "great fizzle." He heralded the seceding antislavery minority for showing that "there is a North," but he also could report that the proslavery Know Nothings were crowing. Albert Pike of Arkansas "rather let the cat out of the bag," announcing to the meeting that the Know Nothing platform voted in Philadelphia, with section 12 intact, "was the first and only platform exclusively Southern that had ever been adopted by a National Convention in the Union." But he allowed that if the Democrats could equal it, he would be voting with them. Southerners had come to Philadelphia to find some protection for slavery in a national party. That effort had indeed fizzled, no matter Pike's bravado.[66]

The Philadelphia convention did not lead directly to the collapse of the Know Nothing movement. It was still the best hope for conservatives north and south who sought a middle ground between proslavery and antislavery extremes. The party recovered in New York, shucked off section 12 (despite Barker's efforts), and won elections in the fall, as they did in Massachusetts.[67] But they won in the North only when they assumed the position of the Philadelphia minority: combining nativism with antislavery. And their future was numbered in months. By the next year they would be essentially irrelevant in national politics. If the Philadelphia convention did not destroy the party immediately, it exposed its fundamental weakness as a national movement. Gamaliel Bailey's question was answered: there was no way to reconcile even moderate proslavery and moderate antislavery elements, south and north. A national union party foundered on the question of slavery.

The failure of the Know Nothings to overcome the division on slavery rested in great measure on the subtle shift in attitudes that Harriet Beecher Stowe, Stephen Foster, and the theater managers had engineered in the northern public between 1851 and 1854. Perhaps they might have succeeded before 1851, but the impetus to organize and nationalize the order emerged in the turmoil over slavery and Nebraska in the spring of 1854. Perhaps paradoxically, much of the party's rapid expansion had come from voters who opposed both slavery and immigrants. In the summer of 1855, the tides of northern opinion were surging against slavery. One of these forces was established, if only recently; one was driven by the logic of legislation. Culture and Kansas, one now a steady background noise, the other a strident emergence, mutually resonating and reinforcing, worked to keep the slavery drama before the northern public.

In late November and early December 1855, the new crisis met the old in cultural performance at the second annual "independent" antislavery series in the Tremont Temple in Boston, which Harriet Beecher Stowe had a hand in founding. Her influence was notable on December 6, when Mary Webb, a noted textual performer of mixed-race background, presented a one-woman show, reading Stowe's latest version of *Uncle Tom's Cabin*, distilled into a dramatic rendition called *The Christian Slave*. Webb would take her performance on the road to the Broadway Tabernacle in New York two weeks later, by way of Worcester, and then on to Buffalo and Cleveland. By August 1856 she was in London performing for the Duchess of Sutherland and her fashionable abolitionist circle.[68]

The first of this series had been given on November 29 and was a two-part event. Surrounded by Charles Sumner and other Boston luminaries, Horace Mann, now president of the new Antioch College in Yellow Springs, Ohio, battled a cold to present an oration on race, equality, and liberty. Then Thomas Starr King, the minister of the Unitarian Hollis Street Church in Boston, rose to read a new poem by John Greenleaf Whittier, "The Panorama." Speaking through the voice of the "Showman," Whittier evoked the vast canvas panoramas of the great West which were still showing in cities and towns across the country, some in performances of *Uncle Tom's Cabin*. In essence, Whittier's Showman presented a place, a choice, and a challenge. The place was Kansas, "the new Canaan of our Israel," and the choice was between

> the homely old-time virtues of the North,
> Where the blithe housewife rises with the day,
> and well-paid labor counts his task a play

and

> The clank of fetter and crack of thong . . .
> A tavern crazy with its whiskey brawls,
> With "*Slaves at Auction!*" garnishing its walls.

The challenge lay with "Men of the North." Would they passively stand by and slowly be reduced to servitude and tyranny?

> If the dark face of Slavery on you turns,
> If the mad curse its paper barrier spurns,

> If the world granary of the West is made
> The last foul market of the slaver's trade,
> Why rail at fate? The mischief is your own.[69]

"The Panorama" challenged the "Men of the North" to connect the enslavement of fellow Americans with their own impending loss of freedom, as Stowe had appealed to "the Mothers of America" and "the Christian men and women of the North" to extend their sympathies to the slave. Both addressed the issue of seeing and building a common cause with the enslaved, seeing and building the confluence of interest and common humanity.

The language of Whittier's "Panorama" built upon a central polarity vividly described in *Uncle Tom's Cabin*, what has been called a battle of the kitchens. In the North, specifically in the Ohio kitchens of Mary Bird and Rachel Halliday, Stowe lovingly imbued freedom with the "homely virtues" of ordered domesticity lightly ruled by free women, whose husbands are engaged in free labor, both supporting the essential neighborhood institutions of church and school. In the South, specifically in the New Orleans kitchen of Aunt Dinah, Stowe tried to evoke the disordered deceptions forced by the slave condition, hung over with dark threats of violence, outrage, and separation. In great measure, the discourse about the choice of an American future in Kansas was presented to the northern public in these terms set forth by Stowe in *Uncle Tom's Cabin*: both an ordered, nurturing freedom and a disordered, destructive slavery now had a material imagery that resonated directly with a constitutional and personal politics of individual autonomy and freedom. "The Panorama" and a wide array of writing about Kansas, well established by November 1855, worked to keep these material-ideological tropes of free society and slave society before the northern public, helping it to discover itself.[70]

In November 1855, Charles Sumner's account "The Slave Oligarchy and Its Usurpations: Outrages in Kansas" was in the public mind in Boston. He had just given this speech at Faneuil Hall, hoping to leave his mark in Boston before the 1855 election and returning to the Senate in December. Reviewing the scope of the efforts by the "Slave Oligarchy" to control the federal government; Sumner described how, "in defiance of the Constitution, it has made Slavery national, when it is in reality sectional." Kansas was the most recent of those "aggressions," in the repeal of the Missouri Compromise, the military rendition of Anthony Burns to slavery, and now, in the autumn of 1855, the removal by President Pierce of Kansas governor Andrew Reeder. The territorial legislature, argued Sumner, "constituted by the overthrow of the electoral franchise" by "hirelings from Missouri," was now free to "overthrow every safeguard of Freedom" by adopting "all the legislation of Missouri, including its Slave Code." Connected by bonds of union and national citizenship, Massachusetts was threatened: "Freedom in Kansas, and our own Freedom here at home, are both assailed. They must be defended."[71]

Sumner spoke to an audience that had been following events in Kansas for a year and a half. In May 1854 there had been about eight hundred white settlers in straggling squatter communities in Indian country west of the Missouri River and the Missouri state line; by March 1855 there were eight thousand whites and 192 slaves in the Kansas territory.[72] They had been without a territorial governor, and thus without authorization to hold elections, until October 1854, when Reeder arrived to take office. The first of the fraudulent elections that enraged the North over the next four years was held in late November, when 1,700 ballots cast by "border ruffians" riding over from Missouri shaped the election of a proslavery delegate to Congress. Settlement in the early months was dominated by Missourians. The first settlement sponsored by Eli Thayer's New England Emigrant Aid Company (NEEAC) began at Lawrence in August 1854, and by the fall, northerners were appearing in sizable numbers. Missourians countered Thayer's organization with their own, with "self-protective associations" and secret "blue lodges" mobilizing both settlers and roving militias of "ruffians" who came to vote. By February 1855, the Free Soilers had organized a "Kansas Legion," armed with Sharpe's carbines—"Beecher's Bibles" some called them—and organized in their own fraternal form, with rituals, a constitution, and a "Grand Encampment" presiding over local regiments.[73] On March 30, companies of proslavery militia crossed over from Missouri by the hundreds to vote in the election for a legislature. With a population of 2,900 legal voters, 6,000 votes were cast, 5,427 for proslavery candidates. After Governor Reeder threw out the results in several districts, the outcome of a second election in May was the same. In April the Free Soilers sent a memorial to Congress begging for relief from "a well matured and settled plan by a large portion of the people of one of the States of our Union, permanently to enslave us, and constitute themselves our masters." In particular, they accused Senator David Atchison of Missouri of being the "leader and captain" of the militias, with "bowie-knife and revolver belted around him," ready to kill "any man who refused to be enslaved."[74] Free Soilers began to meet in conventions, first in June, then in August at Lawrence and in September at Big Springs. Overcoming internal divisions, they met in a constitutional convention in Topeka in October and November, establishing a second, Free Soil government. By the time they elected a governor, Charles Robinson, in January 1856, spiraling confrontations had led to a guerrilla struggle known as the Wakarusa War, and the siege of Lawrence.

These events were unfolding as Sumner gave his speech at Faneuil Hall, and as Whittier's "Panorama" and Stowe's *Christian Slave* were being performed in Boston, Worcester, and New York in late 1855. In the larger picture, these were the preliminaries to the main event: the ravaging civil war that engulfed Kansas in the spring and summer of 1856, including the proslavery assault on Lawrence, John Brown's massacre on Potawatomie Creek, and the ensuing battles at Black Jack, Franklin, Osawatomie, and Hickory Point. When the second territorial governor failed, his successor, John White Geary, a Mexican War veteran and recently mayor of San Francisco, deployed federal troops to end the violence, if not the bad blood between slavery advocates and Free Staters.[75] The crisis over the fraudulent proslavery Lecompton Constitution, which would turn Stephen Douglas against the South, lay further in the future. But the northern press covered events carefully and in detail continuously from May

1854, aided by the flow of stories coming over the telegraph from participant-correspondents, like William Phillips for the *New York Tribune* and James Redpath for the Free Soil *St. Louis Democrat*.[76] Through early 1856, the struggle in Kansas overlapped with the end of the Crimean War, the first major European land war in forty years, and the two narratives fed symbiotically off each other in newspapers all over the country. The scale of coverage was a taste of what was to come starting in 1861 in the Civil War.

The rhetoric of bleeding Kansas was somewhat divorced from its hardscrabble reality. Kansas homesteads were mud cabins, not idylls of domesticity, and in reality New Englanders were in a distinct minority. In 1860, with the first detailed federal census, out of the 82,000 inhabitants born in the older states, only 4,200 were from New England. Over 60 percent of the population came from the Midwest and the Mid-Atlantic. They were not necessarily in the main ardent abolitionists. Rather, most were probably Douglas Democrats, eager to take up land in the West, to exclude the slaveholders and their slaves, but just as eager to exclude free people of color.[77]

None of this stood in the way of antislavery adopting the cause of bleeding Kansas as its own and building an ideological synthesis with its drama, fused with the structure of antislavery culture already so powerfully articulated. The performances of Whittier's "Panorama" and Stowe's *Christian Slave* were events in the ongoing blizzard of antislavery lectures, bazaars, and association meetings— the machinery of institutional and entertainment antislavery that continued to operate, and may have intensified, during the nativist surge. The performances at Boston's Tremont Temple were the first and second events of the 1855–1856 season of the "independent" lecture series that Stowe had started in February 1854. There had been a long season of lectures in the winter of 1854–1855, in which antislavery leaders had circulated around the Northeast. Emerson presented a new address, "American Slavery," at the Tremont Temple in January, and then over the next month took it on the road to Worcester, the New York Tabernacle series, the Pennsylvania Antislavery Society in Philadelphia, the Ladies' Anti-Slavery Society series in Rochester's gleaming new Corinthian Hall, and finally to Syracuse. Henry Ward Beecher and Charles Sumner (repeating his address at fourteen locations) followed in April and May. Sumner shared the roster for the annual meeting of the American Anti-Slavery Society in New York with Henry Wilson, now Sumner's colleague in the Senate, and a few months away from his subversion of the Know Nothings in Philadelphia.[78] Wendell Phillips had done the circuit in winter of 1854–1855, was in Pittsburgh in December 1855, and was on the roster for an early 1856 address at the Tremont Temple. Horace Mann took his November 1855 address from Boston to the Buffalo series on his return to Antioch in December, to be followed by Theodore Parker and Frederick Douglass, both of whom had spoken at Rochester the year before, Douglass presenting his "Anti-Slavery Movement." All three were on the roster for a series in Haverhill, Massachusetts, Whittier's home territory, in the winter of 1855–1856, and Parker and Emerson were on the schedule for a series in Salem, Ohio. The mere personal appearance of these great figures in antislavery circles in far-flung locations worked to reanimate the partisans, and it made a little money for local organizations and speakers alike. So too did the antislavery bazaars which met every year. And beyond this star circle, workaday lecturers plied the local circuits in these months, discussing the imperative of abolition and the events of the day in a long-established antislavery institutional structure.[79]

Kansas was front and center in musical and poetic anti-slavery long before Whittier's "Panorama" was performed at the Tremont Temple in November 1855. The Hutchinson Family was performing a song called "Neb-Rascality" in the spring of 1854, a foot-stomper of seven stanzas set to four different tunes.[80] On June 3, days after the signing of the bill, the *New York Tribune* published a shorter poem titled "Nebraska," which demanded that "the Pirate Crew must haunt no more the homesteads of the free," and featured Loker and Legree, slaver villains from *Uncle Tom's Cabin*, cheering for President Pierce and Senator Douglas.[81] By August, Whittier was out with a poem, "The Kansas Emigrants," beating the drum "for a wall of men on Freedom's southern line" to "make the West as they the East, the homestead of the free." Whittier's poem, set to "Auld Lang Syne," was sung by an Emigrant Aid company setting out from Boston that month. With these songs and poems in mind, the New England Emigrant Aid Company announced a competition for "the best Kansas emigrants' song," set to a common tune; Lucy Larcom, a former millworker and labor activist in Lowell who by 1854 had become a teacher at a female seminary, won the competition with her "Call to Kansas," out in the newspapers by February 1855, and included by the Hutchinsons in their 1858 songbook.[82]

Implicitly or explicitly, these verses all trumpeted the polarity of North and South so dramatically rendered in Stowe's kitchens of the free and the slave. They were also the cutting edge of a new wave of publications about "Kanzas" that began to hit the market in the fall of 1854. Edward Everett Hale had a gazetteer of history, geography, and "account of the emigrant aid companies" out by the end of September, and the NEEAC issued its own *Information for Kanzas Immigrants* in twelve editions between 1854 and 1857. More travel accounts and geographies followed in 1855 and 1856, along with firsthand accounts of events, such as William Phillips's *The Conquest of Kansas, by Missouri and her Allies* and Sara Robinson's *Kansas, Its Interior and Exterior Life*, and then the first Kansas troubles novel, *Western Border Life: or, What Fanny Hunter Saw and Heard in Kanzas and Missouri*, written by an anonymous abolitionist woman and in print by August 1856.[83]

It was in this climate that *The Christian Slave*, dramatized "*Expressly for the Readings of Mrs. Mary E. Webb*," was put out in print in November 1855, followed by Whittier's "Panorama" in March 1856.[84] Thus the new genre of the Kansas crisis was mixed in the bookstores with the established genre of the slave drama. Whereas the writing of anti-*Tom* plantation novels dropped off after 1853, the production of long antislavery texts continued apace.[85] A regular stream of long and well-advertised volumes appeared in 1855. Three were nonfiction by prominent black activists: William C. Nell's *Colored Patriots of the American Revolution*, Frederick Douglass's

My Bondage, My Freedom, and a Boston republication of William Wells Brown, *The American Fugitive in Europe*. Others were in the slave/fugitive melodrama or travelogue tradition: *Our World, or the Slaveholder's Daughter, Ellen, or the Chained Mother*, and *An Inside View of Slavery; or a Tour among the Planters*, with an introduction by Stowe and publicized by John Jewett for "Anti-Slavery Men and Women!" with *The North-Side View of Slavery: Canadian Refugees' Own Narratives*.[86]

In the melodramatic vein, Mary Pike's best-seller *Ida May: A Story of Things Actual and Possible*, published in November 1854, probably had the greatest impact. Her story was drawn from accounts of kidnapping on the Pennsylvania border near the site of the Christiana riot. Ida May is a white girl who is kidnapped, blacked up a bit, and sold into bondage in South Carolina, where she suffers as a slave for fifteen years until she is eventually liberated by her future husband.[87] Rumors circulated that Pike's book was written by Stowe. By the spring of 1856 it was on stage at Barnum's American Museum, with Cordelia Howard as "Ida May, or the Kidnapped Child." This story had already taken a turn into antislavery publicity when Charles Sumner had discovered Mary Botts, the virtually white daughter of a fugitive in Boston. Purchasing her freedom from slavery in Virginia, Sumner had her photograph widely displayed and presented her at antislavery meetings in Massachusetts.[88]

If stories of white slave girls struck a chord with the northern public in the years of bleeding Kansas, it certainly did not push *Uncle Tom's Cabin* out of the theaters. To some extent, this was a matter of time and money invested: the theaters and companies had productions and scenery for *Uncle Tom's Cabin* well in hand, and though it may no longer have drawn the big crowds, it was still a way to make a living. In particular the Howard family, who had launched the Aiken version in Troy in the fall of 1852, made *Uncle Tom's Cabin* their ongoing livelihood. In the summer of 1854, two months after they closed in New York at Purdy's, they were at the National Theater in Boston, where Harriet Beecher Stowe probably saw their performance; by January 1855 they had toured their way to Chicago via Albany, Syracuse, Buffalo, Cleveland, and Detroit. In February 1855 they were in Philadelphia, then moved on to Baltimore, and by the summer they were back on Alexander Purdy's stage in New York, playing *Uncle Tom's Cabin* and *Hot Corn*, followed by a series in Brooklyn.[89] Philadelphia actors put on their own show in March 1855, and Joseph C. Foster was back in Pittsburgh in November with a revival, showing with Charles Shiras's *Invisible Prince*. Presumably both shows featured Stephen Foster's music. Other companies were playing in Boston in March 1855 and again in February 1856, in Poughkeepsie in February 1855, in Milwaukee in August, in Detroit in November. The Howards put on further revivals in 1856 in New York, at Purdy's and at Barnum's, and late in the year they departed for an English tour under the management of Barnum.[90] *Uncle Tom's Cabin*, for better or worse, was now part of the fabric of American life and culture.

ON THE sixth of December 1855, when Mary Webb was performing Stowe's *Christian Slave* at the Tremont Temple in Boston, Harriet Tubman was back in Dorchester County, Maryland, moving the few whom she could to freedom in the North through William Still's safe house in Philadelphia. The newspapers were full of ads for the book of the season. Mary Pike, now writing under a pseudonym, had put out *Caste: A Story of Republican Equality*. Cincinnati's *Star of the West* put *Caste* in the tradition of leading "anti" books with *Uncle Tom's Cabin* and Pike's own recent *Ida May*. In Kansas, the free state capital at Lawrence was besieged by Missouri guerrillas, and letters from the front flooded into Washington offices. "Kansas is invaded by an armed force from Mo.," one settler wrote that day to Charles Sumner. "Her citizens are in arms to defend the dearest rights of Americans. Lawrence is the point of attack... Give Reeder a seat in Congress—admit us as a state and our prosperity is certain. Admit us not and we are but slaves." Three days before, on December 3, the 34th Congress opened its first session in Washington.[91] That

December and January a political structure finally coalesced, ending the liminal crisis at last.

Congress had been in recess since August, and now a newly elected membership faced a new political landscape; once again the rhythm of the political calendar began to drive events. These events were dominated by the ongoing crisis in Kansas, but Congress could not act until it had organized itself, and that would take nine weeks, in one of the epic struggles over the election of the Speaker of the House. Over these nine weeks, two absolutely critical gains were achieved: an antislavery politician was seated as Speaker, and a new national political party was launched. Both were fundamental steps in the coalescence of a permanent structure of political antislavery.

A dinner meeting on Christmas Day brought together many of the key players. Francis Preston Blair Sr., an old Jacksonian from Missouri who had abandoned the Democrats and was moving toward the emerging antislavery coalition, invited a small group of antislavery partisans to his mansion in Silver Spring, Maryland: Charles Sumner, senator from Massachusetts; Gamaliel Bailey, the editor of the *National Era*; Salmon Chase, recently elected as a Fusion Republican to the governorship of Ohio; Preston King, an antislavery Democrat narrowly defeated in a recent key race in New York State; and Nathaniel P. Banks, a representative from Massachusetts.[92] Efforts had been under way for months to plan for the launch of a national Republican Party, and the Silver Spring meeting put these plans in motion. There would be a preliminary party convention, really a mass meeting, in Pittsburgh on Washington's Birthday, February 22, followed by a nominating convention in Philadelphia in June. Blair suggested as nominee John C. Frémont, a fellow Missourian and acclaimed as hero of the Mexican War and various explorations of the mountain West. After some delay waiting for signatures, a convention call went out on January 17 signed by state chairmen from Ohio, Massachusetts, Pennsylvania, Vermont, and Wisconsin, along with a circular from the Washington Republican Club calling for the creation of local organizations "in every city, town, and village in the Union."[93]

These efforts would succeed: the Republican Party would convene, nominate Frémont, and come very close to winning the presidency ten months later. Eighteen months before, antislavery politicians had failed to meet this challenge, as the Nebraska bill was being voted on and signed, in sharp contrast to the success of the Know Nothings. In June 1854 antislavery had a powerful grip on the northern imagination. But the Know Nothings succeeded in organizing hundreds of thousands of voters, at least briefly, because they tried, and because they had a vehicle for accelerated organization close at hand in the form of the secret fraternal lodge. The inability—or unwillingness—of the antislavery men who gathered briefly in Washington in 1854 to form a new party and to organize as aggressively as did Barker and the Know Nothings has to rank as one of the great failures of political imagination in American history. While the known leaders of the 1854 meeting were conspicuously absent from Blair's Christmas dinner, Bailey, King, and Banks had all been involved.[94] Belatedly or not, they now took action.

How had circumstances changed since 1854? Some features of the public landscape were unaltered. The popular culture of the antislavery argument was now part of the northern woodwork, a constant background presence. This had also been the case in 1854. In particular, the issue of fugitives was not going away. From July to November 1855, a fugitive case involving a mother and two children spirited away from a southern diplomat on his way to Central America via Philadelphia had been litigated in the courts, and a white abolitionist named Passmore Williamson was indicted for giving aid. That fall Williamson was nominated for canal commissioner by acclaim at a fusion convention, until a Know Nothing conclave reversed this and other nominations.[95] In Illinois, Abraham Lincoln wrote in August 1855 to his old friend Joshua Speed, "You ought rather to appreciate how much the great body of the Northern people do crucify their feelings, in order to maintain their loyalty to the constitution and the Union." That spring, Frederick Douglass, in his Rochester address, was of the same opinion.

> The Fugitive Slave Bill has especially been of positive service to the anti-slavery movement. It has illustrated before all the people the horrible character of slavery toward the slave, in hunting him down in a free State, and tearing him away from wife and children, thus setting its claims higher than marriage and parental claims. It has revealed the arrogant and over-bearing spirit of the slave States toward the free States; despising the principles—shocking their feelings of humanity, not only by bringing before them the abominations of slavery, but by attempting to make them parties to the crime. It has called into exercise among the colored people, the hunted ones, a spirit of manly resistance, well calculated to surround them with a bulwark of sympathy and respect hitherto unknown.[96]

It is not unlikely that some of Blair's Christmas dinner guests—certainly Bailey—remembered quietly that William Chaplin and several fugitives had been apprehended on the road opposite the Blair mansion in the late summer of 1850, just before the radical convention at Cazenovia.[97] Within a month they would be reminded again by the awful circumstances of the recapture of Margaret Garner in Cincinnati on January 27. Faced with re-enslavement, she immediately killed her daughter in front of the posse. Sold down the Mississippi, she may have drowned another child. Disappearing into the maw of the slave system, she would not so condemn her children. Her case would be discussed in the antislavery papers to the end of the decade. Some readers of *Uncle Tom's Cabin* might have connected Garner with Cassy on Legree's plantation, who kills her son to keep him out of slavery.[98]

What was new was the struggle in Kansas, which had turned into a shooting war with the murder of a free state settler on November 21, and now in December had evolved into a proslavery siege of the town of Lawrence. In the midst of this war the free staters adopted a constitution, and in January elected a governor, establishing two dueling governments in the territory. The emerging Republican leadership hoped to make Kansas a key part of its campaign strategy for the 1856 election, but the signs coming from the fall 1855 elections were not good. The northern secession in Philadelphia had seemed to have killed the chances of a national Know Nothing party, but by late 1855 things again looked complicated. A November convention of northern Know Nothings patched things up with the national group by inviting Edward B. Bartlett of Kentucky, the president of the order, to join them at their meeting in Cincinnati.[99] This conciliatory gesture was grounded in the impressive Know Nothing results of 1855 elections in both North and South. In the North, Know Nothings had won regular state elections in four New England states, including Massachusetts, and in New York. In Ohio, Salmon Chase had won as a nominal Republican, but every other statewide officer on his ballot was a Know Nothing. Democrats had won state elections in Pennsylvania, Indiana, and Illinois; Republicans had won convincingly only in Maine, Vermont, and Wisconsin.[100]

As the new Congress got under way in December 1855, there were a variety of calculations of the path to a House majority. Clearly, with the electoral slaughter of the northern Democrats, the national Democrats had lost their simple majority, so Jacksonian party discipline would not do the trick. It would have to be a coalition, and the northern Know Nothings held the key. If they adhered to the majority platform and combined with southerners (and the few surviving northern proslavery Democrats), a proslavery-nativist coalition might elect a Speaker and control the House. But if northern Know Nothings united with northern Whigs and the various anti-Nebraska representatives elected on Fusion, Peoples, or Anti-Nebraska Democratic tickets, an antislavery-nativist coalition could do the same.

Thus the Silver Spring meeting in late December was something of a gamble. But though the outcome was hard to foresee, buried in the tea leaves were hints that the Know Nothings were something of a bubble. In New York they claimed to have 180,000 members, but even with stellar organization, they could get only 148,000 votes for the Know Nothing candidate for secretary of state.[101] If the antislavery politicians could overcome their pathetic indecision, they could attract many Know Nothings and meet the conservatives head-on. Thus the attendance at the Silver Spring meeting was critical. While Bailey was quietly uncomfortable and Sumner strategic, the meeting was dominated by Blair, Chase, and Banks. These three were onetime Democrats, and two of them had consorted with the Know Nothings. Seward twice declined an invitation because he did not want to be tarred by association with nativism.[102]

For the moment, emergent Republicans needed to swallow their principles and move northerners hovering between antislavery and the Know Nothings to their side. And having failed to contest the 1854 elections for Congress effectively, they now had to act decisively. The battle over the Speakership and then the 1856 presidential contest were high-stakes national contests that played to their advantage. Slavery was a national issue—a grand moral drama that would shape the future of the country. Temperance, nativism, and anti-Catholicism were issues that really resonated at the local and state levels.[103] And they acted in the nick of time. The future, about which they could only guess, would smile upon them; whether by luck, "contingency," or the inexorable force of Seward's "irrepressible conflict," those national winds would start to blow with hurricane force.

By the time of the Christmas meeting at Silver Spring, some of the tea leaves were beginning to form a pattern. Nathaniel Banks was at the meeting because he held the key to the future. Known to many as the "Bobbin Boy of Waltham" (a reference to the job of changing bobbins of thread in textile mills), he had come up the hard way from laboring origins, and in recent years had shifted among Democrats, antislavery, and the Know Nothings. But on December 25 Banks had led the pack in the race for the Speakership by a wide margin, though he could not quite reach a majority. If the contest was deadlocked for the moment, Banks and his floor managers had already assembled an antislavery coalition in Congress.[104]

The battle over the Speakership had begun on December 3, and the antislavery managers had settled on a plan: they would start with Lewis Campbell of Ohio, and if he failed, move to Banks, and then on to Alexander Pennington of New Jersey. All had Know Nothing affiliations of one sort or another. Campbell started off well against the Democrat William Richardson of Illinois, but within two days and ten ballots, Banks had hit one hundred votes, and Campbell reluctantly dropped out on December 7. Banks's support would hold steady for the next two months, just short of a majority. The first vote on December 10 (the thirty-fourth ballot) provides a snapshot: Banks had a hundred votes, Richardson had seventy-four, and forty-seven were scattered among a number of mostly Know Nothing candidates, led by Thomas Fuller of Pennsylvania with thirty-one. Fourteen representatives were not voting, leaving a quorum of 210, of whom 106 would have decided the election for Banks. Southerners supported Richardson, Fuller, and a handful of Know Nothing candidates. The potential deciding votes were a group of eleven Whigs and Know Nothings from conservative districts in New York and Pennsylvania who held out for Fuller (nine votes) and two others. Among them was Thomas Whitney of New York City, who had arrived in Washington trumpeting "the 'National' character of the 'American' party in the North" and extolling the proslavery Know Nothing "Philadelphia platform, twelfth section inclusive."[105] But the voting was remarkably consistent for weeks, with Banks and his floor managers maintaining his coalition, and the notion of a national, proslavery union of Know Nothings and Whigs faded quickly and permanently. The southerners and a small cadre of northern Democrats were united behind William Aiken of South Carolina. Neither Banks nor Aiken could prevail under a majority rule, given a small group of conservative northern Know Nothings who refused to break toward either candidate. Finally, the House decided to invoke the plurality rule which had allowed the election of a Speaker in 1849, and Banks was elected on February 2. (See Appendix, tables 12 and 13.)

The state of the Speakership vote in December, promising if as yet indeterminate, suggested to the committee meeting at Silver Spring that the moment was right for a national Republican Party. The northern seats in the 34th Congress mostly had been decided by November 1854, in an election in which antislavery had miserably failed to organize itself, leaving the field to the Know Nothings. But over the intervening thirteen months, and coalescing in the hothouse of the Speakership battle, the mass of non-Democratic members from the North moved toward the option of an antislavery coalition with nativist undertones. As Gamaliel Bailey wrote to Charles Francis Adams in late January, "Some who came here more 'American' than Republican are more Republican than American." A few days later Joshua Giddings was of a similar opinion regarding Republican coalescence: "We have got our party formed, consolidated, and established. This I regard of far more importance than the election of a speaker."[106] Emerson's "Anti-Slavery Society" was finally taking shape.

The assessment of contemporaries and of historians was and has been that the election of Nathaniel Banks in February 1856 was a defining moment for the emergence of the Republican Party.[107] Banks's election was a disaster for the union nativists, since the Speaker controlled committees in the House. Antislavery figures across the North were thrilled, and a chorus of voices announced that "there is a North." A few northern papers joked that the influence of the North was finally being felt, both in Banks's victory and in a frigid cold snap that was felt deep down the Mississippi Valley.[108] A friend wrote to Sumner on the fourth: "I rejoice in Banks's election. There is a North." Another had just heard the news the night before: "It is almost too good news to be true. It will be a grand thing for Kansas." The next day Sumner echoed these sentiments on the rise of the North: the star that he "fancied" was "glittering over his head" was presumably the *North Star*. An antislavery representative from New York's Burned-Over District wrote to his brother on February 6 that from Banks's election "the South can date the downfall of the slave power."[109]

Joshua Giddings was serious and reflective in a series of letters that he fired off to his daughter Lura Maria back in Ohio. On the first he wrote: "All is bustle, excitement, and confusion in the Hall. There is a nervousness among the members more intensified [than] at any former time . . . Indeed the election of Banks would constitute a triumph too important and too great to be hoped for at this time." Forty-eight hours later he was stunned, in part from lack of sleep, in part from the enormity of "the glorious result." His career was close to an end, but he had had a direct hand in the great moment: "At 7 oclock last evening I administered the oath of office to Mr. Banks in the presence of more than 3000 people amid the cheering of men, the flourishing of ladies handkerchiefs, and universal demonstrations." The public swarmed the House chamber, offering congratulations, "shaking me and others by the hand." Mobbed by well-wishers in his lodgings until midnight, Giddings went to bed still excited. "Sleep had no charms" that night. "I lay in my bed and[,] looking forward to coming generations[,] wrote out the history of the last two months." Writing to Lura the next morning, he admitted, "Today I feel the want of sleep."[110]

CHAPTER 8

Confirming and Consolidating New Structures

The Rise of the Republican Party

ON THE fifteenth of July 1856, a great mass meeting of Republicans assembled in Indianapolis to support John C. Frémont, nominated for the presidency a month before by the Republican convention in Philadelphia. Calvin Fletcher let his sons and farmhands off at noon; they all trooped into town to take part in the afternoon's grand march, performing in a "burlesque Company" that—echoing the tone and message of the *Uncle Tom's Cabin* stage shows—mocked the Missouri "border ruffians" assailing the Free State settlers in Kansas. That month Harriet Beecher Stowe was feverishly finishing a new novel for the election campaign season: *Dred: A Tale of the Great Dismal Swamp*. On sale by early September, *Dred* was being performed by the Howard family before the end of the month on Alexander Purdy's stage at New York's National Theater. And that September, Harriet Tubman, having recovered from a case of pneumonia contracted on an arduous rescue mission in May, was back on the road, making her way south from Philadelphia to Baltimore and into rural Maryland to bring more people out of slavery and into freedom.[1]

That November, in an amazing surge of Republican energy, the vote across the North would almost carry Frémont into the presidency. Though he lost the election, it was by a surprisingly narrow margin—thirty-five electoral votes—for a party that had been organized less than a year before. Democrat James Buchanan won the election over Frémont and Millard Fillmore, the American Party candidate, with 45 percent of the popular vote and 174 electoral votes, sweeping the South and winning five northern states with their essential sixty-two electoral votes. Of these, the large states of Pennsylvania, Illinois, and Indiana were pivotal; everyone knew that if the Republicans could turn them, they could carry the Electoral College. Four years later Abraham Lincoln would win a narrow victory over three other candidates, earning just under 40 percent of the national popular vote but 180 electoral votes, thanks to a virtual Electoral College lock on the northern states.[2]

Lincoln's victory rested on a relatively small expansion of the antislavery vote. In 1852 John P. Hale had won 7 percent of the northern electorate, while Lincoln won with 53 percent in 1860. The great expansion of the antislavery presidential vote came with Frémont's showing, 45 percent of the total northern vote, in 1856. Certainly this was much higher than the 20–25 percent of the North voting for Republican and fusion candidates in the elections for the 34th Congress in 1854–1855. But opinion had changed dramatically by December 1855, when Nathaniel Banks constructed the enduring core of his support for the Speakership of the House. On December 10, Banks was backed by one hundred free state representatives, out of the 144 members of the House. We know that Republican voters were thrilled with Banks's election in February, and certainly there is no evidence that they punished their representatives for this vote. In sum, the one hundred representatives supporting Banks on December 10 had received the votes of 41 percent of the 1854 northern electorate. If we add some voters unhappy with their representatives' refusal to support Banks, this antislavery bloc was quite close to the Frémont and Lincoln votes in 1856 and 1860. The reality was that the North was and would remain divided. Democrats and other conservatives, about half of the electorate, were ambivalent or indeed opposed to the antislavery cause. But the antislavery bloc now controlled the northern agenda and would prevail—against vociferous opposition from most northern Democrats through the war and into Reconstruction. (See Appendix, table 14.)

Banks's election thus stood at the critical juncture in the rise of political antislavery. Abolitionist and even free soil arguments had attracted only small minorities across the North through 1850. Then a broad cultural structure penetrated far more widely throughout the northern public between the two political crises of 1850 and 1854. If late 1854–1855 was a period of uncertain coalescence, the political structure of an antislavery party was established in early 1856. The ground of antislavery had been transformed; what remained was confirmation and consolidation.[3]

That consolidation was achieved in the assembling of an electoral bloc, suggested by the Speakership battle, manifested in the 1856 election, and victorious in 1860. The confirmation would unfold in a flow of events that all reinforced the Republican argument that the southern Slave Power would do anything it could to extend the reach and grip of slavery. The Republican Party was indeed the "favored child of destiny." From the spring of 1856 into the secession winter of 1860–1861, the public affairs of the nation all reinforced and confirmed the established Republican interpretation of the looming threat of slavery to northern liberties.[4] Public drama, court decisions, and presidential manipulation all made it clear that the Slave Power would advance its cause by any means; the way forward would be through the cultural understandings and political structures that antislavery had constructed since the signing of the Fugitive Slave Act in September 1850. And once that cultural and political way forward had coalesced by February 1856, the range of options for national politics changed fundamentally. The possibility of compromise controlled by enduring southern national power—the essential structure of 1787–1854—had been dramatically narrowed, if not entirely eliminated. The establishment of the Republican Party in a seat of national power suddenly left little room for maneuver for "old Union" sentiment. Despite their force and drama, the events unfolding between the spring of 1856 and the spring of 1861 would simply confirm the transformation that had been under way since the summer of 1850.

"This triumph is worth all it cost in time, toil, and solicitude," New York party boss Thurlow Weed wrote to Nathaniel Banks as he received news of his election as Speaker over the wire. "The Republican Party is now inaugurated. We can work with a will."[5] Banks and state politicians did "work with a will," trying to make up for time lost in organizing a party over the previous eighteen months.

Banks's first priority was appointing committee chairs and assigning them committeemen; the result was solid Republican control of the machinery of the House.[6] But if the Republican core held together in roll calls, the Know Noting and Whig allies in the Banks coalition were harder to keep in line, given the failure to establish a general caucus early in the session. Many found it difficult—or inconvenient—to break long-standing alliances.[7]

A general enthusiasm, if not formal state nominations, guided the "mass meeting" of Republicans in Pittsburgh, where about four hundred delegates gathered on Washington's Birthday, February 22. The key item on the agenda was simply establishing the procedures for calling a formal nominating convention, to meet in June at the Musical Fund Hall in Philadelphia. But in just managing a meeting on Washington's Birthday, the Republicans stole press from the Americans, who had scheduled their national council meeting for that same day. Over the next four months the state parties worked effectively to build the party ranks and pools of delegates who would attend the Philadelphia nominating convention that June. Debate in the Senate, pitting Douglas against Seward, kept the issue of Kansas before the public, though it was legislatively deadlocked. The results of local elections in Connecticut, Rhode Island, New York, and Ohio, however, were cause for considerable alarm, suggesting that the Know Nothings were deeply entrenched.[8]

At the same time, a drumbeat of events continued to reinforce and confirm the antislavery message, among them fugitive cases. Hundreds of fugitives passed through Philadelphia and New York, as attested by detailed records kept by Vigilance Committee leaders.[9] Margaret Garner's flight and violent rendition back to slavery continued to be reported; Passmore Williamson, convicted in the Philadelphia fugitive case in July 1855 and sentenced to ninety days, triumphantly attended the February Republican convention.[10]

Three great dramas that confirmed the threat of the Slave Power came in May and involved not fugitives but slavery's assault on the white North. They also centered on Kansas. After an early winter lull, tensions had been mounting in both Washington and the territory. The emigrant aid companies encouraged a spring settlement of Free Staters, and competing initiatives were launched in Congress to admit Kansas as a state. As Douglas and Seward introduced bills for the admission of Kansas in March and April, proslavery authorities in Kansas renewed their efforts to enforce warrants against Free State men in the town of Lawrence. After the arresting sheriff was wounded in a night attack on April 22, proslavery forces converged to besiege Lawrence for the second time in five months. A month later, on May 21, led by the proslavery sheriff, recovering and vengeful, the proslavery militias rode into Lawrence, cannonaded the brick Free State Hotel, destroyed the presses of the *Herald of Freedom*, and set the town afire.[11]

A second drama was unfolding in Washington. Massachusetts senator Charles Sumner had been receiving reports from Kansas regularly all spring, as well as complaints from home that he was—again—being too quiet. The Know Nothings had won the governorship again in 1855, and Sumner was pressed by reports that Governor Henry Gardner was campaigning to take his place in the Senate. Faced with these pressures from home and opportunity to the west, Sumner developed a long oration, "The Crime against Kansas," which he delivered over two days on May 19–20. This was his first major Senate speech on slavery since his efforts against the Kansas-Nebraska bill and the Fugitive Slave Law in the last Congress, and he was out to settle some scores. To packed Senate galleries on the nineteenth, he reviewed the events in Kansas and defended the free state partisans. On the twentieth he pitted a proslavery "Remedy" of "Tyranny," "Folly," "Injustice and Civil War" against a free state "Remedy of Justice and Peace." Along the way, he mocked his longtime opponents in the Senate, Stephen Douglas, James Mason, and Andrew Butler. Butler in particular was a "Don Quixote" among the slaveholders (and Douglas his "Sancho Panza"), whose "mistress" was "the harlot slavery." The entire state of South Carolina, mired in its "shameful imbecility from slavery," meant less in the scale of civilization than the Kansas Free Ftaters' brief but "valiant struggle against oppression." On the twenty-second, Butler's cousin, Representative Preston Brooks, took his revenge for insults on his kin and community, repeatedly striking Sumner on his head and shoulders from behind with a cane as he sat writing at his desk on the Senate floor.[12]

The third drama unfolded two nights later, when Captain John Brown led his men down Pottawatomie Creek in Kansas, killing five proslavery settlers in revenge for the "Sack of Lawrence." But it was the assault on Sumner that shocked northern opinion, far outstripping coverage of either Lawrence or Pottawatomie.[13] Brooks's attack on Sumner viscerally epitomized the threat of arrogant slaveholders and the Slave Power, fully confirming and amplifying the argument that abolitionists and Free Soilers had been making for years, and around which Republicans had finally coalesced early that year—confirming and amplifying, but not transforming. The culture and structure of the Republican Party had been established, even if its political prospects seemed a bit shaky that spring. But the Republicans were now ready to exploit the events of May 1856—and the failures of their opponents.[14]

The first of these failures had already happened, and was the inevitable result of an earlier failure. The American Party—once seemingly so favored—again could not unite northern and southern nativists, this time at its February 22 convention in Philadelphia. Its National Council had already met and adopted a plank that seemed to paper over the division around section 12 and slavery which had splintered the June 1855 convention. But in open convention the proslavery faction persevered, restoring section 12 and its requirement of adherence to the Kansas-Nebraska Act. Once again, large numbers of northern delegates withdrew, and the convention quickly nominated Millard Fillmore, the conservative Whig former president who had signed the Fugitive Slave Law. There was hope that Fillmore would be a unifying "American" candidate of national stature. But very soon it became clear that his candidacy was doomed and that nativism was fatally split.[15]

The Democrats and the new North American seceders held their conventions in June, soon after the assaults on Sumner and Kansas, offering promises and pitfalls to the new Republicans. The Republicans hoped that their candidate would be opposing either President Franklin Pierce or Senator Stephen Douglas, the apparent Democratic front-runners, both of whom were compromised in much of the North by their central roles in determining the fate of Kansas. The Democrats met in early June in Cincinnati, approving a full platform supporting the proslavery agenda. They sidestepped both Pierce and Douglas, however, in the course of seventeen ballots and settled on James Buchanan of Pennsylvania, a reliably pro-southern Democrat who had been ambassador to Great Britain in 1854. He would be a strong candidate; Douglas was quietly promised the 1860 nomination.[16]

The Republican convention met in Philadelphia from the seventeenth to the nineteenth of June, a week after the rump convention of the North American nativists opened in New York on the twelfth. The North Americans set their sights on Banks, nominated him on the sixteenth, and then joined the Republicans at their invitation at the Musical Hall in Philadelphia. Here once again they were blindsided. David Wilmot chaired the platform committee, which, in a well-oiled plan, produced a platform heavy with antislavery planks, offering nothing to nativists. Then on the convention floor the delegates quickly nominated Frank P. Blair's candidate, John C. Frémont.[17]

A month later, on July 15, Indiana's Republicans ratified Frémont's nomination with great fanfare, in a grand parade that illustrates the ways in which Republican mobilization was embedded in the new antislavery culture forged over the previous few years. Hundreds of delegates from all over the state were streaming into

Indianapolis on horseback, by the wagonload, and in railroad cars; the people of Indianapolis and Marion County turned out to watch the procession. The county delegations marched along under swaying banners, led by fifes and brass bands, their glee clubs performing from wagons. One team rolled a twelve-foot-high ball, last seen in the Whig–Log Cabin parades of the 1840 campaign, painted to represent the Republicans' plank supporting a Pacific railway. One float carried a printing press complete with printers printing off sheets from a Frémont "songster" and scattering them to the crowds. All of these were common features of Frémont parades that summer, as was the rolling canoe full of young women waving banners representing the Union and the Kansas territory. The Kansas banner, which was draped in black, proclaimed that the girls were "opposed to old Bachelors," a reference to Buchanan, otherwise derided as "old Buck."

Calvin Fletcher's sons and farmhands marched with an elaborate "Equestrian Burlesque Troupe" known as the Earthquakes. Organized by Calvin's twenty-seven-year-old son Miles at his house in town, the Earthquakes had performed on the Fourth of July and were "received with cheers and shouts of approval." Led by the devil Beelzebub and Belial, declaring, "My works do follow me," the cast performed a series of skits that mocked the great Democratic politicians—Pierce and his cabinet, Buchanan, Lewis Cass—then depicted an auction of slaves, the tribe of Kansas Ruffians attacking Lawrence, and Brooks's assault on Sumner. Tellingly, Douglas was presented arm in arm "with a darky" under a motto, "This is my beloved." Here and elsewhere, blacked-up figures ambiguously represented both slaves and the Slave Power.[18]

Throughout these performances there were references not only to the Republicans' challenge to the Slave Power but also to the new cultural framework that undergirded this challenge. One of the Earthquake's skits lampooned the Mormon leader Brigham Young and his harem of celestial wives, standing for the Republican plank, approved in Philadelphia, demanding that Congress defend the territories against the "twin relics of barbarism—Polygamy and

Slavery." This plank, and the young women representing the states plus Kansas, were symbolic of the more general Republican stance as defenders of the consensual domesticity that Harriet Beecher Stowe had linked with antislavery in *Uncle Tom's Cabin*. As significantly, though not yet in evidence in Indianapolis in July, the 1856 Republican campaign celebrated the marriage of their candidate and the beautiful, accomplished, and politically savvy Jessie Frémont, the daughter of Missouri Democrat Thomas Hart Benton, as the living emblem of their cause, and its connection to the morality and virtue of American women, completing the restoration of women's voice and agency to the antislavery fight which Stowe had begun in 1851.[19] In Indianapolis, Miles Fletcher, with some of his brothers and his sister Lucy, had gone to the Marsh family production of *Uncle Tom's Cabin*, and perhaps to the rawer version put on by the Robinson Athenaeum. The Earthquakes' skits certainly reflected this antislavery theater with all of its racial ambiguity. But Miles and two of his brothers had also joined Know Nothing lodges, and some of the nativists' fraternal mummery was probably reflected in the Earthquakes' performances. Certainly the torchlight parade that closed the ratification events that evening had its nativist analogues.[20]

Republican mass meetings for Frémont like the one in Indianapolis were repeated across the North all summer and into the fall of 1856. Cultural actors worked hard to support the cause, following the script established since *Uncle Tom's Cabin* was first launched in the *National Era* in 1851. Stowe's next novel arrived in late August. *Dred* was a somewhat turgid story of a declining gentry family in Virginia, their slaves, and a legendary self-liberated rebel living in the swamps. It was a more militant version of the emancipatory tale in *Uncle Tom's Cabin*, but without quite the same structure of martyrdom, and abandoning the colonization message. The Howards performed *Dred* at Purdy's National Theater for five weeks, interspersed with revivals of *Uncle Tom's Cabin* and *Ida May*, before they departed for London with P. T. Barnum in November on the Collins Line's S.S. *Baltic*. Other New York performances of *Dred* competed at the Bowery and Barnum's own Museum, and it was soon playing in Boston, in Buffalo, at Joseph Foster's theater in Pittsburgh, and by one inflated report "at most of the Theatres in the smaller cities of the country."[21]

The theatrical output was matched by the press's production of antislavery melodramas and biographies, with *Dred* matched virtually page for page by Harriet Bigelow's *Curse Entailed*, Mary Pike's *Caste: A Story of Republican Equality*, and a biography of Anthony Burns that John P. Jewett put out, in addition to Benjamin Drew's *Northside of Slavery*. These would share the reading table with the host of new books on Kansas, Lydia Maria Child's "Kansas Emigrants," serialized in the *New York Tribune* in late October, and Charles W. Upham's campaign biography of Frémont, published in Boston by the fourth of July.[22] Stephen Foster toed the familial Democratic line, writing songs for his in-law by marriage James Buchanan. But his tunes were borrowed and transfigured for the *Republican Campaign Songster*, perhaps the same book printed on the parade float in Indianapolis that July. After advertising the publisher's list of antislavery books, the *Songster* led off with a lyric set to the tune of the "Star-Spangled Banner," "The North Is Discovered," with its opening refrain, "The free North, *protected by FREMONT the brave!*"[23]

As the Slave Power rhetoric surged to a peak in the fall of 1856, southern leaders darkly threatened secession if Frémont were to be elected—in James Mason's words, "immediate, absolute, and eternal separation."[24] Meanwhile, the new governor of Kansas, John W. Geary of Pennsylvania, a Mexican War veteran, arrived in September and rapidly mobilized federal troops, suppressing the warring militias and establishing a modicum of civil peace. His efforts briefly deflated worries about the Kansas troubles, and may well have saved the election for Buchanan.[25] When Pennsylvania and Indiana tilted to the Democrats in the state election in mid-October, it was reasonably clear that Frémont would not win, and such was in fact the case in November, as northern Democrats held the line against him.[26]

In the 1852 election, Fletcher's Indianapolis had supported the Democrat Pierce over the Whig Scott by roughly three hundred votes out of 2,400 cast, with fewer than a hundred for the antislavery Hale. Fusion candidates won by two hundred votes out of 2,700 cast in 1854. In the 1856 election, despite the best efforts of the Earthquakes, Buchanan edged out Frémont, 2,098 votes to 2,082, with Fillmore the fading spoiler at 152. In 1860, Lincoln would sweep the field. But in 1856, Indianapolis was a rough mirror of the North, with the Republicans surging to a "victorious defeat," winning the plurality of the northern popular vote but losing the key states of Pennsylvania, Indiana, and Illinois. The lesson was obvious to all: if the Republicans could attract enough nativists, they could win the election in 1860. The handwriting was on the wall.

In the meantime, the resurgent if minority Democratic vote in the North elected fifty-three congressmen to the 35th Congress, more than doubling the twenty-three in the 34th Congress, returning the House to Democratic control. Despite these setbacks, the flow of events continued to confirm the structure of political culture that antislavery had been constructing since 1850, now fully ratified in the results of the 1856 election. Governor Geary's efforts in Kansas suddenly collapsed following the election, and he resigned after being targeted for assassination by proslavery militias. Returning to Washington in late March to report to Buchanan, he met with a range of northern politicians in his hotel room, warning of the Slave Power threat in Kansas.[27]

Three weeks before, Roger Taney's Democratic majority on the Supreme Court had issued their decision in the case of Dred Scott, a slave who sued for his freedom on the strength of having been taken by his master into the Minnesota territory. Taney's seven-judge majority ruled that Scott's slave status under Missouri law was not altered by his residence in the territories, and, more important, claimed that blacks had never held citizenship rights anywhere in the United States and thus had no standing to sue. Adding insult to injury, Taney also argued that the Missouri Compromise of 1821, excluding slavery from the northern sections of the territory, had been an unconstitutional violation of slaveholders' rights to property. Two northern justices were scathing in their dissent, and the

Dred Scott decision was widely rejected across the North as illegitimate, and further evidence of the reach of the Slave Power. Linking a rejection of the citizenship of free men with the slaveholders' relentless march to nationalize slavery, Taney's decision inflamed northern option.[28]

In Congress, the struggle was over Buchanan's last-ditch effort to admit Kansas as a slave territory at all costs. Late in December 1857, the proslavery convention held in Lecompton, Kansas, voted through a constitution that was rejected by the voters in January. Despite this, Buchanan demanded that it be debated and voted on in Congress. The Lecompton struggle put northern Democrats in a box from which they never escaped. Reaching the end of their own patience with the Slave Power, a large faction led by Stephen Douglas cut their ties with Buchanan in an effort to save their seats from a wrathful northern public. Approved by the Senate on a sectional vote, the Kansas legislation was rewritten in the House with the proviso (known as the English amendment for its sponsor, Congressman William English) that it be ratified by the Kansas voters, who rejected it in a landslide in August 1858.[29]

Confirming the worst fears of committed antislavery voters and alienating yet another slice of the northern electorate, the *Dred Scott* decision and the Lecompton battle also threw the booming business in land in the northern plains into a crisis, with free state settlers—and investors—suddenly backing away from a potentially slavery-ridden region. The result was a sharp depression in the national economy, which in turn fed a widespread religious revival that continued in 1858. Both the depression and the revival were critical precursors to the coming war, but neither fundamentally reshaped the Republican message.[30]

Douglas's debates with Abraham Lincoln, unfolding in the summer and fall of 1858, with Douglas's Senate seat the prize, further clarified the sectional division in the Democratic Party, as Douglas stood by his popular sovereignty policy regarding Kansas, now anathema to slaveholders, who demanded enforcement of Taney's vision that their property rights in slaves be recognized. From 1858 forward it was increasingly clear that the Democrats would be divided into two sectional parties.

Lincoln's arguments in his debates with Douglas centered on the question of racial equality and the nation's founding document. Speaking in Chicago in July and appealing to voters of German and Irish descent who might be on the fence, Lincoln had turned to a binary of slavery and freedom, championing the verities of equality in "the old Declaration of Independence," and urged his audience to "discard all this quibbling about this man and the other man—this race and that race," and to stand with the Founders for a universal equality. Out on the debating stands across Illinois that autumn, Douglas attacked Lincoln's invocation of the Declaration, forcing him back to his tricornered position in Peoria: blacks were entitled to natural rights, but not to civil rights equal to those of white men in Illinois. Practical Republican operatives were happy with this retreat, which resonated with more conservative voters. But—as Douglas himself warned—the ambiguities of the distinction between civil and natural rights made this boundary far less certain than the boundary between slavery and freedom.[31] The outcome of the 1858 election was a Pyrrhic victory for Douglas: though he won the gerrymandered vote in the Illinois House, Lincoln had won the popular vote.[32] Again, Lincoln's positions reflected both the strengths and the limitations of the antislavery consensus.

Otherwise throughout the 1858 debates, Lincoln methodically built a binary view of slavery and freedom. And in his "House Divided" speech to the Illinois Republican state convention in June, echoed by Seward's "Irrepressible Conflict" speech in October, Lincoln argued that the country stood at the edge of this binary: "I believe this government cannot endure, permanently half *slave* and half *free*. I do not expect the Union to be *dissolved*—I do not expect the house to *fall*—but I do expect it will cease to be divided. It will become *all* one thing, or *all* the other." The solution lay in the resolute action of "the Republicans of the nation[,] mustered over thirteen hundred thousand strong" in 1856. Nevertheless, while they both pointed to what Lincoln blandly called the "advocates" of slavery and Seward called "the designs of the slave-holders," neither invoked the language of the Slave Power, the Jacksonian rhetoric of a secret political conspiracy. Indeed the use of the term "Slave Power" in the press had peaked with the Kansas-Nebraska Act and the 1856 election, and rapidly faded away, seemingly a function of the consolidation of culture and institutions that had already taken shape. In the final years before the critical 1860 election, then, the Republican message retreated from both sentiment and conspiracy to party, policy, and geopolitics.[33]

In these final years leading up the 1860 election, writers and theater producers continued to contribute to building an antislavery culture. *Uncle Tom's Cabin* played regularly across the North; a revival by the Howards was on tour from the summer of 1859 into the fall of 1860. Publishers continued to put out volumes on the slave experience. Martha Griffin Browne's *Autobiography of a Female Slave*, published in New York in 1857, was widely noted. Early northern advertisements for Browne's account proclaimed that "the evils of a slave's life are depicted by no feeble hand," second only to Stowe; southern papers said it was "of vastly deeper infamy."[34] Yet these performances on the page and on the stage were now simply reinforcing the construct established in the early 1850s, which had contributed to the forging of the Republican Party. They were now an established routine, not a transformative force.

In fact, innovative cultural action was more obvious among the unionists hoping to stand between antislavery and proslavery partisans, who wrapped their cause in the memory of Washington. The preservation of Mount Vernon had been bandied about in Congress since at least 1850, when Henry Clay had tepidly advanced a proposal in the opening of debates on the Compromise. In 1853 a group of southern women, designated by 1858 as the Mount Vernon Ladies Association of the Union, had started a fund-raising campaign and recruited a star orator to their cause. Edward Everett was a Massachusetts Webster Whig, briefly Fillmore's secretary of state in 1852, before being elected to the Senate, where he had feebly opposed the Kansas-Nebraska Act before resigning in May 1854. In

1856 he commenced an arduous round of speechmaking in the cause of the memory of Washington and preservation of Mount Vernon, earning the money for the purchase of the estate. Mount Vernon would be the symbol of the united nation—in the face of dark but realistic fears of a "house divided" by an "irrepressible conflict." In the process, he laid the ground for the Constitutional Union Party, for which he would be the vice presidential candidate in 1860. It would draw a dwindling number of old Whigs and nativists. This was a swath of the public that overlapped with the constituency of the 1857–1858 revival, dominated by Old School Presbyterians, who banned any references to slavery.[35]

These efforts were too little and too late. When in December 1859 Captain John Brown brought the Kansas struggle to Harper's Ferry, positions hardened in South and North. Broadly, across the South, the threat of Brown's call for a mountain insurgency of blacks against slavery confirmed the slaveholders' worst fears, suppressed by two generations of control over the federal agenda. This was the South's liminal moment; the response was a militia mobilization that would lay the groundwork for secession and war. Across the North, Brown's supporters, including Gerrit Smith, Frederick Douglass, and several of their circle, departed abruptly for Canada in fear of arrest.[36] But Brown's quick trial and execution under Virginia law created a martyr whose power transcended that of the cult of Washington which Everett was struggling to construct. "John Brown meetings" erupted in December 1859 and continued until after the election; he would be immortalized in song in the coming years of war.[37]

John Brown, then, not Edward Everett, set the dominant tone for the 1860 election. The structure of the election was laid down in an epic sequence of party conventions meeting between April and June. Using contradictory party rules, William Lowndes Yancey of Alabama engineered the collapse of the Democrats in Charleston in April, as a southern-dominated committee produced a slavery extension platform that northern Democrats were now bound to reject. Out of this smashup Stephen Douglas was nominated by the national party, reconvened that June in Baltimore, while John C. Breckinridge of Kentucky was nominated by a New Southern Democratic Party. The conservative Whig-nativist remnant, now the Constitutional Union Party, met in Baltimore in early May to nominate John Bell of Tennessee and Edward Everett of Massachusetts. The Republicans met in Chicago a week later, and after three quick ballots, Lincoln emerged as the winner, defeating both Chase and Seward.[38]

As soon as the field was set in mid-June, there was a growing sense of the inevitability of Lincoln's election among Republican operatives. There had been eastern doubts about Lincoln as an unknown westerner, but these had been overcome in his speech in New York at Cooper's Union in February. The platform committee had carefully protected party interests, blending antislavery planks with a traditional Whig developmental agenda for river and harbor improvements and a transcontinental railroad. The committee had not, however, put a nativist plank in the platform, gambling that protecting immigrant rights would trump nativism, and that progress in converting the nativist vote in the state since 1856 would carry forward. As the campaign unfolded, however, key nativists like Daniel Ullman of New York were recruited to bring in the rank and file. At the same time, Garrisonians, especially in Massachusetts, had been reviving the petition campaign against the Fugitive Slave Law, and this renewed focus on the rights of the self-liberated resonated with the Republican's first substantive plank, upholding the uncompromising language of the Declaration of Independence that "all men are created equal."[39] Excitement was running high. In New York City, on the Monday before the election, George Templeton Strong wrote to "confidently predict that Lincoln will be elected by the people." He also predicted the secession of the Deep South and warned that "the question may have a grim solution in an uprising of the slaves." The next day he "voted for Lincoln."[40]

As in 1856, the results of the 1860 election were settled for many when key states voted for Republicans in their state elections in October. On October 9, Calvin Fletcher in Indianapolis wrote, "This has been an exciting day [and] a day I think long to be remembered."

Indiana and Pennsylvania "give majorities for the Republicans or near so as to give the plurality vote to Lincoln in November." On election day a month later, he wrote of how the "great excitement" before the October vote had "died away," replaced by a "careful watching."[41] The results in Indianapolis roughly reflected the nation as a whole. The Republican vote jumped from two thousand in 1856 to more than three thousand. The Democrats—Douglas and Breckinridge combined—lost about two hundred voters. The small 1856 vote for Fillmore mostly went to Bell and Everett. The big story was the nine hundred new voters—either newcomers or young men coming of age—who voted for Lincoln, among them presumably Calvin Fletcher's sons.[42]

Indianapolis's surge to Lincoln was an exaggerated version of the national story. The Republicans won a solid Electoral College victory, with just under 40 percent of the total national popular vote, in a sectional triumph. While Breckinridge lost Missouri to Douglas and Virginia and Kentucky to Bell, Lincoln swept the North, and 180 of its 183 electoral votes, twenty-eight more than the 152 necessary to win. Even so, Lincoln's 53 percent of the northern vote was not fundamentally greater than Frémont's 45 percent in 1856. He did add almost 500,000 votes to Frémont's 1.3 million, and roughly 320,000 might have been nativist voters in 1856. But the rest were new voters, mainly young men who had not voted in 1856. Young first-time northern voters tipped almost two-to-one for Lincoln over all of his opponents.[43]

The surge of first-time voters in Indianapolis was probably considerably stronger than in the North at large. These young Republican voters, many rejecting the conservative Whig affiliations of their parents, shared a common generational experience. They had been between the ages of thirteen and seventeen in 1852, and, like James Garfield and Harford Toland, they were in the prime years for an impressionable first reading of *Uncle Tom's Cabin*. Of Fletcher's sons in this cohort, Ingram had gone with his older siblings to see the Marsh family production of *Uncle Tom's Cabin* in early 1854, and with his younger brothers William and Keyes had performed in the

Earthquakes' Kansas Ruffian sketch in July 1856. Presumably they joined one of the Republican clubs that formed in the summer of 1860, the Wide Awakes or the Lincoln Rail Maulers, and marched in the grand parade that drew fifty thousand to Indianapolis in late August, on a day that ended in a "torchlight procession and illumination." Miles, who had organized the Earthquakes, was on the Republican ballot himself in 1860, stumping for the ticket and winning statewide to become the superintendent of public instruction.[44] We might imagine some of the first-time Republican voters, teenagers in 1854 and now Wide Awakes, humming Foster tunes as they voted in November 1860.

The election of Lincoln led within six months to an all-consuming war to save the Union and end slavery. Before the war, and indeed its immediate cause, the Deep South states seceded from the Union. They had threatened to secede if Frémont had won in 1856, and in fact had been threatening disunion since the days of the Continental Congress.[45] Now Lincoln's election gave them their final excuse. They were led by the South Carolina convention on December 20, which filled their "Declaration of the Immediate Causes" with a discourse on the settlement of 1787, a complaint that the northern states had failed to uphold their "constitutional obligation" to return fugitives, and the final insult of "the election of a man to the high office of President of the United States, whose opinions and purposes are hostile to slavery." All of the seceding southern states would similarly make clear that they valued their property in slaves far more than they did the union of the young republic.[46]

Conservative Old Whig unionists from both sections worked all through the winter to forge a compromise, and even William Seward wavered, offering guarantees for slavery in the hope of preserving the Union. But efforts to save union and slavery collapsed quickly with the inevitable failure of the Crittenden Compromise, which would have guaranteed slavery in the South and extended it to California. Introduced in a special Senate committee on December 18, this initiative was tabled by the thirty-first. Voting for secession convention delegates was already under way, and over the next month, South Carolina fired on a ship attempting to resupply Fort Sumter and southern militias occupied federal installations. By February 1, 1861, six Deep South states had followed South Carolina's unilateral secession, announcing a provisional constitution in February and forming the Confederate States of America in March. A Peace Commission met in February, but went nowhere, while the Corwin Amendment, guaranteeing slavery in the states where it existed already, repeated the terms of the Republican platform. Clearly the failure of the Crittenden Compromise opened wide the door to regional secession.[47]

Why did compromise fail? While many in the upper South held out hope, fire-eating southerners, dreaming of an empire of slavery, were adamantly opposed. But if some Republican politicians like Seward—with deep ties of collegial experience in Washington—wavered, the rank-and-file Republican voters did not. As the most authoritative study of the North during the secession winter makes clear, ordinary Republicans deluged wavering senators and representatives with a flood of letters and petitions, demanding that they stand against any compromise on the expansion of slavery into the federal territories, the common ground of the antislavery movement. And Abraham Lincoln, attuned to the center of free soil Republican sentiment, stood with them, refusing any concessions on slavery and rejecting the legitimacy of secession. In his inaugural address on March 4, he invoked the Constitution to declare that the Union was perpetual, and governance in that Union must be grounded in majority rule. "Plainly," Lincoln argued in an assault on the memory of John C. Calhoun, "the central idea of secession is the essence of anarchy."[48] War would follow when South Carolina attacked the United States garrison at Fort Sumter, and Lincoln called for 75,000 volunteers to suppress the rebellion.

EPILOGUE

Into the War

As JOHN Quincy Adams had predicted in 1820, war followed secession, and with war came "the extirpation of Slavery from this whole Continent."[1] In these events, beyond the root existence of "the destined sword" of slavery, the fundamental causal arrow was forged in the North, in the emergence between 1850 and 1854 of a large, ultimately determinative bloc of northern opinion against the compromise of 1787 that fused union with slavery. The abolitionists had been their vanguard, but until the early 1850s they were embattled and isolated, unable to mobilize a decisive antislavery majority.

I have argued that the transformative impact of culture in fiction, song, and theater in the liminal space between the twin crises of 1850 and 1854 played a powerful role in this final antislavery mobilization. How powerful is hard to say. We will never know whether the Fugitive Slave Law and the Kansas-Nebraska Act alone could have generated the antislavery convictions that would have carried the Republicans to Lincoln's election, through the war, and into early Reconstruction. We do know that culture intervened and weighed heavily in the judgment of contemporaries. For Henry Wilson, *Uncle Tom's Cabin* was "a revelation and a summons," a "needful preparation" for the "rich fruitage" of votes cast for Frémont and then for Lincoln. James Ford Rhodes, a leading historian of the postbellum period, was certain that "one of the most important causes" explaining the sudden rise of the Republican Party "was the publication of *Uncle Tom's Cabin*," critical "in bringing about the immense revolution in public sentiment between 1852 and 1860." And Frederick Douglass in his 1881 *Life and Travels* kept the flame alive in his account of the early 1850s: "In the midst of these fugitive slave troubles came the book known as *Uncle Tom's Cabin*, a work of marvelous depth and power. Nothing could have better suited the moral and humane requirements of the hour. Its effect was amazing, instantaneous, and universal."[2]

Certainly the book and its author loomed over the Union effort: Chandra Manning has found that *Uncle Tom's Cabin* was—after the Bible—the most commonly mentioned book in the letters that Union soldiers wrote home to their families.[3] Visiting Washington late in 1862, a month before the Emancipation Proclamation took effect, Harriet Beecher Stowe went with Henry Wilson to meet with Lincoln at the White House; Lincoln is supposed to have joked that she had caused the war.[3] That December she visited her son Frederick, a lieutenant in the First Massachusetts Artillery, and glimpsed her younger brother James C. Beecher riding at the head of his own regiment, the 141st New York. He would later command black troops fighting in South Carolina and Florida. The theater made some sacrifices too. Actor William J. Le Moyne, who had started playing in *Uncle Tom's Cabin* with the Howards at Troy in 1852 and then toured the Midwest with the Marsh family, commanded a company in the Twenty-eighth Massachusetts until he was severely wounded in Virginia in late 1862.[4] Alcohol hung over Stephen's Foster's circle of "Nice Young Men" during the war. One of them, a captain in the Fifth Pennsylvania, was court-martialed for drunkenness in 1862. Foster scrabbled by in New York, drinking hard and writing sentimental Union songs, until his sudden death in 1864.[5]

Thousands of young men and women immersed in the antislavery culture of *Uncle Tom's Cabin*, readers and theatergoers, were swept up in the war. Calvin Fletcher's younger sons Ingram, William, and Keyes, Earthquake ruffians in 1856, all served in Indiana regiments in the western theater. In hard campaigning with the Thirty-third Indiana at the Cumberland Gap, Keyes Fletcher had reason to remember the exquisite fiddling of the fugitive Londen at Christmas in 1849.

Passing slaves toiling at a saltworks in September 1862, he noted that they had "seen these very same fellows" months before, "singing their corn songs," adding: "One fellow, that I saw dance the jigg at Colwells, knew some of our boys, & seemed as glad to see them as a brother. He walked with us about a mile." In 1863 his sister Lucy—who had gone with Ingram and their older brothers to see *Uncle Tom's Cabin*—married Cyrus Hines, colonel of the Fifty-seventh Indiana, recently wounded at the battle of Stone's River.[6] In London, Ohio, the young theater critic Harford Toland—uncle of "Little Eva"—stayed home while his younger brother Aquilla enlisted in the 113th Ohio with Eva's father, forty-year-old Toland Jones. These brothers-in-law survived a series of horrific battles from Chickamauga to Kennesaw Mountain to Bentonville. Toland Jones ended the war as the commander of his much-reduced regiment. In 1917 Eva and her sisters failed in an effort to recover his back pay.[7]

The experience of Union soldiers in the South gave a visceral reality to the political confluence of oppressed black and antislavery white. Private Ransom Bedell of the Thirty-ninth Illinois was disgusted by a society in which "a slave dealer can complacently sell his own children as chattel property." Corporal James Miller of the 111th Pennsylvania was of the same opinion, writing home from Virginia in 1863 that a slaveholder nearby was known to have sold children who were "his flesh and blood." He was appalled that "public sentiment is so corrupt" that these sales were widely accepted in the neighborhood. Lecturing his stay-at-home younger brother, Miller declared that "Uncle Tom's Cabin[,] as bad as it was[,] fell far short of portraying the evils of slavery in as bad a light as they realy [*sic*] exist." He admitted that he was "getting to be a radical Abolitionist," and argued that "these two years of war have made more Abolishonists [*sic*] than the lectures" by Wendell Phillips, Gerrit Smith, or William Lloyd Garrison "would have made in one hundred years."[8]

Both Bedell and Miller served in the bitter fighting in the Shenandoah Valley of Virginia, which produced some of the most radicalized white soldiers in the Union Army. Bedell would reenlist, and was killed at Richmond in November 1864.[9] Miller would survive Antietam, Chancellorsville, and Gettysburg to be wounded in a night battle near Chattanooga; he was killed at the battle of Peach Tree Creek outside Atlanta in July 1864. Miller had reenlisted with his regiment six months before as a "Veteran Volunteer." His division, the "White Stars," was celebrated as one of the very few to reenlist en masse, "an entire veteran division." Their commander, John White Geary, the once solid Democrat who had pacified Kansas for Buchanan in 1856, predicted approvingly to his wife, Mary, in October 1864 that "nine-tenths of the soldiers in this Army will vote for Lincoln." Miller's 111th exceeded this margin, voting in camp near Atlanta twelve days before moving out on Sherman's six-week campaign to Savannah.[10] Running for governor of Pennsylvania as a Republican in 1866, Geary was depicted in blackface in Democratic campaign broadsides and attacked for supporting "negro suffrage." In 1867 he and Mary named their youngest daughter Eva Louisa.[11]

These were men once of the Second Corps of the radicalized Union Army of Virginia, commanded by Nathaniel P. Banks of Massachusetts, whose election to the Speakership of the House had turned the tide of Republican fortunes. Banks was one of many white men playing parts large and small in the transformation of political culture in the early 1850s who went on to command black Union troops in the Civil War. Reassigned to the Mississippi Valley, Banks commanded the first black troops to serve after Lincoln's authorization in May 1863, including several regiments of an established "Louisiana Native Guards" and a newly recruited Corps d'Afrique. In May 1863 the Louisiana Guards led an assault on Port Hudson, the first major combat by black troops in the war. Banks had forced out most of the black officers serving in these regiments, but in the wake of the assault he wrote that the black soldiers had "fought splendidly." A few weeks after the Port Hudson assault, Harriet Beecher Stowe's brother James began to train a black regiment in New Berne, North Carolina, recruited from local fugitives; as the Thirty-fifth United States Regiment of Colored Troops (USCT), they saw hard fighting in Florida and the siege of Charleston, serving alongside the Fifty-fourth Massachusetts. Robert Gould Shaw, himself a veteran of the fighting in the Shenandoah with Banks, commanded the Fifty-fourth until his death at Fort Wagner. As a teenager he had educated himself about slavery by carefully reading *Uncle Tom's Cabin* and *The Key*. Another Massachusetts colonel of an all-black regiment, the First South Carolina Volunteers, abolitionist Thomas Wentworth Higginson had been wounded in the effort to rescue Anthony Burns in 1854. He had congratulated Stowe in 1852 for writing "the most efficient of anti-slavery tracts." One of the literati himself, Higginson sprinkled his journals and reminiscences with references to *Uncle Tom's Cabin* and *Dred*. To read *Uncle Tom* with the regiment, however, he later noted, "would have seemed tame[:] any group of men in a tent would have had more exciting tales to tell."[12] Or women. In 1862 Harriet Tubman joined the Union effort in South Carolina, supporting the Port Royal Experiment, helping to recruit black soldiers, scouting Confederate-held territory, and leading an expedition up the Combahee River. Following a leave that took her to fugitive committees in Canada, she tended the wounded after the battle of Olustee in Florida in 1864.[13]

In Indianapolis, Calvin Fletcher helped to raise black recruits and lent some of his fields for use as "Camp Fremont"—a training base for black troops in Indiana's Twenty-eighth USCT. In late July 1864, men of this regiment would fight and many would die in the battle of the Crater at Petersburgh, among them Richard Blakely, who was working on Fletcher's farm in 1850. Another private in the Twenty-eighth, Garland H. White, subsequently commissioned as chaplain, wrote four weeks later to the AME *Christian Recorder* to defend the bravery of the troops and their officers at the Crater, mourning the men who "sleep in the sin-cursed soil of Virginia."[14]

Garland White had been born into slavery in 1829 near Petersburgh in Hanover County, but had been sold as a boy to Senator Robert Toombs of Georgia. He was one of the two men whom William Chaplin was helping to escape in the summer of 1850 when they were arrested in Silver Spring, on the road outside the Blair mansion. White came to know Seward in Washington, and was licensed as an AME minister in the 1850s; he escaped to Canada early in 1861, as Toombs was preparing to leave Washington for Richmond. In April 1865, as the Twenty-eighth USCT led the Army of the James into a burning Richmond, White spoke before a "vast multitude," announcing the arrival of freedom. In a crowd of "broken-hearted mothers looking for their children," an "aged woman" appealed to men of the Twenty-eighth, who hurried her to meet White, thus reuniting mother and son for the first time in twenty years. White wrote later that week, "I cannot express the joy I felt at this happy meeting of my mother and friends"; he informed the *Recorder*, "I have witnessed several such scenes among other colored regiments."[15] Some families torn apart by slavery were finally being brought back together.

SUCH WERE some of the harsh realities and dramatic outcomes of the Civil War antislavery alliance of black and white to destroy the Slave Power. This alliance, fraught and complex, distantly echoed Stowe's idealized "Freeman's Defense"—in which the black George Harris and the white Phinehas Fletcher had stood on a rocky Ohio hilltop against the slave hunters. More important, it was the central thrust of what has been called a black war for freedom, continuous with and extending a longer history of resistance and rebellion.[16] Black leaders Frederick Douglass and Martin Delany, each with very different opinions about a political alliance of white and black in the 1850s, stood together during the war. Demanding a role in the war for African Americans against Lincoln's resistance through 1862, Douglass and Delany with other black leaders worked to recruit black soldiers as soon as Lincoln signed the authorization. Both had sons in the Fifty-fourth Massachusetts; Lewis Douglass was the first regimental sergeant major. Converging, if briefly, in their politics, both Douglass and Delany held meetings with Lincoln, and in 1865 Lincoln commissioned Delany as a major in the army, authorized to both raise black troops and appoint black officers to command them. Delany seems to have proposed raising a black army of liberation to march through the South, echoing the themes of his novel *Blake*, published on the eve of the war. He arrived in occupied Charleston in April 1865 and rapidly raised the 104th USCT from local men of color.[17]

What of the complex, ambiguous hints of cultural creolization that seem to have been at work, a cultural convergence operating on and within this political convergence, and the breakthrough to interracial sympathy, empathy, and identification? As throughout American history, this creolizing dynamic was fleeting and halting, moving in fits and starts, with overt reversals. If it played a role in the early 1850s, however superficially, whites were in full denial of any such exchange by the end of the decade and during the war itself. Indeed Barbara Hochman has cogently argued that there was a great distinction in emotional response between the first-time readers of *Uncle Tom's Cabin* in the mid-1850s and those who took up the book in the years and decades to come. Those reading in 1851 and 1852 were reading quite literally in the liminal moment, under the unresolved stress of the overpowering sense of deep and endless crisis, and their tears, their late-night binges, suggest that the book was its own crisis point in a wider reformation of their understanding of their place in the larger national crisis. But this was a generational experience in a liminal moment that had passed, an emotional experience impossible to transfer or replicate. And those who went through this conversion process, if far greater in numbers than the abolitionist circles, were not a majority even in the North: Frémont's 45 percent of the northern electorate might be a very optimistic guess. Even this large minority had a field of view shaped by a romantic racialism, shaping at best a cultural opacity that would harden and solidify as the century rolled into the next. As significantly, Stowe's novel, with its colonizationist twist and deep implication in the dominant racist constructs of nineteenth-century minstrelsy, was not the strongest ideological vehicle for the coming postwar struggle, the conversion of emancipation's natural rights into full citizenship and civil and political rights for black Americans. These later readings of the novel, enmeshed with the intensified racism of the minstrel show and theater, would play a role in justifying an end to Reconstruction and the rise of Jim Crow "Redemption" regimes in the South.[18]

But in the late antebellum moment, the cultural construct that Harriet Beecher Stowe had set in motion was one of enormous power. The antislavery white minority, allied with a rising black multitude, changed the nation. The sympathetic breakthrough in the experience of antislavery culture in the 1850s played a central role in carrying the North through emancipation and early Reconstruction, before exhaustion and contrary forces set in. At its core, the message of that cultural construct resonated forcefully with political realities and deep fears: barring organized resistance at all levels, the Slave Power had a plan to enslave everyone in the nation. By the 1850s, the proslavery ideologues were blatantly specific in their claim: whites who were not of independent means were better off enslaved. Such was the message of both the plantation novels and the southern journals of political economy; such was the message of the occasional story in the newspapers of whites being enslaved. Such was the overwhelming message of the shallow, tenuous boundary between free white and slave black in the enslavement of "mulattos" of every complexion. The antislavery writers saw the power of this dissolving boundary between white and black and used it at every opportunity: in Hildreth's *Archy*, in Sumner's *White Slavery in the Barbary States*, in Stowe's self-liberating mulatto hero and heroine George and Eliza Harris, in the wider Stowe-Beecher and abolitionist celebration of the light-skinned Edmundson sisters, in *Ida May*, about a white girl kidnapped into slavery, in *Clotel*, "the president's daughter." Such direct and implied threats to white liberty certainly inspired "greasy mechanics" in Sherman's Army to burn more than a few plantation houses in Georgia and the Carolinas during the closing months of the war.[19]

The prevailing message was one of universal liberty, the end of slavery for all, everywhere, which these same soldiers announced on these plantations. Individual freedom from slavery and coercion had been the central message of the radical abolitionists, and Stowe's *Uncle Tom's Cabin* had woven this message into the wider antislavery culture of the early 1850s: slavery was an assault upon basic human rights and the inherent dignity of all people. As the Republican Party began to emerge, this core abolitionist belief was proclaimed as party principle, grounded in the language of the Preamble of the Declaration of Independence. In July 1854 the first convention of Republicans in Michigan resolved that "slavery is a violation of the rights of man as man; that the law of nature, which is the law of liberty, gives no man rights superior to those of another: That God and nature have secured to each individual the inalienable right of equality."[20] In 1856, the national Republican convention meeting in Philadelphia—blending "the principles promulgated in the Declaration of Independence and embodied in the Federal Constitution"—similarly resolved, "We hold it a self-truth, that all men are endowed with the inalienable right to life, liberty, and the pursuit of happiness." When a cautious drafting committee left the 1856 invocation of the Declaration out of the 1860 platform, Joshua Giddings marched out of the Chicago convention hall in protest, and the Republican delegates rose en masse to reinsert this language by acclamation. In his first inaugural address in March 1861, Lincoln focused on the threat of secession and war to a perpetual union rather than on transcendent ideals of individual liberty, except for a passing remark that "the only substantial dispute" at issue was that "one section of our country believes slavery is right and ought to be extended, while the other believes it is wrong and ought not to be extended." A few days before, however, he had stood in Philadelphia's Independence Hall and spoken of his commitment to "the sentiments embodied in the Declaration of Independence" and its promise "that in due time the weights would be lifted from the shoulders of all men, and that all should have an equal chance." When in April 1865 he briefly suggested on the White House steps that the nation should give the vote to the black soldiers who had turned the tide in war, he soon would be shot down by an assassin's bullet.[21]

If Lincoln was restrained in the early months of the war, other Republicans took a far more militant stand. Lincoln's associate on the Illinois circuit, Orville Browning, was among these. Later to be on the relatively conservative side of the Republican spectrum, Browning was a radical in the spring of 1861. Writing in late April after Fort Sumter's surrender, Browning urged Lincoln to call up 300,000 men and to wage war "with the utmost possible vigor." If that were to "bring the rebels to reason," that would be an end to it. But failing a quick end, Browning predicted a long war that would end slavery. "Whenever our armies march into the Southern states, the negroes will, of course, flock to our standards—They will rise in rebellion, and strike a blow for emancipation from servitude, and to avenge the wrongs of ages. This is inevitable." What would happen once slavery was ended? Browning's answer was direct and to the point, and grounded in colonizationist assumptions that the black nationalist Martin Delany might have approved: the only solution for the freed peoples was to "give up the cotton states to them" to form an independent republic under a United States protectorate. "This done[,] our troubles are at an end, and our government planted on the rock of ages."[22]

Such was one vision of an immediate end to slavery, with steps toward a "reconstruction" of southern society, circulating among many in the North in 1861. When Lincoln reprimanded Generals John Frémont and David Hunter for freeing slaves as they carried the war into the South, he was barraged with letters of protest, evidence of a strong emancipationist sentiment in the North in the summer of 1861.[23] Representative James Ashley of Ohio was circulating a plan only slightly less radical than Browning's, urging that the reconquered southern states be reduced to the status of territories before their reconstruction and restoration to the Union; two years later Ashley would write the Thirteenth Amendment, abolishing slavery in the United States.[24] As William Seward himself had suggested in his "Higher Law" speech of 1850, Lincoln now had the power to emancipate slaves immediately by military fiat in the states in rebellion, rather than waiting for the slow, peaceful extinction of slavery by excluding it from the territories. Such would be the policy announced in the Emancipation Proclamation in the autumn of 1862.[25]

But these were military measures, not transcendent principle. Lincoln would meet with Harriet Beecher Stowe in December 1862, and he had sat down with Ralph Waldo Emerson in February; he would meet with Frederick Douglass in August 1863, after Gettysburg and the martyrdom of the Fifty-fourth Massachusetts at Fort Wagner.[26] That November he went to the Gettysburg battlefield and, in quietly soaring language, rhetorically inserted the Declaration of Independence into the Constitution, promising the dead and the living that the nation "shall have a new birth of freedom." This had been the central message of the antislavery culture that had swept the northern states—in shock from the implications of the Fugitive Slave Act—since the spring of 1851. His words at Gettysburg, and the subsequent hard-fought amendments to the Constitution, were the final bridge beyond the liminal rupture to the restructuring of myth and institutions that followed in a second American constitutional revolution.[27]

Appendix of Tables

TABLE 1. Votes for president, 1840–1860, and Congress, 1854–1855
TABLE 2. Antislavery petitioning to Congress, 1833–1845
TABLE 3. Selected Senate votes, 31st Congress, 1st session, on the Compromise of 1850
TABLE 4. Selected House votes, 31st Congress, 1st session, on the Compromise of 1850
TABLE 5. Petitions regarding slavery to the 31st Congress, December 1849–March 1851
TABLE 6. Ohio counties and the petitioning to the 31st Congress, 1st session
TABLE 7. Girls named Eva born 1840–1860, by region
TABLE 8. African American narratives and antislavery literature published, compared with "Anti-Tom" proslavery novels: Page counts and advertising
TABLE 9. Petitions to 33rd Congress, 1st session, on the Kansas-Nebraska bill, January–August 1854
TABLE 10. House Votes on the Kansas-Nebraska Act, 33rd Congress, 1st session, March 21 and May 22, 1854
TABLE 11. Free states: House vote on Kansas-Nebraska Act, May 22, 1854, and reelection to the 34th Congress
TABLE 12. Vote for Speaker of the U.S. House of Representatives, Ballot 34, December 10, 1855
TABLE 13. Free state votes for Speaker, 34th Congress, December 10, 1855, and February 2, 1856
TABLE 14. The 1854–1855 free state voters and the election of Nathaniel Banks

Table 1. Votes for president, 1840-1860, and Congress, 1854-1855

	TOTAL VOTE	ANTISLAVERY PARTIES*		WHIG PARTY	AMERICAN, CONSTITUTIONAL UNION	DEMOCRATIC PARTY	SOUTHERN DEMOCRATIC PARTY	OTHER
1840		Birney		Harrison		Van Buren		
Free states	1,718,152	7,453	0.4%	900,423		810,276		
Slave states	720,303	0		375,160		319,369		
UNITED STATES	2,438,455	7,453	0.3%	1,275,583		1,129,645		
1844		Birney		Clay		Polk		
Free states	1,902,482	62,054	3.3%	911,374		926,979		
Slave states	805,010	0		388,783		412,591		
UNITED STATES	2,707,492	62,054	2.3%	1,300,157		1,339,570		
1848		Van Buren		Taylor		Cass		Other
Free states	2,028,529	291,264	14.4%	924,009		810,531		2,725
Slave states	848,289	211		436,226		411,822		30
UNITED STATES	2,876,818	291,475	10.1%	1,360,235		1,222,353		2,755
1852		Hale		Scott		Pierce		Other
Free states	2,331,976	155,450	6.7%	1,019,467		1,153,294		3,709
Slave states	827,664	349		366,951		452,649		7,715
UNITED STATES	3,159,640	155,799	4.9%	1,386,418		1,605,943		11,424
Votes for the 34th Congress, 1854-1855		Anti-Nebraska/ Republican/ Fusion		Whig	American	Democratic		Other
Free states	2,116,975	518,649	24.5%	494,348	211,550	866,871		25,557
Slave states	1,058,095	36,200	3.4%	4,842	460,936	539,790		16,327
UNITED STATES	3,175,070	554,849	17.5%	499,190	672,486	1,406,661		41,884
1856		Fremont			Fillmore	Buchanan		Other
Free states	2,962,268	1,340,073	45.2%		395,195	1,227,000		0
Slave states	1,086,243	595	0.1%		477,508	608,140		0
UNITED STATES	4,048,511	1,340,668	33.1%		872,703	1,835,140		3,094
1860		Lincoln			Bell	Douglas	Breckinridge	Other
Free states	3,404,279	1,829,598	53.7%		75,184	1,218,558	280,399	540
Slave states	1,276,988	26,395	2.1%		515,762	163,386	571,445	0
UNITED STATES	4,680,727	1,855,993	39.7%		590,946	1,381,944	851,844	540

* 1840–1844: Liberty; 1848: Free Soil; 1852: Free Democrat; 1854: Republican, Fusion, Anti-Nebraska Democrat; 1856–1860: Republican.

SOURCES: The American Presidency Project, https://www.presidency.ucsb.edu/statistics/elections (accessed May 2016); Michael J. Dubin, *United States Congressional Elections, 1788–1997: The Official Results of the 1st to the 105th Congresses* (Jefferson, N.C.: Harrison, 1998).

Table 2. Antislavery petitioning to Congress, 1833–1845

	PETITIONS	SIGNATURES				
PETITIONING BY CONGRESS	Total petitions	Total	Women	Percentage of women	Men	Signatures/petition
23rd Congress (1833–1835)	79	7,051	2,053	29.1%	4,998	89
24th Congress (1835–1837)	79	8,897	2,221	25.0%	5,098	113
25th Congress (1837–1839)	5,437	598,066	312,176	52.2%	275,486	110
26th Congress (1839–1841)	1,601	147,864	55,475	37.5%	88,796	92
27th Congress (1841–1843)	809	50,942	12,937	25.4%	38,005	63
28th Congress (1843–1845)	665	51,428	7,888	15.3%	37,626	77
TOTAL	8,670	864,248	392,750	45.4%	450,009	100
FOCUS OF PETITION						
Mixed focus: D.C./slave trade with gag rule/slave states, territories	1,431	146,725	74,807	51.0%	70,307	103
Slavery in D.C. only and D.C./slave trade	1,592	173,131	100,766	58.2%	68,866	109
Slave trade only	508	46,769	21,690	46.4%	23,364	92
Gag rule only	978	78,827	24,743	31.4%	53,699	81
Gag rule and slave states and territories	324	30,246	12,609	41.7%	17,579	93
Slave states and territories only	2,878	294,395	129,916	44.1%	157,448	102
Other/unknown	959	94,155	28,219	30.0%	58,646	98
TOTAL	8,670	864,248	392,750	45.4%	450,009	100

SOURCE: Carpenter-Moore dataset, https://dataverse.harvard.edu/dataset.xhtml?persistentId=doi:10.7910/DVN/27176 (accessed Nov. 12, 2015).

Table 3. Selected Senate votes, 31st Congress, 1st session, on the Compromise of 1850

	SENATORS IN 31/1	UTAH TERRITORY, JULY 31, 1850 (NO. 170; P. 1485-1)			TEXAS LEGIS., AUG. 9, 1850 (NO. 222; P. 1555-3)			ADMIT CALIFORNIA, AUG. 13, 1850 (NO. 230)			NEW MEXICO LEGIS., AUG. 15, 1850 (NO. 235; P. 1588-3)			FUGITIVE SLAVE ACT, AUG. 23, 1850 (NO. 246; P. 1630-2)			CALIFORNIA SENATORS SWORN IN SEPT. 10	ABOLISH SLAVE TRADE IN D.C., SEPT. 16, 1850 (NO. 281; P. 1830-3)		
		Yea	Nay	Did not vote	Yea	Nay	Did not vote	Yea	Nay	Did not vote	Yea	Nay	Did not vote	Yea	Nay	Did not vote		Yea	Nay	Did not vote
FREE STATES																				
Democrat	15	11	3	1	11	2	2	15	0	0	10	3	2	3	3	9	17	16	0	1
Free Soil	2	0	2	0	0	2	0	2	0	0	0	1	1	0	1	1	2	2	0	0
Whig	13	0	11	2	7	4	2	11	0	2	1	6	6	0	8	5	13	9	0	4
Subtotal	30	11	16	3	18	8	4	28	0	2	11	10	9	3	12	15	32	27	0	5
SLAVE STATES																				
Democrat	18	13	0	5	5	10	3	2	14	2	9	0	9	15	0	3		2	12	4
IR*	1	1	0	0	0	0	1	0	1	0	1	0	0	0	0	1		0	1	0
Whig	11	7	2	2	7	2	2	4	3	4	6	0	5	9	0	2		4	6	1
Subtotal	30	21	2	7	12	12	6	6	18	6	16	0	14	24	0	6		6	19	5
TOTAL	60	32	18	10	30	20	10	34	18	8	27	10	23	27	12	21		33	19	10

* IR: "Independent Republican" [Pratt, Maryland]

SOURCE: GovTrack: Tracking the United States Congress, https://www.govtrack.us/congress/votes#session=80 (accessed June 23, 2016).

Table 4. Selected House votes, 31st Congress, 1st session, on the Compromise of 1850

	REPRESENTATIVES IN 31/1	TEXAS-NEW MEXICO LEGIS. SEPT. 6, 1850–TO PASS S. 307 (NO. 357; P. 1764-3)			ADMIT CALIFORNIA SEPT. 7, 1850–TO PASS S. 169 (NO. 363; P. 1772-1)			UTAH TERRITORY SEPT. 7, 1850–TO PASS S. 225 (NO. 364; P. 1776-1)			CALIFORNIA REPRESENTATIVES SWORN IN SEPT. 11	FUGITIVE SLAVE ACT SEPT. 12, 1850–TO PASS S. 23 (NO. 377; P. 1817-1)			ABOLISH SLAVE TRADE IN D.C., SEPT. 17, 1850–TO PASS S. 226 (NO. 395; P. 1837-3)		
		Yea	Nay	Did not vote	Yea	Nay	Did not vote	Yea	Nay	Did not vote		Yea	Nay	Did not vote	Yea	Nay	Did not vote
FREE STATES																	
American	1	1	0	0	1	0	0	1	0	0	2	0	1	1	1	0	1
Democrat	50	31	13	6	46	0	4	30	13	7	51	28	15	8	47	0	4
Free Soil	9	0	9	0	9	0	0	0	9	0	9	0	9	0	6	0	3
Whig	77	24	45	8	67	0	10	10	48	19	77	3	51	23	66	0	11
Subtotal	137	56	67	14	123	0	14	41	70	26	139	31	76	32	120	0	19
SLAVE STATES																	
Democrat	62	27	29	6	10	46	6	32	15	15		54	0	8	2	45	15
Whig	28	25	1	2	17	10	1	24	0	4		24	0	4	2	14	12
Subtotal	90	52	30	8	27	56	7	56	15	19		78	0	12	4	59	27
TOTAL	227	108	97	22	150	56	21	97	85	45		109	76	44	124	59	46

SOURCE: GovTrack: Tracking the United States Congress, https://www.govtrack.us/congress/votes#session=80 (accessed June 23, 2016).

Table 5. Petitions regarding slavery to the 31st Congress, December 1849–March 1851

	1ST SESSION						2nd Session Dec.–Mar. 1851	31st Congress TOTAL
	Dec. 1949–Feb. 1850	Mar.	Apr.	May	June–Sept.	1st session total		
Abolish slavery and the slave trade in D.C.	35	134	311	131	55	666	7	673
Oppose fugitive slave bill	3	126	307	161	57	654	469	1,123
No slavery in territories, no new slave states	13	233	641	354	98	1,339	1	1,340
Slavery in D.C., territories	10	4	1	4	6	25	23	48
Fugitive slave bill, territories	0	2	1	1	0	4	0	4
Slavery in D.C., fugitive slave bill, territories	0	0	12	1	4	17	0	17
Other issues*	45	3	21	4	8	81	11	92
TOTAL	106	502	1,294	656	228	2,786	511	3,297
Proslavery, pro-Compromise, or colonizationist petitions	3	7	6	1	28	45	8	53

* Other issues: abolish slavery, abolish the domestic slave trade, dissolve the Union, relieve the free states from the burden of slavery, free Drayton and Sayres, return territory to Mexico, allow black men to serve in the militia and to carry the mails, reform the passport laws for black seamen.

SOURCE: House and Senate journals, 31st Congress.

Table 6. Ohio counties and the petitioning to the 31st Congress, 1st session

	COUNTIES KNOWN* TO HAVE SENT PETITIONS	ALL OTHER COUNTIES
Total counties	40	48
Counties with AASS Societies by 1838	32	18
Number of AASS Societies in 1838	171	47
Average Liberty vote in 1844	3.5%	1.0%
Average Free Soil vote in 1848	16.3%	3.9%

* Many of the petitions recorded in the House and Senate journals are not identified by town or county of origin, so this is a minimal count.

SOURCES: *Annual Report of the American Anti-Slavery Society*, 1836–1838; House and Senate journals, 31/1; County Voting Data, Inter-university Consortium for Political and Social Research.

Appendix of Tables

Table 7. Girls named "Eva" born 1840–1860, by region

	EVAS BORN BETWEEN 1841 AND 1850	EVAS PER 10,000 FEMALES BORN BETWEEN 1841 AND 1850	EVAS BORN BETWEEN 1851 AND 1860	EVAS PER 10,000 FEMALES BORN BETWEEN 1841 AND 1850	PERCENT OF REGION'S FREE POPULATION BORN IN GERMANY
New England	102	3.2	739	20.9	0.8%
Mid-Atlantic and Middle West	683	4.1	4596	21.4	6.9%
South	165	1.7	470	3.8	2.8%
Plains and Far West	1	0.3	66	10.8	5.3%

SOURCE: U.S. Census for 1860.

Table 8. African American narratives and antislavery literature published, compared with "Anti-Tom" proslavery novels: Page counts and advertising

	Total books published	Books per year	Total page count	BOOKS OF LESS THAN 200 PAGES			BOOKS OF MORE THAN 200 PAGES			
				Books published	Hits in AHN† for all books	Hits in AHN† per book	Books published	Percent of total books published	Hits in AHN† for all books	Hits in AHN† per book
African American narratives and antislavery literature published										
1826–1842	30	1.8	3,003	26	NC‡	NC‡	4	13%	NC‡	NC‡
1842–1851	26	2.6	2,519	24	61	2.5	2	3%	4	2
1852–1856	31	6.2	8,819	12	100	8.3	19	61%	1,144*	60.2
1857–1861	14	2.8	3,122	6	29	4.8	8	57%	136	17.0
"Anti-Tom" proslavery novels										
1852–1856	22	4.4	7,412	2	58	8.0	20	91%	978	48.9
1857–1861	10	2.0	3,889	0	—	—	10	100%	461	46.1

* Searching for "Uncle Tom's Cabin" produces 3,275 hits; searching for "Uncle Tom's Cabin, or Life among the Lowly" produces 65 hits; the lower number is used here.

† Hits in AHN: Number of results in search of America's Historical Newspapers "defined word string" from title in publication year and following year. This measure is dominated by advertisements (accessed May 2017).

‡ NC: Not calculated.

SOURCES: American Narratives and Antislavery Literature: North American Slave Narratives, accessed Nov. 2013, http://docsouth.unc.edu/neh/index.html (accessed Nov. 2013); The Antislavery Literature Project, http://antislavery.eserver.org/prose/ (accessed Nov. 2013), with the addition of Weld, *American Slavery as It Is*; Stowe, *Uncle Tom's Cabin* and *Key to Uncle Tom's Cabin*; Sumner, *White Slavery* (both editions). "Anti-Tom" Proslavery Novels: as listed in Gossett, *Uncle Tom's Cabin and American Culture* (Dallas: Southern Methodist University Press, 1985), 430–31, and discussed in Joy Jordan-Lake, *Whitewashing Uncle Tom's Cabin: Nineteenth-Century Women Novelists Respond to Stowe* (Nashville: Vanderbilt University Press, 2005), 1–24.

Table 9. Petitions to the 33rd Congress, 1st session, on the Kansas-Nebraska bill, January–August 1854

	PETITIONS TO THE SENATE				PETITIONS TO THE HOUSE				
	Jan.–Feb.	Mar.–May	June–Aug.	SENATE TOTAL	Jan.–Feb.	Mar.–May	June–Aug.	HOUSE TOTAL	SENATE AND HOUSE TOTAL
Preserve Missouri Compromise (only language)	122	140	0	262	67	735	0	802	1064
Preserve Missouri Compromise, oppose Nebraska bill, and/or other opposition to slavery extension	9	0	0	9	0	310	0	310	319
Oppose Nebraska bill, and/or other opposition to slavery extension	76	98	1	175	63	267	3	333	508
Repeal Fugitive Slave Act	12	4	26*	42	16	47	9	72	114
Other antislavery †	16	3	3	22	39	142	2	183	205
TOTAL	235	245	30	510	185	1501	14	1,700	2,210
Proslavery petitions				8				4	12

* Eleven petitions from Massachusetts.

† Other antislavery: predominantly against the slave trade, and against slavery and the slave trade in the District of Columbia.

SOURCE: House and Senate journals, 33rd Congress.

Table 10. House votes on the Kansas-Nebraska Act, 33rd Congress, 1st session, March 21 and May 22, 1854

	VOTES TO COMMIT NEBRASKA BILL TO THE COMMITTEE OF THE WHOLE, MAR. 21, 1854 (111–95) (YEA = VOTE TO STOP BILL)						
	Yea		Nay		Did not vote		Total
FREE STATES							
Whig	44	92%	0	0%	4	8%	48
Democrat	53	59%	26	29%	11	12%	90
Free Soil and Independent Democrat	6	100%	0	0%	0	0%	6
SLAVE STATES							
Whig	6	25%	15	63%	3	13%	24
Democrat	2	3%	54	82%	10	15%	66
TOTAL	111	47%	95	41%	28	12%	234
	VOTES ON THE KANSAS-NEBRASKA ACT, MAY 22, 1854 (113–100) (YEA = VOTE TO PASS BILL)						
	Nay		Yea		Did not vote		Total
FREE STATES							
Whig	44	92%	0	0%	4	8%	48
Democrat	42	47%	44	49%	4	4%	90
Free Soil and Independent Democrat	5	83%	0	0%	1	17%	6
SLAVE STATES							
Whig	7	29%	13	54%	4	17%	24
Democrat	2	3%	56	85%	8	12%	66
TOTAL	100	43%	113	48%	21	9%	234

SOURCE: Govtrack: Tracking the United States Congress, https://www.govtrack.us/congress/votes#session=80 (accessed July 9, 2017).

Table 11. Free states: House vote on Kansas-Nebraska Act, May 22, 1854, and reelection to the 34th Congress

	VOTES IN KANSAS-NEBRASKA ACT, MAY 22, 1854			REELECTED TO 34TH CONGRESS, BY 1854 VOTE ON KANSAS-NEBRASKA ACT		
Free State representatives	Yea	Nay	Did not vote	Yea	Nay	Did not vote
Whig	0	44	4	0	23	0
Democrat	44	42	4	8	8	0
Free Soil and Independent Democrat	0	5	1	0	3	0

SOURCES: GovTrack; Tracking the United States Congress, https://www.govtrack.us/congress/votes#session=80 (accessed July 9, 2017); Dubin, *United States Congressional Elections, 1788–1997*.

Table 12. Vote for Speaker of the U.S. House of Representatives, Ballot 34, December 10, 1855

	Total representatives, 34th Congress	BALLOT 34, DEC. 10, 1855				
		Banks, Republican (Mass.)	Fuller, Know Nothing (Pa.)	Richardson Democrat (Ill.)	Other	Did not vote
FREE STATES						
Whig	46	40	5	0	1	0
Know Nothing	27	18	4	1	1	3
Democrat	25	2	2	15	4	2
Fusion*	46	40	2	0	2	2
TOTAL	144	100	13	16	8	7
SLAVE STATES						
Whig	6	0	3	2	0	1
Know Nothing	27	0	15	2	8	2
Democrat	57	0	0	53	0	4
TOTAL	90	0	18	57	8	7

* Includes one Anti-Nebraska Democrat.

SOURCE: *House Journal*, 34th Congress, 85–87.

Table 13. Free state votes for Speaker, 34th Congress, December 10, 1855, and February 2, 1856

		BALLOT 133, FEB. 2, 1856			
		Banks, Republican (Mass.)	Aiken, Democrat [S.C.]	All Other	Did Not Vote
BALLOT 34, DEC. 10, 1855	Banks	94	1	1	4
	Richardson	1	13	1	1
	Other	6	2	7	6
	Not voting	2	2	0	3
	TOTAL	103	18	9	14

SOURCE: *House Journal*, 34th Congress, 85–87, 442–44.

Table 14. The 1854-1855 free state voters and the election of Nathaniel Banks

	TOTAL FREE STATE VOTES IN 1854-1855 ELECTION, BY PARTY	FREE STATE REPRESENTATIVES IN 34TH CONGRESS	REPRESENTATIVES VOTING FOR BANKS, DEC. 10, 1855		VOTES IN 1854 FOR REPRESENTATIVES VOTING FOR BANKS, DEC. 10, 1855	
Whig	494,348	46	40	87%	315,704	64%
Know Nothing/ American	211,550	27	18	67%	139,674	66%
Democratic	866,871	25	2	8%	18,831	2%
Republican and Fusion	518,649	46	40	87%	377,163	73%
TOTAL	2,091,418	144	100	69%	851,372	41%

SOURCES: Dubin, *United States Congressional Elections, 1788–1997*; *House Journal*, 34th Congress, 85–87.

Notes

Abbreviations

CES: Calvin E. Stowe

CG: *Congressional Globe* (cited by Congress/session; App. indicates that the document is in the appendix to that session's minutes)

CS: Charles Sumner

CWAL: *Collected Works of Abraham Lincoln*, 9 vols., ed. Roy P. Basler, Marion Dolores Pratt, and Lloyd A. Dunlap (Springfield, Ill.: Abraham Lincoln Association; New Brunswick: Rutgers University Press, 1953)

DCF: *The Diary of Calvin Fletcher*, 9 vols., ed. Gail Thornbrough, Dorothy L. Riker, and Paula Corpus (Indianapolis: Indiana Historical Society, 1972–1983)

DGTS: *The Diary of George Templeton Strong*, 4 vols., ed. Allan Nevins and Milton Hasley Thomas (New York: Macmillan, 1952)

DOHB: *Diary of Orville Hickman Browning*, 9 vols., ed. Theodore Calvin Pease and James G. Randall (Springfield: Illinois State Historical Library, 1925)

Era: *National Era* (Washington, D.C.)

HBS: Harriet Beecher Stowe

Hedrick, *Stowe*: Joan D. Hedrick, *Harriet Beecher Stowe: A Life* (New York: Oxford University Press, 1994)

House Journal: *Journal of the House of Representatives of the United States* . . . (Washington, D.C., 1826–) (cited by Congress/session)

HSP: Historical Society of Pennsylvania

HU: Harvard University

LC: Library of Congress

LLRWE: *The Later Lectures of Ralph Waldo Emerson, 1843–1871*, 2 vols., ed. Ronald A. Bosco and Joel Myerson (Athens: University of Georgia Press, 2001)

MHS: Massachusetts Historical Society

NA-SS: *National Anti-Slavery Standard* (New York)

Odell, *Annals*: George C. D. Odell, *Annals of the New York Stage*, 15 vols. (New York: Columbia University Press, 1927–1949)

Senate Journal: *Journal of the Senate of the United States* . . . (Washington, D.C., 1820–) (cited by Congress/session)

Stowe, *Life*: Charles Edward Stowe, *Life of Harriet Beecher Stowe compiled from Her Journals and Letters* (1889; repr., Detroit: Gale Research, 1967)

UTC: Harriet Beecher Stowe, *Uncle Tom's Cabin; or, Life Among the Lowly* Citations are to the two-volume 1852 edition (Boston: John W. Jewett, and Co., 1852) by volume, chapter, page; available at the University of Virginia "Uncle Tom's Cabin and American Culture" website, http://utc.iath.virginia.edu/uncletom/uthp.html.

Preface and Acknowledgments

1. This early version has appeared as "Party, Nation, and Cultural Rupture: The Crisis of the American Civil War," in *Practicing Democracy: Popular Politics in the United States from the Constitution to the Civil War*, ed. Daniel Peart and Adam I. P. Smith (Charlottesville: University of Virginia Press, 2015), 72–95.

Introduction: Confluence, Creolization, Liminal Crisis, and the Antislavery North

1. Daniel Webster, "Speech at Marshfield" (Sept. 1, 1848), in *The Writings and Speeches of Daniel Webster*, 18 vols. (Boston: Little, Brown, 1903), 4:135; *CG* 31/1, App., 269–76.
2. *CG* 31/1, App., 768.
3. *Boston Daily Atlas*, Feb. 8, 1856; *NA-SS*, Feb. 9, 1856; CS to Charles Francis Adams, Feb. 5, 1856; Theodore Parker to CS, Feb. 16, 1856; Sumner Papers, HU; *Manchester (N.H.) Daily Mirror*, Mar. 26, 1856.
4. *DGTS*, 3:67.
5. *DGTS*, 3:67–68.
6. *Frederick Douglass's Paper*, Mar. 23, 1855, 3. See also Frederick Douglass, *The Anti-Slavery Movement. A Lecture by Frederick Douglass, before the Rochester Ladies Anti-Slavery Society* (Rochester: Lee, Mann, and Co., 1855), 39–40.
7. Abraham Lincoln, First Inaugural Address, Mar. 4, 1861; Second Inaugural Address, Mar. 4, 1865, Avalon Project website, Yale Law School, http://avalon.law.yale.edu/subject_menus/inaug.asp.
8. Declaration of the Immediate Causes Which Induce and Justify the Secession of South Carolina from the Federal Union, Dec. 24, 1860, Avalon Project website, Yale Law School, http://avalon.law.yale.edu/19th_century/csa_scarsec.asp.
9. For several recent indications of a new departure, see Nicholas P. Wood, "Jefferson's Legacy, Race Science, and Religious Violence in Jabez Hammond's Abolitionist Fiction," *Early American Studies* 14 (2016): 568–609; John Frederick Bell, "Poetry's Place in the Crisis and Compromise of 1850," *Journal of the Civil War Era* 5 (2015): 399–421; and Michael E. Woods, *Emotional and Sectional Conflict in the Antebellum United States* (New York: Cambridge University Press, 2014).
10. Christopher J. Smith, *The Creolization of American Culture: William Sydney Mount and the Roots of Blackface Minstrelsy* (Urbana: University of Illinois Press, 2013).
11. *DGTS*, 3:68.
12. James M. McPherson, *Abraham Lincoln and the Second American Revolution* (New York: Oxford University Press, 1991), 3–42; Garry Wills, *Lincoln at Gettysburg: The Words That Remade America* (New York: Simon & Schuster, 1992); Christopher L. Tomlins, *Freedom Bound: Law, Labor, and Civic Identity in Colonizing English America, 1580–1865* (New York: Cambridge University Press, 2010), 509–69; Richard Franklin Bensel, *Yankee Leviathan: The Origins of Central State Authority in America, 1859–1877* (New York: Cambridge University Press, 1990); Michael Vorenberg, *Final Freedom: The Civil War, the Abolition of Slavery, and the Thirteenth Amendment* (New York: Cambridge University Press, 2001).
13. For excellent reviews of the long literature on Civil War causation, see Kenneth M. Stampp, "The Irrepressible Conflict," in *The Imperiled Union: Essays on*

the Background of the Civil War (New York: Oxford University Press, 1980), 191–246; Frank Towers, "Partisans, New History, and Modernization: The Historiography of the Civil War's Causes, 1861–2011," *Journal of the Civil War Era* 1 (2011): 237–64; Michael E. Woods, "What Twenty-first-Century Historians Have Said about the Causes of Disunion: A Civil War Sesquicentennial Review of the Recent Literature," *Journal of American History* 99 (2012): 415–39.

14. *The Irrepressible Conflict: Speech by William H. Seward, delivered at Rochester, Monday, October 27, 1858* ([New York]: Republican Executive Congressional Committee, 1858), 1–2.

15. The classic texts in the fundamentalist genre are Eugene D. Genovese, *The Political Economy of Slavery: Studies in the Economy and Society of the Slave South* (New York: Vintage Books, 1965); Eric Foner, *Free Soil, Free Labor, Free Men: The Ideology of the Republican Party before the Civil War* (New York: Oxford University Press, 1970); for overviews, see Stampp, "The Irrepressible Conflict"; Towers, "Partisans, New History, and Modernization"; and Woods, "What Twenty-first-Century Historians Have Said about the Causes of Disunion."

16. David Goldfield, *America Aflame: How the Civil War Created a Nation* (New York: Bloomsbury Press, 2011), is one example. For a review, see Yael A. Sternhell, "Revisionism Reinvented? The Antiwar Turn in Civil War Scholarship," *Journal of the Civil War Era* 3 (2013): 239–56.

17. See the essays in L. Diane Barnes, Brian Schoen, and Frank Towers, eds., *The Old South's Modern Worlds: Slavery, Region, and Nation in the Age of Progress* (New York: Oxford University Press, 2011); Sven Beckert and Seth Rockman, eds., *Slavery's Capitalism: A New History of American Economic Development* (Philadelphia: University of Pennsylvania Press, 2018); and James L. Huston, *Calculating the Value of the Union: Slavery, Property Rights, and the Economic Origins of the Civil War* (Chapel Hill: University of North Carolina Press, 2003); Joshua D. Rothman, *Flush Times and Fever Dreams: A Story of Capitalism and Slavery in the Age of Jackson* (Athens: University of Georgia Press, 2012); Walter Johnson, *River of Dark Dreams: Slavery and Empire in the Cotton Kingdom* (Cambridge: Harvard University Press, 2013); Edward E. Baptist, *The Half Has Never Been Told: Slavery and the Making of American Capitalism* (New York: Basic Books, 2014).

18. Andrew Delbanco, *The War before the War: Fugitive Slaves and the Struggle for America's Soul from the Revolution to the Civil War* (New York: Penguin, 2018); R. J. M. Blackett, *The Captive's Quest for Freedom: Fugitive Slaves, the 1850 Fugitive Slave Law, and the Politics of Slavery* (New York: Cambridge University Press, 2018); Manisha Sinha, *The Slave's Cause: A History of Abolition* (New Haven: Yale University Press, 2016); Eric Foner, *Gateway to Freedom: The Hidden History of the Underground Railroad* (New York: W. W. Norton, 2015); Cheryl Janifer LaRoche, *Free Black Communities and the Underground Railroad: The Geography of Resistance* (Urbana: University of Illinois Press, 2013); Scott Hancock, "Crossing Freedom's Faultline: The Underground Railroad and Recentering African Americans in Civil War Causality," *Civil War History* 59 (2013): 169–205; Steven Hahn, *The Political Worlds of Slavery and Freedom* (Cambridge: Harvard University Press, 2009).

19. Edward Ayers, *What Caused the Civil War? Reflections on the South and Southern*

History (New York: W. W. Norton, 2005), 132–42, quote from 138. See also the discussions in Elizabeth Varon, *Disunion: The Coming of the American Civil War, 1789–1859* (Chapel Hill: University of North Carolina Press, 2008), 3–4.

20. Here see the arguments on "forces" and contingency made by James L. Huston in "Did the Tug Have to Come? A Critique of the New Revisionism of the Secession Winter," *Civil War History* 62 (2016): 247–83, esp. 276–83.

21. Here see Staunton Lynd, "The Compromise of 1787," *Political Science Quarterly* 81 (1966): 225–50; and a vast more recent literature: Paul Finkelman, *An Imperfect Union: Slavery, Federalism, and Comity* (Chapel Hill: University of North Carolina Press, 1981); Donald Robinson, *Slavery in the Structure of American Politics, 1765–1820* (New York: W. W. Norton, 1971); Don E. Fehrenbacher, *The Slaveholding Republic: An Account of the United States Government's Relations to Slavery* (New York: Oxford University Press, 2001); Matthew Mason, *Slavery and Politics in the Early American Republic* (Chapel Hill: University of North Carolina Press, 2006); David Waldstreicher, *Slavery's Constitution: From Revolution to Ratification* (New York: Hill and Wang, 2009); George Van Cleve, *A Slaveholders' Union: Slavery, Politics, and the Constitution in the Early Republic* (Chicago: University of Chicago Press, 2010); Sean Wilentz, *No Property in Man: Slavery and Antislavery at the Nation's Founding* (Cambridge: Harvard University Press, 2018).

22. For the key work in what can be called the "Slave Power" interpretation, see Richard H. Sewell, *Ballots for Freedom: Antislavery Politics in the United States, 1837–1860* (New York: Oxford University Press, 1976); Leonard L. Richards, *The Slave Power: The Free North and the Slave Power, 1780–1860* (Baton Rouge: Louisiana State University Press, 2000); Fehrenbacher, *The Slaveholding Republic*; Van Cleve, *A Slaveholders' Union*; David F. Ericson, *Slavery in the American Republic: Developing the Federal Government, 1791–1861* (Lawrence: University Press of Kansas, 2011); James Oakes, *Freedom National: The Destruction of Slavery in the United States, 1861–1865* (New York: W. W. Norton, 2013); James Oakes, *The Scorpion's Sting: Antislavery and the Coming of the Civil War* (New York: W. W. Norton, 2014); Corey M. Brooks, *Liberty Power: Antislavery Third Parties and the Transformation of American Politics* (Chicago: University of Chicago Press, 2016); Carl Lawrence Paulus, *The Slaveholding Crisis: Fear of Insurrection and the Coming of the Civil War* (Baton Rouge: Louisiana State University Press, 2017). Michael Perman, *Pursuit of Unity: A Political History of the American South* (Chapel Hill: University of North Carolina Press, 2009); Brian Schoen, *The Fragile Fabric of Union: Cotton, Federal Politics, and the Global Origins of the Civil War* (Baltimore: Johns Hopkins University Press, 2009); Matthew Karp, *This Vast Southern Empire: Slaveholders at the Helm of American Foreign Policy* (Cambridge: Harvard University Press, 2016)); Alice Elizabeth Malavasic, *The F Street Mess: How Southern Senators Rewrote the Kansas-Nebraska Act* (Chapel Hill: University of North Carolina Press, 2017); Adam I. P. Smith, *The Stormy Present: Conservatism and the Problem of Slavery in Northern Politics, 1846–1865* (Chapel Hill: University of North Carolina Press, 2017); Elizabeth R. Varon, *Armies of Deliverance: A New History of the Civil War* (New York: Oxford University Press, 2019).

23. Michael F. Holt, *The Fate of Their Country: Politicians, Slavery Extension, and the Coming of the Civil War* (New York: Hill and Wang, 2004), 106–7; William E.

Gienapp, *The Origins of the Republican Party* (New York: Oxford University Press, 1987), 72; Foner, *Free Soil*, 94–95; Varon, *Disunion*, 107. Quote from "Appeal" in *CG* 33/1, 281–182. For important reviews of the political histories of the Kansas-Nebraska Act, see Roy F. Nichols, "The Kansas-Nebraska Act: A Century of Historiography," *Mississippi Valley Historical Review* 43 (1956): 187–212; Dick Johnson, "Along the Twisted Road to Civil War: History and the 'Appeal of the Independent Democrats,'" *Old Northwest* 4 (1978): 119–41; and Yonatan Eyal, "With His Eyes Open: Stephen A. Douglas and the Kansas-Nebraska Disaster of 1854," *Journal of the Illinois State Historical Society* 91 (1998): 175–216.

24. Quotes from Holt, *The Fate of Their Country*, 107; Huston, *Calculating the Value of the Union*, 195; Stephen E. Maislish, "The Meaning of Nativism and the Crisis of the Union: The Know-Nothing Movement in the Antebellum North," in *Essays on American Antebellum Politics, 1840–1860*, ed. Stephen E. Maizlish and John J. Kushma (College Station: Texas A&M University Press, 1982), 185; William E. Gienapp, "The Crisis of American Democracy: The Political System and the Coming of the Civil War," in *Why the Civil War Came*, ed. Gabor S. Boritt (New York: Oxford University Press, 1997), 102. See also Gienapp, *Origins*, 448, where he called it a "remarkable performance." Mark Neely is not as convinced about the impact of the "Appeal"; see "The Kansas-Nebraska Act in American Political Culture: The Road to Bladensburg and the *Appeal of the Independent Democrats*," in *The Nebraska-Kansas Act of 1854*, ed. John R. Wunder and Joan M. Moss (Lincoln: University of Nebraska Press, 2008), 13–46.

25. This is, of course, not entirely new news; the great revisionist David Potter wrote that "the northern attitude toward slavery was never quite the same after reading *Uncle Tom's Cabin*." David Potter, *The Impending Crisis, 1848–1861* (New York: Harper & Row, 1976), 140. He and a host of historians have made passing reference to this cultural transition. I make the shape of this shift and its impact on politics the central problem.

26. For my wider thinking here, see John L. Brooke, "Consent, Civil Society, and the Public Sphere in the Age of Revolution and the Early American Republic," in *Beyond the Founders: New Approaches to the Political History of the Early American Republic*, ed. Jeffery L. Pasley, Andrew W. Robertson, and David Waldstreicher (Chapel Hill: University of North Carolina Press, 2004), 207–50.

27. Arnold van Gennep, *The Rites of Passage*, trans. M. B. Vizedom and G. L. Caffee (Chicago: University of Chicago Press, 1960); Victor Turner, *Dramas, Fields, and Metaphor: Symbolic Action in Human Society* (Ithaca: Cornell University Press, 1974); Victor Turner, *The Forest of Symbols; Aspects of Ndembu Ritual* (Ithaca: Cornell University Press, 1967); Victor Turner, *The Ritual Process: Structure and Anti-Structure* (Ithaca: Cornell University Press, 1977). The term "betwixt and between" is Turner's (*Forest of Symbols*, 93). Bjørn Thomassen, *Liminality and the Modern: Living through the In-Between* (Farnham, Surrey: Ashgate, 2014), 21–88, provides the most comprehensive review of the intellectual history of liminality theory.

28. William H. Sewell Jr., *Logics of History: Social Theory and Social Transformation* (Chicago: University of Chicago Press, 2005), 225–70; Arpad Szakolczai, "Liminality and Experience: Structuring Transitory Situations and Transformative Events,"

International Political Anthropology 2 (2009): 141–72; Arpad Szakolczai, *Comedy and the Public Sphere: The Rebirth of Theatre as Comedy and the Genealogy of the Modern Public Arena* (New York: Routledge, 2013); Bjørn Thomassen, "Notes towards an Anthropology of Political Revolutions," *Comparative Studies in Society and History* 54 (2012): 679–706; Thomassen, *Liminality and the Modern*.

29. Turner, *Dramas, Fields, and Metaphors*, 25–32; Marshall D. Sahlins, *Historical Metaphors and Mythical Realities: Structure in the Early History of the Sandwich Islands Kingdom* (Ann Arbor: University of Michigan Press, 1981); Sewell, *Logics of History*, 197–224. On how antebellum Americans viewed their own time in terms of crisis and "normalcy," see Smith, *The Stormy Present*, 14–16.

30. Sewell, *Logics of History*, 244–56, 262–69; Turner, *Dramas, Fields, and Metaphors*, 37–42, 275–94; Turner, *The Ritual Process*, 94–130; Turner, *Forest of Symbols*, 93–111; Max Weber, *The Theory of Social and Economic Organization*, trans. A. M. Henderson and Talcott Parsons (New York: Free Press, 1947), 358–78, 386–92. See also the essays in the "Special Section: Logics of History," *Social Science History* 32 (2008): 535–95; Robin Wagener-Pacifici, "Theorizing the Restlessness of Events," *American Journal of Sociology* 115 (2010): 1351–86; Sabini Mihelj, "National Media Events: From Displays of Unity to Enactments of Division," *European Journal of Cultural Studies* 11 (2008): 471–88; Thomas Scheffer, "Event and Process: An Exercise in Analytical Ethnography," *Human Studies* 30 (2007): 167–97; Elizabeth S. Clemons, "Toward a Historicized Sociology: Theorizing Events, Processes, and Emergence," *Annual Review of Sociology* 33 (2007): 527–49; Michael D. Kennedy, "Evolution and Event in History and Social Change: Gerhard Lenski's Critical Theory," *Sociological Theory* 22 (2004): 315–27. With the exception of Turner's *Forest of Symbols* and *Ritual Process*, all of these works and others cited earlier develop the premise that liminality can be at work in large-scale modern societies.

31. For a few examples, see *Detroit Free Press*, July 22, 1854; *Sauk County (Wisc.) Standard*, Aug. 30, 1854; *Jackson (Mich.) American Citizen*, Oct. 25, 1854.

32. There is now a veritable school of slavery borderland studies, including Blackett, *The Captive's Quest for Freedom*; Patrick Rael, *Black Identity and Black Protest in the Antebellum North* (Chapel Hill: University of North Carolina Press, 2002); James Oliver Horton and Lois E. Horton, *In Hope of Liberty: Culture, Community, and Protest among Northern Free Blacks, 1700–1860* (New York: Oxford University Press, 1998); LaRoche, *Free Black Communities*; David G. Smith, *On the Edge of Freedom: The Fugitive Slave Issue in South Central Pennsylvania, 1820–1870* (New York: Fordham University Press, 2013); Mathew Salafia, *Slavery's Borderland: Freedom and Bondage along the Ohio River* (Philadelphia: University of Pennsylvania Press, 2013); Max Grivno, *Gleanings of Freedom: Free and Slave Labor along the Mason-Dixon Line, 1790–1860* (Urbana: University of Illinois Press, 2011); James J. Gigantino, *The Ragged Road to Abolition: Slavery and Freedom in New Jersey, 1775–1865* (Philadelphia: University of Pennsylvania Press, 2014); Andrew K. Diemer, *The Politics of Black Citizenship: Free African Americans in the Mid-Atlantic Borderland, 1817–1863* (Athens: University of Georgia Press, 2016); Richard S. Newman, 'Lucky to be born in Pennsylvania': Free Soil, Fugitive Slaves and the Making of Pennsylvania's Anti-Slavery Borderland," *Slavery & Abolition* 32 (2011): 413–30.

33. Charles B. Dew, *Apostles of Disunion: Southern Secession Commissioners and the Causes of the Civil War* (Charlottesville: University of Virginia Press, 2001); Hancock, "Crossing Freedom's Faultline"; William A. Link, *Roots of Secession: Slavery and Politics in Antebellum Virginia* (Chapel Hill: University of North Carolina Press, 2003), 97–120.

34. John Ashworth, *Slavery, Capitalism, and Politics in the Antebellum Republic*, vol. 2 (New York: Cambridge University Press, 1995), 35–44; William Freehling, *The Road to Disunion*, vol. 1, *Secessionists at Bay, 1776–1854* (New York: Cambridge University Press, 1990), 17–19, 74–76, 333–35, 497–510. Woods, "What Twenty-first-Century Historians Have Said," 433–35, provides a synthesis of the Freehling-Ashworth thesis. For white "free soil" racism and hostility to abolitionism, see Eugene H. Berwanger, *The Frontier against Slavery: Western Anti-Negro Prejudice and the Slavery Extension Controversy* (Urbana: University of Illinois Press, 1967); for the new Slave Power synthesis, see the works by Sewell and others cited earlier. For white southerners, see Victoria E. Bynum, *The Free State of Jones: Mississippi's Longest Civil War* (Chapel Hill: University of North Carolina Press, 2001).

35. The definition of hybridity, ethnogenesis, or "creolization" is a complex terrain in the current literature. My essential premise is that all societies in the wider imperial Atlantic world were "creole," in the sense that they developed in new face-to-face combinations of peoples, languages, and power. I use "creolization" rather than "hybridity" or ethnogenesis," two important related frameworks, because the latter two suggest a degree of completeness and finality, while I mean to invoke an uneven, incomplete, and very much contested developing process. For the specifics of the argument for the United States, I am indebted to Smith, *The Creolization of American Culture*. Brian Roberts, *Blackface Nation: Race, Reform, and Identity in American Popular Music, 1812–1925* (Chicago: University of Chicago Press, 2017), can be read as an account of "creolization," stressing, however, terms of hierarchy, appropriation, and containment. For important statements of the wider discussion of creolization, see James Sidbury and Jorge Cañizares-Esguerra, "Mapping Ethnogenesis in the Early Modern Atlantic," *William and Mary Quarterly*, 3d ser., 68 (2011): 181–208, and the forum responses in the same issue; and the articles in Ralph Bauer and José Antonio Mazzotti, eds., *Creole Subjects in the Colonial Americas: Empires, Texts, Identities* (Chapel Hill: Omohundro Institute of Early American History and Culture by the University of North Carolina Press, 2009).

36. For this essential insight, see Eric Lott, *Love and Theft: Blackface Minstrelsy and the American Working Class* (New York: Oxford University Press, 1993), 111.

37. Douglass, *The Anti-Slavery Movement*, 39–40.

Chapter 1: Structures Challenged

1. Thomas Jefferson to John Holmes, Apr. 22, 1820, Jefferson Papers, Founders Online, National Archives, https://founders.archives.gov/.

2. Martin Van Buren to Thomas Ritchie, Jan. 13, 1827, Martin Van Buren Papers, Library of Congress, reprinted in *The Age of Jackson*, ed. Robert Remini (Columbia: University of South Carolina Press, 1972), 3–7, quote from 5–6.

3. William W. Freehling, *The Road to Disunion*, vol. 1, *Secessionists at Bay, 1776–1854* (New York: Oxford University Press, 1990).

4. T. H. Breen, "Making History: The Force of Public Opinion and the Last Years of Slavery in Revolutionary Massachusetts," in *Through a Glass Darkly: Reflections on Personal Identity in Early America*, ed. Ronald Hoffman, Mechal Sobel, and Frederika J. Teute (Chapel Hill: University of North Carolina Press, 1997), 67–95.

5. George William Van Cleve, *A Slaveholder's Union: Slavery, Politics, and the Constitution in the Early American Republic* (Chicago: University of Chicago Press, 2010), 38.

6. Steven M. Wise, *"Though the Heavens May Fall": The Landmark Trial That Led to the End of Human Slavery* (Cambridge: Da Capo Press, 2005).

7. On Mansfield and the Declaratory Act, see P. D. G. Thomas, *British Politics and the Stamp Act Crisis* (Oxford: Clarendon, 1975), 196, 244, 246; on Somerset in the nineteenth century, see Paul Finkelman, *An Imperfect Union: Slavery, Federalism, and Comity* (Chapel Hill: University of North Carolina Press, 1981); William M. Wiecek, *The Sources of Antislavery Constitutionalism in America, 1760–1848* (Ithaca: Cornell University Press, 1977).

8. James Oakes, *The Scorpion's Sting: Antislavery and the Coming of the Civil War* (New York: W. W. Norton, 2014), 115–31.

9. Van Cleve, *A Slaveholder's Union*, 38–39, 52–56, 168–69; David Waldstreicher, *Slavery's Constitution: From Revolution to Ratification* (New York: Hill and Wang, 2009), 21–56; David Waldstreicher, "The Mansfieldian Moment: Slavery, the Constitution, and American Political Traditions," *Rutgers Law Journal* 43 (2013): 471–84.

10. C. C. Pinckney in Jonathan Elliot, *The Debates in the Several State Conventions on the Adoption of the Federal Constitution*, 5:357 (July 23), https://memory.loc.gov/ammem/amlaw/lwed.html; Van Cleve, *A Slaveholder's Union*, 169.

11. *Debates which Arose in the House of Representatives of South Carolina on the Constitution framed for the United States* . . . (Charleston: A. E. Miller, 1831), 28, 30; Sean Wilentz, *No Property in Man: Slavery and Antislavery at the Nation's Founding* (Cambridge: Harvard University Press, 2018), 136–40.

12. *Annals of Congress*, 6th Cong., 1st sess., 231. See Don E. Fehrenbacher, *The Slaveholding Republic: An Account of the United States Government's Relations to Slavery* (New York: Oxford University Press, 2001), 11.

13. Richard Newman, "Prelude to the Gag Rule: Southern Reaction to Antislavery Petitions in the First Federal Congress, *Journal of the Early Republic* 16 (1996): 571–99; Van Cleve, *A Slaveholder's Union*, 191–203; Robert G. Parkinson, "'Manifest Signs of Passion': The First Federal Congress, Antislavery, and Legacies of the Revolutionary War," in *Contesting Slavery: The Politics of Bondage and Freedom in the New American Nation*, ed. John Craig Hammond and Matthew Mason (Charlottesville: University of Virginia Press, 2011), 49–68; *Annals of Congress*, 1st Cong., 2nd sess., 1242–46 (James Jackson, William L. Smith, Feb. 12, 1790).

14. Stanley Elkins and Eric McKitrick, *The Age of Federalism: The Early American Republic, 1788–1800* (New York: Oxford University Press, 1993), 136–53; Joseph Ellis, *Founding Brothers: The Revolutionary Generation* (New York: Knopf, 2000), 48–119.

15. Maeva Marcus et al., eds., *The Documentary History of the Supreme Court of the*

United States, 1789–1800, vol. 7, *Cases: 1796–1797* (New York: Columbia University Press, 2003), quote from 404 (*Hylton v. United States*, 358–505).

16. Matthew Mason, "'Necessary but Not Sufficient': Revolutionary Ideology and Antislavery Action in the Early Republic," in Hammond and Mason, *Contesting Slavery*, 11–32; Richard S. Newman, *The Transformation of American Abolitionism: Fighting Slavery in the Early Republic* (Chapel Hill: University of North Carolina Press, 2002), 16–59; David N. Gellman, *Emancipating New York: The Politics of Slavery and Freedom, 1777–1827* (Baton Rouge: Louisiana State University Press, 2006).

17. Matthew Mason, *Slavery and Politics in the Early American Republic* (Chapel Hill: University of North Carolina Press, 2006), 36–62; Leonard L. Richards, *The Slave Power: The Free North and the Slave Power, 1780–1860* (Baton Rouge: Louisiana State University Press, 2000), 28–51.

18. Nicholas Guyatt, *Bind Us Apart: How Enlightened Americans Invented Racial Segregation* (New York: Basic Books, 2016), 247–80; P. J. Staudenraus, *The African Colonization Movement, 1816–1865* (New York: Columbia University Press, 1961).

19. Manisha Sinha, *The Slave's Cause: A History of Abolition* (New Haven: Yale University Press, 2016), 131–44; James Oliver Horton and Lois E. Horton, *In Hope of Liberty: Culture, Community, and Protest among Northern Free Blacks, 1700–1860* (New York: Oxford University Press, 1997), 125–54.

20. Sinha, *The Slave's Cause*, 137–40.

21. These congressional petitions were just the tip of the iceberg of a massive volume of petitions recorded in the Race and Slavery Petitions Project, Digital Library of American Slavery, UNC Greensboro, https://library.uncg.edu/slavery/petitions/.

22. Sinha, *The Slave's Cause*, 144–59; Newman, *The Transformation of American Abolitionism*, 89–96.

23. *Freedom's Journal*, Mar. 16, 1827, Dec. 19, 1828, Mar. 14, 28, 1829; David Walker, *Walker's Appeal, in Four Articles; Together with a Preamble, to the Coloured Citizens of the World, but in Particular, and Very Expressly, to Those of the United States of America, Written in Boston, State of Massachusetts, September 28, 1829*, 3rd ed. (Boston, 1830), 49, 85, 86; Timothy Patrick McCarthy, "'To Plead Our Own Cause': Black Print Culture and the Origins of American Abolitionism," in Timothy Patrick McCarthy and John Stauffer, *Prophets of Protest: Reconsidering the History of American Abolitionism* (New York: New Press, 2006), 114–44.

24. David F. Allmendinger, *Nat Turner and the Rising in Southampton County* (Baltimore: Johns Hopkins University Press, 2014), 3; Louis P. Masur, *1831: Year of Eclipse* (New York: Hill and Wang, 2001), 9–21.

25. Robert Pierce Forbes, *The Missouri Compromise and Its Aftermath: Slavery and the Meaning of America* (Chapel Hill: University of North Carolina Press, 2007), 33–120; John R. Van Atta, *Wolf by the Ears: The Missouri Crisis, 1819–1821* (Baltimore: Johns Hopkins University Press, 2015); Richards, *The Slave Power*, 49–54, 74–80; Mason, *Slavery and Politics*, 177–212; Van Cleve, *A Slaveholder's Union*, 225–66.

26. James L. Huston, *Calculating the Value of the Union: Slavery, Property Rights, and the Economic Origins of the Civil War* (Chapel Hill: University of North Carolina Press, 2003), 27–30.

27. Martin Van Buren, Washington, D.C., to Thomas Ritchie, Richmond, Jan.

13, 1827, Martin Van Buren Papers, Library of Congress; for a general discussion of parties and slavery, see Michael Holt, *The Political Crisis of the 1850s* (New York: W. W. Norton, 1978), 17–38.

28. Jeffrey L. Pasley, *"The Tyranny of Printers": Newspaper Politics in the Early American Republic* (Charlottesville: University Press of Virginia, 2001).

29. Joel H. Silbey, *The Partisan Imperative: The Dynamics of American Politics before the Civil War* (New York: Oxford University Press, 1985); Joel H. Silbey, *The American Political Nation, 1838–1893* (Stanford: Stanford University Press, 1991). Quote from Joel Silbey, "'To One or Another of These Parties Every Man Belongs': The American Political Experience from Andrew Jackson to the Civil War," in *Contesting Democracy: Substance and Structure in American Political History, 1775–2000*, ed. Byron E. Shafer and Anthony J. Badger (Lawrence: University Press of Kansas, 2001), 68.

30. Donald Ratcliffe, *The One-Party Presidential Contest: Adams, Jackson, and 1824's Five-Horse Race* (Lawrence: University Press of Kansas, 2015).

31. Implied in Taylor on the Carriage Tax (Marcus et al., *Documentary History of the Supreme Court*, 7:404); explicit in Nathaniel Macon to Bartlett Yancy, Mar. 8, Apr. 15, 1818, in Edwin Mood Wilson, *The Congressional Career of Nathaniel Macon*, no. 2 of *James Sprunt Historical Monographs* (Chapel Hill: University of North Carolina Press, 1900), 46–47, 48–50 (cited in Mason, *Slavery and Politics*, 162–63). On Jackson's policies, see Sean Wilentz, *The Rise of American Democracy: Jefferson to Lincoln* (New York: W. W. Norton, 2005), 359–91.

32. Martin Van Buren, Washington, D.C., to Thomas Ritchie, Richmond, Jan. 13, 1827, Martin Van Buren Papers, Library of Congress; Duff Green to William Snowden, Nov. 16, 1827, and Van Buren to Worden Pope, Jan. 4, 1828, as quoted in Forbes, *The Missouri Compromise*, 215. Here and later in this chapter I follow Donald J. Ratcliffe, "The Decline of Antislavery Politics, 1815–1840," in Hammond and Mason, *Contesting Slavery*, 267–90.

33. *Genius of Universal Emancipation*, Jan. 8, 15, 1830; Henry Mayer, *All on Fire: William Lloyd Garrison and the Abolition of Slavery* (New York: St. Martin's Press, 1998), 82–94, 127–31, 171, 173–77.

34. Mary Hershberger, "Mobilizing Women, Anticipating Abolition: The Struggle against Indian Removal in the 1830s," *Journal of American History* 86 (1999): 35–40; Richard R. John, "Taking Sabbatarianism Seriously: The Postal System, the Sabbath, and the Transformation of American Political Culture," *Journal of the Early Republic* 10 (1990): 517–67; Michael P. Young, *Bearing Witness against Sin: The Evangelical Birth of the American Social Movement* (Chicago: University of Chicago Press, 2006).

35. Bertram Wyatt-Brown, *Lewis Tappan and the Evangelical War on Slavery* (Baton Rouge: Louisiana State University Press, 1969), 142–45, 149–63; Newman, *The Transformation of American Abolitionism*, 131–75. Petition numbers are from the Carpenter-Moore dataset, https://dataverse.harvard.edu/dataset.xhtml?persistentId =doi:10.7910/DVN/27176; see Daniel Carpenter and Colin D. Moore, "When Canvassers Became Activists: Antislavery Petitioning and the Political Mobilization of American Women," *American Political Science Review* 108 (2014): 379–498. I am indebted to Kevin Vrevich for locating this dataset. These numbers are congruent with both an analysis of the petitioning to the 25th Congress, as reported in the

House and Senate journals, conducted by myself and Cameron Shriver, and with the petition signature numbers reported in the *Fifth Annual Report of the Executive Committee of the American Anti-Slavery Society with the minutes of the meetings of the society for business, and the Speeches Delivered at the anniversary meeting on the 8th May, 1838* (New York: William S. Dorr, 1838), 48.

36. *Fifth Annual Report of the Executive Committee of the American Anti-Slavery Society*, 133–45, 147–51.

37. Petition numbers are from the Carpenter-Moore dataset, Carpenter and Moore, "When Canvassers Became Activists"; William Lee Miller, *Arguing about Slavery: The Great Battle in the United States Congress* (New York: Knopf, 1996), 301–5; Newman, *The Transformation of American Abolitionism*, 152–75; Susan Zaeske, *Signatures of Citizenship: Petitioning, Antislavery, and Women's Political Identity* (Chapel Hill: University of North Carolina Press, 2003), 90–92, 97–103, 119. The classic account of the 1836–1839 petitioning campaign is Gilbert H. Barnes, *The Antislavery Impulse: 1830–1844* (1933; New York: Harcourt, Brace, and World, 1964), 121–45.

38. David Grimsted, *American Mobbing, 1828–1861: Toward Civil War* (New York: Oxford University Press, 1998), 3–71; Leonard L. Richards, *Gentlemen of Property and Standing: Anti-Abolition Mobs in Jacksonian America* (New York: Oxford University Press, 1970); David Grimsted, "Rioting in Its Jacksonian Setting," *American Historical Review* 77 (1972): 361–97.

39. Richard R. John, *Spreading the News: The American Postal System from Franklin to Morse* (Cambridge: Harvard University Press, 1995), 257–80; Susan Wyly-Jones, "The 1835 Anti-Abolition Meetings in the South: A New Look at the Controversy over the Abolition Postal Campaign," *Civil War History* 47 (2001): 289–309.

40. Wilentz, *The Rise of American Democracy*, 410–12; "Report of the Postmaster General," Dec. 1, 1835, *CG* 24/1, App., 8–9.

41. Miller, *Arguing about Slavery*, 139–49 and passim; Richards, *The Slave Power*, 128–33.

42. John R. McKivigan, *The War against Proslavery Religion: Abolitionism and the Northern Churches, 1830–1865* (Ithaca: Cornell University Press, 1984), 18–55; Glenn C. Altschuler and Jan M. Saltzgaber, *Revivalism, Social Conscience, and Community in the Burned-Over District: The Trial of Rhoda Bement* (Ithaca: Cornell University Press, 1983).

43. *North Star*, Oct. 27, 1848; *Frederick Douglass' Paper*, Mar. 23, 1855, 3.

44. Rhys Isaac, *The Transformation of Virginia, 1740–1790* (Chapel Hill: Institute of Early American History and Culture and University of North Carolina Press, 1982), 84–86; Peter H. Wood, *Strange New Land: Africans in Colonial America* (New York: Oxford University Press, 2003), 62–65; Philip D. Morgan, *Slave Counterpoint: Black Culture in the Eighteenth-Century Chesapeake and Lowcountry* (Chapel Hill: Omohundro Institute of Early American History and Culture and University of North Carolina Press, 1998), 418–19, 581–94; Christopher J. Smith, *The Creolization of American Culture: William Sidney Mount and the Roots of Blackface Minstrelsy* (Urbana: University of Illinois Press 2013), 38, 58, 61; Melvin Wade, "'Shining in Borrowed Plumage': Affirmation of Community in the Black Coronation Festivals of New England, ca. 1750–1850," in *Material Life in America, 1600–1860*, ed. Robert Blair St. George (Boston: Northeastern University Press, 1988), 171–82.

45. Adam Rothman, *Slave Country: American Expansion and the Origins of the Deep South* (Cambridge: Harvard University Press, 2005); Peter Way, *Common Labour: Workers and the Digging of North American Canals, 1780–1860* (New York: Cambridge University Press, 1993); Paul E. Johnson, *Sam Patch, the Famous Jumper* (New York: Hill and Wang, 2003); Cheryl Janifer LaRoche, *Free Black Communities and the Underground Railroad: The Geography of Resistance* (Urbana: University of Illinois Press, 2013).

46. Hawkins's nephew, William Sydney Mount, who grew up with him on Catherine Slip, recorded the creolized performative traditions of the area in a vast archive reaching in the 1860s. See Smith, *The Creolization of American Culture*, 84–92; and David Waldstreicher, *In the Midst of Perpetual Fetes: The Making of American Nationalism, 1776–1820* (Chapel Hill: Omohundro Institute of Early American History and Culture and University of North Carolina Press, 1997), 327–28.

47. John William Ward, *Andrew Jackson: Symbol for an Age* (New York: Oxford University Press, 1955), 13–22; Noah M. Ludlow, *Dramatic Life as I Found It: A Record of Personal Experience* . . . (St. Louis: G. L. Jones, 1880), 319–26, 390–97, 416–18; T. Allston Brown, *A History of the New York Stage, From Its First Performance in 1732 to 1901*, vol. 1 (New York: Dodd, Mead, 1903), 84–90, 100; W. T. Lhamon Jr., *Raising Cain: Blackface Performance from Jim Crow to Hip Hop* (Cambridge: Harvard University Press, 1998), 160–92.

48. *Louisville Public Advertiser*, May 20, 21, 24, June 12, Sept. 22, Oct. 5, 1830. See also *Hagerstown (Md.) Torch-Light and Public Advertiser*, Aug. 28, 1828; *Knoxville Register*, June 30, 1830.

49. Lhamon, *Raising Cain*, 181–86; *New Orleans Bee*, Mar. 21, 28, 1831.

50. *Washington National Intelligencer*, Nov. 1, 1833; *Charleston Courier*, Dec. 21, 1833; *Newark Daily Advertiser*, Mar. 10, 11, 15, 17, 18, 1834; *New York American*, Mar. 27, 1834.

51. Morrison Foster, *Biography, Songs, and Musical Compositions of Stephen Collins Foster* (Pittsburgh: Percy F. Smith, 1896), 10–11; Ken Emerson, *Doo-dah! Stephen Foster and the Rise of American Popular Culture* (New York: Simon & Schuster, 1997), 55; Evelyn Foster Morneweck, *Chronicles of Stephen Foster's Family* (Pittsburgh: University of Pittsburgh Press, 1944), 111–12.

52. For critical examination, see Brian Roberts, *Blackface Nation: Race, Reform, and Identity in American Popular Music, 1812–1945* (Chicago: University of Chicago Press, 2017).

53. *New York American*, Oct. 6, 1832; *Carolina Observer* (Fayetteville), Oct. 9, 1832; *Boston American Traveler*, Oct. 12, 1832; *Poulson's American Daily Advertiser*, Oct. 10, 1832; *Alexandria Gazette*, Oct. 18, 1832; *Pawtucket Chronicle and Manufacturers' and Artisans' Advocate*, Oct. 19, 1832; *Charlotte Miners' and Farmers' Journal*, Oct. 20, 1832; *Newport (R.I.) Mercury*, Oct. 20, 1832 (citing original in *Pennsylvania Village Record*); *Maine Working Men's Advocate*, Nov. 7, 1832. I am indebted to Sarah Schuetze, "More Than Death: Fear of Illness in American Literature, 1775–1876" (Ph.D. diss., University of Kentucky, 2015), 145–207, for an excellent discussion of the cultural impact of the 1832 cholera epidemic.

54. *Macon Telegraph*, July 31, 1833.

55. *Charlotte Miners' and Farmers' Journal*, Aug. 31, 1831; *Pensacola Gazette*, Feb. 25, 1833.

56. *Raleigh Register*, Feb. 14, 1838; *Alexandria Gazette*, July 16, 1833; *Portland (Me.) Advertiser*, Jan. 31, 1837.

57. *New York American*, July 18, 1833; *New-Hampshire Statesman and State Journal* (Concord), Aug. 17, 1833.

58. *New York American*, July 10, 1834; Wyatt-Brown, *Lewis Tappan and the Evangelical War on Slavery*, 70–73, 116–22.

59. *New York American*, Dec. 12, 1834; *New York Herald*, Dec. 9, 1826; see also *Liberator*, Dec. 17, 1836.

60. *Liberator*, Jan. 7, 1837, Aug. 21, 1838; *North Star*, July 14, Oct. 27, 1848; see also Robert S. Levine, *Martin Delany, Frederick Douglass, and the Politics of Representative Identity* (Chapel Hill: University of North Carolina Press, 1997), 41.

61. *New York Herald*, July 18, 1837.

62. Michael P. Young, *Bearing Witness against Sin: The Evangelical Birth of the American Social Movement* (Chicago: University of Chicago Press, 2006); Robert H. Abzug, *Cosmos Crumbling: American Reform and the Religious Imagination* (New York: Oxford University Press, 1994); Jonathan Earle, "The Making of the North's 'Stark Mad Abolitionists': Anti-Slavery Conversion in the United States, 1824–1854," *Slavery and Abolition* 25 (2004): 59–75; David Brion Davis, "Emergence of Immediatism in British and American Antislavery Thought," *Mississippi Valley Historical Review* 46 (1962): 209–30.

63. Timothy Patrick McCarthy and John Stauffer, eds., *Prophets of Protest: Reconsidering the History of American Abolitionism* (New York: New Press, 2006); Robert Fanuzzi, *Abolition's Public Sphere* (Minneapolis: University of Minnesota Press, 2003); Douglas M. Strong, *Perfectionist Politics: Abolitionism and the Religious Tensions of American Democracy* (Syracuse: Syracuse University Press, 1999); Lawrence J. Friedman, *Gregarious Saints: Self and Community in American Abolitionism, 1830–1870* (New York: Cambridge University Press, 1982); Lewis Perry, *Radical Abolitionism: Anarchy and the Government of God in Antislavery Thought* (Ithaca: Cornell University Press, 1973).

64. John Stauffer, *The Black Hearts of Men: Radical Abolitionists and the Transformation of Race* (Cambridge: Harvard University Press, 2002), 15, quoting Gerrit Smith.

65. Here I follow the useful sociology of the abolitionist movement presented in Friedman, *Gregarious Saints*.

66. Friedman, *Gregarious Saints*, 43–67; Nancy A. Hewitt, *Women's Activism and Social Change: Rochester, New York, 1822–1872* (Ithaca: Cornell University Press, 1984); Perry, *Radical Abolitionists*.

67. Friedman, *Gregarious Saints*, 68–95; Corey M. Brooks, *Liberty Power: Antislavery Third Parties and the Transformation of American Politics* (Chicago: University of Chicago Press, 2016), 25–42; Carpenter and Moore dataset, Carpenter and Moore, "When Canvassers Became Activists."

68. Julie Roy Jeffrey, *The Great Silent Army of Abolitionism: Ordinary Women in the Antislavery Movement* (Chapel Hill: University of North Carolina Press, 1998), 96–133; Stacey M. Robertson, *Hearts Beating for Liberty: Women Abolitionists in the Old Northwest* (Chapel Hill: University of North Carolina Press, 2010), 91–126; Melinda

Lawson, *Patriot Fires: Forging a New American Nationalism in the Civil War North* (Lawrence: University Press of Kansas, 2002), 14–39.

69. Friedman, *Gregarious Saints*, 96–126; Wiecek, *The Sources of Antislavery Constitutionalism*, 202–27, 249–75.

70. Friedman, *Gregarious Saints*, 35–39; Hedrick, *Stowe*, 93, 105–9.

71. Joseph A. Del Porto, "A Study of the American Anti-Slavery Journals" (Ph.D. diss., Michigan State University, 1953), provides the best overview of the antislavery press.

72. Carpenter and Moore dataset, Carpenter and Moore, "When Canvassers Became Activists."

73. In a series of letters on the election in the Martin Van Buren Papers, Library of Congress, there is "A Chart, showing the progress of the Great Political Tornado which swept over the Empire State during the 6th, 7th, & 8th November, 1837."

74. *Speech of the Hon. Thomas Morris, of Ohio, in the Senate of the United States, February 6, 1839, in reply to the Hon. Henry Clay* (New York: Piercy & Reed, 1839), 10, 34. See Brooks, *Liberty Power*, 20, 25–27; Richards, *The Slave Power*, 23–24; Jonathan H. Earle, *Jacksonian Antislavery and the Politics of Free Soil* (Chapel Hill: University of North Carolina Press, 2004), 43–48. Earle points out that Morris used the framework of the slave power argument in April 1836 but not the rhetoric until 1839.

75. On Adams, Slade, and Gates as Anti-Masons, see Leonard L. Richards, *The Life and Times of Congressman John Quincy Adams* (New York: Oxford University Press, 1986), 48–53; Michael J. Dubin, *United States Congressional Elections, 1788–1997: The Official Results of the 1st to the 105th Congresses* (Jefferson, N.C.: Harrison, 1998), 101, 105, 106, 110, 111; *Batavia (N.Y.) Republican Advocate*, Feb. 6, 1829, Oct. 30, 1831.

76. Theodore Dwight Weld [pseud. "Wythe"], *Power of Congress over the District of Columbia* (New York: John F. Trow, 1838), 40–47; Finkelman, *An Imperfect Union*, 70–180; Wiecek, *The Sources of Antislavery Constitutionalism*, 172–275; James Oakes, *Freedom National: The Destruction of Slavery in the United States, 1861–1865* (New York: W. W. Norton: 2013), 1–48; Oakes, *The Scorpion's Sting*, 104–465.

77. Brooks, *Liberty Power*, 47–72.

78. Fehrenbacher, *The Slaveholding Republic*, 219–25, Brooks, *Liberty Power*, 70–71; Thomas D. Morris, *Free Men All: The Personal Liberty Laws of the North, 1780–1861* (Baltimore: Johns Hopkins University Press, 1974), 79–84; Bruce Laurie, *Beyond Garrison: Antislavery and Social Reform* (New York: Cambridge University Press, 2005), 78–80.

79. Eric Foner, *Gateway to Freedom: The Hidden History of the Underground Railroad* (New York: W. W. Norton, 2015), 91–118; Robertson, *Hearts Beating for Liberty*, 143, 149, 161–82; Stanley Harrold, *Border War: Fighting over Slavery before the Civil War* (Chapel Hill: University of North Carolina Press, 2010), 55–116.

80. *Tocsin of Liberty* (Albany), Nov. 24, 1841, quoted in Brooks, *Liberty Power*, 82.

81. Brooks, *Liberty Power*, 34–42, 90–94.

82. James Brewer Stewart, *Joshua R. Giddings and the Tactics of Radical Politics* (Cleveland: Case Western Reserve University Press, 1970), 70–76.

83. Alasdair Roberts, *America's First Great Depression: Economic Crisis and Political Disorder after the Panic of 1837* (Ithaca: Cornell University Press, 2012); Jessica M. Lepler, *The Many Panics of 1837: People, Politics, and the Creation of a Transatlantic*

Financial Crisis (New York: Cambridge University Press, 2013); Paul G. Faler, *Mechanics and Manufacturers in the Early Industrial Revolution: Lynn, Massachusetts, 1760–1860* (Albany: State University of New York Press, 1981), 84, 90.

84. Edward E. Baptist, *The Half Has Never Been Told: Slavery and the Making of American Capitalism* (New York: Basic Books, 2014).

85. Robert Fogel has argued that native non-farm workers in the North—eventually a key constituency for both the Know Nothings and the Republicans—"suffered one of the most severe and protracted economic and social catastrophes of American history" between the late 1830s and the early 1850s. Robert W. Fogel, *Without Consent or Contract: The Rise and Fall of American Slavery* (New York: W. W. Norton, 1989), 354–69; see also Marc Egnal, *Clash of Extremes: The Economic Origins of the Civil War* (New York: Hill and Wang, 2009), 101–22; Allen Pred, *Urban Growth and City-Systems in the United States, 1840–1860* (Cambridge: Harvard University Press, 1980), 142–65.

86. Robert L. Thompson, *Wiring a Continent: The History of the Telegraph Industry in the United States, 1832–1866* (Princeton: Princeton University Press, 1947), 240–43; David M. Henkin, *The Postal Age: The Emergence of Modern Communications in Nineteenth-Century America* (Chicago: University of Chicago Press, 2006), 2–3, 21–41. For an accessible overview of the rise and impact of the telegraph, see Tom Standage, *The Victorian Internet: The Remarkable Story of the Telegraph and the Nineteenth Century's On-line Pioneers* (New York: Walker, 1998).

87. Dale T. Knobel, *America for the Americans: The Nativist Movement in the United States* (New York: Twayne, 1996), 1–87; Noel Ignatiev, *How the Irish Became White* (New York: Routledge, 1995).

88. Holt, *Political Crisis of the 1850s*, 101–20; John Joseph Wallis, "Constitutions, Corporations, and Corruption: American States and Constitutional Change, 1842–1852," *Journal of Economic History* 65 (2005): 211–56; John Joseph Wallis, "Founding Errors: Making Democracy Safe for America," work in progress, Dec. 2008.

89. Amy Greenberg, *A Wicked War: Polk, Clay, Lincoln, and the 1846 U.S. Invasion of Mexico* (New York: Knopf, 2012).

90. C. C. Goen, *Broken Churches, Broken Nation: Denominational Schisms and the Coming of the Civil War* (Macon: Mercer University Press, 1985), 113–40. Richard J. Carwardine, *Evangelicals and Politics in Antebellum America* (New Haven: Yale University Press, 1993), 159–74, 245–47, 287–88, 290–91; McKivigan, *The War against Proslavery Religion*, 81–92.

91. Brooks, *Liberty Power*, 105–24; Richards, *The Slave Power*, 146–55; Michael A. Morrison, *Slavery and the American West: The Eclipse of Manifest Destiny and the Coming of the Civil War* (Chapel Hill: University of North Carolina Press, 1997), 41–65.

92 Brooks, *Liberty Power*, 137–53.

93. Fergus M. Bordewich, *America's Great Debate: Henry Clay, Stephen A. Douglas, and the Compromise That Preserved the Union* (New York: Simon & Schuster, 2012), 48–49; Michael F. Holt, *The Rise and Fall of the American Whig Party: Jacksonian Politics and the Onset of the Civil War* (New York: Oxford University Press, 1999), 412.

94. The Carpenter-Moore dataset counts about 450,000 signatures by men on the petitions of the late 1830s. Assuming that men typically signed two petitions, this comes to about 225,000 signers. Carpenter and Moore, "When Canvassers Became Activists."

95. Joel H. Sibley, *Party Over Section: The Rough and Ready Presidential Election of 1848* (Lawrence: University Press of Kansas, 2009), 152–56, quote from 153. For a rather different understanding of the state of sectional politics as of 1848, see Andrew Delbanco, *The War before the War: Fugitive Slaves and the Struggle for America's Soul from the Revolution to the Civil War* (New York: Penguin, 2018), 4, 189–215.

96. Thomas Jefferson to John Holmes, Apr. 22, 1820, Jefferson Papers, Founders Online, National Archives, https://founders.archives.gov/; *John Quincy Adams Diaries*, vol. 1, *1779–1821*, ed. David Waldstreicher (New York: Library of America, 2017), 576 (Nov. 29, 1820).

Chapter 2: Structure Defended

1. Leonard L. Richards, *The California Gold Rush and the Coming of the Civil War* (New York: Alfred A. Knopf, 2007), 62–92; Fergus M. Bordewich, *America's Great Debate: Henry Clay, Stephen A. Douglas, and the Compromise That Preserved the Union* (New York: Simon & Schuster, 2012), 48–56.

2. Kate Clifford Larson, *Bound for the Promised Land: Harriet Tubman, Portrait of an American Hero* (New York: Ballantine, 2004), 72–88.

3. Mary Kay Ricks, *Escape on the Pearl: The Heroic Bid for Freedom on the Underground Railroad* (New York: Murrow, 2007), 25–30, 54–62, 74–86, 90–126; J. F. Pacheco, *The Pearl: A Failed Slave Escape on the Potomac* (Chapel Hill: University of North Carolina Press, 2005), 48–91; Stanley Harrold, *Subversives: Antislavery Community in Washington, D.C., 1828–1865* (Baton Rouge: Louisiana State University Press, 2003), 116–45.

4. Ricks, *Escape on the Pearl*, 172–81, 198–200; Harrold, *Subversives*, 126–45; *CG* 30/1, 649–56; *CG* 30/1, App., 501–10.

5. On the politics of the 30th Congress, first session, see David Potter, *The Impending Crisis: 1848–1861* (New York: Harper, 1976), 64–76; Robert W. Johannsen, *Stephen A. Douglas* (New York: Oxford University Press, 1973), 221–25; Michael F. Holt, *The Rise and Fall of the American Whig Party: Jacksonian Politics and the Onset of the Civil War* (New York: Oxford University Press, 1999), 334–38.

6. Bordewich, *America's Great Debate*, 25–28; *CG* 30/2, 3–7, 21. For the second session of the 30th Congress, see Potter, *The Impending Crisis*, 82–89; Holt, *Rise and Fall*, 384–90.

7. *CG* 30/2, 38, 39, 55–56, 83–84.

8. Quote from *Washington Union*, Jan. 28, 1849, 2, col. 3; Potter, *The Impending Crisis*, 83–86; Holt, *Rise and Fall*, 386–88; Charles M. Wiltse, *John C. Calhoun: Sectionalist, 1840–1850* (New York: Bobbs-Merrill, 1951), 374–93.

9. Johannsen, *Stephen A. Douglas*, 241–48; Potter, *The Impending Crisis*, 82–83; *CG* 30/2, 188, 210–16, 415–16, 604–9, 682–91.

10. *Baltimore Sun*, Nov. 13, 1849.

11. Corey M. Brooks, *Liberty Power: Antislavery Third Parties and the Transformation of American Politics* (Chicago: University of Chicago Press, 2016), 155–60; Jeffery A. Jenkins and Charles Stewart III, *Fighting for the Speakership: The House and the*

Rise of Party Government (Princeton: Princeton University Press, 2013), 155–64, 341–45; *CG* 31/1 (Dec. 12, 1849), 21–22.

12. Zachary Taylor, Annual Message, Dec. 4, 1849, the American Presidency Project, http://www.presidency.ucsb.edu/ws/?pid=29490.

13. *CG* 31/1 (Jan. 3, 1850), 98–99, 119–20.

14. *CG* 31/1 (Jan. 3–4, 1850), 99, 103, (Jan. 22, 24, 28, 1850), 210, 228, 233–38, App., 79–83; a parallel bill was announced on January 7 by William Ashe (*CG* 31/1, 131); Bordewich, *America's Great Debate*, 126–27; Stanley W. Campbell, *The Slave Catchers: Enforcement of the Fugitive Slave Law, 1850–1860* (Chapel Hill: University of North Carolina Press, 1968), 15.

15. *CG* 31/1 (Jan. 21, 1850), 195; Bordewich, *America's Great Debate*, 128–29.

16. *CG* 31/1 (Jan. 23, 24, 1850), 220, 225–27, (Jan. 29, 1850), 244; Bordewich, *America's Great Debate*, 129–33.

17. *CG* 31/1 (Feb. 5–6, 1850), App., 115–27.

18. This summary, and the discussion that follows it, is based on Bordewich, *America's Great Debate*, 182–357; Holman Hamilton, *Prologue to Conflict: The Crisis and Compromise of 1850* (New York: W. W. Norton, 1966), 84–165; William J. Freehling, *The Road to Disunion*, vol. 1, *Secessionists at Bay, 1776–1854* (New York: Oxford University Press, 1990), 487–510; Holt, *Rise and Fall*, 458–543; Elizabeth R. Varon, *Disunion! The Coming of the American Civil War, 1789–1859* (Chapel Hill: University of North Carolina Press, 2008), 210–31. More recently, Stephen E. Maizlish, *A Strife of Tongues: The Compromise of 1850 and the Ideological Foundations of the American Civil War* (Charlottesville: University of Virginia Press, 2018), focuses on the language of sectional struggle over the territories in the Compromise debates.

19. *CG* 31/1 (Apr. 17, 1850), 762–63; Joanne B. Freeman, *The Field of Blood: Violence in Congress and the Road to Civil War* (New York: Farrar, Straus and Giroux, 2018), 151–76.

20. For Calhoun's speech, see *CG* 31/1 (Mar. 4, 1850), 451–55. See also Bordewich, *America's Great Debate*, 156–58.

21. For this argument, made as early as John Taylor on the federal Carriage Tax (1796), see Maeva Marcus et al., eds., *The Documentary History of the Supreme Court of the United States, 1789–1800*, vol. 7, *Cases: 1796–1797* (New York: Columbia University Press, 2003), 404 (case of *Hylton v. United States*, 358–505).

22. *CG* 31/1 (Mar. 4, 1850), 455–56.

23. *CG* 31/1 (Mar. 7, 1850), App., 269, 273, 275, 276. See Bordewich's account in *America's Great Debate*, 165–70.

24. *CG* 31/1 (Mar. 7, 1850), App., 274.

25. *CG* 31/1 (Mar. 7, 1850), App., 276.

26. *CG* 31/1 (July 17, 1850), App., 1268, 1270.

27. Hamilton, *Prologue to Conflict*, 133–42, 155–61; Bordewich, *America's Great Debate*, 302–16, 330–55.

28. See Paul Finkelman's critique in "The Appeasement of 1850," in *Congress and the Crisis of the 1850s*, ed. Paul Finkelman and Donald Kennon (Athens: Ohio University Press, 2012), 36–79.

29. Discussion based on an analysis of the Senate vote regarding Utah on July 31 and the ten other Compromise votes in August and September listed in Hamilton,

Prologue to Conflict, 191–92, 195–200; roll calls (Senate: nos. 170, 222, 230, 235, 246, 281; House: nos. 357, 363, 364, 377, 395; see Appendix, tables 3 and 4). See discussions in Hamilton, *Prologue to Conflict*, 142–49, 161–65; Michael Holt, *The Political Crisis of the 1850s* (New York: W. W. Norton, 1978), 88; Holt, *Rise and Fall*, 539–43. On Douglas, see James W. Sheahan, The *Life of Stephen A. Douglas* (New York: Harper & Brothers, 1860), 161.

30. Northern Whig senators (8 of 13) and congressmen (47 of 77) either voting nay or not voting on the Utah bill, and voting nay on the fugitive slave bill (Senate: nos. 170, 246; House: nos. 364, 377; see Appendix, tables 3 and 4).

31. *North American and United State Gazette* (Philadelphia), Feb. 22, 23, 1850; *Boston Daily Atlas*, Feb. 26, 1850; *Savannah Daily Morning News*, Feb. 26, Mar. 4, 1850; *Daily National Intelligencer*, Feb. 27, 1850; *New York Spectator*, Feb. 28, 1850; *Liberator*, Mar. 1, 1850; *Raleigh Register*, Mar. 2, 6, 1850; *Chilicothe Scioto Gazette*, Mar. 5, 6, 1850.

32. *Daily National Intelligencer*, Feb. 28, 1850; *New York Spectator*, Feb. 28, 1850: *The Diary of Philip Hone, 1828–1851*, ed. Bayard Tuckerman, vol. 2 (New York: Dodd, Mead, 1889), 2:375.

33. *Boston Advertiser*, Apr. 3, 10, 13, 1850; Maurice G. Baxter, *One and Indivisible: Daniel Webster and the Union* (Cambridge: Harvard University Press, 1984), 417.

34. *House Journal*, 31/1, Dec. 31, 1849, 203, 205, 210. Thaddeus Stevens of Pennsylvania repeated the Crowell motion on January 19, 1850, 373.

35. *Senate Journal*, 31/1, Jan. 8, 1850, 64–65; *CG* 31/1, 119–23 (quotes from 120, 123); Bordewich, *America's Great Debate*, 124–26.

36. Root, Feb. 15, 1850: *CG* 31/1, App., 105–9; Stevens, Feb. 20, 1850: *CG* 31/1 App., 141–43; Mann, Feb. 15, 1850: *CG* 31/1, App., 218–25.

37. Seward, Mar. 11, 1850: *CG* 31/1, App., 260–69 (quotes from 262, 263, 265, 268). On gradual and immediate emancipation, and peace and war, see James Oakes, *Freedom National: The Destruction of Slavery in the United States, 1861–1865* (New York: W. W. Norton, 2013).

38. *CG* 31/1, App., 1054–65 (Hale); 468–80 (Chase).

39. Petitions listed in House and Senate journals, 31st Cong. Accounts of northern opposition to the Compromise typically mention the protest meetings that erupted in various antislavery constituencies in the fall of 1850, after its final passage, but the petitioning to Congress in the winter and spring of 1850 is rarely mentioned. For example, see Edward Magdol, *The Anti-Slavery Rank and File: A Social Profile of the Abolitionists' Constituency* (Westport, Conn.: Praeger, 1986), 130–31; Campbell, *The Slave Catchers*, 25. Campbell does not mention petitioning until his discussion of the Kansas-Nebraska Act in 1854 (84). Hamilton, *Prologue to Conflict*, 123, mentions only a massive (25,000-signature) petition from New York City in June 1850. Susan Zaeske, *Signatures of Citizenship: Petitioners, Antislavery, and Women's Political Identity* (Chapel Hill: University of North Carolina Press, 2003), 161–62, has, at this writing, the only recent description.

40. *House Journal*, 31/1, Jan. 14, 1850, 308.

41. Senate and House journals, passim. On the Senate gag rule, see Daniel Wirls, "'The Only Mode of Avoiding Everlasting Debate': The Overlooked Senate Gag Rule for Antislavery Petitions," *Journal of the Early Republic* 27 (2007): 115–38.

42. *Senate Journal*, 31/1, Feb. 7, 1850, 136; *CG* 31/1, 319–23.

43. Analysis of petitions listed in Senate and House journals, Jan. 14–Feb. 28, 1850. The petitions mentioning Drayton and Sayres were presented on Jan. 15, 28, Feb. 4, 8, 11, 21, 1850.

44. *CG* 31/1, 210, 236 (Seward, Jan. 28, 1850).

45. Early reports of Seward's amendment are in *Daily National Intelligencer*, Jan. 29, 1850; *Emancipator and Republican*, Feb. 7, 1850; *North Star*, Feb. 8, 1850; *Liberator*, Feb. 15, 1850. The AFASS circular was printed in *New York Evening Post*, Feb. 16, 1850; *North Star*, Feb. 22, 1850; *Emancipator and Republican*, Mar. 14, 1850; and reported in *Annual Report of the American and Foreign Anti-Slavery Society . . .* (New York, 1850), 26–27. See Zaeske, *Signatures of Citizenship*, 161.

46. *Senate Journal*, 31/1, Mar. 4, 1850, 190, Mar. 5, 1850, 193. Two from Vermont and Ohio, arriving on February 27 and 28 and referred to committee on March 5, were signed on exactly the same printed forms. Petitions from Youngstown, Ohio, and Danville, Vermont, HR31A-G9.5, Committee on the Judiciary, Slavery, Jan. 10–Mar. 13, 1850, National Archives. See also *House Journal*, 31/1, Mar. 5, 1850, 633.

47. *CG* 31/1, 524–27.

48. *Senate Journal*, 31/1, June 11, 28, 1850.

49. *Senate Journal*, 31/1, June 11, 1850.

50. "Proceedings of a Meeting," *Pennsylvania Freeman*, Feb. 21, 1850.

51. *Daily Sanduskian*, Feb. 9, 1850.

52. *Liberator*, Mar. 29, Apr. 5, 1850.

53. *North Star*, Apr. 5, 1850.

54. *National-Anti-Slavery Standard*, Aug. 29, Sept. 9, 1850; see Ricks, *Escape on the Pearl*, 216–24; Harrold, *Subversives*, 257–59; Bordewich, *America's Great Debate*, 326–28. Preston King presented most of the Drayton-Sayres petitions, many from Smith's turf in Madison County, New York; King was a Free Soil Democrat who would become a Republican from St. Lawrence County. Several of these petitions also focused on the problem of passports for African Americans, an issue for sailors and shipping interests on Lake Ontario.

55. *National-Anti-Slavery Standard*, Sept. 9, 1850.

56. *Liberator*, Sept. 20, 1850.

57. *Liberator*, May 17, 1850.

58. *Boston Evening Transcript*, May 28, 30, 1850; *Emancipator and Republican*, June 6, 1850.

59. Horace Mann to CS, Jan. 9, 1850, Charles Sumner Papers, HU.

60. Benjamin D. Silliman to CS, Jan. 14, 1850, Charles Sumner Papers, HU.

61. Joshua R. Giddings to CS, Dec. 24, 1849, Feb. 8, Apr. 15, June 21, 1850, Charles Sumner Papers, HU.

62. *CG* 31/1, App., 768.

63. *CG* 31/1, App., 1124–28.

64. *CG* 31/2, App., 238.

65. *CG* 31/1, App., 1024; 1581–1630; Bordewich, *America's Great Debate*, 318–30.

66. On Seward's departure from Washington, see Walter Starr, *William Seward: Lincoln's Indispensable Man* (New York: Simon and Schuster, 2012), 130.

67. *CG* 31/1, App., 1299–1302 (quotes from 1301 and 1302).

Chapter 3: Liminality Erupting in the First Crisis

1. W. Porter Ware and Thaddeus C. Lockard, *P. T. Barnum Presents Jenny Lind: The American Tour of the Swedish Nightingale* (Baton Rouge: Louisiana State University Press, 1980), 5–6, 29–34; *DGTS*, 2:19.

2. *Baltimore Sun*, Sept. 30, 1850; Harriet A. Jacobs, *Incidents in the Life of a Slave Girl, Written by Herself*, ed. Jean Fagan Yellin (Cambridge: Harvard University Press, 1987), 191; Stanley W. Campbell, *The Slave Catchers: Enforcement of the Fugitive Slave Law, 1850–1860* (Chapel Hill: University of North Carolina Press, 1968), 115.

3. Kate Clifford Larson, *Bound for the Promised Land: Harriet Tubman, Portrait of an American Hero* (New York: Ballantine, 2004), 89–90.

4. *Era*, August 29, 1850; *Boston Bee*, Oct. 1, 1850; *Boston Liberator*, Oct. 19, 1850. For two accounts of these events, see Gerald G. Eggert, "The Impact of the Fugitive Slave Law on Harrisburg: A Case Study," *Pennsylvania Magazine of History and Biography* 109 (1985): 537–69, esp. 540–44; Todd Mealy, *Biography of an Antislavery City: Antislavery Advocates, Abolitionists, and Underground Railroad Activists in Harrisburg, PA* (Baltimore: PublishAmerica, 2007), 127–72. For the definitive account of the impact of the Fugitive Slave Law, see R. J. M. Blackett, *The Captive's Quest for Freedom: Fugitive Slaves, the 1850 Fugitive Slave Law, and the Politics of Slavery* (New York: Cambridge University Press, 2018); for his account of the events in Harrisburg, see 278–93.

5. *Pittsburgh Post*, Sept. 25, 1850.

6. *Pittsburgh Post*, Sept. 25, 26, 1850; *Cleveland Plain Dealer*, Sept. 28, 1850; *Daily Sanduskian*, Sept. 28, 1850; *Boston Daily Bee*, Sept. 28, 1850; *Albany Evening Journal*, Oct. 1, 1850.

7. *New Lisbon (Ohio) Anti-Slavery Bugle*, Oct. 12, 1850.

8. *Washington (Pa.) Reporter*, Oct. 16, 1850; *Boston Evening Transcript*, Oct. 2, 1850; *Boston Daily Bee*, Oct. 2, 1850; *Boston Atlas*, Oct. 2, 1850; Campbell, *The Slave Catchers*, 199.

9. *New York Commercial Advertiser*, Sept. 27, 28, 1850; *New York Evening Post*, Sept. 28, 1850; *Baltimore Sun*, Sept. 30, 1850; *Newark Advertiser*, Oct. 1, 1850.

10. *New York Evening Post*, Oct. 1, 2, 1850; *Boston Bee*, Oct. 2, 1850; *Boston Atlas*, Oct. 2, 1850; *Boston Evening Transcript*, Oct. 2, 1850; *Albany Evening Journal*, Oct. 3, 1850; *Liberty Party Paper*, Oct. 3, 1850; *Washington Union*, Oct. 4, 1850; *Boston Liberator*, Oct. 4, 1850; *Schenectady Reflector*, Oct. 11, 1850; *Trenton State Gazette*, Oct. 7, 1850.

11. *Boston Liberator*, Oct. 4, 1850; Springfield meeting resolves: *NA-SS*, Oct. 17, 1850.

12. *Boston Bee*, Oct. 2, 1850; *Boston Atlas*, Oct. 2, 1850; Wilbur H. Siebert, "The Underground Railroad in Massachusetts," *Proceedings of the American Antiquarian Society*, n.s., 45, pt. 1 (1935): 91–93; see also *Boston Evening Transcript*, Oct. 2, 1850; *New York Evening Post*, Oct. 2, 1850; *Liberator*, Oct. 4, 1850; *Liberty Party Paper*, Oct. 3, 1850; *Gloucester Telegraph*, Oct. 10, 1850.

13. *NA-SS*, Oct. 17, 1850; *Washington Union*, Oct. 4, 1850; *Albany Evening Journal*, Oct. 4, 1850.

14. *Philadelphia Ledger*, Oct. 1, 1850; *New York Evening Post*, Oct. 2, 1850; William J. Switala, *Underground Railroad in Pennsylvania* (Mechanicsburg, Pa.: Stackpole Books, 2001), 86–87.

15. *New York Evening Post*, Oct. 2, 1850; *Boston Herald*, Oct. 4, 1850; *Schenectady Reflector*, Oct. 11, 1850; *New Lisbon Anti-Slavery Bugle*, Oct. 26, 1850.

16. *Newark Daily Advertiser*, Oct. 2, 1850; *Baltimore Sun*, Sept. 30, Oct. 8, 1850; *NA-SS*, Oct. 10, 1850; *Schenectady Reflector*, Oct. 11, 1850; *Boston Liberator*, Oct. 25, 1850.

17. *Boston Liberator*, Oct. 4, 25, Nov. 11, 1850; *Albany Evening Journal*, Oct. 3, 1850; *Washington Union*, Oct. 4, 1850; *Boston Emancipator and Republican*, Oct. 10, 17, 24, 1850; *NA-SS*, Oct. 17, 24, 31, 1850; *Anti-Slavery Bugle*, Oct. 19, 26, 1850; *Rochester North Star*, Oct. 24, 1850; *Xenia (Ohio) Torch-Light*, Nov. 7, 1850.

18. *Rochester North Star*, Oct. 3, 1850; *Syracuse Liberty Party Paper*, Oct. 3, 1850; *NA-SS*, Oct. 17, 1850.

19. *Anti-Slavery Bugle*, Sept. 28, Oct., 5, 12, 19, 26, 1850; *Boston Emancipator and Republican*, Oct. 24, 1850; *Rochester North Star*, Oct. 24, 1850; *Worcester Massachusetts Spy*, Oct. 18, 1850.

20. *Boston Emancipator and Republican*, Oct. 17, 1850; *Boston Liberator*, Oct. 18, 25, 1850; *NA-SS*, Oct. 24, 1850; *Rochester North Star*, Oct. 24, 31, 1850; Gary Collison, *Shadrach Minkins: From Fugitive Slave to Citizen* (Cambridge: Harvard University Press, 1997), 81–82.

21. *Rochester North Star*, Oct. 24, 31, 1850; *Boston Liberator*, Oct. 19, 25, 1850; *Anti-Slavery Bugle*, Oct. 19, 26, 1850.

22. *Hartford Times*, Oct. 19, 1850; *The Proceedings of the Union Meeting, held at Brewster's Hall, Oct. 24, 1850* (New Haven: William Stanley, Union Safety Committee, 1850); *Albany Evening Journal*, Oct. 31, 1850; *Baltimore Sun*, Nov. 1, 1850; *Daily National Intelligencer*, Nov. 2, Dec. 27, 1850; *Pennsylvania Inquirer*, Nov. 2, 4, 1850, Feb. 28, 1851; *Boston Evening Transcript*, Nov. 11, 1850; *Portsmouth (N.H.) Gazette*, Nov. 26, 1850; *Christian Observer*, Nov. 30, 1850, Jan. 4, 1851; *New York Weekly Herald*, Dec. 14, 28, 1850; *Salem (Mass.) Observer*, Dec. 21, 1850.

23. *The Proceedings of the Union Meeting, held at Castle Garden, October 30, 1850* (New York: Bedford and Hobbs, Union Safety Committee, 1850), 3, 27–62; *DGTS*, 2:24.

24. *Pennsylvania Inquirer*, Sept. 26, 1850; *New York Weekly Herald*, Jan. 11, 1851.

25. *Rochester Daily American* Oct. 11, 1850; *Christian Observer*, May 1, Sept. 7, Nov. 16, 23, 30, Dec 21, 1850, Jan. 18, May 3, 1851. See also Richard J. Carwardine, *Evangelicals and Politics in Antebellum America* (Knoxville: University of Tennessee Press, 1997), 180–86; Laura L. Mitchell, "'Matters of Justice between Man and Man': Northern Divines, the Bible, and the Fugitive Slave Act of 1850," in *Religion and the Antebellum Debate over Slavery*, ed. John R. McKivigan and Mitchell Snay (Athens: Ohio University Press, 1998), 134–65; John R. McKivigan, *The War against Proslavery Religion: Abolitionism and the Northern Churches, 1830–1865* (Ithaca: Cornell University Press, 1984), 153–54, 268n36; Campbell, *The Slave Catchers*, 63–79.

26. *The Proceedings of the Union Meeting, held at Castle Garden*, 6, 10, 16. For just some reports, see *Albany Journal*, Nov. 1, 1850; *Trenton State Gazette*, Nov. 1, 1850; *Boston Daily Atlas*, Nov. 1, 1850; *Daily National Intelligencer*, Nov. 2, 1850; *Salem (Mass.) Register*, Nov. 4, 1850; *Worcester National Aegis*, Nov. 6, 1850; *New Hampshire Patriot and State Gazette*, Nov. 7, 1850.

27. Millard Fillmore, First Annual Message, December 2, 1850, the American Presidency Project, http://www.presidency.ucsb.edu/ws/index.php?pid=29491.

28. *CG* 31/1, App., 1302; *CG* 32/2, App., 237–38; *Liberator*, July 11, 1852.

29. "Calamity" from Mann, *CG* 31/2, App., 239.

30. Campbell, *The Slave Catchers*, 114–15, 199; *Daily National Intelligencer*, Oct. 22, 1850; *NA-SS*, Oct. 24, 1850.

31. Campbell, *The Slave Catchers*, 199–200; Collison, *Shadrach Minkins*, 107.

32. Collison, *Shadrach Minkins*, 91–100; Richard J. M. Blackett, *Beating Against the Barriers: Biographical Essays in Nineteenth-Century Afro-American History* (Baton Rouge: Louisiana State University Press, 1986), 87–90; *Boston Emancipator and Republican*, Oct. 31, 1850; *NA-SS*, Oct. 31, 1850; *Liberator*, Nov. 1, 1850. Campbell does not discuss the Crafts' case, nor does he include them in his list of arrests.

33. Collison, *Shadrach Minkins*, 110–65; Blackett, *Beating Against the Barriers*, 91–95.

34. Collison, *Shadrach Minkins*, 190–91; Leonard W. Levy, "Sims' Case: The Fugitive Slave Law in Boston," *Journal of Negro History* 25 (1950): 39–74.

35. On liminality and the figure of the fugitive, see William L. Andrews, *To Tell a Free Story: The First Century of Afro-American Autobiography, 1760–1865* (Urbana: University of Illinois Press, 1986), 167–204; Nancy Kang, "'As if I had entered a Paradise': Fugitive Slave Narratives and Cross-Border Literary History," *African American Review* 39 (2005): 431–57. See also Kevin Dawson, "Enslaved Ship Pilots in the Age of Revolutions: Challenging Notions of Race and Slavery between the Boundaries of Land and Sea," *Journal of Social History* 47 (2013): 71–100.

36. For recent discussions of northern unionism, see Adam I. P. Smith, *The Stormy Present: Conservatism and the Problem of Slavery in Northern Politics, 1846–1865* (Chapel Hill: University of North Carolina Press, 2017), esp. 3–20, 44–48, 65–67; Graham A. Peck, *Making an Antislavery Nation: Lincoln, Douglas, and the Battle over Freedom* (Urbana: University of Illinois Press, 2017), 101–8; Matthew Mason, *Apostle of Union: A Political Biography of Edward Everett* (Chapel Hill: University of North Carolina Press, 2016).

37. For examples, see *Liberator*, Oct. 4, 1850; *Trenton State Gazette*, Oct. 9, 1850.

38. Excitement: *New York Evening Post*, Sept. 25, 1850; *Cleveland Plain Dealer*, Sept. 27, 1850; movement: *Boston Bee*, Oct. 2, 1850; *New York Commercial Advertiser*, Oct. 2, 1850; flight: *Antislavery Bugle*, Oct. 12, 1850; *Philadelphia North American and United States Gazette*, Sept. 25, 1850; stampede: *Concord (N.H.) Independent Democrat*, Oct. 3, 1850; *Syracuse Liberty Party Paper*, Oct. 3, 1850; emigration: *Philadelphia Public Ledger*, Sept. 26, 1850; *Trenton State Gazette*, Sept. 26, 1850; *Boston Semi-Weekly Atlas*, Sept. 28, 1850.

39. *Pittsburgh Post*, Sept. 26, 1850.

40. *Cleveland Plain Dealer*, Sept. 28, 1850.

41. Walter Johnson, *Soul by Soul: Life inside the Antebellum Slave Market* (Cambridge: Harvard University Press, 1999); Walter Johnson, ed., *The Chattel Principle: Internal Slave Trade in the Americas* (New Haven: Yale University Press, 2004); Maurie D. McInnis, *Slaves Waiting for Sale: Abolitionist Art and the American Slave Trade* (Chicago: University of Chicago Press, 2011).

42. *CG* 31/1, App., 1032 (Henry Putnam, July 30, 1850); *Burritt's Christian Citizen* (Worcester, Mass.), July 20, 1850; *New York Evening Post*, Aug. 12, 1850; William Craft, *Running a Thousand Miles for Freedom; or, the Escape of William and Ellen Craft from Slavery* (London: William Tweedie, 1860), 27.

43. *Milwaukee Sentinel and Gazette*, May 18, 1850.

44. *Liberator*, Oct. 8, 1850; *Dedham (Mass.) Norfolk Democrat*, Oct. 10, 1850; *Boston Emancipator and Republican*, Oct. 24, 1850; *Liberator*, April 4, 1851; Larson, *Bound for the Promised Land*, 89.

45. Ralph Waldo Emerson, "Address to the Citizens of Concord on the Fugitive Slave Law, 3 May 1851," in *LLRWE*, 1:260, 263.

46. *CG* 31/1, 195 (Taylor message to the House, Jan. 21, 1850).

47. Ralph Waldo Emerson, "Seventh of March Speech on the Fugitive Slave Law, 7 March 1854," in *LLRWE*, 1:341–42.

48. *Cleveland Plain Dealer*, Sept. 28, 1850, *Liberator*, Oct. 4, 1850.

49. *NA-SS*, Oct. 3, 17, 31, 1850; *New York Evening Post*, Oct. 2, 1850; *Boston Emancipator and Republican*, Oct. 10, 17 , 24, 1850; *Rochester North Star*, Oct. 24, 31, 1850.

50. *Anti-Slavery Bugle*, Sept. 28, 1850; *NA-SS*, Oct. 3, 1850.

51. *Burritt's Christian Citizen*, Oct. 12, 1850.

52. *NA-SS*, Oct. 17, 1850.

53. [Samuel May], *The Fugitive Slave Law and Its Victims*, rev. and enlarged ed. (New York: American Anti-Slavery Society, 1861), 11–37.

54. Lydia Maria Child to Joseph Carpenter, Aug. 24, 1851, in *Lydia Maria Child: Selected Letters, 1817–1880*, ed. Milton Meltzer and Patricia G. Holland (Amherst: University of Massachusetts Press, 1982), 160.

55. For the definitive analysis of the operation of the Underground Railroad, see Blackett, *The Captive's Quest for Freedom*. The standard count for fugitive arrests is in Campbell, *The Slave Catchers*, 199–207. Blackett revises some of his figures (69–70). The estimate of total escapes comes from two sources. The U.S. Census office recorded 1,101 fugitives in 1849–50 and 803 in 1859–60; *Statistical View of the United States . . . being a Compendium of the Seventh Census*, comp. J. D. B. Debow (Washington, D.C.: Tucker, 1854), 64; *Statistics of the United States . . . in 1860; Compiled from the Original Returns and being the Final Exhibit of the Eighth Census . . .* (Washington, D.C.: Government Printing Office, 1866), 337–38. See also "The Fugitive Slave Law," *New York Times*, Dec. 10, 1860. By this estimate, roughly ten thousand fugitives arrived in Canada in the 1850s. Looking at Canadian census estimates, Fred Landon argued for a figure of fifteen thousand to twenty thousand in "The Negro Migration to Canada after the Passing of the Fugitive Slave Act," *Journal of Negro History* 5 (1920): 22–36.

56. John Greenleaf Whittier to John Abbot Douglass, June 2, 1856, in *The Letters of John Greenleaf Whittier*, vol. 2, *1846–1860*, ed. John B. Pickard (Cambridge: Harvard University Press, 1975), 296.

57. Jonathan H. Earle, *Jacksonian Antislavery and the Politics of Free Soil, 1824–1854* (Chapel Hill: University of North Carolina Press, 2004); Sean Wilentz, *The Rise of American Democracy: Jefferson to Lincoln* (New York : W. W. Norton, 2005), 564–65, 483–585, and 547–706 passim; William E. Gienapp, "Who Voted for Lincoln?," in

Abraham Lincoln and the American Political Tradition, ed. John L. Thomas (Amherst: University of Massachusetts Press, 1986), 50–97.

58. *Boston Daily Evening Transcript*, Oct. 16, 1850.

59. *DGTS*, 2:16, 22, 24, 26–27, 29–30.

60. Abraham Lincoln to Joshua F. Speed, Aug. 24, 1855, in *CWAL*, 2:320. See also *CWAL*, 1:126, 2:21; James Brewer Stewart, *Joshua R. Giddings and the Tactics of Radical Politics* (Cleveland: Case Western Reserve University Press, 1970), 167–80; Michael Burlingame, *Abraham Lincoln: A Life* (Baltimore: Johns Hopkins University Press, 2008), 357.

61. *DOHB*, 1:16, 27–28.

62. *DCF*, 4:61–62, 64, 66, 90–91, 140, 146, 157, 163, 180n30, 237–38, 249, 303–4.

63. *America of Yesterday: As Reflected in the Journal of John Davis Long . . .* , ed. Lawrence Shaw Mayo (Boston: Atlantic Monthly Press, 1923), 39, 42.

64. Henry James, *A Small Boy and Others* (New York: Charles Scribner's Sons, 1913), 249–50.

65. William J. Freehling, *The Road to Disunion*, vol. 1, *Secessionists at Bay, 1776–1854* (New York: Oxford University Press, 1990), 481–86; Elizabeth R. Varon, *Disunion! The Coming of the American Civil War, 1789–1859* (Chapel Hill: University of North Carolina Press, 2008), 223–31.

66. Frederick J. Blue, *The Free Soilers: Third Party Politics, 1848–54* (Urbana: University of Illinois Press, 1973), 152–87.

67. Michael J. Dubin, *United States Congressional Elections, 1788–1997: The Official Results of the Elections of the 1st through 105th Congresses* (Jefferson, N.C.: McFarland, 1998), 155, 161–62; *The Letters of Ralph Waldo Emerson*, ed. Eleanor M. Tilton, vol. 10 (New York: Columbia University Press, 1995), 235–37.

68. David Donald, *Charles Sumner and the Coming of the Civil War* (New York: Ballantine, 1960), 189–204; Blue, *Free Soilers*, 115–24.

69. H. L. Trefouse, *Benjamin Franklin Wade: Radical Republican from Ohio* (New York: Twayne, 1963), 64–67; Stephen E. Maizlish, *The Triumph of Sectionalism: The Transformation of Ohio Politics, 1844–1856* (Kent: Kent State University Press, 1983), 159–60.

70. Trefouse, *Benjamin Franklin Wade*, 62–64.

71. Larson, *Bound for the Promised Land*, 89.

72. Virtually all of the petitions are identified in the House and Senate journals only by their state of origin.

73. Theodore Parker to CS, Feb. 19, 1851, Sumner Papers, HU.

74. Petition of twenty-three citizens of Wayne County, Indiana, HR31A-G9.5, National Archives.

75. See Appendix, table 5.

76. *Era*, Jan. 9, 1851. See also *Era*, Nov. 21, Dec. 5, 19, 1850, Jan. 16, 23, Feb. 6, March 20, April 3, 1851.

77. *CG* 31/2, App., 237–49 (Mann), 252–56 (Giddings), 293–96, 305, 308, 309, 311, 322 (Chase, Hale); Notes to Emerson, "Address to the Citizens of Concord" (1851), in *LLRWE*, 1:259; *Speech of the Hon. Horace Mann, on the Fugitive Slave Law, delivered at Lancaster, Mass., May 19, 1851* (Boston: Office of the Commonwealth, 1851);

Speech of Senator Chase, delivered at Toledo May 30, 1851, before a Mass Convention of the Democracy of north-western Ohio (printed at the Ben Franklin Book and Job Office, n.d.); *Pennsylvania Freeman*, Jan. 1, 2, 9, 1851; *Era*, Jan. 23, July 10, 31, 1851, Oct. 9, 1851; *North Star*, Jan. 9, Mar. 20, 1851; *Liberator*, May 9, 16, 23, June 6, 13, 1851; *NA-SS*, Mar. 6, 20, May 15, 22, 29, 1851; Angela F. Murphy, *The Jerry Rescue: The Fugitive Slave Law, Northern Rights, and the American Sectional Crisis* (New York: Oxford University Press, 2016), 110–13; William S. McFeely, *Frederick Douglass* (New York: Simon and Schuster, 1991), 168–70; Robert S. Levine, *Martin Delany, Frederick Douglass, and the Politics of Representative Identity* (Chapel Hill: University of North Carolina Press, 1997), 71–72.

78. Larson, *Bound for the Promised Land*, 90–93.

79. Murphy, *The Jerry Rescue*, 1–5, 104–7, 77–79, 114–23; Angela Murphy, "'It Outlaws me, and I Outlaw it!': Resistance to the Fugitive Slave Law in Syracuse, New York," *Afro-Americans in New York Life and History* 28 (2004): 48–55; *The Diary of Ellen Birdseye Wheaton*, ed. Donald Gordon (Boston, 1923), 89–90; Ralph V. Harlow, *Gerrit Smith: Philanthropist and Reformer* (New York: Henry Holt, 1939), 297–303, 313. For a sample of the early Jerry Rescue coverage, see *Buffalo Morning Express*, Oct. 2, 1851; *New York Evening Post*, Oct. 2, 1851; *Newark Daily Advertiser*, Oct. 2, 1851; *Baltimore Sun*, Oct. 3, 1851; *Alexandria Gazette*, Oct. 4, 1851; *Wilmington (N.C.) Daily Journal*, Oct. 4, 1851; *Cleveland Plain Dealer*, Oct. 4, 1851; *Columbus Daily Statesman*, Oct. 6, 1851; *Daily National Intelligencer*, Oct. 7, 1851; *Milwaukee Sentinel*, Oct. 7, 1851.

80. Thomas P. Slaughter, *The Christiana Riot and Racial Violence in the Antebellum North* (New York: Oxford University Press, 1991), 43–75.

81. Slaughter, *The Christiana Riot*, 59–76; Stanley Harrold, *Border War: Fighting over Slavery before the Civil War* (Chapel Hill: University of North Carolina Press, 2010), 149–57.

82. Michael F. Holt, *Forging a Majority: The Formation of the Republican Party in Pittsburgh, 1848–1860* (New Haven, 1969), 102; Ronald P. Formisano, *The Birth of Mass Political Parties: Michigan, 1827–1861* (Princeton: Princeton University Press, 1971), 210.

Chapter 4: Creative Liminality

1. George Julian to Anna Julian, July 9, 19, Dec. 4, 1850, Jan. 2, 11, 1851, in Grace Julian Clarke, "Home Letters of George W. Julian, 1850–1851," *Indiana Magazine of History* 29 (1933): 139, 141, 150, 153, 156. On the Bailey salon, see Stanley Harrold, *Gamaliel Bailey and Antislavery Union* (Kent: Kent State University Press, 1986), 125–27, 133–34, 141; Stanley Harrold, "Gamaliel Bailey, Antislavery Journalist and Lobbyist," in *In the Shadow of Freedom: The Politics of Slavery in the National Capital*, ed. Paul Finkelman and Donald R. Kennon (Athens: Ohio University Press, 2010), 72–73; Jonathan Earle, "Saturday Nights at the Baileys': Building an Antislavery Movement in Congress, 1838–1854," in Finkelman and Kennon, *In the Shadow of Freedom*, 83–86, 93–96; Grace Greenwood, "An American Salon," *The Cosmopolitan: A Monthly Illustrated Magazine* 9 (1890): 437–48.

2. Harrold, *Gamaliel Bailey*, 81–90, 141–42; Corey M. Brooks, *Liberty Power:*

Antislavery Third Parties and the Transformation of American Politics (Chicago: University of Chicago Press, 2016), 59–72, 132–34.

3. Harrold, *Gamaliel Bailey*, 141–42; Earle, "Saturday Nights at the Baileys'," 83–85; George Julian to Anna Julian, June 15, 26, July 9, 19, Aug. 17, 25, 1850, Jan. 2, 22, Feb. 20, 25, 1851, in Clarke, "Home Letters," 136–161; Kevin J. Hayes, "Grace Greenwood (Sara Jane Clarke Lippincott)," in *Nineteenth-Century American Women Writers: A Bio-Critical Sourcebook*, ed. Denise D. Knight (Westport, Conn.: Greenwood, 1997), 180–85; Amy E. Hudock, "E.D.E.N Southworth (Emma Dorothy Eliza Nevitte Southworth)," in Knight, *Nineteenth-Century American Women's Writers*, 368–76.

4. George Julian to Anna Julian, June 26, 1850, in Clarke, "Home Letters," 138.

5. *New York Commercial Advertiser*, Oct. 24, 1849; *Salem (N.H.) Register*, Dec. 10, 1849.

6. Gamaliel Bailey to CS, July 27, 1850, Sumner Papers, HU.

7. Jane Weiss, "Susan Warner," in Knight, *Nineteenth-Century American Women's Writers*, 452–62; Joyce W. Warren, "Fanny Fern (Sarah Payson Willis Parton), in Knight, *Nineteenth-Century American Women's Writers*, 123–30; *New York Evening Post*, Apr. 24, 1852. For the rise of this generation of women writers, see Mary Kelley, *Private Woman, Public Stage: Literary Domesticity in Nineteenth-Century America* (New York: Oxford University Press, 1984).

8. Vincent Harding, *A Certain Magnificence: Lyman Beecher and the Transformation of American Protestantism, 1775–1863* (Brooklyn: Carlson, 1991), 284–84, 297–98, quoting Beecher in the *Boston Recorder*, Jan. 5, 1831.

9. See Harding, *A Certain Magnificence*, 288–94, 298–327 (on Beecher and the Lane Seminary), 361, 399–402 (on the *Plea* and the Ursuline Convent); *The Autobiography of Lyman Beecher*, ed. Barbara M. Cross, vol. 2 (Cambridge: Harvard University Press, 1961), 250–53; on Foote, see Hedrick, *Stowe*, 72–73. See also Ray Allen Billington, *Protestant Crusade, 1800–1860* (Chicago: Quadrangle, 1938), 70–73; Nancy Lusignan Schultz, *Fire & Roses: The Burning of the Charlestown Convent, 1834* (Boston: Free Press, 2000), 116–17, 160, 165–66.

10. Kathryn Kish Sklar, *Catharine Beecher: A Study in American Domesticity* (New York: W. W. Norton, 1973), 116–17; Hedrick, *Stowe*, 68, 91–92, 170–71; Edward Beecher, *The Papal Conspiracy Exposed, and Protestantism Defended, in the Light of Reason, History, and Scripture* (Boston: Stearns, 1855); Neil Meyer, "'One Language in Prayer': Evangelicalism, Anti-Catholicism, and Harriet Beecher Stowe's 'The Minister's Wooing,'" *New England Quarterly* 85 (2012): 468–90.

11. Lawrence Friedman calls the evangelicals "half-way abolitionists." Lawrence J. Friedman, *Gregarious Saints: Self and Community in American Abolitionism, 1830–1870* (New York: Cambridge University Press, 1982), 35–39.

12. If they were "immediatist" relative to the "halfway" abolitionism of the Lane faculty, Weld and the Lane rebels were allied with the Tappans, and more pragmatic than the Garrisonian wing. Friedman, *Gregarious Saints*, 29–35.

13. Harding, *A Certain Magnificence*, 347–74, 377–89; Robert S. Fletcher, *A History of Oberlin College from Its Foundation through the Civil War*, 2 vols. (Oberlin, Ohio: Oberlin College, 1943), 1:150–66.

14. Cheryl Janifer LaRoche, *Free Black Communities and the Underground Railroad:*

The Geography of Resistance (Urbana: University of Illinois Press, 2013); Wilbur H. Siebert, *The Underground Railroad in Ohio*, ed. A. W. McGraw (Columbus, 1895; repr., 1993).

15. Leonard L. Richards, *Men of Property and Standing: Anti-Abolition Mobs in Jacksonian America* (New York: Oxford University Press, 1970), 92–100, 122–29; Stacey M. Robertson, *Hearts Beating for Liberty: Women Abolitionists in the Old Northwest* (Chapel Hill: University of North Carolina Press, 2010), 14–15; Hedrick, *Stowe*, 147–48.

16. John Niven, *Salmon P. Chase: A Biography* (New York: Oxford University Press, 1995), 42–83; Stephen Ellingson, "Understanding the Dialectic of Discourse and Collective Action: Public Debate and Rioting in Antebellum Cincinnati," *American Journal of Sociology* 101 (1995): 100–144; William M. Wiecek, *The Sources of Antislavery Constitutionalism* (Ithaca: Cornell University Press, 1977), 191–93; Paul Finkelman, *An Imperfect Union: Slavery, Federalism, and Comity* (Chapel Hill: University of North Carolina Press, 1981), 156–72.

17. Niven, *Chase*, 42, 60; Harrold, *Gamaliel Bailey*, 26; Hedrick, *Stowe*, 82–88.

18. Hedrick, *Stowe*, 106–8.

19. Hedrick, *Stowe*, 104–5, 108–9.

20. Sklar, *Catharine Beecher*, 99, 132–37; Hedrick, *Stowe*, 58–59, 109; Mary Hershberger, "Mobilizing Women, Anticipating Abolition: The Struggle against Indian Removal in the 1830s," *Journal of American History* 86 (1999): 25.

21. Catharine Beecher to the Beecher family (Jan. 24–Feb. 18, 1838), Acquisitions, Circular Letters, Stowe-Day Library, Hartford, quoted in Hedrick, *Stowe*, 93.

22. Hedrick, *Stowe*, 230; E. Bruce Kirkham, *The Building of Uncle Tom's Cabin* (Knoxville: University of Tennessee Press, 1977), 102–3.

23. Robertson, *Hearts Beating*, 95–100.

24. Harrold, *Gamaliel Bailey*, 17–18, 41–69; Niven, *Chase*, 60–67.

25. Hedrick, *Stowe*, 133–42; Kirkham, *Building*, 41–57.

26. Hedrick, *Stowe*, 173–93.

27. Debby Applegate, *The Most Famous Man in America: The Biography of Henry Ward Beecher* (New York: Doubleday, 2006), 136–93; Halford R. Ryan, *Henry Ward Beecher: A Peripatetic Preacher* (New York: Greenwood, 1990), 22–25; *New York Evangelist*, Jan. 2, 1845.

28. Applegate, *The Most Famous Man in America*, 193–96; Mary Kay Ricks, *Escape on the Pearl: The Heroic Bid for Freedom on the Underground Railroad* (New York: Murrow, 2007), 190–93, 206–10; *New York Independent*, Feb. 21, Mar. 21, 1850; Hedrick, *Stowe*, 194; Kirkham, *Building*, 62; Forrest Wilson, *Crusader in Crinoline: The Life of Harriet Beecher Stowe* (1942; repr., Westport, Conn.: Greenwood, 1972), 230–40. In 1848–49 Salmon Chase was representing Lyman Beecher in another court case with the trustees of the Lane Seminary; Niven, *Salmon P. Chase*, 118–20.

29. Hedrick, *Stowe*, 205–6.

30. Hedrick, *Stowe*, 187–88; Charles Beecher, *The Incarnation; or, Pictures of the Virgin and Her Son* (New York: Harper, 1849).

31. *New York Evangelist*, June 12–19, 1851; Kirkham, *Building*, 70.

32. HBS to CES, Dec. [27?], 1850, in Stowe, *Life*, 146; see also Hedrick, *Stowe*, 206–7.

33. Hedrick, *Stowe*, 155–56; Stowe, *Life*, 145–49. A year later Isabella had complaints about Harriet's conversion: "She was so absorbed in the dawn of her own ideas, she did not once remember that in common with others of our family she had doubted the wisdom of such practice." Isabella Beecher Hooker to John Hooker, June 20, 1852, Isabella Beecher Hooker Project, fiche 10, quoted in Allyn Van Deusen, "Partners in Reform: Isabella Beecher Hooker and John Hooker" (Ph.D. diss., State University of New York at Binghamton, 2013), 62.

34. HBS to CES, Jan. 12, 1851, in Stowe, *Life*, 148.

35. See the comment by Melissa Homestead, "*Uncle Tom's Cabin* in the *National Era*," https://nationalera.wordpress.com/further-reading/missed-installment-comment-by-melissa-homestead/.

36. HBS to CES, Jan. 27, 1851, in Hedrick, *Stowe*, 206. Kirkham, *Building*, 64–65, dates the letter Jan. 25.

37. HBS to Gamaliel Bailey, March 9, 1851 [typescript], William Lloyd Garrison Papers, Boston Public Library.

38. *Era*, April 17, May 8, 15, 29, 1851.

39. "A Word of Commendation," *Era*, July 17, 1851; Claire Parfait, *The Publishing History of Uncle Tom's Cabin, 1852–2002* (Burlington, Vt.: Ashgate, 2007), 24–26, 30; Harrold, *Gamaliel Bailey*, 139; Michael Winship, "'The Greatest Book of Its Kind': A Publishing History of 'Uncle Tom's Cabin,'" *Proceedings of the American Antiquarian Society* 109 (1999): 309–32. On authors and readers of serialized novels, see Claire Parfait, "The Nineteenth-Century Serial as a Collective Enterprise: Harriet Beecher Stowe's *Uncle Tom's Cabin* and Eugène Sue's *Les Mystères de Paris*," *Proceedings of the American Antiquarian Society* 112, pt. 1 (2002): 127–52.

40. Parfait, *Publishing History*, 26–27.

41. HBS to Gamaliel Bailey, Mar. 9, 1851 (typescript), William Lloyd Garrison Papers, Boston Public Library.

42. John C. Havard, "Fighting Slavery by 'Presenting Facts in Detail': Realism, Typology, and Temporality in *Uncle Tom's Cabin*," *American Literary Realism* 44 (2012): 249–66.

43. This seems clearly to be the case for December 18, 1851. See comments by Melissa Homestead, Michael Winship, and Barbara Hochman about missing installments on August 21, October 30, and December 18, 1851, in "*Uncle Tom's Cabin* in the *National Era*," https://nationalera.wordpress.com/table-of-contents/.

44. Harrold, *Gamaliel Bailey*, 143.

45. Kirkham, *Building*, 105–9; *Liberator*, Oct. 18, 1850.

46. Kirkham, *Building*, 111–12; Niven, *Salmon P. Chase*, 77–83. The Bird family of the novel had been "Burr" in the *Era* serial.

47. Here see in general Steven Deyle, "The Domestic Slave Trade in America: The Lifeblood of the Southern Slave System," in *The Chattel Principle: Internal Slave Trades in the Americas*, ed. Walter Johnson (New Haven: Yale University Press, 2004), 91–116, arguing that the slave trade became a particularly important vector of concern for abolition in the final antebellum decades.

48. Hedrick, *Stowe*, 199–201; Ethan L. Kytle, *Romantic Reformers and the Antislavery Struggle in the Civil War Era* (New York: Cambridge University Press, 2014), 137–50.

49. Of the eleven divided chapters, there is one (chapter 9) set in Ohio and ten in New Orleans and Arkansas. In the third section, Stowe and Bailey were clearly struggling to have St. Clare's killing take place in a continued chapter that would run on New Year's Day, with a suspense-building gap on December 18. Publishing four full chapters on November 13 and 20 put the *Era* on schedule for this holiday cliff-hanger.

50. *UTC*, vol. 2, chap. 41, p. 284.

51. Harriet Beecher Stowe, *A Key to Uncle Tom's Cabin* . . . (1853; repr., Mineola, N.Y.: Dover, 2015), 133.

52. *UTC*, vol. 2, chap. 45, pp. 314, 317, 319.

53. *UTC*, vol. 1, chap.. 9, p. 121.

54. [George Holmes], "Uncle Tom's Cabin," *Southern Literary Messenger* 18 (December 1852): 721. See discussions in John L. Thomas, "Antislavery and Utopia," in *The Antislavery Vanguard: New Essays on the Abolitionists*, ed. Martin Duberman (Princeton: Princeton University Press, 1965), 242; Eric J. Sundquist, introduction to *New Essays on Uncle Tom's Cabin*, ed. Eric J. Sundquist (New York: Cambridge University Press, 1986), 31.

55. This discussion is indebted to a large body of literature on *Uncle Tom's Cabin*: Gillian Brown, "Getting in the Kitchen with Dinah: Domestic Politics in *Uncle Tom's Cabin*," *American Quarterly* 36 (1984): 503–23; Jane Tomkins, *Sensational Designs: The Cultural Work of American Fiction, 1790–1860* (New York: Oxford University Press, 1985), 122–46; Sundquist, introduction to *New Essays*, 1–44; Janet Fagan Yellin, "Doing It Herself: *Uncle Tom's Cabin* and Woman's Role in the Slavery Crisis," in Sundquist, *New Essays*, 85–106; Elizabeth Ammons, "Stowe's Dream of the Mother-Savior: *Uncle Tom's Cabin* and American Women Writers before the 1820s," in Sundquist, *New Essays*, 155–95; Alexander Saxton, *The Rise and Fall of the White Republic: Class Politics and Mass Culture in Nineteenth-Century America* (New York: Verso, 1990), 227–41; Amy Kaplan, "Manifest Domesticity," *American Literature* 70 (1998): 581–606; Jim O'Loughlin, "Articulating *Uncle Tom's Cabin*," *New Literary History* 31 (2000): 573–97; Lora Romero, *Home Fronts: Domesticity and Its Critics in the Antebellum United States* (Durham: Duke University Press, 1997), 70–88; Michael D. Pierson, *Free Hearts, Free Homes: Gender and American Antislavery Politics* (Chapel Hill: University of North Carolina Press, 2003), 61–69. See also the wider literature on the abolitionist publicity surrounding gender and the violence of slavery, most formatively Elizabeth B. Clark "'The Sacred Rights of the Weak': Pain, Sympathy, and the Culture of Individual Rights in Antebellum America," *Journal of American History* 82 (1995): 463–93; and Carol Lasser, "Voyeuristic Abolitionism: Sex, Gender, and the Transformation of Antislavery Rhetoric," *Journal of the Early Republic* 28 (2008): 83–114.

56. Joy Jordan-Lake, *Whitewashing Uncle Tom's Cabin: Nineteenth-Century Women Novelists Respond to Stowe* (Nashville: Vanderbilt University Press, 2005), 1–8; Susan J. Tracy, *In the Master's Eye: Representations of Women, Blacks, and Poor Whites in Antebellum Southern Literature* (Amherst: University of Massachusetts Press, 1995), 141–74.

57. Sarah Meer, *Uncle Tom Mania: Slavery, Minstrelsy, and Transatlantic Culture in the 1850s* (Athens: University of Georgia Press, 2005), 21–50; O'Loughlin, "Articulating *Uncle Tom's Cabin*," 579–90; Michelle Anne Abate, "Topsy and Topsy-Turvy Jo: Harriet Beecher Stowe's *Uncle Tom's Cabin* and Louisa May Alcott's *Little Women*," *Children's Literature* 34 (2006): 59–82.

58. *UTC*, vol. 2, chap. 45, pp. 317–20.

59. *Liberator*, March 26, 1853. Here and throughout this discussion see Thomas F. Gossett, *Uncle Tom's Cabin and American Culture* (Dallas: Southern Methodist University Press, 1985), 170–74; and Robert S. Levine, *Martin Delany, Frederick Douglass, and the Politics of Representative Identity* (Chapel Hill: University of North Carolina Press, 1997), 69–89.

60. *Pennsylvania Freeman*, Apr. 29, 1852; *Frederick Douglass' Paper*, May 20, June 17, 1852.

61. *Pennsylvania Freeman*, May 6, 1852; *Frederick Douglass' Paper*, Apr. 1, May 6, 1852.

62. *Frederick Douglass's Paper*, Apr. 8, May 27, Aug. 13, 1852; see Levine, *Martin Delany, Frederick Douglass, and the Politics of Representative Identity*, 73–76.

63. Douglass to HBS, Mar. 8, 1853, *Frederick Douglass' Paper*, Dec. 2, 1853; "The Heroic Slave," *Frederick Douglass' Paper*, Mar. 4–25, 1853; Levine, *Martin Delany, Frederick Douglass, and the Politics of Representative Identity*, 83–85.

64. *Pennsylvania Freeman*, May 3, 1852, May 30, 1853; Levine, *Martin Delany, Frederick Douglass, and the Politics of Representative Identity*, 144–76.

65. *DCF*, 2:164, 271, 339–40; 3:259, 326, 330–31, 403; 4:303–4, 443–44.

66. In Friedman's analysis in *Gregarious Saints*, this audience encompassed the "half-way abolitionists" and the colonizationists. Here also see the analysis in David S. Reynolds, *Mightier Than the Sword: Uncle Tom's Cabin and the Battle for America* (New York: W. W. Norton, 2011), 129–31.

67. Lydia Maria Child to Susan Lyman Lesley, Mar. 29, 1852, in *Lydia Maria Child: Selected Letters, 1817–1880* ed. Milton Meltzer and Patricia G. Holland (Amherst: University of Massachusetts Press, 1982), 264, quoted in Barbara Hochman, *Uncle Tom's Cabin and the Reading Revolution: Race, Literacy, Childhood, and Fiction* (Amherst: University of Massachusetts Press, 2008), 87.

68. Hedrick, *Stowe*, 214–16, quote from 215. See also Tomkins, *Sensational Designs*, 133–35; Sundquist, introduction to *New Essays*, 5–6; Dawn Coleman, "The Unsentimental Woman Preacher of *Uncle Tom's Cabin*," *American Literature* 80 (2008): 265–92.

69. *UTC*, vol. 2, chap. 45, p. 322.

70. HBS to Earl of Carlisle, Jan. 7, 1852, in Stowe, *Life*, 169.

71. Hedrick, *Stowe*, 211–12.

72. *The Journals and Miscellaneous Notebooks of Ralph Waldo Emerson*, ed. Ralph H. Orth and Alfred R. Ferguson, vol. 8 (Cambridge: Harvard University Press, 1977), 121.

73. See the discussion in the introduction.

74. Hochman, *Uncle Tom's Cabin*, 14–17, 78–130.

75. *Boston Emancipator and Republican*, Oct. 17, 1850, 5; Parfait, *Publishing History*, 33–42; Kirkham, *Building*, 140–49.

76. James L. Birney to HBS, Jan. 12, 1853, in *Letters of James Gillespie Birney, 1831–1857*, ed. Dwight L. Dumond, vol. 2 (New York: Appleton, 1938), 1161. On borrowing, see also discussions of farm laborers Charles Cobb and Carrol Norcross in Ronald J. Zboray and Mary Saracino Zboray, *Everyday Ideas: Socioliterary Experience among Antebellum New Englanders* (Knoxville: University of Tennessee Press, 2006), 123, 185, 249.

77. Frances M. Jocelyn Diary, Sept. 27, 1852, Jocelyn Family Papers, Connecticut Historical Museum, quoted in Zboray and Zboray, *Everyday Ideas*, 132.

78. Joseph Sill Diary, Apr. 25, 1852, HSP.

79. James L. Birney to HBS, Jan. 12, 1853, in *Letters*, 2:1161.

80. Anna Thaxter Quincy Cushing Diary, Apr. 13, 1852, American Antiquarian Society, quoted in Hochman, *Uncle Tom's Cabin*, 82.

81. Maria Woodbury to Lucy Marshall, June 4, 1852, Marshall Papers, American Antiquarian Society, quoted in Hochman, *Uncle Tom's Cabin*, 14.

82. Ellen Douglas Birdseye Wheaton, *The Diary of Ellen Birdseye Wheaton* (Boston: Privately published, 1923), 131 (Apr. 16, 1852).

83. Charles William Holbrook Diary, Oct. 1–4, 1852, in David D. Hall, "A Yankee Tutor in the South," *New England Quarterly* 33 (1960): 89.

84. Joseph Sill Diary, May 2, 1852, HSP.

85. Carrol Norcross Diary, Aug. 26–27, 1852, Cargill-Knight-Norcross Family Papers, Maine Historical Society, quoted in Zboray and Zboray, *Everyday Ideas*, 249–50.

86. *The Diary of James A. Garfield*, vol. 1, *1848–1871*, ed. Harry James Brown and Frederick D. Williams (East Lansing: Michigan State University Press, 1967), 145–46 (July 17, 1852), 181 (Mar. 4–5, 1853).

87. Hochman, *Uncle Tom's Cabin*, 83–84, citing "Harriet Beecher Stowe Dead," *Philadelphia Times*, July 2, 1896; Henry Ward Beecher, "Tribute to Harriet Beecher Stowe," in *Modern Eloquence*, ed. Thomas B. Reed, vol. 1 (Philadelphia: Morris, 1900), 52.

88. Anna Thaxter Quincy Cushing Diary, Apr. 13, 1852, American Antiquarian Society, quoted in Hochman, *Uncle Tom's Cabin*, 84.

89. Mary Pierce Poor to Lucy Pierce Hedge, Apr. 18, 1852, Poor Family Papers, 1791–1921, Schlesinger Library, Radcliffe Institute, HU, quoted in Zboray and Zboray, *Everyday Ideas*, 258.

90. Joseph Sill Diary, Apr. 25, 30, 1852, HSP.

91. Maria Woodbury to Lucy Marshall, June 4, 1852, Marshall Papers, American Antiquarian Society, quoted in Hochman, *Uncle Tom's Cabin*, 15.

92. Elizabeth Cady Stanton to Elizabeth Smith Miller, Nov. 21, 1852, in *Elizabeth Cady Stanton, as Revealed in Her Letters, Diary and Reminiscences*, ed. Harriot Stanton Blatch and Theodore Stanton, vol. 2 (New York: Harper, 1922), 45–46.

93. Henry Wilson, *History of the Rise and Fall of the Slave Power in America*, 2nd ed., vol. 2 (Boston: James R. Osgood, 1875), 519.

94. Henry James, *A Small Boy and Others* (New York: Scribner's, 1913), 159–60.

95. Wendell Philips, *The Philosophy of the Abolition Movement: Speech of Wendell Phillips, at the Melodeon, Boston, Jan. 27, 1853* (New York: American Anti-Slavery

Society, 1860), 29, 32. See the similar construction in Holman Hamilton, *Prologue to Conflict: The Crisis and Compromise of 1850* (New York: W. W. Norton, 1966), 171.

96. For the Senate debates in December: *CG* 32/1, 30, 34–39, 92–96, 112–20, 125, 128, 133–40; Richard H. Sewell, *Ballots for Freedom: Antislavery Politics in the United States, 1837–1860* (New York: Oxford University Press, 1976), 233.

97. *CG* 32/1, 50–51.

98. Greenwood, "An American Salon," 8–9.

99. "G," "Uncle Tom's Cabin," *Era*, Oct. 30, 1851.

100. "S.E.M.," *Era*, Jan. 29, 1852; see Brooks, *Liberty Power*, 170.

101. *Chicago Free West*, Feb. 1, 1852, quoted in Brooks, *Liberty Power*, 170.

102. Leonard Woods to CS, Mar. 26, 1852, Sumner Papers, HU; Edward Jarvis to Horace Mann, Apr. 19, 1852, Horace Mann Collection, MHS.

103. John Jay to CS, July 5, 1852, Sumner Papers, HU; Brooks, *Liberty Power*, 169–70.

104. Wilmot and Dixon in *CG* 29/2, 354, and App., 334, quoted in Elizabeth R. Varon, *Disunion! The Coming of the American Civil War, 1789–1859* (Chapel Hill: University of North Carolina Press, 2008), 186.

105. *CG* 32/1, 394 (Fowler, Mar. 31, 1852); Jewett ad, *Boston Congregationalist*, May 28, June 11, 18, 1852; *New York Evangelist*, May 27, 1852.

106. *CG* 32/1, 531–35, 659–60; see also 700–701.

107. *CG* 32/1, 770, App., 772–76; *House Journal*, 32/1, 470.

108. *CG* 32/1, 901–2; Sewell, *Ballots for Freedom*, 239.

109. *CG* 32/1, 976–96; Sewell, *Ballots for Freedom*, 233.

110. Donald Bruce Johnson, comp., *National Party Platforms*, vol. 1, *1840–1956*, rev. ed. (Urbana: University of Illinois Press, 1978), 17, 21; William E. Gienapp, *The Origins of the Republican Party: 1852–1856* (New York: Oxford University Press, 1987), 15, 18.

111. This discussion is indebted to Sarah Purcell, "All That Remains of Henry Clay: Political Funerals and the Tour of Henry Clay's Corpse," *Common-Place* 12, no. 3 (April 2012), http://www.common-place-archives.org/vol-12/no-03/purcell/.

112. Gienapp, *Origins*, 17.

113. Johnson, *National Party Platforms*, 1:18–20; Sewell, *Ballots for Freedom*, 244–45.

114. *CG* 32/1, 50–51 (Kossuth), 32/1, App., 134–36 (Iowa). Here and throughout the discussion I follow David Donald, *Charles Sumner and the Coming of the Civil War* (New York: Random House, 1960), 210–21.

115. "Pardoning Power of the President" (May 14, 1852), in *Charles Sumner, His Complete Works*, vol. 3 (Boston: Lee & Shepherd, 1900), 219–33.

116. *CG* 32/1, 1474–75, 1934, 1950–53.

117. *CG* 32/1, 2371; *CG* 32/1, App. 1102–13 (Sumner, Aug. 26), quotes from 1103, 1112; Sewell, *Ballots for Freedom*, 239; Donald, *Charles Sumner*, 227–39; *Washington Republic*, Aug. 28, 1852; *Worcester Palladium*, Sept. 1, 1852; *NA-SS*, Sept. 2, 1852; *Era*, Sept. 2, 1852; *Liberator*, Sept. 17, 1852; *Concord (N.H.) Independent Democrat*, Sept. 23, 1852; James W. Stone to John Jay, Sept. 28, 1852, Jay Family Papers, Columbia University.

118. *CG* 32/1, App., 1076.

119. *Proceedings of the Colored National Convention, held in Rochester, July 6th, 7th,*

and 8th, 1853 (Rochester: Office of Frederick Douglass' Paper, 1853), 4, 33–38; *Frederick Douglass' Paper*, Apr. 1, 14, 29, May 6, 30, Aug. 26, Oct. 28, Nov. 18, Dec. 2, 1853; Levine, *Martin Delany, Frederick Douglass, and the Politics of Representative Identity*, 77–90.

120. Joseph R. Hawley and Joseph Wood Hooker to Gerrit Smith, Nov. 5, 1852; Bradford R. Wood to Gerrit Smith, Nov. 5, 1852; Gerrit Smith Papers, Syracuse University; Bradford R. Wood to CS, Nov. 10, 1852, Sumner Papers, HU. See Ralph V. Harlow, *Gerrit Smith: Philanthropist and Reformer* (New York: Holt, 1939), 287–88; Brooks, *Liberty Power*, 176.

121. David L. Child to CS, Feb. 8, 1853, Sumner Papers, HU, quoted in Brooks, *Liberty Power*, 176.

122. John Jay to CS, Dec. 20, 1852, Sumner Papers, HU.

Chapter 5: Transforming Culture

1. Hedrick, *Stowe*, 223–24; Claire Parfait, *The Publishing History of Uncle Tom's Cabin, 1852–2002* (Burlington, Vt.: Ashgate, 2007), 104–8.

2. Mary Kelley, *Private Woman, Public Stage: Literary Domesticity in Nineteenth-Century America* (New York: Oxford University Press, 1984), 180–249; Nancy Isenberg, *Sex and Citizenship in Antebellum America* (Chapel Hill: University of North Carolina Press, 1998), 41–74; Ronald J. Zboray and May Saracino Zboray, *Voices without Votes: Women and Politics in Antebellum New England* (Lebanon, N.H.: University Press of New England, 2010); Julie Roy Jeffrey, *The Great Silent Army: Ordinary Women in the Antislavery Movement* (Chapel Hill: University of North Carolina Press, 1998).

3. Erkki Huhtamo, *Illusions in Motion: Media Archaeology of the Moving Panorama and Related Spectacles* (Cambridge: MIT Press, 2013); David Nasaw, *Going Out: The Rise and Fall of Public Amusements* (New York: Basic Books, 1993); Albert F. McLean, *American Vaudeville as Ritual* (Lexington: University of Kentucky Press, 1965).

4. Leo Braudy, *The Frenzy of Renown: Fame and Its History* (New York: Oxford University Press, 1986), esp. 450–515.; Amanda Adams, *Performing Authorship in the Nineteenth-Century Transatlantic Lecture Tour* (Burlington, Vt.: Ashgate, 2014), 1–85; Grahame Smith, *Charles Dickens: A Literary Life* (New York: St. Martins, 1996), 1–19, 89–128; Brenda R. Weber, *Women and Literary Celebrity in the Nineteenth Century: The Transatlantic Production of Fame and Gender* (Burlington, Vt.: Ashgate, 2012), 1–100.

5. These events are discussed in Hedrick, *Stowe*, 225–30; the details are in the *New York Independent*, Oct. 7, 1852; and the *New York Times*, Oct. 6, 8, 15, 16, 19, 1852.

6. Thomas F. Gossett, *Uncle Tom's Cabin and American Culture* (Dallas: Southern Methodist University Press, 1985), 176–80, 185–238; Sarah Meer, *Uncle Tom Mania: Slavery, Minstrelsy, and Transatlantic Culture in the 1850s* (Athens: University of Georgia Press, 2005), 73–102; Joy Jordan-Lake, *Whitewashing Uncle Tom's Cabin: Nineteenth-Century Women Novelists Respond to Stowe* (Nashville: Vanderbilt University Press, 2005).

7. Hedrick, *Stowe*, 229–30, 441n53; *New York Independent*, Oct. 7, 1852.

8. Weld-Hamilton Mss. Reminiscences, quoted in Gilbert H. Barnes, *The Antislavery Impulse, 1830–1844* (1933; New York: Harcourt, Brace, 1964), 231n21.
9. CES and HBS to CS, Dec. 21, 1852, Sumner Papers, HU; Hedrick, *Stowe*, 44In.
10. HBS to Gerrit Smith, Oct. 25, 1852, Gerrit Smith Papers, Syracuse University.
11. HBS to CS, Nov. 7, 1852; CS to William I. Bowditch, Dec. 15, 1852; John Jay to CS, Dec. 20, 1852; William Bowditch to CS, Dec. (undated) 1852; William Bowditch to CS, before Jan. 6, 1853; CES and HBS to CS, Dec. 21, 1852, all in Sumner Papers, HU; Leonard W Bacon to James Birney, Dec. 28, 1852, Jan. 22, 1853; Birney to HBS, Jan. 12, 1853, in *Letters of James Gillespie Birney, 1831–1857*, ed. Dwight L. Dumond, vol. 2 (New York: Appleton, 1938), 1159–63; Leonard W. Bacon to Horace Mann, Jan. 10, 1852, Horace Mann Collection, MHS.
12. Bradford R. Wood to CS, Nov. 10, 1852; CS to HBS, Nov. 12, 1852, Sumner Papers, HU.
13. John P. Jewett to CS, Jan. 18, 1853; CES, Andover, to CS, Jan. 19, 1853, Sumner Papers, HU.
14. John P. Jewett to CS, Mar. 1, 1853, Sumner Papers, HU.
15. John Jay, New York, to CS, Dec. 20, 1852; CS to William I. Bowditch, Jan. 18, 1853, Sumner Papers, HU; James Birney to HBS, Jan. 12, 1853, in *Letters of James Gillespie Birney*, 2:1160.
16. Maurice G. Baxter, *One and Indivisible: Daniel Webster and the Union* (Cambridge: Harvard University Press, 1984), 493–500; Theodore Parker, *A Discourse Occasioned by the Death of Daniel Webster: Preached at The Melodeon on Sunday, Oct. 31, 1852* (Boston: B. B. Mussey, 1853); Parker Pillsbury, "Letter from Massachusetts," *Lisbon (Ohio) Antislavery Bugle*, Dec. 18, 1852.
17. On Stowe's meeting with Millie Edmundson, see Stowe, *Life*, 179–82.
18. Sarah L. H. Gronningsater, "'On Behalf of His Race and the Lemmon Slaves': Louis Napoleon, Northern Black Legal Culture, and the Politics of Sectional Crisis," *Journal of the Civil War Era* 7 (2017): 206–41; Sarah Levine-Gronningsater, "Delivering Freedom: Gradual Emancipation, Black Legal Culture, and the Origins of Sectional Crisis in New York, 1759–1870" (Ph.D. diss., University of Chicago, 2014), 304–61 (for Hooker, see 338n84); Eric Foner, *Gateway to Freedom: The Hidden History of the Underground Railroad* (New York: W. W. Norton, 2015), 140–42; on successful escapes, see *Statistical View of the United States . . . being a Compendium of the Seventh Census*, comp. J. D. B. Debow (Washington, D.C.: Tucker, 1854), 64; *Statistics of the United States . . . in 1860; Compiled from the Original Returns and being the Final Exhibit of the Eighth Census . . .* (Washington, D.C., 1866), 337–38.
19. Benedict Anderson, *Imagined Communities: Reflections on the Origins and Spread of Nationalism*, rev. ed. (New York: Verso, 2006).
20. Hedrick, *Stowe*, 233–25; Parfait, *Publishing History*, 36, 67–89.
21. Donald S. Spencer, *Louis Kossuth and Young America: A Study of Sectionalism and Foreign Policy, 1848–1852* (Columbia: University of Missouri Press, 1977), 59–62.
22. Anna Matilda McNeill Whistler to Catherine Jane McNeill, Apr. 27, 1853, Anna Matilda Whistler Papers, 1850–1876, LC.
23. Jo-Ann Morgan, *Uncle Tom's Cabin as Visual Culture* (Columbia: University of Missouri Press, 2007), 3, 10n28, 31, 74–82, 189; Stephen A. Hirsch, "Uncle Tomitudes:

The Popular Reaction to *Uncle Tom's Cabin*," *Studies in the American Renaissance* (1978): 317–19, 322 (citing *New York Tribune*, Oct. 23, 1852); *Bangor Daily Whig & Courier*, Dec. 25, 1852; *Liberator*, Sept. 8, 1854; see game at http://utc.iath.virginia.edu/tomituds/game3f.html.

24. Salmon P. Chase Journal, Jan. 9, 1853, in *The Salmon P. Chase Papers*, vol. 1, *Journals, 1829–1872*, ed. John Niven et al. (Kent: Kent State University Press, 1993), 233–34, esp. 233n80, citing Salmon P. Chase to Sarah Bella Chase, Dec. 10, 1851, Chase Papers, LC.

25. James W. Stone to CS, Dec. 27, 1852, Sumner Papers, HU. Stone was a good judge of the "Market," having just put out a narrative of the sensational Parkman murder, James W. Stone, *The Trial of Prof. John White Webster* (Boston: Phillip Sampson & Co., 1850).

26. *A Philadelphia Perspective: The Diary of Sidney George Fisher Covering the Years 1834–1871*, ed. Nicholas B. Wainwright (Philadelphia: Historical Society of Pennsylvania, 1967), 246 (Fisher wrote a review conciliatory to southern feelings, "*Uncle Tom's Cabin* and the Amelioration of Slavery," *North American Review* 77 [Oct. 1853]: 466–93); *The Diary of Ellen Birdseye Wheaton*, ed. Donald Gordon (Boston, 1923), 154 (Jan. 30, 1853).

27. Stowe, *Life*, 189–90; Parfait, *Publishing History*, 106–8; Forrest Wilson, *Crusader in Crinoline: The Life of Harriet Beecher Stowe* (1942; repr., Westport, Conn.: Greenwood, 1972), 325–28.

28. CES and HBS to CS, Dec. 21, 1852; HBS to CS, Dec. 25 [est.], 1852, Sumner Papers, HU.

29. Wilson, *Crusader*, 328.

30. HBS replies are printed in Stowe, *Life*, 164–74. Shaftesbury's first publication of the address, dated November 5, was published in *The Times* of London, Nov. 9, 1852, and republished in the *NA-SS* on Dec. 2, 1852. CES and HBS to CS, Dec. 21, 1852, Sumner Papers, HU.

31. HBS to CS, Dec. 25 [est.], 1852, Sumner Papers, HU.

32. Hedrick, *Stowe*, 240, 246–48.

33. HBS to Gerrit Smith, Oct. 25, 1852, Gerrit Smith Papers, Syracuse University.

34. Publication date of the *Key* estimated from advertisements in the *Boston Recorder*, May 5, June 2, 1853.

35. Hedrick, *Stowe*, 232–50; Wilson, *Crusader in Crinoline*, 340–93.

36. Stowe, *Life*, 160, 178–84.

37. Adams, *Performing Authorship*, 1–56.

38. *Chains and Freedom: The Life and Adventure of Peter Wheeler: A Colored Man Yet Living, A Slave in Chains, A Sailor in the Deep, and a Sinner at the Cross*, ed. Graham R. Hodges (Tuscaloosa: University of Alabama Press, 2009); Nicholas P. Wood, "Jefferson's Legacy, Race Science, and Religious Violence in Jabez Hammond's Abolitionist Fiction," *Early American Studies* 14 (2016): 568–609.

39. Alexander Saxton, *The Rise and Fall of the White Republic: Class Politics and Mass Culture in Nineteenth-Century America* (New York: Verso, 1996), 230–35, describes Hildreth's Enlightenment-informed *Archy* as "out of phase" with mid-nineteenth-century culture, relative to *Uncle Tom's Cabin*. Wendell Philips, *The Philosophy of the Abolition Movement: Speech . . . at the Melodeon, Boston, Jan. 27, 1853* (New York: American Anti-Slavery Society, 1860), 29, called *Archy* "a work born out of due time."

40. For this correspondence, see HBS to CS, Nov. 7, 1852; CS to HBS, Nov. 12, 1852; John P. Jewett to CS, Dec. 18, 1852; CS to Edward L. Pierce, Jan. 13, 1853; John P. Jewett to CS, Mar. 1, 1853; Frances A. Seward to CS, Mar. 1, 1853; John P. Jewett to CS, Mar. 24, 1853; Edward L. Peirce to CS, Jan. 10, 1854, Sumner Papers, HU.

41. James W. Stone to CS, Dec. 27, 1852, Sumner Papers, HU.

42. *Frederick Douglass's Paper*, Apr. 29, 1853; Diary of James Lakey, June 24, 1853, Jan. 27, 1854, Cincinnati History Library & Archives.

43. *Liberator*, Nov. 4, 1853, Feb. 3, 1854; *Pennsylvania Freeman*, Dec. 29, 1853; *NA-SS*, Jan. 21, 1854.

44. *Washington Daily Evening Star*, June 22, 1853; *New York Herald*, quoted in *Western Reserve Chronicle* (Warren, Ohio), June 23, 1852; *Liberator*, Feb. 17, 1854.

45. William R. Taylor, *Cavalier and Yankee: The Old South and American National Character* (New York: Harper Torchbooks, 1961), 299–324; Gossett, *Uncle Tom's Cabin and American Culture*, 185–238; Meer, *Uncle Tom Mania*, 73–102; Jordan-Lake, *Whitewashing Uncle Tom's Cabin*.

46. Excerpts from *Aunt Phillis* were published in the *Washington Southern Press* on July 20 and reprinted in the *Charleston Courier*, July 23, 1852. An early ad was published in the *Baltimore American and Commercial Advertiser* on August 11. On the author of *Aunt Phillis's Cabin*, see Rena Neumann Coen, "Mary Henderson Eastman: A Biographical Essay," in Mary Henderson Eastman, *Dahcotah, or, Life and Legends of the Sioux around Fort Snelling* (Afton, Minn.: Afton Historical Society Press, 1995), xxiii–xxv. Eastman's proslavery credentials were tempered by her husband's and son's Union service in the Civil War; she wrote a minor contribution to sentimental unionism, *Jenny Wade of Gettysburg* (Philadelphia: Lippincott, 1864).

47. For this discussion, see sources cited in table 8.

48. James W. Stone to CS, Dec. 27, 1852, Sumner Papers, HU.

49. Abraham Lincoln, "Hon. A. Lincoln's Address, Before the Springfield Scott Club, in Reply to Judge Douglas' Richmond Speech, August 14, 26, 1852," in *CWAL*, 2:157.

50. *DCF*, 4:159, 163.

51. But see Christopher J. Smith, *The Creolization of American Culture: William Sidney Mount and the Roots of Blackface Minstrelsy* (Urbana: University of Illinois Press, 2013).

52. A search of the America's Historical Newspapers database reveals that references to "sheet music" grow first between 1839 and 1843 and then in 1851–1853, stabilized through 1865, and then rise to a peak in 1909.

53. Dale Cockrell, *Demons of Disorder: Early Blackface Minstrels and Their World* (New York: Cambridge University Press, 1997), 149–55, citing the *New York Herald*, Feb. 6, 1843; Hans Nathan, *Dan Emmett and the Rise of Early Negro Minstrelsy*, 2nd printing (Norman: University of Oklahoma Press, 1977), 113–19.

54. Robert C. Toll, *Blacking Up: The Minstrel Show in Nineteenth-Century America* (New York: Oxford University Press, 1974), 50–51; Meer, *Uncle Tom Mania*, 37–40.

55. William J. Mahar, *Behind the Burnt-Cork Mask: Early Blackface Minstrelsy and Antebellum American Popular Culture* (Urbana: University of Illinois Press, 1999), 355–63; Nathan, *Dan Emmett*, 147.

56. Mahar, *Behind the Burnt-Cork Mask*, 352–53; Eric Lott, *Love and Theft: Blackface Minstrelsy and the American Working Class* (New York: Oxford University Press, 1993), 206–7; Cockrell, *Demons of Disorder*, 160–62. The America's Historical Newspapers database produces 597 results in a search for "minstrels" in 1850; 407 of them are in northern newspapers.

57. Scott Gac, *Singing for Freedom: The Hutchinson Family Singers and the Nineteenth-Century Culture of Reform* (New Haven: Yale University Press, 2007), passim but esp. 4–21, 124–48, 177–82; Brian Roberts, "'Slavery Would Have Died of That Music': The Hutchinson Family Singers and the Rise of Popular-Culture Abolitionism in Early Antebellum-Era America, 1842–1850," *Proceedings of the American Antiquarian Society* 114, pt. 2 (2004): 301–68; Cockrell, *Demons of Disorder*, 153.

58. "The Hutchinson Family—Hunkerism," *Rochester North Star*, Oct. 27, 1848.

59. Frederick Douglass, *The Anti-Slavery Movement. A Lecture by Frederick Douglass, before the Rochester Ladies Anti-Slavery Society* (Rochester, 1855), 40; originally published in *Frederick Douglass's Paper*, Mar. 23, 1855. See Gac, *Singing for Freedom*, 203–5.

60. Carter is identified as "J. P." or "James P." in the Harvard cataloging of *Carter's Melodies*, but as "J. A. Carter" in Mahar, *Behind the Burnt Cork Mask*, 355, 356. A "James P. Carter," a white wigmaker age twenty-five, born in Virginia, was living in New York City's tenth ward in 1850, with two teenage Irish girls and neighbors including a musician (George R. Solomon), engravers, a bookseller, and an agent (David Owens). U.S. Census for 1850.

61. *Carter's Melodies. As sung by him and The Virginia Serenaders at their Concerts Throughout The United States with Unbounded Applause* (Boston: Keith's Music Publishing House, 1844).

62. *Songs of the Virginia Serenaders* (Boston: Keith's Music Publishing House, 1844); *Boston Evening Transcript*, Mar. 16, 19, 29, 1844; *Boston American Traveler*, Mar. 19, 1844.

63. *Boston Atlas*, Feb. 13, 1844, *Boston Evening Transcript*, Mar. 13, Apr. 2, 1844; *Salem (Mass.) Register*, Apr. 4, 6, 8, 22, 1844.

64. *Philadelphia Public Ledger*, June 18, 1844.

65. *Baltimore Sun*, 18, 20–23, 25–27, 29, 1844.

66. Ken Emerson, *Doo-dah! Stephen Foster and the Rise of American Popular Culture* (New York: Simon & Schuster, 1997), 27–32, 82–84.

67. Evelyn Foster Morneweck, *Chronicles of Stephen Foster's Family* (Pittsburgh: Published for the Foster Hall Collection by the University of Pittsburgh Press, 1944).

68. *Pittsburgh Daily Post*, May 9, 11, 12, 15, 16, 18, 24, 30, 1843; Morneweck, *Chronicles*, 261–64; Joanne O'Connell, "Understanding Stephen Collins Foster: His World and Music" (Ph.D. diss., University of Pittsburgh, 2007), 114–16.

69. Emerson, *Doo-dah!*, 116–21. For minstrels in Cincinnati, see O'Connell, "Understanding Stephen Collins Foster," 137–47; and *Cincinnati Commercial Tribune*, Feb. 17, 18, 20, 21, 1846; *Cincinnati Enquirer*, Sept. 3–11, 1847, Apr. 19, Oct. 19, 28, Dec. 12, 21, 1849.

70. Here I follow Emerson, *Doo-dah!*, 104–6; Matthew Shaftel, "Singing a New Song: Stephen Foster and the New American Minstrelsy," *Music & Politics* 2 (2007): 7–8.

71. Emerson, *Doo-dah!*, 127–35; Shaftel, "Singing a New Song," 10–15.

72. Emerson, *Doo-dah!*, 149–151, 274, 309; unknown correspondent to Evelyn Foster Morneweck, May 31, 1933, Foster Hall Collection, Center for American Music, University of Pittsburgh.

73. Emerson, *Doo-dah!*, 146–47; Shaftel, "Singing a New Song," 16–27; Lott, *Love and Theft*, 187–201; Meer, *Uncle Tom Mania*, 53–58. But see the partial critique in Steven Saunders, "The Social Agenda of Stephen Foster's Plantation Melodies," *American Music* 30 (2012): 1–27.

74. Stephen Foster to E. P. Christy, May 25, 1852, Foster Hall Collection, Center for American Music, University of Pittsburgh.

75. Saunders, "The Social Agenda," 285–86.

76. Morneweck, *Chronicles*, 283–84; Morrison Foster, *Biography, Songs and Musical Compositions of Stephen Collins Foster* (Pittsburgh: Percy F. Smith, 1896), 12–14; Emerson, *Doo-dah!*, 104–6.

77. Victor Ullman, *Martin R. Delany: The Beginnings of Black Nationalism* (Boston: Beacon Press, 1971), 20–103, esp. 33, 79, and 114–21; William J. Switala, *Underground Railroad in Pennsylvania* (Mechanicsburg, Pa.: Stackpole, 2001), 81–89; Emerson, *Doo-dah!*, 63–64, 82–83, 110–11, 121–22, 133.

78. Reinhard O. Johnson, *The Liberty Party, 1840–1848: Antislavery Third-Party Politics in the United States* (Baton Rouge: Louisiana State University Press, 2009), 151–58, 247–49; Switala, *Underground Railroad in Pennsylvania*, 24, 70–71, 76–78; Morneweck, *Chronicles*, 303, 330, 360, 390, 418; Emerson, *Doo-dah!*, 170.

79. John Burt, "The Poet of the Iron City: Charles P. Shiras (1824–1854)," *Carnegie Magazine* 67, no. 7 (1987): 20–25; Emerson *Doo-dah!*, 104, 122, 154, 163; Shaftel, "Singing a New Song," 16; *Pittsburgh Daily Post*, Oct. 1, 1850; *Antislavery Bugle*, Oct. 26, 1850.

80. J. E. Snyder, *Harry T. Burleigh: From Spiritual to the Harlem Renaissance* (Champaign: University of Illinois Press, 2016), 16–18; Switala, *Underground Railroad in Pennsylvania*, 81–89; Frank A. Rollin, *Life and Public Services of Martin R. Delany* (1883; repr., New York: Arno, 1969), 76; Morneweck, *Chronicles*, 375–79; Emerson, *Doo-dah!*, 162–63.

81. Douglass, *The Anti-Slavery Movement*, 39.

82. Harford Toland memorandum book, Mar. 7–9, Apr. 28, May 15, July 4, Aug. 2, 1854, Ohio Historical Society. Toland identifies this as the Shires production, which received a rave review for its subsequent Toledo performance later in the month: "Theatricals in Ohio," *Spirit of the Times* (New York), Apr. 15, 1854. Was Eva (Toland) Jones named after Stowe's Eva? The fictional Eva first appears in chapter 14, published in the *Era* on September 11, 1851; Eva Jones was born June 26, 1851. Perhaps her naming was delayed, or she was renamed in September. Perhaps she was named for Eve Hume, who went with Harford's mother to Cincinnati in April 1854 and visited the family in May, and is probably the "Eva Hume" in the 1860 census, an unmarried milliner, age thirty-two, living in the village of London, Ohio. Or perhaps Harford's niece was named for the "precious little Eva" in Fanny Green's poem "A Cradle Song," published in the *Dollar Magazine*, June 7, 1851, or "Annie Gray's Journal," in the *Child's Friend and Family Magazine*, May 1, 1850, potential sources for Stowe's Eva as well. The Jones and Toland

families, prominent in London, Ohio, for decades, would have been able to subscribe to either publication. Eva Jones Graham's birthdate is from her 1926 death certificate, Columbus, Franklin County, Ohio; family details from *The History of Madison County, Ohio* . . . (Chicago: W. H. Beers, 1883), 431–32, 890–92.

83. Victor Turner, *From Ritual to Theatre: The Human Seriousness of Play* (New York: Performing Arts Journal Publications, 1982), esp. 121–22.

84. Bruce A. McConachie, *Melodramatic Formations: American Theatre and Society, 1820–1870* (Iowa City: University of Iowa Press, 1992), 162–74; Nasaw, *Going Out*, 14–18.

85. *New York Evening Post*, cited in the *Buffalo Daily Republic*, May 15, 1854.

86. *CG* 32/2, App., 39.

87. Gossett, *Uncle Tom's Cabin and American Culture*, 261.

88. Hirsch, "Uncle Tomitudes," 320; Harry Birdoff, *The World's Greatest Hit: Uncle Tom's Cabin* (New York: S. F. Vanni, 1947), 20–21, 107–8; John W. Frick, *Uncle Tom's Cabin on the American Stage and Screen* (New York: Palgrave Macmillan, 2012), 31.

89. T. Allston Brown, *A History of the New York Stage, From Its First Performance in 1732 to 1901*, vol. 1 (New York: Dodd, Mead, 1903), 84–90, 297–315.

90. W. T. Llamon, "Turning Around Jim Crow," in *Burnt Cork: Traditions and Legacies of Blackface Minstrelsy*, ed. Stephen Johnson (Amherst: University of Massachusetts Press, 2012), 22–23, 27–28, 30; Odell, *Annals*, 6:229.

91. Odell, *Annals*, 6:228–33; Meer, *Uncle Tom Mania*, 115–19; Frick, *Uncle Tom's Cabin on the American Stage and Screen*, 31–33; Birdoff, *The World's Greatest Hit*, 24–26; *New York Herald*, Sept. 3, 1852.

92. Birdoff, *The World's Greatest Hit*, 118; *Cleveland Daily Herald*, May 11, 1853; *Baltimore American and Commercial Advertiser*, Dec. 28, 1852.

93. *Liberator*, Oct. 8, 1852.

94. Frick, *Uncle Tom's Cabin on the American Stage and Screen*, 33–44; Birdoff, *The World's Greatest Hit*, 40–54; Cordelia Howard MacDonald, "Memoirs of the Original Little Eva," typescript, 1928, 5–7, George C. Howard Collection, Harry Ransom Center, University of Texas, Austin; *Troy Daily Times*, Oct. 15, Nov. 13–16, 1852. I am indebted to Sarah Levine-Gronningsater for collecting material from the Troy papers.

95. Frick, *Uncle Tom's Cabin on the American Stage and Screen*, 73–82, 84–86. Kimball's stage manager, William H. S. Smith, a conservative Whig, probably dismissed the politics of the production but was happy with its box office income. By 1854 he had converted, condemning the passage of the Kansas-Nebraska Act. Adena Spingarn, "When Uncle Tom Didn't Die: The Antislavery Politics of H. J. Conway's *Uncle Tom's Cabin*," *Theatre Survey* 53 (2012): 205.

96. *Boston Evening Transcript*, Nov. 15, 1852. Birdoff, *World's Greatest Hit*, 86; Frick, *Uncle Tom's Cabin on the American Stage and Screen*, 87–88. Kimball's stage manager, William H. S. Smith, a conservative Whig, probably dismissed the politics of the production, but was happy with its box-office income. By 1854, he had converted, condemning the passage of the Kansas-Nebraska Act. Adena Spingarn, "When Uncle Tom Didn't Die," 205.

97. Huhtamo, *Illusions in Motion*, 172–91; Stephan Oettermann, *The Panorama:*

History of a Mass Medium, trans. Deborah Lucas Schneider (New York: Zone Books, 1997), 314–42; Jeffrey Ruggles, *The Unboxing of Henry Brown* (Richmond: Library of Virginia, 2003), 69–77.

98. *Baltimore Sun*, Dec. 27, 1848.

99. *Washington Daily National Intelligencer*, Aug. 2, 1852; *Baltimore American and Commercial Daily Advertiser*, Sept. 27, 1852; *Newark Daily Advertiser*, Aug. 2, 1852; *Burlington Free Press*, Aug. 16, 1852; *Milwaukee Sentinel*, Sept. 27, 1852; *New London Daily Chronicle*, Aug. 7, 1852; *Schenectady Reflector*, Aug. 20, 1852; *Detroit Free Press*, Aug 2, 1852; *Columbus Daily Ohio Statesman*, Sept. 8, 1852; *Kalamazoo Gazette*, Sept. 17, 1852; *Brooklyn Evening Star*, Aug. 4, 1852; *Albany Evening Journal*, Aug. 16, 1852; *Boston Daily Atlas*, Aug. 21, 1852; *Cincinnati Enquirer*, Sept. 23, 1852; *Augusta Farmer*, Aug. 26, 1852; *Philadelphia Inquirer*, Sept. 21, 1852. For a list of panoramas in operation in New York City from August to September 1852, see Odell, *Annals*, 6:262–63.

100. *Troy Daily Times*, Nov. 12, 1852.

101. Ruggles, *The Unboxing of Henry Brown*, 75–159.

102. *Boston Herald*, Apr. 27, 1853; *Cincinnati Daily Commercial*, June 29–July 9, 1853; *Cleveland Daily Herald*, July 11, 30, 1853; *Cleveland Plain Dealer*, June 10, July 18, 1853; *Columbus Ohio Statesman*, July 12, 1853; *Zanesville Courier*, July, 16, 18, 1853; *Syracuse Daily Standard*, Aug. 5–9, 1853; *Conneaut (Ohio) Reporter*, Nov. 3, 1853.

103. Hirsch, "Uncle Tomitudes," 316; *Buffalo Commercial*, July 6, 1853; *Buffalo Daily Republic*, July 8, 9, 1853; *Liberator*, Aug. 5, 1853; *New York Evening Post*, Nov. 20, 1853; *LaFayette (Ind.) Daily Journal*, Mar. 14, 1854; *Bennington State Banner*, Nov. 8, 1853, May 26, 1854; Ronald J. Zboray and Mary Saracino Zboray, *Literary Dollars and Social Sense: A People's History of the Mass Market Book* (New York: Routledge, 2005), 162.

104. See http://utc.iath.virginia.edu/onstage/lantern/lanternhp.html.

105. Odell, *Annals*, 6:237–38, 309–11; Frick, *Uncle Tom's Cabin on the American Stage and Screen*, 44–50.

106. Henry James, *A Small Boy and Others* (New York: Charles Scribner's Sons, 1913), 165; *The Diary of Elisabeth Koren, 1853–1855*, ed. David T. Nelson (Northfield, Minn.: Norwegian-American Historical Association, 1955), 62 (Nov. 22, 1853).

107. Odell, *Annals*, 6:306, 316–17; Frick, *Uncle Tom's Cabin on the American Stage and Screen*, 97–105, 108–9.

108. Birdoff, *The World's Greatest Hit*, 108–10; *Philadelphia Daily Pennsylvanian*, Sept. 19, 29, 30, Oct. 28, 1853, Feb. 14, 1854.

109. Ellen Tucker Emerson to Ralph Waldo Emerson, Dec. 29, 1852, in *The Letters of Ellen Tucker Emerson*, vol. 1, ed. Edith W. Gregg (Kent: Kent State University Press, 1982), 8–9. Ralph Waldo Emerson had delayed his reading, but on January 11, 1853, wrote to his wife, Lidian, "I have read Uncle Tom's Cabin." *Letters of Ralph Waldo Emerson*, ed. Ralph L. Rush, ed., 4 vols. (New York: Columbia University Press, 1931), 4:342–43. Susan J. Baily Diary, Oct. 8, 15, 22, 1853, HSP. Unfortunately Baily did not indicate which show they went to see.

110. Joseph Sill Diary, HSP, Oct. 25–27, 1853 (quotes from 10:274 and 377). In these years Sill went frequently to the Chestnut Street Theater, the Walnut Street Theater, and the Arch Street Theater.

111. James, *Small Boy and Others*, 160–61.

112. "The Theatres," *Philadelphia Sunday Dispatch*, Sept. 11, 1853.

113. William Lloyd Garrison to Helen E. Garrison, Sept. 5, 1853, in *The Letters of William Lloyd Garrison*, vol. 4, *From Disunionism to the Brink of War, 1850–1860*, ed. Louis Ruchames (Cambridge: Harvard University Press, 1975), 248; "'Uncle Tom' on Stage," *Liberator*, Sept. 9, 1853, 142.

114. "Abolition Dramatized," *New York Tribune*, Aug. 8, 1853; see also "'Uncle Tom' among the Bowery Boys," *New York Daily Times*, July 27, 1853.

115. John Jay to Horace Mann, n.d., 1853 [misdated 1852], Horace Mann Collection, MHS; *NA-SS*, Aug. 13, 1853; John Jay to CS, Sept. 3, 1853, Sumner Papers, HU.

116. "The Theatres," *Philadelphia Sunday Dispatch*, Sept. 11, 1853. This review notes that Barmore/Harris used the characters Phinehas Fletcher and Deacon Perry, implying that this version was something of a reproduction of the Aiken-Howard version.

117. For Stowe at the Conway version in Hartford, see Birdoff, *The World's Greatest Hit*, 86–87; for Stowe at the Aiken-Howard version in Boston, see Francis H. Underwood quoted in Florine Thayer McCray, *The Life-Work of the Author of Uncle Tom's Cabin* (New York: Funk & Wagnalls, 1889), 121–22; and Gossett, *Uncle Tom's Cabin and American Culture*, 266, 274; *Boston Herald*, July 3, 1854.

118. Letter of 1853 quoted in Stowe, *Life*, 192.

119. The discussion that follows is drawn from the arguments made in Les Harrison, *The Temple and the Forum: The American Museum and Cultural Authority in Hawthorne, Melville, Stowe, and Whitman* (Tuscaloosa: University of Alabama Press, 2007), 126–66; Lott, *Love and Theft*, 213–33; Meer, *Uncle Tom Mania*, 103–30; David S. Reynolds, *Mightier Than the Sword: Uncle Tom's Cabin and the Battle for America* (New York: W. W. Norton, 2011), 136–46; Spingarn, "When Uncle Tom Didn't Die"; Edward Kahn, "Creator of Compromise: William Henry Sedley Smith and the Boston Museum's Uncle Tom's Cabin," *Theatre Survey* 41, no. 2 (2000): 71–82; Bruce McConachie, "Out of the Kitchen and into the Marketplace: Normalizing *Uncle Tom's Cabin* for the Antebellum Stage," *Journal of American Drama and Theatre* 3 (1991): 5–28; Heather S. Nathans, *Slavery and Sentiment on the American Stage, 1787–186: Lifting the Veil of Black* (New York: Cambridge University Press, 2009), 133–211.

120. "Henry J. Conway, "Uncle Tom's Cabin: A Drama in Five Parts," 5.3, unpublished MS, Boston, 1852, http://utc.iath.virginia.edu/onstage/scripts/conwayhp.html.

121. Harrison, *The Temple and the Forum*, 147.

122. On minstrelsy, see Lott, *Love and Theft*, 216–20; Meer, *Uncle Tom Mania*, 123–24; Harrison, *The Temple and the Forum*, 154–60.

123. Meer, *Uncle Tom Mania*, 129.

124. "Uncle Tom's Cabin" from the *Boston Commonwealth*, in *Frederick Douglass' Paper*, Dec. 3, 1852.

125. Parker Pillsbury, "'Uncle Tom's Cabin' at a Boston Theatre," *Lisbon (Ohio) Anti-Slavery Bugle*, Nov. 27, 1852; "Speech of Theodore Parker at the Annual Meeting . . . Jan. 23, 1853," *National Antislavery Standard*, Feb. 24, 1853; William Lloyd Garrison to Helen E. Garrison, Sept. 5, 1853, in *Letters of William Lloyd Garrison*, 248.

126. Harrison, *The Temple and the Forum*, 140, 147 (quote).

127. *Chicago Tribune*, Dec. 20, 22, 1852, Nov. 14 1853, Jan. 9, 1854; Birdoff, *The World Greatest Hit*, 118–20.

128. *Buffalo Daily Republic*, Mar. 11, 1853; *Rochester Daily Advertiser*, July 28–30, 1853.

129. *Philadelphia Daily Pennsylvanian*, Oct. 28, 1853; *Cincinnati Daily Commercial*, Dec. 19, 1853–Jan. 21, 1854.

130. *Cincinnati Daily Commercial*, Nov. 28, 1853–Feb. 3, 1854; *Cincinnati Daily Enquirer*, Nov. 27, 1853–Feb. 7, 1854.

131. Odell, *Annals*, 6:229, 277; *Buffalo Daily Republic*, Sept. 21, 26, 1853; *Syracuse Daily Standard*, Oct. 3, Oct. 24–Nov. 4, 1853; *Indianapolis Morning Journal*, Jan. 30–Feb. 21, 1854. See Angela F. Murphy, *The Jerry Rescue: The Fugitive Slave Law, Northern Rights, and the American Sectional Crisis* (New York: Oxford University Press, 2016), 146–54; *Indianapolis Morning Journal*, Jan. 30–Feb. 21, 1854.

132. *Cleveland Daily Herald*, Nov. 7–30, 1853; *Buffalo Daily Courier*, May 15–26, 1854.

133. Odell, *Annals*, 6:140, 191; MacDonald, "Memoirs of the Original Little Eva," 6, 9; Birdoff, *The World's Greatest Hit*, 46–48; *Indianapolis Morning Journal*, Jan. 30, 1854. William Le Moyne was apparently not a close relation of the abolitionist family of the same name in Pittsburgh.

134. *Pittsburgh Daily Post*, Nov. 15–Dec. 3, 1853; Morneweck, *Chronicles*, 432–39; Emerson, *Doo-dah!*, 204–5.

135. Birdoff, *The World's Greatest Hit*, 49; MacDonald, "Memoirs of the Original Little Eva," 10. "My Old Kentucky Home" and "Uncle Tom's Religion," a song by George Howard that would be used in many Aiken productions, were advertised together in the *Albany Journal*, Feb. 17, 1853, which suggests that they may have been sung in the brief Albany run of the Howard-Aiken play. For some of the wider associations, see Hirsch, "Uncle Tomitudes," 311–15; Emerson, *Doo-dah!*, 199–200; Lott, *Love and Theft*, 218. See the following playbills posted on the University of Virginia "Uncle Tom's Cabin and American Culture" (hereafter UVa UTCAC) website, http://utc.iath.virginia.edu/onstage/bills/billshp.html; National Theatre, New York, playbill, July 26, 1853, Harry Birdoff Collection, Harriet Beecher Stowe Center, University of Virginia; National Theatre, New York, playbill, Oct. 6, 1853, Ransom Center Collections, University of Texas, Austin; Chestnut Street Theater, playbill, Nov. 21, 1853, Harvard Theater Collection, Houghton Library, HU; Sanford's Opera House, playbill, Oct. 11, 1853, Barrett Collection, University of Virginia.

136. Hedrick, *Stowe*, 224–25; *Cleveland Morning Daily True Democrat*, June 29, 1852; *Concord (N.H.) Independent Democrat*, July 1, 1852; *Salem (Mass.) Register*, July 1, 1852.

137. Sanford's Opera House, playbill, Oct. 11, 1853, Clifton Waller Barrett Collection, University of Virginia; Philadelphia Continental Theatre, playbill, Feb. 13, 1862, Library Company of Philadelphia. Both posted on the UVa UTCAC website, http://utc.iath.virginia.edu/onstage/bills/billshp.html.

138. Emerson, *Doo-dah!*, 198, 237; Meer, *Uncle Tom Mania*, 67–68; Mark E. Neely Jr., *The Boundaries of American Political Culture in the Civil War Era* (Chapel Hill: University of North Carolina Press, 2005), 97–128. For the more established understanding, see Jean Baker, *Affairs of Party: The Political Culture of the Northern Democrats* (Ithaca: Cornell University Press, 1983), 213–47.

139. *Boston Investigator*, Aug. 11, 1875.

140. Neely, *Boundaries of American Political Culture*, 97–128; Melinda Lawson, "Imagining Slavery: Representations of the Peculiar Institution on the Northern Stage, 1776–1860," *Journal of the Civil War Era* 1 (2001): 25–55, esp. comments on 47.

141. Foster, *Biography, Songs, and Musical Compositions*, 14. Here I am indebted to

Steven Saunders, who cites this passage to make exactly this point in the conclusion of "The Social Agenda," 285–86.

142. *North Star* (Rochester), Oct. 28, 1848; *Mystery* (Pittsburgh), discussed in *Pennsylvania Freeman* (Philadelphia), Feb. 19, 1846.

143. Douglass, *The Anti-Slavery Movement*, 39–40.

144. Martin Robison Delany, *The Condition, Elevation, Emigration, and Destiny of the Colored People of the United States* (Philadelphia: published by the author, 1852), 107, 120–21, 124–26, 141–43.

145. *Pittsburgh Post*, Apr. 25, 1853; *Ravenna (Ky.) Star*, May 11, 1853; *Danville (Ky.) Courier*, May 20, 1853.

146. *Louisville Daily Courier*, Dec. 26, 1853; *Brooklyn Evening Star*, May 31, 1855.

Chapter 6: Guarantees Violated in the Second Crisis

1. *CG* 33/1, 2; Jeffery A. Jenkins and Charles Stewart III, *Fighting for the Speakership: The House and the Rise of Party Government* (Princeton: Princeton University Press, 2013), 174–77.

2. John Jay to CS, Dec. 20, 1852, Sumner Papers, HU.

3. David Potter, *The Impending Crisis, 1848–1861* (New York: Harper & Row, 1976), 149–54; William W. Freehling, *The Road to Disunion*, vol. 1, *Secessionists at Bay, 1776–1854* (New York: Oxford University Press, 1990); Robert W. Johannsen, *Stephen A. Douglas* (New York: Oxford University Press, 1973), 390–95; Corey M. Brooks, *Liberty Power: Antislavery Third Parties and the Transformation of American Politics* (Chicago: University of Chicago Press, 2016), 189; *National Era*, Apr. 17, 1853; *CG* 32/2, 539–43; *House Journal*, 32/2, 271–73.

4. Johannsen, *Stephen A. Douglas*, 382–86.

5. Harriet Beecher Stowe arrived in London on May 1–2, left for France on June 4, and left Paris on June 22. *Harriet Beecher Stowe in Europe: The Journal of Charles Beecher*, ed. Joseph S. Van Why and Earl French (Hartford: Stowe Day Foundation, 1986), 69, 142, 185. Douglas arrived in Liverpool on May 14 and had dinner with Thomas Baring on June 10 and with Richard Monkton Milnes in Genoa by June 20; Johannsen, *Stephen A. Douglas*, 382–83.

6. Anna Matilda McNeill Whistler to Catherine Jane McNeill, Apr. 27, 1853, Anna Matilda Whistler Papers, 1850–1876, LC.

7. Johannsen, *Stephen A. Douglas*, 296, 353; James W. Sheahan, *The Life of Stephen A. Douglas* (New York: Harper & Brothers, 1860), 161; *New York Times*, Oct. 31, 1853; *Washington Union*, Nov. 3, 1853; *Phelps' New York City Guide; being a Pocket Directory for Strangers and Citizens . . .* (New York: T. C. Fanning, 1853), 55, 93, 94.

8. Stephen A. Douglas to Charles H. Lanphier, Nov. 11, 1853, in *The Letters of Stephen A. Douglas*, ed. Robert W. Johannsen (Urbana: University of Illinois Press, 1961), 267; Lanphier to Douglas, Nov. 21, 1853, quoted in Johannsen, *Stephen A. Douglas*, 387. On the mystery, see Potter, *The Impending Crisis*, 167–71; William Freehling, *The Road to Disunion*, 1:557.

9. For important reviews of the political histories of the Kansas-Nebraska Act, see Roy F. Nichols, "The Kansas-Nebraska Act: A Century of Historiography," *Mississippi Historical Review* 43 (1956): 187–212; Dick Johnson, "Along the Twisted Road to

Civil War: History and the 'Appeal of the Independent Democrats,'" *Old Northwest* 4 (1978): 119–41; Freehling, *The Road to Disunion*, 1:536–65; Yonatan Eyal, "With His Eyes Open: Stephen A. Douglas and the Kansas-Nebraska Disaster of 1854," *Journal of the Illinois State Historical Society* 91 (1998): 175–216; John R. Wunder and Joann M. Ross, "The Eclipse of the Sun: The Nebraska-Kansas Act in Historical Perspective," in *The Nebraska-Kansas Act of 1854*, ed. John R. Wunder and Joann M. Ross (Lincoln: University of Nebraska Press, 2008), 1–12; Alice Elizabeth Malavasic, *The F Street Mess: How Southern Senators Rewrote the Kansas-Nebraska Act* (Chapel Hill: University of North Carolina Press, 2017), 10–18.

10. The details of this discussion can be followed in Johannsen, *Stephen A. Douglas*, 405–16; Potter, *The Impending Crisis*, 154–59; and, more recently, in Malavasic, *The F Street Mess*, 81–142.

11. Stanley Harrold, *Gamaliel Bailey and Antislavery Union* (Kent: Kent State University Press, 1986), 158–60; David Donald, *Charles Sumner and the Coming of the Civil War* (New York: Fawcett, 1960), 250–52; *CG* 33/1, 186.

12. The details are in Johnson, "Along the Twisted Road to Civil War," 136–39; Potter, *The Impending Crisis*, 162.

13. *CG* 33/1, 221–22, 239–40, 275–82; Johannsen, *Stephen A. Douglas*, 411; Donald, *Charles Sumner*, 250; John Niven, *Salmon P. Chase: A Biography* (New York: Oxford University Press, 1995), 149–50. Seventeen papers carrying preliminary notices of the "Appeal" have been identified, including the *Albany Evening Journal*, Jan. 19; *Boston Daily Atlas*, Jan. 20; *Baltimore Sun*, Jan. 20; *Pittsburgh Gazette*, Jan. 23; *Glasgow (Mo.) Weekly Times*, Jan. 26; *Salem (Ill.) Weekly Advocate*, Jan. 26; and *Hillsborough (N.C.) Recorder*, Feb. 5, all 1854.

14. For arguments that an important political impact of the "Appeal" was to alienate more moderate southerners who might not have supported Douglas and the F Street group, see Potter, *The Impending Crisis*, 169; Michael F. Holt, *The Rise and Fall of the Whig Party: Jacksonian Politics and the Onset of the Civil War* (New York: Oxford University Press, 1999), 816–21.

15. Language of the "Appeal" taken from *CG* 33/1, 281–82.

16. Historians virtually uniformly term the "Appeal" a piece of "effective" "propaganda" but see it as a standalone piece: Elizabeth R. Varon, *Disunion! The Coming of the American Civil War, 1789–1859* (Chapel Hill: University of North Carolina Press, 2008), 253–56; William E. Gienapp, *The Origins of the Republican Party* (New York: Oxford University Press, 1987), 71–73; Michael F. Holt, *The Fate of Their Country: Politicians, Slavery Extension, and the Coming of the Civil War* (New York: Hill and Wang, 2004), 106–8; Potter, *Impending Crisis*, 162–64; Eric Foner, *Free Soil, Free Labor, Free Men: The Ideology of the Republican Party before the Civil War* (New York: Oxford University Press, 1970), 94–95. More recently, Corey Brooks, in *Liberty Power*, 190–91, situates the "Appeal" in the unfolding rhetoric of the Liberty movement and challenges Mark Neely's argument that the "Appeal" had little significant impact (281n8). My discussion of Chase's February 3 speech and its impact on the press extends Brooks's critique. See Mark E. Neely Jr., "The Kansas-Nebraska Act in American Political Culture: The Road to Bladensburg and the *Appeal of the Independent Democrats*," in Wunder and Ross, *The Nebraska-Kansas Act of 1854*, 13–46.

17. Though I do not agree with all of their conclusions, this discussion draws upon Potter, *The Impending Crisis*, 163–65; and Kathleen Diffley, "'Erecting Anew the Standard of Freedom': Salmon P. Chase's 'Appeal of the Independent Democrats' and the Rise of the Republican Party," *Quarterly Journal of Speech* 74 (1988): 401–5.

18. On January 10 Bailey's *National Era* published a challenge to the Nebraska bill's then implied overturning of the Missouri Compromise as a violation of "faith plighted," closing with a mocking jab: "This is honor, this is good faith, this is chivalry!" This piece may well have been an early version of Chase's "Maintain Plighted Faith." "The Case Truly Stated," *Era*, Jan. 10, 1854.

19. *CG* 33/1, App., 133–40, quotes from 134, 139, 140.

20. On honor in the Nebraska debates, see Neely, "The Kansas-Nebraska Act in American Political Culture."

21. A search in America's Historical Newspapers (accessed June 12, 2017) produced hits for the year 1854 as follows:

Anti-Nebraska and meeting	893
Anti-Nebraska	2261
Nebraska and sacred compact	760
Nebraska and sacred pledge	348
Nebraska and plighted faith	710

See figure 10.

22. *Cleveland Daily Herald*, Jan. 26, 1854; *Hudson (Ohio) Observer*, Feb. 1, 1854; *New York Weekly Herald*, Feb. 4, 1854; *Boston Atlas*, Feb. 24, 1854.

23. John Jay to CS, Dec. 20, 1852, Sumner Papers, HU.

24. John Jay to CS, Jan. 9, 13, 16, 19, 20, 24, 25, Feb. 1, 1854; CS to John Jay, Jan. 12, 22, 1854, Sumner Papers, HU. See Brooks, *Liberty Power*, 191–92; Susan Hayes Ward, *The History of the Broadway Tabernacle Church* . . . (New York, 1901), 103.

25. Petitions recorded in journals of the House and Senate, 33/1.

26. The evidence for a universal invocation of the Missouri Compromise in the petitions, speeches, and the press undermines Neely's implication that northerners were primarily concerned about southern efforts to go beyond the "final settlement" of the 1850 Compromise. See Neely, "The Kansas-Nebraska Act in American Political Culture," 38.

27. Petitions in HR 33A-G24.2, Committee on the Territories—Kansas Bill, Petitions against, National Archives.

28. *Washington Union*, Mar. 17, 1854; *New York Times*, Mar. 27, 1854; *Buffalo Daily Republic*, Mar. 28, 1854; *Alton (Ohio) Weekly Telegraph*, Apr. 27, 1854. Douglas is claimed to have said in August, "I could travel from Boston to Chicago by the light of my own effigy," adding, "All along the Western Reserve of Ohio I could find my effigy upon every tree we passed." Quoted in Johannsen, *Stephen A. Douglas*, 351.

29. Searches in *UTC* and the *Key* in the website "Uncle Tom's Cabin and American Culture: A Multimedia Archive," http://utc.iath.virginia.edu/ (accessed Nov. 18, 2010).

30. *Free West* (Chicago), Feb. 2, 1854, quoted in Brooks, *Liberty Power*, 191.

31. Notices that *Sunny Memories* was in preparation began in the *Era*, Mar. 3, 1854, and it was advertised in the *Boston Atlas*, July 11, 1854.

32. HBS, "An Appeal to the Women of the Free States," *New York Independent*, Feb. 23, 1854.

33. HBS to Edward Everett Hale, Feb. 15, 28, 1854, Kansas Historical Society; *NA-SS*, Feb. 4, 1854; *Liberator*, Mar. 3, Apr. 28, 1854.

34. HBS to William Lloyd Garrison, Feb. 18, 1854, Boston Public Library; CES to CS, Feb. 20, 1854, Sumner Papers, HU; *Senate Journal*, 33/1, 210 (Feb. 24, 1854); Hedrick, *Stowe*, 257. There is no record that the Andover men's petition was ever presented.

35. HBS to William Lloyd Garrison, Feb. 18, 1854, Boston Public Library; HBS to CS, Feb. 23, 1854, Sumner Papers, HU; Henry M. Dexter to CS, Feb. 23, 1854, Sumner Papers, HU.

36. "To the clergy of New England: Dear Brethren: Upon another page you find a protest which explains itself. It is sent simultaneously to every clergyman of every name in New England . . . Please tear off, sign, fold, seal and return to us the annexed protest by the next mail to this city, directed to 'Rev. John Jackson, Boston, Mass.' He will combine all the answers received into one great protest, which will be immediately forwarded to Congress." Charles Lowell, Lyman, Beecher, Baron Stow, and Sebastian Streeter to the Clergy of New England, Feb. 22, 1854, Boston, cat. rec. 211807, American Antiquarian Society.

37. *CG* 33/1, 617–23, quotes from 617–18; Donald, *Charles Sumner*, 259; Susan Zaeske, *Signatures of Citizenship: Petitioners, Antislavery, and Women's Political Identity* (Chapel Hill: University of North Carolina Press, 2003), 164–66. Sumner and many others were incensed by Everett's handling of this affair, and he told Charles F. Adams several days later that he had introduced a "supplementary memorial." He also on March 15 presented "a petition of women of New England, remonstrating against slavery in Nebraska." It is possible that Stowe had had a hand in this petition. CS to Charles Francis Adams, Mar. 14, 1854; CS to Theodore Parker, Mar. 22, 1854, Sumner Papers, HU; *Senate Journal*, Mar. 14, 15, 1854. See Matthew Mason, *Apostle of Union: A Political Biography of Edward Everett* (Chapel Hill: University of North Carolina Press, 2016), 205.

38. Frederick William Seward, *Seward at Washington as Senator and Secretary of State: A Memoir of His Life, with Selections from His Letters, 1861–1872* (New York: Derby and Miller, 1891), 226; *Era*, Apr. 7, 1854.

39. Senate Debate, Mar. 2–4, 1854, *CG* 33/1, App., 279–342; *CG* 33/1, 531–32.

40. *Massachusetts Spy* (Worcester), Mar. 15, 1854; Eli Thayer, *A History of the Kansas Crusade: Its Friends and Its Foes* (New York: Harper, 1889), 23–26; Nicole Etcheson, *Bleeding Kansas: Contested Liberty in the Civil War Era* (Lawrence: University Press of Kansas, 2004), 35–36.

41. Ralph Waldo Emerson, "Seventh of March Speech on the Fugitive Slave Law, 7 March 1854," in *LLRWE*, 1:334, 341–42, 347. On this speech, see Lynck C. Johnson, "'Liberty Is Never Cheap': Emerson, 'The Fugitive Slave Law,' and the Antislavery Lecture Series at the Broadway Tabernacle," *New England Quarterly* 76 (2003): 259–324; and Len Gougeon, *Virtue's Hero: Emerson, Antislavery, and Reform* (Athens: University of Georgia Press, 1990), 191–99.

42. Notes to Emerson, "Seventh of March Speech," 1:333.

43. Notes to Emerson, "Seventh of March Speech," 1:342. James Oakes, *Freedom National: The Destruction of Slavery in the United States, 1861–1865* (New York: W. W. Norton, 2013).
44. *Boston Daily Atlas*, Sept. 15, 1853; *Boston Daily Bee*, Sept. 19, 1853; *Boston Herald*, July 2, 5, Nov. 16, 1853.
45. Harry Birdoff, *The World's Greatest Hit: Uncle Tom's Cabin* (New York: S. F. Vanni, 1947), 93–94, 98–99, 101; John W. Frick, *Uncle Tom's Cabin on the American Stage and Screen* (New York: Palgrave Macmillan, 2012), 49, 53–54; *New York Times*, Dec. 5, 1853; Odell, *Annals*, 6:309–11.
46. Odell, *Annals*, 6:306; *Spirit of the Times* (New York), Mar. 11, 1854.
47. *North American and United States Gazette* (Philadelphia), Oct. 22, 1853; *Philadelphia Dollar Newspaper*, Jan. 4, 1854; *Philadelphia Daily Pennsylvanian*, Feb. 10, 13, 1854; Birdoff, *The World's Greatest Hit*, 141–43.
48. *Philadelphia Daily Pennsylvanian*, Mar. 1, Apr. 25, 1854; *Boston Herald*, Apr. 3–20, 1854; Odell, *Annals*, 6:32, 327.
49. *Manufacturers' and Farmers' Journal* (Providence), Jan. 17, 1853; *Bangor Daily Whig and Courier*, June 9, 1853; *Boston Daily Atlas*, Oct. 29, 1853; *Boston Herald*, Feb. 25, 1854; *Burlington Free Press*, Apr. 5–18, 1854; *Hartford Courant*, May 6, 1854.
50. *Philadelphia Public Ledger*, Nov. 24, 1853, Jan. 21, 1854; *Trenton State Gazette*, Jan. 5, 11, 12, 1854; *Philadelphia Daily Pennsylvanian*, Nov. 15, 1853; John Fanning Watson and Willis Pope Hazard, *Annals of Philadelphia, and Pennsylvania...*, vol. 3 (Philadelphia: Edwin Stuart, 1884), 379.
51. *Philadelphia Public Ledger*, Feb. 18, 1854; *Harrisburg Morning Herald*, Feb. 25, 1854; *Lebanon Courier and Semi-Weekly Report*, Mar. 31, 1854.
52. Gerald G. Eggert, "The Impact of the Fugitive Slave Law on Harrisburg: A Case Study," *Pennsylvania Magazine of History and Biography* 109 (1985): 537–69, esp. 546–53, 561–65; UTC ads: *Harrisburg Morning Herald*, Feb. 25–Mar. 16, 1854; Nebraska meetings reported: *Harrisburg Morning Herald*, Feb. 27, Mar. 3, 1854; renditions listed in Stanley W. Campbell, *The Slave Catchers: Enforcement of the Fugitive Slave Law, 1850–1860* (Chapel Hill: University of North Carolina Press, 1968), 201–2, 199–201.
53. *Chillicothe Scioto Gazette*, Feb. 14, 15, 17, 1854; *Cleveland Daily Herald*, Apr. 12, 15, 18, 20, 1854; *Ohio State Journal* (Columbus), May 22, 1854; *Cleveland Daily Herald*, May 31, 1854; *Chillicothe Scioto Gazette*, June 13, 16, 1854; *Lancaster Gazette*, June 29, 1854; *Summit County Beacon* (Akron), July 26–28, 1854; Birdoff, *The World's Greatest Hit*, 114–16; Stephen A. Hirsch, "Uncle Tomitudes: The Popular Reaction to *Uncle Tom's Cabin*," *Studies in the American Renaissance* (1978): 325.
54. *Cincinnati Enquirer*, Apr. 19, Sept. 15, 1854; *Dayton Journal*, Apr. 27, 1854; *Indiana Herald* (Huntington), May 10, 1854; *Perrysburg Journal*, June 3, 1854; *Buffalo Daily Republic*, Aug. 1–14, 1854; *Summit County Beacon* (Akron), Aug. 23, 1854; *Ravenna Portage Sentinel*, Aug. 30, 1854; *Cleveland Herald*, Sept. 4, 1854.
55. *Ohio State Journal* (Columbus), Feb. 8–21, 1854; *Zanesville Courier*, Feb. 23, 1854; Harford Toland memorandum book, Mar. 8–9, 1854, Ohio Historical Society; *Sandusky Register*, Mar. 11, 1854; *Toledo Blade*, Mar. 17–23, 1854; *Spirit of the Times* (New York), Apr. 15, 1854. For Shires, see *Cincinnati Enquirer*, Jan. 22, 1844, Dec. 23, 1855, June 11, 1856; and James F. Dunbar, "Queen City Stages: Professional

Dramatic Activity in Cincinnati, 1837–1861" (Ph.D. diss., Ohio State University, 1954), 26–31, 951.

56. *Sandusky Register*, Mar. 11, 1854; *Toledo Blade*, Mar. 17, 1854; *Portage County Democrat*, Apr. 12, 1854; *Summit County Beacon* (Akron), Apr. 12, 19, 1854; *Jackson (Mich.) American Citizen*, Mar. 29, 1854; *Detroit Free Press*, Apr. 14, 1854.

57. *Indianapolis Morning Journal*, Jan. 30, Feb. 2–21, 1854; *Indianapolis Locomotive*, Aug. 20, Sept. 3, 24, 1853, Jan. 28, Feb. 11, 1854; Proceedings of the Indianapolis Common Council and City-County Council, Feb. 7, 1854, https://journals.iupui.edu/index.php/ccci/issue/view/512 (accessed June 19, 2017); Roger H. Van Bolt, "Fusion Out of Confusion, 1854," *Indiana Magazine of History* 39 (1953): 357–59, citing *Western Christian Advocate*, Jan. 25, 1854; *DCF*, 5:177, 180, 181, 183; *Milwaukee Daily Sentinel*, Mar. 3, 1854.

58. *Milwaukee Daily Sentinel*, Mar. 3, 9, 11, 1854. H. Robert Baker, *The Rescue of Joshua Glover: A Fugitive Slave, the Constitution, and the Coming of the Civil War* (Athens: Ohio University Press, 2006), has an excellent discussion of the impact of the Marsh troupe performance in Milwaukee but states that they started performing on March 13.

59. This reconstruction is derived from Baker, *The Rescue of Joshua Glover*, 1–10, 17–23.

60. There are no times indicated in the first ads, but on Monday March 13, the *Milwaukee Daily Free Democrat* advertised that the doors would open at 7:00 and the curtain would rise at 7:30.

61. *Milwaukee Daily Free Democrat*, Mar. 16, 1854. The reference to "shooting down the Slave-Catchers" may be evidence that the Marsh troupe was weaving elements of the Conway production into the original Aiken version.

62. *Weekly Racine Advocate*, Apr. 3, 1854.

63. *Detroit Free Press*, May 3–14, 1854; *Buffalo Daily Republic*, May 15–26, 1854; *Buffalo Daily Courier*, May 15–26, 1854. According to the *Nashville Union*, Apr. 30, 1854, the Marsh troupe was performing in Chicago.

64. *Summit County Beacon* (Akron), Apr. 19, 1854; *Lisbon Anti-Slavery Bugle*, Feb. 4, 1854; *Galena Jeffersonian*, quoted in the *Janesville (Wisc.) Daily Gazette*, Sept. 8, 12, 1854.

65. *New York Evening Post*, quoted in the *Buffalo Daily Republic*, May 15, 1854; *New York Times*, May 1, 1854. See the assessment of the impact of the theater in Adena Spingarn, *Uncle Tom's Cabin: From Martyr to Traitor* (Stanford: Stanford University Press, 2018), 51–78, esp. 74–75.

66. *Weekly Racine Advocate*, Apr. 3, 1854. See Holt, *Rise and Fall of the Whig Party*, 820 (Apr. 27 quote from Connecticut senator Truman Smith: "This vile measure . . . is just as good as dead! dead!"); and Roy F. Nichols, *Blueprints for Leviathan: American Style* (New York: Atheneum, 1963), 104–21.

67. *CG* 33/1, App., 492–500, 519–30, 661–68, 972–76, 986–89.

68. Holt, *Rise and Fall of the Whig Party*, 820; Nichols, *Blueprints for Leviathan*, 117–18.

69. Votes from www.govtrack.us.

70. *CG* 33/1, App., 768–74, 784–88.

71. Albert J. Von Frank, *The Trials of Anthony Burns: Freedom and Slavery in Emerson's Boston* (Cambridge: Harvard University Press, 1998).

72. Jonathan Earle, "The Making of the North's 'Stark Mad Abolitionists': Anti-Slavery Conversion in the United States, 1824–1854," *Slavery and Abolition* 25 (2004): 59–75, esp. 70–72 (quote from Amos A. Lawrence to Giles Richards, June 1, 1854, Lawrence Papers, MHS); see also Douglas C. Stange, "From Treason to Antislavery Patriotism: Unitarian Conservatives and the Fugitive Slave Law," *Harvard Library Quarterly* 25 (1977): 481–88; Von Frank, *The Trials of Anthony Burns*, 259–301.

73. *Burlington Free Press*, May 26, 1854; *Brooklyn Daily Eagle*, May 26, 1854; *Hartford Courant*, May 27, 1854; *Daily Pennsylvanian* (Philadelphia), May 27, 1854; *Milwaukee Daily Free Democrat*, May 29, 1854; *Milwaukee Daily Sentinel*, May 29, 1854; *Indianapolis Daily Journal*, May 30, 1854.

74. *Senate Journal*, 33/1, 450, 464, 471, 475, 487, 492, 511, 520, 547.

75. *Senate Journal*, 33/1, 450, 458, 464; *CG* 31/1, 1472, 1513–19, 1549–59.

76. Donald, *Charles Sumner*, 262–66; *CG* 33/1, 1471–72, 1513–19, 1552–59; 33/1, App., 1011–15, 1024–26.

77. *CG* 33/1, 2021–23.

Chapter 7: Restructuring Coalescence

1. Ralph Waldo Emerson, "Seventh of March Speech on the Fugitive Slave Law, 7 March 1854," in *LLRWE*, 1:347.

2. *DOHB*, 1:132–160; *CWAL*, 2:285–86.

3. *Illinois Daily Journal* (Springfield), July 18–22, 1854; *Springfield Sangamo Journal*, July 18–22, 28, 1854.

4. Michael Burlingame, *Abraham Lincoln: A Life*, 2 vols. (Baltimore: Johns Hopkins University Press, 2008), 1:357–62, 369–403; Jeremy J. Tewell, *A Self-Evident Lie: Southern Slavery and the Threat to American Freedom* (Kent: Kent State University Press, 2013), 21–28; Eric Foner, *The Fiery Trial: Abraham Lincoln and American Slavery* (New York: W. W. Norton, 2010), 65–66, 331–32. For Lincoln's 1854 speeches, see *CWAL*, 2:226–306; quotes from Peoria on 255, 266, 276.

5. On Lincoln's Senate ambitions, see *CWAL*, 2:287–88, 304–6; William E. Gienapp, *The Origins of the Republican Party, 1852–1856* (New York: Oxford University Press, 1987), 123–24; Beveridge, *Abraham Lincoln, 1809–1858*, 2:275–76; *Herndon's life of Lincoln; the history and personal recollections of Abraham Lincoln, as originally written by William H. Herndon and Jesse W. Weik*, with a newly revised intro. and notes by Paul M. Angle (Greenwich, Conn.: Fawcett Publications, 1961), 300; Mitchell Snay, "Abraham Lincoln, Owen Lovejoy, and the Emergence of the Republican Party in Illinois," *Journal of the Abraham Lincoln Association* 22 (2001): 83–99.

6. John Jay to CS, Dec. 20, 1852, Sumner Papers, HU.

7. Anna Ella Carroll, *The Great American Battle; or, The Contest between Christianity and Political Romanism* (New York and Auburn: Miller, Orton & Mulligan, 1856), 270–71.

8. For different approaches, see Tyler Anbinder, *Nativism and Slavery: The Northern Know Nothings and the Politics of the 1850s* (New York: Oxford University Press,

1992); Michael F. Holt, *The Political Crisis of the 1850s* (New York: W. W. Norton, 1976); Gienapp, *Origins*; Mark Voss-Hubbard, *Beyond Party: Cultures of Antipartisanship in Northern Politics before the Civil War* (Baltimore: Johns Hopkins University Press, 2002), 178–216.

9. On sentimental unionism, see François Furstenberg, *In The Name of the Father: Washington's Legacy, Slavery, and the Making of a Nation* (New York: Penguin Press, 2006); Matthew Mason, *Apostle of Union: A Political Biography of Edward Everett* (Chapel Hill: University of North Carolina Press, 2016).

10. *DCF*, 5:251, 253, 267–68, 273, 309.

11. Robert W. Fogel, *Without Consent or Contract: The Rise and Fall of American Slavery* (New York: W. W. Norton, 1989), 354–69; Michael F. Holt, "The Politics of Impatience: The Origins of Know Nothingism," *Journal of American History* 60 (1973): 309–31; Voss-Hubbard, *Beyond Party*, 17–37; Allen Pred, *Urban Growth and City-Systems in the United States, 1840–1860* (Cambridge: Harvard University Press, 1980); Mark Tebeau, *Eating Smoke: Fire in Urban America, 1800–1950* (Baltimore: Johns Hopkins University Press, 2003).

12. Owen Stanwood, *The Empire Reformed: English America in the Age of the Glorious Revolution* (Philadelphia: University of Pennsylvania Press, 2011); Jenny Franchot, *Roads to Rome: The Antebellum Protestant Encounter with Catholicism* (Berkeley: University of California Press, 1994); Jon Gjerde, *Catholicism and the Shaping of Nineteenth-Century America*, ed. S. Deborah Kang (New York: Cambridge University Press, 2011).

13. Gienapp, *Origins*, 60–64, 93–95; Anbinder, *Nativism and Slavery*, 24–31; Ray Allen Billington, *The Protestant Crusade, 1800–1860: A Study of the Origins of American Nativism (Chicago: Quadrangle, 1964)*, 300–303; *DCF*, 5:251. For a detailed description of the Bedini demonstrations in Cincinnati, see Bruce Levine, *The Spirit of 1848: German Immigrants, Labor Conflict, and the Coming of the Civil War* (Urbana: University of Illinois Press, 1992), 188–91. For longer perspectives, see Steven Conn, "'Political Romanism': Re-evaluating American Anti-Catholicism in the Age of Italian Revolution," *Journal of the Early Republic* 36 (2016): 521–48; and Don H. Doyle, *The Cause of All Nations: An International History of the American Civil War* (New York: Basic Books, 2015).

14. Carl F. Brand, "The History of the Know Nothing Party in Indiana," *Indiana Magazine of History* 18 (1922): 59; Anbinder, *Nativism and Slavery*, 31n33; M. W. Cluskey, *The Political Text-Book, or Encyclopedia* . . . (Philadelphia: Jas. B. Smith, 1859), 65.

15. George W. Julian, *Political Recollections, 1840 to 1872* (Chicago: Jansen, McClurg, 1884), 141–42, quoted in Richard H. Sewell, *Ballots for Freedom: Antislavery Politics in the United States, 1837–1860* (New York: Oxford University Press, 1976), 267–68.

16. Dale T. Knobel, *America for the Americans: The Nativist Movement in the United States* (New York: Twayne, 1996), 92; Bruce Levine, "Conservatism, Nativism, and Slavery: Thomas R. Whitney and the Origins of the Know-Nothing Party," *Journal of American History* 88 (2001): 455–88; Louis Dow Scisco, *Political Nativism in New York State* (New York: Columbia University Press, 1901), 97–100, 118; *New York Tribune*, Sept. 13, 1842, Mar. 24, 1843, Jan. 18, 1851.

17. *The Golden Rule and Odd Fellows' Family Companion, Popular Literature*,

Instruction, and Amusement (hereafter *Golden Rule*) (New York: E. Winchester), 4, no. 7 (Feb. 1846): 114; 6, no. 23 (June 5, 1847): 382; *New York Evening Post*, June 7, 1847; *The Gazette of the Union, Golden Rule, and Odd Fellows' Family Companion: A Saturday Journal of General Literature, Odd-Fellowship, and Amusement* (hereafter *Gazette and Rule*) (New York: Crampton and Clarke), 10, no. 5 (Feb. 5, 1849): 79; 10, no. 10 (May 26, 1849): 333; 10, no. 24 (June 16, 1849): 381; 12, no. 24 (June 15, 1850): 384; 14, no. 24 (June 14, 1851): 385; Carroll, *The Great American Battle*, 271.

18. *New York Tribune*, June 5, 1849; *Golden Rule* 5, no. 14 (Oct. 3, 1846): 216; W. W. Wallace, *The Odd Fellows' Keepsake: A Concise History of Odd Fellowship in the United States* . . . (New York: Mirror of the Times, 1850), passim (lodge data by state for 1850); *Gazette and Rule* 15, no. 12 (Sept. 20, 1851): 182. Thanks to Richard Bensel for reference to the *Keepsake*. Data for 1854 from *Washington Daily National Globe*, Sept. 11, 1854.

19. Mark C. Carnes, *Secret Ritual and Manhood in Victorian America* (New Haven: Yale University Press, 1989); Lynn Dumenil, *Freemasonry and American Culture, 1880–1930* (Princeton: Princeton University Press, 1984); Knobel, *America for the Americans*, 66–68; David T. Bieto, "'This Enormous Army': The Mutual-Aid Tradition of American Fraternal Societies before the Twentieth Century," in *The Voluntary City: Choice, Community, and Civil Society*, ed. David T. Bieto, Peter Gordon, and Alexander Tabarrok (Ann Arbor: University of Michigan Press, 2002), 182–203.

20. *Gazette and Rule* 12, no. 9 (Mar. 2, 1850): 144, 145; 12, no. 15 (Apr. 13, 1850): 244.

21. C. C. Goen, *Broken Churches, Broken Nation: Denominational Schisms and the Coming of the Civil War* (Macon, Ga.: Mercer University Press, 1985); Mitchell Snay, *Gospel of Disunion: Religion and Separatism in the Antebellum South* (New York: Oxford University Press, 1993), 113–15; John L. Brooke, "Cultures of Nationalism, Movements of Reform, and the Composite-Federal Polity: From Revolutionary Settlement to Antebellum Crisis," *Journal of the Early Republic* 29 (2009): 1–33.

22. For the anti-Masonic origins of much of the antislavery leadership, see Ronald Formisano, *For the People: American Populist Movements from the Revolution to the 1850s* (Chapel Hill: University of North Carolina Press, 2008), 103–55; David Donald, *Charles Sumner and the Coming of the Civil War* (New York: Fawcett, 1960), 20; Sewell, *Ballots for Freedom*, 55–56, 83–84; Lurton D. Ingersoll, *The Life of Horace Greeley* . . . (Philadelphia: J. E. Potter, 1874), 73–74; William Preston Vaughn, *The Antimasonic Party in the United States, 1826–1843* (Lexington: University Press of Kentucky, 1983), 27–129 passim; Leonard L. Richards, *The Life and Times of Congressman John Quincy Adams* (New York: Oxford University Press, 1986), 48–53; *Batavia (N.Y.) Republican Advocate*, Feb. 6, 1829, Oct. 30, 1831. The exception was Joshua Giddings, who was a Freemason; *Masonic Review* 29 (1864): 235–37.

23. Knobel, *America for the Americans*, 68–72; Levine, "Conservatism, Nativism, and Slavery"; Scisco, *Political Nativism*, 62–63.

24. Knobel, *America for the Americans*, 49–64; Billington, *Protestant Crusade*, 142–237; Scisco, *Political Nativism*, 32–61.

25. Anbinder, *Nativism and Slavery*, 21–22; Cluskey, *The Political Text-Book*, 63–68.

26. Anbinder, *Nativism and Slavery*, 79; Hendrick Booraem, *The Formation of the Republican Party in New York: Politics and Conscience in the Antebellum North* (New

York: New York University Press, 1983), 57–59; Scisco, *Political Nativism*, 111–24; *New York Times*, Oct. 7, 1854, May 22, 1855.

27. Carroll, *The Great American Battle*, 270–71; *Proceedings of the Grand Lodge of New Jersey* (n.p., January 1857), 205; *I.O.O.F Proceedings of the Grand Encampment of Ohio, 1839–June 1847* (Cincinnati, 1847), 30, 31, 61, 67, 69; *The Symbol, and Odd Fellows Magazine* . . . , vols. 3 and 4 (Boston: Thomas Prince, 1844–45), 3:428, 4:43–665 passim. Albert Pike, one of Freemasonry's great nineteenth-century writers, was a delegate from Arkansas to the 1855 Philadelphia Know Nothing Council; *New York Times*, June 9, 1855.

28. *Gazette and Rule* 10, no. 10 (May 26, 1849): 334–35; *Richmond Dispatch*, May 18, 1855.

29. *Golden Rule* 5, no. 17 (Oct. 24, 1846): 266; *Gazette and Rule* 9, no. 14 (Sept. 30, 1848): 240; 10, no. 5 (Feb. 5, 1849): 79; 10, no. 24 (June 16, 1849): 381; 12, no. 24 (June 15, 1850): 384; *New York Tribune*, June 7, 1847, Nov. 6–7, 1854; *New York Evening Post*, Sept. 19, 1849; *New York Times*, Nov. 7, Dec. 4, 1854, Feb. 27, 1855, Mar. 16, 1855; *Shipping and Commercial List and New-York Price Current*, Jan. 30, 1856.

30. A rough analysis of the relationship in New York State between Odd Fellows lodges listed in Wallace, *Odd Fellows' Keepsake* (1850), 254–68, and the vote for governor in 1854 (ICPSR data, United States Historical Election Returns, 1824–1968, ICPSR 1, https://www.icpsr.umich.edu/icpsrweb/ICPSR/studies/1), hint at this pattern. Counties where there were more nativist voters than Republican voters had more than thirteen lodges on average; the counties where Republicans outnumbered nativists had fewer than eight lodges.

31. Joseph B. Tucker (typescript) diary, HSP, 9, 10, 28, 29, 40, 71-a, 72, 74, 79–81, 83, 84, 89–91, 94–95, 100–101, 103, 108–14, 118, 130–31.

32. Sewell, *Ballots for Freedom*, 268–70.

33. Debby Applegate, *The Most Famous Man in America: The Biography of Henry Ward Beecher* (New York: Doubleday, 2006), 124.

34. Anbinder, *Nativism and Slavery*, 89.

35. Gienapp, *Origins*, 89–90; Stanley Harrold, *Gamaliel Bailey and Antislavery Union* (Kent: Kent State University Press, 1986), 160–64; Corey M. Brooks, *Liberty Power: Antislavery Third Parties and the Transformation of American Politics* (Chicago: University of Chicago Press, 2016), 194; Sewell, *Ballots for Freedom*, 264; *Daily National Intelligencer*, June 22, 1854.

36. On the grip of party, see Rachel A. Shelden, *Washington Brotherhood: Politics, Social Life, and the Coming of the Civil War* (Chapel Hill: University of North Carolina Press, 2013); and Joel H. Silbey, "'After the First Northern Victory': The Republican Party Comes to Congress, 1855–1856," *Journal of Interdisciplinary History* 20 (1989): 1–24.

37. Ronald P. Formisano, *The Birth of Mass Party Politics: Michigan, 1827–1861* (Princeton: Princeton University Press, 1971), 239–51; Gienapp, *Origins*, 104–6; Brooks, *Liberty Power*, 196.

38. Gienapp, *Origins*, 107–21; Roger H. Von Bolt, "Fusion Out of Confusion, 1854," *Indiana Magazine of History and Biography* 49 (1953): 354–89, esp. 278–384; Stephen E. Maizlish, *The Triumph of Sectionalism: The Transformation of Ohio Politics, 1844–1856* (Kent: Stent State University Press, 1983), 189–201.

39. Gienapp, *Origins*, 122–25.

40. Anbinder, *Nativism and Slavery*, 55–56; Gienapp, *Origins*, 48–52, 129–33; Scott, "Creating the 34th Congress," 212–31.

41. Booraem, *The Formation of the Republican Party in New York*, 37–59; Scott, "Creating the 34th Congress," 778–96; Anbinder, *Nativism and Slavery*, 75–83; Gienapp, *Origins*, 147–60.

42. Gienapp, *Origins*, 133–39; Anbinder, *Nativism and Slavery*, 87–92; Kevin Sweeney, "Rum, Romanism, Representation, and Reform: Coalition Politics in Massachusetts, 1857–1853," *Civil War History* 12 (1976): 116–37; John R. Mulkern, *The Know-Nothing Party in Massachusetts: The Rise and Fall of a People's Movement* (Boston Northern University Press, 1990), 29–86.

43. Gienapp, *Origins*, 139–147; William E. Gienapp, "Nebraska, Nativism, and Rum: The Failure of Fusion in Pennsylvania, 1854," *Pennsylvania Magazine of History and Biography* 109 (1985): 425–71; Anbinder, *Nativism and Slavery*, 57–61; Scott, "Creating the 34th Congress," 525–68.

44. Results for 1854–55 from Michael J. Dubin, *United States Congressional Elections, 1788–1997: The Official Results of the 1st to the 105th Congresses* (Jefferson, N.C.: Harrison, 1998), 169–75.

45. *DCF*, 5:309.

46. *DCF*, 5:427–28, 486.

47. *Providence Tribune*, quoted in *Harrisburg Herald*, Dec. 24, 1854, quoted in Anbinder, *Nativism and Slavery*, 99; see also 44–45, 52–102; Bruce Laurie, *Beyond Garrison: Antislavery and Social Reform* (New York: Cambridge University Press, 2005), 279–82; Voss-Hubbard, *Beyond Party*, 127–28, 171–75; Formisano, *The Birth of Mass Political Parties*, 242–43.

48. George F. Hoar, *Autobiography of Seventy Years*, vol. 1 (New York: C. Scribner's Sons, 1906), 189.

49. *New York Tribune*, Nov. 11, 1854, see Booraem, *The Formation of the Republican Party in New York*, 63.

50. *Era*, Nov. 23, 1854.

51. Joshua Giddings, circular letter to constituents, comments in *Era*, Apr. 19, 1855.

52. *Era*, Nov. 23, 1854.

53. *Washington Daily Globe*, Nov. 17, 1854; *Raleigh Weekly Standard*, Nov. 22, 1854, both citing stories in the *New York Herald*.

54. Scisco, *Political Nativism*, 136–37; Anbinder, *Nativism and Slavery*, 62–163. *New York Times*, June 9, 1855, quoting from the *Cleveland Plain Dealer*, June 6, 1855. Horace Greeley continued his vendetta against Barker by spreading false rumors that he had been ousted as the National Council president; *New York Tribune*, Nov. 27, 1854; *Washington Evening Star*, Nov. 28, 1854.

55. Scisco, *Political Nativism*, 137–39; Anbinder, *Nativism and Slavery*, 147–49; *The Know Nothing Almanac, Or True American's Manual* (New York: DeWitt & Davenport, [1855]), 53–54.

56. Anbinder, *Nativism and Slavery*, 146, 150–57, 163–65; Scisco, *Political Nativism*, 143.

57. *New York Times*, May 17, 1855; on Syracuse, see *New York Times*, Feb. 27, Mar. 8, 1855.

58. Amasa Walker to CS, Mar. 14, 1855, Sumner Papers, HU.

59. In this discussion I am indebted to the detailed accounts of the Philadelphia convention in Gienapp, *Origins*, 179–87; and Anbinder, *Nativism and Slavery*, 166–72. The *Tribune* correspondent was Samuel Bowles of the *Springfield (Mass.) Republican*; Gienapp, *Origins*, 182.

60. Henry Wilson, *History of the Rise and Fall of the Slave Power in America*, 9th ed., vol. 2 (Boston: Houghton Mifflin, 1874), 424.

61. Wilson, *History of the Rise and Fall*, 425.

62. *New York Tribune*, June 7, 8, 9, 11, 1855; *Augusta (Ga.) Chronicle*, June 10, 1855 (June 5 *Herald* report).

63. Report of Wilson's June 12 speech in *New York Tribune*, June 16, 1855.

64. *New York Tribune*, June 9, 12, 1855.

65. *New York Tribune*, June, 14, 15, 1855; *New York Times*, June 16, 1855; Anbinder, *Nativism and Slavery*, 169–72; Gienapp, *Origins*, 183–87.

66. *New York Tribune*, June 19, 1855; *Washington Evening Star*, June 22, 1855; *NA-SS*, July 7, 1855 (quoting from the *Tribune*).

67. *New York Tribune*, Aug. 30 1855.

68. *NA-SS*, Dec. 15, 22, 1855, Aug. 23, 1856; *Worcester National Aegis*, Dec. 12, 1855; *Buffalo Christian Advocate*, Jan. 3, Mar. 13, 1856; *Cleveland Leader*, Feb. 11, 1856; Eric Gardner, "Stowe Takes the Stage: Harriet Beecher Stowe's *The Christian Slave*," *Legacy* 15 (1998): 78–84.

69. John G. Whittier, *The Panorama and Other Poems* (Boston: Ticknor and Fields, 1856), 5, 8–9, 13. See the excellent reading of "The Panorama" in David Grant, *Political Antislavery Discourse and American Literature of the 1850s* (Newark: University of Delaware Press, 2012), 65–90.

70. Gillian Brown, *Domestic Individualism: Imagining the Self in Nineteenth-Century America* (Berkeley: University of California Press, 1990), 13–60; David Grant, "*Uncle Tom's Cabin* and the Triumph of Republican Rhetoric," *New England Quarterly* 71 (1999): 429–38; Grant, *Political Antislavery Discourse*, 68–70; Eric Foner, *Free Soil, Free Labor, Free Men: The Ideology of the Republican Party before the Civil War* (New York: Oxford University Press, 1970), 11–72; James L. Huston, *The British Gentry, the Southern Planter, and the Northern Family Farmer: Agriculture and Sectional Antagonism in North America* (Baton Rouge: Louisiana State University Press, 2015), 183–239.

71. Charles Sumner, *The Slave Oligarchy and Its Usurpations. Outrages in Kansas. The Different Political Parties. Position of the Republican Party. Speech of Hon. Charles Sumner, November 2, 1855, in Faneuil Hall, Boston* (Washington, D.C.: Buell & Blanchard, Printers, 1855), 3, 6, 8–9.

72. This summary of the struggle in Kansas through January 1856 is drawn from Nicole Etcheson, *Bleeding Kansas: Contested Liberty in the Civil War Era* (Lawrence: University of Kansas Press, 2004), 28–92, esp. 28–25, 52–61, 69–75.

73. *New York Tribune*, Dec. 12, 1855.

74. "Memorial from the Inhabitants of Kansas to Congress," *New York Times*, May 11, 1855 (dated Apr. 30). See Etcheson, *Bleeding Kansas*, 59.

75. Etcheson, *Bleeding Kansas*, 137–43; John H. Gihon, *Geary and Kansas: Governor Geary's administration in Kansas: with a complete history of the territory until July 1857* . . . (Philadelphia: Charles C. Rhodes, 1857).

76. Craig Miner, *Seeding Civil War: Kansas in the National News, 1854–1858* (Lawrence: University Press of Kansas, 2008), 36–37; Gienapp, *Origins*, 298; John R. McKivigan, *Forgotten Firebrand: James Redpath and the Making of Nineteenth-Century America* (Ithaca: Cornell University Press, 2008), 19–42.

77. Etcheson, *Bleeding Kansas*, 28–29, 71–72; *Statistics of the United States . . . in 1860; Compiled from the Original Returns and being the Final Exhibit of the Eight Census . . .* (Washington, D.C., 1866), liii–liv, lxi–lxii.

78. *Liberator*, Mar. 3, Nov. 3, 1854; *Frederick Douglass' Paper*, Nov. 17, 1854; *NA-SS*, Dec. 2, 16, 23, 30, 1854, Jan. 13, 20, 27, Feb. 3, 17, 24, Mar. 3, 17, Apr. 14, 21, 1855.

79. *Liberator*, Nov. 3, Dec. 8, 15, 22, 1854, Oct. 5, Dec. 7, 1855; *Frederick Douglass' Paper*, Nov. 17, 1854, Mar. 25, 30, 1855; *Salem (Ohio) Anti-Slavery Bugle*, Feb. 24, Nov. 3, 1855; *Pittsburgh Gazette*, Nov. 8, 1855; *NA-SS*, Jan. 20, Feb. 24, May 19, 1855; *Buffalo Christian Advocate*, Jan 3, 1856;

80. *Liberator*, May 19, 1854. For Emerson's 1855 tour, see *LLRWE*, 2:1 (notes); for the impact of lectures and bazaars in the 1850s, see Julie Roy Jeffrey, *The Great Silent Army of Abolition: Ordinary Women of the Antislavery Movement* (Chapel Hill: University of North Carolina Press, 1998), 108–26, 196–209.

81. *New York Tribune*, June 3, 1854 (p. 6, col. 4); see Grant, "*Uncle Tom's Cabin* and the Triumph of Republican Rhetoric," 429–30. This poem should not be confused with a longer poem of the same name, published by Jewett for George W. Bungay, who published anonymously. *Nebraska: A Poem, Personal and Political* (Boston: J. P. Jewett, 1854), advertised in the *Liberator*, Apr. 21, 1854. This poem condemned the Nebraska bill and contrasted the horrors of slavery with the natural beauties of Nebraska rather than the virtue of northern society. http://antislavery.eserver.org/poetry/nebraska/nebraska.html.

82. *Providence Manufacturers' and Farmers' Journal*, Aug. 3, 1854; *Boston Christian Watchman*, Aug. 10, 1854; *Northfield (Vt.) Christian Messenger*, Sept. 6, 1854; *Lays of the Emigrants, as Sung by the Second Party for Kanzas, on their Departure from Boston, Tuesday, August 29th, 1856* (Boston: Alfred Mudge & Son, 1854); *Era*, Oct. 5, 1854; *New York Tribune*, Feb. 22, 1855; *Liberator*, Feb. 23, 1855. For "Call to Kansas," see Lucy Larcom, *The Kansas Prize Song . . . awarded the Prize Offered by the New England Emigrant Aid Company . . .* (Boston: C. C. Mead, 1855); *Book of Poetry by the Hutchinson Family* (Boston: S. Shism, 1858), 62.

83. Edward Everett Hale, *Kanzas and Nebraska: The History, Geographical and Physical Characteristics, and Political Position of Those Territories; An Account of the Emigrant Aid Companies, and Directions to Emigrants* (Boston: Philips, Sampson, 1854); Thomas D. Webb, *Information for Kanzas Immigrants* (Boston, 1854–1857); William A. Phillips, *The Conquest of Kansas, by Missouri and her Allies: A History of the Troubles in Kansas, from the Passage of the Organic Act until the close of July, 1856* (Boston: Phillips, Sampson and Company, 1856); Sara T. D. Robinson, *Kansas, Its Interior and Exterior Life: Including a Full View of its Settlement, Political History, Social Life, Climate, Soil, Productions, Scenery . . .* (Boston: Crosby, Nichols and Co., 1856); [Mrs. W. H. Corning], *Western Border Life: or, What Fanny Hunter Saw and Heard in Kanzas and Missouri* (New York: Derby & Jackson, 1856), advertised in the *Hartford Courant*, Aug. 13, 1856. See Michael D. Pierson, *Free Hearts and Free Homes: Gender and American Antislavery Politics* (Chapel Hill: University of North Carolina Press, 2003), 150, 152, 156–59.

84. *New York Tribune*, Nov. 2, 1855; *New York Times*, Mar. 26, 1856; *The Christian Slave, A Drama. Founded on a Portion of UNCLE TOM'S CABIN. Dramatized by Harriet Beecher Stowe, Expressly for the Readings of Mrs. Mary E. Webb* (Boston: Phillips, Sampson and Company, 1855).

85. Of the plantation novels listed in Thomas F. Gossett, *Uncle Tom's Cabin and American Culture* (Dallas: Southern Methodist University Press, 1985), 430–31, and discussed in Joy Jordan-Lake, *Whitewashing Uncle Tom's Cabin: Nineteenth-Century Women Novelists Respond to Stowe* (Nashville: Vanderbilt University Press, 2005), 1–24, there were fifteen published in 1852 and 1853 and seven between 1854 and 1856.

86. William Cooper Nell, *The Colored Patriots of the American Revolution . . .* (Boston: Robert F. Wallcut, 1855); Frederick Douglass, *My Bondage and My Freedom*, pt. 1, *Life as a Slave*, pt. 2, *Life as a Freeman* (New York: Miller, Orton & Mulligan, 1855); William Wells Brown, *Three Years in Europe: Or, Places I Have Seen and People I Have Met* (Boston: Jewett, 1855); Mary B. Harland, *Ellen, or the Chained Mother, and Pictures of Kentucky Slavery Drawn from Real Life* (Cincinnati: Applegate, 1855); Francis Colburn Adams, *Our World, Or, the Slaveholder's Daughter* (New York and Auburn: Miller, Orton, and Mulligan, 1855); Charles G. Parsons, *An Inside View of Slavery or, a Tour among the Planters* (Boston: Jewett, 1855); Benjamin Drew, *A North-Side View of Slavery. The Refugee: or the Narratives of Fugitive Slaves in Canada . . .* (Boston: Jewett, 1856); *Liberator*, Dec. 21, 1855.

87. Mary Langdon [Mary Hayden Green Pike], *Ida May: A Story of Things Actual and Possible* (Boston: Phillips, Sampson, 1854); *Boston Traveler*, Nov. 4, 1854.

88. *Washington Evening Star*, Jan. 2, 1855; *Frank Leslie's Illustrated Newspaper*, Apr. 12, 1856; Odell, *Annals*, 6:475; Cordelia Howard MacDonald, "Memoirs of the Original Little Eva," typescript (1928), 11, George C. Howard Collection, Harry Ransom Center, University of Texas, Austin. For Mary Botts, see Jessie Morgan-Owens, *Girl in Black and White: The Story of Mary Mildred Williams and the Abolition Movement* (New York: W. W. Norton, 2019); and Mary Niall Mitchell, "The Real Ida May: A Fugitive Tale in the Archives," *Massachusetts Historical Review* 15 (2013): 54–88.

89. *Boston Daily Atlas*, June 19–July 4, 1854; *Chicago Tribune*, Jan. 25, 1855; *Philadelphia Public Ledger*, Feb. 19, 1855; *New York Tribune*, June 19, 1855; *Brooklyn Evening Star*, Aug. 25, 29, Sept. 7, 1855; Odell, *Annals*, 6:377–78, 419–20; MacDonald, "Memoirs," 14; Harry Birdoff, *The World's Greatest Hit: Uncle Tom's Cabin* (New York: S. F. Vanni, 1947), 112–14.

90. *Poughkeepsie Journal*, Feb. 17, 24, 1855; *Boston Daily Atlas*, Mar. 21–Apr. 18, 1855; *Philadelphia Daily Pennsylvanian*, Mar. 15, 1855; *Pittsburgh Daily Post*, May 3, Nov. 22, 1855; *Daily Milwaukee News*, Aug. 11, 1855; *Detroit Free Press*, Nov. 6, 1855; Birdoff, *The World's Greatest Hit*, 110–12.

91. Kate Clifford Larson, *Bound for the Promised Land: Harriet Tubman, Portrait of an American Hero* (New York: Ballantine, 2004), 125–26; *Star of the West*, Dec. 1, 1855; Henry P. Waters to CS, Dec. 6, 1855, Sumner Papers, HU.

92. My account of the Silver Spring meeting is indebted to Gienapp, *Origins*, 250–51; Harrold, *Gamaliel Bailey*, 171–75; Sewell, *Ballots for Freedom*, 277; and Brooks, *Liberty Power*, 216–17.

93. *Era*, Jan. 17, 1856; *New York Tribune*, Jan. 17, 1856; *Proceedings of the First Three*

Republican National Conventions of 1856, 1860, and 1864 (Minneapolis: Charles W. Johnston, 1893), 4–6.

94. The only names that survive from the 1854 meetings are those of the president and secretaries of the meetings. Solomon Foot was a Republican senator from Vermont from 1851 to 1866, Daniel Mace was an Indiana Democrat who was reelected in the 1854 election as a People's (Fusion candidate, and Reuben E. Fenton was a New York Democrat who did not run in 1854 but was reelected as a Republican in 1856. *Daily National Intelligencer,* June 22, 1854. On Bailey, King, and Banks, see Harrold, *Gamaliel Bailey,* 161.

95. Stanley W. Campbell, *The Slave Catchers: Enforcement of the Fugitive Slave Law, 1850–1860* (Chapel Hill: University of North Carolina Press, 1968), 142; Gienapp, *Origins,* 210–11.

96. Abraham Lincoln to Joshua F. Speed, Aug. 24, 1855, in *CWAL,* 2:320; Frederick Douglass, *The Anti-Slavery Movement. A Lecture by Frederick Douglass, before the Rochester Ladies Anti-Slavery Society* (Rochester: Lee, Mann, and Co., 1855), 42–43.

97. Mary Kay Ricks, *Escape on the "Pearl": The Heroic Bid for Freedom on the Underground Railroad* (New York: Murrow, 2007), 218.

98. Nikki M. Taylor, *Driven toward Madness: The Fugitive Slave Margaret Garner and Tragedy on the Ohio* (Athens: Ohio University Press, 2016); Campbell, *Slave Catchers,* 142–45.

99. Anbinder, *Nativism and Slavery,* 196. The details of this meeting are in the *New York Times,* Nov. 21, 1855.

100. Gienapp, *Origins,* 189–237; Anbinder, *Nativism and Slavery,* 172–93; *The Tribune Almanac and Political Register for 1856* (New York: Greeley and McElrath, [1856]), 53–57, 62, 64.

101. On Republican pessimism in late 1855, see Gienapp, *Origins,* 235–40; for the New York optimism and figures, see Anbinder, *Nativism and Slavery,* 187; Gienapp, *Origins,* 231; *The Tribune Almanac for 1856,* 54.

102. Harrold, *Gamaliel Bailey,* 168–74; Donald, *Charles Sumner,* 276; Gienapp, *Origins,* 235–36, 248–53.

103. Gienapp, *Origins,* 235 (citing Artemas Carter to CS, Nov. 16 1855, Sumner Papers, HU).

104. The Speakership battle is covered in detail in Jeffery A. Jenkins and Charles Stewart III, *Fighting for the Speakership: The House and the Rise of Party Government* (Princeton: Princeton University Press, 2013), 177–92; Brooks, *Liberty Power,* 207–11; Gienapp, *Origins,* 240–48.

105. *New York Tribune,* Dec. 21, 1855.

106. Gamaliel Bailey to Charles Francis Adams, Jan. 20, 1856; Adams Paper, MHS, cited in Foner, *Free Soil,* 247; Joshua R. Giddings to L. M. [Lura Maria] Giddings, Feb. 1, 1856, Giddings-Julian Papers, LC.

107. For historians' opinions, see Fred H. Harrington, "The First Northern Victory," *Journal of Southern History* 5 (1939): 186–205; Foner, *Free Soil,* 247–48; David Potter, *The Impending Crisis, 1848–1861* (New York: Harper & Row, 1976), 255–59; Gienapp, *Origins,* 246–48; Michael F. Holt, *The Rise and Fall of the Whig Party: Jacksonian Politics and the Onset of the Civil War* (New York: Oxford University Press, 1999),

962; Brooks, *Liberty Power*, 211. More recently, Joanne B. Freeman demonstrates that with the 34th Congress, antislavery congressmen began to meet southern violence in kind, a symptom of the wider shift in northern sentiment; Joanne B. Freeman, *The Field of Blood: Violence in Congress and the Road to Civil War* (New York: Farrar, Straus and Giroux, 2018), 208–64.

108. *Boston Daily Atlas*, Feb. 8, 1856; *St. Albans (Vt.) Messenger*, Feb. 7, 1856; *NA-SS*, Feb. 9, 1856; *Milwaukee Sentinel*, Feb. 14, 1856.

109. Barzilai Frost to CS, Feb. 4, 1856; George Livermore to CS, Feb. 4, 1856; CS to Charles Francis Adams, Feb. 5, 1856, Sumner Papers, HU; Richard Morgan to Edwin B. Morgan, Feb. 6, 1856, Edwin Barber Morgan Papers, cited in Gienapp, *Origins*, 247; on Morgan, see Elliot G. Storke, *History of Cayuga County, New York* (Syracuse: D. Mason, 1879), 406. See the discussions and citations in Gienapp, *Origins*, 247–48; Sewell, *Ballots for Freedom*, 276; Harrington, "First Northern Victory," 204.

110. Joshua R. Giddings to L. M. [Lura Maria] Giddings, Feb. 1, 3, 1856, Giddings-Julian Papers, LC. The first letter is subscribed to "L. M. Giddings" in Giddings's hand; from the tone, and the longer series of letters to "L. M. Giddings," I assume that the second letter is to her as well.

Chapter 8: Confirming and Consolidating New Structures

1. *DCF*, 5:546–47; *Indianapolis Morning Journal*, July 15, 16, 1856; *Indianapolis Locomotive*, July 19, 1856; Hedrick, *Stowe*, 258–64; Kate Clifford Larson, *Bound for the Promised Land: Harriet Tubman, Portrait of an American Hero* (New York: Ballantine, 2004), 126–29, 131–36; Eric Foner, *Gateway to Freedom: The Hidden History of the Underground Railroad* (New York: Norton, 2015), 190–94.

2. See table 1; William E. Gienapp, "Who Voted for Lincoln?," in *Abraham Lincoln and the American Political Tradition*, ed. John L. Thomas (Amherst: University of Massachusetts Press, 1986), 50–97. See also Michael F. Holt, "Making and Mobilizing the Republican Party, 1854–1860," in *The Birth of the Grand Old Party: The Republicans' First Generation*, ed. Robert F. Engs and Randall M. Miller (Philadelphia: University of Pennsylvania Press, 2002), 29–59.

3. For suggestions of confirmation and consolidation, see Elizabeth Varon, *Disunion: The Coming of the American Civil War, 1789–1859* (Chapel Hill: University of North Carolina Press, 2008), 269, 305; William E. Gienapp, *The Origins of the Republican Party, 1852–1856* (New York: Oxford University Press, 1987), 246–48; Thomas G. Mitchell, *Anti-Slavery Politics in Antebellum and Civil War America* (Westport, Conn.: Praeger, 2007), 123–40. Corey Brooks closes his detailed account with the Speakership election in *Liberty Power: Antislavery Third Parties and the Transformation of American Politics* (Chicago: University of Chicago Press, 2016); Michael Holt closes his analysis with the passage of the Kansas-Nebraska Act in *The Fate of Their Country: Politicians, Slavery Extension, and the Coming of the Civil War* (New York: Hill and Wang, 2004).

4. This phrase "favored child of destiny" is from Don E. Fehrenbacher, "The Republican Decision in Chicago," in *Politics and the Crisis of 1860*, ed. Norman Graebner (Urbana: University of Illinois Press, 1961), 33, in which he cautions against the argument presented here. Gienapp reversed Fehrenbacher's caution but focused on the period after the 1856 election, which he terms a "remarkable turn-around" and

"an astounding performance": "Few parties have ever been handed more advantages or been aided to a greater extent by their enemies than were the Republicans between 1857 and 1860." See William E. Gienapp, "The Crisis of American Democracy: The Political System and the Coming of the Civil War," in *Why the Civil War Came,* ed. Gabor S. Burritt (New York: Oxford University Press, 1996), 102–3.

5. Thurlow Weed to Nathaniel P. Banks, Feb. 3, 1856, Banks Papers, LC, cited in Gienapp, *Origins,* 247n34.

6. Jeffery A. Jenkins and Charles Stewart III, *Fighting for the Speakership: The House and the Rise of Party Government* (Princeton: Princeton University Press, 2013), 194–208.

7. Joel Silbey, "After 'The First Northern Victory': The Republican Party Comes to Congress, 1855–1856," *Journal of Interdisciplinary History* 20 (1989), 1–24; see generally Rachel A. Shelden, *Washington Brotherhood: Politics, Social Life, and the Coming of the Civil War* (Chapel Hill: University of Carolina Press, 2013).

8. Gienapp, *Origins,* 254–59, 264–94; Allan Nevins, *Ordeal of the Union,* vol. 2, *A House Dividing, 1852–1857* (New York: Scribner's, 1947), 419–28; *Proceedings of the First Three Republican National Conventions of 1856, 1860, and 1864* (Minneapolis: Charles W. Johnston, 1893), 7–13.

9. Foner, *Gateway to Freedom,* 193–210; William Still, Journal C of Station no. 2 of the Underground Railroad, 1852–1857, Black Abolitionist Papers series, HSP.

10. *New York Tribune,* Feb. 4, 1856; *Pittsburgh Daily Post,* Feb. 23, 1856.

11. Nicole Etcheson, *Bleeding Kansas: Contested Liberty in the Civil War Era* (Lawrence: University Press of Kansas, 2004), 100–105.

12. David Donald, *Charles Sumner and the Coming of the Civil War* (New York: Fawcett, 1960), 274–97; *CG* 34/1, App., 529–44; on Sumner's "Remedies," see 539–42; on Butler and South Carolina, see 530–31, 543.

13. A search of the America's Historical Newspapers database for May–July 1856 produces 316 hits on "Charles Sumner" and "Brooks," combined, twenty-nine hits on "Sack of Lawrence," and one hit on "John Brown" and "Pottawatomie" combined.

14. For historians who see the Sumner assault as pivotal, perhaps transformative, see William E. Gienapp, "The Crime against Sumner: The Caning of Charles Sumner and the Rise of the Republican Party," *Civil War History* 25 (1979), 218–45; Manisha Sinha, "The Caning of Charles Sumner: Slavery, Race, and Ideology in the Age of Civil War," *Journal of the Early Republic* 23 (2003): 233–62; Michael E. Woods, "'The Indignation of Freedom-Loving People': The Caning of Charles Sumner and Emotion in Antebellum Politics," *Journal of Social History* 44, no. 3 (Spring 2011): 689–705; and Brooks D. Simpson, "'Hit Him Again': The Caning of Charles Sumner," in *Congress and the Crisis of the 1850s,* ed. Paul Finkelman and Donald R. Kennon (Athens: Ohio University Press, 2012), 203–21. For a general statement of the role of the events in May as a "turning point in the Republican Party's struggle for political survival," see Gienapp, *Origins,* 295–303; compare with his assessment of "the crucial importance" and "magnitude of the Republican accomplishment" in electing Banks in February (246–48).

15. Tyler Anbinder, *Nativism and Slavery: The Northern Know Nothings and the Politics of the 1850s* (New York: Oxford University Press, 1992), 206–18.

16. Gienapp, *Origins,* 305–7; Nevins, *Ordeal of the Union,* 2:452–60.

17. Gienapp, *Origins*, 307–46; Anbinder, *Nativism and Slavery*, 206–18; *Proceedings of the First Three Republican National Conventions*, 14–82.

18. *Indianapolis Daily Journal*, July 16, 1856.

19. Michael D. Pierson, *Free Hearts, Free Homes: Gender and American Antislavery Politics* (Chapel Hill: University of North Carolina Press, 2003), esp. 74–80, 115–50, 150–63; David Grant, *Political Antislavery Discourse and American Literature of the 1850s* (Newark: University of Delaware Press, 2012), 153–84.

20. *DCF*, 5:176–77, 181, 267–68.

21. Odell, *Annals*, 6:547–48, 557–58, 565–66; *New York Tribune*, Sept. 17, 22, 1856; *New York Times*, Sept. 23–Oct. 24, 1856; *Buffalo Daily Courier*, Oct. 21, 1856; *Pittsburgh Daily Post*, Nov. 25, 1856; Cordelia Howard MacDonald, "Memoirs of the Original Little Eva," typescript, 1928, 16–19, George C. Howard Collection, Harry Ransom Center, University of Texas, Austin.

22. *Liberator*, Jan. 4, 18, Sept. 19, Oct. 10, 1856; *New York Tribune*, July 3, Oct, 24, 28, Nov. 4, 1856.

23. Ken Emerson, *Doo-dah! Stephen Foster and the Rise of American Popular Culture* (New York: Simon & Schuster, 1997), 233–38; *The Republican Campaign Songster* (New York and Auburn: Miller, Orton, and Mulligan, 1856), 3.

24. David Potter, *The Impending Crisis, 1848–1861* (New York: Harper & Row, 1976), 262–63, Mason quoted 262.

25. Etcheson, *Bleeding Kansas*, 131–43; Tony R. Mullis, "John Geary, Kansas, and the 1856 National Election," *Heritage of the Great Plains* 25 (Winter 1992): 13–24.

26. Gienapp, *Origins*, 401–405.

27. Allan Nevins, *The Emergence of Lincoln*, vol. 1, *Douglas, Buchanan, and Party Chaos, 1857–1859* (New York: Scribner's, 1950), 139–41.

28. Don E. Fehrenbacher, *The Dred Scott Case: Its Significance in American Law and Politics* (New York: Oxford University Press, 1978), 322–448.

29. Kenneth M. Stampp, *America in 1857: A Nation on the Brink* (New York: Oxford University Press, 1990), 82–109, 295–331; Etcheson, *Bleeding Kansas*, 139–89; Potter, *The Impending Crisis*, 267–328; Leonard L. Richards, *The Slave Power: The Free North and the Slave Power, 1780–1860* (Baton Rouge: Louisiana State University Press, 2000), 202–5.

30. Jenny Wahl, "Dred, Panic, War: How a Slave Case Triggered Financial Crisis and Civil Disunion," in Finkelman and Kennon, *Congress and the Crisis of the 1850s*, 159–202; Kathryn Teresa Long, *The Revival of 1857–1858: Interpreting an American Religious Awakening* (New York: Oxford University Press, 1998).

31. Allen C. Guelzo, *Lincoln and Douglas: The Debates That Defined America* (New York: Simon & Schuster, 2008), 81–84, 112, 120–23, 165, 168, 190–201, 220–29, 259–63; Eric Foner, *The Fiery Trial: Abraham Lincoln and American Slavery* (New York: W. W. Norton & Co., 2010), 104–10; quotes from Lincoln at Chicago in *CWAL*, 2:499, 501.

32. Foner, *Fiery Trial*, 110–11.

33. *CWAL*, 2: 461; *The Irrepressible Conflict: Speech by William H. Seward, delivered at Rochester, Monday, October 27, 1858* (n.p., 1858). See figure 1.

34. For a sample of the productions of *Uncle Tom's Cabin*, see *Chicago Tribune*, Feb. 13, 1857, July 27–28, 1859; *Worcester Palladium*, Apr. 1, 1857; *Philadelphia Public Ledger*, Mar. 23, 1857, Jan. 6, 1858, Oct. 11–12, 25, Nov. 16, 1860; *Brooklyn Daily Eagle*, July 24,

1858, Oct. 31–Nov. 22, 1859; *Bloomington (Ill.) Pantagraph*, Oct. 14, 1857; *Manufacturers and Farmers Journal* (Providence), Dec. 3, 1857; *Boston Evening Transcript*, Dec. 12–16, 1857; *Cape Ann Light* (Gloucester), Apr. 17, 1858; *Detroit Free Press*, Dec. 1, 1858; *Wheeling Daily Intelligencer*, July 2, 1859; *Hartford Courant*, Aug. 8, Oct. 26, 1859; *Pittsburgh Daily Post*, Nov. 24, 1859, Apr. 9, June 20, Oct. 4, 1860; *Buffalo Morning Express*, Dec. 23, 1859, Feb. 24, 1860. For Browne notices, see *Ohio Farmer* (Cleveland), Dec. 27, 1856; *Alexandria Gazette*, Jan. 3, 1857.

35. Matthew Mason, *Apostles of Union: A Political Biography of Edward Everett* (Chapel Hill: University of North Carolina Press, 2016), 216–55; Robert E. Bonner, *Mastering America: Southern Slaveholders and the Crisis of American Nationhood* (New York: Cambridge University Press. 2009), 194–205. On the religious context, see Long, *The Revival of 1857–1858*, 111–16; Peter J. Wallace, "'The Bond of Union': The Old School Presbyterian Church and the American Nation, 1837–1861" (Ph.D. diss., University of Notre Dame, 2004). The Mount Vernon initiative was a classic case of a unifying national media event, as discussed in Sabini Mihelj, "National Media Events: From Displays of Unity to Enactments of Division," *European Journal of Cultural Studies* 11 (2008): 471–88.

36. Steven A. Channing, *Crisis of Fear: Secession in South Carolina* (New York: W. W. Norton 1974), 17–57; Stephen B. Oates, *To Purge This Land with Blood: A Biography of John Brown* (New York: Harper, 1970), 229–361.

37. A search in the America's Historical Newspapers database between November 21, 1859, and December 31, 1860, produces 205 hits; Christian McWirter, *Battle Hymns: The Power and Popularity of Music in the Civil War* (Chapel Hill: University of North Carolina Press, 2012), 41–50.

38. Douglas R. Egerton, *Year of Meteors: Stephen Douglas, Abraham Lincoln, and the Election That Brought on the Civil War* (New York: Bloomsbury, 2010).

39. On the growing sense of inevitability see Egerton, *Year of Meteors*, 119, 132, 143, 157, 164, 170–71, 174–75, 188, 193, 199, 201–2, 208; on nativism, see Anbinder, *Nativism and Slavery*, 246–70; on the fugitive petition movement, see Mark Voss-Hubbard, "The Political Culture of Emancipation: Morality, Politics, and the State in Garrisonian Abolitionism, 1854–1863," *Journal of American Studies* 29 (1995): 159–84, esp. 172–78.

40. *DGTS*, 3:58–59.

41. *DCF*, 6:611, 625–26.

42. Election returns from the *Indiana Sentinel* (Indianapolis), Nov. 9, 1860.

43. On age and northern voters, see Gienapp, "Who Voted for Lincoln?," 75–81; Peter Knupfer, "Aging Statesmen and the Statesmanship of an Earlier Age: The Generational Roots of the Constitutional Union Party," in *Union and Emancipation: Essays on Politics and Race in the Civil War Era*, ed. David W. Blight and Brooks D. Simpson (Kent: Kent State University Press, 1997), 57–78; and Anne C. Rose, *Victorian America and the Civil War* (New York: Cambridge University Press, 1992), 214–15. If Lincoln's vote was not fundamentally larger than Frémont's, it was strategically larger, leaving him with a lock on the election in his domination of large northern states. See Egerton's electoral calculations suggesting that he would have prevailed in a two-way race, in *Year of Meteors*, 335–41.

44. *Indianapolis Daily Journal*, Aug. 14, 18, 24, 29, 30, 1860; Kenneth Stamp, *Indiana*

Politics during the Civil War (Indianapolis: Indiana Historical Bureau, 1949), 44–46; Charles Zimmerman, "The Origin and Rise of the Republican Party in Indiana from 1854 to 1860," *Indiana Magazine of History* 13 (1917):349–412; Rose, *Victorian America and the Civil War*, 214–15; Jon Grinspan, "'Young Men for War': The Wide Awakes and Lincoln's 1860 Presidential Campaign," *Journal of American History* 96 (2009): 357–78; Jon Grinspan, *The Virgin Vote: How Young Americans Made Democracy Social, Politics Personal, and Voting Popular in the Nineteenth Century* (Chapel Hill: University of North Carolina Press, 2016), 115–19.

45. On the secessionist threat in 1856, see Potter, *The Impending Crisis*, 262; Varon, *Disunion*, 274–75.

46. "Declaration of the Immediate Causes which Induce and Justify the Secession of South Carolina, Dec. 24, 1860," Avalon Project website, Yale Law School, http://avalon.law.yale.edu/19th_century/csa_scarsec.asp; Charles B. Dew, *Apostles of Disunion: Southern Secession Commissioners and the Causes of the Civil War* (Charlottesville: University Press of Virginia, 2001).

47. William J. Cooper, "The Critical Signpost on the Journey toward Secession," *Journal of Southern History* 77 (2011): 3–16; William J. Cooper, *We Have the War upon Us: The Onset of the Civil War, November 1860–April 1861* (New York: Alfred A. Knopf, 2012), 101–11, 131–36.

48. Abraham Lincoln, First Inaugural Address, March 4, 1861, Avalon Project website, Yale Law School; http://avalon.law.yale.edu/subject_menus/inaug.asp. For Lincoln and the Republican voters, see Russell McClintock, *Lincoln and the Decision for War: The Northern Response to Secession* (Chapel Hill: University of North Carolina Press, 2008), 79–83, 92–95, 142–52, 158–64, 278–79; Daniel W. Crofts, *Lincoln and the Politics of Slavery: The Other Thirteenth Amendment and the Struggle to Save the Union* (Chapel Hill: University of North Carolina Press, 2016), 165–84. For wavering Washington politicians, see Cooper, *We Have the War Upon Us*, 56–81, 104–5; Shelden, *Washington Brotherhood*, 167–91; Joan E. Cashin, *First Lady of the Confederacy: Varina Davis's Civil War* (Cambridge: Harvard University Press, 2006), 92–106.

Epilogue: Into the War

1. *John Quincy Adams Diaries*, vol. 1, *1779–1821*, ed. David Waldstreicher (New York: Library of America, 2017), 576.

2. Henry Wilson, *History of the Rise and Fall of the Slave Power in America*, 7th ed., vol. 2 (Boston: Houghton Mifflin, 1874), 519; James Ford Rhodes, *History of the United States from the Compromise of 1850*, vol. 1, *1850–1854* (New York: Harper, 1896), 278–79; Frederick Douglass, *Life and Times of Frederick Douglass* (1881, 1892; New York: Macmillan, 1962), 282.

3. Chandra Manning, *What This Cruel War Was Over: Soldiers, Slavery, and the Civil War* (New York: Vintage, 2007), 120.

4. Hedrick, *Stowe*, 305–6.

5. Frederic E. McKay and Charles E. L. Wingate, eds., *Famous American Actors of To-day*, 2 vols. (New York: Crowell, 1896), 2:261; Thomas Wentworth Higginson,

comp., *Massachusetts in the Army and Navy during the War of 1861–65*, vol. 2 (Boston: Wright & Potter, 1895), 309.

6. Evelyn Foster Morneweck, *Chronicles of Stephen Foster's Family* (Pittsburgh: University of Pittsburgh Press, 1944), 532; Thomas P. Lory, *Curmudgeons, Drunkards, and Outright Fools: Courts-Martial of Civil War Union Colonels* (Lincoln: University of Nebraska Press, 1997), 103–5.

7. For the Fletchers during the Civil War, see *DCF*, 7:x–xiv, 8:x–xiii. Quotes from "The Civil War Journal of Stephen Keyes Fletcher," *Indiana Magazine of History* 54 (1958): 185. Fletcher regularly referred to his fellow soldiers as "our boys."

56. Francis Marion McAdams, *Every-day Soldier Life: Or A History of the One Hundred and Thirteenth Ohio. Volunteer Infantry* (Columbus: Chas. M. Cott, 1884), 172–78; United States Congressional serial set, no. 7243, 64th Cong, 2nd sess., doc. 1960.

8. Ransom Bedell, "American Slavery," Ransom Bedell Papers, Illinois State Historical Library, quoted in Manning, *What This Cruel War Was Over*, 120; James T. Miller to Joseph Miller, Sept. 7, 1863, in *Bound to Be a Soldier: The Letters of Private James T. Miller, 111th Pennsylvania Infantry, 1861–1864*, ed. Jedediah Mannis and Galen R. Wilson (Knoxville: University of Tennessee Press, 2001), 109–10.

9. John H. Matsui, *The First Republican Army: The Army of Virginia and the Radicalization of the Civil War* (Charlottesville: University of Virginia Press, 2016); Zachery A. Fry, *A Republic in the Ranks: Loyalty and Dissent in the Army of the Potomac* (Chapel Hill: University of North Carolina Press, forthcoming). For Bedell, see Ransom Bedell Widow's Pension Record, Apr. 23, 1865, in *Report of the Adjutant General of the State of Illinois*, comp. J. N. Reece, vol. 3 (Springfield: Phillips, 1901), 125, 139–43.

10. For Miller, see Mannis and Wilson, *Bound to Be a Soldier*, 119 and 31–197 passim. On the 111th Pennsylvania's reenlistment and 1864 vote, see John R. Boyle, *Soldiers True: The Story of the One Hundred and Eleventh Regiment Pennsylvania Veteran Volunteers, and of Its Campaigns in the War for the Union, 1861–1865* (New York: Baton & Mains, 1901), 189–93, 251–52; *Pittsburgh Daily Commercial*, Jan. 11, 1864; John W. Geary to Mary Geary, Oct. 19, 1864, in *A Politician Goes to War: The Civil War Letters of John White Geary*, ed. William Alan Blair (University Park: Pennsylvania State University Press, 1995), 210; Joseph T. Glatthaar, *The March to the Sea and Beyond: Sherman's Troops in the Savannah and Carolinas Campaigns* (New York: New York University Press, 1985), 47, 200–202.

11. "The Two Platforms," Clymer vs. Geary broadside, 1866, Broadside Collection, portfolio 159, LC; Collection notes, Geary Family Papers, 1846–1913, HSP.

12. Noah Andre Trudeau, *Like Men of War: Black Troops in the Civil War, 1862–1865* (Boston: Little, Brown, 1998), 29–46, 114, 137–51, 314, 321–33, James G. Hollandsworth Jr., *Pretense of Glory: The Life of General Nathaniel P. Banks* (Baton Rouge: Louisiana State University Press, 1998), 145–53; Russell Duncan, ed., *Blue-Eyed Child of Fortune: The Civil War Letters of Colonel Robert Gould Shaw* (Athens: University of Georgia Press, 1992), 6–8; *The Complete Civil War Journal and Selected Letters of Thomas Wentworth Higginson*, ed. Christopher Looby (Chicago: University of Chicago Press, 2000), 48–49, 64, 160, 213, 292, 319; Thomas Wentworth Higginson, *Army Life in*

a Black Regiment (1870; Williamstown, Mass.: Corner House, 1971), 246–47. Daniel Ullman, the New York nativist, served under Banks in the Shenandoah and followed him to the Mississippi Valley with a competing commission to recruit black soldiers; he eventually commanded the Louisiana Corps d'Afrique.

13. Kate Clifford Larson, *Bound for the Promised Land: Harriet Tubman, Portrait of an American Hero* (New York: Ballantine, 2004), 203–28.

14. George P. Clark and Shirley E. Clark, "Heroes Carved in Ebony: Indiana's Black Civil War Regiment," *Traces of Indiana and Midwestern History* 7, no. 3 (Summer 1995): 4–16; Trudeau, *Like Men of War*, 232–52; U.S Census Manuscripts, 1850; *Report of the Adjutant General of the State of Indiana, 1861–1865* (Indianapolis: Samuel M. Douglas, 1866), vol. 3, 379, and vol. 7, 660; *Christian Recorder*, Aug. 20, 1864

15. Trudeau, *Like Men of War*, 417–24; *Christian Recorder*, Apr. 22, 1865; Josephine F. Pacheco, *The Pearl: A Failed Slave Escape on the Potomac* (Chapel Hill: University of North Carolina Press, 2005), 219–22; Edward A. Miller, "Garland H. White, Black Army Chaplain," *Civil War History* 43 (1997): 201–18.

16. Steven Hahn, *The Political Worlds of Slavery and Freedom* (Cambridge: Harvard University Press, 2009), 55–114; Gregory P. Downs, *After Appomattox: Military Occupation and the Ends of War* (Cambridge: Harvard University Press, 2015).

17. William S. McFeely, *Frederick Douglas:* (New York: Simon & Schuster, 1991), 223–27; Victor Ullman, *Martin R. Delany: The Beginnings of Black Nationalism* (Boston: Beacon Press, 1971), 282–307; Robert S. Levine, *Martin Delany, Frederick Douglass, and the Politics of Representative Identity* (Chapel Hill: University of North Carolina Press, 1997), 191–223; Douglas R. Egerton, *Thunder at the Gates: The Black Civil War Regiments That Redeemed America* (New York: Basic Books, 2016), a history of the Fifty-fourth and Fifty-fifth Massachusetts, contains extensive details on the Douglass and Delany sons.

18. Here I would suggest that Hochman, *Uncle Tom's Cabin and the Reading Revolution*, 131–230, and John W. Frick, *Uncle Tom's Cabin on the American Stage and Screen* (New York: Palgrave Macmillan, 2012), 110–223, read with David W. Blight, *Race and Reunion: The Civil War in American Memory* (Cambridge: Harvard University Press, 2001), and Brian Roberts, *Blackface Nation: Race, Reform, and Identity in American Popular Music, 1812–1925* (Chicago: University of Chicago Press, 2017), present a more realistic view of the postbellum uses of the book and the play than David Reynolds's seemingly more positive view in *Mightier Than the Sword: Uncle Tom's Cabin and the Battle for America* (New York: W. W. Norton, 2011), 169–273.

19. On the threat of white slavery and the message of universal liberty, I am particularly indebted to Jeremy J. Tewell, *A Self-Evident Lie: Southern Slavery and the Threat to American Freedom* (Kent: Kent State University Press, 2013); see also Manning, *What This Cruel War Was Over*, 120–21.

20. Michigan Republican Party platform, July 6, 1854, in *History of U.S. Political Parties, 1860–1910: The Gilded Age of Politics*, ed. Arthur M. Schlesinger (Philadelphia: Chelsea House, 1973), 1185.

21. *CWAL*, 4:240–41. See Tewell, *A Self-Evident Lie*, 132–39; Graham A. Peck, *Making an Antislavery Nation: Lincoln, Douglas, and the Battle over Freedom* (Urbana:

University of Illinois Press, 2017), 156–83; Eric Foner, *The Fiery Trial: Abraham Lincoln and American Slavery* (New York: W. W. Norton & Co., 2010), 155, 331–32.

22. Orville H. Browning to Abraham Lincoln, Apr. 30, 1861, Lincoln Papers, LC.

23. Foner, *Fiery Trial*, 176–81, 206–8.

24. Robert F. Horowitz, *The Great Impeacher: A Political Biography of James M. Ashley* (New York: Brooklyn College Press, 1979), 65–67, 72–74, 91, 97–98.

25. For Seward's speech of March 11, 1850, see *CG* 31/1, App., 268; James Oakes, *Freedom National: The Destruction of Slavery in the United States, 1861–1865* (New York: W. W. Norton, 2013); Louis P. Masur, *Lincoln's Hundred Days: The Emancipation Proclamation and the War for the Union* (Cambridge: Harvard University Press, 2012); Allen C. Guelzo, *Lincoln's Emancipation Proclamation: The End of Slavery in America* (New York: Simon & Schuster, 2004).

26. Hedrick, *Stowe*, 305–6; Stephen Cushman, "When Lincoln Met Emerson," *Journal of the Civil War Era* 3 (2013): 163–83; McFeely, *Frederick Douglas.* 226, 229–30.

27. Garry Wills, *Lincoln at Gettysburg: The Words That Remade America* (New York: Simon & Schuster, 1992), 90–147; James M. McPherson, *Abraham Lincoln and the Second American Revolution* (New York: Oxford University Press, 1991), 23–42.

Index

References to figures and tables are indicated in italics. References to illustrations and captions in gallery pages are indicated as G#.

abolitionism: in early republic, 28–31; African American, 29–31; spectrum of abolitionist factions, 46–49; and liminal outsidership, 45–46; political outsiders, 55–59; "Jim Crow" minstrelsy used against, 45; opposition to, 45–46; southern fear of, 20; activism after Fugitive Slave Act, 97, 103–4; Fugitive Slave Law condemnation by, 94–95; against slavery, nativism, and proslavery Union, 234. *See also* Garrisonian immediatists; "halfway" abolitionism; Liberty Party; Smith circle; Tappanites
Adams, Charles Francis, 2, 62, 274
Adams, John, 26
Adams, John Quincy, 34, 38, 51–53, 55, 62–63, 244, 295
"Address of the Southern Delegates in Congress," 68
African American: abolitionists, 29–31; convention, 156–57; geographic movement as liminal, 66, 101–2, 128–29, 131, 134, 340n35; leadership, 138–39, 156; publications, 138, 166, 168–69, *172*, 180–81, 188, 200, 265, 266, 301, *313*; rights and citizenship 288–89, 303–5. See also *Frederick Douglass's Paper; North Star*
Aiken, George, 186, 192, 194–97, 266. *See also* Aiken-Howard *UTC* script
Aiken, William, 273
Aiken-Howard *UTC* script, 188–90, 192, 194–97, 219–21, 266, 359n116, 340n135, 366n61
Allen, William, 138
American and Foreign Anti-Slavery Society (AFASS), 47, 54, 83, 117, 138, 225
American Anti-Slavery Society (AASS): convention, 112; Garrisonian control, 52, 86; Kelly presiding officer, 47; militant group, 20; organized by Garrison, 35–36; Wendell Phillips praise for *UTC*, 149; postal campaign, 49; Sumner speaks at meeting, 264; Wilson address, 255. *See also* Garrison, William Lloyd; Garrisonian immediatists
American Colonization Society, 29, 39, 49, 120
American Fugitive in Europe, The (W. W. Brown), 266
American Missionary Association, 93
American Museum (Barnum's), New York, 189, 192, 205, 266–67, 284, *G10*, *G12*
American Revolution: British offer of emancipation, 25–26; liminal moment, 24
American Slavery As It Is (Weld & A. Grimké), 123, 125, 161, 163
Amistad case, 52
anti-abolitionism: riots, 37–38, 43–44, 66, 121–22, 184, 191; and "Jim Crow," 43–44, 180; against *UTC*, 184
anti-Masonry, 51, 369n22

antislavery constitutionalism, 51–53. *See also* Liberty Party; Smith circle
Anti-Slavery Convention of American Women, 37
Anti-Slavery Movement, The (F. Douglass), 3–4, 174–75, 200, 264, 269–70
antislavery media: books and serial stories, 3–4, 118, 119–50, 160–65, 168–70, *172*, 200, 214, 259, 262–67, 276, 284–85, 289, 301, 302, *313*; lectures and speeches, 44, 47, 95, 159, 167, 205, 211, 215, 217–18, 230, 258–61, 263–64, 267, 280–81; music, 4, 18, 21, 39, 164, 171–82, 184, 194–99, 220, 264–65, 283, 285; newspapers, 30, 35, 49–50; poetry, 101, 117, 126, 181, 259–60, 264–65, 285, 373n81; theater, 182–201, 218–25, 266–267, 284–85, 289; toys and merchandising, 164–65, *G6*; and creolization, 20–21, 142, 159–61, 173–79; and capitalism, 160, 164–65, 167–70, 199–200, 202–3; and sympathy, 4, 101–2, 104–5, 133–37, 142, 149–50, 152, 175, 179–80, 190–91, 199–200, 225, 260, 270, 301–2. *See also* Jewett, John P.; *Liberator*; liminality; *National Era*; *North Star*; public sphere; *Uncle Tom's Cabin*
antislavery media event of early 1850s, xii, 6, 90–115, 159–61, 258–61; 1850–1852 cycle, 92–96, 100–101, 116–19, 122–58, 164–65, 171–82, *172*; 1852–1854 cycle, *172*, 182–201, 213–15, 217–25; 1855–1856 cycle, 258–67, 270, 276, 282–85, 295; 1857–1860 cycle, 289, 292; and Civil War, 296–99, 301–2, 305; as first modern media event, xii, 161; contemporaries on impact of, 148–58, 203, 295–96. *See also* liminality: of early 1850s for northern public
antislavery movement: antislavery societies, 35–37; black Americans' role, 5; blackface minstrel shows, 4; failure against Know Nothings, 252; interracial movement, 7; literature of, 3; natural rights militancy, 35; political strategy, 54; popular support for, 105–7; response to A. Jackson's election, 34–35; story of white slave girls, 266; sympathetic breakthrough, 302. *See also* political antislavery

antislavery petitions. *See* petitions to Congress
antislavery resolutions: District of Columbia, 68; southern response, 68
antislavery voters, 13, 54–55, 148, 252, 277, 287, *308*, *317*. *See also* elections
anti-Tom novels. *See* proslavery media
"Appeal of the Independent Democrats, An," 14, 207–11, 213–14, 323n24, 362n14
Appeal . . . to the Coloured Citizens (Walker), 30–31, 35
"Appeal to the Women of the Free States, An" (H. B. Stowe), 214–15
Archy: The White Slave (Hildreth), 168, 302
Articles of Confederation, 26
Ashley, James, 304
Astor House, 205, *G10*, *G12*
Atchison, David, 204, 206, 262
Aunt Dinah, 260
Aunt Phillis's Cabin; or, Southern Life as It Is (Eastman), 170
Autobiography of a Female Slave (Browne), 289
Avery, Charles, 181, *G9*
Ayers, Edward, 9–10

Bacon, Leonard, 49, 162
Bacon, Leonard W., 162
Bailey, Gamaliel: antislavery salon, 116; antislavery caucus in Congress, 216; female celebrities and, 118, 127; H. B. Stowe and, 122, 126; Know Nothings on slavery, 252–53; at Lane Seminary, 121; launch of a national Republican Party, 268–71; L. Tappan and, 117; *National Era* becomes a daily, 207; *National Era* begins publication, 50; party reconciliation impossible on slavery, 258; proto-Republican Party, 248; on Republican Party, 274; Republican Party formation, 245; serial publication of *UTC*, 128–29, 131, 143, 150; Washington move, 116
Bailey, Margaret, 116–17, 123, 129; as *UTC* reader, 151
Baily, Susan J., 190, 358n109
Banks, Nathaniel P., 2, 22, 268–69, 272–74,

277–79, 282, 298–99, *G15*. *See also* elections: House Speaker (1855–1856)
Banneker, Benjamin, 30
Baring, Thomas, 204
Barker, James W., 238, 241–43, 246, 253–57, 269, 371n54
Barmore, Wesley (Samuel E. Harris), 189–90, 195–96, 220–22
Barnum, P. T., 89, 118, 189, 219, 267, 284
Barry, E. H., 251
Bartlett, Edward B., 256, 271
Bedell, Ransom, 297
Bedini, Gaetano, 236
Beecher, Catharine, 122–23, 139, 143, 159
Beecher, Charles, 126, 140
Beecher, Edward, 122, 126, 245
Beecher, Eunice, 145
Beecher, George, 122, 124
Beecher, Harriet, 49; anonymous essay on free speech, 122–23; in Cincinnati, 121–22. *See also* Stowe, Harriet Beecher
Beecher, Henry Ward, 122, 125, 132, 139, 145, 161, 264; nativist views, 245
Beecher, Isabella, 126
Beecher, James C., 296, 298
Beecher, Lyman, 2, 49, 119–22, 139, 162, 216, 245
Beecher, William, 122
Bell, John, 291–92
Benton, Thomas Hart, 73, 284
Bibb, Henry, 85
Bigelow, Harriet, 285
Bigler, William, 114
Birney, Elizabeth, as *UTC* reader, 143
Birney, James, 48–50, 52, 121–22; as *UTC* reader, 143–44, 146, 162; despised nativism, 244
Black Hawk, 43
Blair, Francis Preston, Sr., 268–70, 272–73, 282
Blake (Delany), 301
Blakely, Richard, 299
"Blood Hound's Song, The" (Shiras), 181
Booth, Sherman, 224
Boston Museum, 186, 192, 194
Boston Vigilance Committee, 98
Botts, Mary, 266
Bowdoin College, 124
Boyd, Linn, 202, 226

Breckinridge, John C., 291–92
Bremer, Fredericka, 118
British law: abolition of slavery, 25, 36, 80; Declaratory Act, 25; slavery, violation of natural law, 25; Stamp Act repeal, 25
Broadway Tabernacle, 86, 211, 259; lecture series, 125, 205, 217, 219, 230
Brooks, Preston, 281
Brown, Henry "Box," 188
Brown, John, 43, 85, 262, 281, 290, 377n13
Brown, William Wells, 169, 266
Browne, Martha Griffin, 289
Browning, Orville Hickman, 107–8, 230–31, 304
Bryant, William Cullen, 117
Buchanan, Edward Y., 177
Buchanan, Eliza, 177
Buchanan, James, 276, 282–83, 285–87, 298
Bungay, George W., 373n81
Burlingame, Michael, 231
Burns, Anthony, rendition of, 225–30, 245, 261, 299
Burns riot, 226–28
Butler, Andrew, 71, 281

Calhoun, John C., 68, 73–76, 109, 294
California: Gold Rush, 65; statehood bill, 67–69, 71; statehood convention, 65, 70
"Call to Kansas," 265
Cameron, Simon, 254
Campbell, James, 236
Campbell, Lewis, 272–73
Canoe, John, 41
Carter, James P., 175–76, 178, 355n60; "Lucy Neal," 175–76, *G7*
Cass, Lewis, 62–63, 283
Caste: A Story of Republican Equality (M. Pike), 267, 285
Catherine Market, 40–41, *G10*
Catholicism and anti-Catholicism, 119–20, 236–38, 241
celebrity culture, 117–19, 159–60, 166–68. *See also* women: as cultural celebrities
Chaplin, William, 85, 95, 270, 299
Charlestown Convent riot, 44, 241, 245
Chase, Salmon P.: alliance with Democrats, 111; in Baileys' salon, 116; antislavery Liberty Party, 123; antislavery oration, 80–81; on "Appeal

Chase, Salmon P. (*continued*)
of the Independent Democrats," 80–81, 112, 207–8, 214; Beecher connections, 122; Free Soil Democrat, 64, 150; on fugitive bill, 87, 112; Fusion party in Ohio, 246; on Kansas-Nebraska Act, 257; launch of a national Republican Party, 268–69; Liberty Party leader, 64; L. Beecher associate, 122–23; "Maintain Plighted Faith" speech, 210–11, 213–14, 363n18; petitions to Congress, 83; on Republican nomination, 291; and *Key to UTC*, 162; Semi-Colon Club member, 122; Senate seat, 111; Silver Spring meeting, 272; Underground Railroad conductor defense, 130; *UTC* reader, 129, 151, 165; Van Zandt defender, 130; wins Ohio as Republican, 271

Chatham Garden Theatre, New York, 40–41, 43–44, 184, *G10, G11*

Chestnut Street Theater, Philadelphia, 43, 190, 196, 198, 220

Child, David L., 157

Child, Lydia Maria, 105, 140, 285

child-naming patterns, and *UTC*: Eva, 146–48, *147, 172, 313*, 356n82

Christian Slave, The (H. B. Stowe), 259, 262–63, 265, 267

Christiana riot, 113–14, 130, *G2*

Christy, Edwin, 173, 179, 197

Christy's Minstrels, 42, 173

Cincinnati: abolitionism, 121–23; economic depression in, 123; importance to S. Foster, 177–78; riots in, 121–22, 236; *UTC* performances, 221–22

Civil War: black troops and politics, 298–301; end of American slavery, 295; losses, human and monetary, 8; questions for Reconstruction, 304; Union soldiers in, 296–98; *UTC* impact on white Union soldiers, 299

Civil War causation: debate, 8–15, 24, 237; role of white South, 1–12; role of African Americans, 12–13, 19–20; role of antislavery North, 4–7, 13–15, 21–22, 295–96

Clark, Myron, 242, 247

Clarke, Sarah Jane (Grace Greenwood), 117–18, 151

Clay, Henry, 34, 72–73, 76–78, 96, 153–54, 289

Clotel: or the President's Daughter (W. W. Brown), 169

coal consumption, *58*

Cobb, Howell, 70

colonizationism, 108, 137, 304; Beecher families' views, 139–40; in *UTC*, 137, 139, 194. *See also* American Colonization Society

colored citizens, 85, 92–93, 99–100

Colored Patriots of the American Revolution (Nell), 265

Committee of Vigilance and Safety, 95

compromise of 1787. *See* Constitution, U.S.

Compromise of 1850, 22; debates, 1, 3, 6, 70–81; votes, 77–78, *310–11*; dispute over finality, 150, 152–53, 202; J. Hale and Chase speeches, 81; Mann's debate speech, 80; Missouri and Vermont resolutions, 71; "omnibus bill" proposal, 73, 76; W. Seward's debate speech, 80–81; slavery debates, 79–81, 87; territorial debates, 3, 70–71, 76. *See also* Calhoun, John C.; Union meetings; Webster, Daniel

Condition, Elevation, Emigration, and Destiny of the Colored People, The (Delany), 200

Congo Minstrels, 174

Conquest of Kansas, The (Phillips), 265

Constitution, U.S.: slavery debates in convention and ratification, 8, 11–13, 24, 26–29, 295; fugitive slave clause, 26–27; slavery in, 48; First Amendment, 51; Fifth Amendment, 48, 52; Thirteenth Amendment, 8, 52, 304, 305; Fourteenth Amendment, 8, 305; Fifteenth Amendment, 8, 305

Constitutional Union Party, 290–91

conventions:

—Anti-Slavery Convention of American Women (1837), 37

—Free Soil (1848), 62, 67

—southern disunion (1850), 109–10

—California statehood (1849), 65, 70

—Cazenovia Liberty (1850), 85–87, 103, 112–13, 146, 157, 270, *G2*

—Friends of Freedom (Cleveland, 1851), 112
—Whig (1852), 153
—Democratic (1852), 153, 156
—Free Democratic (1852), 154
—African American: Syracuse (1853), 156–57
—Republican (Wisconsin, 1854), 230, 245–46
—Republican (Michigan, 1854), 245–46, 303
—Whig (New York, 1854), 242, 246
—Fusion (Indiana, 1854 & 1855), 246, 251
—Free Soil and Know Nothing (Massachusetts, 1854), 247–48
—Whig and Know Nothing (Pennsylvania, 1854), 248
—Know Nothing (American) in 1854, 1855, & 1856: (*see* Order of the Star Spangled Banner: National Council meetings)
—North American (1855), 271
—Free Soiler (Kansas, 1855), 262
—Fusion (Pennsylvania, 1855), 269
—North American (1855 & 1856), 271, 282
—Republican (Feb. 1856), 22, 279–80, *G9*
—Republican (June 1856): planning for, 268, 279; undermined nativists, 282; John Frémont nomination, 276, 282; antipolygamy and antislavery planks, 283–84; and Declaration of Independence, 303
—Republican (Indiana, 1856), 246, 276, 282–83; parades for John Frémont, 276, 283–84
—Democratic (1856), 282
—Lecompton (Kansas, 1857), 287
—Republican (Illinois, 1858), 288
—Democratic (1860), 282, 290–91
—Republican (1860), 290–91, 303
—South Carolina secession (1860), 5, 7, 293
Conway, Henry, 189
Conway *UTC* script, 192–95, 219, 362n61
Cornish, Samuel, 30
Corwin Amendment, 294
Craft, William and Ellen, 98, 101, 126, 227, 340n32
Crane, Henry, 242

Creole case, 52, 55, 158
creolization, interracial: xii, 6–7, 18–21, 40–42, 142, 160, 301, 325n35; minstrel music, 39–42, 173–79; on New York Lower East Side, 40–41; F. Douglass's creolizing alliances, 3–4, 6, 21, 38–40, 42, 156–57, 174–75, 179, 200–201, 296; and *UTC* performances, 185, 225, 301. *See also* political confluence
Crittenden Compromise failure, 293–94
Crowell, John, 79
Crystal Palace, New York, 188, 190, 191, *G10*
Curse Entailed (Bigelow), 285
Cushing, Anna, as *UTC* reader, 144–45

Davis, Jefferson, 72, 80–81
Death of Tom, The (G. Aiken & G. Howard), 186
Declaration of Independence, 8, 30–31, 231–32, 288, 291, 303, 305
Delany, Martin R.: in Pittsburgh, 180–81, *G8, G9*; editor of the *Mystery*, 180, 200; critiques minstrelsy, 200; subject of riot, 44; Western Reserve of Ohio abolitionist tour, 180; Fugitive Slave Act protest meetings, 181; A. McDowell and Harvard Medical School controversy, 180; *North Star* editor, 44, 138, 180–81; leadership struggle with F. Douglass, 138, 139, 156; vs. H. B. Stowe and *UTC*, 138, 139, 156; militant black nationalist, 138–39, 180; *Condition*, 200; and Civil War, 300–301, 304
Democratic Party: J. Buchanan presidential nomination, 282; factional splits after victory, 206; "Hunker" Democrats, 110; national convention (1852), 153; national convention condemnation of slavery, 154; new economy, 61; opposition to Bank of the United States, 61; southern, 12, 77, 150, 291; victory of 33rd Congress, 203; welcomed immigrants, 61. *See also* conventions: Democratic; Independent Democrats; Van Burenite Barnburners
Democratic Party, northern: W. Aiken support for speaker, 273; aligned with

Democratic Party, northern (*continued*)
South, 54–55; helped defeat John Frémont, 285; on Kansas-Nebraska bill, 226–27, 250; losses in Congress, 271; Mexican War and, 61; rejection of proslavery platform (1860), 290; on slavery, 68, 77–78, 148, 229, 277, 287–88; support for "gag rules," 38

Deshler, Charles, 242

DeWitt, Alexander, 208

Dickens, Charles, 160, 167

District of Columbia: congressional bill on slavery, 67–68, 79; slavery in, 36–37, 50, 52

Dixon, Archibald, 207

Dixon, George W., 41–42

Dixon, James, 152, 254

Douglas, Stephen A., *G15*; and Compromise of 1850, 76, 77, 126; European tour, 167–68, 204–5, 361n5; out of touch with domestic affairs, 205–6; and Kansas-Nebraska Act, 3, 14, 158, 160, 205–8, 213, 215, 216, 219–20, 225, 226, 231, 279–80; debates with Lincoln, 231, 287–89; burned in effigy, 213, 363n28; 1848 California statehood bill, 67–68; 1850 "omnibus bill" proposal, 73, 76; introduces Nebraska bill, 160, 203, 219–20; Missouri Compromise repeal, 207; final version of Nebraska bill, 208; on ministers opposition to Nebraska bill, 216; Nebraska bill voting, 226; Lincoln challenges, 231–32; mocked by Sumner, 281; mocked by Earthquakes, 283; in "Nebraska" villains cheer, 264; Kansas debate, 280; Lecompton Constitution and, 262; popular sovereignty for Kansas, 287; possible 1856 Democratic presidential candidate, 282; 1860 presidential nomination, 290; railroad bills linked with Louisiana Purchase, 206; transcontinental railroad bills, 204; won 1858 senate election, 288

Douglass, Frederick: *G2*, *G3*, *G7*; at Free Democratic convention, 154; backing for Wilmot Proviso, 62; to Canada after Harpers Ferry, 290; at Cazenovia meeting, 85–86; and H. B. Stowe and *UTC*, 3, 6, 38–39, 156–57, 200–201, 296; and minstrel songs ("heart-songs"; "national music"), 4, 21, 39–40, 42, 174–75, 179, 200; connection between H. B. Stowe and minstrelsy, 181–82, 198; cultural creolization, 18; and G. Smith, 85–86, 113; *North Star* editor, 44, 50; Western Reserve of Ohio tour, 180–81; editor of *Frederick Douglass's Paper*, 112–13; leadership struggle with Delany, 138, 139, 156; disavows Garrisonians' disunionism, 112; Faneuil Hall meeting, 94–95; and Fugitive Slave Law, 14; Fugitive Slave Law and antislavery movement, 269–70; lecture tour in England, 167; and Liberty, Free Soil, and Republican parties, 18, 20; and Civil War, 300; meeting with Lincoln, 305; and Syracuse Convention, 156–57; and money for "industrial college," 138–39, 156, 166; at Tremont Temple, 264. See also *Antislavery Movement, The*; *Heroic Slave, The*; *My Bondage, My Freedom*

Douglass, Lewis, 300

Drayton, Daniel, 82, 154

Dred: A Tale of the Great Dismal Swamp (H. B. Stowe), 139, 276, 284–85

Dred Scott decision, 286–87

Durkheim, Émile, 16

Dylan, Bob, 175

Earle, Jonathan, 227

Earthquakes, 283–84, 286, 293

Eastman, Mary Henderson, 354n46

economy, American, 59–61, 235–36; "King Cotton" and cotton production, 8, 11, 31; "Schumpeterian" surge, 59

Edmundson sisters (Mary and Emily), 85, 125, 132, 163, 302

elections:
—presidential (1824), 34
—presidential (1828), 34
—presidential (1832), 43
—presidential (1840), 48, 52, 55, *308*
—presidential (1844), 48, 53, *308*
—presidential (1848), 13, 58, 62–63, 105, *308*
—presidential (1852), 277, 285–86, *308*
—presidential (1856), 105, 267–77, 285–86

—presidential (1860), 105, 289, 291–93, 379n43; antislavery vote, 277; Constitutional Union Party, 290; Lincoln elected, 2, 12, 291; South secedes following, 293; tone set by J. Brown, 290; voting results of, 277, 291–93, *308*
—presidential (1864), 298
—congressional (1832), 51
—congressional (1842), 55
—congressional (1850): antislavery candidates, 110–11; Free Soil candidates, 110; Free Soilers diminished, 110–11; southern disunion convention, 109–10
—governor's (Pennsylvania, 1851) 114
—congressional (1852): antislavery congressmen elected, 157; Democratic majorities, 202
—congressional (1854), 246–53, *308*, *315*, *317*
—congressional (1856), 14, 286
—congressional (1858), 288
—House Speaker (1847), 69–70
—House Speaker (1849), 69–71, 79, 86–87
—House Speaker (1853), 202
—House Speaker (1855–1856), 2, 22, 268, 271–75, 277–79, *316*, *317*, 381–82n12
Ellen, or the Chained Mother (Mary B. Harland), 266
Ely, Alfred B., 242, 254
Emancipation Proclamation, 52, 304
Emerson, Ellen, 190
Emerson, Ken, 178
Emerson, Ralph Waldo: on *UTC* reading, 141, 358n109; on finality, 97; speeches for Palfrey (1851), 102, 111; Tabernacle address (1854), 103, 216–19, 220, 228, 230; on the "Anti-Slavery Society," 230, 232, 244, 274; Tremont Temple address (1855), 263; met with Lincoln, 305; on lecture circuit, 112, 190, 264
Emmett, Dan, 173–74, 198
English Chartist movement, 63
entertainment technologies, 160
Essay on Slavery and Abolitionism (Catharine Beecher), 123
Ethiopian Serenaders, 175
"Eva" (Whittier), 164
"Eva to Her Papa" (G. Howard), 198
events, reinforcing structure and transformative liminality, 16–18

Everett, Edward, 289–92; ministers' opposition letter introduced, 216

F Street Mess, 206–8
family violence by slavery, 100–102; in *UTC*, 134–137
Fillmore, Millard: assumes presidency, 73, *Pearl* crew pardon, 67; signed fugitive slave bill, 76–78, 89–91; on finality, 96–97; on Missouri Compromise, 97, 108; slave family sold, 101; nomination battle with Scott, 153; Know Nothing (American) Party presidential nomination, 282; election loss to J. Buchanan, 277, 286, 292
Finney, Charles Grandison, 36
Fisher, Sidney G., 353n26
Five Points, 219, *G9*
Fletcher, Calvin: Free Soil Whig, 108; free soil antislavery, 223, 234; colonization opinion, 139; and Londen's music, 171; and John Freeman, 223; and *UTC* performance, 223; hostile to Catholics and slavery, 244–45, 251; hostility to Catholics, 237; and Know Nothing encampment, 253; and John Frémont parade, 276, 283; and 1860 election, 291; and Twenty-eighth USCT, 299
Fletcher, Ingram, 171, 292, 296–97
Fletcher, Keyes, 292, 296
Fletcher, Lucy, 284, 297
Fletcher, Miles, 283–85, 293
Fletcher, William, 171, 292, 296
Foote, Henry S., 72–73, 77, 150
Foote, Samuel, 120
Formisano, Ronald, 114
Fort Sumter, 12, 294, 304
Foster, Dunning, 177
Foster, Jane (McDowell), 178–80
Foster, Joseph C., 197–98, 267, 285, *G9*
Foster, Morrison, 177, 181; on Stephen Foster, 199–200
Foster, Stephen: in Pittsburgh, 176–82, *G8*, *G9*, minstrelsy, 176–79; in Cincinnati, 177–78, 182; familial Democratic patronage, 177, 285; marriage to Jane McDowell, 178–80; F. Douglass's

Foster, Stephen (*continued*)
heart-songs, 4, 29, 175, 179; and creolization, sympathy, and antislavery opinion, 6, 160, 179–80, 199–200, 258; abolitionist friends, 180–81; "Five Nice Young Men," 180–81, 296; influence of *UTC* on, 181–82. *See also* Foster, Stephen: music and songs

Foster, Stephen, music and songs: "Lou'siana Belle," 178; "Oh Susanna," 178–79, 200; "Uncle Ned," 179, 200; "Nelly Was a Lady," 179; "Massa's in the Cold Ground," 179, 197; "My Old Kentucky Home," 179, 182, 197; "Old Folks at Home," 179, 222, 226; "Wilt Thou Be Gone, Love?" 181; "Camptown Races," 198; songs used in stage productions of *UTC*, 160, 184, 198–99, 226; music in Marsh troupe performances, 222; music for *The Invisible Prince*, 197, 267; songs for Democrats, 285. *See also* minstrelsy, blackface: songs

Foster, William, 177
Fowler, Orin, 152–53, 156
Franklin, Benjamin, 27
Franklin Theatre, New York, 208, *G10*
fraternal societies, 238–43
Frederick Douglass's Paper, 113, 169
Free Democratic Party, 154, 157
Free Soil Party: 1848 convention, 62, 67, 93; 1848 election, 13–14, 55, 58, 63, 105–6; members in 30th House, 64, 70, 86; losses in 31st House, 110–11, 150; Bailey invitation, 116, 126; attempted repeal of Fugitive Slave Act, 229; Cazenovia Convention condemnation, 85; in 1854–1855 election, 246–47; reelection to 32rd House (1854–1855), 250; crisis meetings, 93; embraced by F. Douglass, 18; fusion with Know Nothings, 248; Nebraska bill, 226; Republican Party and, 246. *See also* Free Democratic Party

Freehling, William, 24
Freeman, Charles D., 242, 257
Freeman, John, 223
Freemasonry, 238–39, 242, 369n22, 370n27
Frémont, Jessie (Benton), 284

Frémont, John C., 148, 268–69, 276–77, 282–86, 292–93, 295, 301, 304
Fugitive Slave Act, 1, 3, 6–7, 14, 22, 78–79; signed, 73, 77–78; slave catchers and, 90–92; flight following, 90–99; protest meetings and conventions oppose, 84–86, 92–95, *94*, 97–98, 103, 112–13, 181, *G10*; liminal disruption, 99–105; nationalization of slavery, 78–79, 103; as violation of northern states' rights, 102–4; petitioning for repeal, 111–12; range of northern response, 19, 90–95, 97, 102, 104, 107–9, 114–15, 295; national press view of, 100–101, 103, 107; and pro-Compromise unionism, 95–97, 107. *See also* slave hunters

fugitive slave bill (1850): introduced, 71, 72; debate, 73–76, 80–81; jury trial amendment, 82–83; petitions against, 81–82, 83–84, *94*, 312; votes in Senate and House, *310–11*. *See also* Compromise of 1850

fugitive slave debates (1849), 68, 69, 107
fugitive slaves, 7, 53–54, 163–64, 279–80, 340n35, 341n55, *G1*, *G2*, *G9*; as term in newspapers, *94*, *106*, *172*; protection in New England, 98–99; Vigilance Committee records, 279–80; Webster's view of, 76. *See also* Fugitive Slave Act; *Pearl* escape and controversy; Tubman, Harriet; Underground Railroad; vigilance committees

fugitive slaves, arrests and renditions of: 26, 53, 79–80, 90–91, 98–99, 103, 105, 113, 115, 163–64, 221; Burns, 225, 227, 230, 261; Hamlet, 93; Garner, 270, 279; Chaplin, 270; Sims, 228

Fuller, Thomas, 273
Furness, William, as *UTC* reader, 144, 146
fusion parties (1854), 246–49, 252

gag rule, 20, 38, 50, 81
Gap Gang, 113
Gardiner, Richard, 105
Gardner, Henry, 248, 280
Garfield, James, as *UTC* reader, 145–46, 292
Garner, Margaret, 270, 279
Garnet, Henry, 98

Index

Garnett, Henry Highland, 62
Garrison, William Lloyd: militant immediatist abolitionist, 35, 39, 46; object of Boston riot, 37; *Liberator* editor, 49, 86; view of Constitution as proslavery, 48; "address to the clergy," 93; Western Reserve of Ohio abolitionist tour, 180–81; *UTC* review, 137; Conway *UTC* version preferred, 191, 195; debate with H. B. Stowe on ministers' views, 216; calls *National Era* "milk-toast abolitionism," 117; against secret societies, 240
Garrisonian immediatists, 46–47, 344n12; AA-SS and, 52, 86; in Cincinnati, 123; colonization views, 139; at Lane Seminary, 120; most radical of abolitionists, 46, 48–49, 117; *National Era* in opposition, 117; newspapers of, 49–50; northern sympathy for slaves, 199; petition against Fugitive Slave Law, 199; rejection by F. Douglass, 112; schism with Tappan circle, 39; vigilance committees and, 53; women's rights in, 47–48
Gates, Seth, 51
Gavazzi, Alessandro, 236
Geary, John White, 262, 285–86, 298
General Colored Association, 30
Germon, Greene C., 197–98, 222, 226
"Get Off the Track for Emancipation" (Hutchinson Family Singers), 174
Gettysburg Address (Lincoln), 305
Giddings, Joshua R.: antislavery Whig, 55; antislavery leadership, 55, 111–12; *Somerset* principles in *Creole* and *Amistad* cases, 52; censured for *Creole* resolutions, 55; on District of Columbia slavery, 67–68; and *Pearl* incident, 66; on Lincoln in 1850, 107; on Compromise debate, 87; in Baileys' salon, 116; and antislavery petitions, 83; on finality debate, 152; on impact of *UTC*, 183; and "Appeal of the Independent Democrats," 207–8; on Nebraska bill, 226; view of Know Nothings, 252; on Banks speakership, 274–75; protest at Republican convention, 303; as Freemason, 369n22

Giddings, Lura Maria, 274–75
Gienapp, William, 14
Glover, Joshua, rescue, 217, 223–24, 226
Gorsuch, Edward, 113–14
Greeley, Horace, 241, 252, 371n54; despised nativism, 244
Green, Duff, 34
Greenwood Leaves (Clarke), 118
Grimké, Angelina, 47, 123, 125, 161, 163, 184
Grimké, Sarah, 47, 125, 161, 163, 184
"Gumption Cute" (Aiken *UTC* character), 193

Hale, Edward Everett, 265
Hale, John P.: antislavery leader, 66, 112; antislavery petitions, 83, 152; antislavery resolutions support, 79; Baileys' salon, 116; on "Appeal of the Independent Democrats," 208; dismal showing in 1850, 157; Free Soil Democrat, 150; Free Soiler, 64; great antislavery oration, 80–81; nomination of Free Democratic Party, 154; northern electorate vote, 277, 286; and *Key to UTC*, 162; voted into Senate by Know Nothings, 254
"halfway" abolitionism, 49, 344n11
Hamilton, Alexander, 28–29, 34, 52
Hamlet, James, 89–91, 93, 98, 101, 104–5
Hammond, James Henry, 38
Hanway, Castner, 114
Harpers Ferry, 85
Harris, Samuel E. *See* Barmore, Wesley
Harrison, Les, 195
Harrison, William Henry, 55
Hartford Convention, 29
Hartford Female Seminary, 122
Hawkins, Micah, 41
Hawthorne, Nathaniel, 117
Hayden, Lewis, 98–99
Hayne, Robert, 75
Hedrick, Joan, 140
Henry, William (Jerry), 113
Heroic Slave, The (F. Douglass), 138, 168
Hickory Hall (Southworth), 127
Higginson, Thomas Wentworth, 299
Hildreth, Richard, 168, 302
Hoar, George Frisbie, 252
Hochman, Barbara, 142, 301
Holbrook, Charles, as *UTC* reader, 144

Holt, Michael, 14
Home Missionary Society, New York, 125
Homestead Act, 63
Hooker, John, 163
Howard, Caroline, 186
Howard, Cordelia, 186, 266
Howard, George, 186, 187–89, 198, 360n135
Howard troupe, 276, 284, 287, 296
Hunter, David, 304
Hutchinson Family Singers, 174, 184, 198, 220, 264–65

Ida May (M. Pike), 266–67, 302
imagined community, 15–16, 109, 115, 140, 141, 164, 199. *See also* public sphere
"Immediate Emancipation" (H. B. Stowe), 125
immediatists. *See* Garrisonian immediatists
immigrants and immigration, 58, 60–61, 235–36; votes of, 236
Improved Order of Red Men, 239
Incarnation, The (H. B. Stowe & Charles Beecher), 126, 140, 245
Independent Democrats, 14, 207–8; fight against repeal of Compromise, 208–9
Indianapolis, Indiana: Fletcher family, 108, 139, 171, 223, 234, 237, 244–45, 251, 253, 276, 283–85, 292–93, 296–97, 299; Freeman case, 223; H. W. Beecher in, 125, 139; Marsh *UTC* performance in, 196, 197, 222–23; 1855 Fusion party convention in, 246, 251; Republican parade in 1856, 276, 282–84; 1856 election in, 285–86; 1860 election in, 291–93; Camp Fremont and Twenty-eighth USCT, 299
Information for Kanzas Immigrants (T. D. Webb), 265
Inside View of Slavery... (Parsons), 266
Invisible Prince, The (Shiras), 98, 197, 267, G9

Jackson, Andrew, 11, 23, 33, 38
Jackson, Francis, 103
Jacksonian populism: assault on "Money Power," 34; attack on eastern Indian tribes, 34
Jacobs, Harriet, 89, 93
James, Henry: on fugitives, 108–9; as *UTC* reader, 148–49; on Barnum's Museum, 189; on *UTC* at the National Theatre, Philadelphia, 190–91
Jarvis, Edward, as *UTC* reader, 151
Jay, John, Jr.: and Lemmon case, 163; on *UTC* and public opinion, 151, 157, 162, 191–92, 203, 211, 232; and 1854 petitioning, 211–12
Jay, John, Sr., 26, 29
Jefferson, Thomas, 8, 63
Jerry Rescue (William Henry), 113, 146, 196
Jewett, Harriet, as *UTC* reader, 143
Jewett, John P., 128, 143, 152, 169, 198, 285, 373n81; bargaining with Charlie Stowe, 164; correspondence regarding *Key to UTC*, 162; H. B. Stowe cuts ties with, 159; profits from *UTC*, 168; prolific antislavery publisher, 170; publicity for antislavery books, 266; *UTC* merchandising, 164–65
"Jim Crow" minstrelsy. *See* minstrelsy, blackface
Johnson, Frank, 177, 200, G9
Jones, Absalom, 29
Jones, Eva, 197, 297, 356n82
Jones, Toland, 297
Julian, George, 87, 97, 116–18, 238
"Jump Jim Crow" dance craze, 20, 41–43

Kansas, Its Interior and Exterior Life (S. Robinson), 265
"Kansas Emigrants, The" (L. M. Child), 285
"Kansas Emigrants, The" (Whittier), 264–65
Kansas territory: "Beecher's Bibles," 261; Civil War in, 203, 216, 227, 258–63, 267–68, 270–71, 280, 285, 287; census of population, 263; fraudulent elections, 261–62; "Kanzas" publications/antislavery media, 264–67; Lecompton proslavery convention, 262, 287; Pottawatomie Creek revenge, 281–82; "Sack of Lawrence," 280–82; slave state, J. Buchanan's effort, 287
Kansas-Nebraska Act, 1, 3, 13–15, 22, 322–23n23; impact of passage and Burns rendition, 228–29; and Know Nothing organization, 133–35; effect on election of 1854–1855, 250. *See also* Kansas-Nebraska bill
Kansas-Nebraska bill: introduced by

Douglas, 160, 206–7; final version of Nebraska bill, 208; debates on, 207–16, 225–29; attacked by "Appeal of the Independent Democrats," 14, 207–10, 212, 214; in the Senate, 216, 224, 226–27; House votes on, 226–27, *315*; protest meetings and language in newspapers, 211–18, *212*, 363n21; petitions to Congress on, 211–13, 215; H. B. Stowe's activism, 214–16; ministers' petition, 216; R. W. Emerson on, 217–18; synergy of Nebraska debate and *UTC* productions, 218–21, 224
Keith's Music Publishing House, 175
Kelly, Abigail, 47
Kendall, Amos, 38
Kennedy, John Pendleton, 135
Key to Uncle Tom's Cabin (*Key to UTC*) (H. B. Stowe), 132, 161–64, 214
Kimball, Moses, 186–88, 195, 219, 357n96
King, Preston, 268–69, 337n54
King, Rufus, 32, 209
King, Thomas Starr, 259
Know Nothing (American) Party: and nativist movement, 233–44; hostility to immigrants and Catholics, 233, 237–38, 241; fraternal societies and, 238–40; accelerated organization, 33, 269; nativist unionism, 234–35, 237–38, 240, 250–51, 253–58; effect on voting in New York, 243–44; in 1854–1855 election, 247–53; and Republicans, 272; struggle with antislavery opinion, 234–35, 253, 254–57, 281–82; 1855 National Council convention split on slavery issue (Section 12), 253–57; Girard Hotel meeting, 257; "great fizzle," 257–58; Barker, leader, 238, 241–43, 246, 253–57, 269, 371n54; Bartlett elected Know Nothing president, 256; fall 1855 local election success, 279; in Michigan and Wisconsin, 246; Miles Fletcher in, 284; nativist encampment, 253–54; nominating convention in New York, 242; OUA, 241; sectional paradox of, 252–53, 281–82; patch up of national group, 271; failure on slavery issue, 281–82; Fillmore presidential nomination, 282; state races (1855), 248; votes in speakership race, 273. *See also* Order of the Star Spangled Banner;

Order of the Star Spangled Banner: National Council meetings
Kossuth, Louis, 150, 154, 161, 164, 167

Lakey, James (reader), 169
"Land of Slaves, The," 101
Lane Seminary, 47, 49, 120–21, 124; Weld debate, 119–21, 344n12
Lanphier, Charles H., 205
Larcom, Lucy, 265
Latimer, George, 53
Lawrence, Amos, 228
Lawrence, Kansas, Sack of, 280, 377n13
Leavitt, Joshua, 53, 117
Lecompton Constitution, 262, 287
Lee, Henry (Light Horse Harry), 27
Lee, Richard Henry, 26
Lemmon family rescue, 163
LeMoyne, Francis Julius, 180–81, 360n133
Le Moyne, William J., 197, 296, 360n133
Liberator, 35, 46, 49, 86, 95, 101, 137
Liberty Party, 48, 52–53, 55, 58, 64, 113, 123, 117
Life, Labors, and Travels of Elder Charles Bowles, The, 169
liminality: and transformative events, 15–18; of early 1850s for northern public, xii, 7, 15, 21–22, 24, 39, 99–115, 118–19, 153–54, 164, 199, 202–3, 219, 295; end of liminal moment, 229, 232, 267–68, 305; 1859–1860 as southern liminal moment, 290; of American Revolution, 24; of blackface minstrel shows, 21, 39–43; of abolitionism, 45–49; of slave trade and fugitive flight, 66, 99–104, 115, 128–29, 131, 134, 340n35; of G. Bailey's *National Era*, 118–19; and *UTC*, 126, 134–37, *136*; reading *UTC* as liminal experience, 140–42, 148–50, 159, 164, 232, 301; of theater and entertainment, 183, 232, 301; and creolization, 39–42, 142; and communitas, sympathy, and creolization, 134, 142, 148–50; and structure, 7, 16–18, 22, 24, 100, *135–36*, 209, 295; and imagined community, 15–16, 109, 115, 140, 141, 164, 199. *See also* antislavery media event
Lincoln, Abraham, *G15*; on slavery and equality, 107, 269, 288, 294, 303, 305; opposed Mexican War, 62; supports

Lincoln, Abraham, (*continued*)
arrests of fugitives, 107; eulogy for Clay, 154; colonization opinion, 232; despised nativism, 244; Whig loyalties, 246; quotes sea chantey on a mulatto, 171; response to Kansas-Nebraska Act, 231–32; debates with Douglas, 287–88; "House Divided" speech, 288; elected president (1860), 2, 12, 277, 286, 291–93, 295; First Inauguration Address, 5, 294, 303; meeting with Harriet Beecher Stowe, 296; meetings with F. Douglass and Delany, 300; Gettysburg Address, 8, 231, 305; 1864 election, 298; Second Inaugural Address, 4–5; suggests citizenship for black soldiers, 303; and Declaration of Independence, 231, 288, 303, 305
Lincoln-Douglas debates, 287–88
Lind, Jenny, 89, 95, 118, 159, 167, 173; children named for, 146–47, *147*, *172*
Little Katie, the Hot Corn Girl, 219
Logics of History (Sewell), 17
Londen (fugitive), as musician, 171, 296
Long, John Davis, 108, 110
Lott, Eric, 20
Louisiana Purchase: antislavery resistance, 207; Democrats on slavery in Nebraska, 206–7; Democrats repeal ban on slavery, 203; Democrats want slavery in, 157–58; musical fusion of minstrel shows, 40; northern section, 3, 14; sectional fight over, 31
Lovejoy, Elijah, 37, 122
Ludlow, Noah, 41
Lundy, Benjamin, 35, 49
Lynch, Thomas, 26
Lynd, Staunton, 11

Mann, Horace: cites *UTC* in Congress, 156; constituent mail on *UTC*, 151; Free Soiler, 70; and Fugitive Slave Act, 97, 112; in House, 86–87; oration on race, equality, and liberty, 259; rejection of finality, 156; at Tremont Temple, 264
Manning, Chandra, 296
Marsh, Mary Guerneau, 196
Marsh, Robert, 196–97

Marsh troupe, 196–98, 202, 366n63; in Indianapolis, 222–23, 234, 284, in Milwaukee, 223–24, 366n58; fusion *UTC* script, 366n61
Mason, James, 71, 73, 75, 84, 281, 285
Massachusetts: Whig and Free Soil conventions in 1850, 93; Free Soil and Know Nothing conventions, 1954, 247–48; Know Nothings in, 252; *Somerset* principles in, 53
Massachusetts Anti-Slavery Society, 103, 170, 194
Matthias and Co. American Dramatic Company, 222
Mayflower, The (H. B. Stowe), 124
McDowell, Alexander P., 180
McDowell, Robert P., 180
media event. *See* antislavery media event
Meer, Sarah, 194
Merrifield, Rose, 220
Mexican territories, 69; congressional slavery fight, 79–80; free soil resolutions, 67
Mexican War, 13, 58, 61–62
Miles, Robert E. J., 221–22
Miller, James, 297–98
Minkins, Shadrach, 98–99
minstrelsy, blackface, 20, 39–45, 171–82, 198, 244, 355n56; audiences, 42; contradictory creolizing messages, 173–75, 199; F. Douglass and, 4, 39–40, 174–75, 182, 198, 200; Delany and, 200; S. Foster's songs in stage productions of *UTC*, 160; minstrel troupe, 173; origin of, 40; *The Saw Mill, or A Yankee Trick*, 41. *See also* Foster, Stephen; minstrelsy, blackface: songs
minstrelsy, blackface:
—"Jump Jim Crow" dance craze, 20, 41–42
—songs: "Zip Coon," 42–43; "Lucy Neal," 175–76, *67*; "Nelly Was a Lady," 179; "Nigger put down dat Jug," 176; "Old Dan Tucker," 173, 198; *Songs of the Virginia Serenaders*, 176; "Yellow Gals," 176
—*See also* Carter, James P.; Christy, Edwin; Foster, Stephen
Missouri crisis and Compromise, 3, 7, 14,

31, 63, 363n26; and Nebraska protests, 211, 224; effect on Kansas and Nebraska statehood, 206; repealed, 207, 210–11; Taney rules unconstitutional in *Dred Scott* decision, 286. *See also* Kansas-Nebraska bill

Mormons, 283

Morris, Thomas, 51

Morse, Samuel F. B., 241

Mount, William Sydney, 330n46

Mount Vernon, 72, 289–90

Mount Vernon Ladies Association of the Union, 289

music: African American, 40, 171, 177, 200; F. Douglass on "national music," 4, 18, 21, 39, 174–75; F. Douglass vs. minstrelsy, 174; blackface, 21, 39–45; Republican Party, 283, 285; sheet music industry, 115, 160, 164, 171–73, 175–76, 198–220, 354n52, *G7*; and antislavery, 4, 18, 21, 39, 164, 171–82, 184, 194–99, 198, 220, 264–65, 283, 285; and racial creolization, 39–42, 173–79, 225; and *UTC*, 164, 184, 194–99, 267. *See also* antislavery media; Carter, James P.; Foster, Stephen; minstrelsy, blackface

My Bondage, My Freedom (F. Douglass), 265–66

Mystery (Delany), 180–81, 200

National Era, 50, 132, 143, 152–53, 284; established, 116–19; abolitionist serials, 127; and "Appeal of the Independent Democrats," 14, 207–10; Clarke article on *UTC*, 151; H. B. Stowe contributions to, 126; letters on *UTC*, 128; H. B. Stowe recruited to write, 119; female writers in, 117–19, 159–60, *G4*

National Theatre, Cincinnati, 196, 201, 221–22

National Theatre, New York, 184, 185, 188, 190–92, 196–98, 219, 276, 284, *G10*, *G11*, *G13*

National Theatre, Philadelphia, 189–90, 195–96

nativism. *See* Know Nothing (American) Party; Order of the Star Spangled Banner; Order of United Americans

"Neb-Rascality" (Hutchinson Family Singers), 264

Nell, William C., 265

New England Emigrant Aid Company (NEEAC), 35, 86, 166, 216, 261, 265

New Mexico, statehood bill, 71

New Southern Democratic Party, 12, 291

New York Manumission Society, 29

New York Odd Fellows Hall, 239, 242, 247

New York State: convention struggles election of 1854–1855, 247; *Somerset* principles in, 53

New York State Anti-Slavery Society, 48, 54

New York State Vigilance Committee, 53–54, 113

Norcross, Carrol, as *UTC* reader, 145

North Star, 44, 50, 95, 138, 174, 180–81, 274

northern states: antislavery coalition, 232–33; constitutional compromise, opinion of, 21; electoral division on antislavery, 277; expanded antislavery public, 203; opposition to slavery and immigrants, 258

Northrup, Solomon, 169–70

Northside of Slavery (Benjamin Drew), 285

Northwest Ordinances, 26, 31

Nullification Crisis of 1828–1832, 73–74

Odd Fellows, Independent Order of (IOOF): and nativism, 238–44, 246, 247, 253, 257, 370n30; Odd Fellows Hall, New York, 238, 239, 242, 243, 247, *G10*, *G12*. *See also* fraternal societies

"Oh I'se So Wicked" (G. Howard), 198

Order of the Star Spangled Banner (OSSB), 232–33, 237–39

—and fraternal societies, 238–39, 242–44

—in politics, 241–44, 246–47

—National Council meetings: New York City (1854), 233, 237–39, 242–43; Cincinnati (1855), 253–54; Philadelphia (1855), 255–58; Philadelphia (1856), 279, 281–82

—*See also* Know Nothing (American) Party

Order of United Americans (OUA), 238, 241–42

Oregon territory, free soil bill, 67

Our World, Or, the Slaveholder's Daughter (Francis Colburn Adams), 266

Palfrey, John G., 66–67, 102, 110–11; despised nativism, 244
"Panorama, The" (Whittier), 259–60, 262–64
panoramas, 160, 187–89, 195
Papal Conspiracy Exposed, The (Edward Beecher), 245
Parker, Joel, 161
Parker, Theodore: attack on Webster, 84, 86; chaplain for nativist-controlled legislature, 254; Crafts hidden, 98; homily on Fugitive Slave Law, 101; militant abolitionist, 2; praise for Kimball, 194–95; rescue for Burns, 228; at Tremont Temple, 264; Vigilance Committee speech, 95; writes for *National Era*, 117
Parker, William, 113–14
Parkman murder, 353n25
Pearl (ship) escape and controversy, 66–69, 82, 116, 132, 154, 163, *G2*; effect on *UTC*, 132; Fillmore pardon, 66–67; fund-raising, 125; ransomed slaves, 85; white men (Drayton and Sayres) on board, 66–67, 85–86
Peck, Frances Jocelyn, as *UTC* reader, 143
Peck, Lucius B., 79
"Penetrate Partyside" (Conway *UTC* character), 193–94
Pennington, Alexander, 272
Pennsylvania: convention struggles election of 1854–1855, 248; Fugitive Slave Law battleground, 90; Harrisburg fugitive incident, 90–91, 221; slave catchers in, 90–91; *UTC* performance incidents, 221
Pennsylvania Anti-Slavery Society, 93
petitions to Congress, antislavery: in 1790–1799, 11, 13, 27–29; in 1833–1845, 36–37, 47, 50–51, *309*, 328–29n35, 333n94; activists and, 36, 47, 50; slavery in the District of Columbia, 36–37, 50; kidnapping and slave trade, 29, 50; and gag rule, 38, 50; anti-Texas, 50–51; First Amendment rights and, 51; in 1849–1851, 81–84, *94*, 111–12, 155–56, 199, 228, *312*, 333n94, 337n54; Drayton and Sayre (*Pearl*) pardons, 82; jury trial amendment, 83; abolition of slavery,

82–84; during Compromise finality debate, 152; in 1854, 211–13, *212*, 215–16, *314*, 364n37; on Missouri Compromise repeal, 212–13
Phillips, Wendell, 95, 228, 264, 297; Rankin's story of escape over ice, 130; on *UTC*, 149–50
Phillips, William, 263, 265
Pierce, Franklin: nomination and election of President, 153, 157, 285–86; leadership questioned, 206; appointed Catholic postmaster general, 236; mocked by Lincoln, 171; in "Nebraska" villains cheer, 264; mocked in Indianapolis, 283; role in Nebraska bill, 14, 207; signs Kansas-Nebraska Act, 225; removal of Governor Reeder, 261; loses nomination to J. Buchanan, 282
Pike, Albert, 257, 370n27
Pike, Mary, 266–67, 285
Pillsbury, Parker, 103, 194
Pinckney, Charles Cotesworth, 26–27
plantation novels. *See* proslavery media
Plea for the West (L. Beecher), 120
political antislavery, 50, 117, 138, 146, 241, 244, 268, 278. *See also* antislavery movement; Free Democratic Party; Free Soil Party; Liberty Party; Republican Party
political confluence, white antislavery northerners and African Americans, xii, 7, 18–21, 51, 62, 104–5, 185, 225, 260, 297, 301. *See also* creolization, interracial
Polk, James K., 61, 67, 70
Pollock, James, 248
Poor, Mary and Lucy, as *UTC* readers, 145
population, *58*
Primary Geography for Children (H. B. Stowe), 122
proslavery media: books, 136, 170–71, *313*, 374n85; theater, 184, 198; complaints about antislavery books, 169–70; on *UTC* performances, 185–86
proslavery South: Congressional "gag rules," 20; electoral advantage, 11–12; Harpers Ferry fears of black insurgency, 290; liminal moment, 290
Protestants, 2, 36; leaders on the

Compromise, 96; ministers to antislavery cause, 215; "Old School Presbyterian" wing, 120; support for American Colonization Society, 120; opinions on immigrants, slavery, and Catholicism, 234; pressure for national unity, 39

public sphere: and imagined community, 15–18, 109; abolitionists and 35–36, 38–39, 155; African Americans in, 29; different forms of action, 15; effect of printed material, 109; A. Jackson blocks discussion of slavery, 34; pro-Compromise dominance of, 78; women and, 118, 159–60, 214–15. *See also* antislavery media; antislavery media event

Purdy, Alexander H., 184–85, 188–89, 191, 198, 220, 267, 276
Purvis, Robert, 138
Putnam, Henry, 101

Queechy (Warner), 118

railroads, *58*, 60, 108, 154, 179, 195, 203, 206, 222, 235, 283, 291
Rankin, John, 130
Ray, Charles B., 85
Redpath, James, 263
Reeder, Andrew, 261–62, 267
Republican Campaign Songster, 285
Republican Party, 2, 14–15, 230, 232–35; organization failure in 1854, 245, 269; and nativism, 244–45; organization of, 245–46, 268–71, 278–79, 303; Black Republicans, 18–19; control of House, 279; Declaration of Independence as principle, 303; formation of, 203, 245–46, 268–69; John Frémont presidential nomination, 268–69, 282–83; A. Jackson candidacy, 23; mid-Atlantic and southerners, 32; nativist vote needed for 1860 election, 286; Pittsburgh mass meeting, 279; political culture of, 281, 286–87, 303; possibility for compromise, 278; presidential election of 1856, 277; radical beginnings of Civil War, 304; Silver Spring meeting, 268, 271–72; against slavery compromise, 294; against southern Slave Power, 278; state parties, 246; traditional Whig planks (1860), 291; *UTC* role in, 295–96. *See also* Slave Power

Retribution; or the Vale of Shadows (Southworth), 118
Rhodes, James Ford, 295
Rice, Thomas D., 41–44, 167, 177, 184–85, 189, 219, *G13*
Richardson, William, 273
riots and violence, 37–38; blackface songs and, 43–44; Catholic convent, 44; Chatham Garden Theatre, 44; New York riot, 44; Ursuline Convent, 120
Ritchie, Thomas, 23–24
Robinson, Charles, 262
Robinson, Sara, 265
Robinson Atheneum, 222, 225, 231, 284
Rochester Ladies Anti-Slavery Society, 3, 263
Rockwell, Julius, 228
Root, Joseph, 79–80, 87
Russwurm, John, 30

Saunders, Steven, 179
Sayres, Edward, 82, 154
Scott, Winfield, 78, 153–54, 163, 171, 250, 285
secession: Crittenden Compromise failure, 293–94; election of, 293; Fort Sumter and Civil War, 294–95; southern defense of, 5; southern disunion convention, 109–10; southern ordinances for, 7
Second Party System, 56, 234
Semi-Colon Club, 122–23
Seward, Frances, 169
Sewell, William, 17–18
Seward, William H.: jury trial for fugitives, 53, 82–84, 87; "higher law" speech, 80–81, 134, 209, 254, 256, 304; opposed Compromise, 110, 152; petitions to Congress, 152; supports Scott, 153; on "Appeal of the Independent Democrats," 208–9; Nebraska bill opposition, 227; despised nativism, 244; and New York Whigs, 247, 254; Barker aims for W. Seward's defeat, 254; declines invitation to Silver

Seward, William H. (*continued*)
Spring meeting, 272; Kansas debate with Douglas, 279–80; "Irrepressible Conflict" speech, 8, 288–89; defeated by Lincoln for nomination, 291; attempts to keep Union whole, 293–94
Shaftesbury, Earl of, 166
Shaw, Robert Gould, 298
Shiras, Charles, 181, 197–98, 267, *G9*
Shires company, 222, 356–57n82
Silbey, Joel, 33, 63
Sill, Joseph: as *UTC* reader, 144, 146; to *UTC* at NYC National Theater, 190; theatergoing, 358n110, *G10*
Silliman, Benjamin, 86
Sims, Thomas, 99, 114–15, 227
Slade, William, 38, 51, 55
slave hunters, 300; activity of, 113; Craft case, 98; Fugitive Slaw Law effect, 1, 88; in Massachusetts, 103–4; in Pennsylvania, 90–92; Underground Railroad and, 53–54; in *UTC*, 130; Webster's speech on, 85
"Slave Oligarchy, The" (Sumner), 259–61
Slave Power, 1, 6–7, 12–13, 34, 208, 232, 274, 322n22; alliance of black and white against, 20–21, 300; Morris on, 51; Texas and Mexico, 54; and Fugitive Slave Act, 71, 79, 86, 102, 104, 154; Whittier on, 105; and minstrels, 173; "Appeal of the Independent Democrats," 209–10; and Kansas, 280–81, 286–87; and Republican ideology, 283; secession threat if John Frémont elected, 285; as term in newspapers, *57, 106, 172,* 230, 285; term fades away, 289; use of any means, 278. *See also* political confluence
slave trade: Atlantic, 26, 101, 102; domestic, 29, 66, 79, 82, 100, 101, 102, 178, *309, 314,* 346n47; in the District of Columbia, 67, 68, 69, 72, 76, 77, 79, 82, *309, 310–12, 314*; in *UTC*, 130, 131, 132, 134, 136, 193
slavery: and the American Revolution, 24–25; image of slavery, 28; slavery compromise in Constitution, 28; threat of disunion, 28; as term in newspapers, *56*; antislavery tracts burned, 38; British law, 25; Constitutional guarantee, 7–8, 11; disunion fears of founders, 63; proslavery riots, 37–38; public meetings against, 84–85; question for respective states, 102–3; resistance of African Americans, 19; value of slaves, 32

Smith, Gerrit, 297; Anti-Slavery Society supporter; 36, Smith/Liberty wing, 48, 50, 52, 54, 113, 138, 146, 157; Cazenovia convention organizer, 85; *Frederick Douglass's Paper* supporter, 113; and Fugitive Slave Act, 138; elected to Congress, 157; H. B. Stowe correspondence, 161–62, 166; on *Key to UTC,* 162; signed "Appeal of the Independent Democrats," 208; on Nebraska bill, 226; and J. Brown, 290
Smith, Venture, 29
Smith, William H. S., 194–95, 357n96
Smith circle, 48. *See also* conventions: Cazenovia Liberty; Liberty Party; Smith, Gerrit
Somerset, James, 25
Somerset decision, 25–26, 51–53, 55, 71, 155
South Carolina: nullifiers, 43, 75; secession, 5, 12, 75, 294
southern states: antislavery party, response to, 10–11; anxiety over issue of slavery, 31; caucus, 68; disunionism, 72, 107, 110, 112, 285, 290; "King Cotton" and cotton production, 8, 11, 31; secession, 5–7, 12, 19–20, 24, 80, 233, 278, 291, 293–94, 295, 303
Southworth, Emma (E. D. E. N.), 117; antislavery theme stories, 127
Speed, Joshua, 107
Stanton, Elizabeth Cady, as *UTC* reader, 146
Stephens, Alexander, 226
Stevens, Thaddeus, 1, 80, 87, 240
Still, William, 267
Stone, James W., 165, 169, 171
Stowe, Calvin, 164; marriage to Harriet Beecher, 121–22; move to Bowdoin College, 124; H. B. Stowe on her writing, 127–28; gradualist and colonizationist, 139; at Andover Seminary, 151, 159; book proposal

for *UTC*, 143; correspondence on antislavery research, 162; trip to England and the Continent, 166–67; Aiken *UTC* script preferred, 192; petitions to Congress, 215–16; Rankin's story of ice, 130
Stowe, Charlie, 124, 131
Stowe, Eliza, 122, 124
Stowe, Frederick, 296
Stowe, Harriet Beecher, G4; in Cincinnati, 121–24; marriage to Calvin Stowe, 121; as writer before 1850, 122, 123–24, 126–27; health, 124; in Brunswick, 125–27; I. Beecher's encouragement to write, 126; and abolitionism, 123, 125–26; "The Two Altars," 126; "The Freedman's Dream," 126, and G. Bailey, 122, 126–29, writing and publishing *UTC*, 127–33; *American Slavery As It Is* inspiration, 123; to Andover, 139, 151, discussion with F. Douglass, 138–39; J. Parker controversy, 161; researching and writing *Key to UTC*, 161–65; to Great Britain and continent, 165–68, 304–5, 361n5; rejects Hutchinson Family Singers' proposal, 184; *Sunny Memories*, activism in 1854, 214–16, 364n37; "An Appeal to the Women," 214–15; organizes Tremont Temple series, 215, 259; and Lincoln, 232, 296, 305; appeal to female culture, 211, 213–15; family and domesticity, 133, 175, 260, 284; book royalties, 159, 168; wealth and celebrity, 160; colonization opinion, 137, 139–40, 156, 284; critique of American capitalism, 134–36, 193; effect of *UTC* on slavery debate, 3, 6, 140–42, 210, 213, 258, 295–97, 299, 301–2; effect on proslavery writers, 161, 170–71; Higginson praise, 299; on Catholicism, 245. *See also* antislavery media event; *Christian Slave, The*; *Dred: A Tale of the Great Dismal Swamp*; *Uncle Tom's Cabin*
Strong, George Templeton, 291; abolitionists outside power structure, 55; ambiguity of, 107; against antislavery protesters, 95–96; antislavery sentiment, 84; on the Fugitive Slave Law, 3–4, 7, 14, 19; on Lind, 89; problems of the 1850s, 6, 109; on slavery, 2
structure: vs. liminality, 8; party as, 23–24, 32–34, 38, 54–59, 61–64; churches as 39; family as, 99–102, 133–35; Constitution as, 102, 133–35
Sumner, Charles, 302; battle for Webster's Senate seat, 111; "Freedom National, Slavery Sectional," 155; cites *UTC*, 155–56; petition for repeal of Fugitive Slave Act, 155–56; constituent mail on *UTC*, 151; correspondence on antislavery research, 162–63; and "Appeal of the Independent Democrats," 207–8; Missouri Compromise repeal, 211–13; ministers' opposition letter introduced, 216; Nebraska bill opposition, 227; and 1854 petitions, 215, 364n37; introduced repeal of Fugitive Slave Law, 228–29; Kansas situation, launch of a national Republican Party, 268–69, 271; on Banks speakership victory, 2, 274; pressure from Massachusetts, 280; "The Crime against Kansas" oration, 280–81; assault by Brooks, 281–83, 377n13; despised nativism, 244; discovers Botts, 266; low profile on slavery issues, 154; on as *UTC* reader, 165; reprint of *White Slavery in the Barbary States,* 168–69; "The Slave Oligarchy and Its Usurpations," 260–62; at Tremont Temple, 264; uncomfortable with secret societies, 240
Sunny Memories of Foreign Lands (H. B. Stowe), 214, 363n31
Sutherland, Duchess of, 167
Sutter, John, 65
Swallow Barn (Kennedy), 135
Swissholm, Jane G., 181
sympathy. *See* antislavery media: and sympathy

Tabernacle lecture series, New York, 205, 211, 217–18
Tallmadge, James, 31
Taney, Roger, 286–87
Tappan, Arthur, 36–37, 44
Tappan, Lewis, 36–37, 44, 47, 52, 121, 138–39; *National Era* sponsor, 117

Tappanites, 47–50, 123, 139; *Emancipator*, abolitionist paper, 86; H. B. Stowe and, 215
Taylor, Charles W., 184
Taylor, John, 28
Taylor, Joseph R., 243
Taylor, Joseph S., 243
Taylor, Zachary: in 1848 election, 58, 62–63, 173; inaugurated, 69; and territories, 70–71, 73, 102–3
technological change, 60, 235–36. *See also* railroads; telegraph; urbanization
telegraph, *58*, 60, 90, 91, 115, 160, 167, 178–79, 195, 218, 235, 241, 263
temperance movement: Chatham Garden Theatre for, 43–44, 184; Democrats split in Maine, 246; depression and recovery response, 60–61; local societies, 36, 251; performances, 219; temperance and abolitionist performers, 174; Allegany City Temperance Arc, 174, 177; and nativism, 236, 246, 272; Whig-Temperance, 222–23, 243
territorial and slavery debates, 30th Congress, 67–69
Texas, admission to the Union, 50–51, 61
Thayer, Eli, 216, 261
theater and entertainment: Civil War participants, 296; gender divide, 183. *See also Uncle Tom's Cabin*, theatricals
Thompson, Benjamin, 111–12
Thompson, George, 112
"To Little Eva in Heaven" (G. Howard), 198
Toland, Aquilla, 297
Toland, Harford, 182, 292, 297, 356n82, *G14*
Toombs, Robert, 299–300
Tremont Temple, Boston, 85; "independent" antislavery lecture series, 215, 258–59, 263–64, 267
Tubman, Harriet (Minty): as fugitive, 65–66, 84, *G2*; as rescuer, 66, 69, 89–90, 101, 111, 113, 150, 267, 276, *G2*; Union agent, 299, *G3*
Tucker, Joseph, 243–44
Turner, Nat, 31, 43
Turner, Victor, 16–18, 142, 183
Twelve Years a Slave (Northrup), 169
Tyler, John, 61

Ullman, Daniel, 242–43, 247, 291, 382n18
Uncle Tom's Cabin (novel) (*UTC*), 3, 140–42, *G4*, *G5*; origins of, 125–27; Fugitive Slave Law and, 133, 141–42, 152–53; serial and book publication, 127–29, 142–43, 159, 164–65, 168, 296, *313*; installments and four-part narrative structure, 129–33, 346n43, 347n49; paradox of, 133–34; as liminal action, 141–42; liminality and structure in, 126–27, 133–37, 141–42, 148–49; characters in, 134–37; slaves as identifiable people, 142; battle of the kitchens, 260, 265; slavery's violation of the family, 128, 132, 133–34, 137, 214; gender in, 141–42; and romantic racism, 137; colonizationism in, 137–40, 194, 301; African American dialect, 182; and plantation novel/minstrel genres, 135–37; martyrdom in, 140; metaphors of Christ, 141–42; Christian influence in, 140; as reading experience, 143–46, 148–51, 301–2; reviews of, 133, 137–38; as media event, 160–61; as term in newspapers, *172*; child naming for Eva after publication, 146–48, *146*, *172*, 298, *313*; contemporaries on impact of, 148–58, 203, 295–96, 301–3; in Civil War, 295–99; and "Jim Crow" Redemption, 301–2
Uncle Tom's Cabin, as panorama, 187–88, 189
Uncle Tom's Cabin, characters in: John Bird, 130, 133, 135, 136; Mary Bird, 134, 136, 260; Cassie, 132, 134, 136, 140–41; Dinah, 260; Emmeline, 132, 134, 136, 140, 141; Phinehas Fletcher, 300; Rachel Halliday, 130, 136, 260; Eliza Harris, 134, 136–37, 141; flight to Canada, 129–30; Emily Harris, 132; George Harris, 130, 132, 134, 136, 137, 300; George Harris, cast as Edward Wilmot, 185; Simon Legree, 132, 134, 136, 140, 193, 264; Col. Arthur Shelby, 130, 132, 134; Emily Shelby, 135–36; George Shelby, 132; Augustine St. Clare, 131–32, 135, 136, 193; Eva/Evangeline St. Clare, 131, 136, 146–47; children named for Eva, 147, *172*,*313*, 356n82; Marie St. Clare, 131–32, 134, 136; Ophelia St. Clare, 131, 136; Uncle Tom,

129–31, 134, 137, 141, 146; Uncle Tom, sold into southern trade, 129–31; Uncle Tom, killed by Legree, 132; Uncle Tom as Christ-like figure, 131, 140; Topsy, 134, 136; John Van Trompe, 130

Uncle Tom's Cabin, theatricals: 182–98, 218–25, 266–67, *G14*
—music industry and, 198–99
—white audience responses, 190–92
—black audience responses, 200–201
—Aiken and Conway scripts, 192–95
—Taylor-Purdy performances, 184–86, *G11, G13*
—Aiken-Howard performances, 186, 187–89, 190–91, 196–97, 219–20, 266, 289, *G11*
—Conway-Barnum performances, 189–219
—Harris-Barmore performances, 190, dispersal to the west, 195–97, 220–25, *G14*
—performances in: Boston, 186; Baltimore, 184; Troy, 186; Albany, New York City, Philadelphia, 184, 189–90, 220; Harrisburg, 220–1; Pittsburgh, 197; Cincinnati, 221–22; Springfield, Ohio, 182–83; Indianapolis, 222–23; Springfield, Illinois, 231; Milwaukee, 223–24, 226
—Aiken version preferred by H. B. Stowe, 192
—Conway version preferred by Garrison, 195
—John Jay Jr., commentary on, 191–92
—Joseph and Jane Sill at, 190
—Fletcher family at, 284, 292–93
—creolization and political confluence, 184
—and northern audiences and antislavery politics, 183–84, 191–92, 195, 199, 218–25, 231
—*See also* Aiken-Howard *UTC* script; Conway *UTC* script; Marsh troupe; National Theatre, New York; National Theatre, Philadelphia; panoramas; Robinson Atheneum

Uncle Tom's Cabin As It Is, 184

Uncle Tom's Cabin merchandising, 164–65, *G6*

"Uncle Tom's Religion" (G. Howard), 198, 226, 359n135

Underground Railroad, 7, 19, 53–54, 65–66, 92, 106, 113, 121, 130, 164, 181, 223, *G2, G9*; in *UTC*, 130. *See also* Chaplin, William; Glover, Joshua; Jerry Rescue; Lemmon family rescue; Tubman, Harriet; White, Garland H.

union meetings (1850), 78, *94*, 95–97, 107, 110. *See also* Compromise of 1850; Webster, Daniel

United States Colored Troops (USCT), 298–301, *G3, G16*

Upham, Charles W., 285

urbanization, *58*, 60

Van Buren, Martin, 23–24, 32, 34, 43, 51, 62–63, 74, 204

Van Burenite Barnburners, 62, 110, 157

van Gennep, Arnold, 16–17

Van Zandt, John, 130

vigilance committees, 19, 71, 92, 98, 279–80. *See also* Underground Railroad

Virginia Minstrels, 42, 173

Virginia Serenaders, 175–76

Wade, Benjamin F., 111
Wade, Edward, 208
Wakarusa War, 262
Walker, David, 30–31, 35
War of 1812: Creeks, campaign against, 11; and minstrel shows, 40
Ward, Samuel, 84
Warner, Susan, 118
Washburn, Israel, 245
Webb, Mary, 259, 267
Webster, Daniel: "constitutional duties" to North, 80; death of, 163; Democratic Party praise, 96; dismisses northern antislavery, 1; R. W. Emerson attacks, 217; H. W. Beecher and, 125; Missouri Compromise discussion with Clay, 72; "not as a Massachusetts man" speech, 75–76, 78; Odd Fellows neutrality and, 240; T. Parker attacks, 84–85. *See also* Union meetings
Weed, Thurlow, 247, 279
Weld, Theodore Dwight, 47, 52, 120, 123, 125, 161, 163, 184. *See also* Grimké, Angelina
Western Anti-Slavery Society, 93, 103

Western Border Life (Mrs. W. H. Corning), 265
Wheatley, Phillis, 29
Wheaton, Charles, 113, 144, 146
Wheaton, Ellen, 144; as *UTC* reader, 165
Wheelbanks, David Green, 95
Whig Party, 1, 43, 53, 57, 61, 64, 107; antislavery conversion, 107; antislavery position, 54–55, 68, 86–87; collapse of, 246; on the Compromise, 96; end of, 229; failing, 163; finality plank at convention, 153; fraternal societies and, 241; Mexican War and, 61–62; national convention (1852), 153; nativist and antislavery divide, 241; nativist-union-proslavery group, 234; neutral on "gag rules," 38; reaction to Burns return to slavery, 227; southerners on slavery, 77–78; and temperance, 223
Whistler, Anna, 165, 205
White, Garland H., 299–300, G2, G16
white slavery, threat of, 266, 302
White Slavery in the Barbary States (Sumner), 168, 302
Whitney, Thomas R., 238, 273
Whittier, John Greenleaf, 105, 117, 164, 198, 259–60, 262–65
Wide, Wide World (Warner), 118

Williams, James Hamilton. *See* Hamlet, James
Williamson, Passmore, 269, 280
Willis, Sara Payson (Fanny Fern), 118
Wilmot, David, 62, 70, 152, 185, 248, 282
Wilmot, Edward (Taylor *UTC* character), 185, G13
Wilmot Proviso, 62, 65, 67, 70, 76, 84, G13
Wilson, Henry, 111, 148, 248, 253–56, 264, 295–96
Winthrop, Robert C., 70, 86
women: and abolitionism, 36–37, 48, 50, 146; abolition and women's rights, 123; as cultural celebrities, 89, 91, 95, 118–19, 146, 157–59, 167, 173, 165–68; challenging gender norms, 159–60. *See also* Bremer, Fredericka; Clark, Sarah Jane; Lind, Jenny; Southworth, Emma; Stowe, Harriet Beecher
Wood, Bradford, 157
Wood, George, 96
Woodbury, Maria, as *UTC* reader, 146
Woods, Leonard, and Mrs. Woods, as *UTC* readers, 151
Wood's Minstrels, 144, 220
Wright, Frances, 159

Yancey, William Lowndes, 290
Young, Brigham, 283

www.ingramcontent.com/pod-product-compliance
Lightning Source LLC
Chambersburg PA
CBHW020216240426
43672CB00006B/334